The Works of
William Sanders Scarborough

Yours most Sincerely.
W. S. Scarborough.

The Works of
William Sanders Scarborough

Black Classicist and Race Leader

Edited by
Michele Valerie Ronnick

Foreword by
Henry Louis Gates Jr.

OXFORD

UNIVERSITY PRESS

Oxford University Press, Inc., publishes works that further
Oxford University's objective of excellence
in research, scholarship, and education.

Oxford   New York
Auckland   Cape Town   Dar es Salaam   Hong Kong   Karachi
Kuala Lumpur   Madrid   Melbourne   Mexico City   Nairobi
New Delhi   Shanghai   Taipei   Toronto

With offices in
Argentina   Austria   Brazil   Chile   Czech Republic   France   Greece
Guatemala   Hungary   Italy   Japan   Poland   Portugal   Singapore
South Korea   Switzerland   Thailand   Turkey   Ukraine   Vietnam

Copyright © 2006 Oxford University Press

Published by Oxford University Press, Inc.
198 Madison Avenue, New York, New York, 10016
www.oup.com/us

Oxford is a registered trademark of Oxford University Press

Library of Congress Cataloging-in-Publication Data

Scarborough, W. S. (William Sanders), 1852–1926.
[Selections. 2006]
The works of William Sanders Scarborough : Black classicist and race leader /
edited by Michele Valerie Ronnick.
p. cm.
ISBN-13: 978-0-19-530962-1 (acid-free paper)
ISBN-10: 0-19-530962-6 (acid-free paper)
1. African Americans—History—1877–1964.   2. African Americans—Civil rights—History.
3. African Americans—Social conditions—To 1964.   4. African Americans—Education—
History.   5. United States—Race relations.   6. United States—Politics and government—
1865–1933.   7. African Americans in literature.   8. Classical literature—History and criticism.
9. Greek language.   10. Scarborough, W. S. (William Sanders), 1852–1926—Travel.
I. Ronnick, Michele V.   II. Title.
E185.6.S33   2006
973'.0496073—dc22   2006016675

For my brothers, Michael and David

"Be ashamed to die until you have won some victory for humanity."

—Horace Mann, Antioch College,
Yellow Springs, Ohio, 1859

Table of Contents

Foreword

When I was an assistant professor of African American Studies and English at Yale in the late 1970s and early 1980s, I would meet the great historian John W. Blassingame Sr. every morning for breakfast at Naples Pizza. Situated near the geographical center of the Yale campus, Naples had become the actual center of African American intellectual life at Yale by the time that I arrived back there in 1975, after graduate school at the University of Cambridge—all because John Blassingame preferred Naples to every other "restaurant" (and I use that term loosely!) in New Haven, for reasons that he took to his grave. So if you wanted to talk to Blassingame, even during office hours, you would have to do so amid the aromas of burning crusts and savory toppings, hot pepper flakes, and grated Parmesan cheese. When he died a few years ago, the owners of Naples even erected a bronze plaque over John's favorite stall.

Every morning John and I would meet, sometimes alone, sometimes with other colleagues, such as the economists Donald Brown and Gerald Jaynes, the philosopher Anthony Appiah, the historian Peter Ripley, the sociologist Hardy Frye, and the anthropologist John Brown Childs—all regulars during their time at Yale. We talked about everything from last night's basketball game to contemporary politics to historical events. We argued as if our lives depended on it over questions such as whether Booker T. Washington and W. E. B. Du Bois could have forged a strategic alliance or whether "Booker T." was an Uncle Tom. When I was in the process of ascertaining the race of Harriet E. Wilson, African American literature's first woman novelist, it was to Blassingame, at Naples, every day, that I would bring the results of my research and seek his counsel about new leads to pursue. It was there that we celebrated with a piece of pepperoni pizza and a glass of beer when Blassingame became satisfied that Wilson was black.

Blassingame was the first African American scholar to write a full-length study of the history of slavery from the viewpoint of the slaves themselves. Using slave narratives, which at painstaking length he attempted to authenticate, "Blass" (as we called him, with enormous affection and respect) re-created the morals and manners and the life and times of what he termed, brilliantly, "the slave community." And it was at Naples that he and I would plot—fantasize, actually—about the future of the fledgling field of African American studies in the decades ahead.

Upon one thing we agreed early on: we had to find a way to map the field with reference works, sophisticated reference works such as biographical dictionaries; encyclopedias of history and culture; scholarly editions of texts; collected works of authors who had published essays primarily in periodicals; collected papers for canonical figures like Booker T. Washington, W. E. B. Du Bois, Marcus Garvey, and Frederick Douglass (whose papers Blassingame was in the process of editing); bibliographies; concordances—in short, all foundational reference works that, taken together, make a field of study, well, scholarly. It is upon reference works such as these that any discipline of study is constructed, and "Afro-Am" (as we called it) would be no exception. Indeed, we were determined that we would be part of the generation that eliminated forever the curse of scholars of African American studies: that each successive generation was forced to reinvent the proverbial wheel, repeating research undertaken by previous scholars of which we remained painfully unaware. It was nothing less than a textual legacy of memory that we hoped to leave to our colleagues and contemporaries, and to our intellectual heirs. So we embarked upon projects such as the Douglass Papers, the Black Periodical Literature Project, the *Norton Anthology of African American Literature*, the *Encyclopedia Africana*, and others, with alacrity and a sense of excitement that is difficult for our students, who now take reference works such as these for granted, even to begin to understand.

Of these various projects, collecting the occasional essays of nineteenth-century public intellectuals and creative writers intrigued me most. Blassingame's genius had been to understand the crucial role that black-edited newspapers and magazines had played in forging an African American intellectual community by the middle of the nineteenth century. Periodicals such as *Freedom's Journal*, Frederick Douglass's newspaper, the *Anglo-African Magazine*, and *The African Methodist Episcopal Church Review*, among many others, were often the sole venue for opinion and thought among an energetic and emerging class of African American intellectuals, scholars, and writers, who were all eager to express their ideas and feelings, and just as eager to reflect upon the ideas and feelings of their contemporaries.

The problem with choosing newspapers and magazines as the principal forum for black expression is their transience: newspapers, then as now, had a short shelf life. One black writer in the middle of the nineteenth century worried about this, calling these periodicals "ephemeral caskets" in which so much that was rich and vital in the thinking of African Americans would be buried, lost, and forgotten, tossed into the dustbin of history. Who keeps newspapers, and for how long? People, then as now, wrap garbage with newspapers. Can you imagine a more fragile, or perilous, repository for the first vital writings of the first generation of black intellectuals, the children of slaves hell-bent on gaining their freedom, literally and figuratively—on gaining a freedom of the mind, the freedom to embrace the republic of letters, a freedom larger than manumission?

It is not that these writers willingly chose to publish their thoughts in such fragile venues as newspapers and magazines directed primarily at a black readership. While they obviously relished the opportunity to speak to "the race" on behalf of themselves, they also knew that these publications were the only conduit available for their writing: other than the abolitionist press that flourished between 1831 and the end of the Civil War, few white publications opened their pages to African American authors. To publish, as a black writer, meant to publish primarily in the black press.

Fortunately, many of these periodicals survive today, against the greatest odds, because of efforts during the 1930s and beyond to microfilm and thus preserve them. Scholars such as James Danky have painstakingly documented the location of extant copies of the originals and library locations of microfilm editions. Using these tools, scholars are now able to piece together the collective "mind" of the African American people as it manifested itself in print in the nineteenth century.

Of the several black writers whose occasional essays cry out to be collected and published, we have chosen to launch Oxford's Selected Black Writings series with the works of W. S. Scarborough, James McCune Smith, and William Wells Brown, all former slaves. Brown, an escaped slave, was one of the two most popular figures on the antislavery lecture circuit, along with Frederick Douglass. The author of a very popular slave narrative, Brown also published fiction, drama, and popular histories, as well as travel narratives. An autodidact, Brown plunged fearlessly into many genres—he was the first African American to publish a novel, and a play, for example—as if he were eager to demonstrate that broad-based political equality for blacks was inextricably intertwined with the manifestation of artistic and intellectual excellence among a small vanguard of the black intelligentsia.

Whereas Brown was self-trained, James McCune Smith was one of the most highly educated human beings of any nationality or ethnicity, earning a B.A., an M.A., and an M.D. at the University of Glasgow in Scotland.

W. S. Scarborough, like McCune Smith, was extremely well educated, earning his bachelor's and master's degrees at Oberlin College after graduating from Atlanta University. Scarborough became a classical scholar at precisely the time when an aptitude—or lack thereof—for mastery of Latin and Greek had become a curious touchstone through which the innate, or genetic, "capacity" of persons of African descent might be determined or measured. For example, Senator John C. Calhoun, an eloquent apologist for slavery and himself a Yale man, once argued that he would make believe that Negroes were even capable of achieving intellectual equality with white men if he discovered one who had mastered Greek and Latin. Alexander Crummell, the first African American to be educated at the University of Cambridge, claimed to have overheard Calhoun's remarks and decided on the spot that he would prove this claim for his black countrymen. Scarborough took Crummell's quest one step further, becoming the first black person to write a

Greek textbook, *First Lessons in Greek,* published in 1881. Scarborough was the consummate black academic, devoting most of his career to the classroom and to academic administration, becoming the first black member of the Modern Language Association and the third black member (after Harvard graduate Richard T. Greener and Edward Blyden) of the American Philological Association. If W. E. B. Du Bois, the antecedent of today's black public intellectuals, himself has an antecedent, it is W. S. Scarborough, the black scholar's scholar. In this remarkably important and seminal collection, the classicist Michele Valerie Ronnick has edited the most vital and compelling examples of Scarborough's writings, demonstrating why the loss of much of this scholar's work for the past century has unnecessarily robbed generations of scholars of one of the most profound thinkers in the history of black letters, and why the publication of this collection of his essays is a tremendous cause for celebration. Because of this series, the works of writers such as Scarborough, McCune Smith, and Wells Brown will never be lost again.

Henry Louis Gates Jr.

Acknowledgments

This volume would not have been completed without the help of many people. For materials in archives and elsewhere, I am much obliged to Candace Pryor and Latoyra Weston at the Interlibrary Loan department of the Purdy-Kresge Library at Wayne State University, Detroit; to Mike Hawthorne, senior clerk at the Circulation Desk of the Purdy-Kresge Library at Wayne State University; to the staff of the Detroit Public Library, including Patrice Merritt of the Friends of the Detroit Public Library; to Julie Odland of the American Academy of Political and Social Sciences, Philadelphia; to Scott Sanders of Antioch College, Yellow Springs, Ohio; to Karen Jefferson of the Robert W. Woodruff Library at the Atlanta University Center; to Sheila Darrow of the Hallie Quinn Brown Library, Central State University, Wilberforce, Ohio; to Leonard Ballou (1926–2004) of Elizabeth City State University, Elizabeth City, North Carolina; to Randall Burkett of the Manuscripts and Rare Book Library at Emory University, Atlanta; to Joseph Greer and Dave Bragg of the Greene County Public Library, Xenia, Ohio; to an unknown hero at the William R. and Norma B. Harvey Library, Hampton University, Hampton, Virginia; to Ida E. Jones, Joellen El Bashir, and Clifford L. Muse Jr. at the Moorland-Spingarn Research Center, Howard University, Washington, D.C.; to Muriel McDowell Jackson at the Middle Georgia Regional Library, Genealogical and Historical Room, Macon, Georgia; to Sue Parker and Floyd Thomas at the National Afro-American Museum and Cultural Center, Wilberforce, Ohio; to Walter B. Hill at the National Archives and Records Administration, Washington, D.C.; to Cathy Ingram of the National Park Service, Frederick Douglass House; to John Aubrey at the Newberry Library, Chicago; to Roland M. Baumann and Ken Grossi at the Mudd Center Library, Oberlin College, Oberlin, Ohio; to Eva M. Greenberg at the Oberlin Pubic Library, Oberlin, Ohio; to Elizabeth L. Plummer, Thomas J. Rieder, and Mathew Benz at the Ohio Historical Society, Columbus, Ohio; to Kitty Oliver and Chris Howard at the Sidney Lanier Cottage, Macon, Georgia; to Cynthia B. Wilson of the Washington Collection at Tuskegee University, Tuskegee, Alabama; to Michael McCormick and Anne Sindelar at the Western Reserve

Historical Society, Cleveland, Ohio; to Jacqueline Brown, Linda Hasting, and Lynn Ayres of Rembert E. Stokes Library, Wilberforce University, Wilberforce, Ohio; and to Jean Mulhern of the Watson Library at Wilmington College, Wilmington, Ohio.

For scholarly support and technical advice, I am indebted to Kim Robinson, Georgia Maas, Heidi Bogardus, and David Bowers of the Oxford University Press; to Norma and Bernard Goldman of Wayne State University; to Murray Jackson (1926–2002); to Walter F. Edwards, director of the Humanities Center of Wayne State University; to Howard Finley, director of the Interdisciplinary Studies Program at Wayne State University; to Robert Sedler of the Wayne State University School of Law; to Dean Robert L. Thomas, Joe Kieleszewski, Melba Joyce Boyd, Alfred L. Cobbs, Todd Duncan, and Bill Harris of the College of Liberal Arts and Sciences at Wayne State University; to Ed Diaz of the African American Association of Historical Research and Preservation; to Robin Sabino of Auburn University, Auburn, Alabama; to Lisa Ruch of Bay Path College, Longmeadow, Massachusetts; to Meyer Reinhold (1909–2002) of Boston University; to Joan Bryant of Brandeis University; to G. T. Johnson and Joseph D. Lewis of Central State University; to James Tatum of Dartmouth College; to David Bright and Niall Slater of Emory University; to Titus Brown of Florida A&M University; to James J. O'Donnell of Georgetown University; to Henry Louis Gates Jr. of Harvard University; to Richard Newman (1930–2003) of Harvard University; to Zeph Stewart of Harvard University; to Richard Thomas of Harvard University; to John T. Quinn of Hope College, Holland, Michigan; to T. Davina McClain of Loyola University at New Orleans; to Tom Sienkewicz of Monmouth College, Monmouth, Illinois; to Dolan Hubbard of Morgan State University, Baltimore; to Wilson Moses of Pennsylvania State University; to Eddie Glaude of Princeton University; to Nell Painter of Princeton University; to Valerie Smith of Princeton University; to Cornel West of Princeton University; to Patrice Rankine of Purdue University; to Richard Janko of the University of Michigan; to Cortez Williams of the University of New Mexico; to Ward W. Briggs Jr. of the University of South Carolina; to Michael Mounter of the University of South Carolina; to Charles Blockson of the Blockson Collection at Temple University; and to Sylvia Hayre-Randolph, Delores Wright, and Terrance Grasty of the Wright-Hayre Fund at the Philadelphia Foundation.

I am indebted to Reverend Calvin H. Syndor III for permission to include in this volume sixteen articles originally published between 1876 and 1911 in the *Christian Recorder*. Three articles originally published in the *A.M.E. Church Review* have been reprinted with permission from Dr. Dennis C. Dickerson, editor and publisher of the *A.M.E. Church Review*, and one article from *Opportunity* has been reprinted with the permission of Lee A. Daniels, vice president for research and publications of the National Urban League.

I am also deeply grateful to my friends, who have encouraged and supported me all along. These are Ada Anderson, Helene Weldt-Basson, Christine Allen-Bruno and family, Lee Carol Cook, Adelaide Cromwell,

Stanley Crouch, Truman Kella Gibson Jr. (1912–2005) and family, Ted Higbee, Janet Webster Jones, Judge Damon J. Keith, Aya Konstantinou, Jack Lessenberry, Robert McCleod and family, Melvin McCray, Suesetta and James McCree and family, Jay and Alice Mulberry, Richard Nettlow, Lou Ann Palmer, Kevin G. Piotrowski and family, Marilynn Rashid, John Russ, Thelma Tournay Slater, Brian and Andrea Stroik, Sheila Gregory Thomas, and Ralph Valdez.

For putting the manuscript into computer files, I must acknowledge the contributions of Cully Sommers, Natalie Carter, Charles Alexander, Amanda Rahya, Jennifer Backer, and two students, Meghan E. Curavo and Stephen M. Walker.

Finally, I thank the members of my family circle: my mother, Elizabeth Ronnick; my brothers, Michael William Ronnick and David Louis Ronnick and my sister-in-law M. Holly Ronnick, my cousins Richard F. Ronnick and S. P. Ronnick; my niece Anna Klein Michaeli and her husband Eitan; Kevin L. Perry; Henrietta Coon and her children Nathan, Caroline, and Gregory; and Sarah A. Grant, Sarah C. B. Scarborough's great-granddaughter.

Introduction

William Sanders Scarborough was born in slavery in Macon, Georgia, in February 1852. He was in truth twice liberated: once by the Emancipation Proclamation, and again by his effort to educate himself. In this work of self-education he was helped by his parents and other well-wishers, both black and white.[1] Scarborough's goal was to be unfettered—both in body and in mind.

He was a secret scholar, however. Under the system of slavery, Scarborough was compelled to break the law in order to study because the law in many places prohibited the education of slaves. After the Civil War ended, Scarborough studied at Lewis High School (also known as Ballard Normal School) in Macon, Georgia, and then enrolled at Atlanta University. His friends at Atlanta included Lucy Laney, Henry O. Flipper, and Richard R. Wright. Scarborough was in the room when Wright uttered the now-famous words, "Tell them we are rising."[2]

As the most advanced student at the university, Scarborough was literally in a class by himself, and he was well aware that the world was watching. He was the only member of the senior class of 1869 and was the first student produced by Atlanta University. He understood from the start that he was part of an experiment in Freedmen's education and that nothing he did from success to failure was his alone. He was studying on behalf of his entire race. After finishing all the college preparatory classes offered at Atlanta University, he completed his bachelor's and master's degrees in classical studies at Oberlin College. Scarborough treasured his years at Oberlin and joyfully returned to participate in reunions of his class of 1875.[3]

At a time when black illiteracy was legally enforced policy, Scarborough stands out as one who managed to transcend the system. But he was not content merely to learn to read and write American English. Fascinated by all forms of language and literature, Scarborough mastered Greek and Latin; he did so even though many people did not believe that a black person could or should do such a thing. His Greek textbook, *First Lessons in Greek* (1881), showed the world that a black person could master these learned languages, vindicating both himself and his race.[4] The textbook was still being talked about five years after its publication. It was, according to the Reverend A. J. Kershaw, "one of the heaviest blows that has ever been given to the false theory that the colored man is intellectually inferior to other men. Let our young [S]olons purchase a copy of this learned work."[5]

Scarborough's overarching achievement was the example that he made of his life: he lived with serious intent as a citizen, race leader, educator, and scholar. He was a lifelong champion of the liberal arts curriculum for people of African descent, as well as for disenfranchised white people. Scarborough "was not simply a devotee of the Talented Tenth ideal; he was its exemplar."[6]

Scarborough courageously confronted Jim Crowism both in society and in the academy. He crossed racial lines in 1881 to marry Sarah Cordelia Bierce (1851–1933), a woman of European descent from Danby, New York, and his kindred spirit. Trained in pedagogy with college work in Greek, Latin, and French at the Oswego Institute, she was his helpmate in the truest sense. During their forty-five years together she published numerous works of fiction and poetry while teaching full time at Wilberforce for forty-four years. In the 1880s the couple joined the Modern Language Association together. Scarborough himself continually sought active participation in learned organizations, black and white, at home and abroad. He gave more than twenty papers at the American Philological Association, one of the oldest learned societies in the United States, and he was the first black member of the Modern Language Association.[7]

Scarborough was also on the original committee of fifty of the National Association for the Advancement of Colored People (NAACP). He spoke at a meeting of the Los Angeles chapter in 1915, one year after the chapter's founding.[8] As the years passed, Scarborough acquired an enormous circle of friends and acquaintances, from Frederick Douglass, Booker T. Washington, and W. E. B. Du Bois to some of the most powerful white men in American politics, including John Sherman, William McKinley, William Howard Taft, Theodore Roosevelt, and Warren G. Harding.

Scarborough was fighting for a better future, and it was a future that he would not live to see. Forbidden to drink water from fountains, told that he could not enter dining rooms or register at conference hotels at which he was to lecture, and ordered to use freight elevators at political gatherings, Scarborough determined nevertheless that he would find a way to quench his thirst for knowledge and drink from the fountains of the world's best literature and cultural achievements.[9]

Scarborough's remarkable life causes us to ask whether it is at all possible to place restrictive covenants not only on parcels of land, as in *Hansberry v. Lee* (1940), but also on the intellect.[10] Can the life of the mind be segregated, too? In Scarborough, we see a wonderful fusion—a merger between the content of character and the content of the cranium—that shows that although such segregation may be accomplished *de jure*, it cannot be enforced *de facto*.

Scarborough was battling alongside the spirit of Rosa Parks, decades before

Mrs. Parks was born, to get a seat on the school bus. He is exactly the sort of person that Henry Louis Gates Jr. had in mind when he was commenting on the fiftieth anniversary of *Brown v. the Board of Education*. Gates said then that "the blackest thing you could be historically was an educated man or an educated woman within the African American community."[11]

Such an educated black man was William Sanders Scarborough. He was doing "civil rights" work before we had the term, doing this work in order to live as he wanted. And that, in fact, is the definition of liberty, according to the Roman orator Cicero: *potestas vivendi ut velis*, "the power of living as you wish."[12] Scarborough was an original freedom fighter and he frequently put his pen to work in his quest for freedom.

Scarborough was prolific. He was engaged in writing, publishing, and editing for more than fifty years. This compilation contains essays collected from twenty-seven different journals and newspapers. Seventeen of these journals and newspapers were race-related enterprises that served black audiences: *A.M.E. Church Review, Atlanta University Bulletin, Christian Recorder, Christian Register, Cleveland Gazette, Cleveland Journal, Competitor, Detroit Plaindealer, Hampton Institute Publications, Howard's American Magazine, Indianapolis Freeman, Opportunity, People's Advocate, Sodalian, Southern Teachers' Advocate, Southern Workman,* and *Voice of the Negro.* The other ten were publications that covered topics of interest to predominantly white audiences: *Annals of the American Academy of Political and Social Sciences, Arena, Education, Forum, Independent, Journal of Education, Leslie's Weekly, Methodist Review, Our Day,* and *Transactions of the American Philological Association.*

No attempt has ever been made to produce a complete or even a partial inventory of Scarborough's papers, let alone publish a compilation of them. And because his writings both crossed the color line and appeared in the United States and abroad for so many years, it is not unlikely that other items may yet be recovered—especially if the item appeared in a serial or newspaper that was not well known, did not last long, or was never indexed. For those reasons, a complete bibliography may never be achieved.

The purpose of this compilation is to give readers a chance to engage directly with many of Scarborough's writings. The compilation will serve not as *le dernier cri* in Scarborough studies, but as an entry point into his life and times. It should also stimulate the creation of fresh interpretations by scholars working in the multitude of fields in which Scarborough himself worked. Throughout this compilation, all of my notes and any modifications I made to the texts have been put in square brackets. I have left out Scarborough's *First Lessons in Greek.*[13] The book deserves a separate treatment and should be reprinted and analyzed as a unit. Such an analysis lies outside the scope of this compilation.

Because the original sources were not given for the longer quotations in foreign languages, I have presented their wording and accent marks with minor corrections as they appeared in Scarborough's originals. Curious readers can then pursue their own *Quellenforschung* and try to determine actual points of origin. Variations in the quotations are not necessarily Scarborough's. They could well have come from the texts he used or they might have been introduced in the publisher's office by various editors, typesetters, and printers. Scarborough left a large and varied body of material that requires categorization. Let us use the topical arrangement set forth in the table of contents as our method of approach.

Scarborough lived through two major wars. His involvement with military affairs began when he was a child during the Civil War. He was both a witness and an unwilling participant, observing Floyds' Rifles practice their drills in Macon[14] and being forced to carry buckets of water to thirsty Confederate soldiers. He saw the Union cavalry officer General George Stoneman taken captive by the Confederate forces, and he watched the citizens of Macon react as General Howard Cobb surrendered the city to the Union forces.[15] At the end of the fighting in 1865, Scarborough saw, from the top of a tree in downtown Macon, the Confederate president Jefferson Davis led away as a prisoner of war.[16]

With the conclusion of the Civil War, Scarborough enrolled as a student at Lewis High School and became an officer in the school's Cadet Corps.[17] He then matriculated at Atlanta University in the autumn of 1869. Among his friends was Henry O. Flipper, who in 1877 became the first black cadet to graduate from West Point Military Academy. During his time at the university, Scarborough and his fellow students spent part of each day tearing down Confederate fortifications that had been left standing on the school's property.[18]

Scarborough published in the *Christian Register* some of his reflections about the position of black soldiers in the United States. He was prompted to do this because of the war with Spain and because of general concern over the future of the United States' new possessions. Descriptions of Scarborough's dealings with military men such as Henry O. Flipper, John Alexander, and Charles Young can be found at various points in his *Autobiography*. In 1917, Scarborough tried without success to help Colonel Young, once the highest-ranking black soldier in the U.S. armed services, return to active duty.[19]

World War I put Scarborough at the center of military matters at Wilberforce University in Ohio, where he was president from 1908 to 1920. Military training had been part of the school's curriculum since 1893. As president of Wilberforce, Scarborough had to oversee the activities of the Student Army Training Corps on campus. The coming of war increased his already heavy workload. Through personal visits to Camp Funston and Camp Des Moines, where he encouraged the young black soldiers, Scarborough learned firsthand about the problems arising in a segregated armed services.[20]

Scarborough shouldered the burdens of leadership on every level. In a short letter to the *New York Times* on March 25, 1916, entitled "Only One Side to Preparedness," he told the country that Arthur Balfour, the former British prime minister, was now sorry "that England did not build Zeppelins before the war began." "Preparedness," Scarborough advised, was "the best policy and the only safe one." Furthermore, "the Mexican imbroglio certainly emphasizes the fact that there is no time in which preparedness should not be the watchword."

At his home at Wilberforce, Scarborough entertained veterans wounded in World War I. Once, after watching the painful efforts of the injured men to get to their feet as the band played the "Star-Spangled Banner," Scarborough was overcome with emotion and had to leave the room.[21] In September 1918 he gave an address at the opening of the school year entitled "Wilberforce in the War," which was later issued as a pamphlet.[22] By 1919, "hoping to arouse public conscience to right wrongs," Scarborough published the essay "Race Riots and Their Remedy," in which he offered what he thought was the only solution—namely, the elimination of race prejudice.[23]

During the course of his lifetime, Scarborough gave many speeches. He addressed audiences of all ages and all colors, both at home and abroad. As a youth he was inspired by Frederick Douglass and "planned to be an orator."[24] Scarborough's first public recitation was at his high school graduation in 1866, when the local paper criticized his recitation of Tennyson's "Charge of the Light Brigade." The reporter commented that the poem "was rattled off as rapidly as the words could be spoken" and concluded that the young man's "specialty" was not "oratory."[25]

Scarborough made his next speech at his graduation ceremony at Oberlin College in 1875. He was the only black student among the thirty-six graduates in the classical course. His oration was entitled "The Sphere and Influence of Genius."[26]

Scarborough's first professional lecture was given not long after he obtained his position as professor at Wilberforce. He was a guest speaker at an African Methodist Episcopal (A.M.E.) Church in Richmond, Indiana, and his lecture was entitled "Outlooks on the Practical." But because of Scarborough's poor penmanship, the circulars that advertised the event read "Outlooks on the Protocol." The audience was too polite to say anything about the discrepancy between title and talk, however, and Scarborough himself, unaware of the misprinted announcements, wondered at the "mystified looks" he received.[27]

Some of Scarborough's speeches survive only as titles or unpublished texts. Others have completely vanished. A notebook entitled "Some Lectures" in the archives at Wilberforce University contains the texts of nine lectures. But there are no details given about the date they were written, when and where they might have been delivered, or if they were formally published at a later time. Other lectures are mentioned in the same archive by title only.[28]

Various newspaper clippings provide us with titles of additional speeches. On May 30, 1891, Scarborough gave a speech entitled "Modern Drift" at Morris Brown College in Atlanta. Reverend A. L. Sherril of the Congregational Church on Peachtree Street was quoted in the *Atlanta Times* as saying that he had "never heard better doctrine than the speech of Prof. Scarborough and had not heard it better rendered, therefore [Sherril] wished it printed and put into the hands of everybody of all races. No race can stay behind that follows the direction of such a speech."[29]

Mentioned in the *Morning News* from Savannah, Georgia, is a lecture that

Scarborough gave at the Georgia State Industrial College on June 4, 1901, entitled "The True Aim of Education." In 1919, the sixty-third session of Wilberforce University opened with Scarborough's address on "The Coming Crucial Years." On February 15 of the following year, Scarborough spoke about "Racial Responsibility" at the Y.M.C.A. on West 135th Street in New York. In January 1922, he gave a speech entitled "Self-Respect and Self-Reliance" at the 31st Annual Tuskegee Negro Conference, and in March 1923 he gave an address in New York entitled "Some Aftermaths of the World War" at the "colored Y.M.C.A. auditorium."[30]

Titles can also be gleaned serendipitously by going through the records of various organizations, such as those of the American Association of Educators of Colored Youth. On the program of this association's meeting in Chicago in July 1893 is a paper by Scarborough entitled "Traits in Negro Character."[31]

Undoubtedly some of Scarborough's lectures were oral presentations of various published papers. For example, his lecture "The Mission of the Educated Negro," given at Morris Brown College in February 1914, must have been an updated version of a paper titled "The Educated Negro and His Mission," which he had delivered eleven years earlier at the American Negro Academy; this paper had also been published by the group in 1903 and is included in this compilation.[32]

One wonders from time to time what impression this popular speaker made *in propria persona* and how he sounded *viva voce*. Was there a trace, perhaps, of middle Georgia dialect in his voice? One witness is the Chicago attorney Truman Kella Gibson Jr. (1912–2005). He met Scarborough in the early 1920s at Scarborough's home at Wilberforce and described Scarborough's voice as "low and measured."[33]

The four speeches in this compilation, ranging in date from 1884 to 1908, provide a good sample of Scarborough's style. Other speeches characteristic of Scarborough are available in printed editions. "The Hawaiian Question," delivered at Wilberforce University and originally published in the *Christian Recorder* of March 15, 1894, was recently reprinted in *Lift Every Voice: African American Oratory 1787–1900*, edited by Philip S. Foner and Robert James Branham (Tuscaloosa: University of Alabama Press, 1998), pp. 791–796. "At the Unveiling of the Monument to Dunbar, Dayton, Ohio, June 26, 1909," was originally published in *Paul Laurence Dunbar: Laurel Decked*, edited by Davis Wasgatt Clark (Dayton, Ohio: Commissioners of the Paul Laurence Dunbar Scholarship Fund, 1909), pp. 13–15, while "President's Address" was originally published in *Wilberforce Night by the Wilberforce University Club of Washington, D.C., March 8, 1910* (Washington, D.C.: Murray Brothers, 1910), pp. 17–23. A speech included in this compilation, "The Party of Freedom and the Freedman—A Reciprocal Duty," was originally published in Alice Dunbar's *Masterpieces of Negro Eloquence* (New York: Bookery Publishing, 1914), a book that was reprinted in 2000 with an introduction by Manning Marable (Mineola, N.Y.: Dover; Scarborough's speech is on pp. 151–161).

Scarborough's interest in communication, via both the spoken and the written word, came early. In 1883, just a few years out of college, he made plans to publish *The Authors' Review and Scrapbook* with his friend and Oberlin classmate Isaac Walton Fitch. But their project ended with Fitch's untimely death.[34] Scarborough had, to be sure, any number of models at hand to emulate in this journalistic work, from Frederick Douglass's *North Star* and Benjamin Tucker Tanner's *A.M.E. Church Review* and *Christian Recorder* to secular publications produced across the country. Scarborough himself was editor for the A.M.E. Sunday School Union for more than three decades.

It was Scarborough's habit to use humor to reveal underlying truths; he once quipped that "we have almost as many factions among us as we have newspapers."[35] Joking aside, he nonetheless understood how crucial it was for black journalists to build firm foundations for and among themselves so as "to present a solid front, make a stronger fight for our rights and thereby demand fair play in the race of life."[36] Scarborough also saw the value in forging alliances with white publications, which he himself did with regularity. In March 1890 he read a paper to this effect at the Conference of Afro-American Authors, "How Our Connections with Anglo-American Publishing Houses Can Be Strengthened."[37]

In the summer of 1891, Scarborough was stripped of his professorship in ancient languages at Wilberforce (Scarborough seems to have annoyed Bishop Arnett, who had much influence at Wilberforce),[38] and he was compelled to earn his living as a journalist. The timing was particularly bad. He was under considerable financial pressure—for instance, his house was not paid for—and he was unable to collect the wages owed to him by the school. During this period, writing became his "sole dependence." But Scarborough and his wife had decided that "under no circumstance" was he to abandon his Greek and Latin studies or "lose connection with the Philological Association." He counted on his wife's salary and the magazine work that came to both of them.[39]

In 1920, the final year of his presidency at Wilberforce, Scarborough oversaw the establishment of a department of journalism. An article dated January 2, 1920, announced, "WU Starts a School of Journalism." The article stated, "A department of journalism under Professor Albert Sidney Beckham has been established at Wilberforce University," and it unveiled plans for a four-page weekly to be called the *Sun-Dial* that the students would produce. Scarborough was quoted: "Journalism has become such a potent factor in our daily life that I would feel as if Wilberforce were negligent in the event it should exclude such an important subject from its curriculum . . . and we intend to have our students informed intelligently as to the methods of news gathering, the styles of presenting and handling news as is characteristic of the metropolitan dailies."[40]

Scarborough himself was a media star. From the time he was a teenager until his death, his name was regularly mentioned in newspapers and magazines.[41] For more than fifty years he was in print, whether he was writing articles for publication or was being written about. Around 1900 he received a telegram from a student that announced, "our school has this day planted a tree in your honor."[42] He was even the subject of a four-stanza poem entitled "Dr. W. S. Scarborough," published by Mrs. Mary Lee Jones of Waxahachie, Texas, shortly after his 1920 resignation as president of Wilberforce.[43] In his memoirs he recalled, "There is scarcely a Negro publication for which I have not written more or less at some time or other. I have considered it a help not only to such, for these were not able to pay except in rare instances, but I deemed it one way to help onward the race as well as give myself desired outlets. Many of these publications have had but a brief existence, but a few have survived the years."[44]

At the end of his life, Scarborough observed with pride, "Concerning the press, I can truly say . . . that if one has the mind to use his pen in the service of the public, it is a great thing to have a medium of communication whose clearness and integrity are unquestionable, and I have always esteemed it an honor to have been permitted to work with men whose journalistic aims were never below the highest."[45]

Scarborough also wrote several introductions to books. His first introduction was written in 1881 for his own book, *First Lessons in Greek*. The book was a notable achievement. No black person had ever written a textbook for the study of the ancient languages, and creating the book contradicted the common prejudice that it could not be done. The date Scarborough placed at the end of the introduction, February 16, 1881, indicates how significant the book was to him. This day was Scarborough's twenty-ninth birthday, and the dating indicates, as I have argued elsewhere, that the book's publication was both a physical and an intellectual anniversary for him.[46]

Scarborough's other five introductions were written for books by men Scarborough knew personally. Wesley John Gaines was born in slavery in Wilkes County, Georgia, in 1840 and became a bishop in the A.M.E. Church in 1888. Gaines founded Morris Brown College in Atlanta, and the college conferred an honorary doctorate upon Scarborough in 1908.[47] Gaines wrote two books: *African Methodism in the South* (1890) and *The Negro and the White Man* (1897). Scarborough described both Gaines and Henry M. Turner, another A.M.E. bishop, as "my friends from childhood and both men of the 'old school' of slavery, self-made, rugged powerful leaders always working for race uplift."[48]

James Monroe Gregory was a professor of Latin at Howard University. In 1885, after the death of Wiley Lane, the school's first black professor of Greek, Scarborough tried without success to get the position, but it was given to a white man.[49] The two classicists Gregory and Scarborough were both members of the American Philological Association. On March 29, 1893, Gregory sent a letter to Scarborough to ask if he would write the introduction to Gregory's new book, *Frederick Douglass, the Orator*.[50] The book was published later that year.

Benjamin Tucker Tanner was a powerful figure in the A.M.E. Church and was elected bishop in 1888. He was the author of a number of books and was the editor of several important A.M.E. Church publications. He started the

A.M.E. Church Review in 1884 after serving as editor of the *Christian Recorder* from 1868 to 1884.[51] Tanner's book *The Color of Solomon* argued that biblical scholars were wrong to think that the son of David was a white man. In 1901, Scarborough sailed with Tanner to England, and they later visited the art studio of Tanner's son Henry in Paris. Scarborough touched briefly on this visit in his *Autobiography*, and he mentioned that Bishop Tanner presented him with one of his son's paintings, "A Fishing Scene in Brittany."[52]

James M. Conner was born in slavery in Winston County, Mississippi, in 1863. His work for the A.M.E. Church took him from his home state to Louisiana, Arkansas, and Oklahoma. He was the author of two books besides *Doctrines of Christ* (1897), the one for which Scarborough wrote the introduction: *The Outlines of Christian Theology* (1896) and *Elements of Success* (1911). Conner was elected bishop of the A.M.E. Church in 1912.[53]

Horace Talbert was Scarborough's colleague at Wilberforce for many years. He taught Latin and became the school's secretary in 1897. He published *The Sons of Allen*, an important history of the A.M.E. Church, in 1906.[54] Talbert and Scarborough are still together: their bodies lie in adjacent plots in Massie's Creek Cemetery at Wilberforce.

Between 1877 and 1900 Scarborough published several book reviews. With the exception of the classical philologist William Gardner Hale, all of the authors whose books Scarborough reviewed were of African descent. Of these, only Booker T. Washington was not affiliated with the A.M.E. Church.

Theophilus Gould Steward, as a young man in his late twenties, tutored Scarborough, who was then in his teens in Macon, Georgia.[55] After a lifetime of work as a chaplain to the 25th Infantry Regiment, Steward retired to Wilberforce University with his second wife, the medical doctor S. Maria Steward.[56] In 1912, Dr. Steward attended Scarborough's mother on her deathbed. When Dr. Steward died in 1918, Scarborough accompanied Reverend Steward as he brought her body back to New York.[57]

Daniel Payne founded Wilberforce University in 1856 and was the sixth bishop of the A.M.E. Church. He was a lifelong advocate for African American education, and he was among the first people that Scarborough met upon his arrival as a new professor at Wilberforce.[58] In the early 1880s, Mrs. Scarborough enlisted Payne's help in setting up a mineral collection for students at Wilberforce.[59] She also compiled the materials included in two of Payne's books, *Recollections of Seventy Years* (1888) and the first volume of his *History of the A.M.E. Church* (1891).

H. M. Turner affiliated himself with the A.M.E. Church in 1858 and was elected bishop in 1880. As postmaster at Macon, Georgia, in the 1860s, he met Scarborough and encouraged his parents to see to his education. Turner's laudatory review of Scarborough's Greek textbook, "Prof. Scarborough's Book," was published in the *Christian Recorder* on September 22, 1881.[60] Turner stepped down as president of the Board of Trustees and chancellor of Morris Brown College in 1908, the year Scarborough was given an honorary degree there.[61]

Hale was a respected classicist who taught first at Harvard University, then at Cornell University, and finally at the University of Chicago (1892–1919). He was the president of the American Philological Association for the year 1892. His *Art of Reading Latin* "advanced the notion that Latin could be read by students like a modern language."[62]

Benjamin Tucker Tanner wrote seven books. His first was *An Apology for African Methodism* (1867). *The Color of Solomon* (1895) was Tanner's fourth book, and Scarborough wrote the introduction to it.[63] Tanner's *Dispensations on the History of the Church* was published in two volumes in 1898 and 1899.

Scarborough was asked by the editor of the *Annals of the American Academy of Political and Social Sciences* to review Booker T. Washington's book *The Future of the American Negro*.[64] The paths of the two men, both born in slavery, crossed frequently during their lives, and while Scarborough did not believe in unilateral programs of industrial education, he recognized the value of Washington's leadership. Scarborough remembered meeting Olivia Davidson when she was a student, before she became Washington's second wife, and in 1914 he had Washington's third wife, Margaret Murray Washington, as a houseguest. In 1915, Scarborough was an honorary pallbearer at Washington's funeral in Tuskegee. "We were," Scarborough said, "always good friends though our work lay in different lines."[65]

Scarborough "reviewed" the lives of two men he greatly respected and showed his admiration by writing their obituaries. Daniel Payne was the third person Scarborough lost among his circle of friends in 1893. Upon his death toward the end of the year, Scarborough exclaimed with grief, "Death had shown its love for a shining mark in leveling his dart at these men."[66] Scarborough had known Payne since Scarborough's arrival at Wilberforce in 1877. "Daniel Payne's chosen work," Scarborough declared, "was Christian education for his race, his platform the Christian pulpit. As such he was a living example of the dignity and force of an educated ministry which he sought to obtain for his people."[67]

William Hayes Ward, meanwhile, was "one of the most vigorous defenders of black higher education."[68] He often used his position as editor of the *New York Independent*—a position he held from 1896 to 1913—to promote this end. Scarborough's own associations with Ward spanned three decades. Their friendship was "renewed" at Yale University in 1885. About that time, Ward was one of several men who interested Scarborough in joining the American Spelling Reform Association.[69] In later years, Ward participated in the activities that marked Scarborough's third commencement as president of Wilberforce, and he gave a lecture entitled "On Forces That Make for Civilization."[70] Ward was also a guest in Scarborough's home. Concerning this visit Scarborough wrote later, "I cannot forget Dr. Ward's observation after lecturing to our University. His eyesight was poor. He said I wish I could see more clearly, yet even my dim eyes saw a beautiful sight in that audience of youth of all shades of color."[71]

Scarborough found inspiration in the lives of men like Payne and Ward, and he studied the lives of people he admired with care. The first book Scarborough remembered buying was in fact a biography, the *Life and Services of Abraham Lincoln*. Scarborough considered this purchase to be "his first great book."[72] He was wide-eyed with curiosity about the lives of influential men, and the end of the Civil War brought him the freedom to read widely—a habit he never lost. Not long "after General Wilson made his headquarters in Macon," Scarborough's job in Burke's bookstore gave him the "opportunity to read" at will. The library at Oberlin was his "chief resort" during his under-graduate years and in later life his own collection of books, marked with his own bookplate, was a refuge for him.[73]

Richard Greener was the first black member of the American Philological Association. Over the years, he gave Scarborough advice and encouragement on the importance of Scarborough's philological work. Toward the end of Scarborough's presidency at Wilberforce, Greener wrote to him saying, "You have not only held a solid course and fought valiantly with pen and voice for our civil rights, but you have upheld the educational side in a royal manner."[74] Greener spoke at Wilberforce's commencement in 1917 and received an hon-orary degree.[75]

Frederick Douglass was a figure known to Scarborough from childhood and later became his friend. In 1888, Douglass asked Scarborough to come to Washington, D.C., to work on a political campaign.[76] In 1893 both men par-ticipated in the Columbian Exposition in Chicago. In 1895, shortly before Douglass died, Scarborough and his wife visited Cedar Hill, where they "were entertained most royally." Douglass "unbent from his dignity and played with gusto his violin to my wife's accompaniment."[77] An autographed copy of Scarborough's Greek textbook remains today in Douglass's library.[78]

Scarborough's article on Henry Ossawa (not Ossian) Tanner in the *Southern Workman* was one of the first written about Tanner, and it is regularly cited by scholars.[79] Solicited by an editor of the *Southern Workman* to write for the publication, Scarborough's contributions to the journal were made when "the journal began to publish book reviews, editorials on race relations and to take note of the work of important African American leaders."[80]

Scarborough's portraits of Alexander Pushkin, Alexandre Dumas, and Paul Lawrence Dunbar sprang from his interest in the literature written by men and women of African descent. Scarborough was not alone in this interest. Dudley Randall (1914–2000) translated one of Pushkin's poems, and Richard Wright (1908–1960) read Dumas. Scarborough's interest in Dunbar was more immediate, however; Dunbar was his contemporary and lived in Dayton, thirty-five miles from Wilberforce.

Theodore Roosevelt and Warren G. Harding were both Republicans and men whom Scarborough endorsed both in print and on the stump. Scarborough felt especially close to Harding and was in Marion, Ohio, when the news came to Harding of his election as president in 1921.[81] Later in Washington, D.C., at the end of a cabinet meeting, Harding "with his usual hearty manner" announced, "I want to introduce Dr. Scarborough to you. Here is a 100 percent American."[82]

Scarborough met Roosevelt in 1906 when a delegation of members from the American Philological Association was invited to meet the president in the Blue Room of the White House.[83] Although he was unhappy with Roosevelt's treatment of the African American soldiers during the Brownville incident in Texas during the same year, Scarborough remained loyal and visited the grave of Quentin Roosevelt (1897–1918) in the American Cemetery at Chateau Thierry in 1921.[84] In closing the penultimate chapter of his autobiography, entitled "Looking Backward and Forward," Scarborough used Roosevelt's declaration, "Laws must be so framed and so administered as to secure justice for all alike, a square deal for every man," to sum up his own hopes for racial parity in the coming years.[85]

It was travel that kept Scarborough up-to-date, in the know, and full of enthusiasm. He wrote "I must have inherited from my father a love for railroad cars and travel which has remained with me through life."[86] His work giving invited lectures as a scholar, carrying out business for Wilberforce University or the A.M.E. Church, and on behalf of the Republican Party kept him on the road. Scarborough traveled frequently to Philadelphia, New York, and Washington, D.C., among many other East Coast cities. On a few occasions he went west to cities such as Kansas City, St. Louis, Chicago, San Francisco, and Los Angeles.[87]

Scarborough's early travel narratives were educational. He shared with the readers of the *Christian Recorder* the beauties of viewing ancient artifacts at the Metropolitan Museum of Art and let them have an inside look into the world of classicists at meetings of the American Philological Association at Ithaca, New York, and at Williamstown, Massachusetts.[88]

In later years, during the summers of 1901, 1911, and 1921, Scarborough made three voyages to England and the Continent, his wife accompanying him on the first two. The voyages were significant to him, and he included a description of all three in his autobiography. He published two articles in the *Voice of the Negro* about his first trip overseas, and he reworked these materials for his memoirs, which were prepared nearly two decades later.[89]

Scarborough's travels were an integral part of a life-long process of self-education and self-improvement. From the start of his career, Scarborough felt the need to broaden his sphere of activity and engage with the larger world on issues of scholarship, curriculum, and educational theory for himself and for his pupils.[90] His travels were an integral part of this process. He worked within his immediate community at Wilberforce, maintaining constant communication with students and faculty there as well as with those at other institutions.[91] His interest in education included a consistent effort to keep up with trends among white educators at all levels. At one point in the mid-1880s he considered becoming a superintendent of the public school system in Brooklyn, New York.[92]

The title of Scarborough's 1886 article "The New College Fetich," an article that showed how harmful the new elective system was to the entrenched classical curriculum, was Scarborough's nod to Charles Francis Adams Jr.'s 1883 Phi Beta Kappa lecture at Harvard University, "A College Fetich," which called for the elimination of Greek from the college requirements. Scarborough's references in his 1903 pamphlet "The Educated Negro and His Mission" to sentiments expressed by James B. Angell, the third president of the University of Michigan, as well as the quotations that Scarborough took from *The Real College* by Guy Potter Benton, twice president of Miami University, provide evidence that he was well read in discussions about education.[93]

For Scarborough there was a moral imperative underlying all systems of education: to develop students of good character who had the strength of mind to apply themselves even in the face of obstacles. Education was not to be pursued in selfish isolation; it meant uplifting the race and leading by example. In this belief Scarborough followed Cato the Elder's oft-quoted maxim about *vir bonus dicendi peritus*, "a good man skilled in speaking."[94] The acquisition of a single skill or trade must be balanced with the higher learning that the liberal arts provide.

During his lifetime Scarborough saw schools and programs that supported industrial education and manual training set up side by side with the classically based liberal arts systems. In African American communities these programs were patterned on the Hampton-Tuskegee model begun in 1868 at the Hampton Institute in Hampton, Virginia, by its founder, Union officer Samuel C. Armstrong. Booker T. Washington, who became Hampton's most famous graduate, later put the principles of his mentor Armstrong into action at his own school, the Tuskegee Institute, which began in 1881 in Tuskegee, Alabama.

The Hampton-Tuskegee Model was criticized, however, for catering to the "needs and interests of the South's dominant white class" and for having educational goals that supported a "racially qualified form of class subordination"—subordination that resulted, in the words of Monroe Trotter, in "the relegating of a race to serfdom."[95] Although Scarborough opposed these one-sided programs of industrial training and saw "the dangers of this over emphasis on industrial training to the exclusion of culture and higher training," he was interested in the activities at Hampton for most of his life.[96]

Scarborough considered himself one of Armstrong's friends, and he mentioned Armstrong's death in his memoirs.[97] He also admired Robert C. Ogden, one of the school's cofounders and a lifelong supporter.[98] Scarborough sent Ogden a copy of his interpretation of Aristophanes' comedy *The Birds* and was invited at different points by both Armstrong and Ogden to visit and lecture at Hampton.[99] Scarborough made his first trip there in 1889, and thereafter he "was a frequent and welcome visitor to the summer conferences instituted by [Armstrong] to talk with the people, not to them."[100] The school's official publication, *Southern Workman* (1872–1939), which attracted contributors like Scarborough, is considered today to be "an invaluable repository of over half a century of post-bellum African American educational and cultural history."[101]

Scarborough participated in a number of Hampton's summer conferences where the discussions about literature, education and current events were as valuable as the papers that stimulated them. His interest in language, includ-

ing folklore, dialect, and comparative studies, as well as their pedagogy anticipated the work of later African American scholars. He was a pioneer in his
quest for professionalization. In 1884 he became the first black member of the
Modern Language Association (MLA). Two years earlier, in 1882, he had
become the third black member of the American Philological Association.

Decades before the birth of Lorenzo Dow Turner, who began the serious
study of Africanisms in Gullah dialect during the 1930s, Scarborough suggested that young men of African descent could apply their training in classics to the study of African linguistics.[102] In 1924, at an event held in his
honor at the New York Public Library's 135th Street branch, Scarborough
called for the creation of a fund "for the purpose of sending to Africa ten of
our best trained young men."[103]

His interest in Haitian language and dialect led Scarborough to try—on
three different occasions—to obtain a diplomatic appointment there. His wife
shared his interest, and she began a blank-verse translation of Alphonse
Lamartine's drama *Toussaint L'Ouverture* in 1881. She also contributed to the
studies that Scarborough made during 1898–1899 of the characterization of
Iphigenia in the plays of Euripides, Racine, and Goethe by translating Racine
for him.[104]

In the late 1880s, Scarborough was invited by William D. Whitney, professor of linguistics and Oriental languages at Yale University, and by Francis A.
March, professor of English at Lafayette College—who "were strict advocates
of phonetic spelling"—to join the American Spelling Reform Association.
But Scarborough "was not as radical as they," and felt that "an extreme position on the subject would be detrimental to the understanding of the origin of
many words that had important etymological relations."[105] March, who was
directing the team of volunteer readers for the *Oxford English Dictionary* in
the United States, also asked Scarborough "to contribute and to offer suggestions in changes of forms of words."[106]

In the final decade of his life, Scarborough became interested in Japan and
joined the Japan Society.[107] As his health broke down, he chose a word from
Japanese that he thought would help his wife to remain calm after his death.
He told her to behave like an *etsu-bo* and mimic the behavior of young
Japanese warriors who upheld the "Samurai ideals of courage, endurance, and
heroism expected of a boy."[108]

But it was the study of Greek and Latin that Scarborough most enjoyed
and it was during the years of Scarborough's greatest activity that classical
studies in the United States really began. As Ward W. Briggs Jr. has observed,
"the outcome of the Civil War was critical to the creation of American classical scholarship."[109] For it was the former Confederate soldier-scholar Basil
Lanneau Gildersleeve to whom credit is given for making classical studies a
serious national field of study in the United States. This began after he left
the University of Virginia for Johns Hopkins University in 1876.[110]
According to Briggs, "If the South had won, Gildersleeve (and equally terri-
torial New Englanders) never would have thought nationally; he would not
have considered how the American temperament (as opposed to the

Southern) had particular advantages for classical study; he would not have been inclined to make an inclusive national journal of philology [namely, the *American Journal of Philology*] nor consider himself an American representative to Europeans."[111]

For African Americans, the defeat of the Confederacy gave newly freed men and women like Scarborough their first opportunity to study classical languages overtly and without fear of legal reprisal. In the immediate postwar era, the curriculum that black people everywhere embraced in eager pursuit of higher learning was the classically based liberal arts curriculum. As James D. Anderson has pointed out, "Black leaders did not view their adoption of the classical liberal arts curriculum or its philosophical foundations as mere imitations of white schooling. Indeed they knew many whites who had no schooling at all. Rather, they saw this curriculum as providing access to the best intellectual traditions of their era and the best means to understanding their own historical development and sociological uniqueness."[112]

Scarborough, like so many others of his generation, leapt at the new educational opportunities. But he and other intellectuals, both black and white, were well aware that many people had doubts about whether a black person could, or even should, study Greek and Latin, the languages at the core of the liberal arts curriculum.[113] As an adult, Scarborough followed a particular interest in the Greek historian Thucydides, an interest developed during his college years.[114] He published his studies in journals read by professional classicists and by educated people of African descent.[115] Scarborough's work in classics showed post–Civil War America and the world what could be achieved.

There was no time in Scarborough's life in which political matters did not affect him in a direct and personal way. As a child during the Civil War, he learned that "Negro human life was cheap," and that "colored boys were always in danger when found on the streets."[116] As he "passed into manhood," he understood that he had "been born into a struggle upward like all" of his "color." This was the epic struggle to gain the civil, social, and political rights of full citizenship.[117]

Scarborough contributed in one way or another to every advancement that African Americans made across the color line during this period. He made progress intellectually by becoming the first truly professional classicist of African descent, and he brought distinction to the educational mission of the A.M.E. Church. He broke new ground socially and racially through his happy marriage to Sarah Cordelia Bierce, a woman of European descent. He moved the political agenda forward by helping Benjamin Arnett abolish Ohio's Black Laws in 1887 and by responding to Frederick Douglass's personal request for assistance a decade later on a campaign in Washington, D.C.[118] Thereafter Scarborough worked tirelessly on behalf of the Republican Party.

For half a century Scarborough commented on a broad range of subjects. As a spokesman to and for his fellow African Americans, he found himself at times in the center of controversy. This happened occasionally by choice, but it was more often the result of a chance event. In 1875, shortly after earning his bachelor's degree at Oberlin College, Scarborough stopped at Princeton to visit his friend and fellow Oberlin graduate Mathew Anderson, who was then a student at the Princeton Theological Seminary. Scarborough's "arrival created some anxiety as well as curiosity on the part of Princeton officials" because "no Negro had ever entered the college proper." And although Scarborough was only "reconnoitering," it was "rumored" that he "had come to take postgraduate work."[119] Later, in 1891, Scarborough encountered a "small cyclone of controversy and of unexpected publicity" when his Oberlin classmate W. H. Tibbals decided to nominate him for membership in the Western Authors and Artists Club in Kansas City in order "to test the club."[120] After Scarborough was rejected amid charges of racism, the incident was discussed in a number of newspapers. And in the early 1920s, at an oyster dinner sponsored by the Bank of Southampton in Virginia, Scarborough gave a fifteen-minute speech to a racially mixed audience. After the speech he received word of what he called a "doubtful compliment" when a fellow African American reported one official's reaction: "He is no Negro. He is a white man with a dark skin."[121] Such racialized controversy threatened to destroy even his domestic life, as happened in 1913 when a bill to forbid mixed marriages was presented to the Ohio state legislature.[122] Had the bill passed, Scarborough's marriage—the vows of which had been taken more than thirty years before in New York City—would have been declared illegal.

In June 1920, Scarborough stepped down as president of Wilberforce University. The plans of Bishop Joshua H. Jones—who was ambitious for himself and for his son, Gilbert, to control the administration of Wilberforce held no place for Scarborough. So instead, Scarborough devoted several months to Harding's campaign for president and then took a trip overseas. Upon his return at the end of October 1921, Scarborough was ready to go back to work, and he began to look for employment.[123] At one point, Mary McLeod Bethune thought that Scarborough could become "an executive secretary" of her school in Daytona, Florida, and locate "people who have money."[124]

Scarborough had all along held hope, however, that he would receive a political appointment from the Republicans as a reward for more than forty years of service to the party. In a series of letters to Senator Frank B. Willis, Scarborough asked for assistance. Willis acknowledged Scarborough's request by saying that he was "deeply appreciative of what you have done for the whole ticket in the main and myself in particular. You have been a loyal effective Republican and I trust that it may be found possible to recognize your services." Willis closed the letter by noting that "it would be personally gratifying to me if the matter could be arranged according to your liking."[125]

Scarborough hoped to be appointed Register of the Treasury. He told Willis that "my fate is in your hands and I am confident that you will take care of me."[126] In the same letter, Scarborough suggested that a diplomatic appointment to Haiti, which he had sought since Frederick Douglass resigned the post in 1891, would be an acceptable alternative.[127] But neither position was offered to Scarborough, and instead he received an appointment as an assistant in the Department of Agriculture. This was not what Scarborough had expected, and the salary was low as well. Nevertheless, he accepted the job and moved to Washington, D.C. He started work at once on a program to develop a farm bureau, and he submitted a nine-page plan of action on September 20, 1922.[128]

The job was not a good fit. Scarborough's supervisor told Willis in February 1923 that Scarborough was "a fine fellow but by training and experience of rather limited capacity for this sort of work."[129] In September 1923, Scarborough suggested to Willis that he might "render valuable service" to the Department of Education.[130] But it was no easy task to align the bureaucracy of the civil service system with particular acts of political patronage, and. there were also problems with the Democrats under Woodrow Wilson. Senator Simeon D. Fess from Yellow Springs, Ohio, expressed concern about Scarborough's situation. In a letter to Willis, Fess wrote that he thought Scarborough might find a suitable place in the Veterans Bureau, commenting that he was "considerably disturbed over [Scarborough's] situation."[131]

But nothing was changed, and Scarborough's job with the Department of Agriculture officially ended on December 31, 1923. He returned to his home in Ohio and began working occasionally for the Speakers Bureau of the Republican National Committee.[132] His political aspirations had come to an end.

In the 1970s, Wilhelmina S. Robinson, associate professor of history at Central State University in Wilberforce, observed that it was humiliating and unjust to offer a trained philologist—one who was also a seasoned university administrator—a low-ranking assistantship. She pointed out that "[t]he Republican party which Scarborough supported throughout his career could only compensate him for his loyalty with a position in the Agriculture Department upon his retirement from Wilberforce University."[133] "Disillusioned and disappointed over his assignment," observed Robinson, "Scarborough tackled [the job] with the best of his ability. Approaching the task with thoroughness . . . he gathered statistics touching on the life and problems of the Negro farmer. One of the major problems was finance, so he turned his attention to securing help from the Federal Farm Loan Bank. He wrote several articles on the subject of the Negro Farmer, but none of his proposals submitted to the Department of Agriculture was acted upon."[134]

Robinson concluded her essay by asserting that "[w]hat Scarborough had learned from his first encounter with the harshness of American politics in 1877 remained true throughout the long years of loyal support to the Republican party" and that "[m]any politicians who professed great love for the race and had made use of the Negro for their own personal aggrandizement in riches and power turned against him."[135]

Scarborough's job with the Department of Agriculture concluded with the death of Warren G. Harding in 1923. In early December Scarborough returned to Wilberforce having held, as he later observed "but two government positions in [his] life—one as postmaster at the beginning of [his] career and this one at the end."[136] Relaxing into an unaccustomed "quiet home life," Scarborough spent time reading, writing and lecturing.[137] He continued to consider the destiny of the "darker races" all over the globe and was following Gandhi's activities in India as well as the problems in the U.S. over the naturalization and citizenship of the Japanese.[138] In November 1924 he was honored with a reception at the 135th Street branch of the New York Public Library. Notables including Nicholas Murray Butler, Franz Boaz and Kelly Miller paid tribute to him.[139] In June 1925 he was one of fourteen alumni out of twenty-five still living who attended the Fiftieth Anniversary of the Oberlin College Class of 1875.[140] It was a turning point for Scarborough, one that reminded him of his mortality, and upon his return to Wilberforce he began "almost unconsciously" to "set [his] house in order."[141] He worked on his autobiography and assembled his philological papers for publication. The projects went unfinished, however. His autobiography, his studies in philology, as well as his manuscript "Questions on Latin Grammar," never left his desk. His health broke down completely and on September 9, 1926, attended by his wife, he died at home.

The community at Wilberforce mourned his loss. His body lay in state on campus in Galloway Hall. Obituary notices appeared across the country; the American Philological Association acknowledged his death; and his wife made plans for a commemorative volume to contain the many letters and telegrams of condolence that she had received.[142]

And then time stood still for Scarborough. His name fell into oblivion and the contributions made by this courageous black classicist and race leader to our nation's history were forgotten—until now when we can at long last count this American original among those "folks" admired by Langston Hughes "who left no buildings behind them—only a wind of words fanning the bright flame of the spirit down the dark lanes of time."[143]

Notes

1 *The Autobiography of William Sanders Scarborough: An American Journey from Slavery to Scholarship*, edited by Michele Valerie Ronnick (Detroit, Mich.: Wayne State University Press, 2005), pp. 24 and 27–28. This title is hereinafter abbreviated to *Autobiography*.

2 *Autobiography*, pp. 43–44.

3 *Autobiography*, pp. 46–54 and 308–311.

4 Michele Valerie Ronnick, "*First Lessons in Greek*: William Sanders Scarborough's Date with Destiny," *A.M.E. Church Review* 118 (October–November 2002): 41.

5 Reverend A. J. Kershaw, "The A.M.E. Church—Its Literature," *Christian Recorder*, May 20, 1886.

6 Kevin Boyle, *Arc of Justice* (New York: Holt, 2004), p. 75.

7 Michele Valerie Ronnick, "William Sanders Scarborough: The First African American Member of the Modern Language Association," *Publications of the Modern Language Association* 115, Special Millennial Edition (2000): 1787–1793. Under the leadership of Dolan Hubbard of Morgan State University, the Modern Language Association estab-

lished a new book award called the William Sanders Scarborough Prize, of $1,000.

8 *Autobiography*, p. 240.

9 *Autobiography*, pp. 134, 157–158, 162–163, 207, and 301.

10 On the NAACP's work against restrictive covenants, see Boyle, *Arc of Justice*, pp. 202–205 and 307–309.

11 "Black, White and Brown," *New York Times Book Review*, May 16, 2004, p. 35.

12 Cicero, *Paradoxa Stoicorum*, 5.

13 Among other items not included in this compilation are these fourteen articles from the *Christian Recorder*: (1–4) "Sketches from Natural History," published in four parts on November 23, 1876, December 28, 1876, January 11, 1877, and March 1, 1877; (5) "A Perambulation around Columbus, Ga.," concerning Elder Gaines, published on April 19, 1877; (6–7) "Grandeur of Character," a two-part article on abstinence from alcohol, food, and tobacco, published on April 26, 1877, and August 16, 1877; (8) "Our Disadvantages," containing in its body a short letter from Scarborough to Benjamin Tucker Tanner, published on August 30, 1877; (9) "The Exodus," a brief response by Scarborough to an attack on him by a man who identified himself as "Rev. B.F.P.," published on September 6, 1877; (10) "Sermons by Rev. Drs. Smith and Waldron," published on October 11, 1877; (11) "Odds and Ends," concerning the start of the new school year, published on October 24, 1877; (12) "The Late Rt. Rev. Bishop W. F. Dickerson, D.D.," an obituary on the man who had officiated at Scarborough's wedding on August 2, 1881, in New York, published on January 29, 1885; (13) "Money as a Factor in Business," a response to an article by William E. Mathews in the *A.M.E. Church Review*, published August 20, 1885; and (14) "A.M.E. Review Begins," concerning the founding of the *Review* the year before, published on September 24, 1885.

14 *Autobiography*, p. 32.

15 *Autobiography*, p. 33.

16 *Autobiography*, p. 35.

17 *Autobiography*, p. 38.

18 *Autobiography*, p. 42–43.

19 *Autobiography*, pp. 248–250. See also Scarborough's *A Tribute to Colonel Young* (Philadelphia: A.M.E. Book Concern, 1922).

20 *Autobiography*, pp. 253–256.

21 *Autobiography*, p. 327.

22 *Wilberforce in the War* (Xenia, Ohio: Eckerle Printing, 1918). See also *Autobiography*, p. 265.

23 *Autobiography*, p. 256. The essay "Race Riots and Their Remedy" is included in this compilation.

24 *Autobiography*, p. 35.

25 "Closing Exercises," *Macon Telegraph*, June 16, 1866. See also *Autobiography*, p. 39.

26 *Autobiography*, p. 54.

27 *Autobiography*, pp. 72–73.

28 On the verso of page 3 in box 1 of the William Sanders Scarborough (WSS) Papers

at the Rembert E. Stokes Library, Wilberforce University, Box 1, is a list of lectures given at Wilberforce University. See also the text of nine other lectures in "Some Lectures," in box 5.

29 WSS Scrapbook, Emory University Archives, p. 59.

30 WSS Scrapbook, Emory University Archives, "The True Aim of Education," p. 172; "The Coming Crucial Years," p. 83; "Racial Responsibility," lecture ticket stub, inside front board; "Self-Respect and Self-Reliance," p. 108. "Some Lectures," in box 5 of the WSS Papers at the Rembert E. Stokes Library, Wilberforce University, contains a fifteen-page typed draft of "Racial Responsibility." See also *Autobiography*, pp. 300 and 393, note 12.

31 Private collection of Sheila Gregory Thomas, Washington, D.C.

32 For more on the American Negro Academy, see "News from Bishops' Council," WSS Scrapbook, Emory University Archives, p. 145, and *Autobiography*, pp. 152–153. The *Cleveland Gazette* article "Professor Scarborough on Colored Democrats" (June 21, 1884) is an excerpt from Scarborough's speech "Our Political Status," given on April 29, 1884, which is included in this compilation.

33 Private conversation by telephone. For an account of Gibson's own distinguished career see Truman Kella Gibson Jr., *Knocking Down Barriers: My Fight for Black America* (Evanston, Ill.: Northwestern University Press, 2005).

34 *Autobiography*, p. 79.

35 "Journalism and Colored Journalists, No. III," *People's Advocate*, February 4, 1882. This was the third part of a series called "The Spirit of the Colored Press." Scarborough may have been thinking of John W. Cromwell, the editor of the *People's Advocate*, which was published in Washington, D.C., and ran from 1876 to 1886. Cromwell fought with his rival William Calvin Chase, the editor of the *Washington Bee*, over political matters. An unflattering article in the *People's Advocate* about Grover Cleveland was brought to Cleveland's attention and led to the end of the *People's Advocate*. See Armistead S. Pride and Clint C. Wilson II, *A History of the Black Press* (Washington, D.C.: Howard University Press, 1997), p. 100.

36 "Opinion of W. S. Scarborough," in I. Garland Penn, *The Afro-American Press and Its Editors* (Springfield, Mass.: Willey, 1891), p. 431.

37 WSS Scrapbook, Emory University Archives, p. 119.

38 See *Autobiography*, pp. 112–113 and note 53.

39 *Autobiography*, p. 115. Mrs. Scarborough wrote many articles for popular magazines such as *Youth's Companion* and *Lady's Home Journal*. Her essays also appeared in the *Christian Recorder* and the *A.M.E. Church Review*. For more, see the William Sanders and Sarah Cordelia B. Scarborough papers at the Western Reserve Historical Society.

40 WSS Scrapbook, Emory University Archives, p. 33.

41 His name first appears in a newspaper article published in the *Macon Telegraph* on June 16, 1866. Entitled "Closing Exercises," the article describes ceremonies at his high school graduation. See also *Autobiography*, p. 39.

42 *Autobiography*, p. 158.

43 WSS Scrapbook, Emory University Archives, p. 90.

44 *Autobiography*, p. 73.

45 *Autobiography*, p. 319. See also Scarborough's sketch of the editor of the *Cleveland Gazette*, "Hon. H. C. Smith," *The Monthly Review*, Christmas number, 1895, pp. 96–99.

46 Michele Valerie Ronnick, "*First Lessons in Greek*: William Sanders Scarborough's Date with Destiny," *A.M.E. Church Review* 118 (October–November 2002): 41.

47 George A. Sewell and Cornelius Throup, *Morris Brown College: The First Hundred Years* (Atlanta: Morris Brown College, 1981), pp. 20–21.

48 *Autobiography*, p. 197.

49 *Autobiography*, p. 112.

50 *Autobiography*, pp. 92–93.

51 *Autobiography*, p. 357, note 5. See also J. W. Gibson and W. H. Crogman, *Progress of a Race* (Napierville Ill.: Nichols, 1929), pp. 540–541.

52 *Autobiography*, pp. 165–166. The painting's location today is not known.

53 R. R. Wright Jr., editor, *Centennial Encyclopedia of the African Methodist Episcopal Church* (Philadelphia: Book Concern of the A.M.E. Church, 1916), pp. 69–70.

54 R. R. Wright Jr., editor, *Centennial Encyclopedia of the African Methodist Episcopal Church*, p. 220.

55 Albert G. Miller, *Elevating the Race* (Knoxville: University of Tennessee Press, 2003), p. 3.

56 "Steward, Theophilus G.," *Dictionary of American Negro Biography*, edited by Rayford W. Logan and Michael R. Winston (New York: Norton, 1982), pp. 570–571.

57 *Autobiography*, p. 381, note 10, and p. 378, note 4.

58 *Autobiography*, p. 63.

59 *Autobiography*, pp. 115 and 70–71.

60 *Autobiography*, pp. 230–231.

61 George A. Sewell and Cornelius Throup, *Morris Brown College: The First Hundred Years* (Atlanta: Morris Brown College, 1981), p. 51.

62 Ward W. Briggs Jr., "Hale, William Gardner," *Biographical Dictionary of Northern American Classicists*, edited by Ward W. Briggs Jr. (Westport, Conn.: Greenwood Press, 1994), p. 251.

63 *Autobiography*, p. 364, note 11.

64 *Autobiography*, pp. 51 and 230. Scarborough also wrote an endorsement at the request of the publisher for Washington's book *My Life and Work*. See the WSS Scrapbook at the Emory University Archives, p. 117.

65 *Autobiography*, p. 241.

66 *Autobiography*, p. 132. Scarborough wrote at least two other obituaries of Payne: "The Late Daniel A. Payne, D.D.," *Independent*, December 28, 1893, pp. 5–6; and "The Late Bishop Daniel A. Payne, D.D.," *Leslie's Weekly*, January 11, 1894, p. 23.

67 *Autobiography*, p. 131.

68 James D. Anderson, *The Education of Blacks in the South, 1860–1935* (Chapel Hill: University of North Carolina Press, 1988), p. 68.

69 *Autobiography*, pp. 93 and 95.

70 *Autobiography*, p. 213.

71 *Autobiography*, p. 213.

72 *Autobiography*, p. 36. Scarborough's copy of the *Life and Services of Abrahman Lincoln* has not been located, nor has *The History of the Great Rebellion* (1866), which was donated by Sarah A. Grant, Mrs. Scarborough's great-great-granddaughter, to the Sidney Lanier Cottage in Macon, Georgia, in the mid-1980s. It bore the inscription, "W. S. Scarborough, Macon, Ga., bought by his father for him during his absence," and the date "Oct. 1. 1870." Another volume, *A History of England* (1827), was located by Muriel McDowell Jackson, archivist at the Washington Memorial Library in Macon, Georgia. It bears three signatures made by Scarborough in pencil, as well as the date November 8, 1864.

73 *Autobiography*, pp. 34, 49 and 312.

74 *Autobiography*, p. 321.

75 *Autobiography*, p. 396, note 8. See also Michael R. Mounter, "Richard Theodore Greener: The Idealist, Statesman, Scholar, and South Carolinian," PhD dissertation (2002), University of South Carolina(UMI Dissertation Abstract #3052060), p. 521.

76 *Autobiography*, p. 100.

77 *Autobiography*, p. 143.

78 See Catalogue no. 3456 in William L. Petrie and Douglas E. Stover, *Bibliography of the Frederick Douglass Library at Cedar Hill* (Fort Washington, Md.: Silesia, 1995), p. 59.

79 See, for example, Dewey Mosby, *Henry Ossawa Tanner* (New York: Rizzoli, 1991), which cites the article on pages 125, 132, 146, 151, 152, and 290. The original article included several photographs of Tanner's paintings, and an image of the studio's interior, but these have been left out of this compilation.

80 *Autobiography*, p. 157. The editorial staff at the time included H. B. Frissell, Helen W. Ludlow, J. E. Davis, and William L. Brown, and it is not known which of them asked Scarborough to write. *The Southern Workman* was begun in 1872 by Samuel C. Armstrong, the founder of the Hampton Institute, and.it ran until 1939. See Daniel J. Royer, "Southern Workman, The," *The Oxford Companion to African American Literature*, edited by William Andrews, F. S. Foster, and Trudier Harris (New York: Oxford University Press, 1997), p. 683.

81 *Autobiography*, p. 280.

82 *Autobiography*, p. 303.

83 *Autobiography*, p. 193.

84 *Autobiography*, pp. 190–191, 204, and 286.

85 *Autobiography*, p. 328.

86 *Autobiography*, p. 28.

87 *Autobiography*, pp. 123, 228, 240, and 242.

88 See "A Summer Outing: American Philological Association," *Christian Recorder*, August 23, 1894.

89 *Autobiography*, pp. 164–185, 214–224, and 282–291. Everything from the two articles is reworked except a single paragraph from"In and about Edinburgh," which appears verba-

tim on pp. 181–182 of the Autobiography. See "From the Thames to the Tiber," *Voice of the Negro* 1, no.10 (1904): 466–475, and "In and Around Edinburgh," *Voice of the Negro* 2, no. 2 (1905): 548–555.

90 *Autobiography*, pp. 69–70.

91 For example, at Scarborough's invitation a student from Lincoln University attended the lecture he gave at the American Philological Association's meeting at the University of Virginia in 1892. See *Autobiography*, p. 121. See also Scarborough's article "The College as a Source of Culture," *Sodalian* 4, no. 1 October 1909): 3–7.

92 *Autobiography*, p. 84.

93 *Autobiography*, pp. 226–227 and p. 380, note 1.

94 Mentioned by Seneca and Quintilian, and later by others such as Augustine and Juan Vives.

95 James D. Anderson, *The Education of Blacks in the South, 1860–1935* (Chapel Hill: University of North Carolina Press, 1988), pp. 31, 82, and 105.

96 *Autobiography*, p. 103.

97 *Autobiography*, p. 132.

98 *Autobiography*, p. 107.

99 Autobiography, pp. 143, 145–146, and 159–160. See also *The Birds of Aristophanes: A Theory of Interpretation* (Boston: Cushing, 1886).

100 *Autobiography*, pp. 105 and 107.

101 Daniel J. Royer, "Southern Workman, The," *The Oxford Companion to African American Literature*, edited by William Andrews, F. S. Foster, and Trudier Harris (New York: Oxford University Press, 1997), p. 683.

102 *Autobiography*, p. 84 and p. 368, note 16.

103 *Autobiography*, p. 307.

104 *Autobiography*, p. 154. See also Scarborough's "One Heroine—Three Poets, Part I," *Education* 19 (December 1898): 213–221, and "One Heroine—Three Poets, Part II," *Education* 19 (January 1899): 285–293.

105 *Autobiography*, pp. 95 and 82.

106 *Autobiography*, p. 95.

107 *Autobiography*, p. 305 and WSS Scrapbook, Emory University Archives, pp. 76 and 201.

108 *Autobiography*, p. 314.

109 Ward W. Briggs Jr., personal communication on January 16, 2006

110 Ward W. Briggs Jr., "Gildersleeve, Basil Lanneau," *Biographical Dictionary of North American Classicists*, edited by Ward W. Briggs Jr. (Westport, Conn.: Greenwood Press, 1994), p. 215.

111 Ward W. Briggs Jr., personal communication on January 16, 2006.

112 James D. Anderson, *The Education of Blacks in the South, 1860–1935* (Chapel Hill: University of North Carolina Press, 1988), pp. 28–29.

113 *Autobiography*, p. 321. Scarborough was also trained in New Testament Greek. See his "The Greek of the New Testament," *A.M.E. Church Review* 1 (1884): 37–45.

114 *Autobiography*, pp. 50, 155, 161, and 192.

115 Besides the twenty-one items printed in this compilation, see also "Fatalism in Homer and Virgil," *Transactions of the American Philological Association* 16 (July 1885): xxxvi–xxxvii; "The Birds of Aristophanes and a Theory of Interpretation," *Transactions of the American Philological Association* 17 (July 1886): vii; *The Birds of Aristophanes: A Theory of Interpretation* (Boston: Cushing, 1886; a major work); "Notes on Andocides," *Transactions of the American Philological Association* 20 (July 1889): v–vi; "The Chronological Order of Plato's Dialogues," *Transactions of the American Philological Association* 23 (July 1892): vi–viii; and "The Roman Coena," *A.M.E. Church Review* 10 (1894): 348–357.

116 *Autobiography*, p. 31.

117 *Autobiography*, p. 26.

118 *Autobiography*, pp. 64 and 100.

119 *Autobiography*, p. 56.

120 *Autobiography*, pp. 111. For newspapers clippings about this, see the WSS Scrapbook, Emory University Archives, pp. 163–165.

121 *Autobiography*, p. 296.

122 "Intermarriage Bill Would Break Up Homes," *New York Age*, March 13, 1913. See also "That Separate Marriage Bill," WSS Scrapbook, Emory University Archives, p. 127.

123 See *Autobiography*, pp. 280–291.

124 July 9, 1920, letter from Bethune to Scarborough, in box 3 (Correspondence, Democracy and Citizenship) of the WSS Papers at the Rembert E. Stokes Library, Wilberforce University.

125 November 8, 1920, letter from Willis to Scarborough, in box 37, folder 5, of the Frank B. Willis Papers at the Ohio Historical Society.

126 March 30, 1921, letter from Scarborough to Willis, in box 37, folder 5, of the Frank B. Willis Papers at the Ohio Historical Society.

127 March 31, 1921, letter from Scarborough to Willis, in box 37, folder 5, of the Frank B. Willis Papers at the Ohio Historical Society. Concerning Scarborough's interest in Haiti, see *Autobiography*, pp. 105–107 and 322.

128 September 20, 1922, letter from Scarborough to the chief of the Bureau of Land Economics, forwarded to Willis on January 1, 1923; box 37, folder 5, of the Frank B. Willis Papers at the Ohio Historical Society.

129 February 3, 1923, letter from Scarborough to Willis, in box 37, folder 5, of the Frank B. Willis Papers at the Ohio Historical Society.

130 September 28, 1923, letter from Scarborough to Willis, in box 37, folder 5, of the Frank B. Willis Papers at the Ohio Historical Society.

131 September 15, 1923, letter from Fess to Willis, in box 37, folder 5, of the Frank B. Willis Papers at the Ohio Historical Society..

132 Letters from Everett Sanders to Scarborough, dated September 8, 1924, and September 20, 1924, in box 37, folder 5, of the Frank B. Willis Papers at the Ohio Historical Society. Scarborough earned an honorarium of $50 per week. Roscoe Simmons called the honorarium a "meager sum which I know is far below the actual value of your

services." See the September 10, 1924, letter from Roscoe Simmons to Scarborough, in box 37, folder 5, of the Frank B. Willis Papers at the Ohio Historical Society.

133 Wilhelmina S. Robinson, "William Sanders Scarborough: Scholar and Disillusioned Politician, 1852–1926," WSS Papers, Ohio Historical Society, PA box 358, folder 26, p. 3.

134 Wilhelmina S. Robinson, "William Sanders Scarborough: Scholar and Disillusioned Politician, 1852–1926," p. 16.

135 Wilhelmina S. Robinson, "William Sanders Scarborough: Scholar and Disillusioned Politician, 1852–1926," p. 17. For Scarborough's view of this period see *Autobiograhy,* pp. 292–298 and 304. For more of Scarborough's work on black farmers see "The Negro Farmer in the South," *Current History* 21 (January 1925): 565–569, *Tenancy and Ownership among Negro Farmers in Southampton, Virginia* (Washington, D.C.: U.S. Department of Agriculture, 1926), and "The Negro Farmer's Progress in Virginia," *Current History* 25 (December 1926): 384–387, which was published posthumously.

136 *Autobiography,* p. 304.

137 *Autobiography,* p. 304.

138 *Autobiography,* p. 304–305.

139 *Autobiography,* p. 306–307.

140 *Autobiography,* p. 308–309.

141 *Autobiography,* p. 311.

142 *Autobiography,* p. 399, notes 4 and 6.

143 Langston Hughes, *The Big Sea* (New York: Hill and Wang, 1993), p. 310.

Military

The Negro as an Army Officer

Christian Register, August 18, 1898, pp. 933–934.

Among the many important questions that have arisen as a result of our war with Spain, the one that heads this brief article has attracted its share of attention. That negro regiments should be officered by men of their own color is affirmed by many, but denied by others.

As a matter of equity, there is but one side: public sentiment presents two. Equity should determine our action in all matters of public policy. It is upon this principle that we should act.

If the negro can enlist as a private in the regular service, there is no reason why he should not be promoted, provided he fulfils the conditions of promotion. If he is worthy and capable, there is no just cause why he should not, as any other man in the same situation, be commissioned as an officer over men of his own color.

In the Revolutionary War and in subsequent wars he evinced courage, and demonstrated his patriotism to a marvellous degree. In our Civil War he proved his efficiency beyond question. In the present crises he exhibits the same interest, the same zeal, the same enthusiasm, the same courage and love of country that characterized him on previous occasions.

Under trained leaders of his own race he will, no doubt, give us valiant service as he would under trained leaders of any other race. Then, too, the appointment of such men would be an inspiration to the race,—an acknowledgment of capability and a recognition of merit.

Our plea is for justice. Show the colored man that there is something to aspire to, even in a military capacity, and I have no doubt that he will show himself equal to the emergency. His fighting qualities are well known. We need to point only to Fort Wagner, Milliken's Bend, Port Hudson, Fort Pillow, and other historic spots where the negro's blood flowed freely in his country's defence.

There is a strong probability that the army of occupation of the Philippine Islands, and other Spanish possessions that will fall into our hands, will be largely made up of negro immunes, who are regarded as better adopted to the tropical climate, and who are less liable to attack by disease and the fevers of these warm countries. Under gallant leaders of their own race the difficulties that might otherwise be encountered are materially lessened.

General Thomas Morgan of New York states the case clearly and correctly when he says:—

"The war with Spain is primarily and professedly a humanitarian crusade, undertaken for the redressing of the wrongs of the Cubans, multitudes of whom are negroes. The republic can hardly afford to incur the sharp criticism of inconsistency by inflicting a wrong upon its own soldiers and perpetuating in its own army an insidious discrimination against brave men while going out ostensibly in the rights of others. I think the keenest thrust which has been made against the republic since it entered upon this new career of humanitarian has been that of the Spanish caricaturists, who represent us as rushing off to liberate negroes in Cuba while lynching negroes at home. This is a real blot upon our national life which ought to be eradicated."[1]

Nothing that the writer may say can add to the force and logic of these words.

Note

1 [Thomas Jefferson Morgan (1839–1902), Indian Commissioner from 1889 to 1893, led African American troops during the Civil War. See his defense of African American rights, *The Negro in America and the Ideal American Republic* (Philadelphia: American Baptist Society, 1898).]

From Spade to Sword

Christian Register, February 23, 1899, pp. 207–208.

"In 1860," says Williams in his History of the Negro Race in America,[1] "there were in the 15 slaveholding States 3,950,000 slaves and 251,000 free persons," and in the 19 non-slave-holding States and 7 Territories, including the District of Columbia, "237,383 free persons of color, making a total of 4,438,283," or thereabouts, as the negro population, in the United States, at the beginning of the Civil War.

When the first call for troops came in 1861, it was thoroughly understood that "the North counted the negro on the outside of the issue," and, as far as his services being required, this state of affairs continued for some time, though there was scarcely a "city in the North from New York to San Francisco," says the same authority, "whose colored residents did not speedily offer their services to the States to aid in suppressing the Rebellion. But everywhere as promptly were their services declined."

Though the nation, for some time, stubbornly refused to admit that slavery was the cause of that war, the slave had to be considered. He was here, there, and everywhere, and something had to be done. The Confederates, in reality, cut the Gordian knot of the question as to what to do with him by setting him to work on rebel fortifications. Gen. [Benjamin] Butler, seeing this, seized upon the opportunity, coined the new word "contraband," and followed this example by putting to work all who came into his lines. This was in May, 1861. It was hardly the camel's head; but it was, at least, the nose that had entered, for in October of the same year the shovel and spade were exchanged for "fatigue duty," when the negro was employed as teamsters, and in the Quarter-master's Department, where he was *paid* and *put in uniform*. He had to prove himself worthy of promotion, however, to bear arms on the Union side, though records show that from the "earliest dawn of the war the rebel authorities did not frown upon the action of local authorities in placing arms into the hands of free negroes." So to the Confederates is also due the recognition of the "first step in the direction of the military employment of negroes as soldiers."

In the spring of 1862, Gen. [David] Hunter surprised the government by directing the organization of a regiment of blacks in South Carolina, under white officers, when the Secretary of War issued an order for the acceptation of all "loyal persons" to aid in defence of the Union. An extended correspondence was carried on over the matter of this interpretation, and there was a flutter among politicians and a buzz among army officers; but in the end the government "fathered the regiment," and the negro, slave, and freeman, was at last "in it." Other regiments followed, and the work of enlisting colored men continued, until by "December, 1863, there were 100,000 colored men in the service and about 50,000 armed and in the field." Finally, the negro was even *drafted* into service; and in 1865 one of the race was commissioned as major[2] while in some regiments the line officers were colored. A total of 200,000 men were at last enlisted.

Over thirty-five years later the war with Spain found the negro an integral part of the United States army forces, with about 3,100 men in four regiments,—two of infantry and two of cavalry. At once the negro militiamen from various States offered their services, and were accepted in large part. This time their patriotism and enthusiasm were not rebuked, nor their "interest declared insolence." These troops, in the regular army, were soon moved to the front, and helped bear the brunt of battle in Gen. [William Rufus] Shafter's command in Cuba. What they did is a matter of record to which the race can point with pride. What the New York *Times* once said of the negro at Port Hudson was repeated at Santiago,—"The deeds of heroism performed by these colored men were such as the proudest white men might emulate."

What has he gained in these years?

He went into the Civil War with a shovel as his sole equipment: he came out wearing the United States blue, adorned with chevrons, even in one case at least commissioned to wear epaulets and bear a sword. He went in not even owning himself: he came out a free man, receiving the wages for his work in his own hands. He went in a most uncertain quantity as to what soldierly characteristics he would develop, and with the press largely questioning the advisability of the step: he came out a hero, and the Republican press unanimous in its endorsement of him in his new rôle.

On the other hand, he went into the late war wearing both chevrons and epaulets: he comes out with promotions for bravery, and entire regiments officered by men of color, while, where he once had to depend upon white spiritual advisers, he has had from the first chaplains of his own race. He went into this war by the desire of the people generally; and he comes out with their heightened respect and gratitude and the indorsement of Congress, which places more men of the race in the field. He went in with the reputation gained at Wagner and Pillow and Milliken's Bend and Port Hudson: he comes out having fully sustained that reputation and added fresh laurels wherever he has been engaged. Where he was once shunned in the older days, he is now welcomed as a comrade. Enlisting just now, even by the side of those who once owned him, he has fought unquestioned by the white man's side in general. They have "drunk from the same canteen," borne each other from the field, vied with each other in deeds of daring, cheered each other on, saved each other's lives, and now give unstinted praise to each other's valor.

What rancor and prejudice may not the war have wiped out, notwithstanding the recent troubles in the South!

The negro's present situation, in view of all these facts, is by no means discouraging. Even the most pessimistic must admit this. It is to be regretted that the negro, as an officer, has not had the opportunity to demonstrate what he can do as a leader as well as one of the "led"; and it is the feeling that such deeds as were performed by these men around Santiago merit as much advancement as other deeds of heroism received, when performed by white soldiers. But, we repeat, these steps in advance are not discouraging to the race; and much may be gained still by the negro troops as a part of the army of occupation. Let them see to it that their conduct is mapped out along most exemplary lines. Let them take for their motto that of King George's Fifth Regiment of Dragoon-guards,—*Vestigia nulla retrorsum*,—considering any retreat from the honorable position gained before the world "pusillanimous and disgraceful." This will go a long distance toward proving to the world at large the negro's unquestionable right to all that the Fifteenth Amendment is supposed to imply in both letter and spirit, and toward further breaking down of that "unnatural bar of separation now existing in the army."

But, at any rate, to pass in less than four decades from the slave to the commander, from the ditch to the head of a regiment, from spade to sword, is no short step for any race.

Notes

1 [George Washington Williams, *History of the Negro Race in America*" (1882), part 7, chapter 14.]

2 Martin R. Delaney, who "received his commission as major Feb. 8, 1865."

Speeches

Our Political Status

a speech delivered on April 29, 1884, at the Colored Men's
Inter-state Conference, Pittsburgh, Pennsylvania, and printed at Xenia, Ohio,
by Torchlight Job Rooms.

MR. PRESIDENT AND FELLOW-CITIZENS:—I am before you to-day to present a
few thoughts on our political status. I come not in the interest of any party or
sect, but in behalf of the rights of the colored people of these United States,
which to me are of infinitely more importance than party or party organization.

As a race we have had an existence of a little more than two hundred
and sixty years in America, either as slaves or as free-men. From the time
the first Dutch vessel landed with its cargo of African slaves on the coast
of Virginia, negro slavery, negro oppression and negro degradation have
cursed the country. The old slave oligarchy, however, after the loss of hundreds of hundreds of precious lives and the expenditure of mints of money,
crumbled and fell, and it was hoped that the darkest days in our country's history had passed, and that a new era had dawned upon us. But
our hopes have not yet been realized. To-day there exist forms of servitude in the Southern States, ostracism and caste in our Northern States
that can only find a parallel in *ante-bellum* times.

The *Act* known as the Missouri Compromise, passed in 1820, showed that
the colored man had become an important factor in American politics, not
actively but passively. As years rolled on, and as the excitement grew in intensity, the philanthropic voices of Gerrit Smith, Wm. Lloyd Garrison, Wendell
Phillips, Charles Sumner, Frederick Douglass and others, were heard in
strong protest against oppression and loudly in favor of liberty and equality.
John Brown, whose body lies mouldering in the grave, while his great soul is
still marching on, died in behalf of the liberty of this same people with whom
we are identified. Surely we cannot remain quiet or inactive at a juncture like
this. Times demand counsel and concerted action on our part. Circumstances
demand that we rise up as one man and strike in behalf of a down-trodden
people. Will we do it? It remains for us to decide now what shall be done for
ourselves and for our country.

The first object to be secured among us is a more perfect unity and a better understanding as to what methods of procedure are best adapted to aid us in changing our present con[di]tion. The specific object of this Conference, I take it, is to promote the more effectually our general welfare; to devise ways and means by which our common interests may be the more sacredly guarded.

This is not a movement that should arouse suspicion, since all races and classes of citizens have had similar gatherings, for similar purposes. Indeed it would be strange, gentlemen, if under the circumstances, we were not moved to take some action in our own behalf. Our civil and political rights are withheld from us; our liberty is placed in jeopardy, and we as a race are ostracised and outraged. Justice is trampled under foot, in the face of the stern fact that the National safety lies in National justice, and that no government is safe that permits such outrages to escape punishment.

"So simple a thing as an unjust tax on tea precipitated the American Revolution. The outrage and inhumanity of slavery produced the greatest civil war in all history. Outrages now practiced upon the colored people of the South will produce like consequences if long tolerated."—*Ohio State Journal, December 26, 1883.*

I am not Jewish enough to advocate an eye for an eye or a tooth for a tooth, but I do insist upon sufficient harmony in our own divided ranks to demand, unitedly, protection, recognition and equality before the law.[1] It is gratifying to observe that after the Supreme Court of the United States has taken the pains to declare the Civil Rights Bill unconstitutional, the States are now beginning, though slowly, to take the matter in hand. This is a step in the right direction, and is the only way to wipe out speedily that *infamous* decision.

We are advised to wait and be patient. We have waited, and we have been patient; yea, more that this, we have, in a sense, prostrated ourselves at the feet of the government and remonstrated with it to give us our rights and protect us in the enjoyment of our freedom. What has been the result? Nothing as yet. In parts of the South the life of a negro is the least valuable of all living creatures. In Kentucky, one Thomas Crittenden killed a colored man for testifying to the truth.[2] In Georgia another was taken from his bed at midnight, tarred, feathered and mercilessly whipped because he dared to raise the wages of negroes by offering them $1.25 per diem, instead of the usual 50 cents, to help him finish a contract.

Negroes are shot down if they testify against white men, and are likewise shot down if they refuse to do so. If they attempt to assert their civil and political rights in any manly way, they are mobbed, butchered and killed. If they nominate or assist in nominating one of their own number for office, the cry is at once heard, "negroes are drawing the race issue."

The following, entitled "Short Staples to the Front," explains itself. It is from a Southern paper:

"A report was current on the street that the negr[o]es will hang out a candidate for mayor, either one of their own number or some white man pledged to run the city at their dictation. Of the two alternatives we prefer the former. Since the step has been taken, the white men of Athens (Ga.) should hold a public meeting and center upon some good man, requesting the other candidates to come down, which they would doubtless do under the circumstances. Now is as good a time as any to draw the race issue, since the negroes have set the example."

This is poor logic, and if true, every time a white man is nominated for an office, the race issue is likewise drawn. If the nomination of a negro man means a race issue, the nomination of a white man means the same, and we as colored citizens of this great Republic have the same ground that our white citizens have to rise up in opposition. The sooner this kind of argument is dispensed with, the better will it be for all concerned. What difference does it make if he does nominate one of his fellows for any legitimate position? Do not other people the same? Strange doctrine is this!

Of the various nationalities that enter as component parts into this complex and heterogeneous government of ours, there is not one citizen who has so little to say as to how the machinery of the government should be run and as to who shall govern, as that citizen of African extraction, the negro. No other people with so much power in its hands, (for we constitute the balance of power in this country so far as parties are concerned,) would for a moment act as we do. I believe, gentlemen, that the negro race is the [mee]kest, the most patient and the most forgiving of any on earth.

In the majority in most of the Southern cities and some of the Southern States, and having the balance of power in many of the Northern States, we submit to treatment that the independent and resenting spirit of our Caucasian brother would oppose instantly, though death quickly follow.

It is a question as to what is the best to be done, as the National Government seems powerless to render the needed protection to our Southern brethren. Under the circumstances, it would *almost* seem best for them to identify themselves with the local issues, and as a unit support that wing of the Democracy that would do most for them, and, after a while, they *may* secure protection. I would advise meeting force with force, but this with the present sentiment against us, would hardly bring about the desired end. But, if, after employing all the legitimate means available to secure domestic tranquility and universal peace and prosperity, they fail, there is no other alternative but to use the same weapons that foes use against them. Let it be understood, once for all, that we demand justice for ourselves and for our brethren in the South.

"Justice is the great end of government, and when this is perfectly administered, all the conditions of prosperity, either State or National, will surely follow."—*Science of Government.*

This is no idle tale or speculative theory, but a matter of fact. We, therefore, ought to hold the government responsible, and rightly too, for allowing outrages, riots, massacres and lawlessness to pass unnoticed.

These cut-throats, highway robbers, wilful murderers, Ku-Klux Klans, Bulldozers, Ballot-box Stuffers, and Negro Maligners ought to be summarily dealt with and punished according to the crimes committed.

A mere investigation of Danville riots and Copiah massacres[3] is not sufficient, unless the guilty parties are made to suffer for these atrocities.

The distinguished Senator from Ohio, the Hon. John Sherman, has played a noble part, however, in that he desired to ascertain the causes of these fiendish acts and place these rascals before the world in their proper light.

In view, then, of the undesirableness of our present condition as citizens of this great commonwealth, the question that concerns us most is: *What shall be done to change our political status? What attitude shall we assume in matters of public policy to insure protection in the exercise of the right of suffrage? To obtain recognition and to have all our rights guaranteed us?* These are vital questions, for upon them hangs our destiny as American citizens. We cannot afford to be rash or indiscreet in any conclusions we may come to. It is easier to avoid mistakes than it is to avoid them after they are made. If we should content ourselves with our present political condition, and should make no efforts to improve it, [we] would exhibit symptoms of rapid decline, and would deserve all the abuse now heaped upon us, and much more. But not so. We cannot be contented. There must be a change and that, too, speedily.

Again I ask, what shall be done? What line of action shall we adopt? An *independent movement* has been suggested as the only way out of this dilemma. Now it depends upon what an independent movement means. If it means standing aloof—giving aid to the Democratic party—nothing will be gained by it, unless there is a radical change in that party, which I hardly expect to occur until after the Day of Judgment. If it means the right to think and act for ourselves, to say i[n] common with others, who shall rule this country and us with it, I regard that as *independentism* and a step in the right direction. While I am a Republican, "dyed in the wool" as some will probably say, I am not blind to the mistakes of that party. The conciliatory and milk-and-water policy of Ex-President Hayes did the country irreparable harm and the negroes great injury, in that it encouraged Southern rascality and Southern outrages, by removing the National rifle and bayonet from the South, and by leaving them to the mercy of their former masters, without protection.

Gentlemen, I speak not as a politician, neither as an office-holder, nor as an office-seeker, but as one desirous of fair play. The colored man is not so different from other people after all. He has desires and aspirations as well as other men. He is generally as ambitious as other men. He desires to better his condition by the acquiring of education and wealth, to the same extent as other men. This is right and laudable, and who will blame him for it? The founders of the grand old Republican party played their part well when they preserved the life of the Nation; gave freedom to all its citizens; reconstructed the Union; upheld the National honor; kept the National faith; advanced the National credit; reduced the public debt; fixed the time for specie payment, and gave the country unparalleled prosperity.

But the work is not yet finished. We ask that such laws be enacted as shall secure to every citizen of the country, regardless of race or color, the full enjoyment of every civil and political right accorded to the most favored, and that all statute-laws discriminating against us as a people, be repealed. The emancipation act brought upon the party new duties and new responsibilities and established new relations between man and man. Therefore it is the duty

14

of this great party, with which we have acted so long, to see to it that no unjust distinctions be made in favor of one class at the expense of another.

"A great part of our political life is but one vast laboratory for sifting and ascertaining the rights, the interests, the duties of the unnumbered and increasing parties to our complex form of social life." Questions of rights and duties, that were never thought of years ago, are now agitating civil society: the rights of negro pauperism; the rights of negro criminals; the rights of negro daily labor; the rights of negroes as citizens of the United States, in restaurants, eating-houses and inns, in barber-shops, public conveyances on land or water, theaters and other public places of amusement; (the provisions of the Civil Rights' Bill,) the rights of negro private property; the rights of negro debtors and creditors; the rights of negro children in schools and else-where; the rights of negro office-holders or office-seekers; the rights of negroes as professional men, whether lawyers, doctors, theologians, educators, journalists, capitalists or common business men. "These questions, with countless other of the same class, are rising by germs and fractions in every newspaper that one takes up." These are questions that should concern the Republican party especially, as the champion of human rights. These are questions that that party, to be true to its original theory, cannot afford to ignore, and I don't believe it will.

The Democrats have never done anything for the negro but enslave him. While, on the other hand, it is true that a large share of the petty offices in the South that are controlled by the General Government, are held by colored appointees. In the North such appointments are rare. I confess that I would like to see a few more, at least, of our most prominent men serving their country as well as their race in this capacity. We are certainly entitled to it, and I think after a little thought the Republican party will come to the same conclusion. We desire that the representative men of the Republican party at the National Convention in Chicago, put none but good men on the ticket; men who know their duty and will not forget it when elected; men who will not overlook the negro as soon as elected. Let them give us some assurance, before election, that our interests will be cared for in common with others. Why not? The German has this; the Irishman has this; the Jew has this, and in fact all other people, except the colored people. We ask this as a matter of justice, not to bolt the party or to create any undue excitement. Did not colored troops display in the late civil war bravery unsurpassed? Did they not march into the very jaws of death, always facing the enemy, never flinching? If you wish examples, turn to Fort Wagner, Milliken's Bend, Port Hudson, Fort Pillow and other historic spots, where the negro's blood flowed freely to save the country from the hands of traitors, and a down-trodden race from an untimely end. Where will you find bravery that surpasses this? Where will you find heroism greater than this? Where will you find an exhibition of greater devotion to race or country than was found in the breast of these patriots, who gave up their lives without a murmur, when great interests were at stake and their country was calling for help? All the negro wants, gentle-men, is a chance. It is not that he desires greater favors than other people. It is not that he is never satisfied, and will always be a disturbing element in Church and State. It is not that he does not appreciate blessings already received, and is not grateful to those by whom they were bestowed. No, not at all. It is that he desires to be protected in the enjoyment of natural rights, whether civil or political, which God has given to every citizen, whether white or black.

Mr. Peter H. Clark, in reply to an article of mine, printed in the *Ohio State Journal* of April 7th, in which I make the "startling" assertion that few negroes with an *iota of common sense* will dare, openly, support the Democratic party, in Ohio or any other State, says: "The writer's 'vaulting ambition' to be known as an oracle 'o'erleaps itself,' and that I fall into grievous error."[4] Then he adds, with the same "vaulting ambition" which he has attributed to me, "to be known as an oracle," *"that it is not true that the colored people of the country are, as formerly, united in matters of public policy; but it is true that thousands with excellent common sense will openly support the candidate of the Democratic party in the coming Presidential election."*

All that I care to say here in reply to this is: that it is a matter to be regretted that the colored people are not more of a unit in "matters of public policy," when, too, their very lives are in jeopardy. And further, no man should be allowed to teach colored youth one hour who has so far forgotten himself as to openly espouse the cause of the Democracy and their Presidential candidates, before he knows who these candidates will be; and further still—when the triumph of the Democratic party of the North means the triumph of the Democratic party of the South, and a re-establishment of the old slaveholding regime, either modified or unmodified, as best answers their purposes. His logic is simply this: That the Bourbon Democrats of the South are exactly right in their treatment of negroes in that section, and that he will give additional impetus to this sort of treatment by aiding the Democracy of the North, whose victories are Southern victories. The Democratic party of to-day is the Democratic party of old, too slippery and treacherous to be trusted. Born in the lap of slavery, nursed and rocked in the cradle of slavery; reared and educated by the fireside of slavery, it has sworn almost eternal hatred to the negro, except so far as it is necessary to utilize him as a stepping-stone to office and to power.

Like Ulysses, with the giant Polyphemus, it caresses and cajoles the poor colored man until it has made him drunk with wine, then it commits its terrible crimes. From public rostrums and from pulpit come scat[h]ing invectives and denunciations. The cry goes forth "crush him out and let him go, for this is a white man's country, and the negro has no rights that other men are bound to respect." The Danville riot is an evidence of this.

Here an outrage upon law-abiding citizens was deliberately planned and as deliberately executed.—Cincinnati Commercial Gazette.

Men were shot down and butchered like beasts, for no other reason than that they attempted to exercise the right of citizenship. Organized bands of Ku-Klux and disguised desperados, banditti and ruffians infesting nearly every Southern town and village, are also an evidence of the truthfulness of my statement. If this is not sufficient to show the Democratic spleen and hatred of the negro, read Bishop

Pierce's *tirade*, a so-called interview with a reporter, and see what a Southern divine thinks of us.[5] Read extracts from the Democratic platforms the country over. Follow closely Congressional legislation. Watch the movements of Democratic and Rebel Congressmen. You will observe that the fight is against the negro in the main, with most other issues as secondary.

At a convention of colored men held in the city of Columbus, Ohio, Dec. 26th, 1883, a letter was addressed to Congressman Cox, of New York, asking him (I was opposed to the suggestion) that he would turn his attention to a question which to all the colored people of the United State is one of greatest importance, viz.: "The unwarranted and cowardly shooting down, in cold blood, of American citizens in the State of Virginia." The letter further stated that he was asked, because of his position as a prominent Congressman and as a humanitarian, to give this question his serious attention, and to give his aid to the passage of such a law as will protect American citizens in their civil rights. Again, this request was made of him because of the humanitarian position taken by him with reference to a citizen of the United States who had violated the laws of another nation. Since he (S[amuel] S[ullivan] Cox) had thus interested himself in one who had thus violated law, surely he would give his attention to the murder of law-abiding citizens at home. What the distinguished gentleman from New York did with the letter I am unable to say. I suppose it was a secret, like the burial of Orontes, and no one knows, perhaps, save the Congressman and a few intimate friends. It was left for the Hon. John Sherman to do what the *humanitarian* treated with contempt.

I referred to Bishop Pierce in the course of my remarks, now I quote from that interview:

"The negroes are entitled to elementary education the same as the whites, from the hands of the State. It is the duty of the Church to improve the colored ministry, but by theological training rather than by literary education. In my judgment higher education, so called, would be a positive calamity to the negroes. It would increase the friction between the races, producing endless strifes, elevate negro aspirations far above the station he was created to fill and resolve the whole race into a political faction, full of strife, mischief and turbulence. Negroes ought to be taught that the respect of the white race can only be attained by good character and conduct. * * * * If negroes were educated inter-marriage, in time, would breed trouble, but of this I see no tendency now. My conviction is that negroes have no rights in juries, legislatures or in public office. Right involves character and qualification. The appointment of any colored man to office by the government is an insult to the Southern people and provokes conflict and dissatisfaction, when, if left, as they ought to be, in their natural sphere, there would be quiet and good order. The whites can never tamely and without protest submit to the intrusion of colored men into places of trust and profit and responsibility."

What think ye of this, gentlemen? This is said to be christianity—Southern christianity, I suppose.

Is not such doctrine as this enough to stir every fiber of one's being and set every nerve in motion? This is the doctrine of the Southern pulpit. This is the

17

doctrine of the Northern Democrat in his efforts to establish Southern supremacy. This is virtually the doctrine, I am sorry to say, of that liberal and conciliatory class of Republicans who are trying to bridge over the bloody chasm at the expense of human rights.

Jeff Davis, in a recent speech before the Mississippi Legislature, made the remark that the South was fast gaining the ground it had lost, and very soon will assume the helm of the government of the United States. This is not very encouraging, though the state of things seem to indicate the truth of the statement. If the country is carried by the Democrats and the old regime is either wholly or partially restored, as colored citizens, we have more to lose than any other class of individuals. White men may divide on tariff, silver coinage, civil service, whisky bills, railroad and standard oil monopolies, appropriations, star routes, pensions, and on local and national issues of greater or lesser importance, but colored men, for the present at least, are narrowed down to civil and political rights—protection before the law. Until these rights are fully assured, all other questions among us, as it seems to me, must of necessity be subordinate. It is a disgrace to the American people that, with all their boasted intelligence, they cannot rise above the infamous color-line. It is on this ground that I favor mixed schools, mixed churches[,] and mixed every-thing-else that will tend to wipe out these i[n]vidious distinctions, and will enable one to live without always thinking about his color,—whether he is white or black. That white Republicans in any State, as in Georgia should issue a circular calling on other white Republicans to assemble in mass meeting to decide what course they should pursue to check the ambition of colored Republicans, who are in a majority, is a serious matter and should be resented in every legitimate way.

The negro is here, and here to stay. The sooner this fact is admitted and legislation is shaped accordingly, the better it will be for the quiet and prosperity of the country, together with all concerned. For my part, I shall not desert the Republican party, as that is the better of the two parties now existing. Nor will I advise any other colored man to do so, *but to stick to the old ship*.

The Democrats of the North opposed emancipation of negroes on the ground that it would throw upon the border Free States an immense number of colored people to compete with and underwork the whites, and to constitute in various ways an unbearable nuisance if suffered to remain. They did not think it just for the Union soldiers to be compelled to free the colored people, to fill the North with a *degraded* population, to compete with these same soldiers on their return to the peaceful avocations of life. They opposed negro suffrage, declared by resolution that negroes are not equal to white men, and that this is a government of white men. They opposed reconstruction on the ground that it would give the negroes control of the South, and place the lives, liberties and fortunes of white men in the hands of a barbarous people and would, hence, lead to the Africanization of the South. They opposed the Fifteenth Amendment, and loudly clamored for universal amnesty with Jeff Davis included.

If, under the circumstances, we should espouse the cause of the Democratic party and either by word or act, directly or indirectly promote its interests or the interests of any party that seeks to trample our rights under foot, we would be unfaithful to ourselves, unfaithful to the race and disloyal to our country.

All that has been done for the negro has been done by the Republican party; and while I am not in favor of tying ourselves to any party—especially as they are now constituted—in such a way as to deprive us of our individuality or manhood, I suggest that a petition, full and comprehensive, expressive of our grievances and with our desires explicitly stated as to protection and recognition, be submitted to the Republican convention that meets in Chicago, June 3rd. Then we shall see what action will be taken in regard to our wishes, and what planks will be put in their platform to meet the demands in our case; what recognition we shall receive as citizens of the United States, and what assurance we shall have that our future will be better than our past, so far as party can assist in helping us in making it so.

Notes

1 [Scarborough describes an unpleasant experience on a trip from Georgia to Ohio with a Jewish merchant who tried to cheat him. His anti-Semitism does not reoccur, and in 1916 he joined the Provisional Jewish Committee. See *Autobiography*, pp. 56–57 and 246.]

2 [Crittenden of Anchorage, Kentucky, killed Rose Moseley for testifying against him in a lawsuit. See the *Nation*, December 21, 1882.]

3 [Riots in Danville, Virginia, on November 3, 1883, and massacres in Copiah County, Mississippi.]

4 [Peter H. Clark (1829–1926), Democrat, was a black politician and activist. See *Autobiography*, p. 97.]

5 [This may be George F. Pierce (1811–1884); elected bishop in 1854, he became the first president of Wesleyan College in Macon, Georgia, in 1839.]

Why I Am a Republican

a speech delivered at the Lincoln Club of Columbus, Ohio, and printed
in the *Detroit Plaindealer*, August 3, 1888.

MR. CHAIRMAN.—If there ever existed in the minds of any the slightest
doubt concerning Abraham Lincoln's "lofty courage and loftier faith in God
and in the final trial of right,["] the solemn invocation with which he closed
the grandest of his executive acts, the emancipation proclamation, should dis-
pel the last lingering trace. Countless men have lived and died who were more
polished, more brilliant, more learned, but none with loftier aims, purer
motives, warmer hearts, deeper sense of his responsibility of trusts confided to
their care, greater love of justice, more unflinching courage, more abiding
faith in right.

Abraham Lincoln was a grand man because the inherent qualities inseparable from grandeur of character, from grandeur of soul, were ingrained in
every fiber of being. No hero that faced unmoved the cannon's mouth ever
towered higher: for he bore himself with the calm intrepidity of a soul lifted
far above this world, though every day life was passed beneath the awful
shadow of impending danger, though he knew the venemous hate and rage of
incensed rebeldom dogged every footstep. Yet he fearlessly faced it all, braving
it by repeated acts which could but increase the malice of his country's foes.
At last their concentrated venom found vent in the assassin's bullet, and
Abraham, whose memory we honor tonight, died a martyr's death—a victim
to his own fearless and uncompromising patriotism, his unyielding determination that right, not might, should prevail. We mourn him as we ever must.
His memory will remain imperishable engraven upon the nation's heart with
that of Washington, Grant and Garfield. Still, with gratitude, we thank God
that the bullet which laid him low was not sped on its terrible errand till his
great life-work was done. Before the hand of that God-fearing man was made
cold in death, it had set the [seal(?)] to what was the most brilliant star in the
diadem of the martyred hero. He lived to see what his hand had accomplished—the yoke lifted and fetters struck from 4,000,000 human beings, and
the South's most cherished institution, human slavery—the blackest, foulest,
most brutal system that ever disgraced a civilized nation—crushed and swept

out of existence from the face of our fair land. He had called forth a whole race to stand up as freemen and had paved the way for those glorious amendments which crown our American Constitution, clothing the beings, brutes but yesterday, with humanity's unalienable rights—manhood, citizenship and the ballot.

Gentlemen, it was that act, the emancipation proclamation, which gave birth to all of the Negro's opportunities in the following quarter century and made it possible for me to have the privilege and honor of standing before you tonight. Every step which the colored race has taken toward the high plan[e] of intelligence, culture, character, dignity and power is centered therein. Human judgment was not at fault, the voice of the people of the United States did not err when with no uncertain sound the great majority spoke as one man and chose Abraham Lincoln as the nation's chief, for he was a fit leader and commander for the party which placed him at the head of the nation, the party which was and is and ever will be the party of principles, of right, of justice, of broad humanity, the greatest and grandest party that ever wielded power in empire or republic—the Republican party of these United States. And because the platform of this party, of which the great emancipator was chief, rests upon such broad, firm and enduring foundations, gentlemen of the Ohio Republican League, I boast tonight with you of being a Republican. With the memory of more than a century of degradation behind me in the past, the knowledges of the broad fields of opportunities spread out in the present and the vision of the boundless possibilities in the perspective of the future, I can be nothing else.

If further reasons are demanded I would say:

I am a Republican because every right, privilege and honor that I can claim today is due the party which upheld the hands of the revered Lincoln in every act during those perilous years; to the party under whose leadership conquests were made and the final victory won, without which the Negr[o]'s freedom would have been a short-lived mockery; to the part in whose ranks have ever been found indomitable champions of the slave—noble men, such as the silver-tongued Phillips and the fiery Garrison, the invincible Sumner and the fearless Chase, our own eloquent Douglass, with the martyred Lovejoy and grand old John Brown.

I am a Republican because that party not only suppressed the rebellion, but out of the darkness of mourning and adversity, brought the sunshine of rejoicing and prosperity in which both North and South, white and black, native and alien, were invited to sha[r]e alike; because I, too, as an American citizen, have a pride in that "national honor and national faith" which that party was the one to uphold throughout the hours of the nation's struggle and perplexity.

I am a Republican because it is the party which believes intelligence and piety to be the pillars of our national greatness; because it has ever taken decided grounds in favor of universal education; because its heroes and heroines planted school houses and churches close upon the foot-steps of advancing armies long ere the clashing swords and whizzing bullets ceased their ghastly music—noble men and women who sowed then the harvest of today's intelligence and who are still spreading the light of knowledge in the benighted South.

I am a Republican because to be everything else is to clasp hands directly or indirectly with the bitterest foe the colored man has ever had—Democracy; to give any influence to a party which has opposed the rising manhood of the race at every step; to sustain by vote and voice the party which disfranchises today the Negro in the South; to give my sanction to all the lawless acts of intimidation, violence and suppression of votes—bull-dozing, shotgun and fraud—the arguments and policy of the Democratic party; in short, to ally myself to thugs, robbers, rascals. There is no middle ground. Mugwump or Independent, Prohibitionist or Labor, he who divides the Republican vote aids but Democracy.

Again, I am a Republican because to make political alliance elsewhere would be to prove myself the veriest ingrate that ever trod the face of this green earth, the meanest poltroon that ever exhibited his moral weakness to the gaze of the public—deserved to be hissed and spit upon by those I had deserted, and treated like a fawning cur, with inward scorn and contempt, by those whose cause I should espouse.

I am not free to leave the grand old party, the one which has aided the Negro all along the line in his battles against caste and prejudice, for his rights. I say I am not free, and yet no one is more so; for I possess the birthright of every man—freedom to do the right, the only true freedom. All other is false. I am not free to do the wrong—to throw aside principle and lick the hands of the enemy for the few stale crumbs let fall from the Democratic table. Noting but the direst pangs of hunger for the paltry recompense could induce a colored man to such a step. I cling to the Republican party, not because it is perfect, not because it has never erred, not because there are no renegades, no bolters, no prejudice in its ranks, but because, despite any imperfections, any mistakes, I have the utmost faith in its soundness of principle, in its integrity, impartiality and justice; in its sagacity to profit by errors, in its proper recognition of the interests and the services of the Negro race, and in its wisdom to conduct the coming campaign with an eye single to the carrying out of its great principles and insuring victory. I cling to it, gentlemen, as the only party in the political field which promises a release from numberless vexations, from retrogression and from the threatened ruin pretended under the present administration, the only one sufficiently well manned to thwart the schemes for Southern supremacy, which now menaces the country; because it counts among its brave leaders Ohio's chief, our brilliant and patriotic Governor, J. B. Foraker, who dared fling back that gross insult to the nation's defenders with the never-to-be-forgotten words: "No rebel flags will be returned while I am Governor;" because those giant stalwarts, James G. Blaine, Senator John Sherman and Gen. Benj. Harrison, are Republicans; because the greatest and best men of the nation belong to that party; because you, gentlemen are members of the same; because it was the party of Lincoln, Sumner, Garfield, Chase, Wilson, Grant and other dead heroes whom we delight to honor.

Are other reasons needed?

Then, Gentlemen, I sum up the million which might be given with these and answer finally. Were I other than a Republican I would be unfaithful to myself, unfaithful to my race, unfaithful to the sainted dead, and disloyal to my country.

The Party of Freedom and the Freedman— A Reciprocal Duty

a speech delivered on February 11, 1899, at the Lincoln Day Banquet, Dayton, Ohio, and printed in *Masterpieces of Negro Eloquence*, edited by Alice Dunbar (New York: Bookery Publishing, 1914).

Slavery has been well called the "perfected curse of the ages." Every civilization, ancient and modern, has experienced its blighting, withering effect, and it has cost thrones to learn the lesson that:

> "The laws of changeless justice blind
> Oppressor and oppressed;"

that

> "Close as sin and suffering joined,"

these two

> "March to Fate—abreast."[1]

Since the world began, freedom has been at war with all that savored of servitude. The sentiment of liberty is innate in every human breast. Freedom of speech and of action—the right of every man to be his own master—has ever been the inestimable privilege sought, the boon most craved. For this guerdon men have fought; for this they have even gladly died.

It was the unquenchable desire for liberty that brought the Pilgrim Fathers to Plymouth Rock. They knew that all that is highest and noblest in the human soul is fostered to its greatest development only under the blazing sunlight of freedom. And it was the same flame burning in the heart of the young nation planted on these Western shores that led to the ratification of the sentiment placed by the hand of Thomas Jefferson in the corner-stone of our American independence: "We hold these truths to be self-evident—that all men are created free and equal, that they are endowed by their Creator with certain inalienable rights; that among them are life, liberty, and the pursuit of happiness." Here were heralded to the nation prophetic freedom for all mankind and for all generations.

However, the years of bondage for Africa's sons and daughters in this fair land stretched on over a half century more before the issue was raised. But at last the grasping arms of the gigantic octopus, that was feeding at the nation's heart, reached out too far, and the combat with the monster was begun. Then that laurelled champion and leader of freedom's cause, Charles S. Sumner, laid his hand upon that Declaration of Independence and declared that the nation was "dedicated to liberty and the rights of human nature."

I count it the glory of that gifted humanitarian that he gave his magnificent talents and energies to the organization of a party that could add to its *amor patriæ* the larger, broader, nobler love of freedom for all mankind; and I count it the glory of that party that it stood for

"the voice of a people—uprisen, awake;"

that it was "born to make men free."[2]

No matter what name has been inscribed on its banner during its existence of a full half century, the cause that the party of freedom espoused has given its standard-bearer a right to claim that it, and it alone, is the legitimate heir to power in this land where the forefathers sought the liberty the Old World denied. Who dares dispute the claim? Who dares challenge the assertion? Time and events have sanctioned it; age has but strengthened it. And to-day, holding as tenaciously the same principles of truth and justice, the party that, among the parties of this Republic, alone stands as the synonym of freedom is the Republican party.

None dare gainsay it. And, among the growing multitudes in this broad land of ours, none know this better than ten millions of Afro-Americans who but for its strong arm of power might still be suffering from "Man's inhumanity to man."[3]

Forget it? The mightiest draughts from Lethe's stream could not blot from the remembrance of the race the deed of that Republican leader enthroned upon the seat of government, the deed of the immortal Lincoln, whose birth we commemorate here to-night, the deed of that second Abraham who, true to his name as the "father of the faithful",[4] struck the chains from the Negro's limbs and bade him stand forever free.

But did the great work stop there? No; the fast following amendments to the Constitution show that the party of freedom never paused; and the bond forged during the long years of struggle and riveted by emancipation was indissolubly welded when that party crowned the freedman with the glorious rights and privileges of citizenship. Ah, what lamentations loud and long filled the land! What dire predictions smote the nation's ear! What a multitude of evils imagination turned loose like a horde of Furies! What a war of

25

opinion raged 'twixt friends and foes of the race that drew the first full breath of freedom! More than three decades have passed. Have these dismal prophecies been fulfilled? No race under the sun has been so patient under calumny, under oppression, under mob violence; no race has ever shown itself so free from resentment.

But it has been said the Negro was not worth the struggle. Not worth the struggle when, at every call to arms in the nation's history, the black man has nobly responded, whether slave or freeman? Not worth the struggle when, in the Revolution, on Lake Erie with Perry, at Port Hudson, at Millikens Bend, in that fearful crater at Petersburg, he shed his blood freely in the nation's behalf? Not worth the struggle, when he won his way from spade to epaulet in the defense of the nation's honor? *The freedmen fathers were neither cowards nor traitors. Nor do the sons disgrace their sires.*

Who saved the Rough Riders from annihilation at Las Guasimas? Who stormed with unparalleled bravery the heights at El Caney and swept gallantly foremost in that magnificent charge up San Juan hill? Comrades, leaders, onlookers—all with one voice have made reply: "The Negro soldier." Aye; the race has proved its worth, and the whole country, irrespective of party or section, owes it a debt, not only for its heroic service on the battle-field in times of national peril, which was its duty, but for its splendid self-control generally, under the most harassing situations, under most inexcusable assaults.

No; the faith of the party of freedom in the Negro has not been unfounded. In all these years the race has been steadily gaining wealth, education, refinement, places of responsibility and power. It might have done far more for the lasting good of all concerned, had it learned that in all things the

> ". . . Heights are not gained by a single bound,
> But we built the ladder by which we rise, . . .
> And we mount to its summit round by round."

But the prophecies of the past are far behind us. The world has passed its verdict on what has been. Mistakes must yield us profit as the problems of the future confront us. We are to look forward with hope. And in preparation for that future:

> "The riddling Sphynx puts dim things from our minds,
> And sets us to the questions at our doors."

As the Republican party and the Negro face the coming years, one question is of equal moment to both. What shall be the mutual relations in the future? Shall the party of freedom declare at an end its duty toward the party it made men and citizens? On the other hand, shall the Negro say: "Indebtedness ceased with our fathers; we are free to make alliance where we will"?

In view of the blood shed so freely for Republican principles by the Negro as slave and freeman; in view of the loyalty, the courage, the patriotism, the strength, and the needs of the race; in view of this country's prospective broadened domain and the millions of dusky wards to be added to the nation o'er which the American eagle hovers to-day; and in view of the principles that inhere in Republicanism, the party of freedom should find but one answer: "It is and shall be our duty to view you ever as men and citizens, to see that no chain of our forging manacles you to lower planes, that no bar is thrown by us across your pathway up the hill of progress, to help maintain your rights, to throw the weight of our influence for fair treatment, for the side of law and order and justice. The Republican party must not forget for a moment the truth of the argument that Demosthenes once made against Philip with such striking force,—"*All power is unstable that is founded on injustice.*" This party cannot afford to be less than just. The Negro should not ask for more.

This duty laid upon itself on the one hand, it becomes incumbent upon the Negro to reciprocate, and the reciprocation calls for his support of the party. This should be a support, wise and open-eyed, born of appreciation and intelligence. It should be a support, steadfast and loyal, based upon faith in the party's motives and the knowledge that it has stood and still stands for all that the Negro holds most dear. It should be a support that frees itself from selfish leaders and ranting demagogues, that puts aside all mere personal gain, and seeks the good of the race as a whole that it, too, may be lifted up. And lastly, it should be a support that looks for no reward but that which comes because of true worth and ability.

Reciprocity becomes a mutual duty, for there are mutual needs. The Negro's strength is not to be ignored by the party; but the race cannot stand alone. It needs alliance with friendly power; and there is no friend like the tried friend, no party for the freedman like the party that stands upon the high, broad platform of freedom and human rights, irrespective of race, or color, or previous condition.

But having said this, I would be false to the race and my own convictions did I not pause to give the warning that, after all, neither parties nor politics alone can save the Negro. He needs to make a new start in his civil and political career. He must pay less attention to politics and more to business, to industry, to education, to the building up of a strong and sturdy manhood everywhere—to the assimilation generally of all that goes to demand the world's respect and consideration. He must lop off, as so many *incubi*, the professional Negro office-seeker, the professional Negro office-holder, and the Negro politician who aspires to lead the race, for the revenue that is in it. The best men, the wisest, the most unselfish, and above all, the men of the most profound integrity and uprightness, must take the helm or retrogression will be the inevitable result. Politics followed as an end has been the curse of the race. Under it problems have multiplied, and under it the masses have remained longer than they should in the lower stages of development. Only in the hands of men of noble mold, and used only as a *means* to an end, can politics accomplish the highest good for all the race.

The Negro can keep all this in view and yet yield loyal support to the party that set him free.

Let the party of freedom and the freedmen recognize and observe these duties as reciprocal, and a force may be created, having its basis on undying principles, that will pave the way for the ultimate success of the highest aspirations of each—a force that will stretch southward and westward bearing, wherever Old Glory floats, the promise to the oppressed: Freedom, equality, prosperity. And though men may apostatize, this mutual righteous cause shall live to sway for unnumbered years the fortunes of this grand Republic, for the God who reared the continents above the seas and peopled them with nations, who gave these nations freedom of conscience and will, and who has watched their rise and fall from the dawn of creation, still guides the destinies of races and of parties, and standeth

> ". . . within the shadow,
> Keeping watch above his own."

Notes

1 [John Greenleaf Whittier (1807–1892), "At Port Royal" (1862), stanza 17, lines 1–4.]

2 [John Greenleaf Whittier (1807–1892), "Ritner" (1894), stanza 7, line 7.]

3 [Robert Burns (1759–1796), "Man Was Made to Mourn," stanza 7, line 7.]

4 [Hebrews 11:8–19.]

The Negro Graduate—His Mission

a commencement address
printed in the *Atlanta University Bulletin,* June 1908.

"Atlanta's First Graduate"

As I stand upon this platform today I am filled with conflicting emotions. Upon these grounds consecrated to Christian education it was my happy privilege and pleasure to present myself for the first time with that small band of students that entered this University upon the first day it began its auspicious career.

The smoke of a terrible civil strife had just cleared away. On this campus yonder rose still the breastworks thrown up when this city was besieged by Sherman's forces on their March to the Sea; and my hands with those of others helped many a day to level and transform that barricade of war into slopes for peaceful academic pursuits.

So to me this invitation to address the graduating classes of 1908 comes bringing thronging memories. More than this. It comes with a peculiar emphasis, standing as I do as the first student sent out from these walls ready to enter higher work. I feel that I may therefore lay a just claim to being Atlanta's first graduate—the first prepared under the personal training of its distinguished founder and first President, Edmund A. Ware—a man who stood as a father to me in the years I spent here—a man who was one of the salt of the earth.

Because of this, in accepting this invitation I have been deeply impressed with the thought that this occasion must be made to form a most fitting link of present with past when the first product of the illustrious father's training addresses the first class sent out under the eminent son.[1] And the impression has deepened into the conviction that, as I stand before you today, I am charged, as it were, to bring you a message from that experience that means so much to me—a word from the life of one who laid it down in consecrated service for the race of which you and I form a part—a word that shall serve to guide your footsteps and mould your actions in that future upon which you launch your boats tomorrow.

29

Education and Usefulness

Negro education is no longer an experiment. The ability of the race to take rank in higher education is no longer questioned by reasonable minds. The facts speak for themselves.

It was a wise provision that placed this higher culture and training in reach of the race in the early sixties. It was a most beneficent philanthropy which made possible this early training of leaders for a weak people so suddenly thrown upon its own pitifully small resources.

In these forty odd years we have seen great changes in opinions and sentiment, and among these changes there is none affecting the race more than that one which has swept over our country in regard to education.

Today the materialistic tendency has everywhere placed scholarship, higher learning, upon the defensive, until even the President of Yale University[2] has been forced to admit that it has to make good its assertion that it has a *raison d'[ê]tre*, and be prepared to prove its usefulness.

This condition is what the Negro graduate has to face. It falls to every one who comes from college walls to prove that his training has not been amiss, that he is no idle dreamer, no vague theorist. He must evidence to the satisfaction of his critics that he has gathered from books and college life the knowledge that counts; that he has drunk so deep from the Pierian spring that his knowledge is not a dangerous thing; that depths of philosophy have led him to wisdom; that in fact this education he has received has done for him what Milton would have education do, "fitting him to perform justly, skillfully and magnanimously all the offices both private and public of peace and war."

Acquirements Expected of the Graduate

It is right and proper that the years spent in obtaining college education should show fruit. The graduate should not be, as Lord Beaconsfield once said, "one who has simply been through college but one through whom the college has been." These years should have afforded not only growth in breadth of culture, but in strength of character; they should have permeated one with the spirit of high ideals; they should have given independence in views which have crystallized into definite aims; they should have produced not only mi[c]roscopic capacity that enables one to see into the heart of things, but that telescopic capacity as well that gives an eagle's vision that can note things from afar; and they should have so shown each one his relation to the world and humanity at large that he feels himself a reforming force for the world's betterment—a propagandist as it were with a message to be delivered which must be heard. In fact, the desirable acquisition gained from college life should be as Dr. Thwing has rightly gauged it: "three-fourths formation and one-fourth information, three-fourths training and one-fourth knowledge."[3]

But the Negro graduate in view of present day problems—economic and otherwise—stands at a place as he reaches this point in his life where he queries as to what he is to do with this training, this culture, this knowledge.

30

Is it after all to be but a vain possession? Is it to be a dead weight upon him in the race of life?—a sort of *impediment* handicapping him at every step as he meets unexpected obstacles? Will he in a moment of discouragement decide he must throw it aside, as something utterly unfit for practical use, and then fall back into primitive manners, ways, thoughts, actions? God forbid that any one of the comparatively few Negroes who have toiled through colleges and universities should ever reach this point.

Service, His Mission

And what does life present to him? It presents to him what it presents to every one. Life is simply service, and it comes to the educated Negro in a wonderfully boundless degree because he is a Negro whose field for exercise of service is, as has been so felicitously denominated by Dr. Mayo, a veritable "plateau of opportunity."

Service is peculiarly the mission of the Negro graduate—the world's work to which he is called. Through his recognition and acceptance of the fact, college training—the higher education of the race—receives its justification; through it he does honor to his Alma Mater, proving at every step that scholarship, instead of being useless and a hindrance, is a necessity and a help.

It is the beauty and utility of education that any one possessing it "cannot hoard its blessings as a miser hoards his gold," as Dr. Angel[1] of Michigan University pertinently observes. "He can hardly enjoy it without in some degree sharing its blessings with others—its very nature is to be outgoing and effusive."[4] So the recipients of this higher education become object lessons to the race, and others are induced to climb upward. The race gains self-respect by the very contact with the life these graduates lead. It sets up higher aims by the very respect it instinctively accords to these accepted leaders. Race pride is stimulated, ambitions are aroused, and the way is opened for higher and better living.

No need is greater than, this need of inspiration. Dr. VanDyke has sagely remarked that true manhood and womanhood cannot exist without an ideal side, that these are the finer feelings which have no market value but which must be kept alive because it means development in the highest sense. The prophet has truly said "Without a vision the people perish."[5] This becomes a literal fact. A life of high example and teaching is an incentive above all others—it is an inspiring vision for any people so long degraded and oppressed. It is this ideal side that is kept before the people through the inspiration that only the educated ones of the race can give.

Boundless Opportunity for Service

The educated Negro cannot live in any community without finding innumerable channels for his helpful influence. We need as a people to labor for the formation of classes of society where culture and refinement, high thinking and high living in its proper sense, are to help make up what one has denom-

31

inated an "aristocracy of intelligence and character that protects the masses from their foes without and from their own folly and unrighteousness." We want no upper classes whose evils are glossed over. We want classes based upon lives and homes of the highest nature. We want a domestic life where there shall be such morality, such Christian living, such culture, such intelligence, that the ideal family shall be reached. This home life is the essential of any race improvement. If we allow social evils to exist among us, we cannot raise high our people. Purity must be demanded. Only by guarding the home can we have better husbands and wives, better fathers and mothers, who shall give the race better sons and daughters—our hope for the future. If ethical, philosophical, æsthetical training means anything it should mean that we must build for that future by gaining all possible on the side of heredity.

It is a wise man who recognizes his weakness; so with a race. In heredity we find a lack. Here we must strengthen, building upon all of good that we possess. We can count some virtues to our credit from our forefathers, but we must determine to multiply them. As for opportunity, there is no lack among us. Poetry and legend that personify opportunity as bald with only a forelock, which, failing to lay hold of as she flits by, one can never expect to grasp again, present a very misleading picture. For on our plateau, opportunity is crowned with abundant locks, and instead of "knocking but once at every gate," as John Ingalls in his fine sonnet would have us believe, we shall find that Walter Malone voiced the truth when he replied that—

> "Every day it stands outside your door,
> And bids us wake and rise and fight and win."[6]

Importance of Versatility Among the Educated

Every field of human endeavor should be entered if service is to tell on all sides. As a teacher, opportunities are manifold. He can discover talent and urge it to exercise; he can direct energies along the lines where success lies; as a minister of the Gospel he can exalt the pulpit by holding "Truth as the highest thing a man can keep," and by living up to the model that Christ gave and that Chaucer and Goldsmith have immortalized in poetry; as a physician he can aid toward clean, wholesome, hygienic living so needed by our people; as a lawyer he may not only help materially to obtain justice for the race but he can also show that honesty and uprightness are not foreign to this much maligned profession; as a business man he is to guard his honor and responsibility. No matter what path the educated Negro enters, each may be made one of benefaction to the race—helping upward by example and advice, and proving to the onlookers that his life counts as a great factor, without which progress would not be possible. There is plenty of active leadership for the Negro college-bred man as a part of his work. There are books to be written; great questions to be studied and solved; investigations to be made; experiments to be tried; conditions to be analyzed: ways and means invented to reach ends. We need the thoroughly trained Negro graduate to do all this. We need thinkers—thinkers wise and discreet—such thinkers we must have. It is to the college and the university that we look to furnish them. This is the work of the educated man or woman—the teacher, the preacher, the man of letters.

Here again arises the need for service. The Negro who has these advantages of culture must be alert to see that higher aspirations toward learning are not laughed down, scorned, ignored, crushed. The shaft of ridicule often hurts more than argument; the merry quip and jest at the study of Latin and Greek often bring discredit upon higher education. This is a serious matter when we consider that the field is white for just such service as the educated man or woman of color alone can give—when we consider that the workers upon whom the service must fall are so few in number—but a handful as compared with the Saxon by our side. There is so much of ignorance and vice to fight, so much prejudice and opposition to overcome, and the cry from the few out in the field today is Macedonian like in its intense imperativeness. "Come over and help us!" So every one joining the ranks is a power; every one who turns his back upon this need is an apostate indeed.

Need for Toil and Sacrifice

But the Negro graduate faces another fact from which he must not shrink. This service calls for unremitting toil and many sacrifices. The Persian poet's warning *to waste not the hour* comes to us with special emphasis. We cannot afford to have idlers in the educated ranks of the Negro people. In fact there is only hope for the race that works as a whole, and if [Thomas] Carlyle looks upon any idle man as a monster, how much more of a monster must the idle educated man be regarded—the man who has so much force which should be utilized? This force, this culture, this discipline—all are for hard use, if success is to be achieved. So incessant labor is to be a part of the task. More than one great mind has become convinced that genius itself is really but a capacity for infinite labor. Nor are these young people who stand on the shore of tomorrow to be discouraged because tasks seem to increase as the days of service go on. They may feel that these resemble that of Sisyphus, that the stone they push upward is ever rolling back—that the work is endless. But unlike that fabled toiler they will see gain, though they must not look for completion of the task on their part. No work is ever completed in this world. The old masters recognized this fact when as was their custom they signed their pictures "*faciebat*," never "*fecit*,"—with the idea that the work was being done but never finished. There is always something beyond. We do our part in the work and leave to those who follow to take it up and carry it forward, and with our race, many must labor to bring recognition and respect and many will pass away before that day arrives; but the service of all has played a part in the uplift.

The Negro graduate who determines to obey this call to service must expect to sacrifice much. He must expect to meet rebuff, discouragement, misinterpretation, criticism, hardships. Substantial rewards may never come, and appreciation will often be lacking on the part of those served, but even this should not deter one from doing his duty. Looking at the needs of our people, at the multitude to be helped to higher lives, and the few to lay hands to the task, this man or woman of education, strong in power and will should take Horace Mann's words to his heart—words spoken by one who turned from riches and honors to serve the cause of education,—last words given to his graduating class:[7] "Be ashamed to die until you have won some victory for humanity."

We need just such Christian consecration today among all our graduates— men and women who are

> "Humble because of knowledge,
> Mighty by sacrifice."[8]

Of those to whom much has been given much is to be expected. Every generation stands on the shoulders of giants in these days of amazing progress along all lines. Much has been added to the sum of human knowledge within a generation, and those who pass from college portals today are the co-heirs with all other races of what the years have amassed. And as a race we must expect more and more as time goes on to tread this path of service for ourselves.

Charge to Graduating Classes

Because of all this, my young friends of the graduating classes, it is a duty that you owe yourselves, your Alma Mater, your race, the world and God to enter upon the path of service for your people.

We welcome you to our ranks, asking you to join hands with those who in the past have been battling for that future that we, who stand facing life's west windows, may not see but for which we purpose to struggle to the end. We would not have you discouraged at the outlook. There is no greater, grander thing on earth than to march forth from college halls exultant in the fact that one is a finished instrument,

> "A sheathen saber
> Ready to flash out at God's call"

in this work of uplifting a people. And we would have you understand that there are compensations. The light breaks here and there; individuals rise from sheer force of worth and power of intellect; we feel the quickening pulse of the ignorant masses; we see a growth and an upward trend. There is a surpassing reward in the fact that you are taking a part in the transformation; but greatest of all is the supreme satisfaction that comes from knowing that you are really obtaining all that can be gotten from life by any one; that is, discipline for self and joy in service for others.

I say to you then in the words once bestowed upon the youthful knight:

"Go forth, be brave, be loyal and successful."

Go forth with a fixed determination that you will make your service tell on your day and generation. Act wisely, cultivate tolerance and forbearance, while not abating your manliness; make friends, but do your duty regardless of enemies; teach all virtues and condemn all vices.

Go forth, determined to convince the world of the worth and necessity of scholarship and learning, to lead our people to higher and better lives, and to an honored place among races.

Notes

1 [Edward Twitchell Ware.]

2 [Arthur Twining Hadley.]

3 [Charles Franklin Thwing (1853–1937), president of Western Reserve University from 1890 to 1921 and noted educator, wrote many works on education, including *A History of Higher Education in America* (New York: Appleton, 1906) and *The College President* (New York: Macmillan, 1926).]

4 [See James B. Angell's commencement address at the University of Michigan, "A Higher Education: A Plea for Making It Accessible to All," June 25, 1879. Scarborough mentioned Angell's statement in "The Educated Negro and His Mission."]

5 [Proverbs 29:18.]

6 ["Opportunity" (1905), stanza 1, lines 1–4.]

7 [At Antioch College in 1859.]

8 [Rudyard Kipling, "The Islanders" (1902).]

Journalism

Journalism and Colored Journalists

People's Advocate, November 12, 1881.

Years before the art of printing was invented, for example—in those days in which Homer sang of wars and rumors of wars, of quarrels and contests among gods and goddesses, of disputes and wranglings among deified heroes and heroines—in those dark days in which the real and unreal, the material and the immaterial were so closely blended that it was utterly impossible to discriminate between fact and fiction, tradition was almost the sole means of preserving the thoughts of another. It is true that forms of writing, however, were known long before this time. We may, for convenience, call these a species of hieroglyphics. Thoth, an Egyptian, is said to have invented writing between 2000 and 2500 B. C., but Josephus informs us that he has seen [an] inscription by Seth, the son of Adam. If this be true, Thoth was not the inventor of writing in the legitimate sense. The first method of printing was a very rude one. It was performed by stamping paper with blocks of wood. To print according to this method every new page required new blocks as the letters were fixed. It was not till the 14th century that we had any improvement in the art. As to whom the honor belongs there is some doubt. The invention of the new method is generally ascribed to Gutenberg, notwithstanding the claims of Faust and Lawrence Kos[t]er.[1] With this as a prelude, we come directly (1) to the press, then (2) to the *educating power* of the *press,* and (3) to the colored journalists. By the word *press,* I do not simply mean a printing machine, not merely the business of printing and publishing, but I refer to the literature of the press in general and newspapers in particular as a component part of our literature. A newspaper is defined as a *periodical publication printed and distributed for the circulation of news.* From a little crude sheet containing the most meager items it has grown to be a very powerful, political, social, moral and intellectual agency for diffusing general information on all subjects. The earliest sheet with which we are acquainted that approaches a newspaper was found in ancient Rome. It was called the *Acta Diurna* or *Acta Publica.* It came out every day and was controlled by the government. Its contents were enumerations of births and deaths, accounts of money put into the treasury and things relating to the supply of corn. The first papers of any consequence of which we have any account were called the *Relationem* and the *Zeitung*. They appeared in Ausburg and Vienna.[2] The earliest English newspapers belong to the reign of James I. These appeared in the form of pamphlets. From this period they began to increase in numbers and to spread from country to country, city to city, village to village and hamlet to hamlet, revolutionizing the world. It was often a question among the first newspaper editors as to how they should fill their columns. Some took passages from the Bible; others announced that blank space was left for any one who wished to write out his own business. During the reign of George II., prosecutions were very common among newspaper writers and editors. A free press was then almost unknown. The first efforts to report Parliamentary proceedings were violently opposed and many persons were imprisoned. Despite this opposition, however, many articles were anonymously published, and to this day, the author of the Junius' letters is unknown.[3] The first newspaper of Scotland began during the civil wars of the 17th century. When a few of Cromwell's troops went to this country in 1[6]32 they took a printer with them. In Ireland the first sheet was printed during a rebellion of 1641; in France, at the beginning of the 17th century, in Belgium, at the close of the 16th century. This gives an idea of the progress of journalism in Europe during the 15th and 16th centuries especially. In the United States the earliest paper was the *Boston News Letter*, printed in 1704. In 1719 the *Boston Gazette* followed. Next came the *New England Courant* in 1721. In 1729 the *Pennsylvania Gazette* was issued. Thus the beginning and growth in the United States. In 1850 there were issued 2,526 newspapers and periodicals, having a circulation of 426,409,978 copies. In 1860 there were 3,519, with a circulation of 927,951,548 copies. In [1870] the number of newspapers exceeded 5,000, with a circulation unascertained. In 1880 the number of papers and magazines issued and in circulation, both literary and political, was said to be about 1,500,000,000. This is a most remarkable showing for so short a period as a hundred and seventy-five years. Some of these journals employ a large number of men and expend thousands of dollars annually. In return the gross receipts of no small number of them are hundreds of thousands. For example take *Scribners Magazine*, now *The Century*. This periodical, though only eleven years old, issues monthly over 100,000 copies, making the gross receipts for subscription merely over $400,000. The expense incurred is enormous. Eugene Schuyler, for his serial Peter the Great, receive[d] the modest sum of $25,000. In addition to this sum the publishers paid $8,000 for the illustrations. A few of the editors of the political dailies and religious weeklies receive as salary amounts all the way from $2,000 to $10,000, and in a few cases even more. [Charles A.] Dana, of the New York *Sun*, Whitelaw Reid, of the *Tribune*, the local editor of the New York *Herald*, [Thomas] Nast, the great caricaturist, can fare sumptuously on the proceeds of their editorial labors. Religious newspapers are of comparatively recent date. At first they were scarcely more than collections of brief religious essays or theological discussions. Finally there sprang up weekly religious journals containing something for nearly all the members of the household, such as the *Independent, Christian at Work, Methodist Advocate, The Congregationalist*, etc., etc.

Notes

1 [John Faust or Fust of Mainz (c. 1400–c. 1466), once partner with Johann Gutenberg, took over Gutenberg's press with his son-in-law Peter Schoeffer. Laurence or Laurens Janszoon Koster or Coster (c. 1370–1440) represents the Dutch claim to have invented printing.]

2 [In 1609.]

3 [Seventy letters about public events of unknown authorship appeared in the *Public Advertiser* between 1769 and 1772.]

Journalism and Colored Journalists, no. II

People's Advocate, November 26, 1881.

The educating power of the press is almost incalculable and its influence is as broad as civilization. The press is indeed a civilizer—it is a motive power which puts thousands of cords in motion and places the world upon wheels. In an age like ours, when books and papers [a]re so widely circulated, there is not the slightest excuse for ignorance. Every man may be his own educator and may occupy an active place in society. He has the material and that, too, in abundance. Henry Ward Beecher says: "Every one must secure as he goes, his own education. One man cannot educate another man. Every man must educate himself. The school gives him a chance."[1] And he might have added that the newspaper does the same. "Teachers facilitate and help, but after all the man is a schoolmaster as well as a scholar. He is both pupil and teacher." Mr. Talmage tells us that few people read books in our day. Take a hundred business men—ninety-nine do not read one book a year. It is the newspapers that are educating the people, either in the right or wrong direction. A bad newspaper is an angel of darkness—a good newspaper is an angel of light.

It is impossible in a short article to give anything like an adequate sketch of the power of the press. We can more nearly approximate it by contrasting that household to which papers are admitted as welcome visitors with that in respect to which the opposite is true. In the former you will find expanded brains—in the latter brains greatly shrivelled; in the former a genuine culture—in the latter the opposite; in the former generally the power to entertain—in the latter the lack of such power; in the former ease resulting from general information and acquaintance with a variety of subjects—in the latter embarrassment arising from ignorance; in the former feeling of equality—in the latter a consciousness of intellectual inferiority; in the latter we often find a feeling of fear that one may be asked his opinion on something that every body else knows and which he ought to know—in the former no such feeling. In a word there is a lack of even ordinary intelligence in that family that rarely sees a newspaper once a year, while high intellectual development is the rule in the reading man's home.

The press is intellectual in the fullest sense. It discusses all forms of literary topics, from the sublime to the ridiculous, from transcendentalism in all its phases to "Jack the giant killer." If you wish to expand and cultivate more fully the thought faculty, read diligently such articles as the *Rights and Duties of Science*, *Final Philosophy*, *Physiological Metaphysics*, *Lectures on Biology*, on *Socialism* and *Communism* as found in the columns of the daily, weekly and monthly press. If you wish to improve your ethical nature you may find moral and social questions discussed most thoroughly. The meetings of the social science are fully reported, in addition to ten thousand other questions bearing directly upon the same subject. Do you wish to cultivate your æsthetical nature, you can find countless number of essays and reviews on the *true and the beautiful*, communication after communication, article after article on art, both ancient and modern, on music, painting and sculpture. If you wish to acquaint yourself with matters pertaining to any of the learned professions, the press gives this opportunity. You will find every branch of knowledge treated in its proper place. Wonderful to say, all of this for a few dollars a year. The annual subscription of a weekly newspaper varies from $1 to $3; of a monthly magazine from 3 to $5; of a daily paper from 8 to $12. If one has not the money to get the best he can take the next and so on down the scale. He who does not read when there are so many inducements offered is worse than the simpleton who took a stone from the pillar of his house and carried it around the town as a sample of the sort of house he had for sale.

Note

1 [Henry Ward Beecher (1813–1887) was pastor of the Plymouth Church in Brooklyn, New York, from 1847 until his death.]

Journalism and Colored Journalists, No. III

People's Advocate, February 4, 1882.

Our third subdivision is journalism as conducted by men of color. Periodicals, owned, managed and edited by colored men are of comparatively recent date. Who has the honor of being the first to venture in this direction I shall not undertake to affirm, but it suffices to say the numbers are rapidly multiplying. The influence of the majority of these journals will be felt in ages to come, and they will doubtless prove a blessing to the race of whose progress they are exponents. Yes, we have some good papers, well managed and edited; some that would probably be the equal of any in the country if they had a good financial backing. On the other hand we have some sheets that are unworthy the name, and are not worth the ink employed in printing them. Their object is to assail the character of our public men because they are not angels, to slander them and under[r]ate their labors, to criticize every movement that does not give this or that editor a soft bed of down and pave the way to the United States Senate for this or that proprietor. A sad state of things is this on the one hand and one to be lamented. It is our hope that this class of periodicals will be blotted out of existence very soon. May they die quickly. Now to the main point, *journalism as it is and ought to be among us*. To conduct any newspaper will require in addition to brains, money. These with skill will give any paper a place among most people, if civilized. The editor must scan well the reading public so as to know their wants, what to insert and what to reject. Too much local gossip upon men and things is entirely out of place for a paper that is designed to be national, and it is this that reduces the circulation of our colored journals in many instances. We want news concerning the Negro in every State, news th[a]t is of vital public interest, news such as we do not get from our white press, news that we as a race ought to know and which will enable us to act in concert on every race issue. As it is we have almost as many factions among us as we have papers, and very little common sympathy. Our journals can do much to heal this breach and I might add right here that THE ADVOCATE is doing much, with a few others, to make us take the proper conception of things. I commend its course to the reading public. It is not he who can read a little and write a little, that can edit a paper. It requires a great deal more than that. It requires tact, and not a little of it[.] This seems to me to be the reason why so many of our journals spring up one day and die the next—the lack of this element. Money is the next indispensable object. Our press must have money to meet its demands. As we are not rich, where is this money to come from? It must come from the subscription. If this is small then its business must be conducted on a small scale, if not entirely closed. There are about 6,000,000 colored people in America. Of this number there ought to be enough to increase the subscription list of our best journals to 100,000 and more. With the proper care on the part of our leading men—ministers and laymen, this can be done. Our best papers would then be set upon the firmest basis financially.

Introductions
to Books

"Preface" to W. S. Scarborough,
First Lessons in Greek
(New York: A. S. Barnes, 1881), pp. iii–v.

The author, in presenting this Elementary Text Book to the consideration of the public, claims for it a place only on its merits. It has been his aim to simplify as far as possible much of the confused matter often found in similar works; to arrange that which has been used before in various shapes, and to illustrate the forms and principles of the Greek syntax to such an extent that the diligent student may have little trouble mastering it.

It is supposed that this, as an introductory book, is sufficient for most purposes in preparatory instruction. Very many of the sentences that make up the exercises are taken from the Anabasis. In this it differs but little from BOISE's, WHITE's, or LEIGHTON's Elementary Lessons.[1] Many extracts in those works will probably be found here with little change or modification. A few suggestions are taken from the admirable little treatise of Dr. HARKNESS, of Brown University (HARKNESS' First Greek Book).[2]

The plan of this work was designed to be in imitation of JONES' First Lessons in Latin; a book that has no superior of its kind.[3] This Text Book is intended to be to the elements of the Greek what "JONES' Lessons" is to the elements of the Latin language: *a clear and concise statement of the rudimentary forms of the language*, with copious notes and references to the Grammars of GOODWIN and HADLEY.[4] The verb is introduced early and is carried through the entire work, so that the student may, by the time the book is completed, have a fair knowledge of it in its several forms.

It may be often found advisable to devote two or more recitations to a lesson; in which case the Greek with vocabulary may be assigned as one recitation, and the English as another. Each lesson, with few exceptions, is intended to be the length of a recitation. The question of length the instructor is to decide for himself, according to the ability of his pupils. The use of the blackboard cannot be too highly recommended. In my own classes I have found its daily use indispensable.

In addition to the works already mentioned, in the preparation of these Elementary Lessons, I have freely consulted the Greek Grammars of

KÜHNER, CURTIUS, CROSBY, and ARNOLD's Greek Prose.[5] Yet there will probably be found mistakes; in respect to which I invite friendly criticism, and shall be glad to note any correction that may be offered. Words that cannot be found in the regular vocabulary of each lesson will be found in the General Vocabulary. Words which occur in the exercises that are not given in the vocabulary, if Greek, are translated in parentheses; if English, they have the Greek given in like manner.

The book is a two-term study and can be easily completed in that time.

Under Part II. I have given a few selections taken from the Anabasis and Memorabilia of Xenophon. The selections from the Anabasis included extracts from the first and sixth chapters of Book I. The selection from the Memorabilia is "*The Choice of Hercules.*" If it is thought best, the entire select reading may be omitted, and the student, as soon as he has completed Part I., may take the Anabasis, though it will be found to be to the advantage of the class to read the selections with constant reference to the Grammar. The Grammar, indeed, should be the student's *vade mecum*, and every article should be carefully studied.

With the hope that these Lessons may meet the public approval and may be found serviceable, I beg leave to offer them to the public.[6]

Notes

1 [James Robinson Boise (1815–1895), *First Lessons in Greek* (Chicago: Griggs, 1870); John Williams White (1849–1917), *A Series of First Lesson in Greek* (Boston: Ginn, Heath, 1876); Robert Fowler Leighton (1838–?), *Greek Lessons* (Boston: Ginn, Heath, 1876).]

2 [Albert Harkness (1822–1907), *First Greek Book* (New York: Appleton, 1860).]

3 [Elisha Jones (1832–1888), *First Lessons in Latin* (Chicago: Griggs, 1870).]

4 [William Watson Goodwin (1831–1912), *An Elementary Greek Grammar* (Boston: Ginn, Heath, 1870); James Hadley (1821–1872), *Greek Grammar for Schools and Colleges* (New York: Appleton, 1859).]

5 [Raphael Kühner (1802–1878), *Grammar of the Greek Language* (New York: Appleton, 1853); Georg Curtius (1820–1895), *A Grammar of the Greek Language* (New York: Harper & Brothers, 1872); Alpheus Crosby (1810–1874), *A Grammar of the Greek Language* (Boston: Crosby, Nichols, Lee, 1861).]

6 [Scarborough added the subscription, "WILBERFORCE UNIVERSITY, Feb. 16, 1881."—his twenty-ninth birthday.]

"Introduction" to Wesley J. Gaines, *African Methodism in the South, or Twenty-Five Years of Freedom*

(Atlanta: Franklin, 1890), pp. ix–xi.

The fact that the color question is *the* question of the day, attracting more or less attention throughout our entire country—North, East, West and South—makes everything pertaining to the negro—his past, his present, his future, his educational, his moral, his financial status—all the more important. In fact, the negro is at present the center of attraction. All eyes are turned toward him and he is served up in short story and in long, in history and in fiction, in prose and in poetry, as it may suit the fancy of men.

Scientists, theologians, men of letters and even the politicians, are all trying to solve what they call the "Negro Problem"—*Whither is the negro drifting? What will eventually become of him? Will he in time lose his identity in the heterogeneity of the American people? or will he maintain his racial characteristics despite circumstances? or finally will he, like the barbarian hordes of the orient, imbibe a migratory spirit and conclude to leave these shores for a more congenial clime?*[1] These are the questions that arise daily by "germs and by fractions" in every paper that one takes up. Some affirm one thing, some another. Suffice it to say, however, despite the discussions, despite the difference of opinion, the negro intends to hold his own. He has a future, and that, too, in America. If not, what mean these twenty-five years of progress in all lines of industry—progress more marked than that of any other people in the same length of time and under the same circumstances? What means our great A. M. E. Church, with its hundreds of thousands of communicants and its thousands of preachers and teachers, its bishops and general officers? Surely the history and growth of African Methodism in these United States are an evidence not only of progress, but of permanence as well. From a small seed—infinitesimally small as it were—has grown a magnificent tree, as wonderful as it is magnificent. In every State and Territory, wherever the negro is found, African Methodism is known.

Its greatest field is in the South. It is here that we find the numbers both as to churches and as to membership—due, of course, to the fact that the colored people are found there in larger majorities than elsewhere.

The present volume, which discusses African Methodism in Georgia and Alabama, is another welcome addition to the Church literature—emanating as it does from the pen of one who grew up as it were in the Church, and who is thoroughly competent to state the facts as he sees and knows them. Our distinguished friend, Rt. Rev. Bishop W. J. Gaines, stood by the cradle of African Methodism in its incipient stages in the State of Georgia—assisted in nursing it until it became able to stand alone, and thereafter a power throughout our Southern clime—whose influence is felt far and wide. No man of my acquaintance has done more for the propagation of the Church of his choice than Bishop Gaines. Go where you will, in Georgia especially, search the records of the African M. E. Churches, examine the scrolls, and the name of Dr. W. J. Gaines will be found to stand out in bold relief, not only as a builder of churches, but as a wise and faithful shepherd; as one who always reposed an unfaltering trust in God, however dark the hour, and therefore, as a pre-eminently successful pastor and teacher. Such, then, is the writer of this volume. Certainly there could not be found one who is more fitted to portray the growth of African Methodism in the South than he whose name this volume bears. Born and reared in that section, a close observer of the many vicissitudes—civil, political and ecclesiastical—through which the South has passed during these twenty-five years, a friend of reforms, a vigorous advocate of the cause of temperance, an unswerving defender of the rights and interests of his race—conservative rather than radical—with a soul smitten with the love of virtue, with a ruling passion for the true, the noble, the good and the beautiful in all the walks of life—the Rt. Rev. Wesley J. Gaines may justly claim the right to be an authority on the subjects discussed in this treatise. We hail it with joy, and trust that it may be instrumental in awakening a deeper interest in the spread of African Methodism in this great country of ours, and that those into whose hands it may fall may be inspired to go forth as doers of the Word and not simply hearers.

Note

1 [In the original introduction, "*barbarian*" is the last word in italics.]

"Introduction" to James Monroe Gregory, *Frederick Douglass, the Orator*

(Springfield, Mass.: Willey, 1893), pp. 5–12.

When it was announced that Professor James M. Gregory of Howard University would edit a volume bearing upon some phase of the remarkable career of one of the most remarkable men of our times, the Hon. Frederick Douglass, all became expectant, and felt that a worthier chronicler of a worthier sire would be difficult to find.[1]

Both the writer of this volume and his hero as well are eminent citizens in their respective spheres, and will doubtless receive the respectful attention they merit—the former as a representative of the younger generation, and hence the product of the new dispensation; the latter, of the older generation, but the product of two dispensations, the old and the new.

Professor James M. Gregory by education and by training is in a high degree qualified for the task he has undertaken. Having passed through the Cleveland (O.) city schools, he became a student of Oberlin College, and then a graduate of Howard University, Washington, D.C., where he took high honors.

Immediately upon graduation he was made tutor of mathematics in the preparatory department of his alma mater. After four years as instructor here he was made professor of Latin in the college department, and was for two successive years dean of that department. He was also instructor of political economy and general history.

Professor Gregory is a forcible writer, a fluent speaker, and an acceptable orator. Aside from this he is a man of sound judgment and great executive ability. As an educator he ranks among the first and easily holds his own. He was the first executive officer of the American Association of Educators of Colored Youth, organized under the auspices of the alumni of Howard University,[2] and has since been annually re-elected to that important office. This in itself is conclusive proof of his eminent fitness for the position he holds.

He also served as a member of the board of trustees of the Washington city public schools for six years, and during that time was chairman of the committee on teachers. Here as in other positions he distinguished himself by his efficient service and strict integrity.

The hero of this volume is too well known for even a reference from me, but a few observations will not be out of keeping with the plan and scope of this work. Without exception, the most celebrated negro now living is the Hon. Frederick Douglass. Born in the lap of slavery and reared by slavery's fireside at least until he succeeded in making his escape from bondage, Mr. Douglass has demonstrated beyond contradiction the possibilities of his race even against the most fearful odds. There are other prominent colored men in America—doctors, lawyers, theologians, orators, statesmen, and scholars—but none of them from a national standpoint has attained the celebrity or the prestige of the "Sage of Anacostia." The pious Mrs. Auld, when she was "learning Fred how to read," little suspected that she, in reality, was shaping the future of him (though then a slave and a member of one of the despised races) who in time was destined to become one of the most distinguished men of his generation. Thus it was.

Mr. Douglass himself tells us, in his autobiography, that he made such rapid progress in mastering the alphabet and in spelling words of three and four syllables, that his old master forbade his wife to teach him, declaring that learning would spoil the best "nigger" in the world, as it forever unfits him to be a slave. He added that he should know nothing but the will of his master, and should learn to obey it. As to Fred, learning will do him no good, but a great deal of harm, making him disconsolate and unhappy. If you teach him how to read, he will want to know how to write, and this accomplished he will be running away with himself. Such in substance was his old master's opinion, and that it was a true prediction the life and career of Mr. Douglass, which have been fully told elsewhere, are a sufficient proof.

Mr. Douglass's superior ability as an orator and as a writer was early recognized by the friends of the race, and from that day to this his services in behalf of his people have ever been in demand. On the other hand he has been ready to sacrifice his own best interests for his race, and he has not failed to make the sacrifice. He is a brilliant orator, a fluent talker, and an interesting conversationalist. He has an excellent memory, and can recall dates and facts of history with perfect ease. A day in his society is a rare treat, a privilege that might well be coveted by America's greatest citizens. The greatness of the man and the inspiration that comes from every word that he utters, make one wonder how it was possible for such a remarkable character to have ever been a slave; and, further, how even now it is possible for any discourtesies to be shown him because of his color. It is nevertheless true, however, that this distinguished American citizen must suffer with the rest of his fellows and share like indignities—and all because of his race.

Socrates used to say that all men are sufficiently eloquent in that which they understand. Cicero says that, though this is plausible, it is not strictly true. He adds that no man can be eloquent even if he understands the subject ever so well but is ignorant how to form and to polish his speech. We take these views for what they are worth, but venture to add that eloquence is a spontaneous outburst of the human soul.

The cause of the oppressed could not have found a more eloquent defender than Mr. Douglass. Himself oppressed and denied the rights and privileges of a freedman, he felt what he said and said what he felt. The negro's cause was his cause, and his cause was the negro's cause. In defending his people he was defending himself. It was here that the brilliancy of his oratorical powers was most manifest. It was here that he was most profoundly eloquent.

Themistocles, Pericles, and Demosthenes may be said to represent the three ages of Greek eloquence. Themistocles was undoubtedly the greatest orator of Athens before the time of Pericles. "His eloquence was characterized," says Cicero, "by precision and simplicity, penetrating acuteness, rapidity, and fertility of thought."

Pericles was a finished orator, the most perfect type of his school, and was regarded by Cicero[3] as the best specimen of the oratorical art of Athens—*eloquentissimus Athenis Pericles*. But the third representative was one whose oratorical greatness seemed destined to remain forever uneclipsed. In Demosthenes political eloquence in Greece culminated. He was without doubt the greatest of all Athenian orators, and, to use the language of Longinus, "his eloquence was like a terrible sweep of a vast body of cavalry." It mowed down everything before it.

Certainly a noble ambition, if, as we learn elsewhere, the sole purposes for which he labored were to animate a people renowned for justice, humanity, and valor; to warn them of the dangers of luxury, treachery, and bribery, of the ambition and perfidy of a powerful foreign enemy; to recall the glory of their ancestors, to inspire them with resolution, vigor, and unanimity, to correct abuses, to restore discipline, to revive and restore the generous sentiments of patriotism and public spirit. Laudable as was this ambition, it was no more laudable than that which actuated Frederick Douglass during all the years of his active life.

The scathing invectives and fiery eloquence of Mr. Douglass were the inevitable outcome of a soul longing for freedom in all that the term implies, not only for himself but for an oppressed race. His sole purpose was to stir the hearts of the American people against the system of slavery and color prejudice; to touch the philanthropic chord of the nation so as to induce it to recognize the brotherhood of man and the fatherhood of God. A tremendous task was his, but he never gave up the struggle. Day and night he pleaded for freedom, for citizenship, for equality of rights, for justice, for humanity. Could a higher sentiment of philanthropy and patriotism pervade a human soul than this?

Lincoln, Grant, Sumner, Morton, Phillips, Garrison, Garfield, Blaine, Wilson, Conkling, Wade, Thaddeus Stevens, Chase, and other advocates of freedom have all passed away, but they have left behind them influences that survive. The echoes of their words in senate chambers and public halls will resound throughout all ages; their heroic lives and their philanthropic deeds will live when time shall have passed into eternity. These, however, were of Anglo-Saxon extraction. On the other side stands one of African extraction, to some extent their co-laborer, the hero of this volume. In point of ability and all the virtues that go to make up a well rounded citizenship Mr. Douglass compares well with them all—the only difference being that they represent white American and he black America.

This grand old patriot will always live in the hearts of his countrymen as one of the greatest of America's noblemen. His hard-fought battles and victories won will prove an incentive to generations yet to come. His virtuous life and noble deeds will always remain to warn us to bestir ourselves in the interest of manhood rights, in the interest of justice to all men regardless of color or nationality.[4]

Notes

1 [James Monroe Gregory (1849–1915), professor of Latin at Howard University and president of the American Association of Educators of Colored Youth, was the fourth black member of the American Philological Association. For Gregory's letter asking Scarborough to write the introduction, see box 8, folder 1890–1899, of the William Sanders Scarborough Papers at the Rembert E. Stokes Library, Wilberforce University.]

2 [In 1890.]

3 [*De Oratore*, 1.50.]

4 [Scarborough dated his introduction "April 18, 1893."]

"Introduction" to Benjamin Tucker Tanner, *The Color of Solomon—What?*

(Philadelphia: A.M.E. Book Concern, 1895), pp. v–viii.

It is one of the irrefutable proofs of the Negro's progress as well as of his ability that he is beginning to investigate and make researches for himself in all lines of literary activity. The day of helpless dependence is no more. A new era has dawned and the colored man has begun to add his own stint of original thought to the forces that determine the character and status of a people. He is rapidly changing his base and is no longer wholly relying upon the testimony of others as the reason for the faith that is in him, but is himself thinking for himself. This is certainly a most hopeful sign.

We need not multiply examples; for the author of this little treatise is ample proof. The Rt. Rev. Benjamin Tucker Tanner, D.D., is not only one of the foremost theologians of our times, but is indeed one of the best specimens of ripe scholarship the race has yet produced. His long years of experience as an editor, his wide, critical and thorough researches in historical, ecclesiastical, and linguistic lines, make what he has to say on any subject of more than ordinary importance. Thoughtful, discriminating and accurate, he writes not simply to carry conviction but to establish the truth with such force that conviction will be the inevitable result. The discussions that make up the following pages must therefore be of interest to all concerned and especially to the seeker after truth.

There are many theories as to the authorship of the Canticles (Song of Solomon), their object and character, and for this reason the subject is all the more difficult to handle. It suffices to say that from all the evidence that we have—external and internal—Solomon was doubtless of both Semitic and Hamitic extraction. Commentators, annotators, lexicographers, and textual critics, for the most part, avoid all references even though warranted by translation that suggest the idea of such extraction. This is one of the weaknesses of so-called modern interpretation—evasion or neglect—when the race question is introduced. It makes research fit the mold of preconceived notions. So much the more joyfully we hail one who seriously sets himself to the task of giving us the impartial discussion warranted by both the original text and context.

The subjects covered by the study of philology and ethnology, archaeology and paleontology, paleography and paleology lead out into fields that are as debatable as they are interesting. There is so much that is conjectural and so much that remains unsettled that philologists and scientists have been unable to find common ground and have, therefore, like the "son of Atreus, king of men, and the god-like Achilles, stood apart wrangling" among themselves.[1] Philology, like ethnology may be considered as still in a transitional state. Neither has reached the dignity of a fixed science and cannot, as long as the origin and development of language and the history and relation of races remain shrouded in such mist.

Modern philologists are no more agreed than those of old as to the origin of speech if we are to judge from the amount of discussion pro and con. Plato and Aristotle, the teacher and the pupil, held opposite views. Plato, the idealist, reasoned as to what language ought to be; Aristotle the realist, discussed it as he found it. The same old story of the φύσει, ("by nature") and the θέσει, ("by assignment," or "agreement") one or both—which? Aristotle declared that language was the result of an agreement. In themselves, words were meaningless and their significance depended upon what men by common consent decided they should mean.

The late Professor [W. D.] Whitney of Yale in his masterly reply to Max Müller on the Science of Language and in an able paper printed in the Transactions of the American Philological Association discusses at some length the φύσει and θέσει theory.[2] He held that words in their individuality exist θέσει, and only θέσει: but the θέσις itself is φύσει if we may include in φύσις not only man's natural gifts, but also his natural circumstances. In this sense only, and with these limitations, it is proper to answer φύσει to the question as to the existence of speech. We might add argument to argument to show the speculative character not only of philological science but ethnological as well.

With the Bible as a starting point and with the light thrown upon the subject by philological and ethnological research we may regard it as pretty well settled that the numerous tribes and classes of men, throughout the earth formed but one species; that they have all come from a single pair—Adam and Eve—and that the differences constituting the variety of race may all be accounted for by natural causes—all of which, to one desirous of information, cannot be otherwise than conclusive.

The Pre-Adamite theory is not only *wholly* untenable but unscriptural. It has nothing to recommend it. It is simply an easy attempt to settle a momentous question. The Jebusites, the Amorites, the Girgashites, the Hittites, the Hivites, the Perizzites, were not at all, *per se*, averse to intermarrying with the Israelites. There was no personal prejudice so far as the people themselves were concerned for they frequently intermingled. Solomon was the son of Bathsheba, formerly the wife of Uriah the Hittite, while he himself married an Egyptian princess, a daughter of Pharoah. In fact both social relations and

58

political relations grew exceedingly close at times throughout Biblical history, and from this and similar practices in ages following it may be reasonably inferred that neither Solomon nor his Egyptian bride possessed unalloyed racial characteristics.

We are told that nearly every complexion is still found in Egypt—"the yellowish Copt, supposed to represent the ancient Egyptian, the swarthy villager, the dark wild Arab, the dead, dusky soft black of the Nubian, the coarser, more jetty black of the Negro and still further, the weather-blacked, spirited and often finely chiseled face of the southern Arab. The natives of Egypt are generally dark and far southward toward Ethiopia, almost black; yet those of high rank, being protected from the sun are pretty fair, and would be reckoned such even in Britain;" at least so says Matthew Henry.[3]

We can hardly bespeak for this little volume a cordial reception, feeling sure that its perusal will not only result in pleasure but in profit, arousing thoughtful minds to give more attention to a line of investigation that should occupy more and more the scholars of the Negro race.

Notes

1 [In book 1 of the *Iliad*.]

2 [See W. D. Whitney, "Φύσει and Θέσει: Natural or Conventional?" *Transactions of the American Philological Association* 5 (1874): 95–116. He disputed with Müller in "A Botanico-Philological Problem," *Transactions of the American Philological Association* 7 (1876): 73–86, and in "On Inconsistency in Views of Language," *Transactions of the American Philological Association* 11 (1880): 92–112.]

3 [Matthew Henry (1662–1714) was a nonconformist minister and Bible commentator.]

"Introduction" to J. M. Conner, *Doctrines of Christ, or The Teachings of Jesus*

(Little Rock, Ark.: Printing Department of Shorter University, 1897), pp. viii–xiii.

Not a great while ago there was found in the library of a monastery of the Most Holy Sepulchre in Constantinople, a MS. said to contain the teaching of the twelve apostles (*Ἡ τῶν Δώδεκα Ἀποστολῶν Διδαχή*.)

The announcement of this discovery created considerable interest, especially among the theologians and New Testament scholars. Philotheos Bryennios, now Metropolitan of Nicomedia, was the finder.[1] The whole MS. was said to contain, aside from the Teachings, a complete text of the two Epistles of Clement of Rome, the Epistles of Barnabas, the Epistles of Ignatius and of Mary of Cassobelæ, and Chrysostom's Synopsis of the books of the Old and New Testaments. Its genuineness has been questioned in some quarters and admitted in others.

Later (1893) we were informed that another discovery had been made— the Gospel of St. Peter, which was said to throw considerable light upon the teachings of Christ and of the apostles. This MS. was regarded as a fragment of a gospel. In this it differs from the Logia.

There have been other discoveries of MSS. of more or less importance bearing upon the teachings of the New Testament. The most recent however, is the Logia Iesou (*Λογία Ἰησοῦ*) the Sayings of our Lord. This document has not yet been sufficiently tested to establish its genuineness. Some are inclined to receive it as authentic and to let it rest at that; others are not. Our own opinion is that we should be very conservative in regard to such "finds" and that we should be slow to accept as genuine any document that has not stood the test of time, and that has not the burden of proof in its favor. Such evidence should preponderate.

The Scriptures are too sacred to be tampered with and therefore the most scrupulous care should be exercised to prevent changes or interpolations whereby their value might be weakened in any sense by the whims and wishes of men. They are the Revealed Word of God to men. We should make it our special aim to study them daily and hourly so as to become more fully acquainted with all that is contained in them; to know the meaning and import of the blessed volume from Genesis to Revelation, God's will concerning ourselves as made known to us in the Old Testament and the words of the blessed Saviour as found in the New Testament.

The relation of the Old and New Testament can only be thoroughly understood by the study of the one in the light of the other. In the words of another:

"The impossibility of any attempt to dissever the revelations of the Old Testament from those of the New appears most clearly when we consider the explicit declarations of our Saviour, and after him the apostles on this point. If we know anything whatever of the doctrines of our Lord Jesus, we know that He constantly taught His disciples that He had come in accordance with the prophecies of the Old Testament. His teachings are so numerous and explicit on this point that, aside from the inspiration of the writers, such an explanation is not to be thought of for a moment. It is with two of them a matter of personal knowledge that, 'beginning at Moses and all the prophets, he expounded unto them in all the scriptures the things concerning himself,' (Luke xxiv: 27;) and with all of them that He said, after His resurrection, in reference to His past teachings: 'these are the words which I spake unto you, while I was yet with you, that all things must be fulfilled which were written in the law of Moses, and in the prophets, and in the Psalms concerning me.' (Luke xxiv: 44.) That in Christ were fulfilled the prophecies of the Old Testament, appears in every variety of form in the gospel narratives. It constituted, so to speak, the warp into which the Saviour wove his web of daily instruction."

To turn to this new discovery again, the Rev. Dr. [Joseph Henry] Thayer takes the proper view of the matter and we, all of us, who have examined the document at all, must agree with him when he says, "as compared with the contents of our canonical Gospels the 'Sayings' strike me as being distinctly of a secondary character. This is indicated by their expansions (see Sayings 6 and 7), the preterits, verbal echoes and combination of No. 3, and especially by the mystical cast of Saying 2. The unexplained use of bold phraseology, such as appears in the second Sayings implies an anterior educative process in the readers. The accredited teaching of Jesus respecting fasting and the Sabbath, corroborated as that teaching is by the very genius of primitive Christianity as set forth in the apostolic writings, excludes the supposition that the fasting and Sabbath keeping here enjoined are to be understood literally * * * But the true significance and value of the new 'find' can be established only after time has been given to trace out its covert relations to the history of the Church and other extant Christian literature."

Mr. Grenfell himself, one of those to whom we are indebted for this new document, advises caution and discretion in making up our conclusion relative to this manuscript.[2]

Light is what we want; light it what we seek and we are ready and willing to use every legitimate means by which this may be acquired. From what we know of the author of this volume—his studious habits, his ambition, his interest in theological subjects and theological research, we believe that with the light of all the resources at hand, it is his endeavor to throw light where light is needed, with a view to strengthen the weak and to make stronger the strong on all points bearing upon the teachings of the blessed Lord. If this shall prove to be his aim and if his ambition shall partake of the spirit of the Divine Master Himself, we say without hesitation that this volume has a mission. *A blessing on both mission and missionary!*

Notes

1 [In 1873.]

2 [See Bernard P. Grenfell and Arthur S. Hunt, *Logia Jesou* (London: Egypt Exploration Fund, 1897).]

"Introduction" to Horace Talbert, *The Sons of Allen*

(Xenia, Ohio: Aldine Press, 1906), pp. vii–ix.

The Reverend Horace Talbert, B.A. M.A., the author of the following pages, is a graduate of Wilberforce University (Classical Course) and is pre-eminently qualified for the task he has taken in hand. He is a man of strong and vigorous mind, of scholarly attainments, and is a logical and forceful preacher—indeed a theologian of no mean type. By education and association a part and parcel of the great Church of Allen and Payne. Professor Talbert is among the strong men of our Zion from whom we may expect great things.

After leaving his Alma Mater, by appointment he went East where he spent several years in Boston, Cambridge and other centers in that section of the country, and where he had special opportunity of adding to an already well stored mind. He did not fail to make the best use of the advantage offered. The experience gained there constituted a grand outfit with which to begin life and was of especial service to him in his future work.

From the East he was called to a Professor's Chair in his Alma Mater, (Classical Department) thence to the responsible position of Financial Secretary and Business Manager of the Institution, a position which he now holds, and one in which he has rendered invaluable service to the University. It was he who secured, through the munificence of Mr. Andrew Carnegie, the beautiful and substantial library building which now adorns the campus of the University. The bequests of Mr. George W. Hardester, of Urbana, Ohio, and Mr. James Callanan, of Des Moines, Iowa, were also secured through him.

It is with great pleasure, therefore, in compliance with the request of the author, that I offer a brief note of introduction to his book. "THE SONS OF ALLEN" is its title, and a more appropriate name could not have been chosen.

Allen and his sons mean much to the Race, much to the world. If Bishop Allen had not lived, we would not have had, possibly, the African Methodist Episcopal Church.

If Martin Luther had not lived we might not have had a Reformation. Yet it is possible to conceive of both without either of the great leaders mentioned.

For if God had willed it otherwise, he would have provided other means, other agencies to accomplish the same end. But he did not. Richard Allen lived, and he lived for a purpose. He played his part well. God had reared him and set him apart for that end. He will, therefore, always live in the hearts and memories of those who are the recipients of his benefactions. Generations unborn, as they come into being, and as they come on the stage of action, will call him blessed. Well may they do so.

Richard Allen was more than a mere reformer, more than the mere founder and organizer of a great Church. He was a man, every inch a man, a man of ideas, of principles, a man of convictions, and the courage of the same. Though without the training of the schools, he had native ability—and best of all hard, common sense. Richard Allen had no superior among his fellows. He was pre-eminently a leader. He despised shams, and hated Race prejudice in all of its forms.

When therefore oppressed because of his Race and color, he seized the opportunity quickly, and as a result the African Methodist Episcopal Church sprang into being, and now, with nearly a million members and communicants its influence is felt the world over.

Who would not be proud of the Sons and Daughters of Allen's Church, its Bishops, its Clergy, its Laity—all that it represents? Here we find some of the ripest and best brain produced by the Negro people. Who would not be proud of a Church that makes it possible for this brain to receive the very highest development in all lives that make for the good of the Race, for the good of mankind; of a Church that knows neither color nor color prejudice? Of a Church that recognizes the Fatherhood of God and the Brotherhood of Man?

God grant that such a Church may have no end of days, and that it may continue to grow and flourish. Its destiny, its future, however is in the hands of its sons and daughters.

It was only when Israel became an apostate—when she refused to heed the advice given her that God forsook her. He plead with her long and patiently through his prophets without avail. She had become wedded to her idols, so God let her alone. History does sometimes repeat itself. Allen's children have a precious legacy. Let them appreciate the responsibility and yet fear God and keep his commandments.[1]

Note

1 [Scarborough dated his introduction "March, 1906."]

Book Reviews

Review of Theophilus Gould Steward's *My First Four Years in the Itineracy of the African Methodist Episcopal Church*

in the *Christian Recorder*, December 13, 1877.

George Eliot, in the third book of Daniel Deronda [1876], takes the following lines from Sterne as the theme of the opening chapter: "I pity the man
who can travel from Dan to Beersheba and say, ''Tis all barren;' and so it is,
and so is all the world to him who will not cultivate the fruits it offers."[1] How
true! Yes, too true! Strange to say that so many pass through the world with
their eyes shut! There is nothing in nature tha[t] pleases them, "'tis all barren."—"Eyes have they but they see not, ears have they but they hear not."—
There are some who learn something from everything, be it animate or
inanimate, simple or complex. These are they who mean to live for some purpose and the influence of whose lives, be it great or small, be it good or evil
will last, will "live somewhere, within some limit and will be operative wherever it is." Reverend T.G. Steward, the author of "My First Four Years in the
Itineracy of the A.M.E. Church," does not belong to that dead fossiliferous
class to be talked about but not heard. He is a wise man and has a wide range
of knowledge; he is a sound philosopher, not as the sophists would use the
term philosopher in that vague sense of speculation, but as a Christian divine.
As a writer, his style is clear, easy and rather flowing, which one will readily
perceive by referring to the little volume above mentioned.

Having read this little work, it is my purpose in this communication to
express some thought in regard to its literary merit. In the first place I shall
state that it is purely biographical in character, giving, in brief, a sketch of the
author, his birth, early manhood, conversion, call to the ministry, *pros* and *cons*
of his ministerial labors in the North and South, etc., etc.

In this apology the author states that this little pamphlet was written in 1868,
probably while he was in the South. He adds further that it is the result of his
leisure hours; an offering from what might be called his boyhood ministry, and
as such is respectfully dedicated to the young men of the church who feel called
to the ministerial work. In the second, third and fourth chapters we have very

interesting accounts of his transfer to South Carolina in 1865, notes by the way, his arrival, scenes around the Se[a] Islands including Hilton Head, Charleston as it appeared then, the churches, the religious situation etc. The writer in speaking of the Islands, says, "Imagine a river, a bank of the richest green—a wide-spread plain, carpeted with the same material, here and there relieved by a palmetto, a group of live oaks or a magnolia, the whole backed by lofty pines, and you have a scene common anywhere among the Sea Islands."

In the fifth chapter the author gives is the following sketch of a trip from Charleston to Hilton Head. "We left Charleston about 4 p.m., and crossed the bar about sunset with a strong southeast wind blowing, which steadily increased until about 11 p.m., when it rose in violence to a perfect gale. Thunder and lightning, with some rain added to the awful grandeur of the scene, while our frail boat was tossed by the proud waves as a thing of utter insignificance. The old feeling returned; I was again sea-sick. About midnight a huge billow struck the vessel, nearly capsizing her, and carrying away several loose spars from the upper deck. Bishop [Daniel] Payne during this time was sleeping in an extempore bed, which we had arranged for him of some baggage, for prejudice denied him a b[e]rth, and in the general alarm I ran to him and called in his ear, acquainting him at the same time with the horrors of the situation. I shall never forget his reply. He lifted his head, saying: "Nothing but the power of the Almighty can save us," and calmly laid himself down again.

Mr. Steward has given us a number of episodes replete with interest and taken from real life[.] I again [quote]: "A white lady, her sister and sister-in-law came to me stating that their house was troubled by spirits and they could not sleep in it at night, a man had lately died in it. They desired me to come and hold prayers in the room which seemed to be troubled most. Thinking I might do some good, I went, read a portion of Scripture, and kneeling down prayed fervently for the Lord's mercy for them, and my prayer was answered according to the desire of their hearts, for the troublesome ghosts never returned.["]

The work of organizing churches and Conferences in the early days, when the condition of the country was greatly unsettled, is discussed [skillfully by] the writer. Among the prominent names mentioned, we notice those of Bishop Payne, Drs. [Benjamin] Tanner, and [Richard H.] Cain, Elders [A. T.] Carr, [George F.] Johnson, [James Anderson] Handy and [Charles L.] Bradwell.

The little work closes with the author's appointment to Macon, Ga. The price of this little quarto volume, is 25cts. It is for sale at the A.M.E. Book Rooms, 631 Pine St., Phila. Pa. I have read the volume and am certain that no one will regret having purchased this little work for so small a sum as we have mentioned. In conclusion, permit me to refer to another from the gentleman's ready pen, a volume just issued, entitled, "Memorial Volume of Mrs. Rebecca Steward."[2] I have not seen a copy of this new book, but judging from the other and my knowledge of the author's ability, I feel assured that it is up to the times and therefore ought to find a large sale. There are two styles of binding; plain and gilt; the former sold at 60cts., and the latter at 75cts. This is also found at the A.M.E. Book Rooms, 631 Pine St., Phila. Pa.

Notes

1 [Laurence Sterne (1713–1768) published *A Sentimental Journey through France and Italy* in 1768.]

2 [This is probably the *Memoirs of Mrs. Rebecca Steward* (Philadelphia: Publication Department of the A.M.E. Church, 1877).]

Review of Daniel Payne's *A Treatise on Domestic Education*

in the *Christian Recorder*, August 2, 1885.

No topic is so little discussed now-a-days as that which heads the valuable volume just issued by the venerable Senior Bishop of the A.M.E. Church. Many are the lights in which education has been viewed, but the fountain, the head waters have been left undisturbed for so long a time that this generation has almost lost sight of the fact that education, like charity, should begin at home. As the result, young America, male and female, exercises an authority over its elders, dangerous in the extreme when we consider to what such sub-version leads. The volume comes to us in an opportune moment—when most needed. It was peculiarly fitting and appropriate that the Rev. Dr. R.S. Rust the Corresponding Secretary of the Freedman's Aid Society of the Methodist Episcopal Church, should pen the introduction.[1] He was a co-laborer with Bishop Payne in Wilberforce University in its early days—being its first President and serving his apprenticeship in the great work of education among the colored people when it required high moral courage to be a teacher among them, even in Southern Ohio. As a staunch friend of the race, a man of family with a broad experience relative to the subject, with age and experi-ence so near the author's own, Bishop Payne could not have chosen one better qualified. From countless reasons, Rev. Dr. Rust could appreciate the work, its necessity and its worth. That he has appreciated it, and that too highly, is evi-dent from the introductory pages.

To review a work written by such a scholarly divine as Bishop Payne is and is not a difficult undertaking. It is difficult on the one hand on account of the hesitancy which a younger and less matured mind must always feel in review-ing the product of years of experience, study and culture. It reminds one of a pigmy overhauling a giant, a piece of presumption to attempt. Yet it is not dif-ficult when one considers the clear, logical style in which the author always expresses himself, and the exhaustive manner in which he treats any subject upon which he writes at length. The present volume is no exception, only an emphatic re-assertion in itself. That the subject is one of the most vital importance is deeply impressed upon the reader by the earnest manner in which it is presented. From the opening chapter on the "Training of Children" to that on "Sacred Songs," the pages are stored full of sage advice, wise counsel, strong common sense, deep piety and fatherly interest in the youth.

The "Four Conditions of Child-training," discussed in as many chapters, show the hand of one who has not only experience, but whose study and research have completely covered the subject in all its bearings.

Who can take away from or add to these four conditions: (1) unity of the father and mother in domestic government; (2) a family church and a fire-side altar; (3) secret prayer of grand consecration or children; (4) self-culture of children? We fearlessly assert that Bishop Payne has touched all the secret springs in these chapters which work for successful child-training. It is next to impossible to select passages from a book in which the whole teems with such fruitful thoughts. He does not arbitrarily say to do so and so, but with the logic of an Aristotle proceeds to give reasons for the laws which he lays down, in such convincing style that he sweeps away every cobweb of objection from the skeptical mind—so powerful and unanswerable is the reasoning.

While the first three conditions are pointedly set forth, the fourth is strongly emphasized on the ground that "the fruit is like the tree." He says: "But we can make exceptions to this rule by changing the circumstances which surround them, and thus change their condition and elevate them above their parentage.—But, the separation of the child from its mother in order that it may be rightly trained seems to be unnatural, and children from their parents abnormal, because the demand of nature is that the parents be the first educators of their children—hence the wisdom of the thought of Vinet, the 'Necessete de l'education des educateurs'—the necessity of educating the educators."[2]

In chapter VI. the Bishop says the training of a child should begin as soon as it comes into the world. Aside from the cleanliness and comfort which he mentions as the first duty in the physical training, he places none too great stress upon the necessity of enforcing "the law of obedience," for the sake of both mental and moral training. We quote: "The third time we repeat, the first lesson to be taught by the mother and to be learned by the child is obedience to order, law, government and authority, which creates law, order and government. By authority I mean the God above the parents." We hardly know where to close the quotations, as every sentence conveys a strong practical thought. In chapters VII to XI. inclusive he discusses the considerations which require such training as the preceding ones have laid down. Beginning with "Family Considerations," he rises successively to race considerations, national considerations, up to ecclesiastical considerations, adding the school considerations. Here shine pre-eminently the strong reasoning powers, the lucid argumentative force of the author, as well as the results of his keen observation and extensive knowledge indicated in the views expressed and the illustrative material used.

"What the families of a race are, the race will be." Again, "Each family of every race, and every race composing the nation, having in itself the elements of wealth, fecundity and longevity, the republic would, at the end of every century, leap upon a higher plane of national power, grandeur and glory!" Still again, "Suppose that Samuel was made to be the incorruptible judge of Israel, and that John was made to be the herald of the Lord of lords and King of kings, are we to infer, therefore, that Christian parents are not to consecrate their children before they are born, and not to train their children in the paths of wisdom and righteousness and usefulness because they are not called to be judges of a nation nor heralds of salvation? Such reasonings are false and destructive."

Drawing directly upon incidents in his own experience he strikingly illustrates the school consideration, and sums up the whole by the forcible statement, "The reign of universal righteousness, which is justice in its highest form can never be realized till from our institutions of learning graduates shall go forth whose character was first molded and first colored by the hands of Christian parents, then polished by the hands of Christian teachers." But we must curb the temptation to quote. Yet when there are so many golden thoughts, like the child in the midst of bright floral treasures, as we turn the pages we are tempted to cull all within our reach. The pages of chapter XII. on the relations of domestic education to the Church, the State and the common school, including higher education and the Sunday school, are filled with striking apothegms. In the next chapter on the nature and scope of the divine command, "Train up a child in the way he should go," he makes the strong conclusion, "From all we have said it is manifest that the command to 'train up a child in the way he should go' is very indefinite. But this indefiniteness illustrates its universality, and its universality is the proof of its divinity. The natural selfishness of man, fostered in to a passion, could never have conceived such a law, especially under the low and narrow sentiments of race superiority. But this divine mandate, in its length and breadth, in its height and depths, like infinite space, takes in all and makes room for all the educational movements of humanity."

This chapter is followed by one on the "Divine Promise," in which he proves that "when the divine mandate shall have been obeyed the divine promise shall be realized." He gives in proof Moses, Samuel and Daniel, of sacred history, with John and Charles Wesley and Jonathan Edwards of modern history; pointing the whole with, "Every child of Adam is born to such a birthright, such an imperishable inheritance." In Chapter XV. he makes "domestic education, under Christian influences, the highest duty of the parent and the citizen." Under other principles he asserts that it can produce but the mere butterflies, the end of whose pleasure-seeking centres in self, or those whose lives will be similar, but on a lower plane, or those whose "lives will be stained by vice, crime and blood," or "selfish, godless, idolatrous financiers." These expanded points lead indisputably to the establishment of Christian influences, principles and sentiments as to the basis of domestic education, which is the highest duty of man.

In the second chapter the venerable Bishop makes unity in domestic government the first consideration of successful child training. In the [Chapter]

XVI[.] he recurs to it and, adding unity in domestic instruction, the leading thought, the mother and father, co-laborers. Here he pays high tribute to the educated, Christian women, while he recognizes the potent influence of the mother for good or evil. He styles the mother the first teacher, the guide, the first commandment.

We are here reminded of an incident related by Julia McNair Wright, in her "Complete Home," wherein a boy, whose mother had granted certain privileges and laid down certain rules which he was told he must obey, replies: "Catch me running the street if I can have boys here to play with and if I know I daren't!" There is sound philosophy in this last idea and the lady author adds the concise remark, "The human heart was made to be controlled by law and it craves law."[3]

Bishop Payne has made a cardinal virtue of obedience to authority in his wise treatise. There is untold safety for the young in law. Woman receives at his hands no lack of appreciation. Her influence in moulding the character of individuals, races and nations is put at its true estimate by his incisive, cautious, but bold pen. In the chapter on the father's work, which is made supplementary to the mother's by his statement, "I believe the mother is the natural molder of character," he exhibits his characteristic wisdom, prudence and love of justice, when, after showing how the father may aid the mother, he calls attention to the command, "Ye fathers, provoke not your children to wrath," etc., and he immediately draws a timely and sharp distinction between strictness and severity.

The discussion of the mother's influence leads up to the crowning chapters devoted to the special training of girls and the Christian graces. As he says, "a girl is born to affect society as a boy never can," which is his only apology for particularizing in sex. Here we find multum in parvo, while the footnotes are as valuable as the text. The gist of the two chapters is a strong appeal for the training of girls in the womanly virtues, obedience, modesty, veracity, honesty, industry, thrift and temperance and the Christian graces—faith, hope, love, humility, self-abnegation, holiness and righteousness. The final chapter is devoted to sacred songs, written by the Bishop himself and set to music by various musicians.

Such is a brief resume of a most interesting book, which must necessarily convey only a very inadequate conception of the valuable contents. Within these pages, numbering nearly two hundred, is stored a mint of excellent advice. The book is well printed on good paper—the type being clear and easily read, and the whole well bound—an ornament to any table or library. By dipping into its riches, here and there, we hope to incite all who may read the RECORDER to peruse its pages. While every colored family should possess a copy, it is by no means limited in its application. It is written upon the broad basis of domestic education and there is not a sentence, not a line which does not embrace all people. It is not a book written by a colored man for the colored people; it is, as it should be, an eminently exhaustive treatise upon a subject which affects the interests of the world at large; written by a scholar of the deepest piety and one whose belief is deeply rooted as the mountains, that "of one blood God made all the nations of the earth."[4] Yet at the same time, every colored home should possess it. Let fathers and mothers read it, and sons and daughters make it their companion. Young and old may gather instruction from its pages; it is full of seed thoughts for all.

As the Independent well says in its review of the same work: "Bishop Payne's treatise is, like himself, the product of a ripe, rich and mellow experience." (Publishers, Cranston and Stowe, Cincinnati, O.)

Notes

1 [Richard S. Rust (1815–1906), Methodist minister and founder of the Freedman's Aid Society, was president of Wilberforce University until 1863, when the A.M.E. Church purchased it.]

2 [See Alexandre R. Vinet (1799–1847), *L'éducation, la famille et la société* (Paris: Meyruies, 1855).]

3 [For this quotation see chapter 12, "Friendships in the Home," in Julia McNair Wright, *Complete Home: An Encyclopedia of Domestic Life and Affairs* (Columbus, Ohio: William Garretson, 1879), p. 280.]

4 [This is attributed to Shelby Moore Cullom (1829–1914), Republican governor of Illinois from 1877 to 1883 and U.S. senator from 1883 to 1913. The line ends Charles Chesnutt's short story "A Matter of Principle," in *The Wife of His Youth and Other Stories* (Boston: Houghton Mifflin, 1901).]

Review of H. M. Turner's
Genius and Theory of Methodist Polity
in the *Christian Recorder*, September 17, 1885.

One of the most active and progressive men among us, whose versatile mind and massive brain reminds us of another Frederich Humboldt, is the Rev. Dr. H. M. Turner. Having filled various positions of honor in Church and in State, with an experience as broad as it is varied, with a knowledge of many subjects (like Ægyptius[1] of Homeric fame), a great reader and an indefatigable student, the Bishop is thoroughly qualified to discuss any topic that he may undertake. The works that have already emanated from his pen are proofs of this, as is also the little treatise that now engages our attention—"Methodist Polity."

"Of making books and printing papers there is no end"[2] is quite a trite saying, yet the amount of good, instructive literature can not be too great; indeed, it is by far too small. Whenever, therefore, a writer gives to the world a good treatise on any subject of importance our attention is at once riveted and we are forced to examine it and make the contents our own. The subject of Methodism is an interesting one and should be more thoughtfully studied and better understood in all of its details than is generally the case among us at best.

In its broadest sense Methodism began with that great religious movement inaugurated by the Wesleys and Whitfields during the earlier part of the eighteenth century. The religious state of Great Britain at this period was at low ebb. Morality was generally at a discount. Men, like [Jonathan] Swift and [Laurence] Sterne, exerted a baneful influence by their coarse wit and humor. Doctrinal controversy constantly agitated the more thoughtful minds. In short, this was an era of religious unrest. The seed sown at this momentous period is now seen in the growth and spread of Methodism throughout the civilized world.

African Methodism began with Rev. Richard Allen, which, with all the pros and cons, is fully discussed in the first chapter of Bishop Turner's book. Here we have a running history, as it were, of the origin of the A. M. E. Church; then follows, more specifically, the polity of said Church.

Every man should have some knowledge of the government and constitution of the church to which he belongs. He may know little of science, art or literature; he may know nothing of linguistics or the science of number, but the doctrine, creed or polity of his church he must understand in most of its details. It is the aim of Dr. Turner, in his book, to bring the subject within the reach of all into whose hands it may fall. For this reason our author has doubtless adopted the catechetical method. The book, as the Bishop states, is intended to supply a want long felt among the neophyte ministry and laity of the A. M. E. Church.

"Even college training," to use the characteristic and significant language of the writer, "seldom, if ever, fits young men for practical work in the Methodist ministry. There is a qualification that comes only through experience, years of toil and hard labor. The young minister, therefore, who allows himself to be flattered into the idea that he is fitted for the pastorate because he happens to understand little about the rules of college life, is laboring under a lamentable mistake and the sooner he rids himself of it, the better for him and the people he may serve." This is true and may be applied not only to the ministry, but to other professions as well. College training is preparatory as well as disciplinary. It fits one to begin life. Here one gets the theory—the practice comes afterward. I shall greet the day, however, when our theological seminaries, one and all, shall not permit a young man to enter until he shall have finished a college course or one equivalent. This is the only way to raise the intellectual tone of a greatly needed reorganized ministry.

In the second, third, fourth and fifth chapters we have the various conferences discussed—their sphere and influence, their constitution and limitations. Here are volumes of general information for laymen as well as ministers. The young theologian who starts out for the first time on his circuit with his Discipline and Turner's Methodist Polity as his vade mecum need not fear of making mistakes as to his duty in reference to church government.

As to the moral and religious influence of the District Conference we quote: "It is good in mutual edification. It is expected at these conferences prominence should be given to religious exercises, such as preaching, prayer-meetings, love-feasts, the administration of the Holy Sacrament. Revivals and protracted meetings frequently grow out of them and always should. Equally removed from the quarterly and annual conferences, larger and more inspiring than the former and less absorbed in business, the District Conference affords the best facilities for effective preaching for Christian fellowship and spiritual development."

Official Boards, Exhorters, Evangelists, Call to Preach, Local and Traveling Preachers, Itinerant Ministers are fully discussed in the same catechetical style in chapters six, seven, eight, nine, ten and eleven. Again we quote in answer to the question, "How is it that exhorters are members of the Official Board?"

"That," says the Bishop, "is a grave question. They were not made members in the act of the General Conference of 1872. They sustained the same relation to the Board as that of a local preacher, and I think it was a clerical mistake which placed them in the list of membership. They, too, are barred by the General Rules which the General Conference has no power to over-ride. The truth is, the General Conference has no power that can legally make either local preachers or exhorters members of the Official Board."

Under the head of Executive and Assistant Executive Departments the subject of the bishopric and duties incident to that office, also the Presiding Eldership, its nature and scope, are fully considered. Following this the trustees, Stewards and Class Leaders come in regular order. Each section is vigorously discussed and the duties and relations of these different officers clearly defined.

This little treatise of 184 pages and twenty-seven chapters closes with a discussion of the following topics catechetically, as before: Literary Associations, Miscellanies, Special Answers to Inquiries, Appeals, Power of the Preacher, Growth of the A. M. E. Church, Questions on Admission, Forms of Quarterly Conference Reports, Rules of General Conference, Historical and Literary Departments, Conference Constitution, Church Constitution and By-Laws. Bishop Turner has done good service in the compilation of this book and deserves the gratitude as well as the thanks of the A. M. E. Church.

Notes

1 [Ægyptius appears in book 2 of the *Odyssey* and speaks with Telemachus. He is weighed down with age and life experience.]

2 [See Ecclesiastes 12:12, "Of making books there is no end, and much study is a weariness of the flesh."]

Hale on the Art of Reading Latin

in *Education* 8 (November 1887): 198–202.

In this preëminently practical age, when men by the mere touch of the hand are seeking to turn everything into gold, any treatise that has to do with the practical, rather than the theoretical, side of public instruction at once excites attention.[1] It is the new education now, as contrasted with the old, the useful rather than the ornamental, that men delight to discuss, because it smacks more of business, perhaps, more of dollars and cents.

In America, as in Germany, *Lehrfreiheit*, *Lernfreiheit*, and *Studienfreiheit* seem to constitute the real ground of the controversy common to the two countries. In 1884 Dr. Friedrich Paulsen, in his Geschichte des gelehrten Unterrichts auf den deutschen [S]chulen und Universitaten, took strong grounds in favor of the movement as then directed against the classics. Dr. Sch[m]eding, Jens L. Christensen, L. Graf von Pfeil, and others of greater or lesser prominence, have directed their shafts against the old, and in favor of new, methods of instruction in the gymnasia. Scholars of our own country, in the meantime, have not been idle, but the work has been slowly and quietly going on, and as one of the results we have the improved Greek series under the editorial management of Professor John Williams White, of Harvard, and Professor T. D. Seymour, of Yale, published by Ginn & Co. of Boston; a similar series of Latin texts, under the editorial management of Professor Smith, of Harvard, and Professor [Tracy] Peck, of Yale, is published by the same company. Then there is another Greek and Latin series under the editorial management of Professor [Henry] Drisler, of Columbia College, published by Harper Brothers. In the same line and under the editorial management of some of the ripest scholars of the present day is a modern language series, published by D. C. Heath & Co. The aim of the editors in every instance seems to be to add interest to the study and aid the teacher in making his instruction more practical, by ennabling him to avail himself of the best results of recent philological research.

Professor W. G. Hale, of Cornell University, himself a thorough scholar and a live teacher, has attempted in his Art of Reading Latin to get out of the well-beaten path of "ye olden times," by showing that Latin is not so dead as many are wont to believe. It is the teacher rather than the language that is really dead. He has succeeded in a remarkable degree; and if his methods are followed, there will doubtless be a revival of interest in the study of the ancient classics. The order is, now, ability to read the text with grammar and lexicon; ability to read at sight; ability to read at hearing; but the most important of the three is that of hearing, while the next is sight reading; and that which seems to be of the least importance is the old grammar drill-method. To be sure, there are reasons for the superior stress attached to the ability to translate at hearing. The object aimed at is a speaking knowledge of the language, which knowledge, of course, is taken for granted, if the student is able to translate when an author is read in his presence. This is the most difficult task of all, and yet the most desirable. The ability to think in a language is the soul of that language, for then the learner is able to grasp the thought without the monotony of a word for word translation, which is now the fashion in all of our schools, from the academy or high school up through the university.

This thought is thus expanded by Professor Hale: "I take up a simple sentence in the fourth oration against Catiline (3, 5): *Hæc omnia indices detulerunt.* I look for my subject. Fortunately, it lies right at hand. It is *hæc*, nominative plural. Next I translate it, these; or, since it is neuter, these things. Then I proceed to find the verb, which again is obvious; namely, *detulerunt*, in the third person plural, agreeing with the subject, *hæc*. Perhaps I have caught from somewhere the happy idea of not looking words up in the dictionary until I have tried my hand at them. So, very properly, I set out with the simplest meaning I can think of; namely, brought. Now I am well started: These things brought. Next I look for the modifiers of the subject, and find *omnia*. I build on it, and have now, All these things, for my subject—All these things brought. Next I look for the modifiers of the predicate; and I find *indices*, witnesses, accusative plural, object of the verb. Everything is straight: All these things brought the witnesses. I pass on; and when I come to the class-room, and the teacher calls on me, I read out: 'All these things brought the witnesses,' prepared to parse it to the last word, only to be told that I am entirely wrong. Now a Roman boy of my age, and much less clever than I, if he could have smuggled himself into the Senate that day, would have understood what those four words meant the instant Cicero uttered the last of them, *detulerunt*. What is the difference between us? Each of us, he and I, knew substantially the meaning of each word; each of us could inflect, and each of us knew all the syntax required. Yet I missed the idea, while he got it. Wherein did he beat me? Why, simply here: I, following the direction of my teachers, first found my subject and settled on *hæc*. The Roman boy did not know whether *hæc* was subject or object. He only knew it as *hæc*. I knew that *detulerunt* was the verb, and so did he when it arrived. I knew that *omnia* agreed with the subject, *hæc*; while he only surmised that it belonged with *hæc*, whatever that might prove to be. I knew that *indices* was the object; while he only felt that *indices* was subject or object, and that it was the opposite of *hæc omnia* (apposition being out of the question), being object if that should turn out to be subject, and subject if that should turn out to be object. Then he heard *detulerunt*, and with that word everything dropped into place as simply as in Milton's sentence following:—

> . . . 'The moon, whose orb
> Through optic glass the Tuscan Artist views.'[2]

The last word resolves our momentary suspense in regard to the relation of orb and artist; which relation would have been precisely reversed, had we found such a word as 'glads.' " Surely the time has come for a change. Not less Latin nor less Greek, but a change in methods of instruction. The time will never come, perhaps, when these grand old tongues will occupy a less conspicuous place than now. We hope, at least, that it will not be in our day, for we are still willing to worship at their shrine and place our gifts at the feet of Demosthenes and Cicero. For we cannot forget that the classical languages constitute the ground-work and, in large part, the superstructure of our own vernacular. Max Müller was right when he affirmed that in learning Greek and Latin as boys, we are learning more than a new language; we are acquiring an entirely novel system of thought; that the mind has to receive a grammatical training and to be broken, so to say, to modes of thought and speech unknown to us from our own language. We shall always cling to the classics, though we may oppose most vehemently the methods adopted in imparting instruction in them.

Again, to use Professor Hale's own language: "I can best indicate what it seems to me you ought to direct your teachers of Latin to do, *mutatis mutandis*, by telling you what I myself do from the time when I first meet my freshmen to the end of the sophomore year. After my little jest about the Romans hunting up first the subject and then the predicate as Cicero talked to them, or first the predicate and then the subject, whichever one thinks the Roman method may have been, I assure them that what we have to do is to learn to understand a Roman sentence precisely as a Roman understood it when he heard it or read it, say in an oration, for example. How the Roman heard or read, first, the first word, then the second, then the third, and so on through sentence after sentence, to end of the oration, with no turning back, with no hunting around. And in doing this he was so guided all the time, by indications of one kind or another in some way shown through each sentence, that when the last word of that sentence had been spoken or read, the whole of the meaning had reached his mind. The process of detecting these indications of meaning was to him a wholly unconscious one. We moderns, however, of course cannot begin so far along. What we are to reach finally is precisely this unconsciousness of processes; but we shall be obliged, for the first few years, explicitly to study the indications, until we come to know them familiarly one after another. We must for some time think out, at every point, as the sentence progresses (and that without ever allowing ourselves to look ahead), all those conveyings of meaning, be they choice of words, or choice of order, or choice of case, or choice of mode, or choice of tense, or whatever else which at that point sufficed for the Roman mind. And when these indications—which, after all, are not so many in number—have come to be so familiar to us that most of them are ready to flash before the mind without our deliberately summoning then, we shall be very near the point at which in Latin graded to our growing powers we shall interpret indications unconsciously. And the moments we do that, we shall be reading Latin by the Romans' own method." This is the only rational method, as it seems to me, to read and interpret Latin as the Romans themselves did. This, in fact, is the only adequate return for the time spent in its study.

The same may be said of Greek, as the rule which may be applied to one is applicable to the other. Both are regarded as dead languages, and both are so taught. Though I believe the time will come when Greek and Latin will no longer be considered as dead, any more than French is dead, or German or Spanish or Portuguese or Italian. This *furore* may be viewed as an exhibition of public disgust in respect to the small returns received as a result from the enormous expense and the length of time required to get through our colleges. The young collegian may be able to read simple Latin prose at sight; he may be able to translate with ease more difficult prose, with grammar and lexicon in hand; but how often does he utterly fail when required to depend upon the ear, to render the simplest forms into English at hearing! Professor Hale has done good service in the interest of classical instruction. He has awakened new interest in the teaching and study of Latin, in that he has thrown a kind of freshness into the language that brings it to life again, and makes it a living, rather than a dead, tongue. Follow Professor Hale's suggestions as to the art of teaching Latin, and the boy will learn more in six months than he will in a year by the old method, and will likewise enjoy the study as well.

Notes

1 The Art of Reading Latin: How to Teach it. By William Gardner Hale, Professor of Latin in Cornell University. Ginn & Co., Boston. 1887. [In the original review, this note comes after the title rather than after the first sentence.]

2 [*Paradise Lost*, book 1.]

Review of Benjamin Tucker Tanner's
Dispensations in the History of the Church

in the *A.M.E. Church Review* 16 (1900): 360–366.

Within the past thirty years many publications emanating from the pen of Negro authors have been put upon the market. Some of these were distinguished for their scholarship and for the research they exhibited; others were equally noteworthy on account of a lack of these. Some not only added to our literature, but clearly indicated the possibilities of the race in literary lines. Others should never have been written. That which deserves to live, however, will live. That which has a mission will not perish until that mission is fulfilled. But that which has no *raison* d'[*ê*]*tre* will speedily find its place—will soon be forgotten and will be cast aside as so much rubbish.

It is not the number of books that one has written, but the quality and character that determine the intellectual strength of its author. The cost intellectually to produce them—the following out to a logical conclusion any line of thought upon which one may have spent years and perhaps a lifetime—are the things that tell. Yet, taking all things into consideration, it may be said that the Negro has fixed his status in many lines of literary activity and that the literary possibilities of the race are no longer a matter of doubt.

Literature of a lighter vein—the short and the long story, the novel, especially that involving the use of dialect and the plantation Negro, has found exponents in [Paul Laurence] Dunbar and [Charles] Che[s]nutt. Being themselves Negroes they should endeavor to improve on the old style and give us something in the utmost harmony with the highest yearnings of the race. Other fields have been entered by members of the race with more or less success. Here they have reflected credit upon themselves, their race and their country. Not all, of course, for some have missed the mark.

Among the successful writers and authors of the race, the author of the "Dispensations," Bishop B. T. Tanner, D.D. LL.D., stands among the first. He is a man of profound piety and rare scholarship. He is amply qualified to discuss the themes suggested by the title of his book. His long years of literary activity as editor and author, his theological training and Biblical investigation and research make him an authority in these especial lines. Indeed in the realms of theological thought he has an acknowledged place, and whatever he says is sure to attract attention.

The Rt. Rev. W. B. Derrick very fittingly introduces the author's work and clearly sets forth why Bishop Tanner is so well qualified for the task he entered upon. Bishop Derrick, after referring to the author's published works and miscellaneous contributions to the press, says of him most appropriately: "He has shown himself to be an able defender, not only of the church of his choice, but of the faith once delivered unto the saints. Patient, plodding, industrious, soaring above the sordid, always alert and with keen eye, he has kept abreast of the times, making the world decidedly wiser and better informed upon many subjects." Then again the Bishop says that this great work will in all probability be the writer's last literary production and that God has graciously prolonged his life that he may give to church and race a monument of sanctified genius and unfeigned devotion to His cause. We trust, however, that his pen will not be laid down while health and strength last.

There are two volumes of this work before us. In the first there are nine preludes which Bishop Tanner is pleased to designate as Excursus. He concludes this first chapter with the First Dispensation (Adamic). The second volume opens with the First Interregnum. Then Dispensations follow, alternating with Interregnums. The subjects discussed are some of the most important in Biblical history and at the same time some of the knottiest in sacred literature. I call them knotty because some of them have given rise to almost interminable debates from the earliest period of our history to the present moment. But the Master's hand is shown in dealing with them. These are some of the themes: *"The Significance of a Dispensation," "Chronology of the Bible," "The Origin of Man," "Descent of the Negro*[;]*" "Ordination of Women," "The Flood," "Division of the Land," "Prophecy and Prophets*[*"*] *"Baptism."* Following these divisions are: *"The Noachic, the Abrahamic, Mosaic and Christian Dispensations."* The Sixth Dispensation is the *"Dispensation of Glory."*

To appreciate this work, to appreciate its merit and the amount of learning and of research it displays, one must possess it; he must read it and study it for himself. Science and theology go hand in hand and Bishop Tanner shows quite conclusively that there is no exception here. Why should there be? In regard to the chronology of the Bible the following lines appear: "Is there such a chronology?" he asks. "That altogether depends upon the definition given, and the phase of it determined upon. Undoubtedly Moses gives us the rule by means of which all true chronology must stand; and not so much a rule as a statement that is both a discovery and a revelation. "And God said, let there be lights in the firmament of the heaven to divide the day from the night and let them be for signs, and for seasons, and for days and years," Gen. i: 14. Herein man is pointed to the only sure foundation of all chronology; for without the help of the sun, moon and stars chronology would be impossible. If, however, is meant what we might call applied chronology after the fashion of those who speak of applied chemistry, then for reasons both special and general we can agree with those—and among them Dean [Henry Hart] Milman—who declare that there is no such thing as Biblical chronology.

On the origin of man the writer is quite as clear, quite as forcible, and his arguments are both able and convincing, especially to him who is seeking light. He says, "The doctrine of the direct creation of man—what witnesses have we to substantiate them?" Our witnesses are Moses, Job, Solomon, Isaiah, Jeremiah and Zechariah. Moses' first testimony is as follows: And God said "Let us make man in our image, after our likeness."

> "Upon this, the first testimony of Moses, it is to be said that there is little of the definiteness we desire. And yet, as it relates to the question at issue, while we could wish, for the sake of discussion, greater details were given, the fact stated is not to be overlooked, that man was made directly by God. And first, it is notice[a]ble that his making is alluded to in a way peculiar to itself. Of the creation of light, God said, 'Let there be light.' Of the creation of the firmament, He said, 'Let there be a firmament.' Of the seas and the earth, 'Let the waters under the heavens be gathered together into one place and let the dry land appear.' Of the great vegetable world, 'Let the earth put forth grass.' Of the heavenly world, 'Let there be lights in the firmament of heaven.' Of all marine creatures, 'Let the waters bring forth abundantly.' Of all terrene animals, 'Let the earth bring forth living creature of its kind.' It was simply: Let the things be done. But when He came to the making of man, an entirely different form of speech was employed. It is no longer, [']Let the thing be done[']—done by long process of development, if you please, but the set phrase is pushed aside and an entirely new one employed: 'Let us make man.' Why this difference? Manifestly for one or two reasons. Either to settle upon the wisdom of such creation itself, or the use of a different method. That it could not have been the first is certain, and for the reason that the general creation had already advanced too far."

I have thus given this long extract because it so beautifully illustrates the rhetorical finish and the logic of the argument employed by the writer. Again

> "But let us listen to Moses' third statement upon the origin of man; for, if we are not mistaken, it throws such a flood of light upon the matter, in that it gives us details, as ought, we think to settle the question at once. Having previously said that God made (*assah*) man, that he created (*bara*) him, as though unwilling to leave a shadow of ignorance as to the *how*, he graciously says—Gen ii: 6., 'and the Lord God formed man of the dust of the ground.' The verb here employed is neither *assah* nor *bara*, but *yatsar*, which signifies to *form, to fashion, to make*. Are we asked to account for the employment of these three distinct verbs? And all, in the space of what is, to

us, this thirteen verses? With but a single exception only one verb is employed in the recital of all other forms of life, whether of the air, the land or the sea. Twice the number of verses and one verb; one half the number of verses and three verbs. Such a fact as this utterly destroys the argument that Moses uses these verbs synonymously."

How strongly and forcibly put are these arguments. The whole book is just so clear in statement. I have seldom read a treatise dealing with such themes that was so fascinating in style from the first page to the last.

The fourth prelude discusses a subject that every Negro school teacher, every Negro clergyman, every Negro scholar ought to read and to study. I call especial attention to it.

A startling proposition has been made by those not in sympathy with the race and by skeptical scientists and theologians that the Negro is not descended from Ham. In fact, that he is the result of a separate and distinct creation—if created at all—that he is a Preadamite. Many theologians and scientists and men of smaller pretensions are seeking data to prove a theory that may accord with their notions. Bishop Tanner discusses this subject thoughtfully, thoroughly and ably and carries his point, as I think.

After referring to the statement of Revs. Drs. J. H. Vincent, J. M. Freeman and J. L. Hulburt: "It is not certain whether or not the Negro race descended from Ham," (Sunday School Journal M. E. Church, Lesson IV. Jan. 23), the Bishop plunges into his subject and shows that the theory is born of prejudice and not of fact, that it is not Scriptural. Says the author:

"That the Negro is of African patrimony the world knows. The dullest blockhead of the most out-of-the-way country school knows that the father of the black fellow whom he is all the time meeting came from Africa. Nor could the most persistent pedagogue get him to believe otherwise. The Negro, then, is of Africa. But who settled Africa—which of the sons of Noah, we mean? The one authoritative voice in the settlement of this question is the Bible, for it alone, as we have said, throws light upon ages declared to be prehistoric by the secular analysts. Is Europe Japhetic? Is Asia Shemitic? Then Africa is Hamitic by one and the same testimony; re-inforced however, we may be allowed to say, by the facts of philology; for while Europe and Asia depend altogether on the statements of history, Africa can call to her help philology. Why should Holy Writ be thought to speak infallibly of two and fallibly of one? Were the writers biased or were the facts more difficult to remember? Neither supposition is to be entertained."

Again, in another place, he says:

"To attempt to assign the Negro another than Hamitic origin is nothing less than an attempt to read the Bible with other than the old time Christian eyes. In the light of those eyes the Bible is an inspired book; if not verbally inspired, certainly plenarily inspired. According to this light the race was a unit, with Noah for its head as one, and Shem, Ham and Japhet as its heads in parts. But in the light of these new eyes, all this is seen to be erroneous."

Thus does the author meet his antagonists step by step with invincible argument. That language was once homogeneous, that it was once a unit and that it sprang from a common source seems settled beyond dispute. If we then accept this as a fact we must conclude that the race was once a unit, that all races sprang from one and that in the diversity of peoples and races language likewise became diversified. This may add a thought to Bishop Tanner's argument in support of one center of creation—though he is abundantly able to maintain his own ground without any assistance from me.

As to the universality of the flood, the author gives reason for his faith in the summary of his arguments, thus: God's mightiness is equal to the emergency. Secondly, supposing the flood to have been universal, the fact could not be communicated to the world if the record already given does not tell us of that fact. Third, all the ages that have since passed, understood the patriarchs, inspired and uninspired, to say that the flood was universal. Fourth, nothing is gained by denying it, but on the contrary, much is lost in that it makes the teachings of the Bible uncertain.

Significant is that chapter on Baptism, and we can only call attention to it. All the quotations I have so far given have been from Volume I. The second volume is equally interesting; especially are those chapters which discuss the patriarchs and the events that cluster about their lives—the prophets and prophetic times. We forbear to indulge in further reference or discussion of this notable book except to say that as the term dispensation implies, the author has given us "what is unfolded in the scripture" with reference to the Divine economy, and royally has he done his work. He concludes the second volume with the Book of Joshua. I have yet to find a work from which I have derived more genuine pleasure and profit in its perusal than the "Dispensations in the History of the Church".

Review of Booker T. Washington's *The Future of the American Negro*

in *Annals of the American Academy of Political and Social Sciences* 16
(July–November 1900): 145–147.

Mr. Booker T. Washington's book on "The Future of the American Negro" is largely a *resumé*, as the introduction intimates, of what this distinguished negro educator has had to say from time to time upon the theme nearest his heart—industrial education.[1] The negro problem, as it is called, still continues to be one of the most absorbing topics of the times, and Mr. Washington's nineteen years of work in the populous Black Belt of the South have afforded him valuable opportunities to observe, compare, and reach conclusions that are of great worth on the subject. To such a spokesman the thoughtful public willingly lends an attentive ear.

Mr. Washington is well known to be a strong believer in industrial education; he asserts unequivocally that "in too large measure the negro race began its development at the wrong end," that "industrial independence is the first condition for lifting up any race," that the negro must become a producer, meeting the economic demands by industrial training. Chapter I is devoted to a brief sketch of the negro's introduction into America, his increase and his part in the country's life from the earliest times to the end of the Reconstruction era. Chapter II aims to show the interdependence of all parts of our common country and of our people—especially in the southland—in connection with a view of the present conditions there. He insists that knowledge will benefit the race little "except as its power is pointed in a direction that will bear upon the present needs and conditions of the race," and he declares himself in possession of a strong brotherly sympathy for the entire South—all classes and races—suffering from the burdens of the situation. Chapter III pictures the prosperous plantation of *ante-bellum* days, and pays tribute to the methods then followed which produced colored men skilled in the trades. This is contrasted with the conditions of the present time and the almost utter lack of such skill which places him at a disadvantage in the industrial world. Chapter IV emphasizes the preceding one by statement of the author's conception of the proper use of education and by illustrations showing to what this lack of skill has led. Chapter V logically follows with the setting forth of the plan of industrial training carried out in the author's own school—Tuskegee, Alabama—which he sums up as aiming at making teachers and industrial leaders who will push forward similar training throughout the Black Belt. The negro conferences for which Tuskegee has become noted are also sketched, with motives and *modus operandi.*

Chapter VI gives the author's views on the franchise. He defines his position as being subservient to the interests of his race and the whole South, and his policy as one of non-activity in party politics. He attributes the present state of affairs to the "unfortunate" beginning during the Reconstruction era and to mutual misunderstandings between the two races in the South. We find here in an open letter to the State Constitutional Convention of Louisiana, what is perhaps the fullest public expression of Mr. Washington's opinion on political subjects,—a manly, sensible, strong appeal for protection of the ballot, for equal voting tests for both races, for the upholding of law. The permanent cure, he affirms, will come most of all through "industrial development of the negro" which will make him a producer, a property holder, a tax payer, and therefore a careful voter, and he prophesies a division of the negro vote on economic issues.

Chapter VII passes by all theories as to emigration and colonization as impracticable. The desirable relations between the races are dwelt upon, and the negro's weak as well as strong points are summarized and analyzed to a certain extent. It is interesting to note that, despite the frequent assertions of a wrong beginning in negro education that led the race away from a proper consideration of the "dignity of labor," we meet at this point the equally emphatic assertion that the negro "is not ashamed or afraid to work." The lynching evil is forcibly treated at the close, showing, as all right thinking persons must admit, that naught but moral deterioration for all races concerned can follow such utter disregard of law. The eighth and last chapter consists of a general summary of the preceding views and of a series of suggestions as to a future policy. Mr. Washington enumerates six dangers: in impatient extremists among the negroes of the North incapable of understanding the southern situation; in the white South's allowing itself without protest to be represented by the mob; in discouragement to the race under present conditions; in exaggerated reports of race troubles; in ignorance and idleness; and in unjust legislation against the race. His remedy is closer identification of the negro with the South and its interests, southern white interest in negro schools to be actively shown by white teachers, and industrial training for the race, concerning which he says "I believe that slavery laid the foundation for the solution of the problem that is now before us in the South." Mr. Washington grants that professional men will be needed, but we gather as his opinion that there will not be a very decided *raison d'être* for them until there is a colored constituency to support them, and also that, after all, leaders must be those largely able to "infuse themselves into agriculture, mechanics, domestic employment and business."

There are three points, in fact, that might be taken to sum up the book as a whole, and upon which the author places from beginning to end continuous, strenuous insistence. First, that the education first given the negro, based on methods used in New England, was a serious mistake and the possible cause of the lack of progress along economic lines. This is only a half truth. When we consider the universally acknowledged, phenomenal progress of the race since the war we question whether the race would have stood where it does to-day in general prosperity, in intelligence and in the respect of the world had industrial training been at all practicable at that date. The second point is the generally admitted necessity of amicable relations between the races, especially in the South. Third, industrial education is the solution of the problem. The unbounded efficacy of this remedy will be doubted by some.

But, taking the book as a whole, it is an earnest, thoughtful, well-wrought plea for industrial training, just such a book as would be expected from Mr. Washington whose heart and soul are bound up in his worthy and magnificent work in the South. It is epigrammatic, anecdotal, persuasive, and abounds in sensible suggestions, not the least of which is that more attention be given to the race history, to collecting relics that mark race progress and to perpetuate in durable form race achievements. Viewed from any standpoint this work of 244 pages makes a contribution of permanent value to the race discussions. There is one defect, however, which must be noted, aside from that of the attempt to marshal all facts concerning a people as logical material to prove any one thing. Considering the title the book bears it is defective in that higher education is not allowed to play any part in this discussion relative to the future of the American negro, except perhaps to "point a moral or adorn a tale," or to illustrate humorously its mistaken uses. The reasoning connected with mental development all trends along the line that such development is worthless except as it can be traded for a material something (p. 76). I cannot believe that either the white or "colored" race is ready as yet to commit itself solely and irrevocably, along educational lines, to the discipleship of materialistic utilitarianism.

Note

1 [See also Scarborough's review of Washington's *Up from Slavery*, in *Annals of the American Academy of Political and Social Sciences* 18 (November 1901): 149–151.]

Obituaries

Bishop Payne as an Educator

Christian Recorder, January 25, 1894.

When that wealthy slaveholder in Charleston, S. C., in 1829, attempted to persuade Daniel Alexander Payne, then a slender youth of eighteen years, to accompany him to the West Indies, offering as an inducement that the knowledge gained by such travel would be far more valuable to him than the paltry wages he was then receiving as a school teacher, and emphasizing the statement with the added thought that the difference between master and slave was nothing but superior knowledge, he then and there unconsciously decided the destiny of the future colored bishop and leader. Said young Payne to himself: "If it is true that there is nothing but superior knowledge between the master and slave, I will not go with you, but rather go and obtain that knowledge which constitutes the master."[1] He was as good as his word.

Having already obtained a rudimentary education under the auspices of a society of free colored men, which was established in 1803, he pursued his studies, sometimes with and sometimes without an instructor, until he had, in reality, mastered what is now equivalent to a scientific course in an average Western college.

In his "Recollections of Seventy Years," he tells us that on one day he bought a Greek grammar, a Lexicon and a Greek Testament; on the next he mastered the Greek alphabet; on the third he learned to write the same, and on the fourth he translated the First Chapter of Matthew's Gospel from the Greek into the English. Next came Latin and French. These he pursued in a similar way until he had acquired a reading knowledge of them. Nor did he neglect other studies. Philosophy, the Natural and Physical Sciences, Mathematics and History, all received due attention, while at the same time he pushed forward his work in "drawing and coloring till he was able to produce a respectable flower, fruit or animal on paper or velvet."[2]

Nor was this all. He continued similar lines of study and made each subject mastered a stepping-stone to something higher. He was himself emphatically a student and had little mercy upon another who was not, especially if he made pretentions to scholarly attainments. He believed in sound training and thorough preparation on the part of those who assumed the important role of teacher. Quality rather than quantity—fitness was more than a mere theory with him. He opposed show and glittering generalities in all forms of education as in other lines. He believed that the workman should be thoroughly up in his line and no man who was not thus qualified should for a moment occupy the position of an instructor. One of the curses of the Negro race today is the number of *incompetent would-be educators. Quality goes for nothing. Quantity for everything.* To this class Bishop Payne was a relentless foe. He was the results and knew that they made the Negro's progress painfully slow and his acquisitions painfully undesirable. A commendable position to take and it is entirely in harmony with our greatest American educators—Harper, Elliot and others. This phase he has emphasized in his will wherein he leaves two fifths of his real estate to the college and three-fifths to the seminary with the proviso that the whole shall be sold and that the amount shall be put at interest till it shall reach a hundred thousand dollars and then certain chairs shall be endowed in both college and seminary and the same shall be filled by the ablest and most competent men in their special lines that can be secured.

Here we see the genuine educator. Here we see the benefactor—a man whose interest in the education and elevation of his race is so intense that he looked beyond the present into the future twenty, thirty or forty years hence, thus insuring what might be otherwise lost. Benjamin Franklin did this and with splendid results. Who will dare say that this was other than wise forethought. Bishop Payne, like Dr. [William] Whewell, was a man of varied attainments. He knew something about many things and though not a specialist in true sense of the term he was a man of great breadth of learning and in this sense a scholar. His acquisitions came from nature, from travel, from contact with men as well as from books.

It was not until he had left Gettysburg Seminary that his real active life began. Then his fight was for an educated ministry among his people and though often made against great odds, he succeeded in revolutionizing the thoughts and actions of many of his contemporaries and co-laborers in reference to an intelligent clergy. He has been called an apostle of an educated ministry from the early efforts put forth by him to blot out ignorance.

It is in connection with Wilberforce University that Bishop Payne stands forth most prominently as an educator. Here was the theatre of his literary activities. It is here that we see in a greater degree than elsewhere the man, the teacher, the preacher. Sternly critical and possessed of marked individuality, though a man of small physique, he was able to impress those committed to his care with his personality, which at once stamped him as an educator that must be obeyed. The result was that every student who left Wilberforce carried with him the impress of Daniel A. Payne.

As an educator he bore the same relation to Wilberforce that Mark Hopkins did to Williams College, and James H. Fairchild to Oberlin College. Who can think of Hopkins or Fairchild without thinking of Williams or Oberlin? It was that profound of profound scholars, S. H. Taylor, that made Andover Academy the idol of every Andover alumnus, that gave character and tone to that justly celebrated school such as Eton and Harrow could scarcely boast of notwithstanding their long list of learned instructors. Though dead Dr. Taylor still lives in Andover and in the heart of every Andover student. Mark Hopkins is no more, yet Williams College stands forth as a monument to his upright character, his exemplary life, his literary activities and his devotion to the cause of Christian education. Bishop Payne is dead, but he leaves behind a Wilberforce and a Payne Theological Seminary that speak louder than tongue or pen.

Could the Church do a more fitting thing than to commemorate the life and character of such a man, such a teacher by a handsome offering? One hundred thousand dollars should be the mark and every man, woman and child of Negro extraction in particular and every citizen who had the honor of his acquaintance should resolve on the day of his memorial services to crown his memory with a fitting tribute which shall perpetuate the institution bearing his name—*Payne Theological Seminary.*

Notes

1 [Daniel Alexander Payne, *Recollections of Seventy Years* (Nashville, Tenn.: A.M.E. Sunday School Union, 1888), pp. 19–20.]

2 [Payne, *Recollections of Seventy Years*, pp. 22–23.]

Obituary of William Hayes Ward

Independent, September 11, 1916.

With keenest sorrow I learn that a valued personal friend and a friend of the negro race has passed to the Great Beyond, and I gladly accept the invitation to give a brief appreciation of Dr. William Hayes Ward's work for the negro. He has virtually devoted his life to the interests of the race, to its emancipation, to its education, to its struggles, to its ambitions, to its possible future, without a particle of prejudice. Believing that God made mankind all of one blood and that the negro should have free enjoyment of the rights and privileges of any human being and of any American citizen, Dr. Ward arrayed himself always on that platform and fearlessly fought the battles of a weak and defenseless people.

Proscription, segregation, mob violence, lynchings, denial of vote, all race distinctions, all the thousand and one indignities, persecutions and cruelties and crimes against the negro wherever practised, have found in him one who denounced vigorously and unsparingly all such as unlawful, unjust, unchristian and inhuman. His work did not stop with his strenuous endeavors to right the wrongs done the negro, but he maintained that the education of the race should be of the highest type; declared and demonstrated its intellectual capacity thru many negro contributions to The Independent on all lines of thought; and encouraged all its ambitions and aspirations as a people. Everything connected with the race won his personal interest, and he never wavered in his allegiance. Public opinion never warped his convictions. Nor did personal interest ever cause him to swerve from the course he deemed right in regard to the race.

There was no mere sentimentalism in this; he was a humanitarian of the most royal type, espousing our cause because he believed it a just one and because we were lowly, weak, defenseless and friendless. So his warm heart, his keen brain, and his facile pen have united for over fifty years to declare thru The Independent and every other possible channel that he was the negro's staunch friend. The negro people have lost a most noble, loyal champion, one they will ever hold in grateful remembrance. May his mantle rest upon and forever enfold The Independent.

Biographies

Prof. Richard T. Greener:
His Commendable Career and
Claims to Recognition

Christian Recorder, February 9, 1882.

I have just finished reading, for the third or fourth time, the speech of our esteemed friend, Professor R. T. Greener, delivered at the "Harvard Club of New York Dinner."[1] The more I read it, the more I admire the Professor and the more do I commend that indefatigable purpose of his to defend the negro under all circumstances whenever his rights are infringed upon and his liberties are curtailed. Every man ought to be protected in the enjoyment of his rights, and the man who will aid in doing this, whether it be popular or unpopular, is the man for the hour. Professor Greener, by a long, thorough and critical course of classical training in Oberlin College and Harvard University (from which he graduated with highest honors) is doubtless one of the best educated, as well as one of the most brilliant, men among us. In addition to being a man of many parts, he is every inch a scholar and a fine lawyer, and therefore he could represent the negro in any department where he might be called as but few of us can. We need such a man at the front. We need such men at the head of our schools. We must have such men to steer our little bark or else we are all wrecked. Our great mistake is the putting of comparatively ignorant men at the helm of institutions of higher instruction. This will prove to be the death knell to our educational system. We must see to it that sound scholarship and accurate training, combined with good judgment, take the lead among us, for we of all other people cannot afford to have it otherwise. Together with those of our representative men already provided for, nothing would please us more than to see Prof. Greener recognized by the Administration in his appointment to some good position. His appointment would be hailed with joy by the whole colored race, as well as by others who honor him. We would call President Arthur's attention to his claims as a representative Republican, as an active, vigilant worker for Republican principles. As colored citizens and as a component part of the American body politic we present his name to the consideration of the Administration.

His career from the beginning has been excellent. Whenever justice demanded his time, money, and the fruit of his long training, Prof. Greener has given all freely and willingly, and has stuck to his client until the crisis was over. Again, he has been an active and energetic defender of the principles of equal rights and has often placed himself in jeopardy by supporting the Republican party. During the most exciting times in the history of the State of South Carolina, when it was almost instant death for a Republican to make speeches in certain parts of the State, when the old Palmetto State was in a period of transition, split almost from centre to circumference, with the legally elected Governor (Chamberlain) on the one side, and Wade Hampton on the other, when war and carnage stared everybody in the face, when, indeed, it was almost a crime to admit that one was a Republican, Prof. R. T. Greener, traveling through various counties, such as Abbeville and Laurens, bravely and nobly clinging to his principles of justice and equality for all men regardless of race or color, advised every Republican to remain true to his colors. This was heroism; this was patriotism. His speeches still ring in the ears of those who heard them as models of thought and oratory. In the midst of insinuations, taunts, jeers, threats and often almost in the midst of a mob, he proclaimed free ballot and popular rights. This is the gentleman we again commend to the consideration of the President. We take pride in such men as Greener, [Blanche K.] Bruce, [Frederick] Douglass and [John Mercer] Langston, as representative men of the race.

This little retrospection calls up many things which occurred at that fearful period in Southern politics. Who can forget Hodge's station, on the South Carolina Railroad? Who can forget Abbeville?[2] Who can forget Cokesbury? Who can forget Laurens, Edgefield, and a number of other places memorable for fiendish deeds? Ask those true and tried Republicans, ask Governor Chamberlain, ask Prof. Greener, ask them to give you an epitome of a day's doings in those parts. They will give you a history that will remain as fixed as the stars in the heavens. We cannot afford to have such a man as Professor Greener ignored and trust that he will be speedily cared for.

Notes

1 [For a full account of Greener's life, see Michael R. Mounter, "Richard Theodore Greener: The Idealist, Statesman, Scholar, and South Carolinian," PhD dissertation (2002), University of South Carolina (UMI Dissertation Abstract #3052060).]

2 [B. F. Randolph, chaplain to the 26th Regiment of U.S. Colored Troops, was killed while campaigning in Abbeville County, South Carolina, on October 16, 1868. Columbia's Randolph Cemetery was named after him, and his gravestone bears the words "died at the hands of assassins."]

Hon. Frederick Douglass: One of the Most Distinguished and Honored Citizens on the American Continent

Cleveland Gazette, March 20, 1886.

Among the great names that America has produced, whether of Caucasian or African extraction, is the honored name of Frederick Douglass. He was born about the year 1817 in the State of Maryland, at a time when our country was weighed down by the terrible incubus of slavery, and when no earthly power could come between the master and the slave. At an early age he learned to detest the heinous evil and to ardently desire freedom. At length the opportunity came to make good his escape, and from the day he landed in New Bedford, Mass., there began for him an active career under a new dispensation—a second life, strange, varied and romantic as the first, and both stranger than any in fiction.

A brief sketch of such a man must be, perforce, very incomplete. His life has been crowded with incidents, coming upon the stage of action as he did, when the country was beginning to feel the throes of the anti-slavery convulsions. With this movement he became connected, and as the years rolled by and the excitement relative to slavery grew in intensity, as howling mobs and fiendish sympathizers with the old slave oligarchy made cities, towns and villages hideous with their cry for blood and Negro oppression, the voice of Frederick Douglass, with those of [William] Garrison, [Gerrit] Smith, [Wendell] Phillips, [Charles] Sumner and scores of other famous names, was heard sounding the clarion key note to freedom.

Twice he was obliged to seek refuge in England; the first time, to avoid recapture by his former master—kind friends then purchased his person and *gave it to himself*—the second time, to escape from the fury aroused by his connection with John Brown and his supposed connection with the Harper's Ferry raid. There was no movement for freedom in which he did not bear a conspicuous part, directly or indirectly. When permission was at last given to raise colored troops, his influence, by tongue and pen, went far toward enlisting the Fifty-fourth and Fifty-fifth Massachusetts colored regiments. His two sons took the father's place on the field where he would have been also, and the Government then dared recognize his services. When slavery and the war came to an end he still pleaded for human rights. He was delegated by the colored delegation, which waited upon President Andrew Johnson, to prepare a speech in reply. It was a masterly effort. Although not wanted in the National Loyalist Convention of 1866, he bravely asserted our rights by maintaining his as a delegate, and there he pleaded for Negro suffrage.

Mr. Douglass has been editor and publisher of two prominent papers. During the most turbulent times for sixteen years he published the *North Star*, in Rochester, N. Y. This name was afterwards changed to *Frederick Douglass' Paper*. He was then induced to remove to Washington and take charge of the *New National Era*. Deceived as to the condition of the Freedman's Bank, he was led to accept the presidency of the swindle when it was all but ready to collapse, while to his own losses as depositor was added much unjust criticism.[1] After the adoption of the Fifteenth Amendment he turned to the lecture field, preferring a literary life to one purely political. As an orator Mr. Douglass has no superior. Age has not dimmed his intellect nor paralyzed his tongue. A veritable Pylian Nestor, from whose lips flow words sweeter than honey, he has justly earned the title of "old man eloquent,"[2] and in listening, one is inclined to believe that the prophecy which old Homer put into the mouth of the blue-eyed goddess, Pallas Athena, when she says to Telemachus:

> "In part thy mind will prompt thy speech; in part
> A God will put the words into thy mouth,"[3]

has descended in some mysterious manner as a legacy to him. The central thought of all his speeches has ever been the amelioration of the condition of the American Negro. What more could be desired? Upright, firm and steadfast, contented to take obloquy and insult, to lose friends and fortune, upheld by the conviction of acting in the right, assailed by mobs of ruffians and deserted by those who should have sustained him, Frederick Douglass has ever recognized the hardest duty as the highest, and triumph has come through all the trials.

His numerous appointments of honor and distinction, civil and political, can not all be mentioned here. He accompanied the San Domingo Commission; he was appointed to a seat in the Council of the District of Columbia; to the U. S. Marshalship by President Hayes; to the office of Recorder of Deeds under President Garfield, which office he still holds; nor should we omit mention of his services in the Underground Railroad.[4]

Every one who rises, by so much lifts up his people. As Frederick Douglass rose to eminence the possibilities of the race were made apparent, as shown by Dr. Talmage in his sermon of January 3, when he says: "Take the African race. They have been under bondage for centuries. Give them a chance and they develop a Frederick Douglass."[5] He fought the battles during the dark days. We of the present, though hampered still, know nothing of the severity of those conflicts. To cause the wrong views and practices of a people like ourselves to yield to those of sounder nature; to reform the habits of a people situated as we are, a direct appeal must be made to each, and each must be made to see the dire results of adhering uncompromisingly to this or that mode of procedure. In keeping with this thought we call attention to one of Mr. Douglass' many excellent speeches, delivered at Rochester, N. Y., last year. If the people could only see the situation as the orator depicted it, and adopt a policy in harmony with it, the American Negro would soon pass this transition period to a point where he would *demand* respect and not simply *ask* for it.

I regard Mr. Douglass as one of the foremost colored men of the world. In public life he has been straight-forward yet discreet, qualities not at all antagonistic but absolutely necessary in order to win confidence and success in such a career. He was the pioneer of the race in the agitation for freedom. From then till now he has been the relentless champion of human rights and a most fearless advocate of equality before the law. He is the veteran hero of past battles and the staunch color bearer of the present. His age, influence, position and, above all, the work that he has done, make him a leader of the race with all that name implies, and there is no country, age or clime where such a *leader* as this will not have power despite opposition.

To such a one, who spoke fearlessly when life and liberty were endangered every moment; who worked literally with a price on his head; who dared public opinion; frantic mobs and the auction block itself for the millions in bondage; who, by the aid of voice and pen, helped make free speech and liberty our present possession; who won friends for the generation in chains and those unborn, and who among the first won recognition for the ability of the Negro race and faith in the possibilities of that race, we all owe an immeasurable debt of gratitude, and to Frederick Douglass the generation now active in public life should ungrudgingly accord most chivalrous recognition.

Notes

1 [Douglass moved to Washington in 1870, and the bank collapsed in 1874.]

2 [This is John Milton's description of Isocrates in his sonnet "To the Lady Margaret Ley," line 8. "Old Man Eloquent" was also a nickname for John Quincy Adams.]

3 [*Odyssey*, book 2.]

4 [Douglass accompanied the San Domingo Commission in 1875, was appointed to the U.S. Marshalship in March 1877, and was appointed to the office of Recorder of Deeds in 1881.]

5 [Dr. T. DeWitt Talmage revised this line to read: "Take the African race. They have been under bondage for centuries. Give them a chance and they develop a Toussaint L'Ouverture." See "Sermon for the Day," *South Jersey Republican*, February 21, 1900, p. 3.]

Henry Ossian Tanner

Southern Workman 31 (December 1902): 661–670.

In its September issue, a leading periodical of Philadelphia began its reproductions of a series of four paintings in oil by a Negro artist—Henry Ossian Tanner, a native of Philadelphia and a son of Bishop B. T. Tanner of the African Methodist Episcopal church.[1] Mr. Tanner has been making a serious pursuit of his art for some fifteen years and has attained a remarkable degree of success. His first crude sketches at Atlantic City one summer drew the attention of friends who discerned the germs of genius in those first efforts and generously lent substantial encouragement to its possessor to continue in the path he has so far followed with most gratifying results.

Mr. Tanner at first pursued his studies in Philadelphia with Thomas Eakins at the Academy of Fine Arts, coming also under the influence of Mr. [Thomas] Hovenden who, good authority asserts, "infused into him a comprehension of and sympathy with the broader and deeper things of life and art." Thence he went to Paris in 1891, after a brief experience as teacher of art in a Southern college for the race.[2] In this Southern experience he tried his hand at modeling and casting in plaster. A bust of the venerable Negro educator, Bishop D. A. Payne, was a very creditable effort, as it seems to the writer, who has before him this reproduction of that well-known prelate's features. Three oil paintings of this early period are upon the walls of Wilberforce University library, the gift of Bishop Payne, who admired most heartily and encouraged steadily this budding genius, as indeed he did all genius in the race. These three are "seascapes" —one somewhat "Turneresque" in its dashing impressionist style of representing a storm at sea, the other two, small panels, rich in coloring, giving thus a hint of future excellence.

In Paris it was Mr. Tanner's fortune to study under the guidance of Jean Paul Laurens and the late Benjamin Constant in the celebrated Julian School of Art. To the latter artist it is evident that the pupil owes much. This master was both teacher and friend to the ambitious Negro student. To-day, among the treasures in a roomy studio in the Latin Quarter of Paris, nothing perhaps is more highly prized by the occupant than a picture of Constant bearing this inscription: "A mon élève Tanner son maitre et ami, toujours confiant dans le succés de son fini."[3]

In the French capital and art center he gained two prizes—one for a sketch of "The Deluge" and another for a sketch made in Brittany. On the writer's wall hangs one of the bits of the results of his first studies in Concarneau, that picturesque spot in Brittany where painters flock to paint the quaint scenes and dresses of this chief center of sardine fisheries. It is a morning scene— "The Going Out of the Fishing Boats from Concarneau." It is a bright, cheery one—a sandy strip and a brown spit of rock in the foreground with a narrow, dim shore line stretching out against the sky in the background, nearly encircling the broad, blue expanse of water on which, near the horizon, rests a misty fleet of departing sails.

On another wall hangs a reproduction of "The Bagpipe Lesson," another scene in Brittany. A hale old peasant clothed in picturesque costume is seated on the edge of his wheelbarrow, watching with amused interest the efforts of the youth, who, with distended cheeks, is grappling with the mystery involved in drawing sound from the uncouth instrument. The greens and grays with a diffused light make a most agreeable color scheme. This picture was exhibited at Earles's galleries in Philadelphia with sixteen others: "Young Orange Trees," a Florida study; "Study of Head, Italian Woman"; "Spring Morning," a scene in Chester Co., Pa., "Scrub-Pine Land", and "Evening on the St. John's," both from studies near Enterprise, Fla.; "Lake Monroe" and "Orange Grove", studies in the same state; "October," "A Sudden Squall" and "The Thankful Poor"; two studies of "Evening" near Pont Aven, Brittany; one entitled "Bois d'Amour", a study from the same point; with three others, also studies in Brittany: "Rocks at Concarneau", "Return of Fishing Boats" and "The Foster Mother". Space will not permit any effort at description of these earlier works. It would be interesting to follow the fortunes of each one. Have they, like early literary efforts, been mostly consigned to the supposed oblivion of some retired corner, perhaps to be dragged forth at a future day to confront their creator? Hardly in every case, we shall see; yet why chagrin should usually follow such a facing of early efforts of any kind we cannot fully comprehend. Such beginnings not only show the road by which one has come perhaps to fame, nor alone the distance traversed, but comparison and analysis disclose many things of value; so why chagrin in either art or literature?

"The Banjo Lesson" is well known to Hampton visitors. This one of Mr. Tanner's early paintings, now in Hampton Library, has received much favorable criticism because of the remarkable handling of "cross lights." The room in which the lesson is given by the old colored man to the lad is lighted up by bright sunlight streaming through the window, while the figures receive the Rembrandt-like concentration of glow from the grate fire. The result is very successful. Four years after Mr. Tanner went to Paris he sent to the Salon "The Sabot Makers" which received favorable attention, and then he dropped what the artistic world calls *genre* painting and adopted another style.

When "The Banjo Lesson" appeared many of the friends of the race sincerely hoped that a portrayer of Negro life by a Negro artist had arisen indeed.

They hoped, too, that the treatment of race subjects by him would serve to counterbalance so much that has made the race only a laughing-stock subject for those artists who see nothing in it but the most extravagantly absurd and grotesque. But this was not to be. The fact had not been taken into consideration that his early home atmosphere had always been strongly religious, neither was it generally known that it had been the wish of his father's heart that his son should paint Biblical subjects—turn his genius into religious channels and thus make his art serve religion, since neither his pen nor voice was to be employed in such service. So Mr. Tanner turned, at this point in his career, to what promised to be his life work.

The first work in this line was "Daniel in the Lions' Den"—"a den; grim, crouching beasts; and a man leaning in the shadow of a brick wall," so it is tersely described by an enthusiastic art critic with the added criticism, "and it was the Orient and it was the Bible, and it was art as modern as that of Whistler." With this hanging in the Salon in Paris in 1896 came the always coveted "honorable mention." Then followed the "Raising of Lazarus," which brought him to the vestibule of fame; for it was bought by the French government for the Luxembourg gallery—the gateway to the Louvre, where hang only those chosen works of dead artists, honored and immortalized by the choice.

Of this picture there could be said what was said of the "Daniel"—"there was race in it," a quality that one critic avers to be new to Biblical painting. Be that as it may, Mr. Tanner studied to put "race in it." His winters spent in the Holy Land were to bear fruit—and it is that fruit we see in his work—the fruit of an originality that indicates genius of a high order. Unlike the German of the story he did not attempt to "evolve" things simply "out of his inner consciousness," but went straight to the real—to the lowly people of Palestine—for his types, and he has succeeded admirably in his masculine subjects in showing us the Jew as he must have lived and looked nearly twenty centuries ago.

It is of interest to note his treatment of the subject selected for this painting. The works of two other artists are brought to mind in this connection. Benjamin West, over a century ago, chose the same subject, representing it in oil on a canvas over ten feet long and exceeding eight in breadth; and James Tissot the French artist who died in the summer of 1902, produced a *bijou* in water color, hardly more than twelve inches in height. In comparing Tanner's painting with West's we are reminded of the coincidence that both were Pennsylvanians, and that both also owed to Philadelphia schools their first training. There is, however, everything to say in favor of the Negro artist's treatment of the subject. Though the figures are not so many nor as clearly defined as in West's, the reality of the scene is impressive. The dark cavern, the pallid face of Lazarus, the grief-stricken sisters, the startled throng, the strong face of the Christ—all impress you with the clearness of a photograph. You feel that these are Jews. In West's painting, which forms a part of the collection in the Wadsworth Athenaeum, Hartford, Conn., you have an eager, exultant, thankful throng—all but one pressing forward to view the miracle. Lazarus occupies the center, supported by one sister, and his uplifted hand clasped by the other. But you feel that he has come back to life before the out-stretched hand of Jesus indicates the call to come forth. Not so with Tanner's Lazarus. You are certain that his struggle back to life begins only when the Saviour stretches His hands above him. The sisters, too, in their attitudes, show a dread of viewing the beloved features. But art has advanced a long way since 1780.

Turning to Tissot's beautiful gem, the idea arises at once that there is a conception somewhat similar in the minds of both the Negro and the French artist. The latter represents Lazarus as raising himself from the tomb, unaided by human help. Standing on the step of the sepulchre is the Saviour with hand upraised as He speaks the magic words. The sisters, too, as in Mr. Tanner's painting, are skilfully placed in contrasting attitudes. One kneeling at one side near his feet, gazes in awed surprise at the scene, the other, sup-porting herself by hands outstretched on the stone before her, leans forward in fearful, amazed expectancy. As for coloring we cannot compare a water color bit with a canvas in oil. Both have beauties.

Another successful painting of our artist is "Nicodemus" which received the "Walter Lippincott" prize of $300 at the 69th annual exhibit of the Pennsylvania Academy of Fine Arts for the best figure painting by an American artist. But it is in his "Annunciation", which followed the "Raising of Lazarus", that we are able to see the finest conception of his genius. The interior of the cottage in Palestine is in every way "very Eastern in type," as are all the details. Here is a young girl seated upon her cot, roused from sleep to meet the mysterious announcement. But the announcement! No convention-alized angel hovers above with even the gauziest of Tissot's angels' wings, but streaming in upon the maiden is a shaft of golden light—in "line with the higher criticism", so it is said.

The praise this picture has received is voiced by such critical comment as the following: "The general tone of the picture is a rich glowing brown, sug-gestive of Rembrandt, but different. * * * It makes all the other pictures in the room look hard and glaring. It is impossible to put into words the beauty and strength of this picture. Absolutely simple and unforced and true, it comes nearer the greatest in art than any other picture in the Salon except one." We wonder and wish to know that other picture.

But to return to the reproductions of the four Biblical paintings representing the "Mothers of the Bible", mentioned in the beginning of this article. Of these "The Ladies' Home Journal" has brought out three at this writing. As they are probably more or less familiar to many who read this article, a detailed descrip-tion is unnecessary. The first, "Sarah", is a picture of a woman still possessing youthful roundness of face, neck and arms, despite the matron's robe and whitened hair of the aged wife of the patriarch—a woman posed with grace before her ancient loom, with eyes bent in adoring love upon the youth kneel-ing at her feet. It is again an Eastern interior and Sarah is the same type as Mary, save with the exchange of expression for one of rapt, credulous surprise. There is repose in the homely scene which Abraham must look upon with satisfied joy. Nor is Hagar depicted as less fair in the second painting, in the drooping figure that listens to Abraham's decree. Rachel follows with the same pensive expression, though now the attitude is changed as she listens to the wooing of Jacob. In each the light is admirable and the setting realistic. A conscientious endeavor is made to make the looker-on feel a power exercised over him as he gazes, and it is successful.

A complete list of Mr. Tanner's works is not at hand. As before intimated, perhaps he would cut from it some of his early efforts but that would hardly be fair or right. They have value. If there is no deterioration at future points in his work he has plenty of time left for a magnificent display of the originality that is admitted to be his, for though he has reached his forty-third year, he is at the period of life where power ripens often into best effort and we may expect something greater yet from him. That he is not an imitator is settled, thus doing away with one calumny concerning the race. It can work on independent lines and it has genius and talent of its own, shown in art by both sexes, for we need not forget that Edmonia Lewis has wrought her genius into sculpture that ranks high. These achievements have as surely brushed aside the color line as have those of Dumas and Pushkin in literature in the past, and time, we trust, will put the stamp of immortality on these of to-day as on those of yesterday.

That Mr. Tanner is ever a student, the close observer instantly feels. It was our personal pleasure, with Mrs. S———, to accompany him and his father one day in London to view an exhibition of Spanish paintings at the Guildhall Art Gallery—a fine loan collection, chief among which was a series of paintings by Velasquez, mostly portraits, and the main attraction for Mr. Tanner. His appreciative comment made it very evident that nothing is allowed to escape his observation, in all that goes to make up technique in art.

The second opportunity to understand his methods, his life and his study, came to us in Paris where he became the *cicerone* to our party for one afternoon. In the Louvre he was at his best, ready to point the uninitiated to the most artistic everywhere, flitting from party to party with what he thought would be best appreciated. We pardoned him when we reached the Pantheon and he laughingly disclaimed ability to describe the pictures that covered the walls of that Valhalla of France. We doubt, however, that our knowledge of real art was increased by turning us over to the tender mercies of the garrulous guide, though he knew by heart the story of St. Genevieve, the patron saint of Paris.

Personally, the artist is most polite and courteous, though he did not conceal a masculine enjoyment that there was one place where ladies could not enter—the Sorbonne—but he atoned for this lack of French gallantry by straightway conducting us to the place we desired above all to see and where a woman could enter—his own studio in the Latin Quarter. So while our *cochers* drank at the café on the sidewalk of the Boulevard San Michel, we turned down with our guide to the "Escalier des Ateliers" and mounted to his workshop. Here we explored and questioned. On one easel stood an evening sketch from near Paris—a bit of night with trees and dark blue skies. There was also the "Preparation for the Flight into Egypt," and heads by Donatelli and Holbein, a chair of Rubens', and an old Roman lamp interested us, while still further inquisitiveness revealed draperies which evoked the information that when Munkacsy died, Mr. Tanner bought nearly all his oriental costumes. And there were tiles from Jerusalem, some of which, bearing remnants of Arabic characters, form a part of the foreign treasures prized by the party to-day.

Reticent and modest, Mr. Tanner lets his work speak for him, and it was with diffidence that he displayed the cherished portrait of Constant, before mentioned. That he has become very much of a Frenchman, by his years of residence in the French capital, is readily seen in manner, dress, appearance generally, and conversation. Indeed, few would take the slender artist for a member of the Negro race, especially when met in the cosmopolitan cities of Europe or even in London. But the race claims him and claims a share in his work. It is the one inspiration that helps the Negro onward and upward—to know that color is no barrier to progress in the upper realms of thought and endeavor—that Negro genius may mount—has mounted, to the upper rounds of the ladder in these spheres. To be a man despite color is worth everything, and a man is a man in those countries across the sea. So, though Mr. Tanner visits his native land from time to time—has done so this year—it will not be strange if he makes his permanent home in France which fosters art or in England which patronizes art. Freedom from baleful prejudice is necessary to the best development of even genius, and surrounded in these lands by all that encourages and affords opportunity we may feel assured that our artist's best work is before him.

One writer speaking of the classes of artists in Paris says there are three— the many who "have started", a very small number who have received recognition and "are coming", and the few who "have arrived." This one places Mr. Tanner in the second class, but at the present rate of progress the Parisian art world will soon agree that he "has arrived."

Notes

1 [For Scarborough's friendship with Bishop Tanner and his son, Henry Ossawa (not Ossian) Tanner, see *Autobiography*, passim.]

2 [Clark College.]

3 To my pupil Tanner his master and friend, always confident of his final success.

Alexandre Dumas

Southern Workman 32 (July 1903): 313–317.

On the twenty-fourth of July, nineteen hundred and two, France celebrated the hundredth anniversary of the birth of Alexandre Dumas, *p[è]re*, the French quadroon historical romancer who was born at Villers-Cotterets, and who has enchanted the world with his story-telling genius. Nor was France alone in the recognition of this event. Tongues and pens in Great Britain and America paid tribute to the man who stands next to Victor Hugo in French imaginative literature, if indeed, he may not be considered first in many respects. The sentiment set in motion by that anniversary has not ceased to exist. The press is still busy giving us reminiscences and entertaining, even elaborate, studies of his life. These, with new editions of his works, are reviving any interest that may have waned since 1870 when at Puys, France, Dumas passed from this world after a little more than sixty-eight years of life.

These years were strenuous years. Dumas could never chain his lively temperament and restless disposition to a placid mode of life, and he early sought a change from the plodding, clerical work that influence had found for him. At twenty-one he left his native town where poverty and few opportunities offered him little hope for the future. In Paris he found the influences that shaped his life. There the theatre invited his aspirations and he began the work that was to lead him to fame in a few short years through a vivid imagination, seconded by boldness in planning and energy in action. From dramas and historical romances his pen traveled to find at last the field where his imagination could revel untrammelled, and where the world at large best knows Dumas.

Three decades have past since his body was given, in the village where he was born, a dignified last burial in the presence of the leading *litterateurs* of Paris. Now a fresh attempt is being made to gauge his powers from a later day standpoint and to endeavor to fix his status positively in the world of letters. Naturally there are two factions engaged in this work—those who think him highly overrated and those who see him still as the prince of romancers. Probably the two will always exist. Dumas has always had his detractors— those who could see nothing in his writings, who looked with contemptuous pity or sneering tolerance on his works and the stir made over them by the pleased public. To-day an Englishman leads the criticism which is still far from being altogether adverse, and because of this seems to be the best one to be chosen as the spokesman against him. Edmund Gosse claims that Dumas's influence on English literature is seen in the minor English novels of adventure which he denominates as "contemptible". He sarcastically calls Dumas "Hercules and Goliath and Sardanapalus", implying that everything in the career of the French novelist is on a "Rabelaisian scale". Yet he is forced to admit that Dumas has produced in "The Three Musketeers" "one perfect flower of his dream of the legendary elegance and ardor of French aristocracy", and he confesses that here is a national writer. And we claim that this was what Dumas was—*a national writer.*

Though he was accused of writing fairy tales rather than history, the truth is that he respected history quite as much as did Sir Walter Scott, that "Wizard of the North," or even Victor Hugo, whom it is conceded that he preceded as a romanticist. Dumas simply had the talent for seeing what was most picturesque in history and in the documents to which he had access. We prefer to reassert what another has declared—that Dumas possessed not only wit of the first order, but "narrative power of the highest degree which owes nothing to the thrilling sensationalism of the cap-and-sword series." Even Gosse finds a charm in his writing for, while he rudely declares Dumas to be a "rampageous schoolboy", in the same breath he says that if he only wrote books for elderly boys, still these are the best boy's books that ever were written. We have chosen Gosse's criticisms as examples because we feel that he has been contending with himself in an honest effort at unprejudiced criticism, for he makes haste to say that Dumas's manner is "admirable", that his rapidity and perfect transparency "are beyond question", and that the reader is carried along "with a triumphant energy"; yet he complains of "lack of substance", "want of art and reserve", "absence of subtlety and penetration"—in short, he falls back at every turn upon the first criticism, declaring that his admirers are so blinded by flood and glow and gaiety and profusion and vital force—not bad qualities to be sure—that they do not see that his qualities are all "child-like, not adult"—not qualities that "call for study of life and possession of stores of mental experience." We can hardly consider this such a fatal criticism after all. We are all more or less children, and what one may lament as a fault, may not seem a defect in eyes of others. [Robert Louis] Stevenson, the delightful Scotch romancer, loved to read Dumas. He boasted that he had read "Vicomte de Bragelonne" six times, and to the character, "D'Artagnan", he pays this tribute: "I do say there is none that I like so wholly."

But he was a Negro. Ah, yes; but who remembers it? Not those who are moved to tears by his pathos, not those who are convulsed with laughter by his wit, not those who are charmed into forgetfulness by his style. That Dumas was a Negro with certain Negro characteristics is a fact to be proud of. Without these characteristics he would not have been able to give us all that he has in his inimitable way. His father's mother was a black woman of San Domingo. His father's father was a French Marquis. One who knew him says that he had "thick, curly, black wool, broad negroid features, and a complexion which was rather bronzed than swarthy" and ascribes to his Negro heredity an extraordinary capacity for work, which was shown in the field of letters. By this same writer the declaration is made that the infusion of African blood with the French stock proved a rare combination. This we agree to, but we cannot accept the further statement in its entirety: that "from the French side came the nimbleness of thought, the exquisite lightness and brilliancy of fancy, the spirit that danced and sparkled like the bubbles in what he calls his '*joli petit vin d'Anjou*'; also the buoyancy that floated him superior to circumstances whenever any temporary pressure was removed." We feel convinced that a certain share of this airiness came from the African strain.

However no Dumas other than the Dumas of daily life could have created for us the fascinating tales that he poured forth. They were the outcome of his personal qualities. And what were these qualities? No one has summed them up better than Cyrus Townsend Brady in a recent review of [Arthur] Davidson's excellent new life of Dumas [1892]. "Prodigal, extravagant, careless, visionary, unreliable, impracticable, irresponsible, but lovable and charming" is the summary, and we would add, tender-hearted, impulsive, generous. Cloak these with an adventurous spirit, a gift for language, an eye for effect, and a boundless imagination, and we have Dumas *p[è]re*. Are these qualities racial? I contend that they are not to be considered as exclusively so. They belong to all genius in a very large measure. In every nation men and women writers may be found in whom, to a greater or less degree, a large share of these qualities may be found united. We refuse to allow the claim that the less admirable qualities are to be pointed out as a racial characteristics of the Negro. We can go further. The immorality charged as resident in certain of Dumas's work can find more than a counterpart in other French works, while English and American fiction abounds with much that suggests the coarse and immoral.

He is called "Porthos", after one of his characters—a man living only in the present, but even here he is far from being alone. He certainly did not know how to keep out of debt, and he knew what it was to be harassed by creditors. Who is not ready to smile at the grim humor exhibited when he was asked to contribute fifteen francs to help bury a certain bailiff? Thrusting double the amount into the hands of the petitioner, he exclaimed volubly: "Take thirty and bury two bailiffs." The cockney expression, "What's the hodds so long's we're 'appy" seems to be admirably fitted to his temperament. He enjoyed life to the utmost. His unfailing good-humor at least was racial. More, his faculty as a story-teller was racial. The African is a born story-teller. Some of the wildest, weirdest, most imaginative tales in folk-lore have come from the lips of the Negro. He is a child of nature, and he lives close to his mother. Uncle Remus has more than one counterpart who told tales long before Joel Chandler Harris made him a character to live in literature. There is a wonderful combination of Aesopian wisdom and imaginative humor in what the African, as a child of nature, has to say. Dumas showed this strain in some ways and the talent is creeping out here and there through other pens of the race. The strain is not lost.

Dumas was very Bohemian in his life and manners, and we are forced to admit that he possessed a goodly quantity of conceit and vanity. Yet while we wish that these qualities were not so marked, again we say that a host of men of genius can be named who were noted for these same faults. Child-like he may have been in may ways, careless as well, but amidst all the personal criticism and the illy disguised laughter regarding his faults and foibles no one has ever said that he was irreverent. On the contrary, he was innately religious. Here again we touch what is perhaps a racial trait. God was real to him; his pious mother's training was not for naught. In an enthusiastic description of the view from the top of Mount Etna he says reverently, "Never had I seen God so near and consequently so great."

We have said that he did not despise his race. He did not forget those who were enslaved. At a time of need President Lincoln received a large sum to help the widows of the men who fought to free his fellows. There were some who saw only characteristic vanity in his sending also autograph slips to aid the same cause, but the material fact remains that these same slips brought $12,000 and to-day could not be purchased for double that sum. There was in his breast an unbounded love of freedom. He showed it, too, as did Pushkin, the great Negro Russian poet. Like him he possessed an irresistible desire to answer the trumpet call when it sounded for battle for freedom's rights whether in the political field of intrigue or the open arena. So Dumas participated in mad exploits in connection with the revolution which dethroned Charles X, and hastened to offer his services to Garibaldi in 1860. Davidson says of his movements in this direction that he entered politics with a shot gun and two hundred bullets.

There is one more charge to face in connection with Dumas. His works are said to have reached the number of 1200—"impossible without help"! This he, himself, freely acknowledges. Though pushed by debt, it was not the payment of obligations that urged him to super-human literary effort as it did Scott. Dumas was simply fired to a constant white heat of enthusiasm by the richness of his materials, his triumphs, and the possession of power to transmute what he touched into imperishable pictures. No one thinks less of Scott's genius because in "Quentin Durward" [1822] he has borrowed a scene from Racine['s "]Bajazet[" 1672]. Then why underrate Dumas if he did likewise? He borrowed skeletons but clothed the dry bones with his own flesh and blood creations, and garbed them as his own fancy dictated. But criticism aside, the fact remains that Dumas's artist brain, to use Thackeray's words, "moulded many a mighty clay to be cast presently in perennial brass." "Monte Christo", "The Musketeers", "Marguerite de Valois", and the "Chevalier de Maison Rouge", would be monuments enough for any one, to say nothing of the beauties that we may find elsewhere in his other works. To create characters in fiction—no matter where the bones come from—so real that they live and move, that we know them, commune with them, love them and mourn them, while we remember them always, is genius of the highest order. So Dumas created those delightful characters, Porthos, Athos, D'Artagnan, Chicot, the jester, and they charm us in their way as much as does that host that Dickens brought into being.

Hated and abused, loved and worshiped, criticized and praised, Dumas yet enjoyed life, numbered the great among his friends while living, and was laid to his final rest in the presence of the great who gathered about that last resting placing to pay the respect that genius commands, no matter what its faults.

Alexander Sergeivitch Pushkin, Part I

Southern Workman 33 (March 1904): 162–165.

At the present time, when the Negro—his abilities, characteristics, everything connected with him—is being made the one great central theme for discussion, it is of interest to consider one of the most interesting personalities ever bound by blood to the race.

Alexander Sergeivitch Pushkin, so often called the "Russian Byron", was born a little more than a century ago (1799) at Moscow, where Lermontoff, another of Russia's poets, also first saw the light. Though a Russian by birth, Pushkin was of unquestionable Negro descent. His great grandfather on his mother's side was a Negro from Abyssinia. Ibrahim Petrovitch Hannibal was a full-blood Abyssinian princeling who had been stolen in infancy by slave dealers and brought to Constantinople. Some say that Peter the Great's Ambassador to the Porte stole the boy again from a Turkish harem, but others say that the pasha gave him to the ambassador because that official was delighted with the child's antics, and he in turn presented the gift to the Russian Czar.

There are no accidents in this world, it has been pertinently remarked. This was no accident. The circumstances which made this great-grandfather of the "poet of the Caucasus"[1] a favorite slave of a ruler who was keen to recognize merit and ability and to become its patron, made up simply a part of those inscrutable leadings of Providence that men are so apt to interpret as mere chance or fate. It was fortunate for Russia that this ancestor was brought within its dominions to give it a grandson who, in later years, would glorify that northern country, give lustre to its literary achievements, and furnish an incontrovertible argument as to the brain capacity of the Negro race. As the prime favorite of Peter the Great, Pushkin's maternal ancestor was given every opportunity to rise. It was his marriage that afforded a theme for one of the poet's stories, "Peter the Great's Negro", easily accessible to the English reader in the volume of translated fiction called "The Queen of Spades" [1833]. Such was this quondam slave's rise to place and power that before he died he held retired rank in the army of Russia as *general-en-chef*.

It was the granddaughter, Nadejda, who was the poet's mother. Authority speaks of her as an able and accomplished woman, though a recent writer calls her also cold, worldly, and unsympathetic, with little understanding of the nature of her poet son even in his childhood. Pushkin's father was a descendant of the old Russian aristocracy, the boyars, the highest class of public officials before Peter's reign. It is claimed that from his father, Pushkin inherited the frivolity and dissipation of his father's class in society. Be that as it may, the family was a powerful one, and with such connections, influential friends at court were never wanting—a most fortunate circumstance during the poet's turbulent years of enthusiasm for and espousal of the cause of Russian liberty.

With such an heredity Alexander Pushkin was born at a time when the Russian court and literary circles had developed a mania for all things French and a consequent contempt for all things Russian. The French language dominated Russian thought and speech. He was born into that circle where, as his biographer says, though shy and reserved in disposition he lent an eager ear to all the brilliant conversation of the men of letters who frequented his noble father's table, and thus became imbued at an early age with the desire to emulate the French classics in lyric and even in drama.

Small things shape our lives. This is shown in Pushkin's school life, which by the smallest chance was chosen for him where he was to be drawn into a more truly Russian atmosphere, a different environment than had been his among his father's French-worshiping friends. Here he found the use of his native tongue. Had it not been for this he might have become but an indifferent imitator of Molière and Corneille, in whose masterpieces he found immense enjoyment. But the routine of school life was irksome. The boy was a caged bird with free flight proscribed. Yet the creative faculty within him, struggling for utterance and opportunity, found both. His mind was even then already filled with the national songs and popular legends of his country—the old Russian folk-lore learned in childhood from his beloved nurse, a serf of whom in the height of his fame he gave tender testimony concerning her great influence over his career. In truth, every writer on Pushkin attributes most largely to this Russian peasant woman the saving of the greatest Russian poet for Russia.

It was out of this fountain of knowledge gained from his nurse's lips that he drew when at last he stood before an audience at Tsárskoyé-Selò to deliver the poem of his class at graduation. It did not matter that his rank in his studies was very low. Even a Russian faculty appreciated that genius was not to be bound down to the Procrustean bed furnished for the average student. [Gavrila] Derjavin, Russia's "inspired bard" up to that time, was present. So Russia's literary past met her literary future. Again a hand intervened to save the poet for his predestined career; and as the boy's future was discussed, it was the aged Derjavin who helped to thrust aside other suggestions and leave him free to be a poet.

But as public life in some form seems to have been a necessity for all men of letters in early days, so Pushkin was placed in an office at Petersburg in 1818 at the age of nearly twenty. Here the true man began to show itself. His literary ambitions took precedence over all else. In fact, in some points of his public career, especially in his love of congenial society and his indifference to public duties, we are reminded of our American Bret Harte, who as a child of the Sierras found it equally difficult, we are told, to be trammeled by the conventionalities and the duties of political positions. In Petersburg Pushkin allied himself at once with a new and growing school of literature, national and realistic, out of which the noted Tolstoi has grown. But the views expressed publicly and privately by these writers were most displeasing to the Russian court, which was ever ready with its censorship. When at last an "Ode to Liberty" was circulated it settled the matter. The Emperor failed to appreciate the brilliancy of the new poet's epigrams, and only powerful influence made his punishment, instead of Siberian exile, simply transference to another place in southern Russia where the active young brain could be kept out of mischief. Still, it speaks much for a strong personality that Pushkin was possessed of the power to turn into an admiring friend the young Emperor Nicholas I, against whose claim to the throne he was suspected of plotting in complicity with others. The ruler is found later calling him the "*most witty man in Russia*". But this banishment had its effect upon him; one similar to that brought upon Byron by the self-exile which that unfortunate genius was experiencing at the same time. Resentful, Pushkin plunged into a life of excess and his poems written then took on a decidedly "Byronic hue". As one writer puts it, "he was overpowered by the Byronic *weltschmertz*. To appreciate this we have only to compare a lament written at the time with one of Byron's written in his later days.

"An aimless future lies before me;
My heart is dry, my mind is void,
My soul is dulled and blighted
By the monotony of life's riot",

wails Pushkin, while Byron moans,

"My days are in the yellow leaf,
The flowers and fruit of love are gone,
The worm, the canker, and the grief
Are mine alone."[2]

Indeed, an official,[3] who at this period advised his removal from the southern post, testily and emphatically called him "only a feeble imitator" of Lord Byron.

This Byronic influence was only to shadow his more youthful efforts, however. He had learned to love English literature and soon fell under the spell of Shakespeare, and, though the Byronic style remained to a certain degree apparent in his work, yet the Byronic mood largely disappeared. He reached the point when he could compare the two with clear vision after delving into the treasure house of the "myriad-minded" poet, and he was forced to exclaim, "How paltry Byron is by his side!" His penetration also showed itself in his conclusion that Byron understood no nature but his own. In no works from

Pushkin's pen is his recovery from false ideals more clearly shown than in his acknowledged masterpiece, "Eugene On[é]gin" and his historical tragedy, "Boris Godunof".

Aside from his pessimistic mood, his southern exile bore excellent fruit. Out of it and a second visit to the same region we have his "Prisoner of the Caucasus." Out of it, when he was pursuing, like Byron, a restless, wandering life for a time, came his poem "The Gypsies", reminding one in some of its strains of "Childe Harold".[4]

After four years came his recall from exile, a change brought about by strong family influence. Then he spent two more years in the quiet of his father's home. They were years of mental growth. Here for the second time the influence of that wonderful peasant nurse was exerted to permeate him with national fervor—the "uncompleted national spirit," the undiluted richness, raciness, and grace of his native language—which was to enter into the remaining decade of his literary work and life, and fix his status in Russian literature.

There was a strong spice of both Byron and Dumas in his composition. For one thing he was a great lover of liberty, and had he then had in Russia the opportunity that came to these two in Greece and Italy respectively he would unquestionably have been found fighting for freedom. We find him everywhere compromised with this national spirit which was eating into the Russian heart. In fact, he possessed the faculty of getting into trouble like many another genius, and embroglios with the government and with his relatives made life a constant excitement, until it ended in that unnecessary duel with the son of the Dutch minister at the court, and his own brother-in-law, who had aspersed his wife's honor, as he thought, or as gossip had led him to believe.

Notes

1 [Mikhail Lermontov (1814–1841) was also called "poet of the Caucasus."]

2 [See line 5 of Byron's poem "On This Day I Complete My Thirty-Sixth Year" (1824).]

3 [Count M. Vorontzov.]

4 [Pushkin's poem "Prisoner of the Caucasus" is from 1822, and his "The Gypsies" is from 1823–1824.]

Alexander Sergeivitch Puskin, Part II

Southern Workman 33 (April 1904): 234–236.

Pushkin's writings must be viewed from all sides if one would clearly discern the qualities that enter into them. These belong both to the man and to his style. The latter can be best known only by those familiar with the Russian language. There is something evanescent in every language that defies translation. So with our Russian Negro poet. As one of the most appreciative critics of his poetry says, "Only a faint echo of its music is caught in the translations, and the full diapason swell is only heard by Neva's frozen shores or where Don and Volga roll." Yet the echo is fine. Turn as we will to English, German, or French rendering of his glowing moods, we discern the power and artistic finish, the keen analysis of character, the rich imagination. Though at a distance from the first source, yet the ear catches the music that has charmed a nation to forgetfulness of all except genius, and we long to know more of him. Turning to look at the man, as we have intimated before, we see the Byronic tendency to reveal himself to a large degree. His misanthropic, pessimistic spirit creeps out here and there, especially in his romantic productions, though an English writer claims that it is a misanthropy of the brain rather than of the heart. It is shown in these lines from his master-piece:—

> "Whoever has lived and thought,
> Must in his soul despise mankind;
> Whoever has felt, must be haunted
> By the phantom of days that can ne'er return."

Madame [Z. A.] Ragozin, one of the many writers on Pushkin during his centennial celebration a few years ago, has shown rare discernment in speaking of this masterpiece—"Eugene On[é]gin." After stating that as a society novel it rivals Thackeray's "Vanity Fair" in "scope, power and grace, vividness and depth", she adds the discovery of a racial attribute in the "undercurrent of pensiveness and pathos", which forms a part of its charm and which, though she is not the first one to state it, belongs to the race irrespective of time and setting. We cannot agree, however, with the further remark of the same writer as to racial attributes. She recalls the frenzy that Pushkin exhibited when, wounded to death, he expressed his sorrow that he had not killed his foe, and claimed another shot. We cannot see in this the "savage spirit due to his fierce African blood." He simply showed that he was a man, possessed of the feelings that actuate all men alike—Saxon, Muscovite, or African—when honor is outraged.

As a poet of nature Pushkin reveled in the Caucasus where

> "Glistening in its diadem of ice
> Elbruss, the mountains' hoary chief,
> Whitens the azure vault of heaven."

The mountains and the steppes were intermingled with forest and sea in his thoughts, seemingly sharing his mind with the dream of the serf for liberty. This leads us to consider the man as shown in the most predominant role in his verse. He had taken into his being the spirit of his country; he had demonstrated in his work the Russian quality of mind and heart, and Russia did not hesitate to recognize it, hastening to claim that this valued poet was "Russian in every fibre". Madame Ragozin asserts that Pushkin is "Russia, all Russia— a national poet in the widest sense"; and she bases this claim upon the great centenary celebration "when each of the numerous political and intellectual factions, from the highest official circles to the reddest radical cliques claimed him for its own and could support its claim from passages in his works and in his life."[1] Even the most superficial observer must see that his works are steeped in the sentiments and life of that mighty northern "Empire of Discontent." [Ivan] Tourguenieff, the Russian novelist who gave us the epithet "nihilist", said Pushkin lived at the very core of Russian life, and [Friedrich M.] Bodenstedt, in his appreciative work on Pushkin and his poetry, bears similar tribute.

No one, in fact, disputes his claim to be the greatest poet Russia has ever known, and it is this national quality in his writings that has earned him this compliment. His characters are thoroughly Russian, drawn with a ready and sympathetic pen. Tatiana, the heroine of "Eugene On[é]gin," is finely portrayed. There is certainly found in this picture of a woman, whose love has been despised, "sentiment without sentimentality"—a thing difficult to attain in romantic writings. Turning to "Marie", a love story of garrison life lately translated, we not only get the very odor of the steppe, but Peter and Marie stand out in bold relief "as pure as their native snows".[2]

Like Dumas, Pushkin also suffered from an accusation of imitation, though the critics did not plainly call him a plagiarist. But on the other hand, they never feigned to see African fancy in his breezy style, in his light and often fantastic touch. He delighted in the poets of other lands, and among them Ariosto and Wieland were favorites. But that neither the Italian's "Roland" nor the German's "Oberon" supplied him with fancy or material for his "Russlan and Ljudmila."[3] Those who are qualified to know warmly assert, contradicting the accusations that a few would make.

Personally Pushkin was a modest man, and that he grew in modesty as he grew in genius is evident to a close reader of his biography. He was sensitive to criticism, however, but only because he felt it to be ignorant. The more we study Pushkin the more we see that he was to Russian literature what Roger Bacon was to science—a man born long before his time. The world of appreciation was not ready for him.

Pushkin's life was a short one. He lived only thirty-seven years. Yet he did much to make Russians "long love their poet's pages." Thirteen years ago his statue was unveiled in Moscow, and four years ago there was a revival of his works, when the European world especially, celebrated the centenary of his birth. More and more his circle of readers is being enlarged, mainly through English translations. In the British Museum to-day one has but to take the catalogues from the shelves and turn to his name to see his position in the literary world. Pages are covered with lists of his works or of those connected with his name through biography or criticism. Among the last the writer found none more interesting to study than an appreciative French work by Jacques Flach (1894), "Un Grand Poète Russe." In that same great storehouse of literature was found also the work of the French writer, Count Henri Gregoire, published in 1808, and entitled "De la litterature des Négres"—an inquiry, as the author states, "concerning the intellectual faculties of the Negro race, their moral qualities, and their literature". In it are given the life and work of Negroes and mulattoes distinguished in science, in literature, and art from Hannibal to Phyllis Wheatley and [Benjamin] Banneker. To-day one would not have to go back to the centuries when Bagay, or Cugoano, or Vassa lived for material concerning the Negro's ability. From Pushkin down, through the last century, the race can show worthy names on its scroll of fame.

Notes

1 [See Z. A. Ragozin, "Pushkin and His Work," *Cosmopolitan* 28 (January 1900), p. 307.]

2 [From the translator's note in Marie H. de Zielinska's translation, *Marie* (Chicago: Jansen, McClurg, 1877).]

3 [The poem "Ruslan and Ljudmila" is from 1820.]

Roosevelt: The Man, the Patriot the Statesman

Voice of the Negro 1, no. 9 (1904): 391–393.

Mr. Roosevelt in his speech to the Republican notification committee in accepting the nomination for the Presidency used the following significant language: "If next November my countrymen confirm at the polls the action of the Convention you represent, I shall, under Providence continue to work with an eye single to the welfare of all our people." Note his words *all our people*. It is not a part of them, *all* of them. Again he further says with equal emphasis: "We have already shown in actual fact that our policy is to do fair and equal justice to all men, paying no heed to whether a man is rich or poor; paying no heed to his race, his creed or his birthplace." Splendid words are these and worthy to be uttered by such a splendid specimen of America's best manhood. Another quotation from this able document will suffice. The President says: "The humblest individual is to have his rights safe-guarded as scrupulously as those of the strongest organization, for each is to receive justice, no more and no less. The problems with which we have to deal in our modern indust[r]ial and social life are manifold; but the spirit in which it is necessary to approach their solution is simply the spirit of honesty, of courage and of common sense."

These, as are all of the President's sayings touching human rights, are golden words and should be indelibly written upon the hearts and memories of all the people. Ours is a complex life—a complex citizenship and it requires a master hand to deal with it—to deal justly with it. Providentially we have the man in the person of President Roosevelt. I believe that God has set him apart for this work to the same extent as George Washington and Abraham Lincoln were chosen for their respective tasks.

The President is a man, every inch a man—a true man in every sense of the word—one of America's greatest and best and I would place him by the side of Washington and Lincoln—the one the founder—the other the preserver of the Republic.

In these strenuous times—in these times of race conflicts and race antagonisms it requires courage to take the stand that Mr. Roosevelt has done in matters of public policy. It requires courage to place duty before policy—right before expediency when public sentiment is drifting in an opposite direction and when the tendency is to crush the weak and uphold the strong and when a clamorous populace demands that justice should be placed upon the scaffold, especially when the rights of the races are in question. But Roosevelt is the man for the emergency, he is a brave man, a good man—an honest [and] an honorable man—an up-right, God-fearing man, and I plead for his election though in fact I am confident that he will receive the suffrage of the people and will be elected.

During the administration of Mr. McKinley the Nation added new territory to its borders and allied to itself new peoples—peoples of the darker races, thereby rendering what was before a complex situation still more so. It seems that America is to be the theatre for the adjustment of the rights and relations of these peoples—including those of the American Negro. The responsibility has fallen upon President Roosevelt and right royally is he performing his duty. It is our duty to help him—not impede him—to stand by him—not desert him. As at San Juan, the Negro will not desert him; the Negro will stand by the Rough Rider as long as he is in the affray.

Mr. Roosevelt is not only a man of conviction—but he is a brave man. The American people as a whole like brave men and I dare say that in the impending struggle there will be many Democrats that will support him. He has been tried and has not been found wanting. He is sound on the money question and is thoroughly in accord with all interests that make for the good of the Republic. All know him—the other man they don't know. The people are not ready to surrender a reality for an uncertainty, for a shadow, for a myth. They are not so foolish.

It is to be regretted that forty years after the Rebellion—when new issues and new policies should engage our attention we should now be compelled to take up again old issues that we had supposed had long been settled as a result of the war. We think we see method in it. We think we see in the revival of the Negro question and the dead issues suggested by it a determination on the part of the black man's enemies to drive him to wall and thus carry to a successful end that which was failed in during the earlier days of the Negro's freedom. To let up now means to lose the opportunity. To give the Negro a chance now means to fail in executing long cherished and well laid plans, to prove the Negro's supposed inferiority. The evidence of this is seen in persistent race proscription and race discrimination regardless of the character of the individuals. How a black man under the ci[r]cumstances can support the Democratic party—with its history—its traditions, its customs and its general attitude towards the race, is a question that puzzles the best of us. But this is a free country and I suppose men ought to be allowed to do as they please provided their action does not infringe upon the rights of others.

The black man may have failed in the past to measure up to the standard set for him, but there is no excuse now for lapses. He has aside from his own experience, the experience of others and he should profit by it. If he fails now—he has none to blame but himself. And aside from this he puts himself in a position to be rightly criticised and to be charged with incompetency. There is too much at stake for the black man at any time to be indifferent to himself, or as to his relation to the body politic, and the sacredness of the ballot.

It was during the Spanish American War that President Roosevelt showed his large patriotism—his love of country when he volunteered to shoulder his musket and at the head of a regiment to take his place on the field of battle in common with the humblest soldier. His career there is well known and is now a matter of history and needs only to be touched upon to call attention to it. The Rough Riders and the gallant Ninth and Tenth played their part well and played it to the honor and glory of the American people. I venture to say if these brave soldiers—these dusty sons of Ham could by a vote elect Mr. Roosevelt to the Presidency they would do it *unanimously* and without hesitation. They love him and they honor him. The same patriotism that kindled the fires in the breast of the Nation's Chief also stirred these black boys to action at their country's call. Patriotism is patriotism whether found under a black skin or a white one and the Negro who is himself a patriot admires it in others.

In all the wars of the country the black man did his part. He spilt his blood freely that his country might be saved. He never turned his back upon the foe but always died face forward. Will the American people now turn their back upon these helpless people in a struggle that means so much to them? Will they not allow them a chance? Will they continue to refuse to grant them this? *I cannot believe they will.*

Mr. Roosevelt has declared himself on this point. His position, like an open book, may be read of all men. As a statesman the President has long since satisfied his claim to that title. Thoroughly conversant with history and all forms of government—a student and a scholar of the first rank, he is admirably qualified to fill the high station to which he has been called by the American people and to deal wisely and well with all public questions touching their interests. The three years of his Administration already past are an abundant evidence of his fitness to handle in a statesman-like manner all the knotty problems growing out of a complex form of government like ours. Never was a man better qualified for the work of this high office than this man. Well may Uncle Sam put his hand gently on the shoulder of the Nation's great Executive and with a smile upon his face, exclaim, "*He is good enough for me.*" Yes, Uncle Sam, he is good enough for all of us. There is none better and we pledge him our support. We believe that he is already as good as elected. Since his able Speech of Acceptance several polls of business men and others interested in pubic affairs have been taken, notably in New York and Philadelphia, and in every instance the sentiment has been overwhelmingly in his favor.

A Philadelphia evening paper in canvassing several leading Exchanges finds out of 137 of its members 111 are for Roosevelt. A similar poll in Wall street shows like results. Other large cities in the North and West return a similar poll. The people know what they want and will have it. The nomination of Mr. Roosevelt means his election, and his election means good government and a continuation of the wise policies entered upon by him.

Daniel Alexander Payne

Southern Workman 33 (December 1904): 683–688.

It is a long way from Haddington in Scotland to Charleston, South Carolina; and from the year 1722 to that of 1811 time measures nigh unto a century. Yet such are the subtle, silent, mysterious influences that come down through the ages that both time and distance are annihilated. John Brown, the self-educated Scotch shepherd from Perthshire and the pastor of Haddington, was the man whose early efforts for an education and whose reputation for learning and piety formed the ether waves of inspiration that crossed the Atlantic and moved a slender lad of color in the far South to a fixed determination to follow his example.

Daniel Alexander Payne was born of free parents in Charleston, February 24, 1811. In his veins ran the blood of three races. An Englishman was his great grandfather on his father's side, and a Catawba Indian woman was his great grandmother on his mother's side. His immediate parents were of brown complexion transmitted from their African ancestry. Bishop [C. S.] Smith has observed that the admixture of African and Indian blood is productive of strong qualities of character. It is true that from this triple heritage came Payne's unusually quick perceptions, his unyielding principles, his gentle manners, his fervent piety. He was left an orphan at an early age and owed his elementary education to a society formed by free colored men in Charleston for the aid of orphan and indigent colored children. When he was thirteen years old he was apprenticed to the carpenter's trade. In the four and a half years spent at this work he passed through the vacillating period of youth, influenced at first by John Brown's Self-interpreting Bible [1778], to which a biographical sketch of the author was appended. He decided to be like Brown, so he read and studied, but ever with Scotch ideals before him. At length Wallace and Bruce became his heroes and he determined to be a soldier and serve his people in Hayti. But the gentler inner pleadings prevailed, and with his conversion came the turning point when hands seemed pressed upon his shoulders and a voice seemed to speak to his soul: "I have set thee apart to educate thyself in order that thou mayest be an educator to thy people." Again he turned to John Brown of Haddington as his ideal. Up to his nineteenth year, when he left the carpentry trade for the teacher's uncertain life, he worked during the day, reading and studying every moment he could snatch from meals, and at four o'clock in the morning the tinder-box, flint, steel, and candle standing by his bedside were called upon to provide light for still earlier study.

Having set out to be a light to his people he let nothing turn him back. He worked, studied by himself, and taught. He learned to read Latin and Greek and French, and he delved into every possible branch of science, especially astronomy, natural history, and botany. He grew in favor with his pupils—the children of Charleston's free people of color. But their progress was his undoing. His methods, brought to the notice of certain persons, aroused a suspicion that this acquirement of knowledge on the part of colored people was dangerous and stirred to action the Legislature of his State. In 1835 an Act was passed that made the penalty of such work as young Payne was doing "imprisonment and the lash."

As we study history we see how mysterious are God's ways in working out His purposes. Daniel A. Payne was to be something greater than a teacher in Charleston, and the Act that drove him northward from that city sent him forth to wider fields of influence. He carried with him strong friendly letters of cheer and counsel from some of Charleston's best white citizens—from Dr. Bachman, from the Palmers, from Dr. Capers and others—letters that he preserved to his death in his album of treasured correspondence. Colored friends consoled him and rallied to his help, furnishing out of scanty purses the means for his journey into exile.

It was a terrible blow to his ambitions, which were centered in the South as his chosen field of activity. He little knew then that one day he could truthfully say with [John] Wesley, "The world is my parish," and that his victory would come when with swelling heart he should stand upon the steamer Arago's deck thirty years later, amid his band of traveling preachers, no longer an unfriended stripling teacher, but a Bishop of the African Methodist Episcopal Church, about to set his foot on his native soil after thirty years of exile, and there plant the flag of his Church. With trembling hand and streaming eyes he has many times turned the pages of his precious letters and pointed out to the writer Miss Mary [S.] Palmer's prayer which he bore from the South and which the years had realized:

"May He open before you an extensive field of usefulness, so that you may have reason to bless His holy name for causing light to spring out of present darkness and when it is well with you, O, remember your brethren whom you leave behind, and do them good."[1]

His early experiences in the North were varied, but at last he found himself in school at Gettysburg under Dr. [Samuel S.] Schmucker of the Lutheran Church—a church that he loved until the day of his death. But because he felt that he could do his brethren most good in another fold he joined at last the A. M. E. Church, though he began his career as pastor in a Presbyterian church in East Troy, New York, at the age of twenty-six. He had found himself unable to remain in school because of the failure of his eyesight, and acting on the advice of friends he turned to the pulpit as the best sphere for use-fulness. About this time he began to enter public life and meet some of the great men with whom he was to have more extended companionship as the years went on. Again a turning point was reached. He faced the question whether he should lay his talents upon the altar of the public platform in defense of liberty and human rights, as urged by Lewis Tappan and others, or pursue his path in the ministry. It was an exciting hour, and prospects were flattering, but he said of it, "Frederick Douglass could not do the work which was assigned to D. A. Payne, nor D. A. Payne the work assigned to Frederick Douglass." It must be said, however, that he had experienced the same subtle constraint to the work of the ministry that had influenced him toward the path of an educator, and though a minister, he never forgot his previous drawing to the life of an educator. So we find him combining the two, teaching private classes and always filling the position of preceptor in manners and morals.

His influence upon the church with which he had identified himself was such that as early as 1843 he had helped to arrange a course of study for the ministry and had written essays designed to convince it of the necessity of education for the pulpit. He never yielded a step thereafter. He saw no good in mere passionate excitement that passed for religion, he deprecated purely emotional songs, and he uncompromisingly opposed immoral leaders in the pulpit. An educated and pure ministry was his ideal and he fought for it with voice and pen for half a century until the day his voice was silenced forever. In progress of any kind he delighted, but the sensational, the fanatical, the recre-ant, the impure in any garb, received the stinging lash of unsparing rebuke. He called for reformers on every hand. Those who worked with him had to be reformers who could not only speak against existing evils, but could also resist them and spare no wrongdoer. While he possessed a species of self-confi-dence which sustained him in the paths he marked out he also had real humil-ity. When the General Conference of 1852 chose him as one of the two bishops elected at the time, he accepted the office with fear and trembling as a man who felt himself wholly unfit for such a holy position. But the Church made no mistake. It never had a man more humble, more single in purpose, more unselfish, more self-sacrificing, more zealous, or more learned.

From the vantage ground of his office he could do still more for his brethren, and as the next four years passed he was led by friends of the M. E. Church to seek a home where it had established a school for the colored peo-ple at Tawawa Springs, Ohio—a noted summer watering place for Ohioans. He little thought at the time that he would stand for eleven years as its President, with virtual control until he died; for from this beginning came Wilberforce University. From the first day that Bishop Payne set foot upon Wilberforce soil, up to the year of his death, there was not hour when his spirit was not in close contact with the school, his influence all-pervading, his interest ever intense to guide, direct, and benefit the school whose high des-tiny was his hope and prayer. He was preacher, bishop, teacher, agent—every-thing in one where it was concerned.

In the pursuance of this life task he shirked no public or private duty. He strove to make friends for the race everywhere. He believed in concentration of effort, but he helped all. His close friendship with such men as Lewis Tappan, Gerrit Smith, Hon. Daniel S. Dickinson, Wendell Phillips, William Lloyd Garrison, was helpful to the race at large. He sought Congress, public men, and those who moved in private life, with the same direct approach—that of a man who believed in the possibilities of his race and in the goodness of friends that God would raise up for it. Honor came to him at home and abroad. He was sent as a delegate to the Evangelical Alliance which met at Amsterdam and to the Ecumenical Conference in London. He sat at John Bright's left and pronounced grace at a banquet to Garrison in St. James Hall in London in 1867. But he bore all these honors and other recognitions of his worth with the same gentle humble appreciation that evinced no unseemly delight, no vain childish boasting. Only the twinkle of the eye and the well-known twist of his lips showed his feeling.

Aside from an educated and pure ministry there was no question of more moment to him than the education of the girls of the race. In fact these two were paramount always. Out of his interest in the training of women grew his treatise on "Domestic Education", a little volume published in 1885 and dedicated "To the thoughtful fathers and the anxious mothers of every race", for his sympathies were broad. He sought to help all races and he had many white friends by whom he was respected and beloved and whom he loved in turn. He felt that to its women the Negro race must owe its future strength, mental, moral and physical. The book should be reissued for its didactic worth as well as for its erudition, as he left nothing unread on the subject in either English or French.

To the young of both sexes he was a father and a patron. Talent, genius, worth, were never suffered to pass his door unhelped. He sought out the gifted, and was one of the first to help the artist [Henry O.] Tanner on his road to success. He knew all about his race, its music, its art, its literature, from the earliest and humblest efforts to those recognized by the world, and he was proud of every upward step. His early love for science grew with the passing years and old age found him as deeply interested in a flower or a butterfly as he was when a youth. With his ever-fresh enthusiasm and appreciation he inspired all about him. His heart kept young. He was social, he loved the play of bright wit and was as keen at repartee as anyone. His pupils, and the young generally, admired and revered him, but the evildoer feared him, and the idle and self-conceited avoided him. He had no tolerance for these. It is a matter of local history that when a pompous student remarked in his presence on the good results to be obtained for the brain from eating fish, he sharply rejoined, "Mr. X, you will need to eat a whale." He was a martinet in discipline. He knew its worth for an undisciplined people especially. Promptness, punctuality, correctness in manner and speech, were required by him from both young and old. If a student preacher overstepped the time limit in his trial sermon, Bishop Payne has been known to rise from his seat, pluck his sleeve, and point with remorseless significance to the clock.

He did not ask others to do what he did not do. His own life was a most systematic one as to sleep and food, recreation and work, "with the happiest effect," as Dr. F. J. Grimké has said, "both upon his personal character and in the results which have flowed from his labors." Physically he was slight, weighing less than a hundred pounds, but his constitution was wiry, and his ability to do mental work to the last was a marvel. He hated hypocrisy and was frank to a fault, though his candor never turned to slander. He was aggressive, a strong friend, and a strenuous foe. He was not pronounced in his likes and dislikes but was ever the gentleman, refined, polished, and intellectual. His religion, as has been well said, was of the Pauline type, consistent and heroic, with the courage of a lion. He had married twice and his home at Evergreen Cottage was the center of a whole-souled, generous hospitality and a Mecca for the many who knew him. He had taken part in the Congress of Religions at the World's Fair in Chicago in 1893, had returned to his home and was preparing, as was his custom, to spend the winter in Florida; but his work was done and, after a short illness, he passed to the Beyond on a gray November day.

As the spirit of John Brown of Haddington had aroused Bishop Payne's soul to usefulness, so he hoped his own strenuous life might arouse others, and to this end he had consented to the compilation of "Recollections of Seventy Years" which volume was published in 1888. In the introduction, Dr. F. J. Grimké makes this pertinent observation: "How eloquently does this life, out of the difficulties with which it had to contend, and the grand results which were the outcome of his earnest, self-sacrificing labors, plead with the young men and women of to-day to seize the flying moments, freighted as they are with priceless opportunities for improvement!" He had desired a "useful life" and his wish had been granted. He lived to see prosper the work of his hands in his beloved school and the ministry, and he left the race a goodly heritage in his life and examples. As he neared his end his thoughts held tenaciously to the work he had so unflinchingly followed and his lips murmured in disjointed sentences: "Therefore, stand firm for that which is true, that which is good; and hesitate not to handle the two-edged sword in cutting off and cutting down evil."

His dust lies in Baltimore but his spirit is marching on by the side of the race, urging and stimulating it to the highest endeavors.

Note

1 [For the entire prayer, see Daniel A. Payne, *Recollections of Seventy Years* (Nashville, Tenn.: A.M.E. Sunday School Union, 1888), p. 38.]

The Poet Laureate of the Negro Race

A.M.E. Church Review 31 (1914): 135–143.

William Dean Howells, Edmund Clarence Stedman, Eugene Field, James Whitcomb Riley, James Lane Allen and Robert Ingersoll were the jury which named Paul Laurence Dunbar poet laureate of the Negro race.

Dr. Davis W. Clark, of Boston, in speaking of our poet, says: "But, when all is said, his true distinction lies in the fact that he interpreted the particular to the universal, the Negro to the whole human race. He demonstrated, too, by his own genius that the Negro also belongs to the divine family on earth, in spite of all prejudiced denial. He easily molded the white man's language into the modes of thought of the black man and *vice versa*; thus showing that they are interchangeable. So the community of genius is illustrated and proven. The accident of his seniority as the poet of his race would alone insure him a permanent place.

He is the first among ten million. Again, he did not inherit, he originated. His race had nothing to transmit in the way of literary or poetic instinct or training. That this young Negro should take up what has heretofore been the white man's own distinctive art, and excel and surpass in it, is the marvel of the hour. The Caucasian's wealth of literary inheritance and training of several millenniums seemed to give him no advantage over the meagerly furnished and heavily handicapped son of Ham. Right worthily, then, is Paul Laurence Dunbar "laurel-decked."[1] Thus does Dr. Clark emphasize the appropriateness of the verdict of these eminent men.

The Unveiling of the Poet's Monument

It was June 26, 1909, that the white citizens of Dayton, Ohio, paid a tribute to the memory of the dead poet by unveiling a monument in his honor erected by popular subscription and locating it in harmony with the poet's expressed wish under a willow, near a pool of water and not beyond the noises of the road. (See "Death's Song.")

It was a beautiful sight, more than a thousand of Dayton's best citizens had gathered at his tomb that beautiful morning in June, seemingly vying with one another in paying respect to the memory of one of their most distinguished dead—Paul Laurence Dunbar. James Whitcomb Riley was there. It was he who whispered his condolence in the ear of the poet's mother over the long distance telephone, "not trusting his pen or waiting for the mail." Others eminent in poetry and prose and national in reputation were present to do honor to his memory. The Philharmonic Society—seventy in number—composed of Dayton's best white musicians, men and women, sang as hymns the poet's words set to music. It was indeed a gathering for an unusual purpose. It was not that a memorial to a great citizen was an extraordinary occurrence, for this is almost a daily happening. But it was a remarkable thing that such a gathering should be in memory of a man not only of humble birth, but one of the darker race—one with a sable skin, the badge of servitude and oppression that has been the Negro's lot for so many years. But on that day race and color were lost sight of and the Gem City of Ohio was proud to honor its distinguished son who had helped to give it fame—to honor him because of his worth, his genius, his work.

The old adage that a prophet is not without honor save in his own country is another instance of the falsity of so many popular sayings; for in that beautiful city where Paul Laurence Dunbar was reared, where he made his home and gathered to himself friends—here he was most highly honored; and in that memorial to him they not only did honor to an individual man of color who had lived and wrought so well as to deserve recognition by his fellows, but they did honor to an entire race, and to mankind regardless of race.

As I considered that splendid tribute to the Negro poet, as I dwelt upon the meaning of such an expression of appreciation of his greatness, my heart swelled with pride and gratitude that in this day and generation such a thing is possible. And I was more and more convinced that, after all, the possibilities of any race are to be finally determined by the heights reached by its men of intellect, of brain, of genius—men of power who are able to touch the hearts and stir the pulses of the world by their marvelous ability for delineation by pen, brush or chisel—men who rise in the realm of the fine arts and command the world to listen, to gaze, to admire, to respect, to praise their efforts. That tribute to Dunbar by his white fellow citizens showed that after all genius is not a matter of race, color or condition, and that it will win its way forward and upward. The men and women who possess it are the ones who will raise a people to higher planes. These are the ones who will give this same people a place among the nations of the earth. These are the ones that we especially praise and honor.

But the Negro race has had such men scattered throughout its history—men of color who have distinguished themselves. We do not need to go back to the centuries when Bagay or Cugoano or Vassa lived for such material to declare the Negro's ability. The last century has given the world a *proud* list from which we may draw examples of Negro greatness in the higher walks of life.

I recall with pleasure the sight of a bronze figure in the *Place Malesherbes* of Paris which was the work of the great artist and sculptor Doré. It is that of

Alexandre Dumas *p[è]re*, France's great Negro historical romancer, who has enchanted the world with his story-telling genius.

Dumas, the father, and Dumas, the son, both have carved a niche for the race where their names are imperishably written, and France is proud to honor them. Twenty-three years ago Russia did honor to another Negro as we did honor Dunbar five years ago. Then the statue of Alexander Pushkin, acknowledged as Russia's greatest poet, was unveiled in Moscow to an admiring people who celebrated thus the literary achievements of the Negro "poet of the Caucasus." Pushkin's name is immortal in Russian hearts.

Down the list we may come to touch Phyllis Wheatley, whose powers drew a tribute from George Washington; to Banneker, who astounded the world with his scientific astronomical calculations—down to the present where the names cluster more thickly, because of honors won; Edmonia Lewis, who from Rome made her fame as a sculptress and Henry Tanner, whose fame as an artist has reached the coveted recognition of the French Government. These, with Douglass and Washington and Du Bois, and a host of others, have proved to the world that the "Souls of Black Folk" differ not from other souls in high impulses, and aspirations, and even genius.

Russia and France are proud of their sable writers, each of whom stamped his own personality upon the literature of his nation, and why should not America possess the same pride?

When we come down to modern times and review the field as it is stretched out before us, there is no literary character that stands higher than Paul Laurence Dunbar. We speak of Longfellow and Whittier and Bryant and Lowell, and other great American poets, and speak of them with rightful pride; but to my mind not one of them was a sweeter singer than Paul Laurence Dunbar. He sang with equal freedom and boldness, he sang with equal musical rhythm, he sang with their grace and beauty, and he sang of the desires, the struggles, the ambitions, the aspirations of a people that seemed to have no future. In his song he has helped pave the way for a future for his race. He has hewn out a path, has trodden the ground for others to follow, and what was possible in his case is possible for others.

The very fact that he made his way to the front from humble origin and against tremendous odds shows *the power of a soul*.

Paul Laurence Dunbar was no prodigy, no bundle of eccentricities, no Blind Tom whose powers in one direction were miraculous and balanced by the dwarfing of all else in his nature and character. He was a normal man in every respect and as such is to be judged as every other man of letters.

In all nations it is an accepted fact that the literature of a people is influenced by four things. The *race* of the writer is to be taken in consideration as well as the epoch in which he lives and the immediate *environment* about him. We do not except from this rule the one whose name we honored at the unveiling of the monument erected by popular subscription by his friends of the white race. Paul Laurence Dunbar was of African ancestry. It could not be claimed that a large percentage of his ability was due to the amount of Caucasian blood in his veins. He represented the Negro in America in letters as few others who have reached eminence could do. I would emphasize that his gift of song was pre-eminently racial. He had the happy gaiety and the weird imagination of his race. He sang from his heart as the race has sung ever since it was brought to these shores. It is shown in his dialect poems where the same wonderful combination of Aesopian wisdom and imaginative humor that have made [Joel Chandler] Harris' African stories so famous is evidenced at every turn.

He felt for his race, and as his race he sang with the heart and tongue of his people. It was not all joy. Sorrow and sadness crept in. The changeful moods were his, and so his poems met the moods of mankind and won a place in hearts, which must be done to win a way to fame. He was a child of nature. The wind dared him to song: the spring warmed in his veins when the

"Grass commence a-comin'
Throo de thawin' groun'"

And summer lured him with the

"Pines a-smellin' in de wood."[2]

Like all other writers, he was also influenced by his *environment*, which here was closely allied to racial influence and had a strong sway over his works, imbuing them with the touch and personality that have made their peculiar charm.

Every phase of Negro life has been caught by his pen as by a camera. The simplest and homeliest life about him threw upon his brain indelible pictures that he transformed to liquid notes of song, sparkling with grace and vivid imagination. The life of the fireside, the field, the cabin, the wood, the stream—all gave him happy themes for his gift to play upon. The peculiar traits of his people, their quaint characteristics, their propensities and inclinations all received a loving, tender tribute at his hand as he wove them into immortal verse.

The third influence—the epoch—shows comparatively little influence over his works. Here and there we find him centralizing thought upon the spirit of the times about him. It was an age of peace in Dunbar's years, so his muse was not stirred to clarion tones, but when the blind rage of mob violence pursued his people, his "Talking Oak" showed how his heart was stirred; and when Frederick Douglass died he mourned in an elegy that showed the true poetic fire ablaze from the friction of life about him, but his prose has shown this influence of the world ideas about him far more than his poetry, for Dunbar's literary fertility was not confined to the poetic field alone.

Largely influenced by *race* and *environment* in his writings, yet one other influence that has always been the *mightiest* in the literature of any people was also his. This was *Genius*. We cannot account for genius in any people. It springs up and no one can trace it. It comes more often from the lowliest surroundings. The soul that comes from Nature's God, that lives close to Nature, that sees life clearly, that knows other souls by mysterious affinity—that soul is born and carries its possessor into the upper realms where but few can follow, and we call it *genius*.

Paul Laurence Dunbar had genius. Only a genius could have sung as he has sung, only a genius could have triumphed as he has triumphed, only a genius could have made a permanent place in American literature for himself as he has done. His death was untimely. His career was not completed. What might he not have done had more years been given him? But God—who took him—knew best. And here we may repeat that whatever definition we may give genius, the fact is that no man possessing such as Dunbar possessed can ever be kept down. Genius forces its way upward. It demands recognition. Dunbar's native powers forced the world to give him place and to sing his praises. I remember in Europe when, on a special occasion, his name was mentioned before an audience, that the people vied in enthusiastic applause for the black boy who had sung himself into prominence by the greatness of his intellectual powers. If this side of Negro life—the literary side—could be dwelt upon more, if the career made by one like Paul Laurence Dunbar could be held up more before the world, if the intellectual progress of the Negro could be taken up for consideration to a greater extent, and if the distance that he has come from the days of slavery to the present could form the subject of more speeches and orations, I feel very sure that the people of America would be willing to grant the black man a hearing and a more favorable consideration in the matters that make for the highest good of the race.

If the literature of Dunbar is taken upon its merits, we feel that both the prose and poetry of others of the race will be likewise favorably regarded, and in that sense the Negro people will be benefited. The lives of such men as Dunbar, Tanner and Du Bois, who have with others made a future for the people along higher lines, should inspire us all. There are many of the race here and there in nearly every city, building slowly but surely in literature and art and are making a way for those who are to follow.

Greatness does not come to every man even though he may work for it, but there are some who by their own power of mind and personality tower above the common people, thereby showing that greatness is limited to no one people and no one class of people. Mr. Dunbar was one of this class. His life, as has been said, was a brilliant one in a literary sense. He was a prolific writer as well. The large number of volumes emanating from his pen and the great interest manifested by the public at large in his works clearly prove that his powers were fed from a perennial spring.

Their freshness and virility both astonished and pleased the waiting public, which continually called, like Oliver Twist, for more, and continually gave a spontaneous meed of praise for every new effort.

He died in harness, so to speak, with a volume incomplete. Why the Creator saw fit to remove him from the scene of his earthly labors at his early age man cannot tell. We feel the loss as a race of a brilliant man and helper of his people. He has dropped his mantle. Upon whose shoulders it will fall, time alone can tell, but it is due his fame to say that we would eagerly applaud the singer of color who may prove worthy to wear it. We have lamented the loss of such men as Douglass and Crum[m]ell and Payne, men on whom the years bore heavily, but Dunbar was young, in his prime, and greater things were to be achieved. We needed him, as we need all strong literary characters, to help a people to a standing place in the world of letters. Yet his life, his work—this memorial—all must ever be an inspiration to every Negro youth to set his feet in the paths for higher things, to be determined to win spurs in some great ambitious effort to compel the recognition of the world for some great achievement.

Every person of color should feel under lasting gratitude to our honored poet for the position he won for his people; and the race must never fail to show that gratitude, not only for this fact, but for every phase of recognition accorded him by other races.

I say his life, with its crown of laurel, should be an inspiration to the Negro people, and I also say that it should be a lesson for the critics of the race. To those who do well, the recognition befitting their merits should be given. As his mother had reason to be proud of such a son, so the City of Dayton had reason to be proud of such a citizen, and this great State of Ohio should feel itself also honored by such a career of such an illustrious citizen.

I considered it an honor that I was able on that occasion to stand over his monument and in the name of the Negro people, and, in the name of humanity, thank all those of that great city who had joined to raise such a memorial to the honor of this sweet American bard, to thank them all regardless of race or color, who had risen to such heights in honoring this poet of sable hue, to congratulate all that race, color or creed was not allowed to dampen ardor or be an obstacle in honoring their fellow-townsman. Ohio was honored by that tribute. America was honored by it, and that day should ever be a proud one in the annals of that city and its people. There Dunbar spent his youth; there he developed his talent; there he laid down his work, and while we add a laurel leaf to the chaplet which fame placed upon his living brow, we declare that

"The great work laid upon his short years
Is done, and well done."

Such lives are blessings in the world at large. God lends them to the world to show that mind knows no race—that we are all brothers, differing from one another only as gifts and graces differ—that the Creator is our common Father through whose gracious kindness such lives spring up, blossom and bear fruit to prove the immortality of the soul.

Dunbar will never die, even though his body lies buried in the earth. His soul of song will continue to re-echo in the hearts of men, and the brightness and beauty, the humor and pathos, the tenderness and sympathy with which he has enriched the world will rest like a benediction upon us all for all time to come. Yes, Dunbar still lives in his songs and in our hearts—the same earnest, sincere, gentle, genial soul that we knew so well in his earthly years. His gentle spirit today hovers over the home he loved so well, and the city dear to his heart, and though he has gone to take his rest, that spirit will be a guardian angel, blessing all for the greatness of heart and soul that has evoked that tribute from a grateful, appreciative people.

His wish was fulfilled. He sleeps among his fellow-citizens, as be begged in his touching "Death Song."

> "Let me settle w'en my shouldahs draps dey load
> High enough to hyeah de noises in de road;
> Fu' I t'ink de las' long res'
> Gwine to soothe my sperrit bes'
> Ef I's layin' 'mong de t'ings I's allus knowed.["]

Notes

1 An extract from the address delivered by Dr. D. W. Clark, of Boston, at the unveiling of the poet's monument in Dayton's most beautiful cemetery and on the most beautiful knoll in that cemetery. The other orator was the writer of this appreciation of the poet.

2 [From Dunbar's poems "Spring Fever," lines 1–2, and "A Summer Night," lines 7–8, respectively.]

Warren G. Harding: A Brand New President with the Old-Fashioned Belief "All Men Up and No Man Down"

Competitor 3 (1921): 7–8.

We present the accompanying article by Dr. W. S. Scarborough, admittedly competent to give us an unbiased opinion of the newly inaugurated President of the United States. As Dr. Scarborough sees him, our president suffers not the least [b]y comparison with Washington, McKinley and Roosevelt.—THE EDITOR

The distinguished subject of this sketch is a man of peculiar fitness for the high position to which he has been elected by an overwhelming vote—a vote unsurpassed in the history of our country. President Harding is a man of broad intelligence, of wide knowledge of men and affairs, of sanity of judgment, of freshness of spirit, and withal a statesman of the highest type. He has not only convictions, but the courage of the same. He is a firm believer in the doctrine of Roosevelt: "All men up and no man down." He is as well intensely American, and[,] like Lincoln, a humanitarian and a Christian gentleman.

President Harding is a fit successor to Washington, Lincoln, Grant, McKinley and Roosevelt. In his efforts to serve his country and the people who elected him, there is no doubt in my own mind that he will measure up so completely to the high standard set by these predecessors, that the people at large will see that no error was made in the choice for this noble son of Ohio for the highest place in the gift of the nation.

I have known the newly elected president long and intimately and can speak of him from accurate knowledge. I have kept in touch with him during all the years of his public life in the State of Ohio. I have studied him at close and at long range and have always found him the same honest, honorable, true upright statesman—a man in whom there was no guile, a man to be trusted, admired, loved. He has always stood for all that was highest and best in our civilization. Having long honored and admired him, it is a matter of pride with me today to have his confidence and to be numbered among his friends—a place I was equally proud to occupy in connection with that other brilliant, loyal, true man—Senator J. B. Foraker.

President Harding and Senator Foraker were warm friends. Both stood for good government and both fought to sustain it. Both believed that the Negro should have his manhood rights accorded him and that he deserved better treatment than he was getting at the hands of the American people, and both were courageous enough not only to express their convictions, but to contend for the principles they uttered. Senator Foraker has repeatedly expressed to me his high regard for the friend who is now the chief executive of the nation—his high opinion of him as a man, as a statesman, as a gentleman. The sturdy unswerving loyalty of this mutual friendship has been an exceedingly fine thing to note. In fact it stands out in the character of both these great men as a most knightly characteristic. Of all the public men I have ever known, I have yet to find a superior to either of these two stalwart Republicans and representative Americans.

Because of this I felt certain from the first that Senator Harding was the man of the hour. I had an unshaken faith that he would be the final character or choice of the convention. I can confidently claim to be the one man of color who, both long before hand and from first to last in the convention, had centered not only hopes, but convictions and efforts on his star as the one in the end to be ascendant over all. And, here it is pertinent to notice that among Senator Harding's friends whose loyalty has been true and consistent, no one has supported him more earnestly and more faithfully than Hon. H. M. Daugherty; no one has given more tangible and unquestioned evidence of this friendship by activity in the Senator's behalf. He was the original Harding man. Even in the critical moments of the nomination, Mr. Daugherty never wavered in his faith as to the outcome. In this ultimate triumph Senator Willis was another staunch friend who shared and held the confidence of Senator Harding.

Note and follow President Harding from the day of his nomination. We see a man whose conception of duty is so broad and so righteous that it compelled the admiration even of those not of his own party. He grew and grew in favor until party lines were completely shattered and the Democratic Party almost wiped out of existence. There may be some fragments still, but they are hard to find.

Wilson and Wilsonism had become a public stench. The people had had enough of Democratic mismanagement and incompetency; and the Negro had become tired of the attempts to Southernize the North, of the determination to keep the Negro in his place, of the contemptible spirit taken across the seas and spread widely at home in regard to the Negro soldier. So all rose up together, and turned to look for a man who should stand for strength and for justice, for right and for truth. They found him and they about annihilated the Democratic party when they placed Warren G. Harding at the helm to guide the Ship of State—a man abundantly able and qualified to pull it off the shoals onto which it had been cast by this outgoing administration.

I was present on that eventful day at Marion when Senator Harding was officially notified that he was the people's choice. I heard his magnificent acceptance speech given with that same dignity, serenity and poise shown afterwards throughout a long trying campaign, I noted the deep undercurrent of feeling bringing sincerity to every word, and I was proud of the eloquent and emphatic words and manner as he gave his dictum on the Negro question:

"I believe the federal government should stamp out lynching and remove that stain from the fair name of America.

"I believe the Negro citizens of America should be guaranteed the enjoyment of all their rights; that they have earned the full measure of citizenship bestowed, that their sacrifices in blood on the battle fields of the Republic have entitled them to all of freedom and opportunity, all of sympathy and aid that the American spirit of fairness and justice demands."[1]

These stirred the whole vast audience to loud and impressive applause.

Here is President Harding's platform so far as the Negro race is concerned. That he will adhere to it and endeavor to see that it becomes a reality as far as in his power lies, I have not a shadow of doubt. It will take time and the Negro must be wise and patient. The race must help and not impede the President in his efforts to serve the work toward the end in view. But as I have said in speeches in the campaign the Negro must depend much upon himself, not alone upon the individual at the head of the party, and he must wisely work to make the party a means to an end.

If there are those believing that President Harding will be dominated by others on his policies, they will find themselves mistaken. He allows no man to think for him. He will listen and weigh well the opinions of others, but the final decision will be his. He will shape his own policy in his own way, and in keeping with his own matured judgement. That he is absolutely sound on all the fundamental questions that are now before the American people argues well for his ultimate actions.

President Harding is a statesman in many ways resembling McKinley. Of the latter it has been said, "He was temperamentally fitted to fill the great office to which he had been called. He possessed dignity of character, a serenity and soundness of judgment which won the confidence of the nation. He always had the patience to hear, the wisdom and courage to decide. He was controlled by reason and not by passion. He had a veneration for the exalted traditions of the executive office and he did great things in a great way. He carried into the office large experience and a full knowledge of public men. He had been an apt student of the country's needs. He sought to establish public confidence, knowing full well that it is the basis of industrial progress and national advancement."

This may be well said of President Harding in the fullest sense and with equal emphasis. He is also a student of history who notes the lessons of the past in all their bearings upon the present and future.

I fully believe, as God gave to this country Washington, Lincoln, Grant, McKinley and Roosevelt to found and preserve our great Republic, so He has given it Warren G. Harding, the equal of any of these predecessors, to continue the work begun by them.

Let him speak for himself in the following brief pithy extracts from his speeches:

"When the country needed the quickening of conscience, the country sought it through the Republican party, led by Theodore Roosevelt. No appeal to Republicanism has been in vain. The party unfailingly has responded to the needs and aspirations of the American people."

"If we want a restored America, we must give America the freedom which made us what we are."

"Proclaimed peace is delayed because our thoughts were fixed on the directing of the world instead of stabilizing at home and restoring the onward march of the American Republic."

His memorial speech delivered before the Lincoln Club of Portland, Me., in February, 1920, we find the following, showing how thoroughly he also believes in the majesty of the law as the guardian of liberty.

Quoting Lincoln on re[v]erence for law, he utters the well remembered words: "Let every American, every lover of liberty, every well-wisher of his posterity, swear by the blood of the Revolution never to violate the laws of the country and never to tolerate their violations by others"; and again, speaking of his own principles: "He did not value the ephemeral opinions of a day, nor the clamor of haste; he clung to the convictions which could appeal to the judgment of posterity. He was neither opportunist nor advocate of expediency. He was mighty in conviction, and clung to the constitution and the supremacy of law as sole assurance of maintained civilization and national life."

Note

1 [See *Autobiography*, pp. 280–281.]

Travel Narratives

Vacation Notes: The Cesnola Collection

Christian Recorder, August 29, 1878.

I remember asking a class of applicants at our regular monthly examinations [at Wilberforce University], in substance: "What it was that made the land of Cyprus so celebrated. Is there any thing now more than usual that gives it distinction." Though several answers were given, covering the ground quite fully, there were none I believe that tallied *in toto* with the one I had in mind. The subject of this sketch is the answer to the questions referred to. Those who have read the opening article in the *National Repository* for June, or who have had the pleasure of visiting the New York Metropolitan Museum of Art, will doubtless agree with me in saying that the "Cesnola Collection," as it is styled, is truly wonderful. Words will not describe the feeling that creeps over one as he stands gazing upon these magnificent works of ancient art. One may behold terra-cotta especially, amphorae—well known to the student of Homer—bowls, plates, rings, armlets, bracelets, beads and ear-rings; helmets, spears and breast-plates in various attitudes; kings and queens, noblemen and women in ancient costume, presenting a grand array of variety, suggesting to the mind the great progress made by those who lived two thousand years ago and more. I must confess that I was awe-stricken, and often found myself soliloquizing in tones, somewhat indistinct: "Wonderful, truly wonderful, it hardly seems possible that such advancement in civilization could have been made in ages we are accustomed to call *rude*." The collection is called Cesnola's, from the name of the dower, General Louis Palma di Cesnola, an Italian nobleman, who after the Crimean war sailed for America. During President Lincoln's administration, General Cesnola was appointed Consul to Cyprus, the result of whose stay on that island is our exhibition at the Metropolitan Museum of [A]rt. Says the *National Repository*: "The explorations and excavations of which this collection is the result occupied a considerable part of ten years, during which General Cesnola was the American Consul for Cyprus. In the course of the explorations he traversed the whole island in every direction.["]¹ Let us briefly sum up the result of his exploration, as noted by Mr. Johns[t]on: "He explored and identified the sites of eight ancient royal cities; he discovered the ruins of eight other royal cities, and of twelve towns mentioned by Strabo, Ptolemy and other ancient geographers,

* * * * It may be worth while to give the numbers of some of the leading classes of objects. There were vases, 14,240; glass vases, cups, etc., 3,719; busts, and heads in marble and terra-cotta, 4,200; statues in stone, marble and terra-cotta, 2,110; terra-cotta lamps, 2,380; coins, gold, silver and copper, 2,310; bas-reliefs in marble, stone and terra-cotta, 138; sculptural sarcophagi in marble and stone, 270; engraved gems, cylinders and scarabaei, 1,090; objects in gold, such as bracelets and rings, 1,509; in silver, 370; in copper and bronze, 2,107."[2] The above is simply a part of a quotation, an abridgement. Many more interesting facts might have been taken to illustrate further the point under discussion.

The indefatigable labors and apparently Herculean task of Gen. Cesnola at Cyprus, and of Dr. [Heinrich] Schlieman[n] at Syracuse, and their results ought, it seems to me, to inspire young men to press forward in whatever undertaking they may be engaged in, and under whatever circumstances until the goal is reached. The only way to greatness; the only way to success; in a word, the only way to bring about a reaction in this country is by cutting through what appears to be "the inevitables." The black man is to make himself, if he is ever made. It is certain that no one else is going to do the work for him even if it were possible.

From the same authority (N. R.) we gather the following in regard to the island itself which lies in the Northeastern part of the Mediterranean, 60 or 70 miles west of Syria, and south of Asia Minor. "Cyprus was the kittim of the Hebrews, the Aphrodisia, Makaria and Paphos of the poets, with half a score of other names. From the earliest times it was noted for the abundance and purity of the copper which it produced; this was especially known as *Chalkos kuprios*, "Cyprus brass," which the Latins shortened into *Cuprum*, whence our word Cypress. * * * * In shape the island was compared by the ancients to a hide stretched out to dry."[3] There seems to be a little discrepancy as to its size, but probably not enough to make any very great difference.[4] Two or three hours spent in examining the above collection could not be more profitably spent, I am sure.

Notes

1 [H. Guernsey, "Cesnola's Cypriote Antiquities," *National Repository*, June 1878, p. 482.]

2 [John Taylor Johnston (1820–1893), railroad executive and art collector, was elected as the first president of the Metropolitan Museum of Art in 1870 and served until 1889. He paved the way for the purchase of the Cesnola collection. Scarborough quotes Johnston from H. Guernsey, "Cesnola's Cypriote Antiquities," p. 482.]

3 [H. Guernsey, "Cesnola's Cypriote Antiquities," p. 483.]

4 [H. Guernsey, "Cesnola's Cypriote Antiquities," p. 483, describes the island as "forty miles long," "scarcely 10 miles in width," and "about thirty-six hundred square miles."]

Summer Saunterings, No. II

Christian Recorder, September 9, 1886.

Among the many public buildings and palatial residences [in Ithaca] apart from the university itself is the McGraw-Fiske mansion, now famous because of the recent lawsuits to deprive the university of a claim it is said to have upon it by the will of the late Mrs. Jennie McGraw-Fiske [1840–1881]. The property, including the household furniture, so far as it is furnished, is valued at more than six hundred thousand dollars, possibly more—a million. The doors of this magnificent mansion were thrown open and the members of the association were taken through all of its gorgeous apartments. Here are rare vases, beautiful mosaics, wedding chests, ivory chairs, Japanese tapestries, Venetian chimney pieces, bric-a-brac picked up from all over the civilized world and costly paintings in the art gallery. By the will of the owner of this property Cornell has already received more than $700,000 in cash, according to the statement of the Register. The Scripture seems to be fulfilled in nearly every case of large gifts to our schools and colleges: "For unto every one that hath shall be given, and he shall have abundance; but from him that hath not shall be taken away even that which he hath."[1] It has been the rule that the richer colleges get money because they are rich, while the poor one must struggle, gradually eking out an existence by hand to mouth living. I believe this state of things will continue until many of the smaller institutions are swallowed up by the larger ones. The trouble is, there are too many colleges and universities. The number needs to be reduced. If in Ohio there were five instead of forty, the quality of education would be improved one hundred per cent. An institution must grow with the years—must have wise and efficient men at its back as well as men of means—even then it is a struggle. I am told that at one time, when Cornell could not realize on all of the lands belonging to the college, the institution was about to lose some of its best men because their salaries were not paid regularly and their services were in demand at other institutions that could pay more money, and that, too, when due. The President ([Andrew] White) and the trustees were called on to face the music. The President gravely said, "I will give one hundred and fifty thousand dollars to help us out of this dilemma provided you, gentlemen, will give one hundred and fifty thousand dollars more. Come, gentlemen, come, let us meet this thing fairly." They came, too. The amount was given, the professors satisfied and the trouble was thus ended without further delay. Men are constantly dying, but their money goes into prescribed channels. Each has his pet scheme, real or ideal, to which he bends his nerves; and when death comes his will tells the tale to the disappointment of many who had hoped otherwise. I learn that during President White's administration it was quite common when the institution "got into a pinch" to give his check for $1000 or $5000, more or less, to aid some professor whose salary was irregular—without note or interest. A good man, indeed!

The University furnishes houses for all of its Faculty, built upon the most improved styles. Cornell, like Yale, Harvard, Dartmouth, etc., etc., also grants one of its Professors in case he has been appointed by the Archæological Institute of America as Director of the American School of Classical Studies at Athens, a leave of absence for one year on half pay by special arrangement. I will add here that the co-operating colleges number thirteen up to date.

Let me return from my digression. Sage Chapel is the gift of Honorable Henry W. Sage [1814–1897]. It is constructed of brick, with elaborately carved stone trimmings, and is of the Gothic order of architecture. The auditorium has a seating capacity of about five hundred. One of the most noteworthy features of the room is the number of memorial windows and tablets. Opening into the auditorium is a smaller chapel so arranged as to be used in connection with it. On the north side is the Memorial Chapel, constructed in the Gothic style of the second or decorative period. It was erected to the memory of Ezra Cornell [1807–1874], John McGraw [1815–1877] and Jennie McGraw-Fiske. On entering the chapel the eye beholds the memorial windows, which are designed not only to commemorate the connection of the benefactors mentioned, but to associate their names with those of some of the greatest benefactors in the cause of education. The north window contains the figures of William of Wykeham, John Harvard and Ezra Cornell; the east window the figures Jeanne of Navarre [c. 1271–1305], Margaret of Richmond [1443–1509] and Jennie McGraw-Fiske; the west window those of Elihu Yale [1649–1721], Sir Thomas Bodley [1545–1613] and John McGraw. Directly beneath the great north window is a recumbent figure of Ezra Cornell, in white marble, of heroic size, by W. W. Story [1819–1895], of Rome. A crypt underneath the chapel contains recesses for the remains of the founders of the University.

The Sage College is for women. It is also the gift of Hon. Henry W. Sage. It is a home for students, not a separate department. In form it is quadrangular—one hundred and sixty-eight feet front, forty-one feet deep and four stories in height. A gymnasium for young ladies connects the wings in the rear. The rooms for the students are eighteen feet by fourteen with a low board partition dividing off one part for a sleeping room. Besides the dormitories, dining hall and parlors it contains lecture and recitation rooms, museum laboratories, with complete equipments for students in botany, with greenhouses and all the necessary facilities for the pursuit of floriculture and ornamental gardening. Among some of the other buildings belonging to the University may be mentioned McGraw building, White Hall, Civil Engineering Building, Astronomical Observatory, Sibley College, Chemical and Physical Building, Gymnasium and Armory, Cascadilla Place, etc., etc. Among the museums may be mentioned the Agricultural, Botanical and Chemical; the museum of Archæology, of Conchology, of Veterinary Science, of Paleontology, etc. The laboratories are as numerous as the museums. In fact, all the facilities necessary to make a well organized University are found here. Nothing is done by halves at Cornell. The General Faculty, numbering over 80 instructors subdivided into several special Faculties, is composed of the most learned men to be found anywhere in America.

The salary of the President is $6,000 (six thousand dollars) annually, and that of the professors is in proportion. The university preachers (on the Dean Sage Foundation) are composed of some of the most distinguished pulpit orators of the country. Apropos to this remark I may add that I believe that much of the scepticism, and many of the forms of agnosticism that we find in colleges are due to poor preaching. At this point students are passing through what may be termed the formation period of their lives. And it seems to me that they should have the best, most intellectual, as well as the most spiritual preaching. Having inferior preachers to fill college pulpits is wrong; it is an infliction of punishment upon both professors and pupils for no reason whatever. For one I must always enter my protest.

One of the most complete departments of the university is the Agricultural. The university farm consists of 120 acres of arable land, the larger part of which is used for experimental purposes and the illustration of the principles of agriculture. Nearly all the domestic animals are kept to serve the same ends. Those portions of the farm and stock not used for experiments are managed with the view to their greatest productiveness. Statistics of both experiments and management are kept on such a system as to show at the close of each year the profit or loss, not only of the whole farm, but of each crop and group of animals of the two barns.

The Professor, I. P. Roberts [1833–1928], M. Agr., in this department is, perhaps, the most genial man, on short acquaintance, that I ever met. It was through his kindness that I received many important facts relative to his department and the general plans and operations of Cornell, and for which the writer is very grateful. Though the questions were numerous, he was always ready to answer them and explain any point that he thought I did not understand. In fact, I found all the professors whom I chanced to meet as courteous as they were learned.

Thursday noon, after the election of officers for next year, and after selecting a place for the next meeting, the association adjourned to meet at the University of Vermont, at Burlington on Lake Champlain, the second Tuesday in July, 1887.[2] There were invitations from Washington, D. C., the University of Virginia, Albemarle county, Va., and possibly three or four other colleges; but the committee agreed upon the one already given. The Modern

Language Association, which holds its meetings during the Christmas holidays, convenes this year at Johns Hopkins, Baltimore. With but few exceptions all the members of the Philological Association are also the members of the American Oriental Society. The American Spelling Reform Association assembled immediately after the Philological Association had adjourned. After preliminaries, reports of the work of spelling reform in the large cities in Americ[a] and in Europe from various auxiliary bodies were read and commented on by the secretary. In the evening an excellent address was delivered by the President, Dr. [Francis Andrew] March, of Lafayette College. After the reading of papers, etc., etc., this organization also adjourned to meet at the University of Vermont. Thus ended two pleasant gatherings of American scholars under the classic shades of Cornell University.

Note

1 [Matthew 25:29.]

2 [The American Philological Association met at Cornell University in July 1886. Scarborough presented a paper "The Birds of Aristophanes: A Theory of Interpretation," summarized in *Transactions of the American Philological Association* 17 (July 1886): vii. For more details, see *Autobiography,* pp. 96, 356.]

Summer Saunterings, No. III

Christian Recorder, September 16, 1886.

The natural scenery around Ithaca is beautiful in all that term implies. Nature has used a lavish hand in beautifying this part of western central New York. Some portions of it suggest the mountainous regions of Tennessee. Then again one is forcibly reminded of the scenery along the Hudson as he sails, on a June morning, from Albany to New York, or as he travels over the Western Maryland Railroad from Hagerstown to Baltimore. In many instances the landscape here seems almost a reproduction of their sublimer parts. If the reader has ever traveled through the Connecticut Valley by way of the Passumpsic route from White River Junction to Lake Memphramagog, he has an idea of the impressions made upon the writer as he beheld from his window Cayuga Lake, lying low in a bottom with massive hills and towering mountains on either side. It seems a little less than a mile from Sage College and but a pleasant walk. The hill slopes and hilltops appear diversified with farm houses and cottages, surrounded by trees in such regularity as to make a beautiful picture. In fact, the old Roman quinceaux is introduced to our thoughts. The trees seem to be placed in rows so that those in each row are opposite the centre of the interval between the adjoining two in the right and left hand rows. Again oblique lines appear with the same Roman regularity. Then the towns are all classic as to nomenclature. Here are Homer and Virgil, Ulysses and Romulus, Ithaca and Attica, Ovid and Brutus, Marathon and Sparta, Camillus, Cicero, Fabius, Lysander, Manlius and Marcellus and many others—all clustered in the same section. I asked a celebrated divine on board of the steamer how it happened that there was such a cluster of classic names in this part of New York. The reply was that there is a legend to the effect that the parties who planned the towns not only took their classical dictionaries with them but made constant reference to them in search of names for their new towns. I suppose this view of it is only a legend. It is hardly a coincidence, however, and must, in some way, be the result of deliberate planning by the founders and their immediate associates.[1]

It is remarkable how many young men (to return to some thoughts on the personnel of the [American Philological] Association) go abroad now-a-days to finish their education. As there is a large number of fellowships in our best colleges, a stay of two years in Germany or Athens is rendered very easy if a student will take the pains to make a good record in college. These fellowships, as is well known, yield generally from $400 to $600 per year, and most any student can live in Europe at Leipsic, Tubingen, Heidelberg, Gottingen or Strasburg on an annual income of that amount. In the Association we have a number of fellows and graduate students who have taken high rank at home and abroad. They are all Ph. D.s or are now studying for that degree, and are doing good work in their line. At my own table, or rather at the table where I sat at Sage College, there were twelve persons, including the writer, representing twelve colleges, each one distinguished in some special line, as an Epigraphist, either Greek or Latin, or in philology generally or it may be in some one of two branches of the great family of languages. Turning to the papers of the American School of Classical Studies at Athens, Volume 1, of the Archæological Institute of America, we find under the directorship of Professor Goodwin, (1882–1883) the following students enrolled:

John M. Crow, A.B. (Waynesburg College) Ph.D. (Syracuse University.) Harold N. Fowler, A.B., (Harvard University.) Paul Shorey, A.B. (Harvard University,) holder of the Kirkland Fellowship of Harvard University. J. R. S. Sterret, University of Virginia, Ph.D., (University of Munich.) Frank N. Taylor, Wesleyan University. J. R. Wheeler, A.B. (University of Vermont) graduate student of Harvard University. Frank E. Woodruff, A.B. (University of Vermont,) B.D. (Union Theological Seminary,) holder of a Fellowship of the Union Theological Seminary[,] Louis Bevier, A.M. (Rutger's College), Ph.D. (Johns Hopkins University.)

American scholarship is far in advance of what it was a few years ago. Special efforts are now made to elevate it still more. I don't think we need to be ashamed of it. The remark was made not long ago by a professor from one of the Southern universities that he thought it would be quite a while before the German professors would recognize American scholars as equal to themselves or as being very erudite. No reply was made by any of the company, though there seems to be a grain of truth in the statement. The German scholars have always been more or less specialists; the American scholars are becoming more and more so, as the work of the different associations plainly shows. The American idea has been to know a little of everything and nothing perfectly; vice versa with the Germans. In the American Philological Association I have known members to begin a line of thought at one meeting and take it through several years. In fact, this practice is quite common, as the transactions will show. Two years ago in New Hampshire, when I read a paper on the "Theory and Function of the Thematic Vowel in the Greek Verb," I was told by a member of the association who had just returned from Heidelberg that he had heard a dozen lectures on that theme while a student there.[2] Evidently, as was expressed in my reply, the treatment must have been an exhaustive one. This also shows the German method of prosecuting a study.

These articles, instead of "Summer Saunterings," should be called "Hodge Podge," for that is what they are.

Note

1 [The names come from Plutarch. See Meyer Reinhold, *Classica Americana* (Detroit, Mich.: Wayne State University Press, 1984), pp. 257 and 263.]

2 [The summary of this paper is included in this volume.]

Summer Saunterings, No. IV

Christian Recorder, September 23, 1886.

In a variety of aspects Atlanta is a Northern city located in the South. That push and activity which characterizes our Northern towns are observed here. Everybody has something to do and seems in a hurry to do it. In this respect it is unlike most Southern cities. The population is over sixty thousand—a wonderful stride from forty thousand, the number of its inhabitants a few years ago. It is not only a commercial but an educational centre as well. The numerous schools and colleges—professional and non-professional—united with the various industries of the city, make it a pleasant place to visit and a desirable place to live in. I think the sentiment of the South has changed much in twenty five years and that there is a greater disposition on the part of the white people to treat the negro kindly and respect him according to his worth. I noticed very carefully the spirit of the Southern people as I moved among them. I did not see that "rampant," bitter feeling so common years ago. In speaking of a colored man it was either Mr. So and so or So and So. While there is a change in feeling and action towards the negro, there are still many unpleasant reminders of "ye olden times." For example, as you enter Atlanta, the Gate City of the South, the first disgusting thing that meets the eye, that kindles every spark of manhood within one, is the threefold waiting room arrangement distinctly placarded, one for ladies, one for gentlemen and one for colored people. This ought to be broken up, and that, too, speedily. These colored waiting rooms are worse than pig-pens—covered with dirt and filth. Surely the colored people of Atlanta, Marion and elsewhere will not submit to this outrage longer. We are not beasts and do not desire to be treated as such. We demand our rights as American citizens. Passing over this picture we shall take up another, very different in kind and more entertaining. I spoke of the educational facilities of Atlanta. I may add here that it deserves well to be called a city of schools. Aside from a large number of schools for white children, there is almost as large a number for colored children, young men and young women. Atlanta University has now acquired a national reputation in its relation to the A[merican] M[issionary] A[ssociation]. Clark University stands equally high and is known most especially through the channels of the

Freedman's Aid Society. To the zeal and indefatigable efforts of our distinguished friend and divine, Rev. Dr. W[esley] J. Gaines, one wing of Morris Brown College is almost finished. It is a four story brick, with recitation rooms large and comfortable. The seats, blackboards and all of its appointments are on the most improved plan. The main building, when erected, will front the boulevard and will make a magnificent appearance. Dr. Gaines kindly took the writer through the building, and with his usual dignity and grace explained the purposes of the trustees when opportunity (financially) permitted. I have seen the recitation rooms of most all of our best colleges in this country and I find none, so far as the fitting out of rooms and adaptation to ends are concerned, superior to Morris Brown College. Rev. Dr. Gaines and the trustees of this school deserve the congratulations of the African Methodist Episcopal Church—of the entire negro race—for the beginning of what is destined to be, if properly and carefully fostered, the college of the South. There is no doubt in my mind as to the success of this enterprise, so wisely begun and judiciously managed. Our good friends seem to have caught the spirit of Horace, when he said, "Dimidium f[a]cti qui coepit, habet" (He who makes a beginning has accomplished one-half of an undertaking) and are vigorously pressing forward "toward the mark for the prize of the high calling of God in Christ Jesus."[1] If he does nothing more than has been done in the founding of this college, Rev. Dr. Gaines will leave behind him a "blessing which will repeat itself in showers of benedictions" upon future generations. There is no office in the gift of the Church to which such a man would not do honor. A servant of truth, a doer of the word, abounding in purity of heart, full of earnestness, characterized by what may be styled a "virtuous enthusiasm, which is always self-forgetful," our friend will always live in the grateful hearts of his Church and people. M[a]cte Virtute (Go on in your valor), the victory is yours.[2] There are other noble men in Georgia whom I shall always esteem among the best for goodness, wisdom, courage and activity. I need not mention their names, for they are known not only in connection with this college as trustees, but in their work of love in their various parishes. It was my pleasure to stop at the beautiful home of our friend Dr. Gaines. Architecturally it is inferior to none in the vicinity. It is a model house with a model family living in it. These are strictly signs of race progress. They are in part the standards by which we may expect to be measured in the struggle for recognition in this country, nor can we afford to ignore these facts. We must not ignore them. There are many colored people in the South I notice who live in what may be called elegant homes. It is frequently the case that as soon as one sees a house he can tell quite accurately whether the inmates are colored or white, but not so here. One lesson which the negro must learn is not to do things by halves. Again, not far away, on Young street, in another beautiful house different in its architecture from Dr. Gaines', lives a man of much learning and of wonderful versatility of mind—Bishop H. M. Turner. The role he played with Elder Gaines and others in the prohibition movement is too well known through the associated press reports to be repeated here. Suffice it to say Atlanta is a "dry" city and to the labors of these gentlemen with others must the result be attributed. They have become a part of Atlanta—a prominent part—and I notice that the best classes of white citizens seem pleased to do them honor. With such men as leaders there is no such thing as failure.

The colored people here are doing well generally—owning large property and fast becoming financiers. They seem to be aware of the fact that money and education are powerful levers in civilization and are getting both. Many are living on their rents and are producers as well as consumers. In Atlanta as in Macon the entire hack line is owned by colored people. The negroes have representatives in all the industrial pursuits. Some are engaged in selling coal and wood and have their own yards; others are busy in mercantile life; some are master mechanics and control their own business; others are farmers, making and selling their own cotton. In fact, the colored people of Georgia are showing that the old theory that the "negro can do nothing but teach or preach, as the avenues to a livelihood are all closed," has exploded.

I met a young man who was formerly connected with the city schools but who lost his position because he refused to have his school take part in the parade during the Jefferson Davis entree. The attitude taken by this young gentleman is a commendable one. It should not be long before he finds employment. Here is a case of principle, not policy. The young man who will act on this line is the one who deserves all the aid and sympathy that we can give him. When the white people of the South fully understand that "a man's a man for all that,"[3] and that color has nothing to do with determining his action with reference to matters of right and wrong, they will act differently; very differently. The change is coming. Let us be thoughtful.

Notes

1 [Horace, *Epistles*, 1.2.40, and Philippians 3:12.]

2 [This is a traditional form of praise. See Virgil, *Aeneid*, book 9, line 641.]

3 [This is a reference to Robert Burns (1759–1796), "A Man's a Man for A' That" (1795).]

Summer Saunterings, Concluded

Christian Recorder, October 21, 1886.

Macon is the central city of Georgia, and per location ought to be the capital. The inhabitants number something over twenty thousand, nearly three fifths of whom are colored. There are plenty of cities that have more wealth, but none more beautiful or picturesque—in parts, at least. The high elevation above the sea makes it beautiful. Like Atlanta, it has the building mania, which has seized all alike, white and black. I venture the assertion that there is no Northern city in which the people as a whole are more thrifty and prosperous than they are in Atlanta and Macon. I doubt whether the State of Ohio can furnish the wealthy Negroes that we find in one city in Georgia. Newspaper reports are usually exaggerated, but the statements that have gone the rounds of the press that the colored people in the State of Georgia have more wealth in proportion to their numbers than is found among those in any other State in the union is, I believe, actually true. Why, there are numbers that live on their income, whether this is derived from their rents or bankable funds. There are farms, plantations, summer seats and winter homes all owned by colored people. Said a white banker to the writer, "I suppose you have observed the rage for building in this city? It has caught black as well as white. Mr. So and So (colored) has a number of houses and is building more. Some of our strong business men are among the colored people. I can name dozens of colored men in this city that are rich and still accumulating. You will find them in all the business ramifications of this town, and we are pro[u]d of them." I must confess that I was surprised to see the prosperous condition of the colored people. W[illiam G[adson] Johnson, Esq., owns, in addition to large property in different parts of the city, a commodious two storied brick building on the corner of Co[t]ton and Washington avenues in which he has three separate stores: grocery, managed by himself and sons; dry goods, by wife and daughters, and a shoe store, in the hands of other parties. He does business on a large scale. Then there is P[ulaski] O. Holt, another substantial merchant and real estate owner in another part of the city. Then there is Edward Wood[liff], whose houses "are all over the city." He also owns property in Cleveland, O. Then again there is [Ar]mstead Bryant, who is behind none of his rivals in point of ease and good living. He is engaged in the wood business. Following him are P. Perkins, W. B. Clark, Thos. [Nunez M.] Sellers, J. W. Brooks (whose rents net him handsomely,) Thos. Screen (the banker and broker), Jackson and many others whose names I cannot now mention.[1] Some of these men migrate every summer to watering places and other fashionable "haunts" for pleasure and comfort. Among the many churches the most prominent are our own, together with the Presbyterian and Congregational churches. To say Elder [E. P.] Holmes is doing excellent work at Steward Chapel and that he is highly esteemed by his people expresses it mildly. A better appointment could not have been made; a more suitable successor to Elders [Wesley] Gaines, [J. T.] Hall, [F. M.?] Johnson and T[heophilus] G[ould] Steward (the founder of this church) could not have been found. I should like to see life size portraits of these divines—especially the founder—hanging upon the walls of the lecture room of this church. This is fitting. The name of Dr. T.G. Steward will never die, but will always live in the hearts of the citizens of Macon. His name is fondly cherished there and the good Doctor himself is ventured as a man of eminent piety and sound scholarship.[2] The Sabbath school numbers over 600. The morning I was there they seemed to have come out in their full strength. The classes were well divided and well arranged. The method of conducting the exercise was a good one. There is one feature in this school that I admire, among many others, and that is the appointment of a member of the advanced classes or a teacher to review with the explanatory and exegetical remarks as to the occasion of and circumstances connected with the lesson. Miss Fanny Pepper executed her work in this line admirably. It was a pleasure to listen to her. Elder Holmes' class is one of the great promise, and here, as in the church, he exhibits the same faithfulness that has characterized his pastoral labors elsewhere. Mr. Green Smith, the superintendent, shows taste and skill in the management of this school. I was pleased to note, also, the progress made in the secular schools of the city. Prof. Hudson, with his corps of teachers, is doing good work and deserves the gratitude of the patrons of his school.[3] If the other city schools were likewise provided for the educational facilities for the colored children would be many percent better. It is astounding that the principal of the colored schools receives such a small compensation as compared with that of the white schools. This should not be. The colored people should rise up en masse against it and demand a hearing in this matter. Here are the figures: $45 (colored), $125 (white)[.] Read and ponder. Fiat justitia ruat caelum.[4]

Notes

1 [The men mentioned were—according to Muriel McDowell Jackson, genealogist at the Middle Georgia Regional Library in Macon—all prominent figures: Johnson later supervised a colored orphanage; in the 1890s, Holt was involved in a newspaper, *Central City Times*; Woodliff, a free colored person from Virginia, purchased his wife's freedom, and in 1865 he became one of Macon's first colored aldermen, and his daughter later opened the

first school in the basement of her parents' home. Sellers was a brick mason and cashier for the Freedman's Bank in Macon. His son, Cassander Sellers, became one of the first black lawyers in the city. Brooks became a teacher; the Brooks School in the Bibb County Educational System bears his name.]

2 [The men mentioned were all active in the A.M.E. Church. Gaines later became a bishop, while Steward was a cashier in the Freedman's Bank in Macon; Steward Chapel (originally named Cotton Avenue A.M.E.) was named for him.]

3 [According to Muriel McDowell Jackson, Hudson High School in Macon was named for Hudson. After merging with Ballard Normal School, it was called Ballard-Hudson.]

4 [Let justice be done, though the sky may fall.]

Education in General

The Utility of Studying the Greek, part 1

Christian Recorder, April 12, 1883.

MR. EDITOR:—In this and one or two other articles, I purpose giving some thoughts on the utility of studying that grand old language, the Greek. Many things, pro et contra, both practical and theoretical, have been written on this subject, and we may expect as many more on the same theme during these transitional stages of thought and literature, and too, when it is by [no] means fixed as to what place the study of Greek and Latin shall occupy in a course of liberal education. The old and new schools are still contending as to what shall constitute liberal culture, whether the classics shall take precedence of modern languages, natural sciences or mathematics, or whether they shall be banished entirely from an academic curriculum. Each of these branches has its part to play in developing the brain, and they, together, make the well-rounded and symmetrical mind. It matters not, however, what may be the drift of the argument, the fact remains that the study of the Greek language is an indispensable element in a course of liberal training. The Greek is a branch of the Indo-European family and was spoken many centuries before our era by Greeks in Europe and Asia Minor—afterward in the colonies on the coast of the Mediterranean Sea. The Greek, the Latin and the Sanskrit are sisters, offsprings of a common parent. This language is one of the oldest known tongues in the world and as Geldart, in his valuable little treatise on the modern Greek, remarks, "It is a language in which there are the loftiest and deepest thoughts of the greatest poets, the wisest thinkers. It is a medium through which the noblest, holiest and best of teachers have directly and indirectly found their utterance in the far off ages of a hoar antiquity. It is animated with the fire of life, and beautiful with the memory of the past."[1] The utility of the Greek is seen in the discipline the study affords. In the Wilberforce Graduate (June, '82) in an article on the classics as a source of mental culture, I advanced and discussed the same idea. With no desire to contrast or discriminate between mathematical and classical study, it is my opinion that the beauties and niceties of the Greek syntax, the difficulties of translation, the discrimination and selection of words as to purity, propriety and precision, tend as largely, in a sense, to develop accuracy of thought and expression, as a problem in English or Playfair.[2] The difficulty of mastering the peculiar and idiomatic forms of the Greek, requires unusual application with the tact and skill, and is in itself a test of more than ordinary ability in him who succeeds best. The object of a college course is ostensibly mental discipline as well as general information, therefore only those branches should be taught that will bring about this end as speedily as possible and at the same time fit the young student for whatever sphere in life the demands of the future may call him to fill. I don't think that the Rev. Dr. Howard Crosby, in his late effusion, means to discard the study of the dead languages at all, but so far as I learn he would have "the special and microscopic mastery of these tongues deferred to a post-collegiate course for such as are to become classical teachers or commentators."[3] For the masses, a practical education is needed for practical life; special courses for specialists. The utility of the Greek is seen in that it is one of the avenues to a thorough understanding of the English language, and, of course, it is indispensable to philological research. The English language, as is well known, is pre-eminently a composite one—words from the Celtic, Greek, Latin, Anglo-Saxon, Danish, Norman, French, with many others, both ancient and modern. A good knowledge of the English, and a facile use of the same, whether with tongue or pen, demand in part, if not wholly, some acquaintance with the Greek use of the elements that enter into it. There are many words in common use to-day of Greek origin, which one who makes any pretensions at all to learning, should know how to analyze and classify. During the conquests of Alexander the Great, the Greek language and Greek influence gained an important place in Asia and Egypt. It soon reached Palestine. The Jews of Alexandria used it almost exclusively, and hence to them it became a vernacular. The first version of the Hebrew Scriptures ever turned into Greek (Septuagint) was executed by these Alexandrian Jews who had adopted the Greek tongue as their own. Even after the downfall of Greece and during the supremacy of Rome the flexible, eloquent and polished language of the Greeks remained permanent, so that at the advent of our Saviour, this tongue was the tongue, and the one most widely known and most generally used. This leads me to observe that the Greek is one of the principal avenues to biblical learning and research, without which our knowledge of the sacred Scriptures would be very limited indeed; and as far as the New Testament alone is concerned, it is a conditio sine qua non for even a passable knowledge of its meaning in multiplied instances. At this period of the world's history and at this juncture of American civilization one cannot well afford to remain passive and accept every interpretation relative to disputed points without being able to search the records and examine the original text for himself. DeQuincy, himself a Greek encyclopædia, affirmed that it is undeniable that the progress of sacred literature is dependent upon that of the profane; that the vast advances made in biblical knowledge and in other parts of divinity since the era of the Reformation are due in great proportion to the general presentation of classical learning.[4] From what has been said it can be readily seen that this is true, and the man who neglects the study of Latin or Greek on the ground that they are dead languages, cannot expect to succeed as a biblicist or as a man of culture

Notes

1 [Edmund Martin Geldart (1844–1885), *The Modern Greek Language in Its Relation to Ancient Greek* (Oxford: Clarendon Press, 1870).]

2 [John Playfair (1748–1819), mathematician and geometrist, wrote a response to Euclid in 1795.]

3 [Howard Crosby (1826–1891), Greek professor and chancellor of New York University from 1870 to 1881, was also pastor at the Fourth Avenue Presbyterian Church.]

4 [Thomas De Quincey was one of Scarborough's favorite authors. Scarborough purchased a set of his works while he was a student at Oberlin. See *Autobiography*, p. 49, notes 13 and 14.]

The Utility of Studying the Greek, part 2

Christian Recorder, August 2, 1883.

In a previous article I spoke of Hellenistic Greek, or the Greek language as used by the Jews during the time of our Saviour. I wish to speak more fully upon this phase of the subject before I return to the classic tongue. Though Rome had become the mistress of the world, and Roman influence and Roman power were felt in every hamlet, yet the Roman and Latin language could not supplant the polished and flexible Greek. Into the very heart of Italy, into every nook of Roman dominion, tributary or otherwise, the Greek language in some form or other made its way, consequently a better medium for the expression and communication of thought could not be found. This is doubtless one, if not the chief reason why the writers of the New Testament chose the Greek as their dialect. Then, too, this language was singularly adapted to the office it was to fill. As all of us are not specialists, the principles of textual criticism will be of interest to only a few, and must not be discussed here. As was intimated in a former communication, there is no substitute that one can adopt that will enable him to understand accurately the different shades of meaning that words often have in sacred Writ; the relation (in the original) that exists between terms and forms of expression which in English seem identical; that will enable him to decide for himself, independently of English translations and commentaries through which horn of dilemma to make his escape amid the discussion of disputed points. The style and language of the New Testament differ greatly from those of classic writers, as for example Xenophon, Plato or Thucydides, but the fundamental laws that govern the structure of the language are the same. Says Dr. Barrows, "To those who study the New Testament in the original, the peculiarities of its language offer a wide and interesting field of inquiry."[1] What poor fellow will regret spending a few years in poring over his Greek Grammar, puzzling his brain with Greek roots and accents, that he may enjoy the results of his labors in after years? The syntax of any language is usually a bore to the beginner. This is a flimsy objection to the study of Greek. It requires just such digging to make boys into strong men—burning midnight lamps over a Greek verb or some difficult construction. That which constituted a liberal education during the mediaeval period of the world's history does not suffice now. President [Charles William] Eliot says that there is not a school in the United States that is worthy of the name of a university. If this be true, what becomes of Harvard, of Johns Hopkins, of Cornell, et al.? During the middle ages an ordinary university course consisted of the trivium (grammar, rhetoric and dialectics) and the quadrivium (arithmetic, music, geometry and astronomy), which, of course, is scarcely equal to a high school curriculum of the present day. It is quite certain that at this advanced stage of human activity no such limitations will meet the demands. What, then, do we want? We want all that our colleges and so-called universities offer and a great deal more. The trivium and the quadrivium were accepted throughout the middle ages, and long after, as the only true program of a liberal education. To enter Harvard now, the applicant is required to pass an examination in Latin grammar (including prosody), Latin composition and Latin at sight; Caesar, Sallust and Ovid; Cicero and Virgil. Greek grammar (with metres), Greek composition (with accents), Greek prose (including Xenophon's Anabasis and the seventh book of Herodotus); Greek poetry (Homer's Iliad, omitting the catalogue of ships). In addition to this there are also arithmetic, algebra, plane geometry, ancient history and geography; modern and physical geography, English composition, French or German, physical science—either botany, chemistry or the rudiments of physics.

It will be observed that Greek and Latin occupy prominent places among these requirements, which also add to the rigidity. It is right here that our modernists raise the hue and cry against the utility of studying the dead languages on the ground that too much time is devoted to other than practical topics. The student who fails to get the drill that Greek and Latin afford is rather poorly equipped for the struggle of life. Is it true that the same amount of discipline can be obtained from a study of German and French that one gets from the dead languages? Experience says not. History in turn confirms the same. Our deep thinkers and profound philosophers, orators and statesmen are—many of them—indebted to classical training for their outfit. Mr. Charles Francis Adams, Jr., in his recent address, delivered before the Harvard Chapter of the fraternity of the Phi Beta Kappa, made some strong thrusts against the methods of teaching Greek in our American colleges, and not without effect.[2] But when Mr. Adams says that the study of Greek in the way it is traditionally insisted upon as a chief requirement to entering college is a positive educational wrong; that it is a language which has no modern uses; that not only is it a dead tongue but it bears no relation to any living speech or literature of value, this we shall have to take with a grain of salt and notice at some future time. We hope the compositors will treat us a little better in this article than was our fortune in the first one.

Notes

1 [See the later publication of Samuel J. Barrows (1845–1909), *Mythical and Legendary Elements in the New Testament* (Boston, 1899).]

[2] [See Charles Francis Adams Jr., "A College Fetich: An Address Delivered before the Harvard Chapter of the Fraternity of the Phi Beta Kappa, in Sanders Theatre, Cambridge, June 28, 1883" (Boston: Lee and Shepard, 1883). See also Scarborough's "The New College Fetich," *A.M.E. Church Review* 3 (1886): 126–135.]

The True Aim of Education

Southern Teachers' Advocate 1, no. 2 (September 1905): 1–5.

(An address delivered at the Commencement exercises of Kentucky Institute, June 7, 1905)

In no preceding period of history has human activity played such a prominent part in all matters of general interest as in the present. In no former times have investigation, improvement, and reform been so rife as now. No previous century has produced such brilliant results, no other age has done so much for the human race, and no former races have looked upon such marvellous things, have beheld such wonderful events and have assisted in such triumphant anniversaries as those born in the century that has just closed.

No matter how tempted we may be to explain otherwise, because we see no good in the present, nor bad in the past, we must agree that the age in which we live is a most earnestly progressive one; that there are most earnest endeavors to philanthropic movements which shall in every way better man's condition.

It is, however, along the line of education that we find much time and attention given. In regard to this subject there has been a growing interest for over a quarter of a century. It is well that in a republic it has been deemed worthy of such attention, because, as Mathew says, "Education dissipates the evils of ignorance, increases the productiveness of labor, diminishes pauperism and crime, and increases human happiness." Where a people must share in government their duty must be done intelligently. No nation can rest in perfect internal security with millions in ignorance. So, rightly does this subject claim our legitimate attention. And that the country at large understands this—the great danger resulting from illiterate masses—is evidenced by the multiplication of schools, the increase of funds for school purposes and the steady appeals for still more aid from those who man the organized efforts to spread learning throughout the land. The many recent gifts of Mr. Carnegie for the founding and sustaining of libraries throughout this broad land is but another evidence of this truth. But with this awakening have come educational reforms and reformers with their theories and strenuous efforts to carry them into effect. The schoolmaster is surely abroad in all the earth. He carries on his endeavors with the same relentless vigor that has characterized all reforms in all ages and with the diligence of a Diogenes, who

"Searched with lantern light to find an honest man."

These movements have each been characterized as the "New Education," but this New Education is a sort of a chameleon. It has taken on almost every shape and hue, every form and size. To-day it is this, to-morrow, that. This week it is a giant which would storm the citadel of instruction and compel it to surrender *vi et armis, nolens volens*—by force and arms, willing or unwilling. Next week it is a little child in humility, speaking as a child, thinking as a child, acting as a child, ready to follow Dame Nature in any paths she beckons. It is apt to mystify the young teacher and to confuse the old.

The term "New Education" has therefore grown to be vague and indefinite. It has had reference to the means and methods employed in developing the mind from infancy through the work of Kindergarten and Normal schools, and a host of educators from Quintilian down have helped on this idea. On the other hand the term has been applied to the conflict that has been waged with varying vigor between classical instruction on the one side, and modern languages and science on the other—whether culture alone should be the aim of education or whether utility should be considered first in education; then again whether that culture might not be gained as well through science and modern language study as through that of the ancient classics—Latin and Greek. So with the arguments *pro* and *con*, a broader opening came into all schools and elective work crept in to enable the question to be fairly met and tested.

Then came the time when the New Education took on another meaning. Its aspect was again changed. From the idea of making utility prominent there was a new and strong outgrowth of sentiment tending to practical lines—to industrial training. It does not require any claim to prophetic power, nor gift as a seer to enable us to see that this phase of education is more than a passing whim. It has fastened itself upon the educational system of the country with a strong hold. It is continually striking a deeper root. It has proved its worth as an educational factor in the school systems at large and is undoubtedly here to stay.

But whether utility in education is to be considered or culture or the mere acquisition of knowledge, one thing seems certain that all will agree that education has a *purpose*, and as Dr. Jebb puts it, *that purpose* is to form good citizens, useful members of society, men capable of bearing their part in it with credit either in public or private life. It is manhood, womanhood after all that is to be formed. So at last we see that there is something beneath all this—a desirable aim above all others when we consider that to make manhood and womanhood requires more than mere mental culture, more than the mere acquisition of knowledge, more than industrial training, though all these may help in the making. Manhood and womanhood, such as the world demands as good citizens, calls for right habits.

Man has been called a bundle of habits. And it is well known that fixed habits are acts that are said to take on the nature of Fate. They determine us.

They become a clog or a spur. They make weak men or strong men, and thus they build character.

Character, then, after all, should be the true aim of all education—*the first aim*. It precedes culture even as culture precedes knowledge in education.

And what is character?

An eminent writer calls it, "The answer to a problem in addition; the sum total of all we think and feel and do." It must then be in reality the foundation stone of all strength; for its scope of power is enormous. Culture occupies but a small portion of self as we view it and knowledge seems to shrink into insignificance beside it.

Roger Ascham saw this three hundred years ago when he declared in those early centuries that we have not to ["]train a soul, nor yet a body, but a man; and we cannot divide him." It fits the case as well today as then. The divinity of mind struggles with the natural proclivities for sluggishness—the clod and dust wage war with the spirit for supremacy, and we have found that every nerve and fiber of being must be called into action if we would build up self and produce strong character.

As we have said, character embraces all that we are within ourselves—good or bad, foolish or wise, weak or strong, noble or ignoble—all that we are in thought, word or deed, and this is the broad and deep foundation that every one must lay in order to produce true manhood and womanhood. The super-structure of life rears itself with little effort, grows like magic upon such a foundation. As skill needs the guiding hand of knowledge, and knowledge the disciplining power of culture, so all these need the influence of strong charac-ter. When these are combined the possessor has almost omnipotent strength with which the effective work of the world may be done.

We may think that muscle, skill and dexterity are sufficient to the artisan or laborer, that the merchant at his desk or the general on the field can hold sway with potential vigor by mere culture or knowledge, but in the end we shall see that no station in life can be found where lasting success is assured without being gauged first of all by character.

Culture and knowledge and skill may stimulate latent talent into activity, and dormant capabilities may be wakened into life by them, but character after all is the spur which urges one on and up to flights at which weak wings, though they may falter, do not fail under its stimulus. Madame [Jeanne-Louise-Henriette] Campan in answer to Napoleon's question, "What does France need most?" replied, "Mothers." In answer to the question, "What does the world need most? what do we need most as a race?" I would reply, *Men and women of character*—men and women who shall use their education, their talent, their culture, their character in the service of God and man, in the service of the race. With such to lead the way to the solution of our vexed questions, with such to throw time and talent on the altar, to enter heartily into the work of uplifting and the breaking down of barriers that surround us like a Chinese wall—with such, I say, it can only be a question of time, when right shall triumph.

With the odds against us, no people need thoroughly educated, thoroughly consecrated men and women more than we in the struggle before us. The true aim of education then should therefore be to make men and women that shall be able to take the lead in all matters that tend to the elevation of the race.

Character is the one thing essential, but after all it is a growth. It does not spring up in a night nor full grown from the head of a Jupiter, like a Minerva. It slowly, year by year, accumulates its force and grows with the exercise of its power. So it becomes exalted, strenuous, authoritative, blending and harmonizing with all else to make a being of perfect balance out of the man or woman who builds thus surely. Then how shall this character that is so desirable be gained, and where shall it be gained, are questions that the student world today needs to dwell upon, for in the school life of the great school world much of this character is to be formed. There must be placed before our youth in this period, noble examples; there must be given noble teaching; there must be held up before them noble ideals.

Character in every quality must largely be determined by our lives, by our associations, and every life in reality determines itself. What each one becomes is most largely a matter of his own choosing. We choose, and we act, and our actions repeated become habits until we have become creatures of habits—mere bundles of habit. No one can throw the responsibility on other shoulders, nor is there such a thing as Fate to be considered in the making of men and women. Manner of life and associates will determine the outcome for each one. Clean lives, contact with noble men and noble minds will give the power to think nobly, feel nobly, do nobly, which at last results in noble character.

The effectiveness of every man or woman will be found in the elements of true character; for they touch all the virtues, and to those persons ambitious to be foremost in the work of the world today these elements of true character must become a constituent part of their being. It should be remembered that,—

"Our lives are measured by the deeds we do,
The thoughts we think, the objects we purpose."

And so all ambitions must be subordinated to worthy ends, all moving along in life must be along those lines indicated to be among the positive forces of the world, to lead and control. It matters not whether it be in the seething world outside or from some place of retirement; some humble calling, everywhere, right influence, though circumscribed, makes a life that does not die; and laurels of some sort await those who thus aspire.

We have said that we live in an age where the possibilities for achievement were never so great as now. In a large sense they increase rather than diminish with advancing years. The youth who stands upon the pedestal of today belongs to that period of life where though they may be able to look back upon a short past of their own, they can look forward to a half century or more with all its glowing prospects stretched out in a broad vista before them. The race has come thus far on the highway to achievement; there need be no great fear that the future holds but little, if manhood grows strong to do, keeps its integrity, and is possessed of a determined will and a stout heart.

I would urge the youth today to set their faces like flint toward the accomplishment of some purpose, to place manhood and womanhood above all else, to combine with character both culture and knowledge, and to these add skill. Let the hand not scorn to do that which is nearest, though on humble lines, but work for the future. Remember the saying that "circumstances are made of India rubber for the strong, of iron for the weak;" so be strong, *be strong!* The race needs this education in strength—the strength that has made the world great. The world will recognize worth, will bow to excellence, will honor power, in time, be it of brain or of muscle.

Those who leave college walls within these days, carry with them hearts beating high with hopes as they prepare to let their boats slip out into the sea of the world beyond the harbor that has been theirs for so long. They are the ones who must first see to it that no day passes without adding to all that has been given them here—without forging links of strength of character while accumulating more of learning and of culture, building up the true manhood and womanhood that must be ours if we *stand* as a race. The life outside will not allow rests. There is no such thing as rest. This life is a strenuous, active one. The world is asking what you are, and what you can do. You must answer these questions by your life and work. There is work somewhere for all. But do not disdain that which is close by, ever thinking there is that which is better, far remote. It is he who seizes that which is nearest and does his best that succeeds. There is too much chasing of will-o'-th'-wisps among us. Get to work, get to earnest work, honest work and bide your time for higher and better things. That all things come to those that know how to wait is no idle saying. It does mean, however, that it must not be idle waiting; it must be energetic, industrious, purposeful waiting.

The one thing to remember is that it is not for yourselves alone that you work and wait. You are not fitting for living in the mere present. As the years come upon you, when you reach the hill-top of life and stand on its summit, when you face life's west windows, you will then best understand why you were so urged to fit yourselves for the duties before you.

It is for the coming years and generations that you must live and work in unceasing preparation, for the years that many may not live to see, but the years in which the sons and daughters of the race must stand shoulder to shoulder for the upbuilding of that life that shall make future generations stronger still. We are at a most important period of our career as a people. To the young, much must be entrusted in the teaching and training. It must be wise teaching, wise training. Let us strive to make honorable men and women, industrious men and women, self-sacrificing men and women, resourceful men and women, men and women who will demand respect for what they are—for their true worth and innate nobility of character.

I repeat, upon the youth of the present day, rests a great responsibility—the education of the race with all that we have shown that education must mean—fitting for duty, making the most of the faculties given them, fitting for wise discharge of all that may fall upon us; in a word, fitting for LIFE. It should be an inspiration to every young man and woman to view the work committed to such hands. There is no grander work before any race, before any man or woman, and there is no work on earth that calls for grander men and women to carry it on. We must not rest upon our oars; we must gird ourselves to uphold law, to eschew vice, to protect virtue, to countenance no crimes, to preach and teach by our own lives the gospel of pure, clean, upright living from the humblest to the most exalted.

The future depends upon this character building that it is ours to look after. We shall see better days. The future holds for the Negro something worth having. With the possession of a strong exalted character each of us can say, "I have erected a monument more lasting than brass and loftier than the kingly elevating pyramids, which the wasting winds and numberless years and the flight of time shall never be able to destroy."[1]

The race must do this for itself. If this is done other things will be added unto it. Wealth will come by honest industry; respect will come through honest worth and in time the doors of labor will open everywhere when excellence knocks. With that education that aims at the development of high moral character we lay the foundation for the next generation that shall count much for truth and righteousness, for a better understanding between man and man, between race and race. With this end in view,

> "Our good bark aground today
> Shall float again tomorrow."[2]

I adjure the young people, blessed with these rare opportunities, to hold this aim of education ever in view. In the slightly changed words of Massey—that prophet poet, whose royal soul included all humanity in his inspiring words of hope and courage,—I say to you:[3]

> "Build up heroic lives, and all
>   Be like a sheathen sabre
> Ready to flash out at God's call
>   For any sort of Labor."

> Triumph and toil are twins; and aye
>   Joy suns the cloud of sorrow,
> And 'tis the martyrdom today
>   Brings victory tomorrow."

Notes

1 [See Horace, book 3, ode 30, lines 1–5: "Exegi monumentum aere perennius / Regalique situ pyramidum altius, / Quod non imber edax, non Aquilo impotens / Possit diruere aut innumerabilis / Annorum series et fuga temporum."]

2 [See Gerald Massey (1828–1907), *My Lyrical Life, Part 2* (1889), "To-day and To-morrow," stanza 2, lines 15–16.]

3 [See Gerald Massey (1828–1907), *My Lyrical Life, Part 2* (1889), "To-day and To-morrow," stanza 6, lines 1–8.]

Personal Influence:
The President's Opening Address

Sodalian 8, no. 1 (October 1913): 1–6.

Thomas Carlyle once said that he regarded the personal influence of great men as the *largest* factor in making a people. Now the blunt Scotch philosopher said nothing which is to be considered as peculiarly unique when he made this statement. The impressive part, however is in the assertion that personal influence of great men is the *largest* factor—not simply a *great* factor, an *important* factor, but the *largest* factor in the making of the people.

I agree with him, and for several reasons I have chosen this topic of "Personal Influence," upon which to say a few words as we enter the new school year.[1]

We as a people are still in the process of making in many ways. This university where we gather to obtain an education is an institution where opportunity comes to be placed in contact with great men and women at one time or another, and a place where we may and do feel their influence. Then, too, the education and training received are great factors in producing great men and women: so that, look at it as we may—whether from the standpoint of being influenced by great men or women, or of becoming great men or women ourselves, it is worth while to consider the subject.

There are therefore, two things to be urged upon the incoming student body. An attitude on its part is needful that will in the first place cause it to desire and to seek contact with the great in every way, and in the second place, to seek to become fired with the laudable ambition to become great in turn if possible, so that we may multiply this greatness among our own people—this largest factor in the making of the race.

I am fully convinced that there would be no Wilberforce University to-day had there been no Daniel A. Payne. The ten thousand persons who have studied here would not have had the opportunity to light and carry forth the torch of intelligence and learning into the dark nooks had it not have been for his influence. These have done much for the uplift of our people and we have great men among them laboring to this end. But if Daniel A. Payne had not in early youth been influenced in turn by the lives of two great characters, there would have been no Bishop Payne as we know him, to inaugurate the work here which has reached such magnificent proportions. His life would have run in other channels no doubt, and he would not have had the impulse to make real the visions that came to him and which we see in these structures about us and the facilities for education that we possess here, if he had not made Napoleon Bonaparte and John Brown of Haddington, Scotland, in turn, his heroes—his ideals. From his own lips I have often heard the assertion as to the wonderful influence each had in shaping his career.

Trifles turn the scales for nations, and the chance meeting of some forceful character, the chance hearing or reading some forceful utterance has in a multitude of cases constituted the turning point that has been the making of those we call great—morally and intellectually great.

Now we need these great ones to build us up as a people, and the youth of the race need to reach out for this contact in every possible way.

And here two ways are open: So, first I would urge these young people who gather in college walls for a new year of work and development to make companions of their superiors everywhere. Cultivate the companionship of your instructors. The spirit of the men and women back of the teaching is, all things considered, the greatest of all the means available in an all around education.

President Henry Churchill King of Oberlin makes the unqualified assertion that without doubt the prime factors in a complete education are always *persons*, not things, not even books. Personality commands, and its spirit is *caught* and not *taught*.

Since Christ came into the world the worth of the individual has been of prime consideration. I cannot forbear quoting a strong passage from President King bearing on this point. He says, "There is no moral or religious education worthy of the name, possible in a college where such reverence for the person does not prevail, for," he continues, *"that reverence deep seated* and *all pervading, is the finest test of culture,* the *highest attainment in character,* and *the surest warrant* for *social efficiency."*

Now look at it both ways. We wish then that the individual student should be studied and helped by those personally who govern and direct and teach, and we also wish these individual instructors to be looked up to, listened to and followed.

No youth could be brought within the radius of the influence of such men as Mark Hopkins of Williams College, McCosh of Princeton, Finney or Fairchild of Oberlin, Samuel Armstrong of Hampton and D. A. Payne of Wilberforce without receiving impressions and impulses that would mark for life.

But as has been said there is the added personal influence coming from books when one cannot be constantly brought face to face with these great men and women. This for the student must become a strong personal force: for students must read and do read. The thoughts and actions, as set forth in books of great lives and the record of their career and achievements, give the ideals which are so needful to the aspiring, growing mind of youth. The all important thing is what to read. One thing is certain, you must *read* up, *never down*. You must read something above your present knowledge, your present attainments. Such reading really educates, for it will make you think, but the other kind will dissipate your mind and weaken it. Then, never read bad books—bad morally, intellectually or spiritually considered. One's physical condition depends largely upon the food eaten. If this is nutritious and wisely chosen the repair work of the body goes on and it is kept in the highest state of efficiency. The same law holds good in reference to the mind. Strong books, stimulating thought, will make a strong mind. It is thus that Plato and Aristotle, Bacon and Emerson, Shakespeare and the countless authors of high repute will influence you—their thoughts passing like iron atoms of the blood into your mental constitution. All that is learned from books is going into one's talk, going into one's character. They are next to the person's self in their influence. It follows too that the lives of the great ones of earth must stand first in the choice to give models for young lives to follow.

This brings us to the use of the library—the workshop of the student. It must be rightly used. It is not a place where the student goes simply to pass away the time. It is not a place where one browses about merely for athletics and fashion. It is not a place where we go to find pleasure in the near companionship of friends and enjoy physical comfort and luxury. The student who turns his steps to the library for the influence it affords, must go with a definite scholarly purpose in view—to gain something, to add to his store of usefulness, to put another cubit to his mental stature; and when he leaves its walls he should carry with him the distinct consciousness that he has grown stronger and is possessed of higher ideals and ambitions. Otherwise there is no reason for going. But he also must take the right attitude toward what he gleans. He is not to be a mere bookworm—revelling in what he gathers. He is to turn this to account. He should become a live wire, ready to send a current of higher impulse at every contact with others. Thus his own influence begins to be felt in turn. And this brings me to the brief consideration of the influence of companionship of one's fellow students.

"Show me a person's companions and I will tell you the sort of person he is," is as pertinent a statement as "Show me the books a man reads and I will tell you the sort of person he is." "Like seeks like," "Water seeks its own level," are all sayings indicating the conclusions the world has reached as to companions, be they people or books.

At college the student body is forced to accept a certain companionship of instructors, and as I have said, it is for the best if that companionship can be made a closer one. But when it comes to the fellow-student, there is no force exercised. It becomes a matter of simple free-will, of mutual attraction, that leads one student to make another a particular chum. Here is where the stronger *will* has the opportunity for good or evil. Here too is where the individual will has a chance to hesitate before deciding and use judgment and common sense in setting up intimate friendships that may help or hinder one.

Friends must be chosen wisely. If the student knows that he is easily influenced, then all the more should that one use judgment and reach out for the companionship of those who are walking on higher planes in all things, and strong enough to stay there. This is not only wise but is the only safe course. Begin right and you are far more apt to end right. Fall in with the lighter element and you will soon feel the dragging weight which brings you to an undesirable condition, an undesirable end.

We seek students possessing this higher influence, but every college has a mixture. If every one would strip self of every undesirable quality of heart and mind on entrance we should have only the best, and this process I would urge upon every one at the opening of the school year. You are responsible not only for yourself but for your influence over others. Make resolutions that point upward in every line of conduct and work and then set about the task of keeping them, and you have a right to ask and expect help from every instructor in the effort. By this method alone can we purge a college of the bad and indifferent whose influence is against the right—against the law and order.

And here I find it well to draw special attention to one form that this close companionship of students takes. It is a form in which the educational world sees great danger to both individuals and institutions. I refer to those secret organizations where students band themselves together for no educational purpose. Such are subversive to all best interests and the influence exerted is hurtful in every way. Here at Wilberforce we purpose to *exterminate* these influences, though it may result in *exterminating* individuals from our midst who *persist* in carrying on such and inducing others to join them. We shall henceforth tolerate *no* sign or *symptom* of such affiliation. We shall tolerate *no influence* exerted in this direction. We desire the influence of the student body to show itself in *high, honorable, open* ways, not in childish, freakish, secret, questionable and forbidden ways. The *basic* thing in this choice of your companionship is *obedience to the law.* There is no greatness possible without obedience. As Aeschylus says, "*It is the mother of success and wedded to safety.*"

You have come to us to gain all that personal influence, through contact and through books, can give you, but there is another side to observe, as I intimated a few moments ago. Every student should ask himself these questions: "What have I brought hither of worth?" "Have I it in me to be a lever for uplift or are there seething within me those lower elements that will poison and ruin those with whom I come in contact?" You owe it to yourselves and to the college to do this. It will help to bring to the surface the best that is in you, and the best that is in others will be called out. You make the school. With the right attitude toward the work here which must result in building up character for every one, there can be but one outcome—you will influence and be influenced in the right way and go on to growing greatness.

We need the influence of great men and women everywhere. All that is of worth in your education will show itself in your lives. You are to mold the future generations in a multitude of ways. What will you take with you when you leave us? This depends upon what you have brought with you here, morally and intellectually, and what you will choose to gather while here.

We want you to have true culture as well as knowledge. We want you to be fully able, not only to "do things"—to have the efficiency that the world demands—but we want you to have also that which is of equal value—the power to appreciate truth and beauty and all the things belonging to cultivated life.

And why are we so insistent each year upon the acquisition of all these things? Because we know what the world outside demands of you—because we know it depends upon yourselves whether you can meet those demands and because we know that we as a race must not lose any part of a generation in our forward march. If a word from lip or pen of a great mind can start an electric current that develops a Lincoln or a Wm. Wilberforce, a Frederick Douglass or a Payne it may do the same in your case.

A student body is a fine and wonderful thing when we view it in the aggregate—a strong, solid mass full of wonderful potentialities—a mass that is at the most impressionable age of existence—a mass that is to go forth out into the world and do the leavening through its personal influence. Then it is clearly evident that you should seek the company of the great in books and in persons, that you should avoid the uncultured, the skeptical, the irreleigious, the unmoral and the immoral, if you are to be of use to our people, for you will sway and be swayed by what President King calls the *"primacy of the person."*

Young people, your *highest* influence is needed, for the greatness of a race like the greatness of a nation does not rest on material resources but in its *"will, faith, intelligence* and *moral forces."* But you remember that these come from the influence that the careers of all the great ones of earth impress upon it. The man may die, but his thoughts and acts remain, and the influence of his individual character extends from generation to generation. *The dead never die.* The soul of some one who has passed has pointed the way for our every *present* act and thought.

As Henry Ward Beecher once said, "The blossom cannot tell what becomes of its odor, and no man can tell what becomes of his influence and example, that roll away from him and go beyond his ken on their perilous mission."

Note

1 [See also Scarborough's "The College as a Source of Culture," *Sodalian* 4, no. 1 (October 1909): 3–7.]

What Should Be the Standard of the University, College, Normal School, Teacher Training and Secondary Schools

(Durham, N.C.: National Training School, 1916).

The subject set forth for this address covers such a very large field that no brief discussion can do anything approaching justice to it in its entirety.

The problems involved are not altogether new. In a general way the educational world has been wrestling with them for a half century or more in an endeavor to obtain better results from schoolroom work along all lines. But it has been only in the last two decades that we may really say that ideals have been put into any concrete form and the attempt made to bring schools up to a general level. This period will undoubtedly go down in educational history as the standardizing period. We are trying to standardize everything. The term has been "hitched" to the term "efficiency" and the two have invaded every circle of life and endeavor. One hundred per cent is declared as the only real unit of measure and the point to which everything must advance.

Standardization is an excellent thing if we do not make an educational fetich of it, as there is a possible danger of doing. It is a good thing to discuss the subject and to discuss it wisely, particularly as it pertains to Negro education. First of all, it seems to me that we are confronted with a preliminary question—as to what is included in the term "standard." As I look at it there are at least two interpretations of the word that must apply to education. One is the setting up of a unit of measure, in comparison with which the accuracy of others is to be determined; and the other has reference to anything regarded as a type or model and, therefore, a thing of the highest order.

Again, before we can decide further as to *what* standards we are to set up in the Negro schools—or any others for that matter—we must go further and reach a conclusion as to the actual type to set up—have a definition, if you will, and one, upon which there can be agreement as to what is a standard University, a standard College, a standard Secondary, or Normal School or Teacher Training School. Here our subject grows more and more complex, and obviously, we can deal only with some general main facts and offer only

178

some general suggestions in the limits that a paper must have before this body.

After search in all quarters and after investigation of the opinions of expert educators, we find one and all confessing there is, as yet, no general agreement, no consensus of opinion, as to what shall be the standard in any of the different kinds of institutions we are considering. We can find nowhere a satisfactory definition of either University or College, to begin with. The American University is "a hybrid institution" everywhere—even the very best institutions of the country are part college and part university if we consider the term "University" as used in the German sense or English sense. The best ones do both post-graduate and undergraduate work—not one of them doing distinctively advanced and research work, except perhaps, John[s] Hopkins University. True, some of the greatest universities have organized with "two *criteria*—first, the quality of the work done in their graduate departments and second, the entrance requirements to those graduate departments that have been set by them." But it stops there.

Then, if we look at Colleges we will find it equally difficult to find a definition of what a college is. A number have been proposed, but not a dozen have gained anything like a general circulation, to say nothing of actual general acceptance. Let me quote from Dr. S. C. Capen of the U. S. Bureau of [E]ducation:

"There are for instance, the definition of the Carnegie Foundation for the [A]dvancement of Teaching, the definition of the New York Education Department, the definition of the North Central Association of Colleges and Secondary Schools of the Southern States, all of which have a wide currency and have influenced the standards of many institutions. The first two are very brief. The New York definition makes no mention of the scholastic preparation of the faculty, the number of hours required for admission and graduation, the financial resources or the physical equipment of an institution. It is intended to be exclusive rather than descriptive. On the other hand, the definition of the Southern Association is of almost equal length but quite different in content." He continues with four pertinent inquir[i]es that we may make applicable to the situation which we must discuss in connection with Negro institutions:

"Which of these is the right definition? Will the Carnegie Foundation accept for its purposes the definition of the Southern Association? Will the North Central Association be willing to judge the colleges of its territory according as they conform to the definition of the New York State Education Department? If not where shall we stand?["] And he adds another; "*Who can tell what a standard College is?*"

This gives us a fair survey of the national situation. So, after reading much on the subject, hearing much and finding the boldest of daring educators showing a certain amount of timidity about asserting what must be in regard to a standard, and noting that the question has been more or less skillfully skirted in all cases by those who have assumed to deliver anything like a dictum on the subject;—altogether considered, it would seem almost like the height of temerity, to say nothing of vanity, and boastfulness, to think that the Negro should dare rush in where others tread so lightly. Yet, I wish we had the breadth of vision and the strength of daring to stand in the vanguard of this movement, and not always follow. But it is such a far reaching question, we also may well hesitate and go cautiously and slowly in reaching conclusions in regard to our own schools.

Right here, then, let me first refer to Doctor David Starr Jordan's recent article in the September Forum, and note what the ex-Chancellor of Leland Stanford University has to say on a point that may well have direct reference to our Negro Institutions for higher learning.[1] He says that, as a country, we have far too many institutions for higher learning, that the schools range from a few institutions ranking high, down to what he denominates "cross-roads schools with one or two professors and no adequate standards or equipment." Then, he gives us further food for thought in some facts presented: "There are now about twenty-five universities [white, of course][2] represented in the University Association. In these, standards and educational methods agree in general, and in all of these generous provision is made for additional study and research; but there are some sixty other institutions with the same academic standards, but mostly without professional schools and offering as a rule scanty facilities for advanced study beyond the four years which lead to the Bachelor's degree." He continues: "The remaining colleges in our lists do some things well and some things poorly."

On the same question of deciding on a general standard in the University, the President of Grinnell College has this to say:[3] that "the *State* University is an attempt to realize the efficiency conception of education for the whole people of the State;" that "it does not venture except in a tentative and cautious way, to impose upon them a method or system of education which might meet a universal standard;" and that, "if such a standard were available, the *state* would hold it in abeyance or reject it entirely." When we consider how many State Universities are serving the people directly in new courses that shatter all previous ideas as to standards for admittance, we see how involved is this question: "What shall be our standard?"

Now, what conclusion must we reach from these facts as applied to our own schools? I think that we must too agree with those who "question the value of extreme emphasis on standardization," and, while we believe in standards, we must further agree that there are many things we must consider before we can deliver anything approaching an *ex-cathedra* assertion as to bringing all of our schools in any given line of work to the *same* standard.

Our Negro Universities and Colleges, as they now exist, may be roughly classified into three classes as to efficient work done—results achieved: "Those that serve a large constituency drawn from different localities, are very well equipped, and measure up well in essentials to some of the best standards set, and are constantly progressing." Then, there are those which, for various reasons, local and otherwise, serve a limited constituency, have only a limited equipment, and while doing fairly well can, for a long time to come, do only a limited amount of work. Then there is a third class consisting of what may be termed "paper schools," doing nothing of a higher character, mere Preparatory schools—some hardly that,—and with such inadequate equipment in every way that they are practically worthless. I am sure all will agree that this class should be eliminated from the ranks of Negro Institutions for higher learning, where only a "paper name" now holds them.

Our Universities should be few. Few of Negro schools should retain this name. Those best equipped should be prepared to offer advanced work and should hold a high entrance requirement, while measuring well up to any one of the standards that have found regional acceptance. We do not need, just now, so many *great* universities, but we do need to sustain a reputable few and to help these to the highest possible standard. As to our Negro Colleges I feel compelled to take the same ground that Doctor Capen[4] takes and apply his general conclusions to our work in particular. As he asserts, "We cannot prove that all colleges should conform to the same standard—all be of the same type." This is especially true of the Negro College as here are varying conditions which affect the race in different sections. The Southern standard cannot be the same as the Northern standard. If the white South has found itself illy prepared to set the same standards as Northern colleges because of its lack of preparatory schools, surely it is perfectly patent that the Negro College must vary because of the same reasons. With the college a local institution, as nearly all are, the Negro college, situated in Southern territory and drawing almost exclusively upon the south for its constituency, is unable to meet the standard set by the north where school systems are well and highly organized.

We must not for a moment forget that the Negro college has its constituency to serve and that there should be no standards set that will hamper educational opportunity in any section where these schools are placed. They could not grow; and as Doctor Winship[5] says "there should be no standard which will stifle growth anywhere. A standard may be a measuring rod or weight, or a rallying point but it is never a barbed-wire fence for the keeping of anybody away from any good thing." I am convinced that for the present, where the educational systems are more backward in providing proper preparatory schools, there must be some latitude allowed that will not be prohibitive to educational opportunity for those in the section to which such schools must especially minister. For this reason, I am inclined to look with favor upon the idea of Junior College work as it is being tried in certain sections—colleges that do only the first two years of real college work but do also the last two years of secondary work—though this varies. I think many of our weaker colleges might find this their legitimate field, doing therein strong work and becoming feeders for the regular and better equipped colleges. Of course there are objections and difficulties to meet in such an arrangement. I throw out this idea merely as a suggestion, but if some adjustment of work could be made, both our strong schools and weak ones would be ben[e]fitted.

Our best colleges—those with the best all-round facilities—can and should be brought to a high uniform standard, with entrance requirements equal to those demanded by the strongest college associations. Here is where the Association of Colleges for Colored Youth will find its field for stimulation and uplift. I think we should favor the standard set up by it and hope for large increase eventually in its membership. Its requirements for admission consist of fifteen Carnegie units of Secondary work—a unit being considered as four recitations a week of one hour each or five of forty-five minutes each, continuing for a period of from thirty-six to forty weeks; two hours of manual training, or laboratory work to be equivalent to one period of class room work; also certain required studies, the details of which it is unnecessary to outline at this moment. For graduation in these colleges we should require a four years course or one hundred and twenty semester hours of work along prescribed lines carefully laid down. We should go further and call for at least the minimum faculty described by Doctor Calvin French in a paper on, "The Efficient College," read before The Association of American Colleges in January, 1916. This calls for at least eight members, including the President, who is to give all his time to administration and promotion, while the other members give their time to the respective seven fields of Mathematics, Science, Modern Languages, Psychology, History, Latin and English, each of the members taking additional assignments as necessary. And at this point, let me say that there is one thing for which I would have a set standard and a high one, and that is for the faculty itself. Every faculty should pass some rigid test as to preparation, ability to instruct and to inspire, as to "character and strong personality, and as to whether the members are a real moral, vitalizing force"; "for the faculty largely makes the college or university.["] A "Mark Hopkins on one end of the log," means much for high standardization in any institution of learning. When it comes to considering endowments as standards we may well pause. I think, as do many others, that we cannot justly set a required standard as yet, as much first class work is being done with comparatively small endowments, and to shut out these schools would be to discourage good work. For this reason The American College Association, of which Wilberforce University is a member, has not set this standard for membership.

Little time is left to consider the other schools included in the subject under discussion and I shall touch them very briefly. Teacher training work must have varying standards because of the regional conditions before mentioned. In sections where rural conditions are low—the schools unorganized and the length of the school term entirely too short—the nature of this work may and should require much modification in preparing teachers for the elementary work. In Northern work it would be different. In this connection I would say that within the last four years the State of Ohio has undergone a revolution in regard to Teacher Training, and has set a high standard for all of its Normal Schools and Training Courses. In accordance with the new state laws we have standardized all such work at Wilberforce University. This calls for fifteen units of secondary work for admission to our Teachers' Training Course (two years) which does not call for a degree. For graduation from this course we require sixty-four semester hours, or ninety-six term credits together with minimum practice and observation of one hour a day for one semester in Primary, or seventh and eighth grades, and a minimum of two units of industrial work. Our actual work however, equals seventy-four semester hours, exclusive of vocational work, with electives for seniors. We are above the standard. This required work places us upon the list of "approved schools for teacher training" as recognized by the State Superintendent; and we thus stand upon the same plane as other State training schools. Our graduates receive a "provisional certificate"—good for four years—to teach in the state and this is recognized in thirty-five states. After twenty-four months of succesful teaching, the holder may have a state life certificate without examination. We also offer in the same work, vocational courses of two years, with the same standard for admission. In our College we have two courses in Education, for those wishing to teach in Secondary schools, four years in length and leading to the degrees of A. B. and B. S. in Education. These courses require fifteen units for entrance. For graduation, the regular one-hundred and twenty semester hours are required as in all our college work; thirty of these semester hours must be professional work—a minimum of fifteen of these being specified work. I have given this as a concrete example of what one Negro institution is accomplishing in standardized Teacher Training courses. Our best equipped colleges and universities should set similar standards for admission and graduation. The same could not be reasonably expected in all sections of the country.

In the necessarily few words on Normal schools, I will say that, in my opinion, they, too, must vary in different localities, as, until there is a fair development of High Schools in a school system, it is not possible for those Normal schools to advance greatly their entrance requirements and get rid of doing the academic work they must offer. A certain amount of this work must be done by them, but differentiated courses for Primary and Upper grade teachers will help toward a higher standard. Stress, however, must be laid on professional work and a specified amount must be covered.

As to Secondary Schools. I am positively convinced that if we need a set standard anywhere, it is here. This work is foundation work, not only for higher attainments, but for life directly, as so many of our boys and girls stop when they gain a diploma from High School. I am not a stickler for the time element *per se*, but I think four years are needed here, with no elective work. The average Negro youth needs this time in which he may obtain culture and a chance for maturity. We are getting too much immaturity in higher educational courses. This Secondary work should, however, be separated entirely from the higher work. There should be separate facilities also. We have accomplished this at Wilberforce University. Separate housing would also be most desirable, if possible. We should be sure of our standards here as most of the Negro colleges and universities for various reasons will doubtless be compelled for some time to keep up such a department.

What I have said must be considered as but hastily sketched suggestions on an almost illimitable subject. I know that I have not said all that could be said upon it, because of the limited time allotted me. Of one thing I am certain, however, in this matter of standards, and I am sure that all will agree with me—that for many reasons connected with the future advancement of the race, and because of the respect in which it is desirable that all Negro

Institutions should be held by the world, it is necessary that all such institutions of learning *set as high a standard as possible, maintain it strictly, do the work well, and continually advance as rapidly as possible.*

Finally, I conclude with the statement of a fact that is probably apparent to all of us—that it is going to be a difficult, if not altogether impossible matter to set a general standard and to classify justly until we have gathered much more important data regarding such work in Negro schools than are at present at our command. We must have far greater knowledge of all significant phases of our educational work. This would call for a kindly, fair and full investigation without prejudice or favor. And right upon this point it is that Doctor Capen sounds a judicious note of warning to all engaged in standardizing education. He stands where he can well know the "results of past endeavors in surveys and attempted classification of schools," and out of wide experience, he says: "Classifications have been attempted, and however successful they may appear to the classifiers, the classified have sometimes had a different opinion, and circumstances have conspired to bring home to the Bureau with peculiar force this opinion." He adds, "Classification should never be based upon guess work or hearsay evidence," and he concludes with the very significant words: "*Sometimes I fear it has been in the past.*"

Notes

1 [See David Starr Jordan "Does the American College Pay Dividends on the Investment?" *Forum* (September 1916): 313 and 314.]

2 [The square brackets around "white, of course" are in the original edition.]

3 [John Hanson Thomas Main, president from 1906 to 1930.]

4 [Samuel P. Capen was the first director of the American Council on Education.]

5 [Albert Edward Winship was the editor of the *Journal of Education.*]

Education of Blacks

Echoes from the South

Christian Recorder, June 28, 1876.

MR. EDITOR:—In a previous communication, I took the opportunity of discussing the merits and demerits of our common school system in rather a general way, showing, as it then existed, that its very purpose and interest was to crush out the colored man whenever possible. Since then there have been some changes which are likely to prove more detrimental to said system, and as I believe, will in the end annihilate it *in toto*. The management of the county schools, especially in Bibb [County, Georgia,] has been transfered, in part or wholly from the supervision of the Grand Jury to that of Commissioners who are elected by the people. Public sentiment on the part of our white brethren is so strongly arraigned against negro education or any undertaking in which his educational interests are involved that we have not only positive grounds for believing but for boldly asserting that within the march of time, the colored American in Georgia if left to the mercy of School Boards, under the immediate control of the democratic machinery, will himself become a useless machine, useless as far as the good of himself or his race is concerned, only to be acted upon by somebody else and therefore always a mere servant. We say that such would be the case, provided these School Boards and Commissioners get a firm hold upon the educational interests of the negro and their plans and purposes are executed as they desire them. But these tactics will not work. There is an independent spirit of manhood about him that is hard to be repressed, though sometimes impugned. His right and his privileges may be denied him, but his manhood still remains. This is evident from the indignation [in the] meetings that have been held here in the city of Macon. The appropriation this year for the support of the common schools of Bibb County has been reduced to $10,000, five or ten thousand less than last year, hardly enough to support them five months out of ten, with incompetent teachers, who work for mere nothing because they are incompetent[,] and inadequate school facilities. Note here that this appropriation is for all the schools both colored and white, and the remark in regard to incompetent teachers and poor school facilities is applicable to the colored schools only as the white schools will be amply provided for at the entire expense of the colored.

Leaving this question for the present, I turn to the "dead line" which was revived at the park the 16th day of May. On that day the Lincoln Guards[,][1] one of the three colored commissioned military companies of the city had its 4th anniversary at the Central Park. Quite a number of days before these were to take place, the Mayor[2] of the city granted the Captain of the company an order for the use of the park on the 4th. This of course gave him exclusive right to it on that day. Thinking he held it securely, he gave himself no further trouble about it. When the appointed day and hour arrived, the company met at the armory, paraded through the principal streets, thence to the target ground. After the prize shooting, they returned and marched to the park.

On arriving there, though they held the order issued by the Mayor, they found it taken by a party claiming to be the rightful owners(?). This party consisted of a number of schools (S. S.) who had gathered from the suburbs and vicinity of the city for the purpose of having a picnic. They took possession of the grounds as aforesaid. When the company reached the gate they marched in without music, but to be met by policemen and directed to certain obscure corners through a wagon high-way, as "the whites held the other portions." Immediately after the company had made its appearance a dead line was drawn by the "negro hating fiends" and no colored person was allowed to cross that line until after a certain hour in the afternoon under the penalty of death. Look at this picture and then read Lamars's patriotic(?) speeches and observe the wonderful consistency(?) between them.[3] The difficulty lies somewhere and can be accounted for. It certainly looks as if Taney when he said "the negro had no rights which white men were bound to respect" gave utterance to no idle fancy.[4] After three o'clock in the afternoon the death line was disbandoned[,] then the company and invited guests had a little more space. But the grounds were not entirely given up to them till about 5 o'clock. This is one of the most dastardly outrages that has been committed against the colored man since the wars (K. K. K., &c., &c., excepted). It was his labor, his money in part that has made the park what it is. This the Mayor himself admits, but yet suffers him to be euchered out of his rights in this way without any cause whatever. If there had been a mistake the two parties might have met together in harmony and union, without insults on the part of the one against the other, had there been a disposition to let the negro have his rights. But in my opinion, there was no mistake. The Captain of the Lincoln Guards had his order first and in face of that, another was granted to other parties, giving them claims to the very same park and portion to which the Lincoln Guards held title. Look on this and tell us whether we are drifting. It is very certain that democratic ascendency means none other than death to the colored man. Let every voter remember it and act accordingly.[5]

Notes

1 [The Lincoln Guards, founded in the 1870s, lasted more than thirty years. They marched in the Atlanta Exposition in September 1895.]

2 [William A. Huff was mayor from 1871 to 1879.]

3 [Lucius Quintus Cincinnatus Lamar (1825–1893), Democrat, studied law in Macon, Georgia, and was later senator and associate justice of the Supreme Court. The three notations (?) in this paragraph are in the original text.]

4 [Chief Justice Roger B. Taney said this in 1857 in the Dred Scott case.]

5 [Scarborough subscribed this article "MACON, June 12, 1876."]

Our Schools and Their Needs

Christian Recorder, March 23, 1882.

This subject has been written on, about and around, most especially the last, by those interested in our schools. If persistence can accomplish anything we may hope in time to bring our schools up to the most approved standard. There are some schools controlled and managed entirely, or nearly so, by the colored race. Great has been the opposition to this work from white and colored. Warm friends and lukewarm ones have withheld encouragement and even money has been but sparingly given, if at all. Every one has looked askance as at an experiment. Failure has been oft predicted. Nothing short of an absolute miracle—or actual bricks without straw—could or can make the majority believe in our ability and capability. In many things we have only ourselves to blame. If we have not confidence in one another we need not expect others to exhibit a very marked degree of it. Much of the criticism has been just and merited. We *have* the schools, though, and there are a few things to be considered if we would keep and sustain them with honor instead of being obliged to drop them, proving true all that has been said and thus bringing an everlasting shame and disgrace upon the race. First of all we must have unity in remote management and control, unity and interest; unity of plan and unity of action, unity in understanding the danger of leaving any school to the management which, except a few, gives no thought to its interest but once a year, and to vagrant chances of receiving money for its benefit and perpetuation. When the remote management is fully alive to this, one of the greatest beginnings is made. But then there is the immediate management from the head down. Shall we be content with second-rate teachers? If so we must expect second rate results and in proportion scathing criticism.

"The most deadly enemy of any school is he who on any pretext assists in putting an incompetent teacher over any class of children and youth." So says a prominent educator, so say we. There is no excuse for such an act. We must put aside internal jealousies which prompt so many to tug at the skirts of those who have climbed higher than others; we must not give way to the favoritism which puts and sustains in positions men who, through lack of merit, have no business there; we must rise above the ignorance which lauds to the highest those of low and narrow ability and puts such in power where high mental acumen, breadth of culture and executive power are demanded.

The day has come when our youth demand the best and if we do not give it in our schools, no love of race, no philanthropic motives, no self-sacrificing spirit will keep them from seeking it elsewhere. Money and good teachers will bring students to any orthodox school. Even let the former be lacking, retaining the latter, if possible, and still you will have students; but lose the latter, displace, remove, put ignorant ones in their places and the students immediately disparage the school, leaving it if possible and giving to it a reputation which prevents further increase. There must be some one at the head who is not afraid to execute laws and rules, one who fears no man in the carrying out of all plans; one whose knowledge of the world of schools and colleges, of men in general, is such as to enable him to guide his own in an enlightened manner; one whose mental culture is sufficient to cover the scope of the work under his control, who rests not, but each succeeding year finds his own particular work on a more elevated intellectual plane. And the same is true of all departments. A teacher must be called to teach. It is as much a Christian necessity as that a man must be called to preach. But many mistake the former call as well as the latter.

Our schools must be well manned and, if I may coin a word, well womanned too. The woman teacher must, as well as the man, be of that degree of culture and education co-ordinate with that found in other schools. We cannot afford to take a teacher who is incompetent because that teacher is white any more than we can because one is colored. The time has come when it is out of taste to be ministered to indiscriminately as by missionaries to the heathen, when we refuse to agree that the minimum amount of learning is sufficient to instruct colored people when *meum* [mine] and *teum* [yours] as regards race is obtruded in our schools. A college education does not unfit one for teaching a primary school, but an elementary education does unfit one to instruct in college courses. Whoever we choose as instructors for our youth must understand well that which they purpose to teach. We want no experimenting on our children and youth. We want no teachers who make us and our schools simply a "stepping stone." We cannot afford it unless we wish to make true that which our white brothers say of our ability; to establish the truth of which is to shut all doors to future advancement and keep us hemmed in, driven back within most narrow limits. A teacher from the head down must be as far as possible a *vade mecum* for the pupil. It is proper to admit one's ignorance, as omniscience is not expected, but the mistake lies in putting over youth that one who is in a chronic state of ignorance. To persist in error and to teach false doctrines to cover ignorance is still worse than admitting the chronic state referred to. Teachers must be gentlemen and ladies in the highest sense of the terms; courteous and polite. Students as a rule mirror their schools. They must have teachers whom they can respect for manners and acquirements, and those who respect them as students.

In a great measure the students are as much the voice of the school as the people are the voice of the nation. They have the right to demand the best possible instruction, and for the sake of our name and race we must furnish such instruction, coupled with other requisites, money and executive ability, necessary to the successful conduct of our schools. Let us place at the helm those whose names and influence will bring honor and prosperity as in other schools. Let us place in all the departments those whose teachings shall be correct instead of false, thorough instead of superficial, collegiate where needed instead of elementary. We cannot prop up broken columns nor allow excuses for poor instruction. There is but one test, competent or incompetent, and that should be rigidly applied. Let us become a unit on this subject, if possible—throw aside all partizanship to meet the common enemy, criticising foes: show to the world what we can do, that we have the material to make our schools a success and that we know how to select it. Whomsoever we put over our children and youth, let that person be thoroughly qualified for the position. "*Verbum sat sapienti.*"[1]

Note

1 [A word to the wise person is enough.]

The New South and Hampton's Part in It

Southern Workman 25 (October 1896): 194–195.

The appearance of Booker T. Washington, Principal of the Tuskegee Normal and Industrial Institute, as one of the orators at the opening of the Atlanta Cotton Exposition has been regarded by many as auguring a new era for the Negro in the South and as a harbinger of a new dispensation for both races. This act of the managers is looked upon as a progressive step—indicating a radical change of sentiment—which shall in time, produce a better feeling on the part of the whites towards the blacks and vice versa.

Be it as it may, if the action of the Cotton Exposition Managers cannot be taken as an expression of Southern sentiment as a whole, it is nevertheless commendable and deserves more than a passing notice. It gave the country, the world, an opportunity to see what the Negro could do when he had a chance; whether he could quit himself like other men under similar circumstances. This is a great deal and portends much. We cannot reform a people in a day. We cannot rid them of notions, that have been years in forming, in a few hours. It is idle to attempt it. All that the Negro can do as things now are, is to make the most of his opportunities and in time matters will right themselves. What the colored boy and the colored girl, the colored man and the colored woman should do is to fit themselves for places of trust and responsibility so that when the opportunity comes they will be ready. This is Hampton's mission as I under[s]tand it and a laudable one it is.

It was a Hampton graduate that took an honorable and conspicuous part in that Cotton Exposition of the South. The selection of Mr. Washington was both fitting and opportune. The occasion was a great one and the orator was equal to the emergency. None knew better than he the demands of the situation and how best to meet them. The sphere of his activities is in the South. His relations and associates are largely Southern. Of necessity he is brought into contact with the southern white man and the southern Negro daily, and therefore knows both their wants and needs. Some of his utterances are worthy of most serious reflection on the part of both races and especially on the part of the whites of the South, but none more than these:

"Casting down your bucket among my people, helping and encouraging them as you are doing on these grounds, to education of head, hand and heart, you will find that they will buy your surplus land, make blossom the waste places in your field and run your factories. While doing this you can be sure in the future as you have been in the past, that you and your families will be surrounded by the most patient, faithful, law abiding and unresentful people that the world has ever seen. As we have proved our loyalty to you in the past, in nursing your children, in watching by the sick beds of your mothers and fathers, and often following them with tear dimmed eyes to their graves, so in the future in our humble way, we shall stand by you with a devotion that no foreigner can approach, ready to lay down our lives, if need be, in defence of yours, interlacing our industrial, commercial, civil and religious life with yours in a way that shall make the interests of both races one."

Notable words are these, Atlanta did well in giving opportunity to express them. Much rests upon the colored people themselves as to what their future shall be. It is they that must carve out their own fortunes and make themselves a respected people. The first step towards becoming a people that others will respect is that they respect themselves while endeavoring to become capable and worthy citizens.

The work of Hampton in molding character and in making good, respectable and productive citizenship is worthy of great praise. Not only the South, but the North as well, needs such citizenship and Hampton is doing much to supply the need. If this school had sent forth but one Booker Washington, that act alone would be sufficient to rally to its support the best element of the best citizens of all the land. The South, the North, the country is feeling the good effects of such training.

The possibilities of the race are developed here as in no other school in the country, as far as I know. The conception that obtains at Hampton of what it takes to make a strong, sturdy, full-fledged manhood and womanhood is here found in the broadest sense; and this conception is furthermore indelibly stamped upon those who go out from its walls, so that the Hampton graduate and under graduate have had and will continue to have a great deal to do in the building up and in the development of the new South.

The dignity that attaches itself to labor cannot be overestimated. It is important that this idea should be kept before us. No system of education is perfect which does not give due recognition to the relation that exists between the head, heart and hand, and which does not adjust the training of a human being accordingly.

In the past, both races in the South through environment and training have held mistaken ideas as to the dignity of the labor of the hand and it has become a part of the mission of the Hampton apostle to correct this erroneous impression—of the Negro, by proving that such industry brings wealth and by fostering a pride in finished products of the hand; of the white man by showing that the skilled hand accompanies the best element of citizenship in the land and that the development of any section is in proportion to the encouragement given to labor.

This of itself is a work not to be under-rated. If the man who shows how to make two blades of grass grow where but one grew before is a benefactor, much more ought one to be called such who shows how to make any vocation command increased respect. In this the student from Hampton is a benefactor and not only he but the race at large should make that institution a Mecca. To this spot the Negro at least should turn with bowed head in thankfulness to God for giving the world its founder, General [Samuel Chapman] Armstrong.

It was he who kindled the torch that should light the dark places and the fire that should consume the dross—refining the gold. It was he who planted the tree, the leaves of which should be in time "for the healing of the nations" of the epidemic—prejudice against the Negro.

The Negro and the Trades

Southern Workman 26 (February 1897): 26–27.

Roger Ascham wrote the first complete treatise, in English, on Education, about 300 years ago. In it he affirmed that we have not to train a soul, nor yet a body, but a man; and we cannot divide him. If true then—much more is it so now. This practical age and the call for practical talent make demands far beyond those of the days of Ascham, and our education must not only include more, but must extend further than then, to meet the present demands.

The various problems agitating our own country and the leading nations of Europe—problems growing out of the various relations of capital to labor—bring this fact home to all of us with tremendous force and startling clearness.

How one is to live in this work-a-day world is the problem, at least, before the masses. The world demands pay for all we get—of rich and poor alike; but it is the toiling masses, however, that feel the burden most—to them it becomes a very serious question.

This brings all to a thoughtful consideration of the sort of education that is best adapted to fit young men and women—black and white—for the active duties of life, and make them, in a measure at least, equal to the emergencies that will inevitably confront them as citizens of a common country.

This should be a matter of great concern to the Negro youth whose scope of activity is necessarily limited. With him it may be "clerks without clerkships, lawyers without clients, clergymen without congregations, physicians without patients and teacher without schools." Other avenues aside from these, must be sought and entered by the Negro boy and girl, because of their peculiar relations to our commonwealth.

America, we are told, is accused by the old world of being sternly practical and prosaic. But these very qualities have enabled her to stand foremost in many ways and in many things. This rigid idea of utility has served her well. The Negro may learn a lesson from what the manual labor of the nation has accomplished. This does not mean however that the cultivation of mind is not to be continued, that there is too much book learning—not at all. Such learning accompanied by a skillful hand is all the more powerful.

It was [James Anthony] Froude, the great historian, who said, "The Ten Commandments and a handicraft make a good and wholesome equipment to commence life with." The Negro boy and girl who stand to-day in the sunlight of youth, will realize more fully as they see the 20th century ushered in, the importance and meaning of this statement.

The Negro has a special aptitude for trades. There is something in the delicate manipulations, the mysterious workings of machinery that appeals powerfully to him, and the trades are bound to contribute much to his future success.

A noted writer, on speaking of the Anglo-Saxon, asserts that a knowledge of varied industries is a necessity if he would rise to be respected and honored. The Negro is not an exception. He too must be included in this statement. It applies to the race so recently enslaved with special force and directness.

False notions of life, however, must be uprooted to have this thoroughly appreciated. The Negro's ideas of gentility are so largely gathered from the circumstances of those whom he has served in a menial capacity, that his aspirations have been largely directed toward being as they, with this difference—that the youth think too much that dress and imitation of manners make the man. Too many of our young men and women to-day allow themselves to be supported and kept in comparative idleness in the school room by the hard-earned dollars of their mothers and fathers, who vainly hope to see their sons and daughters move in a different sphere from that they are compelled to occupy. A laudable ambition of course—but too often are the children undeserving and ungrateful!

All cannot receive the higher education, desirable as it may be—all have not the capacity. Then too the limitation of the Negro's opportunities for employment in teaching and the professions should play some part in the selection of courses as laid down in our schools.

It is becoming fashionable among our white friends to learn trades. It must become likewise a fixed fashion among the Negroes. One discouraging feature has been the attitude of trades unions relative to colored labor. Avenues of employment, after the war, closed so rapidly that it became a serious question where the Negro could learn trades.

But what were the results of shutting the doors, thus, in the Negro's face? Friends rose up, philanthropists opened their purses, and here and there throughout the Southland, where Negro schools and colleges were planted were also planted the germs of such work, that grew into a plant in more senses than one and for which the race in particular and the country in general have great reason to be eminently grateful. The race will be the more so when it comes to a full realization of what this means for the welfare of all.

All praise and honor to such benefactors as John F. Slater, George Peabody, Daniel Hand, C. P. Huntington, Morris K. Jesup and a host of others who have always been mindful of the lowly and who especially had regard for the needs and interests of the sable sons of Adam—"the despised Negro."

Some are gone, but their memories are fondly cherished. Their money, their benevolence, their high Christian humanitarianism have made such work possible, and have placed the Negro under a debt of gratitude that he can never pay except by *showing himself worthy of what has been done for him.*

Such a building as the Armstrong and Slater Trade School Building at Hampton means more for the race than tongue can express. There is an eloquent tongue in every nail and in every bolt that rivets its parts together, that tells of the coming prosperity of a people whose privilege it is to enjoy such advantages.

The race has had to be dependent and there is not a man in it but recognizes with gratitude—or ought to do so at least—what good such schools supported by friends have done, since the guns of Sumpter were fired and the note of freedom sounded.

Notwithstanding the progress made, the race cannot be wholly independent of help in these special lines, though it is hoped that the time will come in which it may be self-reliant. It takes time. The Negro is still in his infancy. He has still many things to learn and many false notions to correct.

These technical schools are doing more to open doors now shut than anything else. They are doing much to check the prevalence of crime, vice, and vagabondage by giving opportunity to the idle to learn methods by which to obtain an honest living. They are doing much toward instilling into the minds of our young people the idea that labor is honorable.

They are doing much toward inculcating in the breasts of others a respect for the Negro. They are making the Negro what he aspires to be—independent, self reliant, and self helpful. In short, by them, more than by any other means, are the Negro youth initiated into the proper realization of this truth that "*triumph and toil are twins.*"[1]

The toil that can move machinery, that can fashion varied implements, that can rear the cottage and the palace, that can span rivers, that can make clothes for the body, that can till the soil so as to make it yield twice or three times its usual amount, is the avenue to triumph—to success for all races and for the Negro in particular. Let the Negro avail himself of all these advantages.

Note

1 [See Gerald Massey (1828–1907), *My Lyrical Life, Part 2* (1889), "To-day and To-morrow," stanza 7, line 5.]

The American Negro Academy
Leslie's Weekly 22 (1897): 264.

There was organized recently, in the city of Washington, a society that will no doubt attract wide attention as soon as its purposes and objects become fully known. It is the American Negro Academy.[1] The name "academy," as generally used and understood nowadays, is somewhat pretentious, but it expresses exactly what the founders of this organization had in mind. Like other institutions of its kind it is exclusive in its character and is intended to be a society for literary men of the race—those engaged in literary pursuits; a society for negro savants. It is established to aid its members in their efforts to advance in the arts, sciences, and literature; to encourage men of letters and stimulate them in their literary aspirations. It further aims to promote the publication of literary and scholarly works written by colored men; to aid colored youth of genius in the attainment of higher culture at home and abroad; to gather into the archives of the society valuable data pertaining to all phases of negro literary life, and the historical and literary works of negro authors in America and Europe; to aid by publications the vindication of the race from vicious assaults in all the lines of learning and culture.

Only graduates of colleges or professors in the same, men of acknowledged literary standing—authors, artists, and distinguished writers—are admitted to membership. A call for the organization of this society was issued towards the close of the winter. The academy held its first meeting in March in Washington, D. C. The Washington *Post*, in referring to the organization, used the following words:

> "The American Negro Academy which is to be organized is composed of authors, scholars, graduates, and writers of African descent for the promotion of letters, arts, literature, and science, and to aid in the publication of works of merit and genius. The membership is limited to forty. Papers will be presented by Professor A. P. Miller, Fisk University; Professor Kelly Miller, Howard University; and Professor W. E. B. Du Bois, assistant in sociology in the University of Pennsylvania.

"Dr. Alexander Crummell, the leading spirit in the new enterprise, has secured the active co-operation of such men as Dr. J. W. E. Bowen, of the Gammon Theological Seminary; Bishop B. T Tanner, D.D.; Professor W. S. Scarborough, M. A.; Chaplain T. G. Steward, of the United States Army; Rev. Dr. F. J. Grimke, Washington, D. C.; Booker T. Washington, of Tuskegee, and a score of other educators and literary men in different sections of the country.

"The meetings will be held in Washington city annually. Among other things the academy proposes the publication of an annual, as well as its proceedings and occasional papers. The first to be sent forth will be a review of 'Hoffmann's Race Traits and Tendencies of the American Negro,' by Professor Kelly Miller, of Howard University."

It will be seen that the plan of this organization is modeled somewhat after the French Academy of Belles-Lettres. This latter body began on a small scale in 1629, when certain patrons of literature in France met weekly at the house of one of their number to discuss literary topics and advance their own literary interests. They finally determined upon a permanent organization, with by-laws and constitution. They elected a publisher who was not a member of their body. The principal function of the academy seems to have been to purify the French language. At first the meetings were informal. They offered, however, an outlet for members of a literary cast of mind to read their own productions and have them criticised. Such a mutual exchange of opinion became helpful and the informal conversations on literary subjects served as an impetus in literary pursuits. This very same idea pervades the American Negro Academy. To what extent the society may be able to carry out its purposes remains to be seen.

Note

1 [See Alfred A. Moss Jr., *The American Negro Academy: Voice of the Talented Tenth* (Baton Rouge: Louisiana State University Press, 1981).]

The Educated Negro and Menial Pursuits

Forum (December 1898): 434–440.

Thirty years have passed since the Negro was made a freeman and a citizen. In these years he has demonstrated to the world at large that he has mental capacity sufficient to cope with a rigid curriculum of studies; that he has industry amounting to thrift, as shown by the Census statistics of the wealth of the colored population; that he is fully as law-abiding as the rest of mankind, not prone to indulge in strikes, to join mobs, to incite riots or become either anarchist or socialist; that he is both brave and patriotic; in short, that while he is by no means a saint, neither is he the worst element of the nation.

Although this has been proved by figures that cannot be disputed, yet questions about the race are constantly arising. The truth is that, in some form or other, the Negro is ever in the public eye. There is one question, however, that confronts the student of economics and sociology,—the question relating to the means by which a livelihood is earned by the educated colored man or woman;—and while this, too, has many sides, one particular phase of it so presents itself that other phases are lost sight of. Still there is an inter-relation that will not admit of discussion of this phase without incidentally at least referring to others.

The particular question may be and is put squarely in this form: "Why is it that so many young colored men and women, after having acquired a high-school or college education, follow menial pursuits?" The question is pertinent, as in fact are all questions which touch a truth. This one is broad as well as pertinent. It cannot afford to be ignored. It suggests much that has to do with the position of the race before the world. It raises many other questions that reach out along several lines of life. It indicates that, despite unparalleled progress in many ways, the race must be perpetually on guard.

But let us see, first of all, whether there is such a broad basis of fact as the question would indicate. Is it really the educated Negro, the graduate, that is found so largely in menial pursuits? A reasonable doubt may be thrown upon the implied assertion, by a reference to some statistics. Taking up the catalogues of two institutions which may be said to represent most fairly Negro higher education and its results, we find in one,—a college in the North largely controlled by colored men and largely taught by colored teachers,—the following facts; viz., out of three hundred graduates from courses ranging from normal, through theological, scientific, and classical, not more than twelve are known to have followed menial pursuits. These graduates are teachers, ministers, secretaries, in the employ of the Government as diplomats, chaplains, post-masters, clerks, mail-carriers, etc., or taking post-graduate courses; while many of the girls are mistresses of their own homes. In the other catalogue, representing a leading school for the race in the South, out of one hundred and fifty graduates not one is found who is in any position other than one far removed from menial occupation. Though without actual statistics before me regarding other schools, yet my personal knowledge of many is such that I feel safe in saying that the proportion of their graduates returning to menial pursuits is at any rate no greater than that found in the institutions I have cited.

There is another view which may be taken of the matter. It is doubtless true that many a graduate desiring to study for a particular profession, or to pursue higher courses, finds himself where the state of his exchequer will not allow him to proceed. Then, for the end in view, the quickest, easiest way for him to replenish it is by some work he knows how to do, which will bring ready returns, and to which he need not be bound longer than to satisfy these needs. It is no reflection on the colored youth that those ways are largely menial: it is simply a reflection on the civilization that holds him so largely to such ways. But that is another topic, which we shall reach in answering the basic question. In such a course the colored boy or girl is not alone; as we find even the poor white boy or girl doing the same at times, though not nearly so often, because of this very civilization to which I have referred. But a careful study will show that the colored youth—no more than the white youth who has such an end in view—does not remain wedded to such pursuits. The writer knows of one recent case that may be taken as a typical one in respect to the Negro. A young medical graduate of a Northern first-class medical college turned his knowledge of the duties of a waiter to advantage at a large gathering in one of our leading cities, in order that he might provide himself with means to take him to Texas, where he purposes to practise his profession. We know he will succeed. No: the Negro boys and girls, as a rule, if found engaged in such pursuits, do not continue to follow them.

There is still another standpoint from which to look at this matter. The colored youth knows and appreciates the value set upon education by the world at large, and especially by the cultured classes with whom he may be thrown in contact. The colored youth is charged with being imitative. Be that as it may, knowing and appreciating the value the world sets on education, there have been instances where he has posed in a borrowed character, and has practised imposition upon those whose short acquaintance with him would not render him liable to exposure. Knowing his public, he has taken an unfair advantage of the unwary philanthropist, or philosophical social economist, and has led him to think that the youth who has been wielding his razor, passing his soup, polishing his russets, carrying his valise, or sweeping the halls, is a graduate because he takes pains to let fall the statement that he "finished at Oberlin." Whether Oberlin *college* or *public school*, or what interpretation is to be placed upon the word "finished," is not always ascertained.

But let us return to our first question, and analyze the supposable situation upon which it is predicated. Thereby we may perhaps furnish an answer that shall at least vindicate the Negro from the charge that his higher education is a mistake, that it is not appreciated at its true worth, that he does not know what to do with it, and that he turns to the "flesh-pots" naturally.

On the hypothesis that the supposedly educated Negro youth does seek to be waiter, caterer, bellboy, porter, bootblack, newsboy, chambermaid, or what not, in the list of callings termed menial, is it a matter of choice or a matter of necessity? If it can be proved to be the former there can be but one view to take of the case; viz., that a thousand-dollar education has been wasted upon a ten-dollar boy or girl. In such a case no inner compelling force is in existence to make the subject mount higher. There is nothing to cause that one to "break the bar of invidious circumstance." There are in every race some such who may be prodded up and on, but in whom, when the prod is removed, lower tastes reassert themselves, the dust triumphs over the "divinity within," and the person sinks into the mire from which he was once raised.

But, if it is a matter of necessity, it is quite another thing. I take the stand that, so far as statistics and experience go to prove anything, the majority of such cases are pushed to this extremity by necessity. This is so far true that, taking it into consideration with all that it implies, it is not only a matter of curiosity to the thinking white man, but is a matter of the deepest perplexity and concern to every thoughtful member of the colored race. It is a matter of moment as to how the colored educated girl or boy shall make a livelihood. It goes so far that even university-trained negroes, when facing the situation, look dubiously upon the long years spent in preparation, and ask themselves in hours of discouragement, "Cui bono?" When such a man, mentally equipped with the wealth of education, finds influence the most potent factor in obtaining recognition where he can put his talents to use; when he sees that fitness so frequently plays only a small part in obtaining positions which he has studied hard and faithfully to fill; that barter is not confined to business solely, he questions himself seriously, as he finds he must either turn to work from which he shrinks, or beg or starve. And here I may say that the colored beggar is seldom seen, as also is the colored tramp. Is it because the Negro prefers to work at anything rather than take up these *rôles*? And, if so, is he lazier than his white brother? These are questions well worth considering.

With the conviction that the situation of the educated Negro as a menial when found in such a position, is most largely one of necessity, let us see why it is so. The Negro boy or girl who has pursued an educational course to completion is in the most literal sense thrown out into the world to sink or swim. Let us look at this world into which a colored youth is thrown. Let us contrast his condition with that of his white schoolmate, and see if we can find a reason for the necessity that confronts him at almost every turn.

Why does he not go into an office, learn his father's business, become a merchant, a business man of some sort, or a clerk[?] Why does he not lead a life of leisure? Why does he not find himself called to the editor's chair, to the presidency of a college, to a professorship, or to a diplomatic position? The colored youth teaches and preaches; but such positions are limited both in number and in scope. He must do something else. Few offices are open to him; and these are besieged. Sometimes he gets a place as clerk, secretary, typewriter, stenographer; more often the only vacancy for him is that of janitor or doorkeeper. He may perhaps study law; but that brings him no income unless he plays the part of the lawyer's office-boy while so studying. As to learning his father's business,—if, fortunately, his father has been able to provide for him thus far, it is usually the case that it has been at the cost of much self-denial on the part of the parent. The father seldom has a paying business into which he can take his son or daughter. When he has, the graduate does not take to menial work.

Again, to become a man of business calls for capital as well as brains; but every educated man is not cut out for a business life. Inclination and adaptability are to be considered here as elsewhere. Travel is out of the question, as a rule, because of lack of means; and the same lack precludes the possibility of the Negro's living a life of scholarly leisure. Should he wield a brilliant, trenchant pen, he can expect his talents to find recognition only as he enters the army of reporters. This he does at times; but a chair in the editor's sanctum is seldom for him. Though he may be a graduate and a post-graduate, he cannot expect the presidency of any but a Negro college. The majority of such positions are held by white men, and the professorships follow largely along the same line. Only the inferior appointments—tutor, instructor, etc.—may possibly be his. The fact that he is a specialist, a post-graduate, makes little difference. The same holds true in regard to diplomatic positions: only minor appointments are his.

When it comes to considering the possibility of a life of leisure, what shall be said? One of luxurious idleness is, happily for the race, out of the question; and a negro tramp, as I have said, is a *rara avis*. As for the enforced idleness of a felon's cell, the fact is that the educated Negro is very seldom a criminal— "Smoking Flax" and such atrocious misrepresentations to the contrary notwithstanding.[1] Unfortunately some are lazy; but the vice of laziness is not particularly the Negro's. If the Negro youth starts out in law or medicine or business he has an exceptionally uphill task. The conditions are, however, growing better in these lines; for the race has more confidence in men of its own color than it once had. The colored lawyer, editor, dentist, physician, and grocer are all better patronized than formerly. It is all a matter of growth; and until a certain healthy maturity comes there will be the blighting influence of discouragement.

These, then, are reasons why the educated Negro youth does not do the things that the educated white youth does so largely. If he becomes pessimistic and thinks it all a mistake—this education he has gained at such an expense of pains and time—and should turn to a trade as a last resort for a livelihood, he finds himself again balked. Trades-unions have shut their doors; and the Labor party has see-sawed so much on the question of his admittance that it is difficult to know where it stands. Here and there he may succeed in attaching himself to a master-workman who will give him work and teach him the trade; but this is the exception. Because of these conditions there are many who, seeing only this phase of life, make the unqualified assertion that the Negro was vastly better off during the Slavery *régime*, when the Negro master-workman was no rarity. But there is light ahead in this respect. Such schools as Hampton and Tuskegee, with their magnificent equipment of industrial shops, are helping to solve this part of the problem. They will give the Negro the knowledge. He must then push out and compete for the work.

But the dark side of the situation is such that it has prompted many to propound other questions, though not always with the humanitarian motive: "Why waste higher education thus? Why not give the Negro industrial training exclusively? Why not give him a pick instead of Latin and Greek?"[2] The answer is, that higher education is not wasted on the race, no matter what facts are found as to his condition brought about by his environment. These facts were, however, to be confronted at some time, and the situation thoroughly canvassed; necessitating careful thought as to how it might be rendered better. It is no more wasted than it would be on white boys and girls, some of whom, with similar advantages, follow pursuits more or less menial in character. It is not wasted, because, even if done from necessity, there is the hope of a future for other boys and girls—a future with better conditions, I prophesy, when the experiences of those enduring the hardships and discomforts of the present situation will be for the advantage of coming generations.

If life is not to be looked upon wholly as a bread-and-butter existence, as our greatest and best philosophers continually assert, there is to be noted the uplifting influence in that home where the educated Negro youth is to be found, though conditions may force the boy or girl into menial walks. That home is the better, the more refined, for the education of some of its members. The race realizes this. It is not pessimistic at heart, though the outlook at times seems gloomy. The people will continue to clamor for the higher education; and the educated porter will heroically help younger brothers and sisters to its advantages, in the hope that there will be found a footing for some one of them, though his own has not been made secure. It becomes an aspiration that is ennobling to the highest degree. Then, who shall say that the educated youth may not bring to his menial task, if found in it, something higher and better out of himself that will have both a subjective and an objective influence?

Though conditions exist that may force the youth into such positions, the case does not present an utterly hopeless aspect; and certainly no friend of the race should become so impressed by it as to find in it an argument against higher education for the Negro. The race must have higher education, just as it must also have industrial training. But good judgment must be used. It does not follow that every boy should be forced into the ranks of higher education, any more than that every one should be taught a trade alone. President Edward C. Mitchell, of Leland University, in an address to the American

Baptist Home Mission Society, in May, 1896, answered those who labor under such false impressions in the following words, which cover the whole situation:[3]

> "Let us teach him what our colleges and universities were founded to teach. Let us teach him the only thing left him to teach. Let us teach the only thing the Negro cannot do as well for himself. Let us teach the thing which the experience of ages and the matured judgment of all true educators have decided to be essential for the full development of manhood. Let us teach the Negro what he is and what he is as God made him in his physical and mental structure. Let us teach him what the world is that God has made for him, with all its elements and powers and forces,—in short let us give him such glimpses of the whole range of science as shall tax his powers to the utmost, while it takes the conceit out of him and brings him nearer to the supreme discovery of Socrates, that he knows nothing."

Let us continue to teach him thus, and trust to the broader views, the wider philanthropy, the higher civilization, to leave the avenues of life's higher work open to him as to others; and then, with justice done, let him rise or fall on his own merits,—his inclination or disinclination to do or to be. With no barriers erected, we should soon listen in vain for even the echo of the questions that the present conditions force upon us.

But, after all, with the knowledge that the whole trend of these thirty-odd years has been upward, and that there has been at least some growth in culture, refinement, wealth, and intellectual achievements, would it not be well to leave these lower walks of life and to ask, "How many of the educated Negroes are following the higher paths?" Would not this question be well worth an answer? Would not the answer be of greater value to the sociologist?

Notes

1 [The phrase from Matthew 12:20, "a bruised reed shall he not break, and smoking flax shall he not quench," refers to weakness. Scarborough refers here to *Smoking Flax* (New York: Neely, 1897), a novel by Hallie Erminie Rives (1876–?) about a black villain.]

2 [See Michele Valerie Ronnick, "'A Pick Instead of Greek and Latin': The African-American Quest for Useful Knowledge," *Negro Educational Review* 47 (1996): 60–73.]

3 [Edward Cushing Mitchell gave the May 26 address, entitled "Higher Education and the Negro," at Asbury Park, New Jersey.]

Booker T. Washington and His Work

Education 20 (January 1900): 270–276.

Were Pope living to-day he might with propriety felicitate himself upon his epigrammatic setting of a belief that seems to be more current at the close of the nineteenth century than when the Elizabethan writers settled upon it.

That "the proper study of mankind is man"[1] is borne out by the avidity with which human nature seizes upon the theme at present, subjecting ideas, customs, habits, motives—everything that concerns the individual, man—in order that knowledge may be broadened on the subject. Especially is this true when one of the species has reached a position where he stands in "that fierce light" that is said to "beat upon a throne."[2] And at the present day we do not lack interesting material for that study, as the events of these years have brought before the public eye many men in many spheres who stand thus conspicuously before the world. These must pay the penalty of such prominence, and submit to be weighed, criticized, praised, fêted, followed, perhaps flouted or condemned. Nothing escapes the attention of on-lookers; every action demands explanation; every thought is searched for its message; every word is tortured for its hidden significance.

Woe to the man who cannot stand the test! The search-light of public gaze is turned upon him with the penetrating quality of X-rays. It discloses the inner being completely. Here and there it flashes until, having clearly diagnosed the whole, it is withdrawn, leaving one so illuminated as to shine with more resplendent light than before, or so withered by the scorching blaze as to be practically blighted, dead—a blackened ruin.

The truly great men of the world have stood the test, and when they have passed away the brilliancy of their record has been found to be immortal, as it were,—left in their works, which live behind them in some form or other.

Every race and every clime in the civilized world has had such men. They have been the heroes which all mankind naturally loves to worship in some fitting degree. The fields in which such men have attained prominence to-day are various, and the men themselves have been largely the result of opportunity. They have been the determined, keen, shrewd, farsighted, swift ones who have caught successfully that much-reached-for forelock, and, resolutely gripping the advantage, have been borne whither the on-marching dame carries those that do not lose their hold. No great wave of any movement has ever rolled over a land but that among its people some one has seen its coming, measured its power and momentum, and with expert agility and ability risen to its crest and rode boldly and bravely at its front.

In epoch-making movements such men become the advisers, counsellors, leaders of the people, whether political, social, religious or educational, and they have in large measure been indispensable to the full success of any phase of action they lead. They become, as it were, the voice of the people as regards that movement; they speak in clarion tones, and the world stops to hear.

In the negro race has been found at various times a voice to speak its wrongs, to contend for its rights, to direct its ways, to counsel its paths. Toussaint L'Ouverture was a man whose life indeed "lay in thought and action, rather than in words," but he was none the less the voice of the struggling race. He possessed the characteristics for leadership; he seized the opportunity and leaped, bound by bound, from slavery's chains to the head of San Domingo's armies.

Frederick Douglass felt within him the stirrings that come with a soul recognition of soul strength and self-reliance, and as events paved the way he, too, stepped to the front and stood for his people and with his people—their counsellor, their leader, until the end came. These two used their lives for freedom from shackles, in defense of the rights of freemen. Then arose another opportunity as time rolled on.

Dense ignorance enshrouded a large belt of the freed race. There was need for an uplifting force, and another stepped forth, one who had walked the same path of slavery and poverty as the others, and, seeing the need, grasped what to his mind was the lever for the purpose. Through the environing influences of a great white leader, who had seen the same vision of need and supply, he entered the black belt whither opportunity had led him. So Booker T. Washington set out upon his career, one which from the undeniable need, the indefatigable energy, the excellent results, has brought him to the forefront as a thinker and a worker along the lines of industrial education as it pertains to the negro.

Tuskegee Institute is the fruitage of his work. It, with its annual conferences and its leader, has become almost synonymous with negro education, so widely have these become known, such an open ear have they gained, such a pleasing impression have they made upon all who watch the development of the race. The almost phenomenal growth of this school from a log cabin in 1881 to the immense plant it has now become has caused all eyes to be fixed upon it and its head. It has become a center with no small centripetal force. Because this is so it is well to consider seriously the question that arises as to what is being done by this man that he and his school should demand such widespread attention: what is this theory? what his policy? what his practice? and the many other questions that belong to this. Other schools than this have been instituted in the South along similar lines.

First of all it must be conceded that Mr. Washington is a man of unquestionably strong personality. Not only is this true, but he is one who has succeeded in convincing those who have the means with which to assist such enterprises that he is not only capable, but sincere, devoted—a man to be trusted. This has gone far to make Tuskegee a success. It has brought the thousands of dollars that have built the many buildings of which it boasts; it has brought the interest that is exhibited in all that is said and done there at the conferences. These last constitute another source of power,—one which up to quite recent date has differentiated this school from others. It was the first to lay hold of this practical, sociological idea that in a sense is as near the true "settlement" plan of help as perhaps it would be wise and profitable just now to carry out in these black belts. So Tuskegee stands as a helpful, uplifting influence. Its visitors come and see a gathering like to no other in the land. To the race itself immediately surrounding it these meetings are an incentive; to the white friends of the North they are seen as a necessity. The novelty, the practical side, the results, the busy beehive itself,—all suggest an enormous activity for good,—a place where economic conditions, sociological problems may be best met face to face and considered conservatively and wisely.

Tuskegee is a growth not of the mushroom variety. This is of itself encouraging. It is a big industrial school with just enough of book-learning work to make the industrial phase profitably intelligible. A reproduction in greater part of the Hampton idea, its environments have favored more rapid increase. Here is a belt pre-eminently fitted to lend itself to the success of this experiment, and one trained in Hampton schools is pre-eminently qualified to carry it out. Without this preliminary training we must confess that Tuskegee as it stands to-day would be an impossibility. Without Hampton influence, Hampton allies, its present glory could not have been attained. And this does not in the least detract from the work of the head, whose stern purpose, untiring zeal and great executive ability have been manifest at every step.

How far this work at Tuskegee is to be considered as a main factor in solving the negro problem is a question that will arise. There can be no question that it is a vast help. The industrial idea that Booker T. Washington carries out undoubtedly has an important place in this solution. The vast numbers of colored people in these congested districts must constitute for a long time a sort of peasantry. Such a class cannot rise to high levels instantly nor by the help of mere brain culture. A higher class in any race is an evolution,—a result of time and growth through lower stages. To let these learn to work wisely and well with the hand is of vast importance. To teach them habits of industry, thrift, prudence is of equal value. These lessons learned the higher planes are before them, and will be reached by the gradual rising of those souls with high aspirations—sensible aspirations. In just so far as the leader of the enterprise at Tuskegee keeps it in view that no great principle must be sacrificed, just so far his work is a most important factor in the endeavor to reach a solution of the questions that vex us all regarding the race. He is a needed leader in this direction. But this is not saying that because of his success in this line all the race must run mad over industrial education, or that because this line is doing much good the whole world must jump at the conclusion that at last has been found the sole sort of education the race as a race should have.

Friends become inimical to the true interests of the Negro when they become short-sighted and narrow. Benefactors cease to become such when they look upon a large part as the whole. The danger is that those who have the means are apt to throw completely both money and influence upon the side of industrial education. The world loves a hobby, and it also likes to hear what it believes. It also likes to follow the crowd, and we would be sorry to see the abandonment of one iota of effort toward higher education for the Negro while pursuing this new belief. It would be a sad thing for rapid development in the future should any one, black or white, reach such a commanding position before the world as to throw the least shadow upon the higher learning, upon those struggling institutions hardly one of which is so well, so magnificently equipped for its work as is Tuskegee for industrial education. Culture is as necessary to make a cultured Negro as to make a cultured white man, and those who have the ability—and there are very many—should have the fullest opportunity. We can become too practical.

Mr. Washington has not reached his eminence unassailed by criticism. He has been called no true educator because he has placed no more stress upon higher education, because he has held to a single idea. He has been denied the appellation of benefactor by those who have seen in the rapid progress of the Negro since freedom the result of this higher education—this attention to culture of intellect. Some refuse to accept the appellation of "leader of the race" because his sphere is limited. He has been called a "trimmer" because he has left other vital issues untouched by voice or pen.

To this I would reply by saying that with certainty he is an educator. He has met the necessity for a certain kind of education in a broad, comprehensive, sensible way. Narrow indeed are those who cannot see the educational value in his work. A trained hand is of need to any people. A certain class must live by this alone. As for being a benefactor: one who makes two blades of grass grow where but one grew before belongs to this class assuredly, and his work in its entirety aims to just such increase both literally and figuratively. As to leadership, it is a foolish thing to discuss. A leader is known by his followers. We cannot make or unmake a leader by declarations. Mr. Washington is leading well a class along industrial lines. He has followers who are striving to emulate him in this respect, and the good work goes on. But the whole race is not absorbed in these lines, not by any means. The race has been growing in wealth, refinement, learning. All these have worked to produce another class where there may be found goodly numbers on the heights where leaders dwell; a class of which he certainly has never claimed to be leader, for whom he has never aspired to speak. Mr. Washington is too conscientious a man to claim to stand for Negro education at large. He may justly claim to stand pre-eminently for Negro industrial education, because his efforts, his success, his well-won recognition, entitle him to this place. The question of "leadership" is discussed by one of the race (Dr. N. F. Mossell) who understands the situation well, and his opinions are given in *City and State*:

"There is a vast difference between the elements of leadership for one who conducts private enterprise, be it ever so large, and one who aspires to be the leading representative of an outraged and oppressed people. A few months ago, in discussing the race problem from the stage of the Academy of Music before thousands of listeners, Mr. Booker T. Washington made this frank admission:—

"'I am heartily sorry that the interests of my work in Tuskegee, Ala., will not permit me to discuss in detail the recent race conflicts in Wilmington, N. C.'

"It was there that Mr. Washington gave the audience to understand by inference, if not by direct charge, that the dominant people in his State would cripple his work there if he dared tell the whole truth.

"Mr. Washington feels that he must get the $8,000 for his school annually from the State Legislature of Alabama, and more if possible. His anecdotes and illustrations are not always of the highest order; they do not always illustrate the highest aspirations and emotions of our people; but like most men who are collecting money for similar work, they appear at times to magnify the degradations of the people whom they seek to elevate. But in this matter he feels himself justified, because he must have larger means to carry on his work. It is here that we must make the differentiation between the leadership of a large industrial school, situated in the heart of the South, and that great race leadership which would justify a man in being called the 'Moses of his race.'"

Mr. Washington stands where he has placed himself, "upon a platform on which the whites of the South and the blacks can stand with full justice to each race." In no way can he enter into the discussion of burning questions concerning the race without endangering this work. In no other way could he have built up Tuskegee. While he limits himself to consideration of nothing but his school and keeps to the platform of his creation, he will continue to be the one great Negro in the eyes of the South, and, indeed, in the eyes of all who believe that fitting the race for practical lines of work is the sole equipment needed by this people.

Had a Booker T. Washington miraculously arisen at the close of the Civil War with his influence and his following, paradoxical as it may sound, another such would have been well nigh impossible. It took the world a long time to be convinced that the Negro of the cotton field, the Negro of dark hue, could receive the higher education. A good share of the world does not know of the educated Negro to-day. He is not met to any degree socially. His work does not appeal to the world at large. It is not objective enough. But it would be a blow to advancement if the labor and opinions of thirty-five years should be overshadowed,—thrown into complete eclipse by the success along industrial lines. The race needs many leaders, as much as do the Saxon Americans. It needs philanthropy to flow along all channels, so that education of whatever kind the race is capable may be at hand. The work of leading and following in science, literature, art, must go on as well as in the lines of manual labor. To stop now and bend all efforts to industrial education would be to bring about a reaction dangerous to its highest interests. All lines should be carried on faithfully and wisely. There should be ample means, ample room, ample influence for fruition of the higher aspirations, without which no people can hope to hold its own other than as a toiling peasantry, a stolid laboring class, a wage mechanic. Neither side should suffer from lack of friends, of interest, of encouragement, of recognition as leaders by race or by the world at large. Let Cæsar have the things that belong to Cæsar. No more can be asked.

But what effect does the educational world think an attempt to engraft higher education upon this plant would have upon Tuskegee, upon the South, upon Mr. Washington himself? There is room here for speculation which might give rise to much both suggestive and beneficial.

Notes

1 [Alexander Pope, *An Essay on Man* (1733).]

2 [Line 27 of the dedication to *Idylls of the King* (1885), by Alfred, Lord Tennyson.]

The Negro and Higher Learning

Forum 33 (1902): 349–355.

The particular part the negro is to play in the development of this great country is a question of the future. But one thing is certain; he is to play some part. It is equally certain that the future of the negro race is irrevocably bound up in its present. And if, as Victor Hugo declared, the nineteenth century made the negro free but the twentieth century is to make him a man, there is no question that higher learning is to be a prominent factor in this process. Accordingly, no lines should be drawn, no limits set, and no boundaries defined, if he is to reach the highest development. If a spirit of restriction were carried into practice, it would be to the ultimate disadvantage of all concerned, both white and black. No country has ever been prosperous or happy where such lines have been drawn. In this country an attempt to draw them would lead to a caste system that would be ruinous. Deterioration would inevitably come to any nation that allowed or encouraged such distinctions. Two systems of civilization would but create an *imperium in imperio*; for in the lower there would be leaders, and there would grow up a power and a system of life which in the end would produce a revolution. A growing body must and will break any bonds that seek to restrain or confine it. It is the law of the world's growth—the law of nature itself.

It is said that the masses of the negro race are ignorant; that they must go slowly; and that they will have to remain largely a laboring class. Handicraft, therefore, is the all-important thing. This does not follow. Perhaps they will so remain; but the handicraft is not the all-important thing, though it has its importance. That the masses must be uplifted is evident; but why limit the plane? Why say "only so far"?

But who is to do the work of elevating to a higher plane? Is it always to be an outer force, the help being given by another race? Are the negroes themselves to take no part in the movement? Are those who believe in the negro's elevation to be pushed aside and those allowed to take the control who declare that the higher education is a mischievous thing, and so hold the race within bounds? Who are those of the race who are to teach the negro in the future? Is it to be simply those who are the educated men of to-day? But what of to-morrow? Shall just the few who have friends or money enjoy the higher courses in our great centers of learning? Whence will come the leaders for higher planes if the higher forces are not to be supplied without limit from the rising generation? Shall we let the masses sleep because perchance they are sleepy? These are questions of vital importance, and we may well pause to reflect upon them.

The negro may be compelled to belong for years largely to the laboring or industrial classes. But whatever is good for the development of one race is good for the development of another. The negro people, as is predicted, may not all rise above the middle classes [that] have given us much of the best material in this, our Anglo-American, civilization. What would have been the result if similar lines had been drawn in former times? The one great boast of this proud Republic to-day is the universal opportunity of education for the poorest and humblest; and the boys and girls of the masses are invited, nay urged, to take the highest and the best training.

But we are met with the assertion that, after all, it is really a mistake, on general principles, to send the poor of any race through college, as the result is disconnect with former modes of life, unhappiness, and in many cases even absolute failure. We answer that this does not deter others of other races from continuing to go to college. That very discontent has often brought new, revivifying elements into the old, narrow life, and has evolved changes for good. Some failures must be expected in the attempt to carry out high ideals, and some wrong ideals may creep in as well. We learn our lessons by experience. A noble discontent is not harmful to either individual or race. It is the harbinger of better things. It is often truly said that satisfaction with the present is the beginning of decline. Other races, as other individuals, have gone through, and are still going through, their series of experiments to success or failure—ever groping for the best, for the right view of life. The negro must do the same. A few sacrifices along the road must not frighten him; a few mistakes, a few blighted prospects, a few instances of unwise choice should not deter the negro people from seeking to reach higher intellectual planes.

The world often reads much falsity into the countless philosophic sayings on education. In fact, each individual reads his own desires and theories into these, and often twists them to suit himself. So a certain class reasons that it is absolutely wrong, even wicked, to fit a man for a place that he can never reach. "Where ignorance is bliss, 'tis folly to be wise"[1] is often quoted at the expense of the negro race.

Where, indeed, would the old world have been had this philosophy found literal acceptance throughout the ages? Where would have been the progress of humanity? Where would have been the arts and sciences, the love of learning, the culture—civilization, in fact, of the present high order—or even the great nations themselves?

Though the negro scholar may not realize all that he would desire in afterlife, though his learning may have little chance to throw its beams afar, yet there is not necessarily any waste of time thereby, neither should there be grave disappointment. The negro should not be criticised for acquiring accomplishments that may seem doomed to lie largely within the folds of the napkin. They are not thrown away. The true worth is in the discipline given, the culture, the strong grasp upon other things that will make life mean more, that will urge on the aspiring soul to higher planes, that will sustain in trying hours, and that will even make avenues to places where these acquisitions will be of financial value. Avenues of all kinds are not always to be closed; and the weaker the race that clamors at the gate for admittance the stronger are the stimuli needed. There will ever be among any people those whom nothing will inspire; there will be those also who may be rendered by study unfit for practical life. But these are the exceptions. It is a part of the general plan that out of the mill of development shall come some imperfect specimens. This, however, does not prove the worthlessness of the mill or lessen the value of the perfect products.

I claim for the race all the latitude in the pursuit of knowledge that other races have, if it is to have a glorious future. I would have every youth follow the bent of his genius; and I contend that the bent of genius is best disclosed through a course of higher study. I would throw open to the negro youth all the avenues of life. I would encourage him to take advanced courses whenever and wherever possible. If a desire is present for specific work, I would encourage him to follow his inclination in that line. I would bid him study himself and his people. I would advise a familiar acquaintance with the ancient classics, with modern languages, with mathematics, with science, with philosophy, and with all other branches of study that go to form a liberal education. I would bid him do, so far as he is able, what others have done in those lines. I would counsel him to distinguish himself by rare attainments, and so advance not only his own interests but those of his race. I would have him inspired to do his best. The study of philosophy could not fail to lead him to wisdom. This done, the future will take care of itself. No one should be forced along these lines if he is incompetent or incapable, and no one should be restrained if he has ability or inclination.

But, with all this, I would have the negro taught the dignity of labor, the nobility of work; that idleness is a crime, and that to every task of hand or brain the best within him should be brought. Then I would have him be content to bide his time; to put his hands to any honest service, and work and wait. The possibilities of the race need not be discussed here. It has its exponents, in all lines, of what the higher life and the higher education can do for it; but it must have many more of such representatives. The future of the race depends largely upon its intellectual advancement. It must have many more and still abler professional men—lawyers, doctors, preachers, instructors, and men of letters, to give it tone and character.

It has been progress on these intellectual lines that has made other peoples stand out prominently before the world. It has always been intellect that has commanded notice. The negro race has been, and will be, measured by the heights reached by its most scholarly and intellectual men; by what these men have done and have said; by their influence on the world at large. Let such men arise at any time, and the world accords them a hearing, and even gives them honor. With the rise of such individuals the race to which they belong goes up in the world's estimation. This will, in fact, be the final test of the negro. Such has been the rule throughout the world's history, and there is no reason to believe that it will be otherwise in regard to the future of the negro people. The race will rise or fall according to the intellectual step that it can keep with other races of the world.

Too long already has the race been compelled to content itself with ignorant leaders. Immediately after the Civil War there was an apology for the lack of educated leaders; there was then an excuse for make-shifts. To-day there is none. No matter what criticism may be given to the education provided for the race at that critical period of its free existence, it served a purpose and laid the foundation for the higher education as we see it now, as well as furnishing capable men to lead in these higher paths. In the future, more than in the past, the negro is to be largely his own instructor. The broad education then begun—an education that will fit him for broad dealing with men, for wise action, for sympathetic relations, and for deep insight—will be the best possible foundation for all this leadership. Longfellow says that great men stand like solitary towers in the city of God, and that secret passages running deep beneath external nature give their thoughts intercourse with higher intelligences which strengthen and console them, and of which the laborers on the surface do not even dream.[2] Such men are not the product of mere mechanical training, of the industrial idea solely. They are rather the products of the broadest culture. We need them for leaders. In fact such men will be leaders.

Negro colleges and universities have sent forth scores of physicians, ministers, lawyers, teachers, and business men. These are the powers that uplift; and the greater the ideal these graduates have had set before them, the greater the work that they will do. Those that have come forth from schools like these do not fill the criminal ranks. They are uplifting influences. They are broad men and women, though they may find their life calling them to other work than the strictly educational. Though they may be compelled even to live close to the soil, they are better fitted for living. They carry into home and family life a higher, finer element, and make wiser mothers and fathers to rear up future generations. These coming sons and daughters will be blessed in many ways through the learning, the aspirations, and the talent of the parents. They will have the inestimable birthright of a heredity so often denied them now.

By this the race will be placed on a higher plane—a plane to which it never could attain were it narrowed down, as one says, "to the learning of any mere individual facts connected with any given line of handiwork." Wealth, honesty, respectability—all are needed, and all may come from the education received in the lower grades of the schools, and even from the manual training alone. But while the negro must have these in order to rise, he must, if he would reach the highest point of civilization, have the other and higher learning as well. The negro race is to be taught that it is to reach upward to the heights, no matter how inferior it may be regarded now, and no matter how much opposition may loom up in its path.

It would be morally wrong even to think of limiting the educational opportunities of the race. Cruelty is a weak word to apply to an attempt to curb the ambition of those that see their greatest future in other than industrial lines. And the negro himself should be the last to advocate such limits, however dark the outlook may seem at times.

Mr. Booker T. Washington does not ignore this fact, for he says: "Mr. Tanner's success as a painter is to me a prophecy of the negro along the higher lines of attainment."[3] Again he says:

> In the years to come we shall have many increasing evidences of the fact that the negro is making his way into all lines of attainment in which other races are prominent. I make this assertion because I believe and know that my race is thoroughly capable of assimilating the higher instruction, and is, when permitted to receive the training, fitted to enter upon any of the pursuits, æsthetic or otherwise, as other men and women are. We have too many successful examples of thoroughly educated men and women who are making their way for me to entertain any belief to the contrary that could be considered a virtual indictment of the mental capacity of my race. The future, in my opinion, is to bring us many colored men and women who will distinguish themselves in art, in science, in literature, and in statesmanship.

But with the rushing sweep of reforms along educational lines, and especially in view of the attempt to narrow the race down to an industrial sphere of education, one serious aspect presents itself and calls for our earnest and careful attention. It is this: The higher education of the negro is in danger of languishing on account of lack of adequate financial support. An appeal made in behalf of Fisk University not long ago, showing the sums given for negro education, is full of suggestion for the thoughtful mind. It says:

> Over thirty million of dollars given to endow institutions of learning in 1899 is a significant fact. That not one-thousandth part of this sum has been given to endow institutions for the race which includes one-tenth of our population is a still more significant fact. Everything for those who have had centuries of civilization behind them, nothing for those whose civilization has not had as many decades, does not accord with an American twentieth-century idea of justice. It is a disparity doubtless in part due to the fact that the institutions of learning for black people are little known.

When we consider that the industrial schools do not and cannot afford this higher education, and that those desiring and deserving it cannot all attend the great colleges of the land, because of the necessary expense, we certainly see that if the race is to be kept upon the upward grade as to scholarship, the day has not yet come for these negro higher institutions of learning to be abandoned either by the race itself or by its white friends.

It is true that there is a growing difficulty in obtaining funds for these schools unless they possess industrial attachments. We realize that the public has often been called upon to contribute to work that never existed, and that the race has thereby been misrepresented and the cause of deserving schools harmed. But we must face the fact of growing apathy everywhere toward helping on work that seeks the higher education of the negro. This apathy must be counterbalanced by the presentation of arguments and cold facts, and by insistence in demanding that the race must have these centres of learning within its reach. Otherwise there will soon be seen a vast difference in our civilization and in the general progress. Without this higher education, the "submerged tenth" of this country's population would soon make its influence felt upon American civilization in a way that would convince every one of the truth of what I have stated.

The relation of higher education to the future of the negro, then, is this: No race can reach high planes without the self-knowledge that comes from years of culture through higher courses of study; no race can hope to hold its own without the broad altruistic knowledge that comes only from the study of humanity through the humanities and correlated subjects; no race can take first rank with the peoples of the earth unless possessing a wide knowledge of its duties to the world and to itself, and the appreciation of the right, the true, the beautiful that comes only through the well-trained mind and the well-disciplined soul.

Higher education is to be the principal factor in forcing recognition through achievement along the lines to which the world pays the highest respect and honor. It will win this for the negro at home and abroad. It will round him out in his manhood and citizenship. It will strengthen his posterity. It will fit him for the varied services to which time and circumstances may call him. It will show to the race values in life that would be all unknown without it, and it will rouse it to its own highest possibilities. It will tend to incite to morality, honesty, sobriety, and industry, by training the intellect, the emotions, and the will to obey the mandates of that highest of monitors—conscience. In short, without in the least undervaluing the sphere and influence of industrial training, we may affirm that this higher education is, after all, to be the most powerful lever in the negro's development and in the ultimate perfection of humanity at large.

Notes

1 [See the last two lines of stanza 10 of "On a Distant Prospect of Eton College" (1742), by Thomas Gray (1716–1771).]

2 [See the opening paragraph of *Kavanagh* (1849), by Henry W. Longfellow (1807–1882).]

3 [See Booker T. Washington, "Henry O. Tanner, Artist," *The Interior* 32 (October 31, 1901): 1371.]

The Educated Negro and His Mission

(Washington, D.C.: American Negro Academy, 1903),
Occasional Paper no. 8, pp. 3–11.

Human thought is like a pendulum. It sways from belief to belief, from theory to theory, from plan to plan, and the length of its vibrations is governed by a multitude of contending forces operating from both within and without. Two of these influences, in the present age, are all potential. One is the ardent desire to find the best ways and means by which the human race may hasten on its varied development, and the other is the strenuous determination to discover what may be styled the "Northwest" passage to that coveted result.

The consequence is that, in this determined reach for all that humanity craves for itself and for its civilization, the oscillations of thought and endeavor are oftimes marked by notable extremes. Especially has this been true in lines of education. Again and again has it been sought to wheel the educational car upon new tracks where exaggerated views, revolutionary ideas, radical methods have caused the eyes of the world to be focused upon the attempt, and no movement within the arc that the world's opinions have traversed has been unnoticed.

These changing sentiments in regard to education have been most noticeable in their bearing upon the Negro race. It is conceded that material tendencies are characteristic of the present age. Romance, sentiment, idealism in life and letters, struggle as they may, are swept aside by the vigorous commercialism that has taken possession of the nation at large. Meat has become more than life and raiment more than body. One question is being intensely pressed forward—*how to learn a living?* and the swing of the pendulum concerning the Negro's education has swept a degree beyond any heretofore measured.

That manual training is needful no one will deny for a moment; that some of all races must inevitably be sons of toil is readily admitted; and that such education has its share in the development of every race there is no contention. We all know that Learning and Labor traveled hand in hand, with the emphasis upon the former, when the Anglo Saxon first wrestled with the wilderness of America. We know too that when the desert wastes were changed to smiling plains the ways of the two drifted apart, and learning took the path for culture and high scholarship, untrammeled, while labor plodded on, gaining slowly comparative ease in its varied lines. It is only when limitation is placed upon a race that objection comes—when one race is selected for more than a fair share of experimentation in the exploitation of a theory. Then danger seems imminent. In this case the danger lies in the tendency to lose sight of Negro scholarship—of Negro higher learning. There are other questions of equal importance to that of how to earn a living, and that college president who expressed it in these words "How to live on what one earns— how to live higher lives," understood well their relative worth when pre-eminence was claimed for the latter, and pointed to a fact too largely ignored—that the lessons which teach these last mentioned come from a different training from that represented by industrial training alone.

We repeat that the suggestions bearing upon the education of the Negro race have caused too decided a swing of the pendulum in many quarters and higher education is in danger of being swallowed up, if not to a great extent abandoned, in the extreme importance attached to that other education we denominate as Industrial.

The error arises in confounding race with the individual, which is not only radically unphilosophic, but morally wrong. The recognition of individual limitation is right and proper, and it is the individual that must be considered. As Dr. [William Hayes] Ward has pertinently observed, "To the man who wants to lift a mass of people out of lower into higher conditions they are people, individual people, not races," and he adds further with just emphasis, "When it comes to nurture and education they are to be considered as individuals, each to be lifted up and their children surrounded by a superior environment." Now, this cannot be done if limitations are set which must by the very nature of things press heavily upon the individual. The race must be left free as air to take in higher learning.

Still, it is true that with a general change in ideas as to education—its use and end—higher education, pure scholarship, has everywhere been placed upon the defensive. President [Arthur Twining] Hadley has felt compelled to say that it must be prepared to prove its usefulness. This being true, so much the more must Negro scholarship be prepared to prove its right to continuance, to support and to freedom of choice.

The educated Negro is an absolute fact. The day is past when his ability to learn is scoffed at. But on the other hand is born that fear that he may go too far—excel or equal the Anglo-Saxon,—and that fear is a prime motive in the minds of many who seek to hedge the onward path of the race. But this path will not be hedged. This educated class, though few in number, has been keeping for years the torch aloft for the race. It must be with us for the future. It has a mission in the world and it is working in a brave endeavor to fulfill that mission. For the good of the whole country this class must multiply, not decrease in number.

There are no two definitions of a scholar to be applied to different races. The Negro scholar must be the same as any other—endowed as Milton would have him "with that complete and generous education, that which fits a man to perform justly, skilfully and magnanimously all the offices, both private and public, of peace and war."[1] And he should have, in order to meet this requirement, what Emerson has emphasized as necessary—"the knowledge that comes from three great fields—from nature, from books and from action."

The Negro like any other scholar is not the man who has simply been through college, but the one "through whom the college has been"[2]—the one who has not only gathered from contact with college life varied stores of knowledge, but who has grown in strength of character and breadth of culture; one who has become imbued with the spirit of high ideals; one who does not scorn the old-fashioned virtues of truth, honesty and virtue; one who has views crystalized into definite aims; one who has a settled purpose in life; one who is strenuously determined to realize a worthy ambition; one who has both microscopic and telescopic capacity, able to look into the minutest details and sweep a broad range with clear vision; and one (slightly changing a potent phrase) whose "reach upward is ever exceeding his grasp."[3] Added to this the Negro scholar above all must be one who makes himself a reforming force for the world's betterment. Here is the Negro's opportunity—to combine in himself those characteristics Mr. Austin mentioned not long ago—the purely scholarly qualities of the German, the statesmanlike qualities of the English and then to be a *propagandist*.

The Negro who is an educated man must be a practical man, and zealous in getting to work to show that thinking and doing go together. If the world needs such men from the white race, so much the more are educated Negroes needed. Educated men are the ones to take a place in affairs, national and municipal, aiding to solve great problems, cure great evils and guide the destinies of a people. What else can it mean when we see such a scholar as President Seth Low step from the administration of college affairs to the administration of the affairs of a great city in a righteous endeavor to help cleanse a corrupt government?[4] Again, President Roosevelt takes up the reins for the entire nation after active service in literature, in camp, on field and in the executive chair of a great state. Still again we instance Dr. Gladden who has shown in the west what a scholar's service may and should be to his city, when he chose to sit in its council.[5] These examples can be multiplied many times to show that the educated man has taken for his motto that highest one—"Ich dien"—I serve—a service by leading and made both necessary and fitting by attainments and worth.

This idea of service to the race is peculiarly the mission of the educated Negro. In no other way can higher education be justified for the race; and Dr. Mayo has well denominated the field before him as a "high plateau of opportunity."

It is a part of his mission to take up the leadership of the race. The day for ignorant Negro leaders is rapidly passing. One of the first services to be rendered along this line is to insist that *seeming* shall no longer be allowed to pass for *being*. No matter where it strikes or whom it strikes, he must help strip away pretense from the vain and shallow, unveil those who masquerade under borrowed, empty, high-sounding titles—those whose vociferous tones, glib tongues and unlimited audacity seek to pose their owners as learned ones under the thinnest veneer. This uncovering of shams, exposure of frauds will save the race many a gibe and sneer.

When there is more of genuine scholarship among members of the race there will be a different attitude assumed towards it. But as long as the Negro prefers to construe owlish looks as wisdom, to bow down to clam-like silence as profound philosophy, to stand agape over blatant mouthings as eloquence, and to measure mental calibre by bodily avoirdupois, he not only gives evidence of weakness in a lack of sound discrimination, but he subjects the entire race to consequent criticism and contempt.

It is to our shame, however, that we are forced to admit that just such shams are so often on "dress parade" before the world that by them the race is too frequently largely judged, and to its detriment. The day has come when the brain of the race must both direct its brawn and expose its brass. Ignorance and charlatanism will seek enlightenment or retreat only when intelligence and learning make a masterly array for leadership.

This mission of leadership has many phases. The educated Negro leads by making himself felt, unconsciously, in many ways. Dr. Angell of Michigan University has truly declared that a man who has any claims to scholarship or learning cannot hoard its blessings as a miser hoards gold, that he can hardly enjoy it without in some degree sharing its blessings with others, that its very nature is to be outgoing and effusive.[6] Because of this truth the Negro scholar is an inspiration to his own people who need just such an object lesson as himself. The race gains self-respect as it sees one of its own on higher planes. It gathers higher aims by the respect it instinctively accords him and its pride is stimulated along higher levels. It is thus that colored men of learning—men of high ideals—are far more influential through the simple contact of their presence than are those of another race.

It is admitted that the race is cursed with not only pretenders but with idlers. So is every other race, but the Negro can least afford it just now. It may be true that some of these hold diplomas indicating completion of courses of higher studies, but they are not really the educated ones, and the fact of their existence does not prove the uselessness of the educated Negro or the failure of higher education for the race. It is to our credit that comparatively few, who have struggled through the long years that lead to culture and scholarship, can be found to give enemies of the race an opportunity for assault from that quarter. Figures will not lie, though they sometimes may stagger one; and statistics show us that the college-bred Negro is far from giving a record for uselessness.

I have said that the educated Negro (and I include both sexes) leads by the inspiration that is radiated. Much as we regret it we cannot refuse to face the fact that grows upon us daily—the fact that there are too many Negro youths to-day, who seem lacking in ambition, in aspiration, in either fixedness or firmness of purpose. We have too many dudes whose ideal does not rise above the possession of a new suit, a cane, a silk hat, patent leather shoes, a cigarette and a good time—too many in every sense the "sport of the gods."[7] It is the mission of the educated Negro to help change this—to see that thoughtlessness gives place to seriousness. Ruskin spoke a basic truth when he said that youth is no time for thoughtlessness; and it is especially applicable to the youth of a race that has its future to make[.] The Negro who stands on the higher rounds of the ladder of education is pre-eminently fitted for this work of inspiration—helping to mold and refine, "working out the beast" and seeing that the "ape and tiger die," rescuing from vice and all that the term implies.[8]

He will help to form classes of society where culture and refinement, high thinking and high living, in its proper sense, draw the line—classes made up of what one denominates as "aristocracy of intelligence and character that protects the masses from their foes without and from their own folly and unrighteousness."

This same influence is to be exercised over those young men and women fresh from college who have two things to learn—that the knowledge they possess is neither altogether new, nor is it patented by them, and further, that one great danger lies ever before those of any race who have won great distinction in college halls—that of total extinction out in the world.

Nothing but true scholarship can lead these young people to take proper measure of self and estimate the things about them at their true value as they stand at that precarious place, the beginning of a career. There they need the warning of Omar emphasized to "waste not their hour."[9] There is plenty of active leadership for this Afro-American scholar as a part of his mission. There are books to be written; experiments to be made; conditions to be analyzed; ways and means invented to reach ends; and we need Negro specialists in all these fields. Great economic results will never come to us, nor will a truly great standing be ours as long as we are content to leave our affairs to the sole direction, however wise or kindly intended, of another race.

So scientists, historians, linguists, sociologists, professional men in all lines are needed, not only that the life and history of the race may be properly presented to the world, but in order that another mission may be fulfilled—that of keeping before the world the fact that the Negro possesses intellect; that he is both able and capable, and that through this possession and training the race purposes to develop its civilization.

The Negro scholar must not be so wrapped up in his own achievements that he cannot see the possibilities in those about him. In this way also he is to help keep the victories of the race at the fore. As a teacher he has a fine opportunity to note and encourage talent, as a writer or journalist he can give credit where credit is due. Petty jealousy is out of place and fear of rivalry is but an evidence of mediocrity. As a specialist in any line he will be able to stand where he can call this talent to his aid and foster its growth.

There are other fields of activity that need the presence and kindly penetrative interest of the educated ones of the race. The slums call for this influence. The growing problems in our northern cities especially call for work at the hands of the intelligent, scholarly men and women. Vice must be checked in the race, and a transformation be effected in the manner of life in the dark portions of the cities. Here we have a problem of our own—to separate poverty from viciousness and encourage the people to better morals and industrious, clean lives. No one knows better than the thoughtful members of the race the difficulties to be faced here where a people is segregated in certain portions—where the good and the bad must perforce live elbow to elbow, in constant contact and often constant contamination. It needs settlement work of the most earnest kind, and only those who have standing and education will be able to do the desired good.

It is so often said to-day that the Negro should let politics alone that many have come to the conclusion that this is a field to be entirely abandoned. But the Negro has his public duties as a citizen to perform unless he proposes to drop out of sight, and in this field he has a duty. Here the man of education should do as it has seemed good for some of the Anglo-Saxon race—lend his help toward purifying the corrupt atmosphere, standing for what is upright and just. It is an incontrovertible fact that the standing one gains demonstrates the capabilities and worth of the race. To be clean-handed in all political dealings, to guard both honor and responsibility in matters of business—in short to quit oneself like a man in all things—must be preached daily as of the utmost advantage to the race. The present attitude of the outside world places the Negro scholar in a most responsible position, for every movement on his part is noticed, criticized, and if he falters or fails higher education receives another blow. Not for one second can the educated Negro men and women afford to be indifferent to an iota of their action or conduct.

With all these spheres calling especially for education and culture there is still another of the most importance, for it holds so much for the future of the race. This is the improvement of domestic life. We want no upper classes where evils are glossed over because there are money and position to be respected. We must work for the ideal family life. Home is the social center for a race, the real center of race improvement, and we want better homes. For this we must have better fathers, better mothers, better husbands, better wives, better sons and daughters. Industry alone does not make for morality. As one has said, "A strict labor diet does not strengthen morals, it only suppresses passions." In the home and for home building is needed that ethical, philosophical, and esthetical training that belongs to the higher education. This training is the great instrument for the present upbuilding of the race which is to do so much in laying foundations for the fine heredity every race covets. I repeat that the seeds of culture are to be sown by the educated Negro and in the home they are never wholly without fruit.

The artisan, the laborer have their niches, but they must work with and not against the educated classes. That the strong working brain must be the guide of the strong working hand, I have ever contended. The masses must move, but it must be the classes that move them if progress upward is to be the order. We must build up an honest, thrifty yeomanry, but we must multiply rapidly our educated men to lead and work and influence in these various fields.

The fact that the Negro scholar is needed for this work shows the demand. We have not enough of them to-day. If Dr. Angell of Michigan University does not consider, when speaking of the Anglo-Saxon, that one college bred person in a thousand in his state "is unwise or inexpedient," why should friend or foe of the Negro consider less than 3000 college bred men and women out of an entire population of nearly 10,000,000, "unwise or inexpedient?" It would be laughable if it were not so pitiful to think of the hue and cry about too much learning for the Negro. The trouble with the race is not too much learning but not enough. A little learning is surely a dangerous thing. Short cuts are too many and do not really educate. They utterly fail to give drill and discipline absolutely necessary to that culture, which comes only after hard labor of years. All honor to Dr. [J. L. M.] Curry when he so bravely declared that the talk of the hopelessness of education or of too much education, or of the inappropriateness of academic education is vain, adding emphatically, "The Negro wants all he can get, and all he gets he profits by."

No; the race is in no danger of going "college mad." Although the early schools for it were generally established upon the broad university plan, yet their work has been largely basic; and they have done far more in laying foundations than in producing a surplus of graduates from higher courses. It is an absurdity to claim there can be too many of the race with learning enough and discipline enough to make themselves useful leaders.

There is room for all kinds of work. There is need of the practical, the industrial, and it is honorable to work with the hands. It will help in weeding out idleness. But at the same time it is easy to ignore and crush higher aspirations. The quiet shaft of ridicule oft-times does more than argument, and many things that are very desirable and necessary are often overshadowed by the skilful juxtaposition that shifts them where they are but dimly seen, while other things stand forth in a strong light and are thus looked upon as all important. So the merry quip and jest at the Latin and Greek studied by the Negro bring far more than a passing laugh—they *really bring discredit upon the whole higher training where none is actually intended*. It causes the old friends of higher learning to pause, and take it far too literally, and then determine that it is after all better to abandon the support of institutions for higher education. The pity of it all is that it is next to impossible to undo the wrong. Like the sped arrow and the lost opportunity such words and their effect cannot be recalled. Even assurance that it is largely jest comes too late. The jest has been all too convincing and the converts have at once arrayed their philanthropy against forwarding the efforts of those who seek the higher courses.

Dr. VanDyke has said that true manhood and womanhood cannot exist without an ideal side; that these are the finer feelings which have no market value but which must be kept alive. Why should we endeavor to keep them alive? Simply because the world at large recognizes that this means development in the highest sense, and we claim that this is an especial need of the Negro race. Then we ask, How are these finer feelings kept alive? and the answer comes that this stimulation must proceed from culture and scholarship.

With our needs pressing upon us we see as no other people the importance of all this to bring about a change in the environment of the race. It has a bearing upon this desired change that the virtues resulting from manual labor alone cannot exert. Industrial training is needed too to teach how to earn a living, but, as intimated in this paper, something else—the higher education—must be counted upon to teach *how to live better lives, how to get the most and best out of life.*

There is much involved in the attempt of the educated Negro to fulfil his mission. The fact that there is such a swing of the pendulum away from higher training for the race, makes it more difficult for those who possess it to-day to carry out the mission. The Negro scholar who sets out to pursue the paths pointed out does it at a great amount of self-sacrifice. He must expect to meet rebuff, discouragement, misinterpretation, lack of recognition, hardships, and these do not by any means come alone from the Anglo-Saxon. The foes are often of his own race. It will take all the philosophy he can summon to contend with the opposition that comes from ignorance, from coarseness, from the unthinking and the malicious. It will need all his self-control and forbearance to move along under grasping, bullying ignorance that seeks to ride rough shod over superior knowledge and breeding; it will demand all his logic to meet the arguments from without that the Negro has no time now for scholarship—that he must get money and get land first; that learning possesses little mercantile value now; that the way to advancement along scholarly lines is barred; that the cook, the carpenter, the shoemaker, are all better paid than the scholar for the use of the sum of their knowledge which costs far less than his. He must face the facts no matter how unjust or inconsistent such things are and meet the final question—*Is it worth striving for?*—*Is it worth while to put ambitions and longings on the altar, to work unceasingly, uncomplainingly amidst stolid indifference, absolute contempt and often open hostility?*

We are face to face with the question whether scholarship pays, whether the educated Negro is to be encouraged to multiply and push forward determinedly on his mission. If there was but the present moment to contemplate, the race might be excused for pausing, for acquiescing in the limitations set for its education, and for saying the game is not worth the candle. But to-day does not end all. There is a *future* and that Negro is lacking in proper manhood who does not determine to help on that future. The future is always bound up in the present and if this future is to make men and women out of the race in coming generations the question is answered. Negro scholarship is worth striving for, because the educated Negro is to lead for that future. Education, learning, scholarship will make the undying lustre of a people—will prove their greatest glory. Thinkers will give an immortality to a people that neither wealth, nor industry, nor strength of arm, nor even virtue can procure for it.

So the educated Negro must keep this in view, must see his mission clearly and stand courageously ready to undertake it—

> "Cleansed of servile panic,
>   Slow to dread or despise,
> Humble because of knowledge,
>   Mighty by sacrifice."[10]

But there must be united effort among the leaders of the race along all lines to this end. Advocates of higher learning and of industrial education must accord respect to each other's opinions and work unitedly, in order that neither may fall a sacrifice to the "Nemesis of Neglect."[11] And the race must sustain its leaders of thought and action. There is no time to lose, none to waste in eternal strife. The field is large enough for all to glean and work in. The race must make a common cause, meet a common enemy and win common friends.

Notes

1 [John Milton, *Of Education* (1644).]

2 [Benjamin Disraeli, Lord Beaconsfield.]

3 [See Robert Browning (1812–1889), "Andrea del Sarto" (1855), lines 97–98: "Ah, but a man's reach should exceed his grasp, / Or what's a heaven for?"]

4 [Seth Low went from president of Columbia University to mayor of New York City.]

5 [Reverend Washington Gladden served a term on the Columbus, Ohio, city council from 1900 to 1902.]

6 [The reference is to "A Higher Education: A Plea for Making It Accessible to All," a commencement address made by James B. Angell, president of the University of Michigan, on June 25, 1879. Angell declared that the graduates were "not taking with them hidden treasures to enjoy in secret as a miser gloats in the solitude of his garret over gold, but rather precious seed which they will sow."]

7 [Compare the title of Paul Laurence Dunbar's novel, *Sport of the Gods* (1902).]

8 [See stanza 118 of Alfred, Lord Tennyson, *In Memoriam* (1850).]

9 [This maxim comes from the *Rubaiyat* of Omar Khayyam (1048–1122).]

10 [See Rudyard Kipling, *The Islanders* (1902).]

11 [This is a symbol of crime. See an image in *Punch*, September 1888.]

The Relation of the Teacher to the Moral and Social Elevation of the Race

Hampton Institute Publications 8 (July 1904): 79–83.

The two great educative factors in the moral and social elevation of a race are the home and the school. Upon the training received in these rests the future of every people. In the home the earliest impressions are made. Every educator therefore recognizes the importance of making that center all that it ought to be in the great work of character formation, which we value to-day as the prime end of education. It is too true that comparatively few Negro parents understand the part they have to perform in this work. Countless homes throughout the land fall far short of what they ought to be. Too many parents are either ignorant or indifferent as to their share in the education of their children. Dr. Thayer asserts that the mass of children and youth in the public schools of our land never receive any moral lessons at home. When we look at the statement in the light of the conditions in many homes, especially those of many of the Negro race, we can but acknowledge the truth of the assertion. Moreover, it is a noteworthy fact that the children of school age to-day, spend far more time under the direct influence of the teacher than under that of the parent.

This being the case, we see that the work of moral and social elevation must be largely done by the schools, and that the onus of its rests preeminently upon the teacher. If, in the formative period of their lives, the boys and girls are trained in the right direction and are brought under wholesome moral influences such as I perceive exist here at Hampton, the results will be shown in better homes and in higher ideals of domestic life, which are in too many instances greatly needed among us.

To assure the future of any people there must be a growth in both thinking and doing[.] The Negro race must learn to think for itself, not let others always think for it. It must learn to do for itself along all lines and not be entirely dependent upon others. The task of leading to such growth is the teacher's. The men and women who are to-day directing our youth are in reality directing the destiny of the race. On them rests the responsibility of inculcating in their pupils all the little things that go to make an honest, industrious class of people, all those correct habits of life that make for morality and decency, neatness, punctuality, accuracy, truthfulness, thoroughness, system—habits that are to so great an extent lacking in the homes of undeveloped peoples.

It devolves chiefly upon them to accentuate those correct views of life which every child must be taught to hold if there is to be progress. Insight, the right perception of relations, the intellectual and moral training that will develop common sense, sharpen intellect, purify soul, and strengthen character—these are needed above all by backward races, and thus do they become the teacher's life work.

In reality the teacher is better fitted in many respects for the performance of this duty than is the parent; for the teacher is stripped in a large degree of that partiality which blinds one to faults and weaknesses, and of that ignorance, ambition, and vanity which cause so many parents to drive children to an unworthy course in life.

The youth of to-day are to learn to be industrious, to learn that hard work hurts no one, that even learning is labor, and that all labor is honorable; that a trained intellect and a trained hand go together to make a perfect man. They are to be taught that the mind must be rightly occupied and that when the hand alone is at work the brain is left free to run riot—a freedom that usually means license to think upon debasing things if the mind has not been inspired by thoughts above the soil.

There has never been a time in the history of the world's education when men and women, looking back over the formative influences that have come into their lives, have not found that their uplifting is due to some teacher. It has been some honorable, enthusiastic, self-sacrificing, noble, virtuous man or woman who has kindled self-respect, fanned to a flame the spark of divinity within, and stirred the fires of ambition to be and to do. Thus the teacher should be the spiritual, mental, and physical adviser of a people, holding a position than which none has a closer relation to the elevation of the race, none a more potent influence for the future. The opportunity is his to lead to higher levels, to point out error, to correct false ideas, to direct to true estimates of life, to bring out the best, to repress the worst, to transform the viciously inclined, to inspire and encourage the dullards, to indicate right channels for eager, brilliant minds.

This being true, what must this teacher be who bears such a relationship to the future of the race? In the first place the moral sense of a race cannot be elevated nor can its social plane be lifted unless its teachers have a high moral sense and the proper comprehension of what differentiates social planes. Example has ever been far more than precept. Negro teachers must be champions of honor and virtue. Loose lives must not be tolerated among them. Gambling, frequenting questionable places of amusement, drinking, should have no place in the lives of those who are to lead the young. The teacher, like the preacher, stands too near the young to be other than thoroughly honorable. Weak, unprincipled, selfish persons with no race pride, no race love, no race hope, should not be found at the teacher's desk. Those who teach must be men and women in whom frivolity finds no lodgment, who are not only above reproach, but who possess such force of character that they make boys and girls strong to discriminate between right and wrong and resolute to follow light and do the right. They must have, too, that personal magnetism that clothes the born teacher with power to carry followers wherever he leads.

This responsible position as a leader calls for preparation along mental lines as well as for moral equipment. An ignorant leader in any cause is a dangerous one. The time is past for entrusting the great work of education to the hands of those who are poorly prepared. A money reward need not be expected by the one occupying the teacher's chair. This most important and responsible position—the opportunity for the formation of character, for the upbuilding of a race—this is the most poorly paid. Neither should teaching be used simply as a stepping stone to something more desirable. No one who has not consecrated his life to his calling, who has not heard with unmistakable clearness the voice that summons to a vocation, has a right to meddle with the immortal work of a teacher, as sacred as any on earth. But with the clear call resounding in the ear, preparation for, as well as interest in, teaching as a life work is absolutely necessary. Breadth of knowledge and varied culture should belong to a teacher. Ethics and philosophy must be studied, for only through a knowledge of these can one know how to cope with the task of training minds. He should be familiar with science and should have wide learning generally. Breadth and depth in these mean elevation as well. But shallow knowledge leads to false ideas. To drink deep of the "Pierian spring" will alone bring one face to face with truth and its clear understanding. The blind cannot lead the blind.

Above all, teachers should be religious, God-fearing, Christian men and women. The Bible should be their standard, and religion a part of their lives, not the frothy kind that has only religious vocabulary without a religious experience, but the kind that can stand the light of fiercest scrutiny. Free thought, liberal religious views, as they are termed, may be one's personal right, but for immature minds to be encouraged or led to such exercise is dangerous in the extreme.

The youth who sit at the feet of their teachers to-day are going to do more than anything else to transform the homes of the race, and elevate Negro citizenship. With cultured homes, and schoolrooms presided over by teachers thoroughly fitted for their work, the trend must be upward. With a steady growth in love of high ideals, with profound contempt for idleness, with pride in work, with a deep-rooted horror of crime, a people always moves on to higher lev[els.] Its moral elevation is secured and with it will come that social elevation which must have its genesis within its own ranks.

If the Negro race is to become a dignified, self-respecting, respected people, the change will come largely from the seed sown in thousands of schoolrooms, from the kindergarten to the university, by those whose learning and culture and Christian lives ever make them the most influential power for uplifting that any age can possess.

Howard University's Semi-Centennial

Independent, March 19, 1917, p. 505.

Howard University has just celebrated the fiftieth anniversary of its founding in Washington, D. C. It was March 2, 1867, that the charter was first approved and signed, and from that time, thru all of its fifty years, Howard University has steadily grown, increased its usefulness, making itself felt as an educative force, till it now has an attendance of fifteen hundred students and has become one of the best institutions for Negro education in all the land.

The spirit of General O. O. Howard—its chief founder—in honor of whom the institution was named, is still seen and felt as one moves about the College Campus. Quite all the schools for Negro higher learning, founded in the Sixties, were in one way or another helped and aided by this prince of good men. He breathed into these movements for Negro elevation—movements dear to his heart—a spirit that has ever since actuated them.

The purpose of this Anniversary was twofold: a review of the past, and a prophecy of the half century to come—another fifty years, "with all of its possibilities of increased usefulness."

It was an occasion that brought together some of the best minds that the University has ever sent forth, and many of the leading educators of the country who were not Howard men.

At a meeting in Convention Hall where the presiding officer was ex-Chief Justice Stanton Judkins Peel, president of the Board of Trustees, the speakers included such men as Bishop Thirkield, a former president of the University, Hon. Franklin Lane, Secretary of the Interior, Dr. Carl Kelsey of the University of Pennsylvania and Prof. H. T. Kealing of Western University.

Dr. James Waring presided over another interesting meeting held at the Congregational Church, to commemorate the birth of the University and the signing of its charter. The speakers were President Newman, Prof. Richard T. Greener and others.

A Sociological Conference also formed a part of this anniversary, with such themes as: Negro Homes, The Negro in Business, The Negro in Health and Sanitation, etc.

I am asked what Howard University stands for. The answer is easy: It stands for the high "Educational Ideals" set by its founders, and up to which it has lived, both in the spirit and in the letter. Then, too, the greatness of any institution is measured by its product, by its graduates—their successes and their achievements. And here, I observe that Howard men and women have generally made good.

Philology in General

The Negro Element in Fiction

summary, *Transactions of the American Philological Association* 21
(July 1890): xlii–xliv.

Several papers bearing upon "Negro speech forms" have been read before this and similar associations. But the aim has generally been to set forth the peculiarities of Negro-English, with special reference to orthography, etymology, and occasionally, when written signs would permit, to the sounds and intonations of said speech. In no instance has there been a close and accurate analysis of the same, either as to variety or the probable ground of difference.

The "Negro dialect" is not a symmetrical whole; nor does one set of speech forms represent the untutored Negro throughout the South. It varies in the several states,—in the mountain regions, on the highlands, and on the coast— more widely than that of the whites of those sections: South Carolina, Georgia, Alabama, Mississippi, and Louisiana have each a peculiar phraseology and intonation. In many instances, it requires not only a difference in spelling, but as a matter of fact, a record of these forms is utterly impossible. This is due to indistinct enunciation,—the clipping and dropping of letters, vowels, and consonants. Examples of aphaeresis, metathesis, epithesis, prothesis apocope, syncope, epenthetic insertions, etc., etc., abound in Negro speech.

The word exemp'men' is almost untraceable, so different is it in etymology from the word for which it is used—"discernment." Indeed, it has no etymology, though it is invariably employed by the most ignorant classes of the Southern blacks—especially those of the highlands—to express the idea of keenness of mental vision, or good judgment. Frequently catching a faint sound of a familiar word, the Negro coins a new word to suit his fancy, without regard to the law of verbal formation. Onomatopoeia unconsciously plays an important part in Negro speech. It helps him out of many difficulties, and enables him to express thoughts that otherwise would remain unexpressed. He hears a sound, or sees a sight, and makes a word to indicate the idea conveyed to his mind. It may be a meaningless term or a confused mass of meaningless expressions, yet it serves his purposes, and at once becomes part of his vocabulary. Some forms of the Negro dialect have been traced to early

English; but where the resemblance is sufficient to justify this conclusion, it is accidental and not intentional. It is original and *sui generis*. Like the plantation melodies, it is the product of his own brain.

The majority of fiction-writers ignore this altogether. It is dollars and cents with them. Philology and the philosophy of dialect go for naught. With an impossible hero and an unheard-of dialect, they venture to throw their literary wares upon the market for what they will bring in pennies. "Out de candle" in one section is "blow dem candal out" in another. "Brudder" in one is "bruder" in another, "brer" in another, and "bruffer" in another. Sometimes we hear "brodder."

"I ez bin er wait fer yer" becomes "I bin er wait a fer yer."

"Kum er long mer seestahs an' he'p ring dem chahmin' (charming) bells" is in another locality "Kum lung me seestahs an' he'p ring doze chahmin' bells."[1]

The point I wish to make is that it is absolutely incorrect to regard these speech forms as homogeneous either in orthography or orthoepy.

Joel Chandler Harris, in his introduction to "Nights with Uncle Remus," gives us a very accurate list of a few of the quaint word forms found in "Daddy Jake's" limited vocabulary. I can vouch for their correctness, as I myself have frequently heard the same on the coasts of South Carolina and Georgia.

These are some of the more prominent:—

"B'er"	=	brother.
"Beer"	=	bear.
"Bittle"	=	victuals.
"Bret"	=	breath.
"Churrah"	=	splash.
"Dey"	=	there.
"Dey-dey"	=	here.
"Enty"	=	aint he.
"Gwan"	=	going.
"Leaf"	=	leave.
"Way"	=	where.
"Yent"	=	isn't.
"Wut"	=	what.
"E"	=	he, she, it.
"Ut"	=	earth.
"Ooua"	=	you, all of you.
"Life"	=	live[.]
"Lil, lila"	=	little.
"Lun"	=	learn.
"Sem"	=	same.
"Shum"	=	see them.
"Tam"	=	time.
"Tankee"	=	thank you.
"Tek"	=	take.
"Tink"	=	think.

"Trute"	=	truth.
"Urrer"	=	other.
"T'row"	=	throw.
"Yeddy"	=	hear.
"Turrer"	=	the other.
"Teer"	=	tear.
"Titter"	=	sister.

Without a glossary it cannot be well understood. The letter *r* is almost invariably omitted where it should be used, and used where it should be omitted, as in "*cornder*" for "*corner*," "*dorg*" for "*dog*" and "*gorne*" for "*gone*."

B is generally substituted for *v*, and "*very*" becomes "*bery*," and "*verse*" "*berse*"; "*vault*," "*bault*"; "*vat*," "*bat*"; "*vex*," "*bex*," etc.

Says "Daddy Jack" in the story of "Old Grinny Granny Wolf,"[2] "Ki! I bin want fer see you bery bahd. I bin-a tell you' nunk Jeem' how fine noung mahn you is. 'E ahx wey you no come fer shum. Fine b'y—fine b'y," etc., etc.

In this extract we have "nunk" for "uncle"; "noung" for "young"; "b'y" for "boy."

Joel Chandler Harris, though more consistent than the average magazine writer in the use of dialect forms, is not always correct. The Negro who says *dis, dat, fer, ter, gwine*, etc., etc., would hardly say *you*, in "wut mekky you do dis"; but "wut mekky yo' or yer do dis," etc., etc.

Judge [Albion] Tourg[é]e's characters in "Bricks without Straw," "Fool's Errand," etc., etc., are far from real life so far as it relates to dialect. The same is true of Thomas Nelson Page, and others that I have recently examined.

Some time ago a popular writer and novelist[3] in one of his publications held up the negro clergy by implication, both by expression and portraiture, in a typical negro minister of his own making. The scene of this novel is laid in Charleston; but all who know the Charleston Negro know his tendency to a peculiar prolongation of the *a*-sound, which is neither our *a* in father nor its Italian sound, but rather *a = ae* as *mae* for "ma." Here also we find the *r* inserted where it should be left out, and *w* substituted for the *v*-sound as well as other peculiarities of dialect which Mr. Roe failed to bring out in his portraitures.

Other inconsistencies lie in the putting of "don't[,]" "doan," "don"; "fore," "foah," "fo"; "think," "tink," "tunk"; "dat," "that"; "the," "de," all in the mouth of the same individual, and that too in Charleston.

The following is an example. Words enclosed in marks of parentheses are my own corrections:—

"Now, frens," resumed Mr. Birdsall, "this (dis) 'mergency of (uf) Miss Buggone's health (helf) has (hab) been (ben) met in (en) de right human (humon) and (an') scriptural (scriprel) spirit (speret). Frens and (an') family (fambly) hab gathered roun' de 'flicted one an' hab paid dar (dah) respects ('spects) ter her usefulness (yoosefulniss) an' value (vahlyer) an' hab shown (shawn) her (or shawn 'er) becomin' sympathy (sampatha). Her own family (fambly) as is also (ahs ez alsah) becomin' hab been (ben) first (fus) ter ease her ('er) up accordin', first (fus) to (ter) the (de) law (lawah) of (uf) primige-neshureship. I knows dat dis is (ez) a long word, but (bot) long words of'en mean (means) a (er) heap, an' dat-s why dey are (is) so (s-) long."

This outline sketch is sufficient to determine the object of this paper.

Notes

1 Lines from a Negro melody.

2 *Nights with Uncle Remus*, p. 322.

3 E. P. Roe, in *The Earth Trembled*.

Function and Future
of Foreign Languages in Africa

Methodist Review 76 (November–December 1894): 890–899.

This is a subject of double interest: first, because of its missionary value, and, secondly, because of its linguistic importance. The influx of foreigners to the Dark Continent—missionaries and explorers—gives the African tongues greater prominence than ever before, while at the same time it adds to their philological significance. Africa, therefore, furnishes a field for the solution of some of the knottiest problems known to man, linguistic as well as religious. The future can only determine the outcome. Again, the recent caustic criticism of Max Müller's position relative to the science of language, by America's greatest authority, the late Professor W. D. Whitney, of Yale, adds new interest to the subject of philology, while it demonstrates beyond contradiction that linguistic science is still in a transition state and that it has not yet reached the status of an exact science. Until this shall take place we may expect differences of opinion in regard to many important philological questions. Whether "the science of language is physical or historical, whether roots constitute a spoken language or are phonetic types that never enter into actual speech, whether isolating languages become agglutinative and agglutinative inflectional, whether dialects precede common language or common language dialects, whether the languages of the world have all been derived from one or two primitive centers or whether they have a diversity of origin,"[1] all seem still to be matters of dispute. Yet, so far as the writer's own investigations have gone, the unity of language is just as much a settled fact as the unity of the race; and no one can doubt the latter but the most avowed skeptic.

Max Müller is reported to have said, at the meeting of the International Oriental Congress, that scholars eschew the question "whether it is possible to account for the origin of languages, or rather of human speech in general, because it is one to be handled by philosophers rather than by students of language." As plausible as this theory seems to be, a better view to take of the subject would be to regard the science of language as belonging to both philosopher and philologist; for, though the former may not always be a philologist, yet the latter must in a large sense be a philosopher. It is not the object of this paper, however, to settle disputed points of philology, but rather to offer some suggestions as to the probable outcome of foreign languages in Africa. The arguments that follow will be based on the presumption that the order of linguistic development is from isolating to the agglutinative, from the agglutinative to the inflectional, or the dropping out of existence of present dialects and forms of speech, and the substitution of others of a more advanced character.

It is generally admitted, we believe, that the majority of all the languages known to linguists are for the most part agglutinative in character, or, in other words, that they are nearest the lowest stages of development, if we take root formations as the starting point; and that the inflectional element is represented by only a small proportion of these. If we adopt Professor Sayce's division of the languages of the world and classify the African tongues[2] accordingly, it will be found that the Hottentot Bushman, with all of its dialects and subdialects, belongs to the agglutinative, isolating, and semi-inflectional groups. The Bantu family, with its numerous dialects, is of the prefix-pronominal class. The Negro group, so far as is known, is agglutinative and isolating. The Nuba Fulah family is also agglutinative. The Hamitic and Semitic families are inflectional. Other scattering African tongues are variously classed as agglutinative, isolating, prefix-pronominal, polysynthetic, semi-inflectional, and inflectional. These divisions are not intended to indicate, because certain families are agglutinative or inflectional, that all are alike in form. Members of the same family differ from one another to a greater or less degree, in proportion to the nearness of kinship. It is generally conceded that languages of the same family pass one from another much more easily and readily than those of different families; for example, the agglutinative to the agglutinative, the isolating to the isolating, the semi-inflectional to the semi-inflectional, the inflectional to the inflectional. In speaking of the changes in language Sayce gives three causes for the same: first, imitation, or analogy; secondly, a wish to be clear and emphatic; thirdly, laziness, sometimes referred to as the law of the least effort. Then the same authority adds that, if we choose to go deep enough, we might reduce the three to one—laziness.

This last suggestion should be somewhat modified, as we have numerous examples of peoples and tribes who gave up their native tongue for other reasons than those of laziness. Love of imitation has played an important part in producing linguistic changes; and yet we are forced to believe that necessity is as potent an element in the changes as either imitation, the wish to be emphatic, or the law of the least effort. How far it is true that the Celts of Cornwall, the Wends of Prussia, or the Huns of Bulgaria gave up their own tongue altogether and adopted that of their neighbors simply because of the love of imitation, and that only, is in our opinion an open question. When a pronunciation is once established it remains more or less fixed. When there is a change there is a reason for it, call it what we may. Philologists have noted instances wherein analogy has altered the whole structural complexion of language; and Sayce himself refers to special cases of the same. We give a few examples: the Coptic language was once an affix language, like the Egyptian or the Semitic tongue. It became a prefix language, denoting by prefixes the relations of grammar. This change is thought to be due to the neighboring Berber and cognate dialects. As an illustration of the desire to be clear and emphatic, the Negro Dinka language has been offered as an example. In this tongue the vowel of the singular is lengthened or sharpened to form certain plurals. For example, *ror,* which is the singular for "wood," has *rōr* for a plural; *nom,* "head," has *nim* for its plural; *lib,* "tongue," has *lyep* for its plural; *tut,* "goose," *tuot,* "geese." To form the passive voice of its verbs the "final *i* of the formative elements is lengthened." This "differentiation"[3] is supposed to be for the sake of clearness. It has been asserted that the origin of the tones in the Chinese language is due largely, if not entirely, to the same cause; and this is probably very near the truth.

The third cause of the change in language, which is attributed to laziness, is not so potential in its influence as the other two, except perhaps among the ruder and more barbarous tribes. That dialects and forms of speech have grown out of it is true; but just how far there is no way of deciding. Dialects seem to be the natural outgrowth of language,[4] whatever be the causes; for every tongue seems to have its dialects, numerous or otherwise. Among the Basques, whose country has less than a million of people, there are no less than eight principal dialects, with a number of subordinate ones, many of which are said to be mutually unintelligible. Civilization determines the character of a language; and wherever this is wanting dialects for the most part abound, as the tendency in language in its natural state is toward diversity. Intermarriage of peoples of different tribes and nations is frequently the basis of linguistic changes. Various influences may operate to modify one's speech, as, for example, climate. Diversity of pronunciation in the same country may be frequently accounted for through the agency of climate.

If, as has been said by a well-known English philologist, it is among the speakers of the agglutinative or polysynthetic tongues, when brought into contact with inflectional languages, that the difficulty of change from one family of languages to another is best exemplified, it is by no means easy to state, even approximately, just what will be the outcome of the contact of African tongues with foreign languages. It is evident that the fittest must survive, and that two unlike languages cannot remain together in the same country and in the same community without one's influencing the other. The so-called American Negro dialect is not a fair example of the mixture of tongues. For the negro has been so long removed from his native speech and native influence as to have lost all traces of either. As an outcast in a foreign country he became easily susceptible to whatever linguistic influences were nearest him; and, therefore, without law or order, he garbled up whatever came within reach and made it distinctively his own. [Alexander von] Humboldt tells us that the South American Indians find great difficulty in learning Spanish, and this is said to result from an embarrassment arising from the impediment they meet in attempting to use a language so different in structure from their own. The Chinese come to this country with no knowledge of English whatever; but necessity compels them to acquire some knowledge of the language, and they attempt it. The kind of English we have as a result is sometimes styled "Pigeon" English, which is neither English nor Chinese. In fact, the blending of these two tongues is utterly impossible, as they are too unlike in genius and structure. It is well known that in their attempt at pronouncing English the Chinese give the sound of *l* wherever the sound of *r* occurs in our language; and we are informed that the Japanese do exactly the reverse. In a recent article in *Scribner's Magazine* we are told that this people put *r* in the place of every *l*.

The Hawaiian language is a branch of the Malayo-Polynesian type, and contains only five consonants—*k, l, m, n, p*—with an aspirate *h*, five vowels, and a vocalic *w*. This is a mere skeleton, as compared with the letters and sounds of our own tongue. One can easily conceive of the difficulty that arises when a native attempts to learn English. Notwithstanding these difficulties efforts will always be made, and there will always be a barbarous and imperfect blending of tongues whenever two or more peoples, distinct, like these, in language and thought, are brought together. As a result there will always be a borrowing of words and phrases, of sounds modified or unmodified, until one yields to the other or one becomes extinct.

The influence of civilization is a mighty lever in shaping the destiny of language. Dialects crumble before it, and the diversity of tongues drifts toward unity. The language of the intelligent must supersede, wholly or in part, that of the unintelligent wherever they come in contact, either by displacing it or fashioning it after its own mold. As the weaker languages and dialects of Europe have disappeared before the light of intelligence, so will the languages and dialects of Africa drop out of existence, one by one, it may be, as the same influence shall quicken and permeate the people. One by one will the stronger swallow up the weak, until the speech of the dominant people shall prevail, jargon first, perhaps, extinction later. Doubtless many more dialects than now exist have passed away, some of them leaving not a relic behind to tell the story of their existence, while of others bare skeletons of speech may be found here and there, but hardly enough to indicate their linguistic relations. The forces that produced these changes are still at work, but in a greater degree; and, though we can make no definite statement as to the results growing out of the invasion of Africa by foreign languages, yet again we believe that the inflectional will survive the uninflectional languages of the world. No artificial language can stand the test of time. In fact, it will hardly gain a foothold, but, like Volapük, will die in its infancy.[5]

Of European languages the Portuguese seems to have had the *entrée* first and to have first become fixed in an African colony. In Angola,[6] on the west coast, and Mozambique, on the east, the Portuguese has exerted an influence that has made itself felt, not only upon the natives as a people, but upon the language of the natives. As new ideas sprang up new words were needed to express these ideas; hence, the adoption of new words and expressions of a foreign character. It is said that travelers in the interior have found hundreds of natives who could speak and write Portuguese. Of course, the Portuguese must have undergone some changes and have become corrupted to the extent of receiving the native accent and intonation and the introduction of new words. It is also said that Brazilian immigrants at Lagos speak a corrupted dialect, filtered through America to Africa. Cust mentions a secretary, a native well versed in Portuguese, who had learned it from missionaries. Many of the natives of Ambaka read and write Portuguese; and their children and grandchildren seem to take it up as if it were their own vernacular.[7] The Spanish colonists in Algeria, Ceuta, and Morocco use the Spanish language, and likewise the inhabitants of the Niger delta. But the Spanish has not made the same progress as the Portuguese. This is certainly not due to any great difference between the two languages, so far as their structural relations are concerned, but rather to the lack of activity on the part of Spanish colonists, missionaries, and explorers in making their linguistic influence felt.

The Dutch language has taken hold on Africa, though in a corrupted form. To use the words of Cust, this language "has undergone considerable dialectal degradation, even among the colonists of whole or half blood; and the form of speech spoken by the Bastards, the Orlam, and the Griqua, as well as by the republican Boers, is very different from the Dutch of Holland, the words being corrupt in form, while there is misappropriation of meaning, barbarous modes of expression, and bold defiance of grammar."[8] The French language and the French people hold sway in large portions of Africa and seem to be on the increase in strength and influence. Even now efforts are being made by the French to secure the republic of Liberia. In French colonies French is the language used, whether pure or corrupt. Senegal and Gabun furnish examples of the influence of this tongue. The French Roman Catholic missionaries are active in the spread of the French language. The Italian is likewise widely diffused, especially on the Mediterranean coast. Like other tongues, it is assaulting the native speech where it is weakest. The Germans are pushing themselves and their language into the interior as far as possible and are determined not to be in the rear. The German authorities have instructed their agents to compile dictionaries of all the native languages spoken in their colonies. The influence and power of these compilations must be the same as those of all similar compilations, and in the end must serve to make the strong stronger and the weak weaker. The influence of missionaries, numerous translations of the Bible in African tongues, and commercial relations must in some way operate in the interest of the foreign languages.

The English language, more powerful than any of its competitors, is vying with its rivals and has made commendable progress wherever English-speaking representatives have found an entrance on African shores. Its influence is felt, not only upon native speech, but upon its rival sister languages as well. In West and South Africa, on the east coast, and in the interior English-speaking missionaries are found in large numbers. In many cases the English is the only medium of communication between native ex-slaves and English-speaking people. Churches, schools, and other agencies for disseminating light and truth dot English-speaking colonies. Cust says:

"Travelers allude to the jargon of Sierra Leone English, and state that the people of Lagos speak a patois of English which closely approximates to Yariba; and the Krumen, so largely employed in English vessels, speak a form of the English language difficult to describe; that the Grebo tribes speak an Anglo-African jargon for purposes of traffic, which is made up of native idioms interwoven with broken English words."[9]

Under such circumstances what may be the future speech of the natives remains to be seen. Possibly the native tongue may after a while become extinct and the interloper, in this as in other instances, take complete sway.

Albert S. Gat[s]chet, of the United States Bureau of Ethnology, has on several occasions discussed the nature and peculiarities of the North American languages before the American Philological Association.[10] In this paper on the affinity of the Cherokee to the Iroquois dialects Mr. Gat[s]chet calls attention to the fact that in illiterate languages, like those of the North American Indian, one and the same term may be correctly pronounced in six or ten or twelve different ways, on account of the alternation or permutability of certain sounds. Then he calls attention to a phonetic law by which one may successfully compare vocables belonging to different languages. Suffice it, however, to say that, difficult as the task may seem, some of these Indians have learned to speak English well enough to make themselves understood, notwithstanding the low degree of civilization which they have attained. The Grebos of Africa are very low in the scale of civilization and possess a dialect so rude that, to indicate the person and tense of their verbs, they make use of gesticulations. Yet there is no reason, if these people or their descendants are only brought under proper influence and proper training, why they, too, may not adopt a new tongue totally unlike their own. We may not be able to conceive of such a tongue at present; but the time may, and we believe will, come when even the Grebo dialect will become extinct and when the people themselves will adopt a new tongue and become, through the power of the Gospel, a new nation in character and language.

We know the law of history, that a conquered nation always forsakes its own tongue for that of the conquerors when the latter are superior in civilization. The Celts who lived in Gaul in the time of Cæsar's invasion did so. On the other hand, when the Germans later invaded the same country they forsook their own speech for that of the conquered but more civilized foe. In Africa we find few armies, as a rule, to enforce the acceptance of any language. Then, too, such armies as there are include a large native contingent. But we do find, in every instance where a foreign tongue has been effectually introduced by an army, that the latter has been superior in civilization to the natives. In Africa, besides, there are no contending classes among the foreign element—an upper and a lower—bringing in two dialects, a literary and a common one, and so lengthening the period before either the native or the foreign must inevitably perish. Missionary and similar efforts, affecting commercial and social relations, make the crystallization of anything that can be called a permanent form of speech likely, from another standpoint, to be extremely slow. The native character in its varied phases is to be considered, as

244

also the fact that the assaults upon the native dialects, though many and from various points and oft repeated, are not delivered with a force determined to conquer, as in the instances we have mentioned. Christianity modifies all warfare, whether it be that of arms or of tongues; and so long as it is not the sole purpose, except in a few instances, to subdue the native tribes, we may expect any movement of change to be one of no very great rapidity.

If we take a still broader and more comprehensive view of language and its influence in all foreign countries to-day we may see the creeping movement of some toward a more universal use than others. While we are not prepared with statistics, we state on the authority of others that the English tongue is gaining a foothold over all others. Be this as it may, the very idea suggests a new difficulty—another knot in the problem before us. If the foreign languages in Africa do so influence the native speech that out of the two grows another new tongue, what influence will these foreign tongues have upon each other during this transformation? Shall we have a new set of dialects or of tongues, which in turn will be called upon to coalesce in their future history by conquering armies, as instanced in the birth of the French language; or will there be such a radical change as to cause existing native tongues to drop out of existence and the almost bodily adoption of the most powerful of the foreign languages?

If one can be said to reach a conclusion in what, from present data, must be largely looked upon as an inconclusive discussion, we may hazard the prediction from what we have before us, judging the present by the past, as to the history of peoples and the history of language, that there will come a day in the march of civilization through the Dark Continent when the agglutinative tongues of the natives, with others, will yield to the more powerful inflectional tongues of foreigners; that the former will become extinct as such, new languages being built up, modified, as in the past, according to all the rules we know to have affected the changing speech of mankind—by necessities, environments, and the strength of the characteristics residing in the peculiar native sounds; and that the areas of these new tongues will in turn be enlarged by conflict and conquest among themselves. In short, the partition of Africa among the nations of the earth has brought this powerful factor of language as a compelling force in all the movements. Africa, on its way to a higher civilization, must and shall tread in the footsteps of Europe, only that the onward march will be a more vigorous and attractive one, lighted up by the arts and sciences of the present high civilization of the intruding powers which have transferred their tongues to its shores; and so, at length, the ancient glory of this continent, so long asleep, shall return to it with all this added modern splendor, so that it shall vie with America, the two being the greatest theaters of future events, as the trend of the present flow of immigration, on the one hand, to America, and, on the other, of conquest and new possession in Africa, would clearly indicate.

Notes

1 [A. H.] Sayce, Science of Language [London: C. K. Paul, 1880].

2 See also special articles on the languages of Africa in the proceedings of the Ethnological Congress on Africa.

3 Sayce.

4 This view presupposes that language precedes dialects.

5 [Volapük, a world language based on English, German, and Latin, was invented in 1879 by Johann Martin Schleyer (1831–1912).]

6 [Robert Needham] Cust's *Modern Languages of Africa* [1883].

7 [*Modern Languages of Africa*], p. 44.

8 *Modern Languages of Africa*, p. 44.

9 [*Modern Languages of Africa*], p. 47. On mixed jargons, see Sayce, Whitney, and Max Müller.

10 [The papers of Albert S. Gatschet (1832–1907) in *Transactions of the American Philological Association* are "On the Syllabic Reduplication as Observed in Indian Languages, and the Klamath Language of Southwestern Oregon in Particular," 10 (1879): 35–37; "On the Substantive Verb in Some North American Languages," 15 (1884): xxvi–xxxiii; "On the Affinity of the Cheroki to the Iroquois Dialects" 16 (1885): xl–xlv; and "Sex-denoting Nouns in American Languages," 20 (1889): 159–171.]

Notes on the Function of Modern Languages in Africa

summary, *Transactions of the American Philological Association* 27
(July 1896): xlvi–xlviii.

It seems to be a universal law that a conquered people shall forsake its own speech for that of the conquerors,—provided the latter are superior in civilization, culture, and refinement. The Kelts in the time of Cæsar's invasion did so. While, on the other hand, the Germans, who later invaded the same country, forsook their own language for that of the conquered but more civilized race. The French language, like the Italian, Spanish, and Portuguese, is derived from the popular Latin,—like them it is the "product of the slow development of the common Roman speech."

The phonetic changes observed in the development or decadence of a language may be attributed in part to the structure of the vocal organs as well as to the difference in race or climate. All of these have their influence. As examples, we note the Langue d'Oïl and the Langue d'Oc of north and south Gaul respectively. What is true here is true elsewhere. What is true of Europe, of America, is true of Africa under the same or similar conditions. It is the survival of the fittest whether in the realm of linguistics or of animal life. Civilization is the mighty power that shapes the destiny of language. Dialects crumble before it and diversity of tongues drift toward unity. The stronger will swallow up the weaker until the speech of the dominant people prevails; jargon at first, perhaps, extinction later.

From an early period, from the time that African ethnology, African linguistics, African folklore, began to attract the attention of ethnologists and philologists to any considerable extent, a scheme of classification of these African speech forms has been a matter of serious study. But in an unexplored field like this, however, difficulties of an insuperable character are wont to arise, making it impossible to arrive at anything definite. A classification of these on a purely scientific basis seems out of the question. Dialects and sub-dialects, the product of ignorance and environment, are so numerous that philologists are baffled to find a starting-point.

247

It is not straining a point to declare that the native African is a linguist of no mean sort—that many of them speak several languages and dialects apart from their own; even the rudest of them seeming to pick up speech wherever they find it. As an example we may mention the Veys and the Deys, the Golahs and the Pessas from the interior, who, from contact with foreign-speaking people, and especially the English, learn the language of their superiors sufficiently to converse intelligently with foreign residents. The Krumen may be taken as another example. Both the Kru and the Grebo tribes belong to the agglutinative speaking class. In the language of [Robert Needham] Cust, "travelers allude to the jargon of Sierra Leone English, and state that the people of Lagos speak a patois of English which closely approximate to Yariba."

Clicks form a curious linguistic feature of the Hottentot group. Sayce speaks of an unpronounceable click not otherwise found in the language, as associated with the folk story of a hare, which story in turn is traced from the Bari of Central Africa, through Melagasy, Swahili, Kaffir, Hottentot, back to the Bushmen. It is well to note here that these clicks are found in connection with beast fables of the backward tribes of southern Africa. He refers to them as the bridge that marks the passage of inarticulate cries into articulate speech; "we may see in them survival of those primeval utterances out of which language was born." Herodotus says of the Ethiopian Troglodytes (IV. 183): γλῶσσαν δὲ οὐδεμιῇ ἄλλη παρομοίην νενομίκασι ἀλλὰ τετρίγασι κα[τ]ά περ αἱ νυκτερίδες. These clicks are expiratory sounds, consonantal in their character. I prefer the classification into dentals, palatals, and laterals, of the three out of the four found in the Hottentot speech. These three clicks are also found in Zulu and in the speech of other tribes who seem to have caught them by contagion. I have found natives of Ama-Xosa, Ba-Suto, Tembu, Zulu, and what is called the Fingo tribe, who spoke English fairly well, using these same clicks—all of which are difficult for a foreigner to incorporate with any readiness into the word he wishes to utter.

C, *q*, and *x* are the characters that the English translator has made use of to represent these clicks. *C* stands for the dental, *q* for the palatal, and *x* for the lateral. The letter *c*, as found in the word *ncapai*, is to our ear nearly like the sound produced by a kiss; but it is made by the compression of the tip of the tongue between the teeth and then drawing it back in haste. The sound represented by *q* is made by placing the tongue against the roof of the mouth and then withdrawing it quickly—the effect being a cracking sound. The letter *x*, representing the third of these clicks, corresponds to the sound we use in clucking to a horse—the tongue unites with the double teeth as in the pronunciation of the word *box*. This sound, in common with the others, does not come at the close of a word, but before the vowels as we find it in the tribal name Ama-Xosa. These clicks are never found in the formative part of a word. The fourth sound in the Hottentot speech, referred to above, not a click proper, is guttural, from the bottom of the throat—rough, and made by contracting the throat, while forcibly expelling the breath, and moving the epiglottis so as to modify it tremulously. It seems almost impossible to be

248

made except by natives. These can drop it with seeming ease, so far as I have observed, and substitute the English sounds for *c*, *q*, and *x*, pronouncing words containing them without hesitancy.

Of all the European people the Portuguese were the first to become established on African soil. Their language soon became fixed and exerted an influence over the native speech that quickly determined the future of the latter. *Piccaninny* is Portuguese in its origin, but of African mold. It is what some would call a loan word incorporated into the native speech. It seems to be from *picade niño* or *pequeño niño, a little infant*. Sifted through the African speech it comes out *piccaninny*, a term that is often applied in the Carolinas and on the coast to a negro child. *Palaver* is Spanish from *palabra*, and usually denotes idle talk or gossip, but, like *piccaninny*, it too became an incorporate part of the native speech, taking on the form, accent, and peculiarities of the same in parts where the Spanish is predominant. The terms for *knife* in the Basque language are all loan words so called—*e.g. ganibeta*, from the French *canif*, and *nabala* from the Spanish *nabaja* (*novacula*—Latin).

As the result of these mixed speech forms we note the jargon of the negro of the Danish West Indies. It is a specimen of broken Danish and is sometimes called Creolese. It seems to have neither gender, number, declension, nor conjugation. Another example is found in the negro-English Dutch, which includes also words from the Spanish, Portuguese, and French.

Thus it will be seen that in the changes resulting from blending all these tongues, the speech forms of the more intelligent survive, though the process of development is slow.

Creole Folk-Tale: Compair Bouki and Compair Lapin

Southern Workman 25 (September 1896): 186.

The word "compair" has the same meaning as our word confederate, an accomplice in some trickery, a pal. Bouki is a the goat, the incarnation of stupidity, as the rabbit, Lapin, is the emblem of cunning. "Compair" has the same force in the creole stories that Brer has in the stories of Uncle Remus. The rabbit and the goat are major characters in creole animal tales. I have selected this story from a number of Bouki and Lapin tales gathered by Prof. [Alcée] Fortier of Tulane University, La.

One day, quite early, Compair Lapin arose, and he felt hunger gaining upon him. He looked everywhere in the cabin and there was nothing to eat. He ran to Compair Bouki and found him gnawing a bone. "Eh, Compair Bouki, I had come to take breakfast with you but I see you have nothing famous to offer me."

"The times are hard, Compair Lapin, there are no more rations in the cabin, only this bone left.["] Compair Lapin thought over it a bit[.] "Well Compair Bouki, if you wish, we shall go hunting for the eggs of the tortoise[.]" "Agreed, let us go right off[.]" Compair Bouki took his basket and his hoe, and they started towards the bayou in the woods. "Compair Lapin, I don't often go hunting for tortoise eggs; I don't know well how to find them." "Don't trouble yourself, Compair Bouki[.] I find all the time a place where tortoise lay their eggs. You will dig them up."

When they arrived at the bayou, Compair Lapin walked slowly, looking well on this side and on that. Soon he came to a dead stop: "Compair Bouki, the tortoise thinks she is cunning. She scratches the ground with her big paw, and she lays her eggs in a hole, then she puts a little sand on them, and then she scatters leaves on her nest. You see this hillock? Take off the leaves, and scratch with your hoe, sure you will find eggs." Compair Bouki did what Compair Lapin told him, and they saw a pile of eggs shining in that hole. "Compair Lapin, you are more cunning than I: I am very glad to have you as my friend." Compair Lapin shared the eggs, he gave half to Compair Bouki.

250

"Compair Bouki, I am very hungry, I am going to eat my eggs immediately."
["]Do as you want, Compair Lapin, I shall take them to my wife to have them cooked."

They went on a long time still, and they found many eggs. Compair Lapin always ate his, Compair Bouki did not like raw eggs; he put them all in his basket. "Compair Bouki, I am beginning to be tired: I believe it is time for us to return home." "I have enough eggs for today. Compair Lapin, let us go back." As they were going towards the river Compair Lapin said to himself: "Compair Bouki does not know how to find tortoise eggs, it is I who found them, they ought all to belong to me. I must make some trick to gain them." As they were nearly arrived at the river, Compair Lapin said: "Compair Bouki, I forgot to take some eggs for old mother. You would be very kind to lend me a dozen. I shall return them to you another time." Compair Bouki gave a dozen, and they went each on his way. Compair Lapin went to put his dozen of eggs in his cabin, then he went to Compair Bouki's. When he came near the cabin of Compair Bouki he began to complain and to hold his stomach with both hands. Compair Bouki came out. "What is the matter with you, Compair Lapin? You don't look well." "Oh, no, Compair Bouki, those eggs have poisoned me."

"I beg of you: quick, run to get the doctor." "I shall run as fast as I can, daddy." As soon as Compair Bouki started, Compair Lapin went to the kitchen and fell to eating tortoise eggs. "Thank you, great Lord, I shall eat to the full today. The physician lives far; I have the time to eat all, before they come." When Compair Lapin had nearly finished eating the eggs, he heard Compair Bouki speaking outside. "Doctor Macaque (Doctor Monkey.) I am very glad that I met you on the road, my friend is very sick." Compair Lapin did not lose any time, he opened the window and jumped out. Compair Bouki came into the cabin: he did not see [C]ompair Lapin. He ran into the kitchen; the shells of the eggs were scattered all about. Compair Lapin was already in the fields. Compair Bouki tore his hair, he was so angry. He started to run after Compair Lapin. Compair Lapin had eaten so many eggs, that he was not able to run fast. When he saw Compair Bouki was pressing him too close, he hid in the hole of a tree.

Compair Bouki called Compair Torti (Tortoise) who was passing on the road. "Compair Torti, pray come to watch Compair Lapin who stole all your eggs. I am going to get my ax to cut down this tree." "Go quickly Compair Bouki, I shall watch the rascal well." When Compair Bouki started Compair Lapin said: "Compair Torti, look in this hole, you will see if I have your eggs[.]" Compair Torti lifted his head, Compair Lapin sent some decayed wood into his eyes[.] Compair Torti went to wash his eyes in the bayou; Compair Lapin ran off immediately. Compair Bouki came to cut the tree, he saw that Compair Lapin had already run away. He was so angry, he went to Compair Torti on the bank of the bayou, and he cut off his tail with his ax. *It is for this reason that the tail of the tortoise is so short to this very day.*

Folklore and Ethnology: Old Saws

Southern Workman 25 (October 1896): 206.

In the opening paragraph of the Folk-Lore Department of the SOUTHERN WORKMAN for September reference was made to the proverbs cited by Prof. Scarborough as being much in vogue among the colored people. One of them was quoted then as the point of illustration in a story. In the following lines we give the others, in Prof. Scarborough's own words.

Proverbs and sayings from Africa and the West Indies.

A pullet always tells where she lays her first egg. (Noisy).
An open door lets in many visitors. (Too free).
When trouble sleeps don't wake it. (Caution).
The tongue of a liar has no bone.
What goes over the back comes under the belly. (Retribution).
Feed the devil with a long spoon (Keep away).
If we lie down with dogs we must rise up with fleas.
If you make yourself an ass the world will ride you.
The man who gets up early fin's de way short.
To have tarry fingers. (Thievish).
He keeps his neighbor's chair too warm.
When a cock-roach makes a dance he nebber invites neighbor fowl.
    (Not too familiar with an enemy).
A chip nebber jumps fur form de block.
If you have a lame toe keep out of a fight.
A tale-bearer keeps the pot boiling.
A locked jaw-bone 's sure to be out of trouble.
When the dumb speaks he is more furious than the devil.
A crooked foot makes a crooked step.
"Greedy chokes puppy." (Ambitious one grasps so much it gripes.)
Trouble-tree nebber blossoms.
If you are in rags keep from fire.
Good fungi never meets with good pepper pot.

Disobedience will drink water with his hands tied to his back.

Walk with a crooked stick until you can get a straight one.
(Contentment).

The pebble at the bottom of the river never feels when the sun is hot. (Unsympathetic).

Give the glutton a dull knife to eat with.

The master holds the handle of the knife but the servant the blade. (Yield).

One pumpkin bothers the basket. (Balance—companionship).

Always leave an egg in the nest.

The eye never sees what the chin does.

When you see the shore strewed with weeds be sure a storm is coming.

When the whale comes on the surface be sure the sea is rough below.

When an alligator comes and tells you news in the river, believe him.

Creole Proverbs

I shall show you who I am.

Great to speak, little to do.

One goes everywhere with fine clothes.

Ox who comes first always drinks clear water.

That is not the baptism of a doll. (No laughing matter).

When the tree falls the goat climbs it.

The best swimmer is often drowned.

When one is very hungry one does not peel the sweet potato.

His tongue knows no Sunday.

I keep nothing hidden in the sideboard. (To keep nothing back).

These have largely their counterpoint in the French tongue, and we may find variants of some of them in various parts of the country here. Of course they lack the quaintness of the creole patois, which is as much needed as a proper setting for these proverbs, in order to show their genuineness, as is the dialect of "Uncle Remus" in Mr. Harris' tales, a necessity to the naturalness of those stories.

I have also selected a few scattering proverbs and sayings, picked up at random, which I am not able to refer to any particular locality; but which may serve to enlarge the collections being made, and, at last, find their place of *being* if not of *birth*.

Set your type before you go and then read it (Have on the tongue what one is going to say).

To be briggity. (Uppish, forward).

To be a regular fly-up-the-creek. (Speaking of one who is uneasy, restless, wild, erratic).

A swampy lookin' pusson.

To have "zemptment." (Discernment, energy, judgment, forethought).

To feed with a long spoon. (To be cautious).

I don' care what ye say, nothin' 'bout it; come day, go day, God sent Sunday with me. (God sends rest day)[.]

Nev'r min'. Dog wants bone more'n once. (Want friends more'n once).

He says every thing but his prayers; them he whispers. (Loose tongued, trifling).

Don't set horses. (Don't agree).

To open her wallet. (To tell all she knows).

To swap the devil for the witch. (To make no improvement in exchange).

Don't bite your tongue. (Say just what you think).

To leave a body in the suds. (To leave one in trouble).

To sing small. (Not to be too conspicuous).

"Mitey-bitey.["] (Good by).

An old formula that children were required to say after meals, has been given me by a friend as belonging to old Virginia times:

"Got 'nough, got plenty,
Don' want no more;
Tank e Lawd, Tank e ma'am,"

This was to be ended with a "churchy," as it was called—a funny little bob of the body in ludicrous imitation of the curtsey.

To wall eyes. (To show the white part of the eye—indicating displeasure).

Negro Folk-lore and Dialect

Arena (January 1897): 186–192.

Three things are looked upon as having contributed to the decline of folk-lore: (1.) Scientific ideas and explanations. These appeal to the judgment and reason, and cause a spread of intelligence that repudiates the idea of being governed by or of indulging in observances or customs that would in any way imply that one was a believer in them. (2.) The clergy, who as a rule have swept away as fast as possible a belief in that which has to do with the supernatural aside from pure religion itself and its accompanying faith. (3.) The great changes that come to a people when civilization takes hold upon it. Commingling, change and improvement in conditions, all conduce to the stamping out of these ideas which we d[e]nominate now under one general head as folk-lore.

Folk-lore in its broadest sense is a record of a people's history. Trench tells us that the word recently borrowed from the German as a substitution for the long and Latinized popular superstitions must be esteemed an unquestionable gain. A knowledge of it aids to a better understanding of all that is ancient in the life of a people. It helps the archæologist, the linguist, the philosopher, and the historian, each in his own line of operation.

But what folk-lore does in general, negro folk-lore does in particular. Here especially the negro has a field to himself, and he should take pride in it, in any effort, to accumulate and give to the world such of the tales, sayings, superstitions, and observances as will throw light upon and best illustrate the evolution of his race.

It is to be regretted that the negro himself seems to stand aloof from anything that connects him with his past. As a consequence we are without much that he knows and could use with advantage to all concerned with reference to his own life and history. He fails to appreciate the importance of such knowledge to the world at large. But it is just what one might expect under the circumstances. He is not wholly to be blamed.

The negro has to-day a rich field for exploration and research; but, set in the midst of a civilization such as we find on the brink of the twentieth century, what is done to preserve these queer, quaint, odd sayings, expressions, and superstitions with the accompanying dialect must be done quickly or else they will be swept away and completely obliterated by the growing intelligence of the descendants of the race, which is now a little over thirty years removed from bondage. Rich will be the record of this people when its full history shall be written in the light of the civilization of the future.

Negro folk-lore is enhanced by negro speech forms, characterized as they are by metaphors, figures, similes, imaginative flights, humorous designations, saws, and sayings. His speech is replete with archaisms, obsolete usage of words, many things that go to form a dialect and which add to its attractiveness in many ways. But there is one thing that makes it exceedingly difficult for the student who seeks for that which is distinctively the heritage of the negro,—that is, the ready adoption by the race of what may properly be called Southernisms as distinguished from expressions and sayings such as are used in other localities of our country. This is true in large measure wherever two races have had many years of life together within a country. The superstitions, the proverbs of the one are more or less sure of readaptation by the other. Yet it is true that the very quaintness of the negro speech has often converted common sayings into gems of originality by the new setting, so to speak, that it gives them. This we shall see to be true in Louisiana, where the Creole proverbs are largely borrowed from the French. We find, too, a similar adaptation in the proverbs—many of them—which are the property of the Bermudan negro.

Prof. Harrison, in a paper on Negro English read before the American Philological Association at Yale College some years ago, truthfully observed that the negro has a talent for dealing with hyperbole, rhymes, picture words, like the poet; his slang being not mere word distortion, but his verbal breath of life, caught from his surroundings and wrought up by him into wonderful figure-speech.[1] It is also true that, as the same authority further observes, the negro humor and naïveté are features not to be overlooked; that much of his talk is baby talk; that he has as well a power of indescribable intonation. In speaking of the negro further he says what we know to be true of all people in a primitive state of development, that to him "all nature is alive, anthropomorphized as it were, replete with intelligence, the whispering, tinkling, hissing, booming, muttering, zooning around him are full of mysterious hints and suggestions which he produces in words that imitate often strikingly the poetic and multiform messages which nature sends through his auditory nerve, thus bringing that onomatopoetic element into his speech found the world over in speech beginning. The primitive negro is on intimate terms with the wild animals and birds, with the flora and fauna of the wild stretches of pine woods among which for generations his habitation has been pitched. His mind is yet in the stage in which ready belief is accorded to the wrangle of shovel and tongs, the loves and hates of dish and platter on the kitchen shelves, the naïve personification of the furniture of his cabin; and for him rabbits and wolves, terrapins and turtles, buzzards and eagles, live lives no less full of drama and incident, of passion and marvels, than his own kith and kin gathered around the pine knot or the hickory fire."

Prof. Harrison of course is describing, and that, too, admirably, the characteristics of a generation passing away, the generation in fact that came up under the dispensation of slavery, that was so situated as to be kept in a primitive stage for a long time, considering its close proximity to the circle of civilization just without its limits. In short we have had, as it were, primitive man with his ideas, beliefs, and all pertaining thereto at the very doors of learning some two centuries or more. The only wonder is that scholarship has not sooner seized hold upon his life and investigated it as illustrative of such life since creation.

It is not the present generation that furnishes us the folk-lore of the race, though it must be largely the gleaners and preservers of it. It is not the present generation which pins its faith on spells and witches, charms and dreams and signs. Much superstition may cling to it, it is true; in fact, will cling as among the most highly civilized; for even at the acme of civilization no people has been known to have freed itself entirely from all the bonds of superstition cast about it by its forebears in primitive days. So we acknowledge that the negro is not so far away to-day from these primitive influences that here and there may not be noted the out-cropping of early beliefs to be seen in old observances and customs, especially in those localities where ignorance has not given way to intelligence and learning.

We find this true in Hayti, in various parts of Africa; it is seen also in Bermuda and among the Creole population in Louisiana; while nearer home there are those isolated spots where superstition lingers as evidenced in both speech and action. These then are the best fields for the student of folk-lore.

"Very many of the sayings found in the Southern States, especially in the South Atlantic States, are traceable to the Elizabethan usage of the early settlers, and in that respect resemble in expression, in archaistic pronunciation, in obsolescent forms, similar ones found as well in Eastern States of the North." The negro not only distorted his words already at hand, but he formed new ones as we have before intimated. He has been truly a Mrs. Partington in his ingenuity and facility along this line.[2] Taking both these facts together, I feel safe in asserting that the negro's natural gift for language, for word using, added to his opportunities, modified in turn by his lack of advantages, would in time have resulted in a new tongue nearly as correctly formed according to the rules that govern the formation of a new language, as were the Romance languages of Europe, of which the French, the Italian and Spanish are most prominent types. Such might have been the probability had no revolution in his status taken place.

In a paper on the French language in Louisiana, Prof. Alcée Fortier makes the following observation:[3]

> While speaking of the French language in Louisiana it is necessary to say a few words about that very peculiar dialect, if it may be called so, spoken by the negroes in lower Louisiana. It is quite interesting to note how the ignorant and simple Africans have formed an idiom entirely by the sound, and we can understand, by studying

the transformation of the French into the negro dialect, the process by which Latin, spoken by the uncivilized Gauls, became our own French. However ridiculous the negro dialect may appear, it is of importance to the student of philology, for its structure serves to strengthen the great laws of language, and its history tends to prove how dialects have sprung from one original language and spread all over the word. The negro's language partakes necessarily of his character, and is sometimes quaint and almost simple. The plantation songs are quite poetical, charming in their oddity. There is no established orthography for the negro French, and this obscure dialect of a Romance tongue is written like the Spanish without regard to etymology and simply by the sound, though the letters in passing from the language to the dialect have not kept their original value.

What we are pleased to call negro dialect, however, is, as Rudyard Kipling would say, another story;[4] yet I venture to point out some of the peculiarities belonging to it—the leading principles of all language formation, which strengthen my conviction about the possibilities of a new tongue evolved by the negro. It also seems pertinent that I should make this point, as the varied forms of folk-lore lose much of their native strength when separated from the accompanying dialect which is the characteristic part; and, too, a proper appreciation of both folk-lore and dialect forms of speech can only be obtained from an understanding of some of the causes that lead to dialect formation the world over.

The negro has simply done as other races—applied the principle of mishearing or *otosis*, as the late Prof. Haldeman of Pennsylvania has termed it.[5] He was further helped to perpetuate this by analogy. In short, he put in practice all the principles linguists classify under aphæresis, when he said *'possum* for *opossum*; under prothesis, when he said *year* for *ear*; under syncope, when he said *cur'us* for *curious*; under epenthesis, when he said *cornder* for *corner*; under apocope, when he said *fiel'* for *field*; under epithesis, when he said *clost* for *close*; under transposition, when he said *ax pervishun* for *ask provision*. These initial and final clippings from words, initial and final additions, medial additions and clippings and transpositions are all found when any ignorant people attempts to speak the tongue of another people with which it is wholly unfamiliar. These belong to the law of mispronunciation; though we would not be understood as saying that they constitute that law, whose strength lies more particularly along the transmutation of sound.

But to return to folk-lore proper. I may add that the interest that has been recently aroused by the investigation of philologists and folk-lorists in this special field is meeting with a general response by many—even among the negroes themselves—who have hitherto paid little or no attention to the subject. I remember, years ago, that the ceremony of "foot-wash" was held in great repute by the negroes of the South—a ceremony which they as industriously performed in their own peculiar, odd, quaint way as it is possible to imagine.

It was as much an occasion of merriment for some as it was a part of the religion of others. To enjoy it one has to see it. A mere description of it fails to convey to the reader what it actually was, and is,—for it is by no means an obsolete custom to-day. The singing and the exhorting are all in the dialect, making the whole affair one of intense interest to the on-looker.

Negro superstitions, beliefs, and sayings hold an equal place with their customs. Signs and omens are innumerable and are religiously observed. The power of witches, witch doctors, and charms gains ready credence. Many of all these are a bequest from African forefathers, while many others have descended to them, as has been noted, through the French in Louisiana and through the Elizabethan influence in other more northeasterly localities. Indeed, some of the charms of these last named are very like those of the early English as seen in the Riddles of Cynewulf. It is true that in either case the native African depends upon oracles, and pins his faith closely to the responses that come from the chosen source of consultation. Geographically speaking, the ancient African was not so far away from Delphi and its oracles; and it opens up a field for considerable conjecture as to whether there was not an influence that filtered down through the ages cropping out in what we may be pleased, perhaps, to call a more degenerate form, as shown in the prophecies of certain soothsayers of the present day among the negroes of this country.

One story will illustrate the credence placed in "hag-riding," as well as show the use of charms or spells and the use of dialect in the telling:

"Yaas, hags is folks sho' 'nuff. I done seed 'em wid dese two eyes. One ole hag dun rid dis chile twell I'se so crawney dat yoh could er seed de bones. I tried eb'ryting. I done put cork in de bottles in de middle ob de floh, den I done put down co'n an' peppah, but dere wan' no res'. Den someting done tole me ter tek de Bible an' put it undah my haid an' tek my shoes off an' tu'n de toes f'um de bed an' dat ole hag she can' jump ober it. Sho' 'nuff dat night it comes jes' lak befo' an' it couldn' jump, an' it stood dar twell day crep slam onter it, so I could er seed it; an', honey, it wan' nobody but Sis Jimson, she dat libs jinin' me. Oh, yaas, ole hags 's people des lak we is."

I append a few sayings that are current in Africa:

"The man who gets up early finds the way short."

"When a cockroach makes a dance, he never invites neighbor fowl."

"The tongue of a liar has no bone."

"Trouble tree never blossoms."

"Good fungi never meets with good pepper pot."

Signs for bad or good luck are numerous, as well as the movements necessary to avert the former. "Ef yer dream ob aigs an' dere ain' none broke, trow salt in de fire soon nex' mornin' or dar gwine be er mighty big fuss; but ef some is broke den de fuss done broke." "Ef yer dream yer teeth's fallin' out, yo'll hear ob a death; an' ef dey be eyeteeth 'twell be in de fambly." No charm seems to be given to prevent this. But again, a specific cure for backache is "when yer hears de firs' hooper-will holl'n, ter git down an' roll on de groun'."

But whether in stories, sayings, signs, or songs, whatever form these characteristic expressions take, there is that quality of nearness to nature and her secrets that we find common to folk-lore the world over. The negro, too, is as epigrammatic in his way as any race, and there is at the bottom of the curiously wrought phrases a fund of sound common sense that shows keenness of insight, a penetrative quality of mind that some are averse to allowing the race as a whole.

The gathering in of this store of material for the use of the future philologist and antiquarian is as yet in its infancy; still with the American Dialect Society interesting itself, the Folk-lore Society actively bestirring itself in this direction and, in turn, levying upon all sources of information through schools and their numerous colored students, there is no reason why valuable additions may not be made to the vast stores already accumulated in the line of the folk-lore of the world's peoples, and thus, incidentally at least, make plain to the negro himself that he has a history of his own in more ways than one.

Notes

1 [James A. Harrison (1848–1911), "Negro English," *Proceedings of the American Philological Association* 16 (1885): xxxi–xxxii. The paper was excerpted from Harrison's "Negro English," *Anglia* 7 (1884): 232–279. See also *Autobiography*, 93–94, 105, 107, and 151.]

2 [Created by Benjamin Penhallow Shillaber (1814–1890), "Mrs. Partington" is a caricature who misuses words.]

3 ["The French Language in Louisiana and the Negro-French Dialect," *Transactions of the Modern Language Association* 2 (1884–1885): 96–111.]

4 [See the first paragraph in Rudyard Kipling (1865–1936), "By Word of Mouth," in *Indian Tales* (New York: Lovell, Coryell, 1890).]

5 [Samuel Stehman Haldeman (1812–1880), professor of comparative literature at the University of Pennsylvania, quoted from Harrrison's American Philological Association paper, p. xxxi.]

Iphigenia in Euripides and Racine

summary, *Transactions of the American Philological Association* 29
(July 1898): lviii–lx.

In viewing the character presented by these two poets, similar scenes are to be compared most closely.[1] The first meeting between father and child, the shock of surprise which comes to Iphigenia upon learning her destined fate, and the announcement of her final resolve to resign herself to it—these afford the basis of proper comparison.

Euripides in the first depicts a happy, care-free, dependent child, unburdened by affairs of the state—one whose questions indicate not only ignorance of existing conditions, but the most childish curiosity concerning them, one upon whom the sense of a father's uneasiness is forced because so very apparent (633–676).

> ὦ μῆτερ, ὑποδραμοῦσά σ᾽, ὀργισθῇς δὲ μ[ή],
> πρὸς στέρνα πατρὸς στέρνα τἀμὰ περιβαλῶ.
> ἐγὼ δὲ βούλομαι τὰ σὰ στέρν᾽, ὦ πάτερ, *etc.*

Racine introduces her as a more mature, more dignified maiden (Act ii. Sc. ii: 531–536, sq.), keenly observant of her father's uneasiness, seeking to divine the motive (Act ii. Sc. ii: 554, 559), and filled with filial love and pride, for example:

> Vous vous cachez, Seigneur, et semblez soupirer;
> Tous vos regards sur moi ne tombent qu'avec peine.
> Avons-nous sans votre ordre abandonné Mycène?

In Euripides she next meets Agamemnon as a frightened, pleading child, weak and terrified (1211); actions in perfect keeping with the character he introduces, evincing none of the "stout-heartedness" (εὐψυχία) so strenuously asserted by some to be the cardinal virtue of Grecian women. In Racine the meeting between the two finds her self-poised, giving but a startled exclamation, "Mon père—Ciel!" (Act iii. Sc. v: 914, 922); then she gathers herself up, more Dorian in type than in the Greek characterization, forgetting herself in defending her father for the part he plays (993–998, 1001 sq.). When in Euripides she declares her determination to die, it is with abruptness and seeming inconsistency when we consider her so recent lament for life; yet the inconsistency is that of the very child he draws (1368), borne up and carried on by her ideas concerning Fate and a sort of swiftly reached, Joan-of-Arc exaltation, sustained by the easy surrender to her resolve which Achilles makes, because no true love fills his heart for her. Racine leads her more gradually to this determination, no less firm, unchanged by a lover's pleading, but sustained by a more womanly idea of the effect of her death upon the future of those she holds most dear—father and lover.

Euripides' character is a child, dependent upon her mother Clytemnestra, who suggests, directs, and manages almost entirely the whole affair, influenced by Agamemnon, her father, who to the last "will or nill" must make the sacrifice, and by a lover who does not seriously combat her determination to become a martyr.

Racine's Iphigenia is a more stately self-poised conception, presenting a more complete woman in the unfolding. This is aided both by the creation of a rival, Eriphile, who develops her generosity, and by a father whose resolve at last to save her, however weakly put forth, gives other root for higher heroism than fanatic exaltation. There is a more independent existence apart from the mother, and a higher motive in the resignation which turns from the clinging resolution of a passionate lover to support a father in whom she trusts. It is true that Racine lets us see more of Iphigenia, but we are to judge from what is placed before us, not from what is concealed. Imagination is capable of conjuring up almost any idea as to what may have had lodgment in the mind of the heroine in the absence of words or acts in support of any theory.

A religious tragedy in both cases; in one the religion is full of pagan characteristics, while the other savors throughout of Christian sentiment. In one, the least religious of Greek poets has portrayed female character—a poet who, like the Attic tragedians of his time as De Quincey declares, knew little about such character in truth because of a lack of opportunity to study it; in the other, the picture is drawn by one whose Port Royal training crops out wherever the theme is religious—by one who had plenty of opportunity to know woman. We conclude that the finer qualities reside in the heroine of the French poet. It is the truly heroic, generous, tender, modest woman we admire, more than the naïve, impetuous, piqued child-martyr of Euripides.

Note

1 [See also Scarborough's "One Heroine—Three Poets: I. Iphigenia at Aulis," *Education* 19 (December 1898): 213–221.]

The Negro in Fiction as Portrayer and Portrayed

Southern Workman 28 (September 1899): 358–361.

Some eight years ago I presented phases of this subject before a body of educators in Nashville, Tenn. Since that time there has been astonishing growth in fiction which deals with Negro life and character, both in quantity and in quality. It therefore seems to me not altogether unprofitable to review what was then said while I note what the passing years may have developed concerning this theme.

This development emphasizes the utterance of Judge [Albion] Tourg[é]e then quoted: that with the conditions resulting from the downfall of slavery, southern life would furnish to the future American novelist his richest and most striking material. We have seen this verified with the Negro in the predominating part. How well it has been done is another story.

Both northern and southern writers have presented Negro nature, Negro dialect, Negro thought, as they conceived it, too often, alas, as evolved out of their own consciousness. Too often the dialect has been inconsistent, the types presented, mere composite photographs as it were, or uncouth specimens served up so that the humorous side of the literary setting might be properly balanced.

A long list could be made of those of our white friends who have attained name and fame through fiction dealing with the Negro. Harriet Beecher Stowe, Judge Tourg[é]e, Thomas Nelson Page, Joel Chandler Harris, Ruth McEnery Stuart, are but few of the names that have gained prominent places in the world of letters largely through their portrayal of the Negro character.

Then comes the list of those who, dilettante like, dabbled in the roles and essayed occasionally to drag in the Negro. Among these we may mention George W. Cable, Donnelly, W. D. Howells, E[dward] P[ayson] Roe, Harry Stillwell Edwards, and Will Allen Dromgoole. A number of other writers of fiction in short and long story have incidentally brought the Negro before the public.

I paid my respects to W. D. Howells' "An Imperative Day [1893]," when I stated that his delineations are essentially street types, with but one excuse,—

that higher types would not allow him to carry out the purpose of the book, which was to analyze the character of a modern American conscience in the matter of living a lie. Of E. P. Roe one can only say that his dialect is a makeshift and his people artificial.

Since then, within comparatively recent years, another species of fiction has sprung up,—the purpose novel, as it deals with the Negro. Judge Tourg[é]e once said, "About the Negro as a man, with hopes, fears, aspirations like other men, our literature is very nearly silent. Much has been written of the slave and something of the freedman, but thus far no one has been found able to weld the new life to the old."

This is no longer true, but with what success the ventures in this direction have met is still another question. Here again the white man has entered the field and "Yetta Segal [1898]," by [Horace Judson] Rollins, reasons out the whole matter of race absorption to a logical, optimistic conclusion. "Harold," while commendable as a literary effort, presents the pessimistic side and gives evidence of its authorship. Mrs. Harper's "Iola LeRoy [1892]" is in similar, somber hues, while "Imperium in Imperio [1899]," a work entirely void of literary merit, deals with an anarchistic view that few Negroes hold, we are happy to say. We hardly feel it worth while to mention [Hallie] Ermin[i]e Rives' "Smoking Flax [1897]," which presents an educated villain and asks the world to take him as a type of the Negro.

We now come to another point. Eight years ago I said that the Negro must come to the front and boldly assume the task of portraying Negro life and character from his own standpoint. We see that the work has already been begun, and aside from those named as colored writers of the purpose novel, we find [Paul Laurence] Dunbar easily among the first of his competitors taking rank in the world of fiction as a portrayer of Negro life and character. [Charles] Chestnutt follows in the same line. There may be others.

And here we pause to see what these have added to our literature, what new artistic value they have discovered. Dunbar and Chestnutt have followed closely the "suffering side," the portrayal of the old fashioned Negro of "befo' de wah"—the Negro that Page and Harris and others have given a permanent place in literature. But they have done one thing more; they have presented the facts of Negro life with a thread running through both warp and woof that shows not only humour and pathos, humility, self-sacrifice, courtesy and loyalty, but something at times of the higher aims, ambitions, desires, hopes, and aspirations of the race—but by no means as fully and to as great an extent as we had hoped they would do.

The Negro has entered the field of fiction as portrayer as well as portrayed, to remain we are sure; to make an honored name for himself and race we trust. It is in his power to do so. Belonging himself to one of the "despised races," he will naturally be better able to depict the feelings and ambitions of his "brother in black," and to represent him more truly in accordance with the facts in the case. He knows from his own consciousness what the situation must necessarily be under the circumstances, and if he is true to nature and to himself, he cannot fail.

The Negro possesses an exuberant imagination; he is a natural story teller. Witness Uncle Remus. He has stood close to nature and she has communed with him as confidentially as Kipling's "Mowgli." One great Negro writer of fiction has stirred the world—Dumas p[è]re; and Dumas fils has not been far behind. The artistic merit that is claimed for the Negro as the portrayed is shown as well in the work that comes from his hand as portrayer.

But there are dangers lurking in the efforts being put forth by the black novelist,—dangers that have overtaken many a writer of the white race. One of these is that in the desire to shine in too many spheres, and in the elation of creation, the real bent of genius may be forced out of its natural order and development; forces may be scattered and literary strength diffused. Some one line well followed is best for all concerned. Another danger is that of degenerating into a writer of "pot boilers," turning off this and that for the money that is in it, leaving crudities here and there, and at last almost losing the art that once resided in hand and brain.

There is still another danger. It is that of imitation pure and simple, the following of lines which gave fame to others; leaving that which is best known to deal with themes and situations impossible to depict with the highest success because of the very force of circumstances. The white man has failed in such attempts and the Negro does the same. Literature is a coy mistress and a jealous one in each line. Very few have the power or ability to be great in several lines; very few can dally here and there or give attention to quantity instead of quality with any hope of success. Deterioration is the price that must eventually be paid for such stupidity.

It has been said by a writer in Lippincott's that in the many possibilities of the world the African has his fair share, and it is hinted that the future novelist of America may be a Negro. But I return to the idea suggested in the article mentioned in the beginning of my paper. What we want is a novelist who possesses the genius to "weld the new life to the old,"—one who can overcome the difficulty spoken of by Judge Tourg[é]e, "the finding himself always confronted with the past of his race and the woes of his kindred."[1]

The demand is for the novelist who will portray the Negro not in the commonplace way that some have done, but one who will elevate him to a high level of fascination and interest; one who can place the old life with the new in such a dramatic juxtaposition that the movement as well as the characters, while absorbing, will yet be true to life. Let the dramatis personae represent the plantation, or the hut in the black belt of the South; or let them be college bred, or from the more refined society of the Afro-American, north or south, but above all let them be true to nature—to fact.

The Negro, I claim, can portray the Negro best if he will. There is an inner circle, a social sphere, that no one else knows so well as he. Others may have looked in upon it; they may have spent hours, days, even years within it, but even then that is not living the life. The onlooker who may perchance remain with us longest can never know all. So we must look to the Negro as the last resort for that portrayal of the Negro character that will attract and please, yet be true to the facts.

We are tired of vaudeville, of minstrelsy and of the Negro's pre-eminence in those lines. We want something higher, something more inspiring than that. We turn to the Negro for it. Shall we have it? The black novelist is like the white novelist, in too many instances swayed by the almighty dollar; in too many instances willing to pander to low tastes and cater to public sentiment for what he can get out of it. Like Esau he is ready to sell his birthright for a mess of pottage.[2]

Let the Negro writer of fiction make of his pen and brain all-compelling forces to treat of that which he well knows, best knows, and give it to the world with all the imaginative power possible, with all the magic touch of an artist. Let him portray the Negro's loves and hates, his hopes and fears, his ambitions, his whole life, in such a way that the world will weep and laugh over the pages, finding the touch that makes all nature kin, forgetting completely that hero and heroine are God's bronze images, but knowing only that they are men and women with joys and sorrows that belong alike to the whole human family. Such is the novelist that the race desires. Who is he that will do it? Who is he that can do it?

Notes

1 [From Albion Tourgée, "The South as a Field for Fiction," *Forum* 6 (December 1888): 409.]

2 [Genesis 25 and 29–34.]

Iphigenia in Euripides, Racine, and Goethe

summary, *Transactions of the American Philological Association* 32
(July 1901): xxxvii–xxxviii.

In a previous paper Iphigenia in Aulis by Euripides and Racine was discussed. The present one is a continuation of the theme and deals with Iphigenia in Tauris as presented by Euripides and Goethe.[1]

Though Aeschylus, Sophocles, Horace, and Lucretius sustain by inference and otherwise the opinion that Iphigenia's blood was really shed in Aulis, both Euripides and Goethe follow the fable that a hind was substituted by Diana, leaving Agamemnon—

δοκῶν ἐς ἡμᾶς ὀξὺ φάσγανον βαλεῖν (1. 785).

As in Iphigenia in Aulis, the endings of the tragedy differ in the Tauris situation. The opening monodies are, however, somewhat alike in some respects, but sounded in two widely differing keys of sentiment. The heroine of Euripides speaks of herself as—

θῦμ' οὐκ εὐγάθητον,

and as—

οἰκτράν τ' αἰαζόντων αὐδ[ά]ν
οἰκτρόν τ' ἐκβαλλόντων δάκρυον (11. 227, 8).

In the dialogue with Orestes, declared by Mahaffy to be the finest left us of any Greek poet, she shows her petulant self in her rage against Helen:—

ὦ μῖσος εἰς Ἕλληνας, οὐκ ἐμοὶ μόνῃ (1. 525).

She is not only hysterical in lament as ever, but ungrateful, equivocal, ready with pretext, deceitful, and so crafty in planning as to draw a doubtful compliment from Orestes:—

δειναὶ γὰρ αἱ γυναῖκες [εὑ]ρίσκειν τέχνας (1. 1032).

She is fluctuating as at Aulis, believes in Fate as a true Grecian, and fears death with the old fear:—

πῶς οὐ θανοῦμαι.

She ventures but few decided opinions concerning mankind. Mistrusting Pylades she says:—

οὐδεὶς αὑτὸς ἐν πόνοις τ᾽ ἀνὴρ
ὅταν τε πρὸς τὸ θάρσος ἐκ φόβου πέσῃ (11. 729, 30).

And she says to the women of the chorus:—

καλόν τοι γλῶσσ᾽ ὅτῳ πιστὴ παρῇ (1. 1064).

She weakly accepts woman's place as she conceives it:—

ἀνὴρ μὲν ἐκ δόμων
θανὼν ποθεινός, τὰ δὲ γυναικὸς ἀσθενῆ (11. 1005, 6).

She is narrow, with a decidedly limited intellectual range, a true woman of antiquity.

Goethe's characterization is far more sharply in contrast with Euripides than is Racine's. We cannot agree with De Quincey that this tragedy as a whole is nearer the Greek model than is Racine's. Goethe gives a type of womanhood to be found in the nineteenth century. This womanhood does not possess the εὐψυχία of the Grecian, but it is made up of a large degree of firmness and independence rooted in lofty sincerity and appreciation of right. This is ingrained in her.

So wirst du, reine Seele, dich und uns
Zu Grunde richten,

says Pylades in recognition of this fact.

And the nearest approach to consent to further a deceitful scheme for escape is found in the sad soliloquy which opens the fourth act:—

. . . Ach! ich sehe wohl,
Ich musz mich leiten lassen wie ein Kind.
Ich habe nicht gelernt zu hinterhalten,
Noch jemand etwas abzulisten;

while her inability to condone falsehood is shown in the lines that savor of sarcasm as she replies to Pylades' pleadings:—

> O, trüg' ich doch ein männlich Herz in mir!
> Das, wenn es einen kühnen Vorsatz hegt,
> Vor jeder andern Stimme sich verschlieszt.

She does not believe in Fate, and reluctantly recalls the Parcae's song: nor has she a Grecian fear of death, which she welcomes instead. She is reflective, philosophical, when she says:

> Ein unnütz Leben ist ein früher Tod.

She is totally antagonistic to the Grecian ideas regarding her sex. She knows woman and her lot, and freely and fearlessly expresses her opinions concerning her:—

> Der Frauen Zustand ist beklagenswerth.
> *   *   *   *   *   *   *   *
> Wie enggebunden ist des Weibes Glück.

She is assertive, and does not hesitate to defend her sex when taunted by Thoas in a rage:—

> Nicht herrlich wie die euern, aber nicht
> Unedel sind die Waffen eines Weibes.

Her independence reaches a climax when she declares for both freedom of thought and action, as no Greek maiden would have dared, as she defies Thoas' command in these words:—

> Lasz ab! Beschönige nicht die Gewalt,
> Die sich der Schwachheit eines Weibes freut.
> Ich bin so frei geboren als ein Mann.
> *   *   *   *   *   *   *   *
> Ich habe nichts als Worte, und es ziemt
> Dem edeln Mann, der Frauen Wort zu achten.

Nobility of character, combined with dignity of action and word, all unite to bring about the release of all by the noble-minded Thoas, a situation wholly at variance with Euripides' *dénouement*, where she is flippant even as she lightly tells Thoas θαυμάσῃς μηδέν, and where her deceptive ruse succeeds, and Minerva intervenes to prevent pursuit.

That Goethe makes much of sentiment does not despoil the tragedy of beauty despite the implied criticism of Mahaffy; and both beauty and effect are found in it, though these do not necessarily come as an echo from Grecian models as stated by Schlegel. We have said before that Euripides' heroine at Tauris is perfectly consistent with the one depicted at Aulis, though De Quincey might find grounds here for saying the Grecian poet did not know women, though we think De Quincey was thinking of womanhood of later centuries. But Goethe evidently knew their sex, knew, too, the true woman soul, *das ewigweibleiche*, better than either Euripides or Racine.

We conclude that though Goethe's type of womanhood is based upon Racine's, it is farther from the Greek model than is Racine's,—it is the Christian girl of Racine, broadened and chastened by suffering, expanded intellectually and spiritually.

Note

1 [See also Scarborough's "One Heroine—Three Poets: II. Iphigenia at Tauris," *Education* 19 (January 1899): 285–293.]

Classical Philology

The Theory and Function of the Thematic Vowel in the Greek Verb

summary, *Transactions of the American Philological Association* 15
(July 1884): vi.

After remarking upon the agglutinative character and complexity in structure of the Greek verb, the writer defined "thematic vowel," and gave illustrations form the Greek, Latin, and Sanskrit. Explanations of the phonetic changes of the vowel, peculiar to each of these languages, were offered. The theories of Bopp, Pott, and Curtius as to the nature and origin of this vowel were passed in review and briefly discussed.[1] Cases of apparent omission in several Greek verbs were presented, and the explanation of omission by syncopation was condemned. The conclusion was drawn that the vowel is an important element in the make-up of the verb for euphonic purposes; that its especial function is to facilitate pronunciation, and that in force it is conjunctive, serving to unite or connect the termination with the verbal base.

Note

1 [Franz Bopp (1791–1867), a German philologist in Berlin, made comparative studies of the grammar of the Indo-European languages. August F. Pott (1802–1889), a German philologist at the University of Halle, worked on Indo-European historical linguistics. Georg Curtius (1820–1885), who held appointments at Prague, Keil, and Berlin, wrote influential works on etymology and Greek grammar.]

On Fatalism in Homer and Virgil

A.M.E. Church Review 2 (1886): 132–138.

The Greek and Roman religion has been justly styled many sided and many colored.[1] The multiplicity of *divinities, sub-divinities, quasi-divinities, allegorical deities* or the so-called *impersonations of moral powers* rendered their system of faith and worship complicated. The polytheistic tendency—"gods many and lords many"—the essence of their creed presents a striking contrast to the doctrine of Divine unity so universally accepted among us of to-day. While this is true we find at times, in opposition to polytheism, appearances and manifestations of a primitive monotheism in the supremacy of Zeus, the father of Gods and king of men (*divûm pater atque hominum rex.*)

Amid the strifes, the struggles and conflicts, whether among Gods, demigods or heroes, the will of Zeus is seemingly fulfilled as the one supreme ruler whose mandates are final as well as unquestionable and whose power is irresistible.

"Διὸς δ᾽ ἐτελείετο βουλή."—Il. I. 5.

There are, in fact, numerous instances in which Homer and Virgil seem to recognize to the fullest extent the authority of the father of the Gods with his associates and represent their heroes as offering sacrifices, sometimes for one thing and sometimes for another, either as a propitiation for sins committed or in token of some blessing desired. Zeus was then doubtless regarded as the dispenser of good and evil, and before him every knee must bow. In confirmation of this view I note the following: Ulysses who was asleep in the wood, was suddenly awakened by Nausicaa the daughter of Alcinous, King of the Phæacians, with her handmaidens. He comes forth and humbly begs aid, food and clothing. The request is granted. The Goddess first addresses him in this language:

"Ξεῖν᾽ ἐπεὶ οὔτε κακῷ οὔτ᾽ ἄφρονι φωτὶ ἔοικας,
Ζεὺς δ᾽ αὐτὸς νέμει ὄλβον Ὀλύμπιος ἀνθρώποισιν,
Ἐσθλοῖς ἠδὲ κακοῖσιν, ὅπως ἐθέλῃσιν, ἑκάστῳ."—Od. VI.
187–8.

("O stranger since thou art not like unto a worthless or foolish man—and Olympian Zeus himself distributes happiness to men—good or bad to each as he chooses," etc., etc.)

Another passage:

" Ἀτρείδη Μενέλαε διοτρεφὲς ἠδὲ, καὶ οἵδε
Ἀνδρῶν ἐσθλῶν παῖδες· ἀτὰρ θεὸς ἄλλοτε ἄλλῳ
Ζεὺς ἀγαθόν τε κακόν τε διδοῖ· δύναται γὰρ
[ἅ]παντα."—Od. IV. 235-7.

("O thou, Jove nurtured Menelaus, son of Atreus and also these sons of brave men—but the God Jupiter gives both good and evil, sometimes to one and sometimes to another; for he is able to do all things.")

Again:

.... "Θεὸς δὲ [τὸ] μὲν δώσει, [τὸ δ']ἐάσει,
[ὅ]ττι κεν [ᾧ] θυμῷ ἐθέλῃ· δύναται γὰρ [ἅ]παντα."—Od. XIV. 444-5.

("For God bestows one thing and refuses another, whatever He wills in His own mind; for He can do all things.")

While these references seem to establish beyond question the sway of Zeus and make his power limitless, and while there are many proofs of the same, there are many others equally as explicit that make even Zeus himself powerless and subject to a *blind impersonal force*, behind the Gods and beyond their power as paradoxical as it may appear, to control the career of mankind; to guide the events of the world; to subject Gods as well as men to its unchanging decree. Another name given to this Force is Fate, μοῖρα, (*fatum.*)

The term Fate may refer to the will of the Gods, or it may refer to that *unknown* power behind them. In this two-fold sense we find it used in both Homer and Virgil as well as in the classic authors generally.

When the Lydians, whom Crosus had sent by permission of Cyrus to bear his fetters to the Gods of the Grecians, had arrived at Delphi and delivered their message, the Pythian is reported to have made this answer:

"Τὴν πεπρωμένην μοῖραν ἀδύνατα [ἐστὶ] ἀποφυγ[εῖ]ν καὶ θεῷ."—Herod., Bk. I, § 91.

("Even the God himself cannot avoid the decrees of Fate.")

Æschylus[2] represents Prometheus as saying in reply to the chorus desiring to know whether Jupiter was less powerful than the Fates (μοῖραι τρίμορφοι):

"Οὖκουν ἂν ἐκφύγοι γε τὴν πεπρωμένην."—Æsch. Prom. 518.

("Most assuredly he can not at any rate escape his Fate.")

Cooper takes exception to giving a double meaning to *fatum* as found in Virgil. He believes that Virgil's notion of Fate was a philosophic one; that he makes Fate to be nothing more than the decrees, purposes or counsels of Heaven pronounced by the mouth of Jove, as the etymology of the word implies. He adds that Virgil often calls destiny *fata deorum*, which can mean nothing else than the Divine decrees. This appears from several passages. And if he gives to Fate the epithets *inexpugnabile* and *inexorabile* he must mean that the laws and order of nature are fixed and unchangeable as being the result of infinite wisdom and foresight, and as having their foundation in the Divine mind which is subject to none of those changes that affect feeble and erring mortals.

I cannot altogether entertain this view. There are numerous passages in Virgil that carry with them *prima facie* evidence that the opposite is true.[3] *It is fated; so it is decreed; just as the Fate wills; wherever destiny leads.* The religious tendency of the Iliad, Odyssey and Æneid is decidedly fatalistic. The grim hand of Fate seems to rule the action of men and sternly though slowly to direct their course in life; taking away the freedom of the will and depriving them of all moral responsibility. On nearly every page of these two great epic writers the fatalistic flavor is to be observed. In fact it is the leaven that leavens the whole lump. Fate is the key-note, the "*motif*" of the Iliad, Odyssey and Æneid. I believe as one writer[4] expressed it, that without this idea in the mind at the outset, the true spirit of any one of these master-pieces will be lost.

Contra fata Deûm, perverso numine poscunt.—Aen. Bk. VII. 584.

Fate here evidently refers to the responses of the Oracle of Faunus and is equivalent in sense as Ruæus suggests to *contra voluntatem deorum.*

In Homer, μοῖρα θεοῦ, μοῖρα θεῶν, as *fata deorum* in the Latin, imply the will of the God or Gods. In meaning it is about the same as *fata Jovis* (Æn. IV. 614): the decree of Zeus. In this I agree with Cooper.

The conception expressed by Fate has prevailed to a certain extent in all religions.[5]

"With the course of Grecian thought this conception became more spiritualized. In Æschylus it is an *inexorable Destiny*. In Sophocles and Plato it is more *of a free and ordering will*. In later forms of Greco-Roman speculation it seems to undergo various modifications. With the Epicureans it becomes identical with Chance, τυχή: with the Stoics it is the opposite of this. In the one case the absolute is a mere blind fatality; in the other it is an imminent necessity of reason, governing with iron sway the apparently accidental phenomena of life. To turn to the two great religions of modern times—Christianity and Mohammedanism—we note that the same conception is found in various forms. In Mohammedanism the *Highest* is conceived as an *arbitrary* and *inexorable law, swallowing up every lower law of activity and per-mitting no scope to freedom of development in human nature.* Whereas in Christianity and forms of belief springing from it, fatalism shows itself more or less in the doctrines of Predestination and Philosophical Necessity."

Not even in the speculations of Cicero[6] am I able to find a fuller and more comprehensive meaning of the mysterious term Fate, than is observable in many other classics writers, though the subject has been widely discussed by this philosopher. I quote:

"Hinc vobis extitit primum illa fatalis necessitas quam εἱμαρμέ νην *dicitis ut quidquid accidat id ex aeterna veritate causarumque continua-tione fluxisse dicatis."*—De Natura Deorum, Bk. I. Chap. 20.

("Hence first arose your fatal necessity which you call *Εἱμαρμέ νην* so that whatever happens you affirm that it flows form an external chain and continuance of causes.")

Further: "Sequuntur quae futura sunt. Effugere enim nemo id potest, quod futurum est. Sæpe autem ne utile quidem est scire, quid futurum sit; miserum est enim nihil proficientem angi nec habere ne spei quidem extremum et tamen commune solacium, praesertim cum vos iidem fato fieri dicatis omnia, quod autem semper ex omni æternitate verum fuerit, id esse fatum. Quid igitur juvat aut quid adfert ad cavendum scire aliquid futurum, cum id certe futurum sit?["]—De Natura Deorum. Bk. III, Chap. 6.

("Now follow events of an inevitable nature. No one can avoid what is to come, and indeed it is often useless to know it, for it is a miser-able thing to be afflicted to no purpose, and not to have even the last, the common comfort, *hope*, which according to your idea none can have; for you say that Fate governs all things and call that Fate which has been true from all eternity. What advantage, then, is the knowledge of the future or how does it assist us to guard against impending evils since it will come inevitably?")

Μεἱρομαι is used by Homer and Hesiod only in the third person, singular Perf. Act. in the form of *ἔμμορε.* In later Epic writers we find *ἐξέμμορον* used as an Aorist *to obtain one's share of a thing,* (followed by the Genitive,) *to receive an allotted portion,* hence *to be fated or destined.*

Μέρος, μερἱς, μοῖρα, μόρος, μόρα, μόρσιμος, μερἱξω, are all derivatives from a common root found in *μεἱρομαι,* and, as such. signify *share, portion* or *fate. Μοῖραι* has the same meaning as the Latin Parcae (*pars,* part). The plu-ral form is used but once by Homer. In every other instance, in speaking of Fate, he employs the singular. In the Theog[o]ny of Hesiod (218), we find the first mention of the three sisters (Fates), whom he calls daughters of Night (Nox): Clotho, *the spinner of the thread of life;* Lachesis, *who determines the lot of life*, and Atropos, the *"inevitable,"* answering respectively to the three stages of human life, *birth*, *years* and *death*. In line 904 of the same book these sisters are spoken of as the daughters of Zeus and Themis. In the former relation, daughters of Night, they are regarded as indicating the darkness and obscurity of human life; in the latter, daughters of Zeus, as indicating the descendants of "high heaven,"—a happy origin. In four places, at least, in Virgil we find Fate (*fatum*) represented by these three sisters (*Parcæ*),—for example:

> *"Talia sæcla, suis dixerunt, currite, fusis*
> *Concordes stabili fatorum numine Parcæ."*—Ecl. IV. 46–7.

> *"Si dant ea mœnia Parcæ."*—Æn. V. 798.

> *". . . . prohibent nam cætera Parcæ [s]cire."*—Æn. III. 379.

> *"Ergo aderat promissa dies, et tempora Parcæ*
> *Debita complerant."*—Æn. IX. 107.

Alcinous addresses the Phæacians, and urges them, after having feasted, to go home and sleep, and on to-morrow to call together more of the elders, to entertain the stranger (Ulysses) in the palace, offer fit sacrifices to the Gods, provide a suitable escort, that the stranger may return rejoicing to his paternal land, that no harm may befall him before he reaches home. There at home he will suffer whatever things Fate and the heavy destinies spun with the thread for him at his birth, when his mother brought him forth:

> *". . . . ἔνθα δ᾽ ἔπειτα*
> *Πείσεται ἄσσα οἱ [αἶσα] κατὰ κλῶθές τε*
> *Βαρεῖαι [γιγνομένῳ] νήσαντο λίνῳ ὅτε μιν*
> *Τέκε μήτηρ."*—Od. VII. 196–198.

In the fifth book of the Odyssey, Jupiter is represented as dispatching Mercury, his messenger, to the island of Calypso, commanding her to send Ulysses away. For, says he, it is fated for him to behold his friends and return to his lofty-roofed house and his own paternal land:

> *"[ὣς] γάρ οἱ μοῖρ᾽ ἐστὶ φίλους τ᾽ ἰδέειν καὶ ἱκέσθαι—*
> *[οἶκον] ἐς ὑψόροφον καὶ ἑὴν ἐς πατρίδα γα[ῖ]αν."*—Od. V. 41–2.

Again: For it is not in accordance with destiny for him (Ulysses) to perish here at a distance from his friends; but it is his (destiny) to behold his friends, etc., etc.:

> *"Οὐ γάρ οἱ τῇδ᾽ [αἶσα] φίλων ἀπονόσφιν ὀλέσθαι,*
> *ἀλλ᾽ [ἔτι] οἱ μοῖρ᾽ ἐστὶ,"* etc., etc.—Od. V. 113–4.

Ulysses, on his return home and finding his house disgraced, slays all the suitors, while twelve of the female servants are hanged by Telemachus and the herdsman. While among the slain, with hands and feet besmeared with blood and gore, Ulysses calls the nurse, saying:

" Ἐν θυμῷ, γρηῦ, χαῖρε καὶ ἴσχεο μηδ᾽ ὀλόλυζε·
Οὐχ ὁσίη κταμένοισιν ἐπ᾽ ἀνδράσιν εὐχετάασθαι
Τούσδε δὲ μοῖρ᾽ ἐδάμασσε θεῶν καὶ σχέτλια ἔργα[·]
Οὔ τινα γὰρ τίεσκον ἐπιχθονίων ἀνθρώπων,
Οὐ κακὸν οὐδὲ μὲν ἐσθλὸν, ὅτις σφέας εἰσαφίκοιτο·
Τῷ καὶ ἀτασθαλίῃσιν ἀεικέα πότμον ἐπέσ[π]ον."—Od. XXII. 411–6.

Ulysses entered the infernal regions; met his mother, who desired to know how he came hither, being alive. To her he replied: "O my mother, necessity led me to Hades to consult the soul of Theban Tiresias:"

"'Ὣς ἔφατ᾽, αὐτὰρ ἐγώ μιν ἀμειβόμενος προσέειπον·
Μῆτερ ἐμή, χρειώ με κατήγαγεν εἰς Ἀίδαο
Ψυχῇ χρησόμενον Θηβαίου Τειρεσίαο·"—Od. XI. 163–5.

Again:

"Τίς νύ σε κὴρ ἐδάμασσε τανηλεγέος Θανάτοιο."—Od. XI. 171.

In reference to an act contrary to Destiny, ὑπέρμορα is used as in the Iliad. Agamemnon proposes a return home, and the people, weary of war, rush to the ships and proceed to draw them into the sea. The intervention of Athena and the activity of Ulysses prevent them form executing their purposes:

"Ἔνθα κεν Ἀργείοισιν ὑπέρμορα νόστος ἐτύχθη,
Εἰ μὴ Ἀθηναίην Ἥρη πρὸς μῦθον ἔειπεν."—Il. II. 155.

Homer often uses μοῖρα as equivalent to death or destruction: μοιρηγενής, child of happy Fate:

"[Ὣς] φάτο, τὸν δ᾽ ὁ γέρων ἠγάσσατο, φώνησέν τε
[Ὦ] μάκαρ Ἀτρείδη, μοιρηγενές, ὀλβιόδαιμον,
Ἦ ῥά νύ τοι πολλοὶ δεδμήατο κοῦροι Ἀχαιῶν."—Il. III. 181–3.

Pious Æneas, impelled by Fate (*profugus fato*) left his native land, came to Italy and settled in Latium; forced to abandon every country in which he attempts to settle till he reaches the destined shores;

"*Desine meque tuis incendere teque querelis
Italiam non sponte sequor*["]—Æn. IV. 360.

279

When he reaches Italy he finds the fated wife foretold by the ghosts of Creusa, his former wife:

> *Hunc illum fatis externa a sede profectum*
> *Portendi generum*—Æn. VII. 255.

Juno, the queen of the Gods, on account of anger and jealousy, persecuted the weary Trojans to the utmost limit but was not able to prevent the founding of another Troy:

> *"Quippe vetor fatis"*—Æn. [I.] 39.

The little band of tempest tossed Trojans through countless perils and various misfortunes made their way toward Latium:

> *"Sedes ubi fata quietas ostendunt."*—Æn. I. 205.

The miserable Dido, the disappointed lover with tears besought the Trojan hero to tarry a little while longer at least till she should bring her mind to bear his loss. But he was moved by none of her tears:

> *"Fata obstant."*—Æn. IV. 440.

Again she saw that the hero was fixed in his purpose and all her entreaties going for naught;

> *"Tum vero infelix fatis exterrita Dido*
> *Mortem orat:"*—Æn. IV. 450.

Again, Æneas having departed from Carthage and while still beholding the blaze of the funeral pile of Dido a violent storm arose and drove them toward Sicily. In the midst of the confusion the pilot Palinurus consoles the crew:

> *"Superat quoniam fortuna, sequamur:*
> *Quoque vocat, vertamus iter."*—Æn. V. 22.

Having reached Italy, Æneas must now overcome his rival Turnus before the marriage alliance can be consummated. Led by Fate he seeks aid from the ruler of the Grecian colony:

> *Optima Grajugenum, cui me fortuna precari,*
> *Et vitta comptos voluit praetendere ramos:*—Æn. VIII. 127.

Eurystheus was king of Mycenæ. To him Hercules was made subject by the Fates for many years. This king, at the instigation of Juno, the unrelenting enemy of her step son, imposed upon him severe labors in order to destroy him:

―― ―― ―― ―― ―― [*"*]*ut duros mille labores*
Rege sub Eurystheo, fatis Junonis iniquae,
Pertulerit."—Æn. VIII. 291.

Here *fatis* should be rendered *through the power of* and the expression *fatis Junonis iniquae* should be taken as equivalent to *fatis potestatem Junonis iniquae*. This gives the term *fatum* a derived meaning (*ad sensum*). We find many examples of the kind in Virgil. I conclude with the statement that Fate as we see it in Homer and Virgil, is a variable quantity. The different terms used to denote this conception in the classics are proof that even in the mind of the writers themselves there was not always a clear, definite idea as to the exact meaning of the word as we have it translated into English. Fate may mean one thing under one chain of circumstances and another under another.

As ὑπέρμορα, it may refer to the misery and misfortune which one, through his own folly, brings upon himself, and for which the Gods are not responsible. As μοῖρα αἴσιμος, Κήρ, *fatum, casus, eventus*, it may be used as an equivalent for θάνατος or *mors*. In the sense, however, of blind, impersonal force silently, though slowly, impelling events and guiding them to their destined end, I regard the Iliad, Odyssey and Æneid as being pre-eminently fatalistic.

Notes

1 This paper was read before the American Philological Association at its last annual session at Yale College, July 7, 1885. [In the original article, this note comes after the title, rather than after the first sentence. See also Scarborough's "Fatalism in Homer and Virgil," summary, *Transactions of the American Philological Association* 16 (July 1885): xxxvi–xxxvii.]

2 The accomplished and distinguished scholar, Prof. W. W. Goodwin of Harvard, Pres. of the A. P. A., is of the opinion that the statement of Prometheus as given by Æschylus, should not be cited as a proof, as he (Prometheus) was a rebel and what he had predicted in his frenzy would not come to pass did come to pass. While I fully concur with Dr. Goodwin I believe, however, that there was a semblance of truth in what he said, though spoken by an enemy. Vide Stanley on the Pythagorean notion of Æschylus.—W. S. S.

3 εἰ μαρται, *fatum est*, etc., etc.

4 Miller, *New England Journal of Education*.

5 Chambers's Encyclopædia.

6 *Vide* Cicero's *De Fato* for arguments in opposition to Stoic doctrine of Fate.

Grote on Thuc. vi. 17 (ἀνέλπιστοι)

summary, *Transactions of the American Philological Association* 18
(July 1887): v–vi.

The speaker aimed to show that Grote's rendering of ἀνέλπιστοι (Thuc. vi. 17; Grote, Hist. Gr., Vol. VII. p. 154, Am. ed., 'desperate'), as 'enemies beyond hopes of being able to deal with' is inaccurate as a matter of history, as well as on philological grounds. Thuc. vii. 4 and 47 could not be adduced to support this rendering, since in the former passage ἀνέλπιστος is active, and in the latter passive. It was maintained that Alcibiades meant to say that the Peloponnesians were never hopeless of success against the Athenians; and supposing them to be otherwise, they can invade Attica only by land, but he can always prevent their attacking the Athenians by sea. ἀνέλπιστος is neuter when applied to things, and active when applied to persons. Examples were cited illustrating a similar transference of meaning: *fidus* (Verg. Aen. ii. 399), *mentita* (Verg. Aen. ii. 422), *benignus, blandus, beatus, durus, incautus, inimicus, iniquus, severus*; φυβερός. ἀνέλπιστος is used by Thuc. 15 times, ἐλπίς 63, ἐλπίζω 49; typical examples were presented and discussed, with instances from other writers. A survey of the historical situation led the speaker to conclude that up to the time of the Athenian defeat there is no reason to believe that Athens and Sparta were uncompromising enemies, though each had a desire, prompted by jealousy, to surpass the other in glory, power, and in extent of territory.

Ancipiti in Cæsar, *B. G.* I. 26

summary, *Transactions of the American Philological Association* 18
(July 1887): xxxviii.

After referring to a number of editions of Caesar and reviewing their interpretations of the passage, the writer took exception to the usual rendering of
ancipiti ('double') and suggested 'doubtful' or some equivalent.

He argued that the sense requires that *anceps* should be translated in such
manner as to express the uncertainty of the struggle between the contending
forces—which was of more importance to Caesar than the position of the
troops could have been: that 'double' is not a primary but a secondary meaning of *anceps*, as its etymology shows. If having "heads all round" (probably the
original meaning of *anceps*) means anything at all, it must mean instability,
uncertainty. It may be reasonably concluded from an etymological standpoint
that *anceps* means 'doubtful' in the sense of 'critical' or 'uncertain,' rather than
'double,' and it is clear that this meaning is most in keeping with the context
of the lines referred to.

Xenophon or Andocides,—Which?

Journal of Education 27 (May 17, 1888): 311.

Xenophon's *Anabasis* has been used so long in our preparatory instruction that it has become, almost, a *conditio sine qua non* for entering college. The continuous, uninterrupted use of this well-known author, is due, possibly, to the fact that no better text has been offered or suggested. With the exception of a few difficult constructions here and there it is easy and attractive, especially when Κῦρος ἐλαύνει occupies section after section. This is one objectionable feature,—too much repetition. The boy glides over this glibly, and thinks it is fun. This is about the only discipline he receives from such passages. Then, as [W. J.] Hickie remarks, there are in many instances a general disregard of Attic usage, inaccuracies of language, and a false use of tenses. Xenophon would make a very good text for the advanced student who would be competent enough to detect and avoid errors as they appear.

As a substitute I regard Andocides as the best Greek text that we could adopt.[1] I refer to his orations as a whole,—*De Mysteriis: De Pace*, etc. The style of Andocides is purely Attic, while the work is well adapted to pupils who have finished the first book (Greek Lessons). The subject matter is another attraction,—The Sicilian expedition, the mutilation of the Hermæ, the profanation of the Mysteries, Alcibiades and the charges brought against him and the prosecutions that took place, etc., etc.

It is an interesting topic, discussed in the simplest manner. I am decidedly in favor of Andocides as a substitute for the *Anabasis*, for the reason that better results will be obtained by its use. If it is thought desirable, the *Anabasis* for sight reading, rather than actual study, might with profit to the student follow Andocides.

Note

1 [See also Scarborough's "Notes on Andocides," summary, *Transactions of the American Philological Association* 20 (July 1889): v–vi.]

Observations on the Fourth Eclogue
of Vergil

summary, *Transactions of the American Philological Association* 19 (July 1888):
xxxvi–xxxviii.

This Eclogue, unlike the remaining nine, has little in common with the pastorals of Theocritus, except, perhaps, casual references to a few rural scenes. In
this respect Vergil has departed from his master and has adopted a style peculiarly his own, which in some respects transcends bucolic limits.

For glow of imagery and exaggerated effusion it stands alone. Between the
human and the divine, there is more of the latter than of the former. It is a
remarkable production, abounding in passages of striking resemblance to many
of the old Messianic prophecies. There is just enough of the maze about it to
confuse the reader and make it doubtful on his part as to the poet's real design.

The date of this poem is said to be about 40 B.C., during the consulship of
Asinius Pollio, a friend of the poet. To him also he was indebted for the
restoration of his property, previously confiscated by an order of Augustus. In
view of this circumstance many critics have supposed that Vergil testifies his
gratitude to Pollio by dedicating these lines to his unborn son, and that v. 17,

Pacatumque reget patriis virtutibus orbem, confirms the theory.

The writer took exception to this view, asserting there is nothing in the line
to support it, as the subject of *reget* is not expressed and is likewise indefinite;
that the prediction was not fulfilled, as the son of Pollio died in infancy; and if
he had lived, it could not have been fulfilled, as the description, taking the
Eclogue as a whole, was not only inapplicable to "the consular dignity of
Pollio," but to mortals generally. It was true that the golden age was earnestly
looked for, and that the theme of the poet was the *age of peace*, and as a result
exaggerated descriptions and highly colored expressions followed as it were
from necessity. As proof many passages from the poets were cited.

Many of the theories held by scholars were briefly discussed, and the view
advanced by a *few* that Vergil wrote under inspiration was objected to. The

writer held that Vergil probably had some knowledge of the Jewish Scriptures, as the Jews were quite widely spread over the Roman Empire about this time, and the Old Testament Scripture had become largely known to Gentile as well as Jew. There seems to have been a general belief that a Messiah would come into the world, and it is not unlikely that the poet may have shared this belief.

The ground of this statement was based mainly upon the resemblances existing between passages in the Eclogue and the language of the prophet Isaiah, especially the eleventh chapter of his prophecies. Other Scripture was also cited and compared with the more striking parts of the Eclogue (notably Gen. iii. 15; Eccl. iv. 24, etc.).

The writer held that neither *coincidences nor the images employed by Hesiod and the poets generally descriptive of the golden age* could be regarded as sufficient to explain these marvellous passages. There seems to be an intentional obscurity, which makes the meaning of the poet difficult to understand and renders a clear exposition impossible. If we accept in explanation Vergil's acquaintance with the Sibylline books of Alexandrian manufacture, then we must conclude that those books reflected Jewish ideas largely.

The writer also held the theory *"that reference is made to the expected offspring of Octavianus and Scribonia"* to be untenable; likewise, *"that the child referred to was the son of Antony and Octavia"* to be without support. In the first place, the child of Octavianus and Scribonia was the wicked and disreputable Julia; in the second place, it is highly improbable that Vergil would make the child of a subordinate person the redeemer of the Roman world. Then, too, Antony was the rival of Augustus, and one whom Vergil would hardly have complimented in this way at the expense of his friend and patron.

If any compliment at all was intended in this poem, the writer suggested the preferable one among various views, the name Marcellus, the son of Octavia by her former husband of the same name (Aen. vi. 861 sqq.). He was born during the consulship of Pollio, was adopted by Augustus, and was intended by him to be his successor. Vergil pays him a glowing tribute in the sixth book of the Aeneid.

Xenophon, Andocides, Cebes,—Which?

Journal of Education 28 (September 20, 1888): 223.

Sometime ago I wrote a brief note to the JOURNAL OF EDUCATION suggesting Andocides as a substitute for the Anabasis, with a few reasons for the change subjoined. I was well aware that my views would not receive a cordial reception and some of my distinguished scholastic friends would more than likely regard it as an innovation and, as a consequence, take issue with me. Therefore I was not surprised to read the laconic but courteous reply of Professor R. L. Perkins, of Boston, in your issue of the 21st of June, under the heading of " Ἐντεῦθεν Ἐξελαύνει."

Mr. Perkins's reasons for the retention of Xenophon are the same as those that I should advance for a change, though his, perhaps, are the views of four fifths of the teachers interested in preparatory instruction.

I hardly think that his comparison between Κῦρος ἐλαύνει, ἐντεῦθεν ἐξελαύνει of the Anabasis and τὴν δ᾽ ἠμείβετ᾽ ἔπειτα, τόν δ᾽ἠμείβετ᾽ ἔτειτα of the Iliad is a happy one. I grant that "*it is a necessity of the narrative in either case,*" but the syntax of the one as a whole is so different from that of the other that the ground for the rejection of the *Anabasis* cannot apply to the *Iliad*. There is much repetition, of course, in Homer, but that does not affect the narrative. The peculiar characteristics of his style, the dialectic forms, and the metrical anomalies etc, all serve to render it an indispensable text in Greek instruction.

Then, again, there is no other work with which I am acquainted that may be taken as an exact equivalent of Homer.

In a recent letter from the accomplished editor of the *Christian Register*, the writer calls my attention to a recently published book, *Cebes' Tablet*,[1] and adds that he finds it easy, full of interest, and of good moral lessons. As it is used in Germany and has been revived in England, the editor thinks it an excellent thing to revive in this country. I simply mention this to show the drift of public opinion relative to the kind of Greek read in our schools.

There is little doubt that the *Anabasis* is seeing its best days, and that after a while a change of some kind will be demanded notwithstanding its long use in the preparatory curricula. I am not prepared to say what the substitute will be,—whether Andocides or Cebes, or some other author. It is simply a question of time.

Prof. George A. Williams, of Cook Academy, Havana, N. Y., in speaking of *Cebes' Tablet* says:[2] "It seems admirably adapted to supplement the regular work in the *Anabasis*, or to take the place of an equivalent of the latter."

Prof. A. K. Wells, of Antioch College, Yellow Springs, O., further says in reference to the same text: "I am well pleased with it, and shall certainly use it next term with my beginning class. The *Anabasis* never seemed to me interesting enough to the average student to make a fit introduction to Greek literature. I think the *Tablet* will meet my needs exactly."

The subject is now beginning to awaken interest, and I am pleased to note it.

Notes

1 Edited by Prof. Richard Parsons of the Ohio Wesleyan University, published by Ginn & Co., Boston.

2 Ginn & Co.'s Catalogue and Announcements for 1888.

"Ancipiti": Cæsar's De Bello Gallico

Book I., Chapter XXVI., Line 1.," *Education* 9 (December 1888): 263–268.

ITA ANCIPITI PRŒLIO DIU ATQUE ACRITER PUGNA-
TUM EST.

Does *ancipiti* in this passage means *doubtful* or *double*? On what ground is one signification preferable to the other? These are the questions that suggest themselves to one's mind as he reads this twenty-sixth chapter, and especially the part quoted with the comments on it. I have examined several editions of Cæsar by various editors, and find that all more or less agree that *ancipiti* should be rendered *double*, on the ground that the battle was fought in two places, at the top and at the foot of the hill.

To be more specific, I quote the language of a few of the editors mentioned:—

"*Ancipiti*, two-headed, thus facing two ways at once."—Allen and Greenough.

"*Ancipiti*, two-fold, because the Romans were fighting in two fronts."—Kelsey.

"*Ancipiti prœlio*, the battle is called *anceps*, *double*, because the Romans were contending with enemies, both in front and in the rear."—Andrews.

"*Ancipiti prœlio*, in a double battle—so-called, because fought on different fronts."—Harkness.

"*Ancipiti prœlio* is equivalent to *dubio marte* (according to Davies), because they were ignorant to which side the victory inclined. Others say the engagement was fought in two places—at the top and at the foot of the hill."—Spencer.

"*Ancipiti prœlio*, in doubtful battle; i. e., victory inclining to neither side."—Bullions.

"*Ancipiti prœlio*, in a double conflict."—Chase and Stuart.

"*Ancipiti prœlio*, in a double conflict."—Leighton, in his extract of the Helvetian war (Latin Lessons).

It will be observed that Spencer is in doubt; forms no opinion of his own, but simply dismisses the subject with (in substance) a remark—some say one thing and some another. Bullions states positively, "in a doubtful battle."

Though the trend of the argument of a majority of these and other commentators favors the rendering of *ancipiti* as *double,* I am of the opinion, after a careful reading of the lines and the context, that *ancipiti* should be translated *doubtful, with the sense of uncertain or critical.* To adopt any other meaning seems to be straining a point to make out a case. The position of the troops, though of importance, is not first as it seems to me; it is the outcome, the result, that is of the greatest moment, and in a hard fought battle like this there was doubtless great anxiety on the part of the Roman commander-in-chief as to which way victory was inclining. And, too, this thought seems to be brought out by the context: "Diutius quum nostrorum impetus sustinere," etc. When they could not withstand the attack of our men longer, one party retreated to the mountains and the other to their baggage and wagons, for during this entire battle, though fought from the seventh hour till evening, no one was able to see the retreating enemy. They fought till late at night, even to the baggage, because they had employed these (their wagons) for ramparts and from vantage-ground were hurling down javelins upon our men (the Romans) while advancing, and some were discharging javelins and darts from below, between the wagons and wheels, and were wounding our men. After a long fight, our men captured the baggage and camp. A daughter and son of Orgetorix were captured. From this battle about 130,000 men survived whom our men, says Cæsar, were not able to follow because of the wounded soldiers and the necessity of burying those already dead. The fact that the Romans did not follow up this victory shows that it must have cost them dearly.

The sense of the passage, then, I should think, requires that we translate *anceps* in such way as to express the uncertainty of the contest. This is not done when we say it was a double contest. We learn from the latter part of the preceding chapter that the Roman army was drawn up in three lines (triplex acies); the first and second lines formed one division which advanced against those who had been defeated and were compelled to retreat, i. e. the Helvetians: the third line sustained the attack of those advancing (venientes) upon them:—

"Romani conversa signa bipartito intulerunt; prima ac secunda acies ut victis ac submotis resisteret; tertia, ut venientes exciperet."

May we not surmise that the battle between the contending parties had been raging for some time, the details of which having been admitted, Cæsar, with his usual vivacity in describing an event, dashes into the subject as here recorded: *Ita ancipiti prœlio . . . . pugnatum est,* thus they fought long and valiantly—with victory inclining neither way[?] *Ita,* in this case, would refer not to the position of any of the contending lines (acies), but rather to the degree or intensity with which the battle was fought. In the seventy-sixth chapter of Book VII., a similar construction occurs:—

"Præsertim ancipiti prœlio, quum ex oppido eruptione pugnaretur, foris tantae copiae equitatus peditatusque cernerentur."

According to some authorities, *ancipiti* in this passage is explained by the two clauses following: "*quum ex,*" etc., "*foris tantae,*" and consequently with the meaning of *double; a double battle.*

[Ethan Allen] Andrews, in his Latin lexicon, says that *anceps* in general has reference to an object whose qualities have significance in two respects—*double, that extends on two opposite sides*; while *duplex* to an object that exists in separate form, twice. "Thus," continues he, "*anceps sententia* is an opinion *which wavers, fluctuates between two decisions*, while *duplex sententia* is a twofold opinion." After giving some examples illustrating this use, he adds, that since everything which oscillates in two different directions has no stability, *anceps* signifies *wavering, doubtful, uncertain, unfixed, undecided*, and further, since hesitation in the issue of an undertaking frequently causes danger, *anceps* also signifies dangerous, perilous, critical. There are examples in Livy, Cicero, Tacitus, Horace, Nepos, Ovid, Sallust, etc., illustrating these different meanings, though, as it seems to me, etymologically speaking, *anceps* ought to convey the one idea of *doubtful* or *uncertain*, i. e., as in No. 3 of Andrews' division.

Anceps is derived from *an-caput*, the *an* being equivalent Greek ἀμϕί, and with *caput* literally meaning "having a head on each side," or "heads all around." There are other words of similar derivation, *præceps*, headlong; *biceps*, two-headed, *triceps*, three-headed, all with *caput* as the radical, and *præ*, *bis*, and *tris* as prefixes. In *anceps* appears the root *cap* which is the same as the Indo-European root *kap*, signifying grasp, and which is also seen in *caput, capitalis, capitolium, capitulum, capillus, capillaris*, and in κεϕαλή, κεϕάλαιος, ἀκέϕαλος of the Greek. The root "*cap*" (kap), as suggested by Professor Halsey,[1] "is probably connected with *cap*" in *capio*. As we find it in *caput* and words derived from it, the meaning seems to be secondary and not primary, for in the primary sense of to hold, to grasp, from the ablant *cap* (kap), come *anceps, particeps, princeps*, and similar words with genitive in *is* signifying birdcatcher, sharer, chief, etc., etc.

Now, if having "heads all around," means anything at all, it must mean *instability, uncertainty*. "A double-minded man," says one of the sacred writers,[2] "is unstable in all his ways." In other words, the man who halts between faith and unbelief is not a safe man, he is not to be relied on; for he is indecisive. The idea I wish to emphasize is the *doubleness*, the *twofoldness*, and hence, the *doubtfulness*, as here implied. In the Vulgate for the expression, a *double-minded man*, we have, *vir animo duplici*; in the ῾Η καινὴ Διαθήκη (Greek New Testament), ἀνὴρ δίψυχος. Doubtless the *vir animo duplici*, the ἀνὴν δίψυχος and *anceps* are similar in thought and may mean the same thing, so far as the result is concerned.

The following are a few passages in which *anceps* seems to have the meaning of *double* according to the authorities consulted and the text itself:—

"Milites Romani perculsi tumultu insolito capere alii, aiii se abdere pars territos confirmare trepidare omnibus locis; vis magna hostium, cælium nocte atque nubibus obscuratum periculum *anceps*." Sall[ust]. J[ugurtha] 38–5.

Some, however, render *anceps* indiscernible, thus, danger was indiscernible, meaning, I suppose, that the struggle was of such a nature as to make it uncertain where the greatest danger lay.

"Talia magniloquo tumidus memoraverat ore, *ancipitemque* manu tollens utraque securim institerat digitis, primos suspensus in artus." O[vid]. M[etamorphoses], 8–397.

"Hic etsi pari prœlio discesserant, tamen eodem loco non sunt ausi manere: quod erat periculum, ne, si pars navium adversariorum Euoeam superasset, *ancipiti* premerentur periculo."—Nepos. Them[istocles] 33.

"Bestiarum autem terrenae sunt aliae partim aquatiles aliae quasi ancipites in utraque sede viventes; sunt queadam etiam, quae igne nasci putentur, appareantque in ardentibus fornacibus saepe volitantes."—Cic[ero]. De Natura Deorum, Bk. I., 37.

"At vero curia, maesta ac trepida ancipiti metu et ab cive et ab hoste, Servilium consulem, cui ingenium magis populare erat, orare, ut tantis circumventam terroribus expediret rem publicam."—Livy, 2, 24.

"Sed quod erant quidam eique multi, qui aut in re publica propter ancipitem, quae non potest esse seiuncta, faciendi dicendique sapientiam florerent, ut Themistocles, ut Pericles, ut," etc.—Cic[ero]. De Oratore, Bk. III., 16.

"In qua velim sit illud, quod saepe posuisti, ut non necesse sit consumere aetatem atque ut possit is illa omnia cernere, qui tantummodo aspexerit; sed etiamsi est aliquando spissius aut si ego sum tardior, profecto numquam conquiescam neque defatigabor ante, quam illorum ancipitis vias rationesque et pro omnibus et contra omnia disputandi percepero."—Cic[ero]. De Oratore, Bk. III., 36.

Watson, in his translation of the orators,[3] renders ancipiti *doubtful*, and not *twofold*, as in the sixteenth chapter. I give his rendering:—

"In regard to which (in qua) I could wish that that were true which you have often asserted, that it is not necessary to consume our lives in it, but that he may see everything in it who only turns his eyes toward it; but even if the view be somewhat obscure, or I should be extraordinarily dull, I shall assuredly never rest, or yield to fatigue, until I understand their *doubtful* (ancipitis) ways and arts of disputing for and against every question."

Again: "Tertium dubitandi genus est, cum pugnare videtur cum honesto id, quod videtur esse utile; cum enim utilitas ad se rapere, honestas contra revocare ad se videtur, fit ut distrahatur in deliberando animus adferatque ancipitem curam cogitandi."—Cic[ero]. De Officiis, Bk. I., 3.

To illustrate further another thought, that *anceps* may have a derived or figurative signification which seems to be in harmony with its etymology, I quote from Virgil a passage in the Æneid, where this word occurs with the peculiar meaning of *treacherous* or *intricate*. It is found in Bk. V., 589. Reference is made to the Labyrinth with its numerous cells, winding avenues, so arranged as to lead back and forth in a maze, thus bewildering those who enter it and preventing their finding their way out of it:

> Ut quondam Creta fertur Labyrinthus in alta
> Parietibus textum caecis iter, ancipitemque
> Mille viis habuisse dolum, qua signa sequendi
> Falleret indeprensus et irremeabilis error.

Another illustration is found in the same book where the poet represents the Trojan matrons excited by Iris (through Juno) as applying the torch to the fleet of Æneas as it lay moored along the Sicilian coast in the port of Drepanum:—

Ab matres primo ancipites, oculisque malignis
Ambiguae spectare rates miserum inter amorem
Praesentis terrae fatisque vocantia regna:
Quum dea se paribus per coelum sustulit alis,
Ingentemque fuga secuit sub nubibus arcum.—Æneid V., 654, etc.

Doubtless the meaning of *anceps* in this passage is the same that of *infestae*, hostile. There are many other similar examples to be found, both in prose and poetry. It may be reasonably concluded (from what has been said that *anceps* has no fixed meaning, but so far as one signification is more permanent than another) from an etymological standpoint, that *anceps* means *doubtful* in the sense of *critical* or uncertain, rather than double, and that meaning is by far more in keeping with the context of the lines quoted from the twenty-sixth chapter of Cæsar's Commentaries.

Notes

1 [Charles H. Halsey,] Etymology of Latin and Greek [1882].

2 St. Paul, Epistle to James (i:8).

3 [J. S. Watson, *On Oratory and Orators* (1881).]

On the Accent and Meaning of Arbutus

Education 9 (February 1889): 396–398.

Shall we say *árbutus* or *arbútus*? Both Webster and Worcester, in the older editions, adopt the latter pronunciation. Professor Fisk P. Brewer of Grinnell, Iowa, at the recent meeting of the American Philological Association, suggested that the accent should fall upon the first syllable, and he has abundant support for his theory.[1] I remember no instance whatever among the classic writers in which the accent is placed upon the second syllable, but it is invariably upon the first.

Horace Bk. I., Ode I,:—

> "Est qui nec veteris pocula Massici,
> Nec partem solido demere de die,
> Spernit, nunc viridi membra sub arbuto,
> Stratus, nunc ad aquæ lene caput sacræ."

> *"One puts not mellow Massic's cups away,*
> *Nor scorns to filch a part from solid day,*
> *His limbs now 'neath the green árbutus spread,*
> *Now by some sacred water's gentle head."*

The meter demands that the first syllable should be accented.

The verses quoted also make it quite evident that the meaning of the word is that of a tree, and *not the common Mayflower*, as popularly used; but a tree under whose lofty shade goats love to graze and idle men, like happy-go-lucky fellows whom Horace describes delight to lie, that they may be protected from the scorching Italian suns.

Virgil, G., II., 69:—

"Inseritur vero ex fetu nucis arbutus horrida."

"The rugged Arbutus is, forsooth, grafted with a scion of that nut tree."

Then again, Virgil, G., III., 300:—

"Post, hinc digressus, jubeo frondentia capris, Arbuta sufficere et fluvios praebere recentes."

"Afterwards, departing from my subject, I ordered (the farmer) to give the goats the Arbutus branches, and supply them with fresh water."

Many similar examples occur in both the *Georgics* and the *Eclogues*, as well as in Horace and Pliny, from which the meaning and size of the arbutus tree may be quite accurately determined. In every instance the demands of the meter place the accent on the first syllable, and where the authority comes from for accenting the second *at any* time I am unable to say.

Ovid, Metam[.], X., 101 sq.:—

Ornique et piceæ, pomoque onerata rubenti
Arbutus, et lentae (victoris praemia) palmæ,
Et succinta comas hirsutaque vertice pinus,
Grata deum metri.

"The mountain-ash, the pitch pine, the arbutus laded with red ripe fruit, and the pliant palms—the reward of the victor, etc., are all agreeable to the mother of the gods."

Professors F. D. Allen, of Harvard University, and T. D. Seymour, of Yale, with other high philological authorities, adopt the same accentuation as Professor Brewer. Arbutus is kindred in meaning with *arbor*, a kind of tree that is very abundant in Italy. Professor Brewer defines it as a small tree or shrub, growing to the height of about twelve feet. In this instance I think the term shrub is inapplicable. Arbor alone may refer to an alder tree (*alnus*), fig tree (*ficus*), fir tree (*abies*), palm tree (*palma*), or the cypress tree (*cupressus*), but never as far as I know to the arbutus.

This species was also well known among the ancient Greeks as far back as the times of Aristophanes. For in his Birds he presents Pisthetærus as saying,—

"An olive tree, again, will be the temple of the august birds; and we shall not go to Delphi or to Ammon, and sacrifice these, but we will stand amid the *arbutus* and the wild olives with barley and wheat and pray to them, holding up our two hands, to grant us some share of blessings. And these shall immediately be ours, when we have thrown to them a little wheat."

We infer that the arbutus here spoken of is a tree and not a shrub as the prefix *arbor* implies, arb-utus. The ending—*atus* occurs with many words in the Latin language, and denotes what the thing has, its qualities or its characteristics. In like manner, the ending—*utus* is also used, e. g., *cornutus, horned; nasutus, large nosed; arbutus, having the properties of the arbor or tree.*

To say, then, that it means, or has at any time meant the common *Mayflower* as popularly known among us, is to have a wrong conception of its etymological relations and to give it a meaning that the ancients never thought of, and philologists will not accept. Lexicographers so far as they have not done so will doubtless correct the mistakes of the old dictionaries and give *arbutus* its proper accent and meaning. The Ericeæ, which contain a number of species,—trees and shrubs of various sizes,—constitute the order of which arbutus is a genus. The fruit is somewhat fleshy, with five cells, and is many seeded. The *Arbutus Únedo* is found in Southern Europe, also in Asia and

America. It grows to the height of twenty or thirty feet. The bark is rugged (*horrida*). The flowers are large; in color, a greenish white.

Another species is seen in the *Arbutus Andrachne*, found in Great Britain as an ornamental plant; though hardy, it is often killed by frosts. Among others may be mentioned the *Arbutus Integrifolia*; *Arbutus Furens*; *Arbutus Aculeata*; *Arbutus Uva Ursi*, sometimes called *Arctostaphylos Uva Ursi*, and the *Arctostaphylos Alpina*—all of which are more or less evergreen, and grow to heights varying from three to twenty feet. The fruit is sometimes eaten, as in the case of the *Arbutus Integrifolia*, in Greece and the Oriental countries. Very few species are found in this country; they are common to Europe and South America. The *Arbutus Aculeata*, which resembles our myrtle, is found on Staten Island, I belive, where is grows in unusual abundance. The species we find in America does not spproach the great size or even the beauty of its European cousins, but it is more on the order of the *bush*—less stately and less attractive—sometimes a "large bush," so called.

Note

1 [See Fisk P. Brewer, "A New Word: Arbútus," summary, *Transactions of the American Philological Association* 19 (July 1888): xxvii–xxviii.]

Observations on the Fourth Eclogue of Virgil

Education 10 (September 1889): 28–33.

This Eclogue, unlike the remaining nine, has little in common with the pastorals of Theocritus, except, perhaps, some casual references to a few rural scenes. In this respect, Virgil has departed from his master and has adopted a style peculiarly his own—"transcending bucolic limits," as it seems to the writer.[1]

For glow of imagery and exaggerated effusion, it stands alone. Between the human and the divine there is more of the latter than of the former. It is a remarkable production—abounding in passages of striking resemblance to many of the Messianic prophecies.

There is just enough of the maze about it to confuse the reader and make it doubtful as to the poet's real meaning. Shakespeare did not err when he said:—

> "The poet's eye in a fine frenzy rolling
> Doth glower from heaven to earth, from earth to heaven;
> And as imagination bodies forth
> The forms of things unknown, the poet's pen
> Turns them to shape and gives to airy nothing
> A local habitation and a name."[2]

The sentiment expressed in these lines is fully verified in this celebrated Eclogue. The date of this poem is said to be about 40 B. C., or 714 A. U. C., during the consulship of Asinius Pollio, a friend of the poet Virgil, and one to whom he was indebted for the restoration of lands which had been formerly confiscated by an order of Augustus. In view of his services many have supposed that Virgil testifies his gratitude to the father by dedicating these lines to the son; further, that the key to the poem is found in verse 17:—

"Pacatumque reget patriis virtutibus orbem."

"He shall rule the world reduced to peace by his father's virtues."

That is, the son of Pollio shall reach the highest honors in the Roman State, and shall rule in great pomp and splendor. His reign shall be an era of peace, and shall be beneficial to all classes—plebeian as well as patrician.

Orbem seems to include the world as then known to the Romans—the Roman empire as a whole. If we accept this interpretation, then the office referred to could not have been that of the consulship alone, but rather that at the head of the empire itself. However, the prophecy was not fulfilled, as the son of Pollio died in nine days after his birth. The chief objection, nevertheless, is, taking the Eclogue in its entirety, that the poet has ascribed to the son of a mere man what might fittingly be attributed to a divine rather than a human being, whether *advocate, senator,* or *conqueror*.[3]

It is true that the golden age was looked for and extravagant expressions indicating its approach marked nearly every page of both prose and poetry, as may be observed in the following verses:

> "Pauca tamen suberunt priscae vestigia fraudis,
> Quae temptare Thetim ratibus, quae cingere muris
> Oppida quae jubeant telluri infindere sulcos.
> Alter erit tum Tiphys, et altera quae vehat Argo
> Delectos heroas: erunt etiam altera bella,
> Atque iterum ad Trojam magnus mittetur Achilles.
> Hinc, ubi jam firmata virum te fecerit aetas,
> Cedet et ipse mari vector; nec nautica pinus
> Mutabit merces: omnis feret omnia tellus."—(Virg. Ecl. IV., 31–39.)

I cannot believe that Doctor [Joseph] Trapp is correct in his interpretation of—

"Aspice convexo mutantem pondere mundum," etc.

"Look with compassion upon a world laboring and oppressed with a load of guilt and misery." I am rather inclined to believe that the poet meant to say,—

"Behold a world reeling to and fro with its vaulted mass, earth, expansive sea and high heaven; behold how all nature rejoices at the approach of the golden age." (Virg. Ecl. IV., 50 Sqq.)

There is a similar thought to be found in the 68th Psalm, 8th v., also 114th, 7th v. The one refers to the coming of the Deity; the other to the earth's trembling at His presence. There are many other parallel passages noticeable in the Eclogues and the Psalms.

Professor [Charles S.] Jerra[m], the English scholar and classical editor, regards the language of verse 17, Ecl., as inapplicable to the consular dignity of Pollio. He thinks it is rather an exaggerated description of consular power. This is doubtless the correct view to take of it. As to vagueness of language and expression, Virgil has succeeded admirably. He leaves the reader to draw his own conclusions as to the real thought of the poet, and to surmise the best he can as to who is the principal hero—the son of Pollio, Marcellus, or the offspring of Octavianus and Scribonia.

If we turn to verse 49,—

"Clara (cara) Deûm suboles, magnum Jovis incrementum!" we observe that the reference is evidently made to the great Julian family—"*divi genus.*" (Vide Aen. VI., 790, etc.)

"Hic vir, hic est . . . Augustus Cæsar," etc., etc.

The *aurea condet saecula qui rursus*, v. 792 of this same book, "he who again shall establish the golden age," etc., is the theme of Ecl. IV.—*the age of peace.* Virgil lays great stress upon this phase of his Eclogue and praises without stint the infant boy (nascentem puerum), who is to be the future ruler of the empire. Says he, "Jove nascenti puero," "Be propitious to the infant boy." As to who this boy is, whence he comes, are questions that have not been settled.

I venture the suggestion, which is by no means a new one, that reference, indirectly at least, is made to the advent of the Messiah, and to the peaceful state of things at that period—the golden age that is to follow.

There seems to have been about this time a general belief that a Messiah would come into the world. His appearance was doubtless looked for by many of the Romans as well as Jews. As is well known, the Jews were spread in considerable numbers over the Roman empire, and the Jewish scriptures had become known to many who were not of Jewish extraction. Virgil probably obtained some knowledge of these sacred writings through some such channels. There is no authority whatever for assuming that the poet was inspired, or that he wrote under inspiration in the same sense as St. Paul and other sacred writers. Whatever else may be drawn from vv. 54, 55, there is no ground for attaching to the passage any such meaning as *divine inspiration.*

Spiritus here means poetic inspiration which the poet desired should remain just long enough to enable him to describe the deeds of his mystic hero. If any such interpretation could be put upon the passage, I am sure that our more recent editors and annotators of Virgil—Allen, Greenough, Frieze, Johnson, Papillon, Jerra[m], etc.—would not have omitted to make some mention of the fact.

If Virgil had no knowledge of the Scripture, we are at a loss how to account for the parallelisms that seem to exist between this Eclogue and the language of the prophet Isaiah and the psalms already referred to. We must not forget that the traditions of a "Messianic kind" were wide-spread, and that it is not assuming too much to suppose that the poet had a traditional knowledge of the Sacred Narrative.

Some have supposed that as the images employed by the poet are common to all descriptions of a golden age, and as abundant parallels are found in the Greek and Latin classics, it is unnecessary to seek further explanation. Usage is sufficient to make what seems obscure perfectly clear. While it is true that Hesiod and many subsequent writers have adopted extravagant figures descriptive of the golden age, there are few passages I believe where the meaning of the writer is so difficult to understand as the Eclogue in question. Other poems of Virgil are a key unto themselves, but this one seems to be a remarkable exception. To show further the resemblance between this Eclogue of Virgil and portions of the Sacred Narrative, I make a few other citations. Says Virgil:—

"Nec magnos metuent armenta leones."

"Nor will the common herds fear the lions of great size," etc.—(Ecl. IV., 22.)

Isaiah speaks thus:—

"And the cow and the bear shall feed; their young ones shall lie down together; and the lion shall eat straw like an ox," etc.—Chap. II., v. 7.

Again in Isaiah (LXV., 25),—

"The wolf and the lamb shall feed together," etc.

Virgil, in his Eclogue:—

"Occidet et serpens et fallax herba veneni occidet," etc.

"The serpent shall die and the deceiving poisonous herbs," etc.—(Ecl. IV., 24).

Another from this Eclogue—

"Jam redit et Virgo, redeunt Saturnia regna," etc.

"And now returns the Virgin (the Goddess of Justice) and the reign of Saturn," etc.

In Genesis we find the following:—

"And I will put enmity between thee (serpent) and the woman, and between thy seed and her seed; it shall bruise thy head and thou shalt bruise his heel."—(Chap. III., 15.)

Remarkable passages are these—strange coincidences. The poisonous herb shall die. There shall not remain one plant whose destructive properties shall injure man or beast. The serpent whose head was to be bruised by the Messiah shall no longer exist, the terror of mankind.

If this coincidence is to be explained by the poet's acquaintance with the later Sibylline books which were manufactured at Alexandria, then those books must have reflected Jewish ideas largely. There is no other alternative.

Some writers hold that the child referred to was that of Antony and Octavia, by whose marriage [in October 40 B.C.] the peace of Brundisium was solemnized. This interpretation according to [T. L.] Papillon, rests upon the "authority of [Quintus] Asc[o]nius Pedia[n]us, and is adopted by [Johann Carl Otto] Ribbeck and Professor [W. Y.] Sellar, but," continues he, "it is difficult to think that Virgil could, under the circumstances, speak of the child of any subordinate person as the regenerator of the Roman world." In truth, it is so difficult as to make it highly improbable.

In the sixth book of the Aeneid, Virgil compliments Marcellus, but this is not sufficient to prove that similar compliment was intended in the fourth Eclogue of his Bucolics. Vide Aen. VI., 861, Sqq.

Marcellus was born during the consulship of Pollio, was adopted by Augustus, and was intended by him to be his successor in the empire.

The closing lines of this Eclogue are exceedingly beautiful:—

"Incipe, parve puer, risu cognoscere matrem;
Matri longa decem tulerunt fastidia menses;
Incipe, parve puer: cui non risere parentes,
Nec Deus hunc mensa, Dea nec dignata cubili est."

"With a smile, dear boy, begin to recognize thy mother," etc., etc., etc.

The child is not yet born, and these lines seems to be of the nature of a prayer, invoking blessings upon it, its mother, and its future career. The child is commanded to smile that its mother may smile in return —a good omen; for him upon whom his mother has smiled, a God will honor at his table and a Goddess will bless with the marriage tie.

Notes

1 [Scarborough is quoting from the summary of his American Philological Association paper (July 1888), "Observations on the Fourth Eclogue of Vergil," and he modifies the phrase "transcends bucolic limits" to "transcending bucolic limits."]

2 [This is from Theseus's speech in *A Midsummer Night's Dream*, act 5, scene 1, lines 12–17.]

3 These terms are used by Horace in his Ode to Asinius Pollio (Bk. II., Ode I.), in which he counsels him to cease writing tragedies until he shall have finished his history.

Bellerophon's Letters, *Iliad* VI. 168 ff.

summary, *Transactions of the American Philological Association* 22
(July 1891): l–liii.

Owing to the lateness of the hour, the paper was read by title only.

Πέμπε δέ μιν Λυκίηνδε πόρεν δ᾽ ὅ γε σήματα λυγρά, etc.
Misit autem ipsum in Lyciam, deditque ei *notas* perniciosas, etc.
The story of Bellerophon briefly told runs thus:—
Bellerophon, a comely and virtuous youth, incurred the displeasure of Antea, the wife of Proetus, king of Argos. She therefore falsely accused him to her husband, charging him with an attempt on her honor. The irate husband, however, refused to lay violent hands upon our hero, but sent him to Iobates, his father-in-law, with letters—"deadly characters" (σήματα λυγρά)—in a sealed package (ἐν πίνακι πτυκτῷ), requesting that the bearer be put to death.

What were these characters, these letters? Were they simply pictorial signs, mere hieroglyphics, crudely conveying the king's wishes to his father-in-law, or what? It is my opinion that they were genuine letters in written characters. This view is based upon the presumption that the art of writing was not wholly unknown in Homeric times; that it was probably employed for general purposes, though crudely; that σῆμα, aside from its ordinary meaning, may express the idea of written characters.

There is a strong presumption that the Greeks had frequent commercial intercourse with the Phoenicians prior to 1100 B.C., and through these relations they obtained some knowledge of written alphabetical characters. It is hardly supposable that a people like the Greeks would not have taken advantage, even in those earlier days, of all the opportunities of developing their civilization, which the social contact with Phoenician life might afford.

The lack of the testimony of monumental inscriptions cannot be taken as an argument against this view, for the reason that many of these inscriptions, and especially those bearing upon this point, both of historical and anti-historical times, have been lost.

[F. A.] Wolf and his school, of course, oppose this view. Hug and others declare that the unity of the Iliad is a strong proof of the use of writing in Homeric times.

"The cramped and awkward characters of the earliest extant marbles," if they prove anything at all, certainly suggest an imperfect knowledge rather than absolute ignorance of the art.

[J. P. B.] Kreuser years ago, in his *Vorfragen über Homeros* [1828], showed that πτυκτῷ implies that σήματα might have been understood by Bellerophon, and that πολλὰ suggests words, and not picture writing.

Wolf, in his vain endeavor to make σήματα mean everything but one thing (γράμματα), gives away his case when, in the 19th chapter of his Prolegomena [1795], he makes this statement:—

> "Sed qui duo sunt apud Homerum loci, in quibus simile quidem scripturae reperitur, accurata interpretatio facile vincet, eos non magis de scriptura accipiendos esse, quam celebrem illum Ciceronis de typographia nostra."[1]

Apollodorus applies the term ἐπιστολή to these σήματα (Il. Z 168), in the following brief manner:—

Προῖτος ἔδωκεν ἐπισκολὰς αὐτῷ πρὸς Ἰοβάτην κομίσειν, ἐν αἷς ἐνεγέγραπτο Βελλεροφόντην ἀποκτεῖναι.

[William Seymour] Tyler, in his *Theology of the Greek Poets* [1887], and Professor Jebb, in his *Introduction to Homer* [1887], are both of the opinion that Homer not only knew the art of writing, but that he himself might have used it as circumstances demanded. This is my own view of the matter.

Σῆμα, though most frequently used by Homer with a meaning equivalent to the Latin *signum*, sometimes has other translations:

Il. X. 466 . . . . . δέελον δ᾽ ἐπὶ σῆματ᾽ ἔθηκεν.
Latin equivalent . . . . conspicuumque *signum* apposuit.

Il. XXII. 455 . . . . λευκὸν σῆμ᾽ ἐτέκηκτο, etc.
Latin equivalent . . . . alba *macula* erat, etc.

Il. II. 308 . . . . . ἔνθ᾽ ἐφάνη μέγα σῆμα. . . .
Latin equivalent . . . . illis apparuit magnum *signum*.

Il. II. 353 . . . . . ἐναίσιμα σήματα φαίνων. . . .
Latin equivalent . . . . fausta *signa* ostendens.

Il. VIII. 171 . . . . σῆμα τιθεὶς Τρώεσσι.
Latin equivalent . . . . *signum* dans Trojanis.

Il. XIII. 244 . . . . δεικνὺς σῆμα βροτοῖσιν.
Latin equivalent . . . . ostendens *signum* hominibus.

Il. II. 814 . . . . . ἀθάνατοι δέ τε σῆμα, etc.
Latin equivalent . . . . immortales autem *sepulcrum*.

Il. XXII. 30 . . . . . σῆμα τέτυκται.
Latin equivalent . . . . *signum* est.

Il. XXIII. 326	σῆμα δέ τοι ἐρέω.	
Latin equivalent	*metam* autem tibi indicabo.	
Od. XIX. 250	σήματ' ἀναγνούσῃ, etc.	
Latin equivalent	*signa* agnoscendi, etc.	
Od. XX. 111..	σῆμα ἄνακτι.	
Latin equivalent	*signum* regi.	
Od. XXI. 231	ἀτὰρ τόδε σῆμα τετύχθω.	
Latin equivalent	at hoc *signum* fiat.	
Il. XXIII. 843	ὑπέρβαλε σήματα πάντων.	
Latin equivalent	jecit ultra *signa* omnium.	

These are simply a few of the numerous examples that might be taken in proof of the indefinite meaning which σῆμα is found to possess.

Herodotus informs us that he himself has seen in the temple of the Ismenian Apollo at Thebes in Boeotia Cadmean letters engraved on certain tripods, for the most part resembling the Ionian. One of the tripods has this inscription:—

"*Amphitryon dedicated me on his return from the Teleboans.*"

These must be about the age of Laius, son of Labdacus, son of Polydorus, son of Cadmus.[2] This was considerably earlier than the Trojan War,—about 1550 B.C.,—the time, according to the myth, Cadmus is supposed to have lived. What these ἐπιγράμματα were we are not told, but we infer that they were real alphabetical letters.

Notes

1 Vide *De Natura*.

2 Vide H[ero]d[o]t[us]. v 59.

On Grote's Interpretation of Ἀνέλπιστοι

Education 12 (January 1892): 286–293.

Καὶ νῦν οὔτε ἀνέλπιστοί πω μᾶλλον Πελοποννήσιοι ἐς ἡμᾶς ἐγένοντο, εἴ τε καὶ πάνυ ἔρρωνται, τὸ μὲν ἐς τὴν γῆν ἡμῶν ἐσβάλλειν [κᾶν] μὴ ἐκπλεύσωμεν, ἱκανοί εἰσι, τῷ δὲ ναυτικῷ οὐκ ἂν δύναιντο βλάπτειν. ὑπόλοιπον γὰρ ἡμῖν ἐστιν ἀντίπαλον ναυτικόν.—Thucyd[ides], VI., 17.

Grote renders this passage somewhat as follows: "As to the Peloponnesians, powerful as they were they were not more desperate enemies (ἀνέλπιστοι) now than they had been in former days: they might invade Attica by land whether the Athenians sailed to Sicily or not; but could do no mischief by sea for Athens would still have in reserve a navy sufficient to restrain them."[1]

In a foot-note he tells us that the construction of ἀνέλπιστοι is not certain. Then he adds, "I cannot think that the meaning which Dr. Arnold and others assign to it is the most suitable. It rather seems to mean the same as in VII., 4, and VII., 47: enemies beyond our hopes of being able to deal with." [Henry] Dale, on the other hand, gives us the following translation: "And as things stand now, never yet were the Peloponnesians more hopeless (ἀνέλπιστοι) with regard to us; and even if they are ever so confident, for invading our country indeed they are strong enough, even though we do not undertake the expedition; but with their naval force they cannot hurt us [though we do not undertake it;][2] for we have a fleet left behind that is a match for them."

A writer in the Journal of Classical and Sacred Philology[3] gives the sense of this passage as follows: "In the first place (τε) the Peloponnesians never were so hopeless of success (ἀνέλπιστοι) against us; and secondly (τε), supposing them to be in ever such good heart, they can but invade us by land, and that we cannot prevent in any case while we shall always have a sufficient naval force at home to prevent their attacking us by sea." This interpretation I have adopted as the one most in accord with the facts in the case, both historical and linguistic, and, therefore, the one most probable.

It is evident that Dale and the writer just quoted, agree as to the construction and meaning of ἀνέλπιστοι, and that both are opposed to the historian Grote.

If we turn to the lines referred to by Grote, we shall find that instead of strengthening the ground taken by him, the passages in question make his position utterly untenable, and consequently, unjustifiable. I quote: προσεῖχέ τε ἤδη μᾶλλον τῷ κατὰ θάλασσαν πολέμῳ, ὁρῶν τὰ ἐκ τῆς γῆς σφίσιν ἐπειδὴ Γύλιππος ἦκεν ἀνελπιστότερα ὄντα.—Thucyd, VII., 4.

The second:—

* * * * Καὶ τὸ χωρίον ἅμα ἐν ᾧ ἐστρατοπεδεύοντο ἐλῶδες καὶ χαλεπὸν ἦν, τά τε [ἄ]λλα ὅτι ἀνελπιστ[ότατα] αὐτοῖς ἐφαίνετο.— Thucyd, VII., 47.

In both instances the adjectives (ἀνελπιστότερα, ἀνέλπιστα) are neuter, and have what may be called a passive signification; while in the passage under consideration the word is used actively, as also in VIII. 1. (ἀνέλπιστοι ἦσαν σωθήσεσθαι).

Dr. Gottfried Boehme[4] says in his note on this passage, "νῦν könnte man aus einer Brachylogie erklären, indem gedacht näre: und jetyt steht die Sache so: nie waren die Pelop. hoffnungsloser: doch besser nimmt man wohl eine Vermischung zueier Redeweisen an: 1) und jetyt sind die Pelop. hoff-nungsloser als je, 2) und noch nie waren die Pelop. hoffnungsloser als jetzt.— ἀνέλπιστοι aktiv. s. 8, 1, 2 und in etwas verschiedenem Sinne 3, 30, 2. In passiver Bedeutung, wie es Kr. erklären enöchte, kommt es bei Thuk. nur von Sachen, nicht von Personen vor (s. Bétant lex.)."

Another passive use of ἀνέλπιστος is found in VI., 33, 34: καὶ οὐκ ἀνέλπιστον ἔμοιγε κ. τ. λ., also, καὶ ἡμῖν οὐκ ἀνέλπιστον τὸ τοιοῦτον ξυμβῆναι κ. τ. λ.—δοκεῖ δέ μοι καὶ ἐς Καρχηδόνα ἄμεινον εἶναι πέμψαι[.] οὐ γὰρ ἀνέλπιστον αὐτοῖς, ἀλλ' [ἀεὶ] διὰ φόβου εἰσὶ μή ποτε Ἀθηναῖοι αὐτοῖς ἐπὶ τὴν πόλιν ἔλθωσιν, κ. τ. λ.

If it is true that when applied to things ἀνέλπι[σ]τος has a passive signifi-cation, as has been stated, it is very doubtful whether an instance can be found where, in its passive sense it is applied to persons. If, however, there are any examples illustrative of this application of the adjective, I have not been able to find them. As in Latin, so in Greek, we find words and especially adjectives used in this double or twofold sense—actively and passively—their significa-tion depending upon the gender of the substantive with which they agree. *Fidus* when spoken of in its relation to persons may be rendered: *faithful, trusty, reliable*, etc., when used with neuter substantives it takes a *transferred* meaning, *sure, safe*, etc.

> *Diffugiunt alii ad nares, et litora cursu*
> *Fidi petunt.*—Verg. Aen., II., 399.

Mentita may be mentioned as another example:—

> *Primi clypeos mentitaque tela*
> *Agnoscunt, atque ora sono discordia signant.*—Verg. Aen., II., 422.

Other examples may be given, and these are only a few of the many that frequently occur in Latin authors: *castus*, of persons, *spotless*—of things, *sacred*, e. g. *nemus castum*; *benignus*, of persons, *friendly, kind, benevolent*—of things, *rich, fruitful, abundant*; *blandus*, of persons, *bland, persuasive, smooth-tongued*—of things, *agreeable, enticing, pleasant*; *beatus*, of persons, *blessed, happy, rich, wealthy*—of things, *splendid, magnificent*, e.g., *gazæ, beatus*; *durus*, of persons, *hard, rude, obdurate*—of things, *irksome, arduous, troublesome*; *inca[u]tus*, of persons, *incautious, unsuspecting*—of things, *dangerous, unsafe*; *inimicus*, of persons, *hostile, unfriendly*—of things, *unfavorable, injurious*; *iniquus*, of persons, *hostile, unfair, unjust*—of things, *hard, severe*; *severus*, of persons, *serious, grave, stern*—of things, *rough, frightful*.

φοβερός, like ἀνέλπιστος, is often employed in a double sense. In Thucyd., II., 3, the translation of φοβερός is *timid*: "when things were in readiness, as far as they could make them so, having watched for the time when it was still night and just about daybreak, they began to go out of their houses against them; that they might not attack them by daylight, when they would be bolder, and on equal terms with themselves, but in the night when they would be more timid (φοβερύτεροι), and fight at a disadvantage through their own acquaintance with the city."[5] In VI., 55, it expresses the idea of terrifying: "But owing to his former habit, both of striking fear (terrifying, φοβερόν,) into the citizens, and of paying strict attention to his mercenaries, he retained his sway with abundant security," etc.[6]

Though we find the terms ἔχθροι and πολέμιοι *seemingly* used indiscriminately in Thucydides as often applied to one party as to another, yet we observe no instance in which ἀνέλπιστος is employed as a synonym of either or both.

The adjective with its noun-forms and verb-forms, simple and compound, is of frequent occurrence in Thucydides with meaning more or less fixed, and there could have hardly been any doubt in the mind of that historian as to its real signification.

(a)—In bk. I., ἀνέλπιστος does not occur; in bk. II., it occurs once; in bk. III., three times; in bk. IV., once; in bk. V., once; in bk. VI., five times; in bk. VII., three times; in bk. VIII., once: *total, fifteen times*.

(b)— Ἀνέλπις (hopelessness) does not occur anywhere in Thucydides.

(c)—In bk. I., ἐλπίς occurs six times; in bk. II., fourteen times; in bk. III., eight times; in bk. IV., five times; in bk. V., five times; in bk. VI., six times; in bk. VII., ten times; in bk. VIII., nine times: *total, sixty-three times*.

(d)—In bk. I., ἐλπίζω, with various forms of the participle, occurs five times; in bk. II., eight times; in bk. III., four times; in bk. IV., eleven times; in bk. V., six times; in bk. VI., five times; in bk. VII., five times; in bk. VIII., four times: *total, forty-eight times*.

WHOLE NUMBER OF INSTANCES, 126.

(a)—As ἀνέλπιστος does not occur in bk. I., there are no examples illustrating its use and construction.

Ἀνελπίζω occurs but once (Bk. 1–70), and that too, with the meaning, *to hope instead* or *in turn*: "Then, if they fail in an attempt at anything by forming fresh hopes in its stead, they supply the deficiency; for they are the only people that succeed to the full extent of their hopes in what they have planned, because they quickly undertake what they have resolved."—ἦν δ᾽ ἄρα του καὶ πείρα σφαλῶσιν, ἀντελπίσαντες ἄλλα ἐπλήρωσαν τὴν χρείαν. κ. τ. λ.

I have examined with some care many Greek authors, and am unable to find ἀνέλπιστος conveying a meaning different from the usual one: *hopeless, something unexpected, unlooked for,* however greatly the object may be desired. For example, in the Suppliants of Aeschylus (319, κ. τ. λ.), the king of the Pelasgians says to the Chorus: "You seem now to me to share this land of old; but how did you dare leave your paternal abodes? What misfortune has come upon you?"

The Chorus responds:

> ἄναξ Πελασγῶν, αἰόλ᾽ ἀνθρώπων κακά.
> πόνου δ᾽ ἴδοις [ἂν] οὐδαμοῦ τα[ὐ]τὸν πτερόν,
> ἐπεὶ τίς ηὔχει τηνδ᾽ ἀνέλπιστον φυγὴν
> κέλσειν ἐς ᾽Άργος κῆδος ἐγγενὲς τ[ὸ] πρ[ί]ν,
> ἔχθει μεταπτοιοῦσαν εὐναίων γάμων;

In Sophocles (Tr. 673), Deianira speaks of a circumstance that occurred as being an unexpected (ἀνέλπιστον) marvel.

Again, in the Electra (186, κ. τ. λ.) of the same author, the following occurs: "But from me the greater part of life hath already passed away *without hope,*" etc., etc.,

> (᾽ἀλλ᾽ ἐμὲ μὲν ὁ πολὺς
> ἀπολέλοιπεν ἤδη
> βίοτος ἀνέλπιστος κ. τ. λ.).

In the Helen of Euripides (411, κ. τ. λ.), the poet puts into the mouth of Menelaus, these words:—

> τρόπις δ᾽ ἐλείφθη ποικίλων ἁρμοσμάτων
> ἐφ᾽ ἧς ἐσώθην μόλις [ἀνελπίστῳ] τύχ[η]
> ᾽Ελέν[η] τε, Τροίας ἥν ἀποσπάσας ἔχω.

Theocritus (Idyll IV., 40–44), makes Corydon, the cow-herd, use the following language:—

> Θαρσεῖν χρ[η], φίλ[ε] βάττ[ε] τάχ᾽ αὔριον ἔσσετ᾽ ἄμεινον
> ᾽Ε ἐν ζωοῖσιν ἀνέλπιστοι δε᾽ θανόντες χ[ώ] κ. τ. λ.

In ἐλπίδες ἐν ζωοῖσιν ἀνέλπιστοι κ. τ. λ., we have two contrasted ideas, "hope in life—hopelessness in death," or, while living there is always hope for the better (ἔσσετ᾽ ἄμεινον), but dead, our hopes are "blasted" (ἀνέλπιστοι θανόντες). The same thought is expressed by the poet, Tibullus:—

> *"Credula vitam*
> *Spes fovet et fore cras semper ait melius."*

It is unnecessary to quote further. Suffice it to say, that examples are to be found in Plato, Xenophon, Demosthenes, Andocides, etc., illustrating a similar meaning and construction of this adjective—all of which prove that Grote has greatly erred in his interpretation of it.

As a matter of history it will not be out of keeping with the design of this paper to give in conclusion a brief summary of the causes and results of this great struggle, as it will aid in our purpose to show that there was no ground, no just ground at least, for asserting that the Athenians regarded the Peloponnesians as desperate enemies before the battle of Aegos Potami. I quote the language of the historian himself:[7]—

"The Peloponnesian war was a conflict between Athens and her allies, on the one hand, and Sparta and her allies on the other. It began in 431 B. C., lasted twenty-seven years, and ended in weakening Greece generally, and in completely destroying the Athenian ascendancy."

"This war was occasioned by the jealousy which the great power of Athens stirred up among many other of the Greek cities; but it had in reality a deeper cause; it was the outbreak of an irrepressible conflict between Ionians and Dorians, between democracy and oligarchy,—Athens being the chief of the Ionian and democratic states, and Sparta the chief of the Dorian and aristocratic states. The immediate occasion of the war was a conflict between Corinth and one of her colonies, Corcyra. Siding with the latter, Athens executed the wrath of the Dorian confederacy; and a Spartan army invaded Attica 431 B. C. During the first ten years of the war, down to 421, the two parties contended with nearly equal success, the Athenians being much the stronger by sea, and the Spartans and their allies by land. A peace was then concluded, called the peace of Nicias (421 B. C.), which was to last for fifty years; but as many of the confederates were dissatisfied with its terms, it was not likely to be of such long duration, and indeed, hostilities were renewed almost immediately."

"The renewal of the war was precipitated through the political influence of Alcibiades,[7] a handsome, dissolute young disciple of Socrates; he possessed brilliant talent, but he was ambitious, and he was eager to renew the war, as affording him an opportunity of personal distinction."

"Alcibiades brought forward a scheme of conquering Syracuse, a city in Sicily. It was a bold scheme, and its successful execution would have given a great preponderance to Athens over Sparta. The Athenians adopted the plan, and in B. C., 415, sent a fleet and force against the Syracusans. Sparta sent aid to the Syracusans, and thus the Peloponnesian war was renewed. In the midst of the enterprise Alcibiades was recalled to Athens on a charge of impiety; but he managed to escape, and went over to Sparta. The Syracusan expedition proved a total failure (413, B. C.), and greatly damaged the power of Athens. During the last eight years the Peloponnesian war was carried on mainly at sea, off the coast of Asia. Sparta allied herself with Persia, and it was Persian gold that afforded Sparta the means to continue the contest against Athens. Athens, however, made a bold front, and under the lead of Alcibiades (who had meanwhile been recalled to the command), kept up the contest with wonderful vigor. But a fatal blow fell when the Spartan admiral, Lysander, surprised the beached galleys of the Athenians at Aegos Potami in the Hellespont, B. C., 405. The siege and surrender of Athens in the following year brought the great Peloponnesian contest to an end."

"The result of the Peloponnesian war left Sparta the greatest power of Greece. Athens sank into the background as a second-rate state; still, while she lost her political supremacy, she became more and more the leader in literature, art and philosophy."

"After the decline of Athens, Sparta stood without a rival in Greece, and for thirty-four years from the victory at Aegos Potami to the defeat of Leuctra (405, 371 B. C.) the Lacedaemonians exercised an undisputed sway in Greece."

From this period, if ever (the downfall of Athens), the two powers, Athens and Sparta, might be regarded as *"desperate enemies"*—["]*enemies beyond our hopes to deal with.*" If this view be accepted as tenable, may we not then assert from an historical standpoint, that Grote's interpretation of ἀνέλπιστος is untenable; and that Alcibiades meant in his speech before the Athenian assembly, convened to hear the report of their commissioners on their return from Egesta, that the Peloponnesians were *"hopeless"* in the sense that they were not powerful enough, had not resources enough to make a successful resistance against the Athenian forces? Up to the time of the Athenian defeat there was no reason whatever for believing that the two contending parties were uncompromising enemies, other than a desire on the part of the one (prompted by jealousy), to surpass the other in glory, in power, and in the extent of conquests; no ground for affirming that deadly hostilities, beyond reconciliation, existed between the rival parties until the lustre of Athens began to wane, while that of Sparta began to increase. Then, and not till then (after the battle of Aegos Potami), it seems to me, are we justified even on historical ground in rendering ἀνέλπιστοι *"enemies beyond our hopes of being able to deal with."*

Notes

1 Vol. VII., P. 154, History of Greece. (Am. Ed.)

2 [The square brackets around "though we do not undertake it;" are in the original article.]

3 Published in London, 1854. [Possibly Edward M. Cope.]

4 Thukydides, fur den Schulgebrauch [1894] erklart von Dr. Gottfried Boehme, Professor und Prorector am Gymnasium zu Dortmund.

5 Dale's translation.

6 Swinton's Outlines of the World's History (Ancient and Modern) [1874], page 100.

7 Vide Grote, also Thucydides.

Hunc Inventum Inveni
(Plautus, Captivi, 442)

summary, *Transactions of the American Philological Association* 24
(July 1893): xvi–xix.

Whether Plautus was purposely obscure or whether the obscurity is due to the license to which Schlegel refers when, in speaking of Terence, he says, "Even his contemporaries reproach him with having falsified or corrupted a number of Greek pieces for the purpose of making out of them a few Latin ones," is in some respects an open question. No one will deny that the Latin comic poets assumed liberties and licenses in attempting to copy the new Greek comedy and to adapt Greek originals.

This may not be due either to indifference, to laziness, or to that "negligentia" which Terence praises and which Dr. West in his excellent edition of Terence says must not be confounded with slovenliness.[1] The liberties referred to may be attributed to some other causes,—to undue haste prompted by the need of money, to the genius and structure of the Roman tongue, possibly to the character of the audience for whom the plays were intended. Whether one of these or all of these, the fact remains the same that Plautus has succeeded well in weaving into his plays here and there an obscure passage that neither context nor the circumstances of the play itself seem to throw much light upon. The passage under consideration is one of them.

In this passage it will be observed the alliterative element appears, to the frequent use of which Plautus was especially addicted. It occurs, indeed, with almost clock-like regularity, and to my mind the indication is that there was method in its use, that it was not merely accidental or a fortuitous coincidence.

Be this as it may, no one can deny its large presence in his plays.

Plautus was not alone in its use. Alliteration was a Latin characteristic. To quote Professor Peck,[2] "Those who to-day doubt, as Lachmann doubted, the presence of alliteration as characteristic in Latin diction, should in this particular compare such contemporary and fairly comparable writers as Lucretius and Catullus, Cicero and Caesar, Virgil and Horace."

But we are forced to the conclusion that in too many instances Plautus sacrificed clearness to the swing of the verse that alliteration enabled him to give. The present passage, in my opinion, is a strong illustration of this.

Let us turn to the act and scene itself.

The personae of the 3d scene (Act II.) of the Captivi are Hegio, the rich old man of Aetolia, Philocrates, a captive, and his slave, Tyndarus (Hegio's own son, but as yet unknown to him as such). Hegio turns to Philocrates, mistaking him for the slave, tells him that his new master desires that he should pay faithful obedience to his former owner in whatever he may wish, and further that he is desirous of sending him to his father in order that he may secure the return of his son.

Philocrates declares himself ready to do anything that he is commanded to do. Tyndarus appeals to Philocrates not to forget him when he has returned to his own country. Philocrates assures him that he will be true to the trust reposed in him. The language of both is designedly ambiguous, as Hegio is standing in hearing distance and it is the purpose of each to deceive the old man. I quote:

"Serva tibi in perpetuom amicum me atque hunc *inventum* inveni."

Some editions have the following:

"Serva tibi in perpetuom amicum me atque hunc *inuentu* inueni."

Hallidie gives the following note on the passage:[3]

"Inuentu *by finding his son*'; so Sch[legel], who refers to Merc. 847, eorum inuentu. The MSS. reading, inuentum, is taken to mean '(on your return) find a friend in this man, in whom we have already found one'; in support of it [Julius] Brix quotes Men. 452, homines occupatos occupat, Cur. 540, subiges redditum ut reddam tibi, Cic. Fam. XIV. 1, uide ne puerum perditum perdamus."

[W. M.] Lindsay says: "*hunc*: i.e., Hegio, 'and do not lose this one you have found.'"

[C. S.] Harrington gives this as his opinion:

"*Hunc inventum inveni.* The meaning of this passage is much disputed. *Hunc* is referred to Hegio and to his son, and to Tyndarus in the character of Philocrates. Some translate, 'And still find Hegio yours, as you have found him'; others, 'Find this young man, already in part found by the information we have given of him'; or, 'Find a friend in this young man, discovered and restored to his father.' Brix says, 'Gain one already gained to be wholly a friend to you.' *Insure Hegio's perpetual friendship by the restoration of his son.*"

It will be seen from the extracts given that editors are not all agreed as to the exact meaning and translation of this line; and no one of them, so far as I have observed, ventures to give an interpretation of his own, but each contents himself with giving what others say.

Dr. [John] Proudfit approaches nearest an acceptable interpretation of the passage in question of any of the editors and annotators of Plautus that I have consulted. He disposes of it as follows:

"*Hunc inventum inveni*. This obscure passage has given rise to many con-
jectures. Some interpret thus: '*Find* a friend in Hegio, *already found*,' *i.e.*, confirm his friendship to you by restoring him his son. Others suppose it to refer
to the son of Hegio: '*Find this* young man, already in part *found* by the information we have given of him.' Both are unsatisfactory. It most probably refers
to the son of Hegio in a different sense, and the whole line may be interpreted
thus: 'Make me your friend forever, and *find* (*gain*) a friend in *this* young man,
discovered and restored to his father.'"

The meaning of this particular line is determined by the antecedent of
hunc. If we make this antecedent Hegio, then it would read, "Find this person,
Hegio, a friend still as you have found him." This is not a common-sense
translation, taking the material we have to make it out of. What ground have
we for declaring that Hegio was ever a friend to either of these, Tyndarus
(though his son) or Philocrates, both of whom were as yet unknown to him at
the time the play begins? Philocrates was a prisoner of war, and was purchased
with others by the old gentleman, who hoped to find his son among the number. Tyndarus was the servant of Philocrates at the time of the purchase. Both
were strangers, at least so far as Hegio's knowledge went, and were thus
regarded till the discovery was made by the return of Philopolemus through
the agency of Philocrates, and till Tyndarus had been sent for to come home
from the quarry to which he had been taken.

Again, no such translation as the following is allowable, neither will the
Latin permit it, whatever be the suggested relations of the words of the passage: "Make this old man, Hegio, a friend and keep him so by finding his son
and returning him to his father." The editors who adopt this view have no
ground for it whatever, it seems to me, and are doing violence to the verse that
they are striving so hard to explain by making it mean what it has never meant
and cannot now mean. I quote the context and a portion of what follows:

> "Scito te hinc minis viginti aestumatum mittier.
> Fac fidele sis fidelis, cave fidem fluxam geras.
> Nam pater, scio, faciet quae illum facere oportet omnia.
> Serva tibi in perpetuom amicum me atque hunc inventum inveni.
> Haec per dexteram tuam te dextera retinens manu
> Opsecro, infidelior mi ne fuas quam ego sum tibi."

If we make *hunc* refer to the son of Hegio, Philopolemus, the meaning is
clear and the interpretation is simple. The thought in the mind of Tyndarus,
doubtless, was the absent Philopolemus for whom Philocrates was now to be
sent. He is not lost, as Hegio supposes, but *found* (*inventum*). The play upon
words comes in the *finding* and the already *found*. To the old man, Hegio, he
was lost, hence the word *find* (*inveni*) could be with propriety used; to
Tyndarus he had already been *found* (*inventum*). The cleverness of Plautus
appears in the use of the two words *inventum* and *inveni*,—the one referring
to one person, the other to another; *inveni* (*find*) from Hegio's point of view
and *inventum* (*found*) from that of Tyndarus. With *hunc* referring to the son of

Hegio, the thought suggested by the passage would be, *and do you now seek out this person whom we have discovered to be in possession of Menarchus. Go fetch him to his father, for we know where he is. He is no longer lost, but found (inventum).* This latter rendering seems to me to be in keeping with the idea intended to be expressed by Plautus himself, and therefore to be the only intelligent and rational view to take of it with the light we have at hand.

It will be observed that I have based the remarks of this paper upon the reading *inventum*, as found in the text of [Charles F. W. A.] Fleckeisen (Teubner series) and upon which Harrington and others based their editions of Plautus, and not upon the reading *inventu*. (Vide Ausgewählte Komödien des T. M. P. für den Schulgebrauch erklärt von Julius Brix, II., 2d ed., 1870 (Captivi); T. M. P. comoediae. Ex recognitione Alfredi Fleckeiseni, 2 vols.; Fr. Ritschl über die Kritik des Plautus, eine bibliographische Untersuchung (1836) in his Opuscula philologica, II., 1868, I sqq.)

Hallidie, who substitutes *inventu* for *inventum*, avails himself, as he tells us, of the *apparatus criticus* in Professor [Fritz] Schoell's edition of Plautus and a collation of V included in his preface to the Casina, 1890.

Inventum is found in all the MSS., B D V E J. This being true, the question arises, How did *inventu* creep into the text? Is it an interpolation, a mistake of the copyist, or did some editor or scholiast insert it to help himself out and to make the text read as he thought it ought to read? I have not accepted the substitution because it lacks MS. authority, so far as I have been able to observe.

With an interpretation based upon *inventu* the translation suggested by this paper would necessarily be modified, and the interpretation given of it by the majority of editors would stand.

Notes

1 [Andrew Fleming West, *Andria et Heauton Timorumenos* (1888).]

2 Transactions American Philological Association, 1884.

3 [Archibald R. S. Hallidie, *The Captivi of Maccius Plautus* (1891).]

The Chronological Order
of Plato's Writings

Education 14 (December 1893): 213–218.

At the meeting of the American Philological Association held at the University of Virginia (Charlottesville), I discussed, in brief, the subject that constitutes the head of this article.[1] I shall now present to the readers of Education the result of subsequent investigation aside from the views presented on that occasion.

That Plato stood in the front rank of the philosophers of his time, few will deny; that as pupil and companion of Socrates, he came nearest of all of his contemporaries, reflecting the views of the great teacher, is equally true; that he was an idealist to all intents and purposes and in many important respects *sui generis* is also conceded, and that his conception of ethics and ethical instruction will always present a field for study not only to the educator but to the general reader as well, needs no proof.

Plato, indeed, is our pioneer educator, from whom many of our educational theories have sprung and to whom we are indebted for many ideas relative to methods and aims in education—only we have failed to give him credit for them.

Our interest in Plato as a teacher, as an expounder of moral truths is in fact the genesis of a similar interest in the chronological order of his writings. Aside from this, the inquiry is of little value.

Thirty-five dialogues and thirteen epistles have been generally ascribed to Plato.[2] *Schleiermacher*, the celebrated German translator of our author, gives us four divisions as follows: "*those of the first class comprehend the elements of philosophy*, as the Phædrus, Protagoras, Parmenides, Lysis, Laches, Charmides and E[u]thyphron; *in the dialogues of the second class these principles receive their application*, as in the Gorgias, Theæte[t]us, Menon, E[u]thydemus, Sophists, Politicus, Phædron and Philebus; in *the dialogues of the third class the investigations are of a more profound character*, as the Timæus, Critias, Republic and Laws: *the fourth class includes the dialogues of circumstance*, so called, as the Crito and the Apology."

Anthon[2] regards this division as ingenious but of little real value, as the first three classes are not based upon such a chronological order as to enable us to see the "system of Plato come into existence, develop itself and attain to maturity."

Socher, another German scholar of considerable note in his *Uber Platons Schriften*, etc., adopts the following grouping: 1. *Dialogues relative to the trial and death of Socrates,*—the E[u]thyphron, Apology, Crito, Phædrus and Cratylus; 2. *Dialogues which form a kind of continuation of each other,*—The Theætetus, Sophists, Politicus, Republic, Timæus and Critias; 3. *Dialogues directed against false philosophy,*—The E[u]thydemus, Protagoras, Gorgias, Ion and Hippias; 4. *Dialogues treating of speculative questions,*—the Phædron, Theætetus, Sophists, Philebus, Timaeus, and Parmenides; 5. *Dialogues devoted to politics or the art of government,*—The Politicus, Minos, Republic, Laws and Epinomis; 6. *Dialogues treating of Rhetorical topics,*—the Gorgias, Menexenus, Phædrus and Banquet; 7. *Dialogues relative to individuals accustomed to associate with Socrates,*—The Theages, first Alcibiades, Laches and Theætetus; 8. *Dialogues in which the question is discussed whether virtue can be taught,*—E[u]thydemus, Protagoras and Menon; 9. *Dialogues in which false opinions are considered,*—The Theætetus, Sophists, E[u]thydemus and Cratylus; 10. *Dialogues, the titles of which indicate particular subjects,*—The Charmides, or of Moderation, Laches, or of Bravery, Lysis, or of Friendship, and E[u]thyphron, or of Piety.

The objection offered to this classification is that the utility of arrangement is destroyed by placing the same dialogue under so many different heads at the same time, according to the point of view from which it is considered.

Some have divided the literary life of Plato into four periods and have attempted to fix a chronological order from that device. This *modus operandi* is certainly preferable to some we have seen, though it failed to establish anything definite or reliable.

Diogenes quotes from Aristophanes of Byzantium—the first possibly to make an attempt at a chronological order of the Platonic dialogues and gives his divisions into trilogies as follows: 1. The Republic, Timæus, Critias; 2. The Laws, Minos, Epinomis; 3. The Theætetus, E[u]thyphron, Apology; 4. Sophists, Politicus, Cratylus; 5. Criton, Phædron and Letters. The remainder of the dialogues was left unclassified.

After these books had been conveyed from the Platonic School at Athens to the Alexandrian library, Aristophanes and Eratosthenes made a critical examination of the same—throwing much light upon them. Of their works very little is now extant. The fact, however, that the genuineness of some of these dialogues has long been a matter of dispute puts out of the question—in a measure at least, tangible evidence as to a definite chronological order of the Platonic writings. But if any evidence at all is produced that may be taken as surely reliable it must come from Plato himself—it must be internal rather than external.

In the absence of dates, a close analytical study will have to be made of the structure, the syntax, the style and the grammatical relations of sentences and the results compared with the usage of the times in which the dialogues are said to have been written as well as with one another.

Socher questioned the genuineness of the Sophist and the Politicus on the ground that they lacked the general characteristics of Plato's style. His position was substantiated by Schaarschmidt. Similar objections were made against the authenticity of the Laws, although Aristotle some time before had declared them genuine. Granting, then, on the testimony of Aristotle, that the Laws are authentic and likewise the other dialogues that approximate those that are received as authentic, Schleiermacher raised the question of the order of these dialogues—chronological rather than logical—(for I do not hold these two terms to be necessarily the same nor necessarily different). I believe with Grote that Plato deliberately intended his compositions as perfectly distinct works and consciously laid aside in each all reference to the rest as regards theory.

We take up the Theætetus and what do we observe? Why that the same characters are present as in the Sophists, but their line of argument is by no means a continuation of any discourse begun in a previous composition.

In a paper in the *Bibliotheca Platonica*, Professor Campbell, of St. Andrew's University, Scotland, makes the statement that he has established the genuineness of the Sophist and the Politicus and has assigned them their proper place in the order of composition of Plato's dialogues. The plan adopted by him is the group system. He collected the traits and characteristics common to the Philebus, Sophist and Politicus and arranged them according to their homogeneity. In the same manner other groups were taken and common traits selected and arranged according to the homogeneity of form. In this way the entire list may have been gone over and the chronological order approximately established. After considerable research I find that many of the formulæ and particles by Euripides, said by some to be exclusively confined to Platonic usage are used by Aeschylus, Aristophanes and one or two other tragic and comic writers.

Again the formulæ and idiomatic expressions as well as the particles referred to by Dittenberger and other German critics may be taken as marking the contrast between the Republic, the Phædrus, Theætetus and the earlier dialogues; hardly more than that.

That τὶ μήν does not occur in some of the dialogues but is frequently employed in the Phædrus, the Theætetus, the Republic, the Sophist, the Politicus, the Philebus and the Laws, proves very little it seems to me. That mannerisms abound in the Platonic dialogues can hardly be denied, but in themselves they are of little moment in fixing either the logical or chronological order of these compositions.

An observable mannerism in Plato is the addition of περ as a suffix to such adverbial forms as μέχρι, ὅπη, ὁσαχή, ὅπου, ὁπόσοι forming the particles, μέχριπερ, ὅπηπερ, ὁσαχηπερ, ὅπουπερ, ὁπόσοιπερ. Instances of this kind may be found throughout the Platonic series. In Sophocles Odipus Tyrannus—1458—we find ὅπ[οι]περ used in the following line:

ἀλλ' ἡ μὲν ἡμῶν μοῖρ' ὅπ[οι]περ εἰσ, ἴτω.

"But for my fate, let it go, which-way-so-ever it will"

For ὅπηπερ, ὅποιπερ is sometimes written, especially in the tragedies, and yet these two forms are not exactly synonymous as to meaning; the one implies the place, *where*; the other, *whither*.

In Soph. Ajax, ὅποιπερ occurs in the following line and with the following meaning:

810. ἀλλ᾽ εἶμι κἀγώ κεῖσ᾽ ὅποιπερ ἂν σθένω.

"But I will begone whithersoever I shall have strength."

An example of the use of ὁποιόσπερ is found in Aesch.[3] Cho. 669.

In the paper referred to in the *Bibliotheca Platonica*, Prof. Campbell calls attention to the fact that Dr. Schanz pointed out in 1886 a curious variation in the comparative use of τῷ ὄντι and ὄντως; the latter though only found in a comparatively few dialogues yet even in these instances seems to have supplanted τῷ ὄντι. The former is a Platonism—pure and simple —and is found only in Euripides aside from Plato, so far as I have observed.

I have not examined all of the forms in Plato and therefore base my authority upon that of another in the following tabulation:

(1) ὄντως is not found in Laches, Charmides, Protagoras, E[u]thydemus, Apology, Crito, E[u]thyphron, Gorgias, Menon, Symposium: τῷ ὄντι is present in all of these except in the Charmides, Crito and Meno. τῷ ὄντι occurs once in Sophist, and not at all in Politicus, Philebus, Timæus[,] Crito etc.

ὄντως is found in

Sophist	21 times
Politicus	11 "
Philebus	15 "
Timæus	8 "
Laws	50 "

Ὀχεδὸν without τι following is regarded by Campbell and others as a Euripidean idiom, and yet I have found examples of a similar use in Homer, Pindar, Herodotus, Demosthenes, and with verbs of knowing, in Sophocles and others.

Many tragic forms are employed by Plato in these dialogues and some Ionic expressions. The Ionic dative plural is found in both the Politicus and the Laws as well as in the Phædrus and Republic. Plato seems to have borrowed from all literature, whether Epic, Lyric, or Tragic. He has also interwoven much of the poetic element—and in the Phædrus it is said that he uses 170 words that do not occur elsewhere in any of his writings—while in the Th[e]ætetus which represents his normal style, 93 words are similarly used. The Phædrus has been assigned a late date for various reasons—one of which is the avoidance of a hiatus—but Blass thinks this is not at all sufficient in itself and I think Blass is right. For one isolated case is not sufficient to prove anything either in regard to their genuineness or the order of composition in point of time.

If we can establish what Plato's latest style actually was and then can trace the transition step by step from his earliest to his latest there will be little or no difficulty in fixing the chronological order of these dialogues.

We know the change[4] in Plato's manner of writing as he grew older; we know also from a careful perusal of his works that his style grew stiff, while the tendency to adopt "new derivatives" and tragic terms seem almost marvellous. Taking this into account and the internal evidence gathered from the style, the syntax, the grammatical relations and structure of sentences together with the subject matter, including the logic, the metaphysics, physics, politics, ethics, etc., etc., etc., we can see nothing strange in saying that a chronological classification is by no means an impossibility. In fact it is a part of the natural order of things with no other data than that given above.

Notes

1 [For a description of that meeting, held in July 1882, see *Autobiography*, pp. 120–122. See also Scarborough's "The Chronological Order of Plato's Dialogues," summary, *Transactions of the American Philological Association* 23 (July 1892): vi–viii.]

2 [Charles] Anthon's Classical Dictionary.

3 Aeschylus Choephorae.

4 Compare Paradise Lost and Paradise Regained.

Cena, δεῖπνον, prandium, ἄριστον

summary, *Transactions of the American Philological Association* 25
(July 1894): xxiii–xxv.

There are few words, perhaps, in classical literature, more variable in meaning than the four selected as the subject of this paper.

Ordinarily we speak of δεῖπνον as a late meal, and, in this sense, equivalent to δόρπον; cf. *Od.* XII. 439; IV. 429; II. 20; vide Aesch. Fr. 181: ἄριστα, δεῖπνα, δόρπα θ' αἱρεῖσθαι τρίτα. Among the three meals mentioned here, δόρπον comes last, and must correspond to our supper, or cena in Latin, when used as a late meal.

δεῖπνον, though sometimes equivalent to ἄριστον, an early meal, varied with the fashion of the day, sometimes early, sometimes late.

The phrase, ἀπὸ δείπνου, found in Homer and elsewhere, may mean *straight-way after dinner*, or simply after a meal, with the idea of *chief meal* implied. Il. VIII. 54. In Il. II. 383, it is simply provender or dry food; vide Aesch. Supp. 801, etc. δεῖπνον is equivalent to prandium, and implies an early meal, Od. IX. 311.

ἄριστον becomes δεῖπνον, the chief meal of the day, Xen. Mem. II. 7, 12.

In Xen. Cyr. I. 2, § 11, there is a difficulty because of the indefinite meaning of ἄριστον. To the superficial or casual reader it is either breakfast or dinner. It has been suggested that ἄριστον, with the meaning of *dinner*, agrees perfectly with the statement that in two days they took the food of but one—breakfast before they left home, supper in place of their dinner, and supper, on the second night, of what they should have eaten on the evening of the first day. In the same section occurs ἀριστήσαιεν, but with the meaning (suggested by the editor[1]) of breakfast. This is only one of many instances of confusion growing out of the doubtful meaning of ἄριστον. As an early meal, vide Il. XXIV. 124, etc.; also Aesch. Ag. 331; Fr. 181.

δεῖπνον, in its relation to the modified root "*dap*" of a shorter form *da*, which carries with it the idea of distribution, means simply a meal. The same root appears in δάπτω, to devour: Il. XVI. 159; Il. XXIII. 183; Aesch. Supp. 70; Soph. O. T. 682; Aesch. Pr. 437.

The later Greeks called breakfast τὸ ἀκράτισμα; luncheon, ἄριστον, or δεῖπνον μεσημβρινόν (Athen. 1, 9, 10, p. 115). It is only with some such modifying word as μεσημβρινός that the meaning of any of these words applied to meals can be determined with any degree of definiteness. This may be said to be due to the fact that the etymology has little or no influence over the popular notion as to what the words should mean.

If we associate ἄριστον with ἕως (dawn), or with ἠέριος (early morn), then we must concede to it the primary meaning of an early meal (our breakfast). In this sense it is etymologically equivalent to prandium, which also primarily meant the first meal of the day. Cf. Thuc. VII. 81; IV. 90; Hdt. III. 26; VI. 78; Aristop. Nubes, 416; Eq. 815; Anab. IV. 6, 21, 22. δεῖπνον in Hellenistic Greek differs little from its classic use. Vide Luke xiv. 12; xvii. 8; xx. 46; xxii. 20; John xii. 2; xiii. 2–4; xxi. 20; Matt. xxiii. 6; Mark vi. 21; xii. 39; Rev. xix. 9; Dan. v. 1. It will be observed that δεῖπνον, in a few of these passages, is rendered feast, e.g. ἐν τοῖς δείπνοις (at feasts). Cf. also Rev. iii. 20; Luke xiv. 16, 17, 24. For ἄριστον, vide John xxi. 12, 15; Luke xi. 37, etc.

Prandium is derived from *pram-(e)d-iio-m, if we accept [Hermann] Osthoff's derivation. Cf. Umbr. prumum primum.

From this we get prandeo, to take breakfast; pransor, he who breakfasts. Etymologically, prandium is an early meal, earlier than midday. It is a morning meal (our breakfast). Its composition agrees with the Greek breakfast—simple. Cf. Plaut. Cap. III. 1, 19, etc.

Varying customs seem to have paid no heed to the etymology, and left it to the whim of the writer or speaker to decide for himself, not only the time but whether he must say: δεῖπνον, cena, ἄριστον, or prandium. Vide Plaut. Menaechmi III. 2, 25; II. 3, 37; Stichus IV. 2, 46; Amphitruo II. 2, 33; Hor. Sat. II. 7. 30; Cic. Mur. 35; Phil. II. 39; Ver. II. 1, 19; ad Fam. IX. 26; Suet. Cal. 58; Seneca, Ep. 83; Quint. VII. 3. 33.

Cena apud antiquos dicebatur quid nunc est prandium, says a Roman grammarian (506 A.D.). Vide Sext. Pompeius Festus, s.v. cena.

Cena is not to be associated with θοίνη, the latter word being connected with Skt. dhinoti satiate, Old Bulgarian doilica nurse. Cena, on the other hand, represents older caesna. In its more general sense, θοίνη means a dinner, a meal or banquet. ἐκ θοίνης, after dinner, occurs in Epicharmus (9, 9, Ahr.), εἰς τὴν θοίνην καλεῖν τινα, in Eurip. Ion 1140, ἐπὶ θοίνην ἰέναι, in Plat. Phaed. 247 B. Cf. Theaet. 178 D, etc.

The conclusion reached from the foregoing observations is that δεῖπνον, like cena, varied as to time from noon to midnight and possibly later, as in the case of banquets or feasts which were not ordinary meals; so, also, ἄριστον, like prandium, from early morn to midday.

Note

1 [John Jason] Owen's edition of the Cyropaedia [1846].

Extracts from Thucydides with Brief Notes, VII. 7, 1; VII. 8, 2; VIII. 29, 2

summary, *Transactions of the American Philological Association* 30
(July 1899): vii–ix.

(1) καὶ [ξ]υνετείχισαν τὸ λοιπὸν τοῖς Συρακοσίοις [μέχρι]¹ τοῦ ἐγκαρσίου τείχους' —VII. 7, 1.

(2) ἢ κατὰ τοῦ λέγειν ἀδυνασίαν ἢ καὶ μνήμης ἐλλιπεῖς [γε]νόμενοι κ.τ.λ.—VII. 8, 2.

(3) καὶ ἅμα ταῖς γοῦν ναυσίν, ἧ πρότερον, ἐθάρσησε κρατηθείς.— VII. 49, 1.

(4) —ὅμως δὲ παρὰ πέντε ναῦς πλέον ἀνδρὶ ἑκάστῳ ἢ τρεῖς ὀβολοὶ ὡμολογήθησαν.—VIII. 29, 2.

(1) And they assisted the Syracusans to complete the remaining wall up to the cross-wall, so as to make one with it (*thus forming a continuous wall*).

(2) Either because of an inability to express themselves clearly or on account of a lapse of memory, etc., etc.

(3) And at the same time—even though he had been defeated—he placed greater (μᾶλλον) confidence in his fleet than before (*an indication that he was by no means discouraged*).

(4) Nevertheless for every five ships more than three oboli were agreed upon for each man.

Possibly few passages in all Thucydides have given rise to a greater number of interpretations or have perplexed editors and expositors more than the lines quoted (VII. 7, 1).

Grote tells us that Dr. Arnold after rejecting various explanations proposed by others, and after vainly attempting to elucidate it in a way convincing to his own mind, pronounces it to be unintelligible at least, if not corrupt (pp. 274–275 Arnold). Grote himself says the words are obscure.

Colonel Leake says, "The Syracusan cross-wall (ἐγκάρσιον τεῖχος) was now united with the enclosure (see map and plan of Syracuse) of Temenitis, and thus largely extended the dimensions of that outwork of Achradina." See notes on Syracuse, p. 67.[2]

[Franz Joseph] Göller and [Connup] Thirlwall are of the opinion that τὸ λοιπόν refers to the completion of the Syracusan counter-wall which had been left unfinished. [Henry] Dale thinks otherwise.

[Samuel T.] Bloomfield suggests that the words μέχρι τοῦ ἐγκαρσίου τείχους may mean beyond the interval where the two walls converged toward each other.

Says [Ernst Friedrich] Poppo, "Haec verba si omnia retinemus, explicationem non habent. Goellero quidem Syracusani prius absolutis extremis muri tunc intermedia quoque aedificando ope Corinthiorum et reliquorum, qui tunc advenissent, videntur explevisse. Sed idem diligentius, quid verbis μέχρι τοῦ ἐγκαρσίου τείχους significari putet," etc.

[Gottfried] Böhme puts it thus: Das dies ein anderer Flügel der Syrakusischen Gegenmauer ist, als der C. 6 beschriebene, scheint mir keinem Zweifel zu unterliegen; denn letzterer hatte auf alle Fälle nicht die Richtung auf die Quermauer zu: wie hätte er sonst das nördliche Ende des athen. Baues überholen können?

Frost in his edition of Thucydides (bks. VI. VII.)[3] says that the allies, on their arrival, built a wall from a fort (τείχισμα) which they had constructed on the high ground of Epipolae to cover the approach to Epipolae by Euryâlus (VII. 43—τὸ τείχισμα ὃ ἦν αὐτόθι τῶν Συρακοσίων αἱροῦσι, i.e. near Euryâlus) down Epipolae (VII. 43—τὸ παρατείχισμα) to join the cross-wall (μέχρι τοῦ ἐγκαρσίου τείχους —VII. 7, 1). Thus the ἐγκάρσιον τεῖχος and the παρατείχισμα formed an uninterrupted line, although no doubt a curved one, from the summit of Epipolae to the Syracusan city wall.

Professor Charles Forster Smith follows [Adolf] Holm (Sic. II. 392–395) and rejects μέχρι. He is of the opinion that it may have sprung from a misunderstanding of πρὸς τὸ ἐγκάρσιον τεῖχος ἁπλοῦν (C. 4, 1).—τὸ λοιπόν is connected with τοῦ ἐγκαρσίου τείχους.—Cf. C. 71, 6.

I fail to see the necessity for rejecting μέχρι or any of the words introduced by it; I have therefore retained it in my translation. I do not regard it as an interpolation, but as a legitimate part of the text. It seems to me that, studied in the light of previous passages bearing upon this part of the narrative and of the plan and topography of Syracuse before and after the arrival of Gylippus, the text becomes both clear and simple.

At this time Syracuse was, as it were, a network of walls and counter-walls, vallations and circumvallations, constructed by both besieged and besiegers. Compare VI. 98–103 inclusive; VII. 4–6 inclusive.—Vide τείχισμα, παρατείχισμα, προτείχισμα. Gylippus built a fort (τείχισμα) on the high ground of Epipolae, at a point that seems to have been the terminus of the new wall of junction (παρατείχισμα) referred to in VII. 43. It was intended to guard the entrance from Euryâlus.

In our next passage (8, 2) some critics substitute γνώμης for μνήμης. In support of their reading they cite the three requisite qualifications of an orator.

The sense, however, requires the retention of μνήμης. *A lapse of memory* is no doubt the meaning of Nikias as represented by the historian.

In the third and fourth passages (VII. 49, 1, VIII. 29, 2) the exact meaning of κρατηθείς and παρὰ πέντε ναῦς has given rise to much confusion. In the light of the context the ordinary meaning of κρατέω seems to me best suited for this passage. If παρά is taken in the sense of εἰς or κατά, as we find it in some editions, then the translation, *for every five ships*, is most assuredly the thought of the speaker.

Notes

1 [The square brackets around "μέχρι"are in the original article.]

2 [William Martin Leake, in *Transactions of the Royal Society of Literature* (London, 1848).]

3 [Percival Frost, *The Sicilian Expedition, Being Books VI and VII* (1867).]

Brief Notes on Thucydides

summary, *Transactions of the American Philological Association* 32 (July 1901): lxxix.

II. 4. 2: τοῦ μὴ ἐκφεύγειν denotes purpose, not result. But it is better to read, with Dobree, τὸ for τοῦ.—II. 5. 7: δ᾿ οὖν means 'nevertheless.' Cp. I. 3. 5.—II. 18. 3: ξυναγωγή is to be taken metaphorically ('war-clouds').—III. 16. 3: ὃς ἔμελλεν κ.τ.λ. is not ambiguous or superfluous. As admiral Alcidas would naturally conduct the expedition.—III. 31. 1: σφίσι is to be construed with γίγνηται.—III. 82. 1: the sense demands either two finite verbs or two participles.

Notes on the Meaning and Use of *φίλων* and *ξένων* in Demosthenes, *De Corona*, 46

summary, *Transactions of the American Philological Association* 33
(July 1902): xx.

Kennedy tells us that, in his translation of this passage, he has made no distinction in meaning between *φίλων* and *ξένων* simply for the reason that the English language furnishes us no equivalent for the latter in the sense in which it is employed here by the orator.

He further adds that the word *ξένοι*, as used here, denotes absent friends—those who would be *φίλοι* if they dwelt in the same place, but being separated can only correspond or occasionally visit each other and exchange hospitality. If we follow his suggestion, the reading would be something like this: "For instead of friends (*φίλων*), as they were named when bribed, they are now called parasites and miscreants (enemies to the gods) and such befitting names." The omission of *ξένων* plainly weakens the thought and, in a sense, destroys the force of the passage. Evidently they were not only friends (*φίλοι*) in a general sense, but friends (*ξένοι*) in a more restricted sense—"plighted" friends—*Gastfreunde*, as some editors translate it—bound one to the other by reciprocal pledges of hospitality. *Mark the time.* It was during the period of bribery. May we not go a step farther by adding that this friendship (*ξενίαν*) was influenced by bribery?

The context seems to suggest, and the sequel seems to imply, this conception of the passage—*For at one time those (whom Philip had deceived and bribed, sc. φίλων καὶ ξένων) were regarded as friends (φίλοι)—friends in the ordinary sense—also friends (ξένοι) in the sense of parties mutually pledged by gifts or otherwise to support each other regardless of the nature of the cause or compact.*

During the period of bribery they (sc. Philip and those who had sold themselves to him) were friends—both *φίλοι* and *ξένοι*—but after that period, after the aspirants for power and influence had gained their object they hated and despised those through whom they had obtained it.—τότε καὶ μισεῖ καὶ ἀπιστεῖ καὶ προπηλακίζει.

Prospectively the term (ξένων) may then refer to the bribe-givers and bribe-takers—Philip and his adherents. I think this is the orator's meaning, and that φίλων and ξένων are used in a derisive sense.

Note the orator's words: εἰκότως· οὐδεὶς γὰρ, ὦ ἄνδρες Ἀθηναῖοι, τὸ τοῦ προδιδόντος συμφέρον ζητῶν χρήματ' ἀναλίσκει, οὐδ' ἐπειδὰν ὧν ἂν πρίηται κύριος γένηται, τῷ προδότῃ συμβούλῳ περὶ τῶν λοιπῶν ἔτι χρῆται· οὐδὲν γὰρ ἂν ἦν εὐδαιμονέστερον προδότου. Ἀλλ' οὐκ ἔστι ταῦτα· πόθεν; πολλοῦ γε καὶ δεῖ sqq.

Notes on Andocides and the Authorship of the Oration against Alcibiades

summary, *Transactions of the American Philological Association* 34
(July 1903): xli.

The genuineness of the Oration against Alcibiades has long been a matter of dispute. Andocidean authorship is rejected by Dionysius, Harpocration, and in modern times by [John] Taylor, [Jeremiah] Markland, [George] Grote, [Friedrich] Blass, and [R. C.] Jebb. The language of the oration is simple and just what one might expect of a man speaking under great stress of excitement and provocation. Mistakes both of fact and history are likely to follow unless the subject is well in hand.

Considering the subject from the standpoint of internal evidence, and comparing the style of this with that of other speeches said to have been delivered by this orator, there is a strong possibility that the author of the Περὶ τῶν μυστηρίων, Περὶ τῆς Καθόδου, Περὶ τῆς Εἰρήνης, and the Κατ' Ἀλκιβιάδου was one and the same man.

Transition (Transitio vocatur, quae quum ostendit breviter, quid dictum sit, proponit item brevi, quid sequatur—Cornificius) is common to all the Andocidean orations. To denote it μέν and δέ, μὲν οὖν and δέ play an important part.

"Ac primum quidem vocibus μὲν οὖν indicatur παλιλλογία vel ὁρισμός tum voce δέ significatur πρόθεσις."—[Carl Wilhelm] Linder, De rerum dispositione apud Antiphontem et Andocidem oratores. The same scholar says:

"Eodem loquendi modo (μὲν οὖν... δέ), sed non eadem vi et significatione aditus ad βεβαίωσιν patefactus est."

In § 10 (or IV.), where μὲν οὖν... δέ occur, the μὲν οὖν do not indicate a repetition (παλιλλογία, recapitulation), but rather a premonition (praemunitionem) whereby the orator prepares the minds of his audience for what is to follow.

Cf. Andocides, IV. 7, περὶ μὲν οὖν τούτων... δέομαι δ᾽ ἱμῶν, κ.τ.λ. This is only one of the many examples that might be mentioned to illustrate the points in question, and to show the common authorship of the four orations.

Notes on Thucydides

summary, *Transactions of the American Philological Association* 37
(January 1907): xxx–xxxi.

I

Κατέκλησαν (v. 83, 14). It is generally agreed that parts of this passage are corrupt, and for this reason many emendations have been suggested. [August] Bekker, [Franz] Göl[l]er, [Stephan] Krüger, [S. T.] Bloomfield, [Ernst] Poppo, [Carl J.] Classen, [Gottfried] Boehme, and others have all proposed corrections and have vigorously defended their position. [Henry] Dale, however seems to be among the extremists. He declares that the whole difficulty centres in κατέκλησαν, and that in this verb lies the root of the evil. Evidently with this thought in view he translates the words, κατέκλησαν δὲ τοῦ αὐτοῦ χειμῶνος καὶ Μακεδόνας Ἀθηναῖοι κ.τ.λ., "The Athenians ravaged (ἐλήϊσαν), too, during the same winter a part of Macedonia," etc. To avoid one extreme, he falls into another, for κατακλείω never means 'ravage.' It cannot have such a meaning. Its etymology will not permit it. Such a translation then is unwarranted, for κλείω with its compounds—in whatever sense used—always carries with it the idea of 'shutting up' or 'shutting in,' hence seclusion, from which we get the thought 'to blockade,' which is the real meaning of κατακλείω in the passage quoted. It cannot mean anything else. It is in this sense that we find it frequently employed by the philosophers, historians, orators, and poets. Dr. Dale evidently misconceives the meaning of the author, when he objects to this signification. Cf. Theocr. 7, 84; 18, 5; Xen. *Cyr.* vii. 2, 5; iv. 1, 18; Herod. i. 191; ii. 128; Thuc. i. 109; iv. 57; Ar. *Nub.* 404; Xen. *An.* iii. 4, 26; iii. 3, 7; *Mem.* ii. 1, 13; Andoc. 24, 19; Xen. *Cyr.* vi. 4, 10; iv. 1, 18; Herod. ii. 128, κ.τ.λ.

In bk. I. 117 (Thuc.) we note these words: ἐλθόντος δὲ Περικλέους πάλιν ταῖς ναυσὶ κατεκλῄσθησαν, "but when Pericles arrived they were again closely *blockaded* by the fleet." In this passage κατεκλῄσθησαν can have no other meaning than the one given it—'blockaded.' Herodotus (ii. 86) in referring to the ancient Egyptian custom of embalming their dead uses the words καὶ κατακλήσαντες οὕτω θησαυρίζουσι, κ.τ.λ., that is, 'and having enclosed the body (of the mummy in a case) they store it in a sepulchral chamber,' etc. These references all show that Dale is not correct when he claims that κατακλείω never means *to blockade*, but that it always "refers to men being shut up in particular places."

II

θαρσῆσει κρατηθείς (*id.* vii. 49, 7). The readings of this passage vary, but even then very little light is thrown upon it. The fact is, as it stands, it is impossible of translation. It has been remarked that this passage in Thucydides is very curious, and so it is. Frost renders the words θαρσῆσει κρατηθείς thus: 'overpowered, as it were, with confidence more than before.' Dale puts it this way: 'because he was influenced by confidence in his fleet at any rate more than before.' Boehme would change the reading by changing the tense of the verb—substituting ἐθάρσησε for θαρσῆσει—but this leaves the sentence just as obscure as before, because the root of the trouble is not in the verb. In fact, all the suggestions of the critics have been rather of the nature of an interpretation than a translation; for as the passage stands, a translation in the usual sense of the word is impossible without completely emending the text.

The Greeks and Suicide

summary, *Transactions of the American Philological Association* 38
(December 1907): xxii–xxiii.

Ο[ὔ] φασι θεμιτὸν εἶναι αὐτὸν [ἑ]αυτὸν ἀποκτιννύναι.—Plato's *Phaedo*, 61 E.

The significance of this passage depends wholly upon the meaning that is given θεμιτόν. Like *fas*, θέμις may express a duty or obligation from a moral point of view—a religious act, *e.g. Od.* xiv, 56, οὔ μοι θέμις ἔστι, κ.τ.λ.—'It is not right for me to dishonor a stranger' (ξεῖνον). It is frequently used with this meaning in Homer. But θέμις (√Θε, τίθημι) like θέσμος (Dor. τεθμός) in its etymological sense refers to an established rule or law—that which is laid down—human or divine. Ancient usage, however, has given it a fixed meaning. It has put upon it a divine seal—the sanction of the gods. In this sense it seems to have been generally employed by Greek writers. Cf. Plat., Xen., Aesch., Soph., Eurip., Pind., Hdt., Dem., etc., etc.; Cicero and Virgil (the fate of Dido).

When Plato therefore represented Cebes as saying, *ο[ὔ] φασι θεμιτ[ὸ]ν,* κ.τ.λ., he evidently meant that it was not the will of the gods—of the Greek deities—that one should take his own life—that it was not in keeping with the theology of the Greeks to do so. Inasmuch as suicide was a violation of divine law, it goes without saying that it was contrary to human law.

Pythagoras, to whom both Greek and Roman writers made copious references and whom they regarded an authority on this subject, took a decided stand against self-destruction. Plato himself drew largely from the philosophy of Pythagoras and accommodated much of it, as he did that of his revered master, Socrates, to his own system and life.

In reply to Cebes Socrates is represented as quoting from Pythagoras: *ὁ μὲν οὖν ἐν ἀπορρήτοις λεγόμενος περὶ αὐτῶν λόγος,* κ.τ.λ. vide *Phaedo*, 62 B. In the *de Senectute*, 73, Cicero says: Vetatque Pythagoras *iniussu imperatoris*, id est dei, de praesidio et statione vitae decedere. Cf. *T. D.* i, 74: *injussu suo.* Rather than submit to Caesar, M. Porcius Cato took his own life.

During the days of the Empire there was so little regard for life that it was a common occurrence—perfectly in keeping with dignified conduct—for one to take his own life to free himself from troubles. During the days of the Republic it was different. The strenuous Roman was otherwise occupied and suicides were fewer.

The drift of public sentiment, even in the earlier days of Greek life, was against αὐτουργία (αὐτοφονία); cf. Aesch. *Eum.* 336.

Politics, Policy, and Prejudice

A Nationality

Christian Recorder, April 13, 1876.

It would be well for the advocate of *en masse* migration, self government, distinct nationality, etc., to put aside the trite theory that this is a white men's government and endeavor to bring about a better state of things here upon this our own continent by harmonizing as far as possible the discordant elements existing among the members of the colored race here in the South at least so that they will work together, and also to inculcate the necessity of educating and requiring wealth if we wish to hold what belongs to us and maintain our independence whether here or in Africa. Education, wealth, harmony and Union are elements, among others absolutely essential to a nationality in the strictest sense of that word. These I claim we as a race have not and are therefore not ready for the undertaking or even its agitation. These views to some, may seem frank and untimely, but nevertheless they are true. It is a fancy, an idle fancy to say because white settlers once left their mother country and came to another for the purpose of building it up we are justifiable in doing likewise. We are not to follow precedent just now. No, time and circumstances do not demand such a movement on our part.

The undertaking would be as wild as it is unreasonable. We have a vital interest in this country and government; for we helped to make it what it is; in part it is the result of our labor, and every effort put forth to euchre us out of this claim is a direct violation of right. That our future is dark and gloomy I am compelled to admit. That we labour under political as well as social disabilities, to an alarming extent is very evident, but I consider even the agitation of this question as much out of place as the undertaking itself would be, viewing it from our present condition, and circumstances. I hope for better things and sincerely believe my hope will not be in vain. Down South we have unfortunately been the dupes of leaders in a very great degree, who were grasping after the almighty dollar forgetful of the interest of their constituents, but mindful (?) of their own. They have been bought and sold for a few pennies; they have gone around with petitions soliciting the names of as many of their colored constituents as they could deceive to remove the disabilities from such men as Hardeman here in Georgia and others who they very well knew, would use their influence to crush the colored man whenever opportunity presented itself.[1] These are among the conspiring influences that have tended to render the colored man's condition not hopeless but *very, very* undesirable. If there had been the right kind of politicians and preachers in days past our condition would have been vastly different from what it is. But it is said that we should let the dead past bury the dead past, so we return to the present. One Alexander G. Murray of Griffin, Ga., advocates *en masse* migration voluntary or compulsory on the ground that it would be better for the country at large.[2] He thinks that ten year's experience has rendered it evident that the two races can not prosper mixed up as one people, and if a separation cannot be brought about, abject poverty and degradation is certain to befall both and this will lead to indiscriminate amalgamation. Hear him in his own language and then you will be convinced that the age of fanaticism has not yet passed. He says: "An all-wise God made the African, implanted in him his nature from which his character and disposition are formed, and placed him in Africa where the spontaneous productions of the earth furnish him food, and where the climate is mild the year round that he will not suffer from cold even if devoid of raiment. God made Africa to suit the negro and the negro Africa; and it was a violation of the laws of nature to take him from his native soil and undertake to citizenize him elsewhere. Africa is his Canaan, and back to Africa he ought to go. He has served out his time here as a slave, and therefore he ought to make his exodus back to his promise[d] land." He thinks it may be necessary to use the purse and power of the nation, but this will be small compared to the mischief he will do it suffered to remain. He thinks further that the government should (insanely) attempt to make him go, whether he wills or not. He thinks further that war is inevitable at no distant day provided he continues to sojourn in the land of his birth etc., etc. This Mr. Murray claims to be a white man loyal to his country and government, and to have voted for Mr. Grant in '68 and '72. We are certainly glad that he has his country at heart, and will therefore let his view go for what it will bring. In regard to bettering our condition, as I have before stated[,] I do not think the proposed plan will do it, though it cannot make it much worse, and its agitation only tends to keep the minds of the people unsettled. I hope every friend to humanity will use his influence toward changing our condition on this our own soil and let migration rest for a while.

From the following outrage it will be seen that injustice still stalks to and fro under guise and the poor colored man knows not when he will become its victim. About three weeks ago a colored man was shot and killed a few miles from Cochran[3] by a young white man named Graham under the most unprovoked circumstances. It is said that Graham and his father were returning from Cochran with a loaded ox wagon which became stalled in a bog. A colored man who was sitting on a fence near by was insultingly ordered by this young Graham to get down at once and come and assist them get the wagon out of the mire. The old man got down but not as quickly as Graham thought he ought to have done. He threatened to kill him if he did not hasten. As the colored man neared the wagon the young fiend (Graham) drew his pistol and fired two shots, one of which produced instant death. The deceased was about sixty five years old and was killed in the presence of his wife. The next question is, what was done with the murderers—for there were two concerned, father and son—they made their escape as usual. But as their escape was somewhat singular, it is believed to be a concocted plan pre-arranged. Graham and son after having been incarcerated for a few minutes asked the keeper to allow them to stop out privately for a short time, which being done, they were never heard of more, at least we have not heard of them since. This is only one of many like occurrences.[4]

Notes

1 [Thomas Hardeman Jr. (1825–1891), Democrat, served in the Confederate army and was later a member of Georgia's house of representatives and a U.S. representative from Georgia.]

2 [Alexander Murray married Martha Weems and had a son, Samuel W. Murray, in 1853.]

3 [Cochran, the seat of Bleckley County, was named for Arthur E. Cochran, president of the Macon and Brunswick Railroad.]

4 [Scarborough subscribed this article "Macon, Ga., March 29, '76."]

The Exodus—A Suicidal Scheme— The Machinations of Disappointed Office Seekers

Christian Recorder, January 3, 1878.

Severing themselves entirely from the traditions, superstitions and precedents of the past; entering upon a new system of philosophy, founded upon intelligence, wealth and union; and at the same time aiming at the establishment of principles of thrift and industry; it is obvious that the colored citizens of this great Republic should not for a moment permit themselves to be decoyed into a scheme that will probably prove suicidal to their best interests. By scheme, I mean the cunningly devised plot to slip to Africa as many as possible of the Southern blacks, on the ground of ameliorating their condition; also on the ground that this is the white man's country and not the negro's as well. By what course of reasoning these conclusions are reached, I am unable to tell but suffice to say, the sooner these disappointed office-seekers divert themselves of these absurd notions, and turn their attention toward educating and lifting up their fellows to a higher plane of civilization, the better it will be for themselves, their race and their country.

In part, these very men who are crying, "*let us come out from under the heel of oppression*," are responsible for this oppression and the abject condition of their race. They have held various positions in church and state; in the latter positions varying from the common sherriffalty to the executive's chair, and the race to-day is only the worse off for it. Such actions are a disgrace to humanity.

In South Carolina it is said, thousands are selling or letting their little farms and homes by way of preparation for leaving America, men, women and children, all have the African mania. My advice to these people now, is this, to pay no attention to these fair promises[;] if they have sold their farms, buy them back if possible; if they have leased their farms, rent others till the lease expires and then return to their own; or if this is not desirable, seek homes in the great west in the land that gave us birth, forgetting color, race, or condition only to rise above it.

And why is this the better plan? The poor ignorant masses will not do as well in Africa as in America. To prove this I quote from Prof. Blyden, in the July number of the Methodist Quarterly Review. He, in speaking of unskilled labor says: "In Liberia there is no lack of the lower kinds of unskilled labor supplied by the numerous aborigines who throng the settlements. The immigrant, who comes from America, is at once made a proprietor. He has land given him by law, but having no capital to employ labor he must enter single-handed upon the work of subduing the forest, and with all the efforts he may put forth, it is with the utmost difficulty that he ever rises above a hand-to-mouth existence. Hence very often men owning this twenty-five acres of land, pressed by their necessities, prefer to leave it a wilderness and go to the arduous, and for new comers, perilous labor of shingle and lumber getting or enter the employ of men, who may be able to keep them from starving but hardly able to give them a start toward self-support on their own lands."[1] When it is remembered that Prof. Blyden is a citizen of Liberia and knows whereof he speaks, there will be no reason to doubt the truth of the above statement. Take it as true and act accordingly.

I regard the Liberia Exodus Association as another Credit Mobilier affair, on a small scale. We judge of an undertaking by the character of the men engaged in it. Now it does not require a profundity of knowledge to tell who and what these men are; what has been their past history, what it is now and what it will probably be in the future. All these we can pretty well determine. It is stated on good authority, that a petition will be sent to Congress praying for aid, the exact amount not being stated.

However I am confident that I express the feeling of hundreds of the better thinking colored citizens, when I say that Congress should make no appropriation for any such pell mell movement. If Congress wishes to make an appropriation for the negro, let it make it with the restrictions that is shall be used to pay off the deficit caused by the sinking of the Freedmen's Savings Bank; or for the purchasing of lands and outfits in the great West, that the Negro may wend his way thither, build up and utilize the hitherto barren country. The time has come in which the black man is to work out his own salvation in this country, by what he "does and dares," cutting through the inevitables in making a niche for himself. He cannot rise by simply wishing. No, not at all.

In further proof of the utter unreasonableness in even supposing that the ignorant masses can emigrate from this country to Africa and succeed better there than here, permit me to again quote from Prof. Blyden, in the July number of the *Review*.

He says in regard to the new comers: "Inferior also in educational training to the peasants, vine-dressers, tradesmen, mechanics and common laborers who go from Germany to the United States and soon better their condition and prospects, the negro immigrant coming to this country—Liberia—in his poverty, can do nothing well but swell the indigence and incompetency which already hamper the progress of the nation.

Such persons driven to Liberia by want of subsistence, that subsistence is all they will care to seek or find in Liberia. Thus we get among us a permanent pauper class." This needs no explanation, is full enough and, in the writer's opinion, is one of the many convincing arguments which may be adduced to show the folly of the present movement and the fanaticism of its leaders.

From this then it may be rightly inferred that while the writer does not approve of the proposed exodus because, among other reasons, it is untimely and uncalled for; because the end sought will not be secured and because it is a useless expenditure of money. I say while the writer[']s opposition to the movement may be inferred, it may also be inferred that he does favor devising some means by which men of color may rise to higher levels in the enjoyment of civil, political and equal rights in America. It is a matter of regret that the moral, intellectual and physical condition of the negro is so low in one portion of the country: not hopeless, as has been termed, but lamentably bad. Will he ever amount to anything in America? is a question too often asked by his enemies, and even those professing to be his friends, and, sad to say, too often answered in the negative. I do not think that there is cause to despair in regard to the future of the colored man in America. Only be charitable towards him, doing unto him as you would have him do to you, and he will come up by and by. No one will deny, that the black man must rise above his present condition largely through himself; that he is to solve the problem of his future, in part through his own indefatigable efforts. These are indisputable points. It is hoped therefore that these men who have the African fever, will speedily cure themselves that the disease may not spread and that the negro's future may be better than the present. As the darkest hour is just before day, it is probable that this is somewhat of a transformation scene through which the nation is passing, preliminary to something better or a brighter era for all concerned, both white and colored. It is well then not to be too hasty. Think before acting!

In conclusion, I append the plan for emigrating, including an outline of the resolutions recently adopted at a meeting of the joint Stock Steamship Company held in Charleston, S. C. It is proposed to raise $300,000 for the purpose of fitting out one or more ocean steamers for transportation. The shares are placed at $10 dollars each, hence 30,000 persons are necessary to the completion of the undertaking. Each person taking a share secures his own passage form Charleston to Liberia, besides holding a life share in the vessel.

The resolutions are, First, that there shall be elected fifteen persons who shall constitute the Board of Directors for the Company and one of them shall be President, another Treasurer, and another Clerk. Second, that the company, through the Board of directors, make proper arrangements for storing away provisions or furniture that may be sent to Charleston before that are ready to take leave of America.

I have written the above in good faith trusting that our citizens may be influenced to condemn this movement *in toto* as fanatical, and therefore detrimental to our best interests.[2]

Notes

1 [See Blyden's articles, "The Republic of Liberia: Its Status and Its Field," *Methodist Quarterly Review* (July 1872), and "Liberia at the American Centennial," *Methodist Quarterly Review* (July 1877).]

2 [Scarborough subscribed this article "Wilberforce, November, 1877."]

The Civil Status of the Southern Negro

People's Advocate, September 11, 1880.

The trains on the Macon and Western Railroad[1] have three distinct coaches for passengers—one for the Caucasian, one for the African, and one for the Caucasian smokers. In the Negro coach it is placarded, "This car is for colored people only." But I noticed as I came up that quite a large number of white persons took refuge in there, often in close proximity with their colored brother. At times they began to smoke, but the conductor asked them to go into the next car, the smoker. Now notice the difference. A white man may go into a car that they call exclusively a Negro car, and sit down while there; if a Negro attempts to return the compliment his head or back pays the penalty. Observe again a feature of Southern justice. Throughout the North there are two grades of tickets, first and second; in the South but one, a first grade ticket. A white man and his black brother will buy the same ticket, for the same point on the same train. His "excellency" goes into the car he pays for. His "nigger" takes his valise into one he did not pay for. You remember that I said in No. 2 that it was rumored that Joe Brown and others of the same temperament said that they, though not Republicans, affiliated with that party in the early days of reconstruction to keep Negroes out of office as much as possible, and so save the State from Negroes and carpet-bag supremacy.[2] I concluded that article by saying: "Whether true or not, an article on the condition of the black man would show that it bears a semblance of truth." I ask the Indiana Democrat, the Ohio Democrat, the New York Democrat—all the Democrats, if there are any conscientious ones among them for an impartial decision on this point. Well, I am wondering and seeking that [which] I won't get. The social and political condition of the Southern Negro is somewhat mysterious. Your correspondent has tried analytically and synthetically to solve the problem, but he, like others, finds no satisfactory solution, unless in a radical change of the Negro's present status, affected by him and through himself. Financially, here in the city of Macon, the colored people are doing well. They own all the hack lines, are acquiring property, some on a small and others on a large scale. A few, in addition to their homes in the city, own plantations, where they spend the summer when heat makes it disagreeable within the city limits.

Notes

1 [Originally chartered as the Monroe Railroad and Banking Company in 1833, this company was reorganized in 1845 as the Macon and Western Railroad. It was later consolidated into the Central Railroad of Georgia.]

2 [Joseph E. Brown (1821–1894) was governor of Georgia from 1857 to 1865 and U.S. senator from 1880 to 1891. After Reconstruction, Brown changed his party affiliation from Republican to Democrat. The article identified as "No. 2" has not been found.]

The Claims of the Colored Citizen
upon the Republican Party

Christian Recorder, June 23, 1881.

WASHINGTON, May 21.—Register Schofield to-day retired from the office of Register of the Treasury, having been commissioned as one of the Judges of the Court of Claims.[1] Before retiring he introduced to the principal officers of his division the newly-appointed Register, ex-Senator Bruce who will assume his official duties on Monday. Among the congratulations received by Register Bruce upon his appointment, none have been extended more cordially and sincerely than those of the Southern Senators and members with whom Mr. Bruce served in Congress. A colored man, in the person of Mr. Bruce, now holds a position under the government where every man in the country will soon have daily ocular evidence of the fact that the colored race has received prominent recognition as a part of the body politic. Every circulating note, whether of the United States or the national banks, every Government bond, and all other forms of national indebtedness, bear the signature of the Register of the Treasury, and from this time onward, while Mr. Bruce continues in his present office, the signature of a man who, twenty years ago, had no rights that white men were bound to respect, will be necessary to give currency to the circulating notes of the United States and national banks, as well as to attest the correctness and completeness of nearly all the transactions of the Treasury of the United States. The signature of Blanche K. Bruce on the circulating notes of the United States furnishes emphatic illustration of the great results that have been accomplished by the war for the suppression of the rebellion.—*New York Times*.

This excerpt from the New York *Times* will doubtless meet the hearty approbation of every colored American citizen. Such distinguished men as [John M.] Langston, [Frederick] Douglass, Bruce and Prof. [Richard T.] Greener, ought to be rewarded not only for their fidelity to the Republican party but also because they are the most conspicuous among the representatives of five millions of newly enfranchised citizens. Not to reward these liberally and generously, is a disgrace to the party now in power and an insult to the negro race. Professor Greener has not been provided for as yet. Why it is and how it is, must be answered by Pres. Jas. A. Garfield. It cannot be that he means to overlook his claims. The professor's active life and services demand recognition, as much, at least, if not more, than any colored man has yet received. The negro does not seek more than belongs to him, nor does he ask for half of that to which he is legally entitled. He only desires to be treated as other men. The motives, impulses and desires that prompt him to action are the same as those of other men, and ought thus to be regarded. Among others whom I would specially mention are Dr. H[enry] H. Garnett, of New York, and the Hon. J[ohn] H. Jackson, of Lexington, Kentucky.[2] The Liberian mission, given to the Rev. H. H. Garnett, a veteran in the cause of civil and political liberty, and a consulate to Mr. J. H. Jackson, would be marked tokens of the high appreciation in which their past services are held by a grateful President and an equally grateful party. A few moments in retrospection:

One year ago, June 2nd, the National Republican Convention convened in Chicago. The weather was fine; the air, though generally sultry, was at times cool and balmy. Four candidates were in the field representing as many factions. O times! O customs![3] The convention understood what a tempest there was ahead, and the 306 saw it. The state of things had almost reached a crisis. The Republican party seemed to have little hope of success. The National Convention, like the Georgia State Convention, seemed destined to break up in a row and without nomination. During this exciting season, the colored members of the different delegations were as firm and decided in their preferences, as their white brother. They acted and voted according to the dictates of their consciences. None, I verily believe, were purchased for gold, although they were courted and favored by various chiefs. It was at the Palmer House where I had my headquarters, not as a delegate, but as a looker-on. Hon. John H. Jackson, who was a delegate-at-large for the State of Kentucky, shared a room with me. Mr. Jackson, aware of the importance of his position, was true to the great trusts reposed in him; he was zealous in carrying forward the wishes of his constituency, and was earnest in all the deliberations and councils relative to the interests of the Republican party. His services as an educator are not only observed but highly appreciated by his fellow-citizens of the State of Kentucky.[4] He is a graduate of Berea College, a child of Oberlin, and has the recommendation of the Faculty, among many others, for a Consulship. We cordially invite the attention of the President to his desires. We have been ignored as a people. Our claims have been overlooked, though we have "petitioned, though we have remonstrated," though we have cast ourselves down at the party's feet, it has all been in vain. A few petty offices, with few exceptions, have been parcelled out as candy to a fretful child, and we have been commanded to be quiet. We are a component part of our great American body-politic. We constitute the balance of power, taking either horn of the dilemma. Our recent elections show this most decidedly. It is not reasonable to suppose that a people with intelligent leaders, knowing that they hold the decisive vote, when great interests are at stake, will always be as "clay in the hands of the potter." This is only a hint. The Jew is recognized, though with difficulty, in some parts of the land. The German is recognized far out of proportion. The Scotchman, the Irishman, the Frenchman, all have their claims favorably considered, but the negro is debarred by reason of his color. *There must be a change.*

Notes

1 [Glenni William Schofield (1817–1891), Republican, was appointed by President Hayes as Register of the Treasury and served from 1878 to 1881. Blanche K. Bruce (1841–1898), born in slavery, served as Register of the Treasury from 1881 to 1885 and again from 1897 until his death.]

2 [John H. Jackson (1850–1919) was a Republican delegate from Kentucky to the Republican National Convention in 1880. Henry Highland Garnett (1815–1882) was U.S. minister to Liberia from 1881 to 1882.]

3 [This is Marcus Tullius Cicero's exclamation, "O tempora, O mores," made in his first oration against Cailine in 63 B.C.]

4 [Jackson, head of the black teachers' association in Kentucky, was the first president of Kentucky State University, which was chartered in 1886. He published *History of Education from the Greeks to the Present Time* (Denver, Colo.: Western Newspaper Union, 1905.)]

Our Distinguished Visitors
Ex-Senator and Mrs. Bruce

Christian Recorder, November 17, 1881.

We have a few distinguished representative men among us whom we delight to honor, whose name and fame we delight to herald. Yes, in imitation of that blind old bard of "Scio's rocky isle,"[1] we feel like invoking the muses to give us tongue and pen that we may paint in full the lives and characters of those who have succeeded, despite the odds against them, in cutting through what seems to be the inevitables in gaining a place for themselves as well as a name. Some time ago Prof. Richard T. Greener said "Young men to the front."[2] Did our honored Professor mean this as advice? If he did it has been well taken, as is fully shown in the case of our distinguished ex-Senator on the one hand—for he is comparatively young—and our learned Professor on the other. Did he mean it as a prediction? If so, it has been fully verified in both cases mentioned, together with many others. The career of Senator Bruce has been as successful as remarkable. He has risen from honor to honor with a quiet and unostentation which are really commendable. Eminence and honorary distinction are death to some persons, but in the case of the subject of this sketch, it is vastly different, a noble example. I take the following from a letter written by one of my most valued correspondents (R. T. G.): "Register Bruce is a rare man; he has much tact, native brains and good business qualities. I know you will enjoy seeing him if you have not met him before. He has made an excellent officer, moves along quietly but surely and is assisted greatly I should judge, by a judicious, shrewd and handsome wife."[3] This gives the writer's impression of the ex-Senator better than he himself could have done it. It is *multum in parvo*. I met Register Bruce (then Senator) in '75 for the first time, during a visit to Washington, D. C. I was favorably impressed at first sight. The next time I had the pleasure of meeting Mr. Bruce was in the same city at an entertainment at the residence of Mr. M. M. Harlan,[4] whither I went accompanied by my friend, Mr. Wm. E. Matthews. My impressions of the gentleman were still more favorable. In fact I desired to know more of Mr. Bruce socially and determined to seize the first opportunity to satisfy this desire. At the National Republican Convention held in Chicago, ex-Senator Bruce was present, gentlemanly and unassuming in all his bearings, though like Ajax of old, he towered head and shoulders above all the rest. He was called to preside for a time over that great body, composed alike of Senators, representatives, governors and officials of every grade. He performed his every duty admirably and in this as in other cases he honored himself, his race, and the nation. Months have elapsed since then. The Presidential election has taken place amid great excitement; the national honor has been preserved. Among the official acts of our lamented President [Garfield] during his short term, was that of appointing Mr. Bruce as Register of the Treasury, which position was in keeping with his former exalted one as Senator of the United States. The recent Ohio campaign, though greatly lulled by the sad events of September, was conducted with some considerable enthusiasm. Among the few speakers who were invited to take part in the canvas was Register Bruce, who spoke most excellently Oct. 4th, at Xenia, Ohio. It was a fine effort. "Senator Bruce made a telling speech last night at the Courthouse"—*Xenia Torchlight*. On the evening of the 5th, through the special invitation of the writer, Register Bruce with Mrs. Bruce (who accompanied him during the campaign in Ohio) in company with lawyer Maxwell and lady, of Xenia, drove out from that city to spend a few hours in visiting "the classic shades" of Wilberforce. The day, though a little cool, was as pleasant otherwise a[s] could be desired. It was a most agreeable meeting. Mrs. S—— and our esteemed friend, Gussie E. Clark, instructor in music here, contributed largely to make our distinguished guests welcome, than whom few understood the art better. After viewing all that was interesting about the University, at our request, Senator Bruce addressed the students assembled in the chapel to greet him. Here again his speech was practical, pointed and well-timed. It doubtless did the good the speaker intended. It was just such food as students need, varying decidedly from many sermons and homilies we are accustomed to hear on state occasions. Many of our divines, public speakers and teachers, often forgetting that student life is a peculiar one, and that students themselves constitute a peculiar class in this busy world of ours, attempt day after day, Sabbath after Sabbath, to cram into them, willing or unwilling, a sort of *fossiliferous theology of antedeluvian times* or some exploded theory of government and its functions, or an exposition of some ancient school of philosophy long ago rejected, or some new system of education as false as it is ridiculous. Register Bruce is not a man of this sort; no, not at all. He understands human nature too well and knows equally well when and how to speak. Hence he succeeds where many fail. Mrs. Bruce well deserves the name the world has given her. Handsome, talented, and highly cultured, she must be an invaluable assistant to her husband in whatever position he is called to fill. Our symposium has now closed; our guests have returned to Xenia for the evening train and I must close my brie[f] by wishing them in their exalted station heaven's best blessing.

P. S.—Very soon I hope to give a series of articles on Wilberforce; its intellectual status, etc. etc.

Notes

1 [Homer is described as the "blind old man of Scio's rocky isle" in canto 2, stanza 2, line 8 of Byron's "Bride of Abydos" (1813).]

2 ["Young Men, to the Front!" *Washington New National Era*, April 24, 1873. For the text see Alice Moore Dunbar, editor, *Masterpieces of Negro Eloquence* (New York: Bookery, 1914; reprint, Mineola, N.Y.: Dover, 2000), pp. 37–39.]

3 [This is likely Scarborough's friend Richard Theodore Greener (1844–1922), the first black member of the American Philological Association.]

4 [John M. Harlan (1833–1911), associate justice of the U.S. Supreme Court from 1877 to 1911, was the only dissenting voice in the *Plessy v. Ferguson* decision. William E. Mathews (1845–c. 1893) opened a real estate and broker's office in Washington, D.C. See William M. Simmons, *Men of Mark* (Cleveland, Ohio: Rewell, 1887), p. 246.]

Frederick Douglass: The Democratic Return to Power—Its Effect?

A.M.E. Church Review 1 (January 1885): 215–216.

It is almost too early to state with any positive assurance what the probable effect of the recent Democratic victory will be upon the colored people of this country.[1] Twenty-four years have elapsed since the last December President occupied the White House. During the interval, between the close of Buchanan's Administration and Cleveland's election, the negro has been made a freeman and a citizen at the hand of the Republican party, with the right to vote and act as any other citizen. All the privileges that the colored man enjoys whether educational, civil or political are the direct results of Republican legislation. The history and policy of the Republican party have, from the beginning, been in accord with the interest of the negro race. This is well understood by every colored man in the country. It is quite natural, then, that there should be doubts and fears as to the new Administration.

The Democratic party fought to keep the negro in slavery. It opposed negro citizenship, negro Suffrage, negro Equality, negro education and negro advancement. In fact the Democratic party has opposed all legislation, more or less, that appeared in any sense favorable to the colored man.

With this record before him the colored man feels that unless there is a radical change in the policy and methods of that party little may be expected from it. Already in parts of the South and North there have been signs trouble between the lower stratum of the Democratic party and citizens of African descent,—the former taunting the latter with the boast that *the Democratic party is now in power and negro rule is at an end*. Such treatment with many outrages will probably increase in the less civilized parts of the South and North, inasmuch as this element of that party will feel that it has the support of the Democratic Administration behind it.

This will make the condition of the negro very undesirable, if not intolerable, in many respects. To talk about re-establishing the old slave oligarchy, of remanding the negro to slavery is all nonsense. This could not be done if the Democrats desired it. The negro has nothing to fear from this source. The colored citizen is now a fixture; he is a component part of the great American body politic and any efforts taken to change this feature of the case would produce an upheaval that has no parallel in the history of civilization. If however the negro will consent to give up his Republican principles, to affiliate with the Democratic party of the South, to divide upon local and sectional issues, voting for one of the two rival Democratic candidates that may be in the field, eschewing northern advice and northern influence, it will go well with him as far as *peace* is concerned; otherwise not unless the new Administration intends to protect the colored man, in common with others without regard to party, in freedom of speech and ballot.

As for my part the only ray of light that I can now discern lies in the supposed conservatism and independence of Governor Cleveland. If he will be the President not only *de nomine* but *de facto* and will not permit himself to be swallowed up by the party which he represents; if the Bourbon element is given to understand that its advice is not needed and that he (Cleveland) intends to co-operate with all law-abiding citizens in seeing to it that no harm befalls any citizen, negro or Caucasian, and that political rights of all are to be held sacred, I entertain some hope for the future. But to do this would be to carry out plans utterly foreign to the principles of the Democratic party heretofore, and would break the backbone of power of the "solid South"—an event too Utopian to dare hope for at present. Still as the recent victory was not, strictly speaking, a Democratic victory, the Independent and Prohibition voters contributing largely to his election, and as his majority was exceedingly small, it is quite probable that the President elect will endeavor to make his administration as popular as possible in order to ensure success to the Democratic party in the future.

The whole, however, is a mere matter of conjecture based upon suppositions which we must wait to see realized before we can make any positive statement as to whether or no[t] the progress of the race will be retarded by the recent election.

Note

1 [The full article on pages 213–250 is made up of many responses; Scarborough's is on pages 215–216.]

Ohio's Black Laws

Cleveland Gazette, February 14, 1885.

Abolish Them—Colored Men Who Oppose the Ely Bill Should be Ostracised.

EDITOR OF THE GAZETTE:—Of the many strange phenomena that are constantly taking place among us the strangest one of the strange, as it seems to us, is the stubborn opposition offered by a few people to legislation made in their own behalf. There are some things that I can account for, but this is one of the *unaccountables*. I am astonished; yes, I am astounded at the daring insolence of that class of people who will attempt to place their own interests over against the interests of a race; who will set aside principle to accomplish their own end. This is no individual matter, it is broader than that—it concerns the whole Negro race.

The fact that there are "black laws" on the statue books of Ohio which discriminate against the Negro, is unmistakable evidence of the feeling that exists in reference to the inferiority of the colored man and the opposition to his citizenship and the rights which this citizenship ought to guarantee. We want no laws discriminating against us. We want these invidious distinctions wiped out. We want the same privileges and opportunities that other men enjoy. We ask for a fair chance in the race of life. Any colored man who openly or secretly opposes Senator Ely's bill[1] or a similar measure, has lost, as it seems to me, all self-respect, and deserves to be regarded as an enemy to his race and hostile to its best interests. *Ostracism* and *boycotting* should certainly follow in close pursuit.

Note

1 [George H. Ely (1844–1925) from Cleveland, Ohio, began work on a bill against black laws; Benjamin Arnett from Greene County carried the bill forward. See John P. Green, *Fact Stranger than Fiction* (Cleveland, Ohio: Riehl, 1920), pp. 179–180, and also *Autobiography*, p. 89.]

The Future of the Negro

Forum 7 (March 1889): 80–89.

The situation of the Negro race to-day presents both a bright and a dark side. It is most encouraging when viewed with regard to the race itself. Within less than a quarter of a century the Negro has made most wonderful progress, and his present, as contrasted with his past, exhibits an astonishing evolution, mentally, morally, physically, and financially. Even his worst enemies, or those who are most indifferent to all that pertains to him, will not attempt a denial of this. The mass stands on a higher plane. To use Mr. Grady's words, "the worthy and upright of his race may be found in every community, and they increase steadily in numbers and influence." No one has more clearly set forth in brief the magnitude of this upward movement than has Mr. G. W. Cable when he answers his own questions, "What has the Negro done? What is he doing?"[1]

But another view presents the dark side, that of his relative situation—a race suspended between a selfish, arrogant, and supersensitive South, and a vacillating, over-sympathetic North. This is said with a full understanding of that "miracle" of "kindly feelings" of which the South boasts as having ever existed between the races in that section, as well as with warm appreciation of all the material aid and sympathy from the North which have helped to make bright the other side of the picture. Still it is true.

With few exceptions the South shows in all discussions the determination to make the Negro bend to its desires, subordinate himself body and soul to what it conceives will make for its own prosperity and happiness, and allow it to exert dominion and power little removed from that of slavery. It proscribes and persecutes him in countless ways. Fraud, intimidation, violence, and constant depreciation of him as a man, are the methods which have been and are still pursued with relentless vigor to make freedom a mockery and life simply a terrorized existence; and then in the refinement of cruel irony it turns from the murder of defenseless blacks to "impress upon him, what he already knows, that his best friends are the people among whom he lives." At every attempt to protect his life and liberty a hue and cry is raised that insurrection is threatened, and his most peaceful efforts to exercise the privileges conferred upon him by the Constitution are construed as a movement toward "Negro supremacy."

On the other side is the North, so divided between its desire to have right and justice meted out to the long-suffering subject race and the wish to deal fairly and magnanimously with its Anglo-Saxon brothers of the South, as to be incapable of decisive action on either side; now determining to relieve the Negro at all hazards, now yielding to the frantic appeal for non-interference and the pleading cry of the "peculiar situation."

It is this situation which makes the dark picture, and it is the true situation wherein is found the menace to the peace and prosperity of the South to-day. The unsettled, seething condition of affairs in that section is due to this situation, which has been made what it is by the stubborn refusal of the South to do the right. The shadow cast over the Negro's pathway by such acts as those mentioned is reflected in gloom upon all sides; nor does the defense of "self-preservation" make the South any the less responsible for what the Negro suffers and what itself endures. His increasing intelligence is blindly ignored, as are his rights, save when it serves some selfish purpose or ulterior design to admit their existence. And if he were not possessed of a steadfastness of purpose worthy of higher recognition and encouragement than it receives, he would feel like giving up the struggle as useless; for, in face of his unquestionable advance, it is a fact to be noted that never before has his presence as a factor in this body politic been so apprehensively looked upon—so generally considered by the South as a serious disturbing factor, conducive to critical complications and dire results.

We may well stop to ask how this is. The North refers the question to the South, which gives back the answer in its reiterated fear of "Negro supremacy," and which endeavors by every possible sophistry to impress upon others the terrors which it claims will result from this dreaded thing. Is there any basis for this fear? None at all. That which the South declares it will not have—Negro supremacy—has no part in the Negro's plans for his future, nor is it desired by him. He simply seeks to exercise undeterred the freedom to enjoy rights guaranteed him as a citizen by the Constitution. He leaves all else to the future evolution of just public sentiment and to private choice. He has no desire to rule over or to harm the whites.

Pushed from the ground of Negro supremacy, the fear takes the shape of "being left to the mercy of an ignorant black majority," and "reconstruction days" are cited by Senator Wade Hampton[2] as proof of the evils in store, and as reason for abrogating the Negro's rights. I answer this by saying that there could now be no such ignorant rule as is claimed to have existed then. The conditions which governed those days have changed. The Negro has in the meantime made a remarkable advance in intelligence and education. The admitted progress of the race has given birth to leaders, younger and better educated, to replace those ignorant and irresponsible ones. This younger class is largely composed of men who know little of the horrors of slavery, who took no part in the strife and cherish no deep settled spirit of revenge for wrongs perpetuated in the past; men who bear a forgiving, kindly feeling in their breasts, who are able to take a calmer, more dispassionate view of all sides than could their elders who were so near the battle's recent heat and so fresh from slavery's wrongs; in short, men who, losing sight of mere narrow race fealty, white or black, are capable of assisting in the adjustment of matters upon higher considerations—the good of all as an American people. And as for being "left to the mercy of the blacks," it is a strange cry to come from a people who left wives, children, honor, and homes to the mercy of the "low, brutal, superstitious," ignorant slave; a strange shrinking is this from the freeman with his developed instincts, his higher aspirations and intelligence, as from a ravening beast bent upon their destruction.

Again, it is not ignorance that is feared. If it were, they might note the poor whites among them—an ignorant mass according to their own statistics, some as unlettered and depraved as the lowest of Negroes. They might note the in-pouring stream of foreigners with which the North and West must cope as well as the South—a swarm of people from every nationality, the largest part ignorant and degraded, with the lowest principles and an utter disregard of all moral, religious, and civil law; the product of immemorial servility in their native lands. Yet these are allowed an astonishing freedom of speech and action, and a large share in the control of the machinery of the government, with no such abhorrence of their presence and rule as is shown of the Negro's, though the latter is a truer patriot in every sense. These are even welcomed and gladly used where their voice and vote may help to shut out the Negro. But this is no proof that black ignorance and corruption are more to be feared than white. No, such is not the point; the cultured, intelligent Negro fares no better at the hands of those who make this outcry than does the low and ignorant.

These fears are groundless and are not at the root of the feeling; but that which does underlie the whole matter and which gives the key to the disturbance is the deep-seated prejudices of color and caste. The South shrinks from the probable civil and political equality of the Negro race before the law, and more so now than ever, as it knows that intelligence cannot be crushed or easily overridden. And with these prejudices may be coupled the fear of loss of political power through the colored adherents of the opposing party. This is hinted at by Senator Colquitt[3] when he says:

> "We thought we saw a determined effort so completely to Africanize our State and the States of the South as to leave for all time to come no doubt of Republican domination on our soil."

It is this which makes the whole southern problem in all its relations what it now is. The Negro has little to hope for from the South, if it adheres to its determination to direct alone the settlement, refusing all aid which does not accord with its desires. That this is its stand is especially discernible from the general expression of public opinion, recently drawn forth by Mr. Murat Halstead, of the Cincinnati "Commercial Gazette," as to the wisest and best course to be adopted by the new administration in dealing with this question. While there is breadth of view and difference of opinion at the North, ranging from a decisive handling of the matter to the most pusillanimous leaving of it to self-adjustment or Southern adjustment, the South is nearly unanimous in its desire to be suffered to deal with it alone, and this desire runs the gamut from the cry of despair, through the whine of sycophancy and the bold demand, to threatening defiance.

Is there not a possibility that the South, in its continued cry for indulgence, is demanding too much forbearance under the circumstances from all parties, the Negro included? Would it not be for its own welfare to have some of its sensitiveness seared over, so that it may not always be pleaded as a ground for non-interference? Then, too, would it not be well for the North so to steel itself that its sympathies may not vibrate too readily when this cry is sounded?

Yet, dark as is this picture of the Negro's relative situation, I am by no means inclined to take a gloomy view of it. I denounce while I deplore the outrages and injustices of which he has been and is still made the victim; but when the question comes, "Watchman, what of the night?" I am constrained to claim in reply, "All is well." There must be pioneers of every race. This and at least the next generation of the blacks must be the pioneers, even martyrs, of the Negro race, opening up the way along paths blazed by blood and fire, but surely opening it to better days for the tramping feet of millions unborn; for the Negro has a future before him in this country, where he has elected to remain, and I believe it to be one of promise despite present discouragements. This view is based upon three facts:

First, his ability to improve even under most adverse circumstances, as shown by his admitted progress—the proof of the possession of inherent power to better his condition as well as the indicator of the upward trend of his desires.

Secondly, his determination to use this power to make that condition one to command the admiration and respect of all. He fully understands the situation with all of its hinderances and its possibilities, and is quick to see and to seize the advantage offered by education and wealth. He has no more idea of sinking into a mere nonentity than he has of becoming again a slave or of overmastering the whites; but he is bent upon being a man, with all that the word implies in a free republic, and this ambition pervades the mass.

Lastly, the awakened conscience of the nation, as evinced in the general admission, irrespective of race, section, or party, that this question, involving the rights of an entire race, is the question of the day, calling for settlement. And, as Mr. Grady asserts, "it dominates all other issues" in the South. But despite super-sensitiveness, bitter rancor, and fire-eating, dogmatic assertions supported by neither facts nor reason, there is a growth of public sentiment even there, as shown in admissions such as Senator Colquitt's:[4]

"Of one thing friends and foes may rest assured, that the people of the Southern States are not so foolish as to believe that their peace, their prosperity, or even their safety can be assured if a moiety of the population is treated with injustice and denied its rights in the state."

This leaven is bound to work, and, I trust, with force sufficient for the salvation of all concerned. At any rate, discussion, which in the past gave rise to decisive action, is an approach to some sort of settlement of this vexed question. But it must be pervaded by justice and cool reason to prevent any further complications, because of existing inequalities between the races in the South, where the solution is to be largely worked out under present conditions. No one, white or black, should desire this to be other than an amicable one, and to this end a practical application of all the wisdom and philosophy at command to govern both speech and action, is needed to grasp and deal with the matter effectively. I am of the opinion that such inflammatory, strongly denunciatory utterances as those of Senator Eustis of Alabama,[5] Mr. Grady of Georgia, Senator [Wade] Hampton of South Carolina, and others, can but postpone this, if not render it impossible. The South, though poor in material resources, can never hope to prosper by repudiating its debt to the Negro and regarding him as a formidable foe to be laid prostrate, annihilated, or driven from its borders; for not only his future, but that of those about him, primarily depends upon whether he be granted his rights, pushed to the wall, or arrayed on the defensive. If the Negro is to remain in the South, this settlement must look to the disposition of the political situation. With this in view, three courses have been proposed, with a possible fourth:

The first, to avail him anything, is dependent upon the justice and sufferance of the whites in granting fair play—allowing him his vote, a fair ballot, and an honest count; using their strength and influence to prevent intimidation, violence, and fraud in any form. It is useless to claim that this is now being done. Facts prove the contrary, no matter how strong the asseveration, or form whatever source it comes, or how fully believed by any of the better class making it. Indeed, it is broadly admitted by such an authority as Mr. [Henry] Watterson when he says:[6]

"I should be entitled to no respect or credit if pretended that there is either a fair poll or count of the vast overflow in States where there is a Negro majority, or that in the nature of things present there can be."

Putting aside the bar sinister found in this closing dictum, it is positively certain that this is the only amicable solution possible, as it is based upon the recognition of the principles of right and a call for voluntary obedience to the law from all under the law. Because of this it could not be productive of evil. The Negro on his part stands ready to do his share toward bringing about peace and harmony upon the adoption and carrying out of this course. It remains for the South to cease its shallow pretense of "fear of an ignorant majority," to divest itself of color and caste prejudice and its determination to solidify. All of these combined have not increased and will not increase its prosperity, while they have retarded the Negro's; and the danger of loss of political power is more imminent the longer this last is persisted in. Mr. Grady recognizes this when he says:[7]

> "To remain solid, therefore, is to incur the danger of being placed in perpetual minority and practically shut out from participation in the government."

He further says, "The solid South invites the solid North." He might have added, the solid Negro; for that is one means for the Negro's self-preservation—as strong a natural law with him as with others.

In case of refusal to adopt this course, the next means to the same end is the appointment of United States marshals and supervisors who shall exercise a strict surveillance over all federal elections, protecting all voters alike. Whichever one is to be followed, neither means "Negro supremacy" nor "ignorant rule," whatever may be the result as to party power.

If the North fails to see this, but one course of action is left—one which disregards the Negro entirely: to nullify the Amendments by legal enactment and disfranchise him. Whether his vote is allowed or disallowed, the thing must be done legally; at the same time the congressional representation according to votes cast must be reduced.

Against this course I enter a stern protest on broad grounds. Congressman [William Calvin] Oates of Alabama is reported to have declared that the disfranchisement of the colored race would be advantageous to both races. I unqualifiedly dissent from this settlement. To disfranchise many hundred thousand Negro voters after these years of suffrage, would not only be rank injustice, but would work injury irreparable to them, depriving them of the only weapon now in their hands for self-defense against oppression, no matter how seldom used; and to permit such to remain within the state, yet not of the state, without voice or vote, would precipitate far more serious trouble than would so-called Negro supremacy. The solid South might be broken, but the solid Negro element, with a gathering enmity intensified by this great wrong, would prove a formidable force against law.

No statesman could delude himself with the belief that this would be a solution in any sense save for the briefest period. It certainly would not be amicable, much less productive of security. No one need delude himself with the idea that the spirit of the Negro can again be easily broken, and reduced through discouragements to the former docile servility. Servility is becoming a thing of his past. The strains of independent blood are asserting themselves and unfitting him for further serfdom. For the first time he would be driven to desperation, and the state presented by such a perspective none should invite. He will aid in every lawful solution but that promising a blight upon his future. Such he could but oppose with manhood's might, for he is not going to remain a mute and passive spectator in that which affects him so vitally. This is well borne in mind. He is no longer in swaddling-clothes; he is nearing his majority, and will not be summarily dealt with. He did not make himself the problem, neither is he alone the problem; his growth has injected some of the complications, but as a return for this he will certainly share in effecting the solution. Hamlet must speak and act in "Hamlet." What will be done with him in the settlement will largely depend upon what he will do himself; and Mr. G. W. Cable has given him pertinent and salutary advice in this connection.[8]

The possible course left would be a division of the Negro vote; but it is not probable that there would be at any time a division of sufficient strength to guarantee him protection, or to placate the South. Compulsion cannot effect it. Mr. Grady sees danger in such a division, which pre-supposes a divided white vote, and he argues against it as a ground for southern solidity. His claim as to "what the Negro vote is," is not only unverified by facts but couched in language too strong to be allowed to pass unchallenged. He says:[9]

> "It is alien, being separated by racial differences that are deep and permanent. It is ignorant, easily deluded or betrayed. It is impulsive, lashed by a word into violence. It is purchasable, having the incentive of poverty and cupidity and the restraints of neither pride nor conviction. It can never be merged through logical or orderly currents into either of two parties."

This is the unproved assertion made in support of the further claim that:

> "The very worst thing that could happen to the South would be to have the white vote divided into factions, and each faction bidding for the Negro, who holds the balance of power."

But the only conclusion to all this must be the one first reached, that the South fears not condition, but color; not loss of "political integrity," but of political power; and the present situation is the result.

If none of these courses can produce a settlement, with the Negro in the South, he must leave it. This is the only alternative fraught with more of good than evil to all, leading to greater promise for himself than he could hope for where conflict is a constant menace. I firmly believe this to be the wisest plan and the one which will ultimately be carried out. The various movements which have taken place when liberty of speech and action seemed purchased at too great a price by remaining, all look to this step. He is beginning to see that vigor and blood are wasted to a large degree by endeavoring to cope with any situation where security is dependent upon either southern sufferance or congressional aid alone. But where will he go? West, where other Americans are turning. He is already noting the breadth of that territory, and the great middle class will see a brighter future awaiting them there.

But this removal must be a voluntary one, and it must not be *en masse*, but gradual. I do not mean by this that the Negro should colonize; far from it. His leaders know that colonization would be his death-knell. The isolation of any race as a distinctive people in one large solid body in any part of a country means retrogression. In this case it would in time become an *imperium in imperio*, and the question which is now considered such a "cancer" would be but shifted from our shoulders to those of our descendants, who, if not vastly wiser grown, would find the cancer of too malignant a type for cure, because of its stronger hold and magnitude.

As a member of that race I believe the Negro is looking over the whole situation as a patriot should view it—with an eye not only to his own prosperous growth, but to that of the American people, of whom he considers himself an inseparable part. With such a view he can but take that step which will lead from present troubles to a fruition of his hopes—to be a man among men and not simply a Negro.

Notes

1 The FORUM for August, 1888. [Henry W. Grady (1851–1889), Atlanta journalist, was known as the "spokesman for the New South."]

2 The FORUM for June, 1888.

3 The FORUM for November, 1887. [Alfred Holt Colquitt (1824–1894) was a Confederate democrat; he served as governor of Georgia from 1876 to 1880 and served in the U.S. Senate from 1883 to 1894.]

4 The FORUM for November, 1887.

5 [James B. Eustis, "Race Antagonism in the South," *Forum* (October 1888): 144–154. Eustis was a senator from Louisiana.]

6 The FORUM for April, 1888.

7 Address delivered at Augusta, Ga., November 29th, 1888.

8 The FORUM for August, 1888.

9 Address delivered at Augusta, November 29th, 1888.

Political Necessity of a Federal Election Law

Our Day 6 (July 1890): 25–33.

The most vital question ever before the American people is the so-called negro problem with all the complications growing out of it. Recent race troubles, largely the result of political differences, make it very evident that peace will never exist between the two races, South, till this question approaches some sort of settlement. Socially and commercially the negro question needs no helping hand, it will adjust itself; politically never. There must be some external influence brought to bear upon the Southern white voter or political manipulator to force him to recognize the colored voter as a political factor. More than once already, the Democratic politicians of the South have publicly declared that they will never tamely submit to the negro's free exercise of the right of suffrage, as that suffrage might result in what is called negro supremacy. From this it may be inferred that fraud, intimidation, and violence will continue in the future as in the past. The negro as a citizen and voter cannot live peaceably unprotected below Mason and Dixon's line. This is a plain statement of the case. It matters not how well educated, how rich and prosperous, how quietly disposed he may be, he must eschew everything savoring of politics or take the consequences. White minorities must rule; black majorities must submit, though in Congressional apportionment they must be counted in. This is the verdict of all Southern Congressmen who have written or spoken on Southern elections. What then? Can we hope or ever expect a change under such circumstances?

"Frank Leslie's Illustrated Weekly"[1] speaks in no uncertain tone and to the point when it says:—

> It is ridiculous to talk of fair elections in Mississippi [and it might have added, in any other Southern state][2] in the light of General [James R.] Chalmers' experience as the Republican candidate for Governor. He has retired from the canvass, and does so because he found that the doors of the court-house and public halls which were readily opened to Democratic speakers were locked against him

whenever he undertook to make an address in the State. He was begged by prominent colored and white Republicans to refrain from making a canvass for fear that as a result negroes would be massacred by Democratic bull-dozers, and their blood would be charged to General Chalmers' canvass. What a condition of affairs this is in "the land of the free and the home of the brave."

And yet Mugwump and Democratic newspapers in the country are perpetually insisting that the ballot and the canvass are as free in the South as in the North. It is a standing reproach to the American people that in any State of the Union free speech is denied and a free ballot is suppressed. If the Republican party in control of this administration and with a majority, small as it is, in both Houses of Congress does not promptly seize the opportunity to right a great wrong, then the Republican party will fall far short of the expectation of its supporters, and will tarnish a record that thus far is without spot or blemish.

It is a matter of deep regret to many that President Harrison in his annual message to Congress did not take more radical ground in regard to Southern elections, and at the same time recommend national control of elections for representatives. Though he has given the country an able document in all other respects, in this he has fallen far below the hopes and expectations of many of his firmest supporters.

As relates to freedmen's rights there is but the following brief statement in the President's message:—

> The power to take the whole direction and control of the election of the members of the House of Representatives is clearly given to the general government. A partial and qualified supervision of these elections is now provided for by the law, and in my opinion this law may be so strengthened and extended as to secure on the whole better results than can be attained by a law taking all the processes of such elections into federal control. The colored man should be protected in all of his relations to the federal government, whether a litigant, a juror, or witness in our courts, as an elector for member of Congress, or as a peaceful traveler upon our interstate railways.

[3]the race question, which clearly shows that he fully realizes the importance as well as the magnitude of the subject. This will doubtless have a soothing effect upon that class of negroes inclined to oppose the administration on the ground that it is indifferent to their wrongs and ignores their grievances.

The President is without doubt sincere, and believes that the desired end will be reached in the manner described by himself, but there is a vast number of the contrary belief—that no tinkering with or extension of existing laws will prove half so effectual as an iron-clad federal election law, placing the entire supervision of said elections under federal control. A partial control will be worse than no control at all; for it will simply exasperate the South and excite an intensely bitter feeling against the blacks who constitute the main-stay of the Republican party in that section.

Race hatred and race antipathy are of such a nature that to deal timidly with this question is simply to invite further violence and encourage an increasing disregard for law.

Shall Congress pass a Federal Election Law? is the question. In light of these and many other facts that I cannot now mention, I answer most emphatically, Yes. To fail to do this would be to commit a greater blunder than the withdrawal of the federal troops from the South by President Hayes.

It is not a question of likes and dislikes, nor is it one of expediency merely, but it is rather the imperative demand of justice to all concerned. The Republican members of Congress should act accordingly, though they may prefer not to touch the subject at all, and may rather see the matter vainly strive to regulate itself to the end that the Southern people be allowed to manage their own political affairs without outside interference. Our past experiences show the fallacy of any such position. Fair play to all men without regard to color or politics is now out of the question. If the negro could be eliminated from the body politic; if his influence as a political factor could in any way be neutralized so as to make him a nonentity, the matter would end there. The bugaboo of so-called negro.[3]

It seems to me that the objections which have been raised, namely, that such a law as Congress is asked to pass will involve a needless expenditure of money, and that it will produce a sort of centralization of power, are all of little force and importance as compared with the great wrong to be righted and the necessity of sustaining such a principle at whatever cost. This, however, is the plea of the Democracy, the Mugwumps, and a class of lukewarm Republicans who are very little interested as a rule in good government or fair elections. It is the negro's desire that there shall be no failure on the part of Congress to act in this matter, and speedily. It is for the interest of the country, North and South; it is for the interest of the American people, black and white, that there shall be in every section of our land a free ballot and a fair count. Many of our Congressmen have fully expressed themselves upon the subject, and have by tongue and pen advocated the passage of a federal election law. The Hon. Cabot Lodge says, among other things, in speaking on this question:

> "There is another matter more important than any tariff can be which is certain to receive the careful consideration of Congress, although it played but a slight part in the last campaign. This is the question of protecting the ballot by suitable legislation. Public attention has been drawn more and more of late years to this vital subject, and several of the States have made great efforts to guard the purity and honesty of the ballot by the most careful and elaborate legislation that could be devised. . . . There is no desire anywhere to revive the sectional animosities of the war, but there is a very general wish and a widespread determination, among the people of the North at least, to have a fair ballot throughout the length

and breath of the land. There is, of course, no doubt of the power of Congress to pass a federal election law for the purpose of regulating the elections which decide the choice of electors and members of Congress. There can be almost as little question of the expediency of a simple but efficient statute which shall make federal elections as honest as it is possible to make them by legal provisions.

If the Republican Congressmen as a whole could be induced to take the same view of the subject as does Mr. Lodge, there is little doubt as to the result. My own views are the same as his, and I believe that every other subject should be made second to this—free elections in the South and fair treatment of the negro. Congress has a duty to perform in this matter and it cannot afford to evade it. The nation looks to it to be saved the disgrace of such wholesale frauds as well as from future complications which are sure to arise from its negligence in this particular. The repetition of a few examples will not be out of place, for while they serve to refresh our minds they will impress the enormity of these frauds and deepen the importance of the measure under discussion. I take South Carolina, General Hampton's own State, as a conspicuous example. According to the census of 1880 we note the following:—

	TOTAL	WHITE	COLORED.	Males of age. White.	21 years and over. Colored.
First Congressional District	118,803	53,811	64,992	12,445	13,884
Charleston County as follows: Parish of St. Philips and St. Michael, including the city of Charleston	57,167	22,874	28,293	5,876	6,738
Township of Mt. Pleasant	783	304	479	80	99
Moultrieville	661	439	202	104	41
Summerville	636	431	205	98	38
Colleton County, as follows:	19,231				
Township of Bells	1,968	1,207	761	241	148
Barns	1,990	760	1,230	189	207
Carns	877	427	450	102	83
Dorchester	2,658	971	1,687	198	354
George	2,028	713	1,315	152	286
Givbam	1,306	403	903	87	206
Heyward	1,748	1,167	581	251	129
Kozer	1,490	641	849	134	165
Sheridan	1,612	776	836	163	170
Verdier	3,554	2,553	2,001	340	449

	TOTAL	WHITE	COLORED	Males of age. White.	21 years and over. Colored.
Orangeburg County, as follows:	27,761				
Township of Branchville	2,010	667	1,343	133	251
Caw Caw	2,881	864	2,017	190	398
Cow Castle	1,149	361	788	71	136
Edisto	1,035	541	494	100	101
Elizabeth	2,116	768	1,358	157	267
Goodland	2,681	1,182	1,499	234	253
Hebron	960	510	450	96	83
Liberty	1,215	621	594	122	141
Township of Middle	1,663	548	1,115	130	211
New Hope	1,267	272	995	57	173
Orange	6,046	1,760	4,286	417	852
Union	1,418	381	1,037	79	184
Willow	1,748	978	770	204	149
Zion	1,572	576	996	94	196
Lexington County	18,564	11,096	7,468	2,346	1,426
Second Congressional District	136,748	51,266	83,482	11,446	16,283
Colleton County, as follows:	4,194				
Township of Broxon	2,317	1,207	1,110	261	168
Warren	2,317	966	911	190	153
Hampton County	18,741	6,286	12,455	1,401	2,427
Barnell County	39,857	13,853	26,004	3,131	4,775
Aiken County	28,112	12,936	15,176	2,873	3,112
Edgefield County	45,844	16,018	29,826	3,590	5,648
Third Congressional District	131,569	62,783	68,786	13,359	12,707
Abbeville Country	40,815	13,172	27,643	3,000	5,053
Newberry County	26,497	8,236	18,261	1,956	3,542
Anderson County	33,612	18,747	14,865	3,865	2,636
Oconee County	16,256	11,955	4,301	2,389	764
Pickens County	14,389	10,673	3,716	2,149	712
Fourth Congressional District	167,230	79,633	87,597	17,670	16,985
Greenville County	37,496	22,983	14,513	4,801	2,834
Laurens County	29,444	11,736	17,688	2,627	3,213
Fairfield County	27,765	6,883	20,880	1,633	3,968

	Total	White	Colored.	Males of age. White.	21 years and over. Colored.
Fourth Congressional District (*continued*)					
Spartanburg County, except Townships of White Plains and Limestone Springs	34,193	22,282	11,910	4,820	2,339
Union County, except Townships of Gowdeysville and Draytonville	18,641	7,459	11,182	1,645	2,069
Richland County, as follows:	19,692				
Township of Centre	3,874	2,164	1,710	449	375
Columbia	13,083	5,135	7,948	1,380	1,838
Uppen	2,735	969	1,766	216	349

These figures explain themselves. In the First and Second Congressional Districts the total population is 118,803 and 136,748 respectively, of which in the First 64,992 are colored, and 53,811 are white; in the Second 85,482 are colored, and 51,266 are white; negro voters in the First, 13,884, white voters 12,445; in the Second, negro voters, 16,283, white 11,446. In the First the excess of negro voters is about 1440, in the Second about 4,837. In the Third District, according to the same census, the white vote exceeds that of the negro by something more than 600; in the Fourth by a little more than 650 votes. It will be observed that, according to the above table, the negro population in the Third and Fourth Districts is greater than that of the white by at least 4,000 and 7,900 respectively, and yet their vote as recorded is less than that of whites. There is evidently a mistake somewhere, and the same methods employed to count the negro out in other portions of that State are adopted in the Districts referred to. I believe that the order of the figures which record the vote ought to be reversed, giving the 600 and 650 votes to the negroes in those two districts.

There are now in the six States of Georgia, Alabama, Arkansas, Louisiana, Mississippi, and South Carolina about 1,720,000 males of voting age, and forty-three representatives in Congress. In 1888 only 785,185 votes were polled, making one representative for every 18,260 votes cast. Turning from the South to the North, we find that it takes about 42,457 votes to send one representative to Congress; that is to say, twelve Northern and Western states with a voting population of about 4,485,000 have only 88 Representatives. This has been justly regarded as a flagrant and open violation of the Constitution, a constant humiliation of the North, a disgrace to a republican government, and a menace to the peace and welfare of the country. If we adopt the Southern ratio, the twelve States of the North ought to have 204 representatives instead of 88. This disparity should not be tolerated, because it is both unjust and unconstitutional. It is due to the evil practices we have[.]

The "Indianapolis Journal" makes these very striking remarks:—

> The Republican party by its origin, its principles, its traditions, and its platforms is committed to deadly war against this gigantic evil, and to right it if possible. . . . The important question is how to right the wrong. The Republican party cannot be true to itself unless it at least attempts to apply some remedy. The failure of the attempt would be far less disgraceful than the failure to make it."

Governor Foraker has on more than one occasion emphasized the same opinion, and has vigorously declared that is the Republican party should at this date neglect to do its duty toward the negro, it would deserve defeat. Senators [John] Sherman, Chandler, and others are on record as having likewise advocated at various times measures looking to a speedy adjustment of Southern election troubles.

These measures ought not to be regarded as partisan, though the Republican party may be forced to take the initiative. They are measures in which all good citizens ought by right to be interested, and to the carrying out of which that ought to feel morally bound to lend a helping hand. It is becoming a serious matter, and the negroes themselves are greatly aroused, to the significant extent of holding special conferences and organizing leagues with special reference to their relative political condition. In this they are perfectly justifiable. Wise and judicious discussion will assist rather than retard any movement. There are many of both races who advocate not only sturdy and unyielding, but even aggressive and retaliatory resistance in these matters. But at no time would I advocate violence where it can be avoided, and where better results can be secured through other channels, as I believe they can. Yet the constant repetition of outrages upon black voters by which the defeat of the Republican ticket is brought about in every Southern State, demands immediate action from authoritative quarters—peaceable if possible, by force if necessary.

As a case in point I take a recent election in Louisiana—the Third Congressional District, where there is a large Republican majority composed chiefly of negroes. If the colored voters had not been terrorized, and if the same freedom of ballot ha[d] been allowed there as in the North, Mr. Minor, the Republican candidate, would have been overwhelmingly elected. But thousands of negroes, simply to save their lives, refused to cast a ballot; to vote was death. This the blacks fully understood. As a result they voluntarily disfranchised themselves. It is said that within a week of the election more than four hundred negroes were flogged to intimidate them and keep them from the polls. The success of this method appears in the Democratic majorities, and the Republican defeat. Many of the most prominent Southern leaders make no denial of these facts, but rather advocate such methods as a matter of necessity. A clear statement of the case from a Southern standpoint is made by Senator Morgan.[4] We are told that to disfranchise the negro is morally right, and we are further made to understand that for the present at least we may expect a continuance of the practices to prevent a fair poll.

These views are not confined to men of Southern birth and breeding alone, but there is a similar feeling in the North. I have observed that when men of Northern extraction do espouse the cause of the South, they as a rule "out Herod Herod" in bitterness and intolerance. This is the condition of things that confronts the American negro to-day.

With a divided North and solid South it is utterly out of the question to suppose that these election difficulties can be settled in any other way than through national intervention. I think it may be regarded as certain that the South does not intend to recognize the negro voter as a political factor either in state or national elections until forced to do so, especially as long as there are negro majorities in any of the Southern States. The demand, therefore, for radical legislative measures to insure honest elections everywhere is all the more imperative.

Notes

1 November 2, 1889.

2 [The square brackets around "and it might have added, in any other Southern state" are in the original article.]

3 [Text has dropped out of the original article in two places, both at the top and at the bottom of page 27.]

4 [John T. Morgan, "Shall Negro Majorities Rule?"] *Forum* for February 1889.

The Race Problem

Arena 2 (October 1890): 560–567.

This question, improperly styled the "Negro problem," is in reality the white man's question. From the negro's standpoint the conditions that usually enter into a problem are absent and therefore the wonder is why all this discussion in regard to the blacks, why this confusion, these sectional differences, this bitter strife concerning the negro's rights,—his citizenship?

The blacks are quietly disposed and inclined to accept any amicable terms of peace that may be proposed by either North or South in the interest of the common good. They are not aggressive, nor vindictive, nor are they hostile to national prosperity. Negro supremacy or negro domination is a thought entirely foreign to their plans, and those who would insinuate that the demand for fair play is a cry for this or social equality surely do not understand the negro or his desires in the matter. His demand for fair play is not unreasonable, and why should the whole country by so stirred up over the subject?

But when we stop to think about it, it occurs to us as not being so very strange, for intolerance is largely a characteristic of the American people,— especially intolerance of race.

So many have flocked to these shores, driven by persecution, that intolerance has become implanted in the minds of all as the sign of superiority. In no other way can we account for this among people of high civilization; for the rule is, the higher the civilization the more tolerant of races, creeds, and all else that may be attacked by the least civilized.

Take the Jews for example—a quiet, inoffensive people, many of whom are the monied kings of the world. Note the discrimination against them. Are they not ostracized? Is not the spirit of intolerance so strong against them in many parts of the world that it is impossible for them to remain and have any interest in the soil or learned profession, or even remove elsewhere? What can be worse than this? It is certainly not on the ground of color that there is such clashing. *It is race.* The Chinese constitute another familiar example of race prejudice which has led to prohibitory legislation. In all these we have a variety of race distinctions, attributable, as it is claimed, to some one or more objectionable racial characteristics said to be possessed by those who do not belong to the more favored race,—"the fair-haired Saxon," or rather the American Caucasian who is largely mixture of nationalities and races. What a commentary upon our boasted American civilization when in the face of all this we read what economists affirm: the more civilized the country, the more tolerant it becomes.

Senators Hampton, Butler, Eustis, Morgan, Colquit[t], and other Southern statesmen, have declared it to be their opinion that the two races can never live here together in peace, and further that there will never be an amicable adjustment of affairs as long as the negro essays to exercise the rights of citizenship. He must be satisfied with the place assigned him, however humble, however menial, despite any ambition to rise above the sphere laid out for him. Is this tolerance? If so, then such condition alone can never solve the race problem to the satisfaction of either party. Twenty-five years of school privileges have changed the negro, virtually making a new creature of him; and it is just as impossible to remand the mass of growing intelligence to former ways of thought and action, as to change his color. From the standpoint involving such a condition, the deportation of the entire race of color is the only alternative by which we may hope for solution of this most vexed question, and it might be as well for the race to rise *en masse* and petition Congress to pass the Butler bill to enable them to go to their fatherland (?) where they are supposed to live in peace and amicable relations with all men.[1]

I have never looked with much favor upon emigration, whether forced or voluntary. I have believed that colonization of any kind meant death to the negro, and therefore would prove to be more serious in the end than all the abuse and insults that may be heaped upon him here; but I do favor removal from the South to the West. A scattering of the population over these United States would, in my opinion, do him untold good within the next twenty-five years. Then if it is found to be impossible to live there, I would favor migration as a whole to Africa, or any point beyond the American influence and government. American prejudice is now almost greater than the negro can bear,—North as well as South. There is very little difference as to quantity.

Judge Fenner, in a recent paper, makes the following pungent remarks:—[2]

"We have had innumerable suggestions as to what people of the North should do, as to what the white people of the South should do, as to what the Federal and State government should do. We have been told that we should educate the negro; that we should provide for transporting the negro to Mexico, to Cuba, to Central America, to Africa, or to some unsettled portion of our own vast territory; that we should do this, that, or the other, for the negro, or with the negro. In all these schemes the negro figures merely as a passive, inert, irresponsible factor, who is to have something done to him or with him, or for him, and who is not called on to consider, or decide, or to act for himself according to his own judgment of what is best for his own interest."

If our friends would act upon this principle, then they would be able to arrive at such conclusions as must bring about the desired end more speedily than by the present alienation process. The recent Mohonk Conference called to consider the moral, intellectual, and social condition of the negro, with the negro *in persona* left out, convinces me that there is a great deal of insecurity on the part of many so-called advocates of the race, and that much of the zeal that we see is the outgrowth of a desire for notoriety rather than for the actual improvement of the condition of the race in question. What makes the affair appear more absurd is that the negro's views of the "negro question" were given by a white man. If social equality were feared by these, then there is little hope for the future. Catering to the prejudices of men only prolongs the conflict, and if the negro's friends expect to really aid him in his struggles upward, they must change their *modus operandi* and adopt a different system of tactics. The blacks are not seeking social equality and if the promoters of that Conference supposed that, they evidently utterly failed to comprehend the negro and had little conception of what such a conference must be to carry with it weight and influence. Why not give the negro a hearing,—let him plead his own cause and give his own views relative to these issues which are as vital to him as to any American citizen?

There must be a common understanding between the two races as to what is desirable and as to the best method of reaching that end. There is certainly something to be done on both sides. The whites should exercise forbearance, the blacks, patience; the whites should exercise justice, pure and simple, in granting the negro all his civil and political rights, the negro should make the most of his opportunities, winning respect and confidence by his intellectual and moral attainments and his financial worth.

A significant and pertinent remark is made by Frank Leslie's Illustrated Newspaper when it says of this "perplexing problem":—

> "It may possibly work out its own solution, but it is incumbent upon all to treat it with circumspection, with justice, and with regard for the rights of all concerned."

The Hon. W. C. P. Breckinridge, of Kentucky, in his able paper on this question in The Arena for June, makes an observation that strikes the thoughtful man as being, in truth, the common ground upon which all must take a stand in this discussion:—[3]

> "The only justifiable postulate for the Christian religion and for free institutions is that God created men of one blood, and that in His likeness, and therefore, Christ, as the son of God, is the Brother of all mankind, and men, as the sons of God, are necessarily free, and, with equal necessity, equal. If this be not true, there is no substantial and unshakable foundation for either the Christian religion, or Christian philosophy, or free institutions. And we must accept this as the fundamental truth in all our attempts to reach the exact

nature of the problem which now confronts us, and by this truth we must measure every proposed remedy for whatever evils we may suffer under."

If Mr. Breckinridge had made his deductions from these premises, instead of switching off on tangents exhibiting more prejudice than calm reason, the following tone of the article would have been in a very different vein. After such a preliminary statement, one cannot judge otherwise when he finds the admission of cruel rigor and injustice in the treatment of races that "have become colored," coupled with its justification on the ground that it is a duty to keep the races separate and "protected in those habitations which God had appointed unto it," while admitting that it is also a duty to be "just and humane." One thing is certain, if both are duties, there is no question in Christian ethics as to the claim of the latter over the former. According to the same writer there is no negro, the "vices of two hundred and fifty years" having produced various degrees of color and "variation of character;" yet, in the same breath, the assertion is made of his being of an alien race, and of his incapacity to control because he is a negro. We are told these things and find ourselves confronted by the statement that assimilation—"the very contemplation of it—was unendurable," side by side with another which affirms the existence of "strong, mutual affections." "Incapable of control," and when consolidated, "more subject to doubtful if not actually vicious influences," it is argued that the "more numerous we could make these families in Africa, the more hopeful the outlook for the redemption of that country." We are told that "you cannot continuously keep any part of America in subjugation," that the "worst possible use you can put a man to is to proscribe him and make him hopeless," and yet seven millions of Americans are to be kept in their habitations which the South has appointed unto them—a state of servile subjugation with which there must be no outside interference.

And then, in the face of all of this, "we look forward to being judged on the same judgment day, by the same Judge upon precisely the same principles,"— all of us, of course, if we are brothers according to the writer's first "postulate."

What is the negro to expect in the face of such inconsistent and fallacious argument? Nothing; for it all points one way,—a cry for non-interference of federal authority when home protection is a farce. All arguments from Southern statesmen seem to point to this as the only remedy, and the discussion about the settlement of the problem seems to be mainly to prove how in the wrong the North has been in its attitude upon the question from the days of the Civil War, as well as how dark were reconstruction days, how unwise, to say the least, the Republican party was in all its movements as regards the South and negro. As in Senator Hampton's article "Bygones" and "Dead Issues" occupy the most of the discussion. He, too, attributes all the "ills" to the enfranchisement of the blacks and what he calls their incapacity for self government, but his statements are not justified by the facts in the case. He cites Hayti, Liberia, San Domingo, in proof, and supports his statements by directing our attention to Froude and Sir Spencer St. John, neither of whose testimony can be deemed reliable, as they, too, were guided by their prejudices rather than by good judgment.[4] Of the former the *Critic* for March has this to say: "Mr. Froude, as is well known, learned his political and social philosophy and his literary art from his Gamaliel, Carlyle," and, like his master, "in his secret soul he despised pretty much all the human race." This accounts for the coloring he gives to the negro's "incapacity" which he tries to *prove* by the reckless statements made by enemies of the colored race who persist in presenting a study of low types as indicative of the race.

That individual denominated the negro to-day, has shown his capacity for the exercise of virtues for which even his enemies give him credit; he has representatives in every profession doing honor to the race; he is being counted among the prosperous men financially; he has for years administered well the affairs of Grenada, which, despite Mr. Froude and others, proves capacity for government. The turbulent spirit in Hayti proves no more against him than the same spirit in France proves against the white race. He gave Senator [Wade] Hampton's State his voice and vote for education, and in this line he has risen marvelously.

But after all, these things are not the question. They are only advanced to prove that the South must be left to manage this as it desires; that it is dangerous to allow the blacks to exercise their constitutional rights, and to rouse resistance against Federal supervision. Right here let me say the bill for this last makes no provisions for usurpation of power such as is claimed by its opponents, and if it did, such usurpation could not take place. It is true that it alone will not solve the problem, though it will eliminate some of the perplexing political features. The main question is *How shall we adjust the present relations between the blacks and the whites, so as to promote the general interests of all?* To this question we should stick, but in passing let me reaffirm what I have said elsewhere as to the matter of suffrage referred to by Senator Hampton.[5] To have failed to give the blacks the right of suffrage or to deprive them of it even now, and at the same time to permit them to remain within the state yet not of the state, without voice or vote, would precipitate far more serious trouble than would the so-called negro supremacy. *The solid South might be broken, but the solid negro element, with a gathering enmity intensified by this great wrong, would prove a most formidable force against law.*

It is not the segregation of the negro that is intensifying his race prejudice, so much as it is the injustice done him in depriving him of his rights, and the cruelties to which he is subjected in forms varying from the mildest ostracism to murder; though I believe with Mr. Breckinridge, that it would be far better for these millions to scatter over this country, and that until this is done, America will be in a state of unrest. As this is not probable, at least at present, the trouble must be met and disposed of in some other way. To accept the inevitable, forget the past, overlook the present mistakes and provide against further ill-feeling and friction, seems to be the only wise and discreet policy which can be carried out.

We must all look largely to the future, letting justice, wisdom, education, and the accumulation of wealth combine with time. "The race problem is the natural outcome of environment, and a change must be made in the environ-ment," says Dr. J. C. Price, the negro orator. This is true and this combination will produce the change. In a professional way it is best for the negro to eschew politics, but justice and wisdom must grant him all the civil and polit-ical rights of a citizen and a man, then education, moral and intellectual, and the accumulation of wealth will work together to insure respect and bring about a different state of affairs.

But to assert arrogantly, not only the present superior advancement of the whites as a race, but the determination not to allow the negro to rise to equal heights, is only to sound continually the tocsin of war, to throw down the gauntlet which a rapidly growing intelligence will pick up and prepare to measure arms in achievements. Let the "subtile" and "irresistible powers" work in each race and let the best win. To quote Mr. Breckinridge again, "Intelligence in the long run will conquer ignorance, even if from the hands of intelligence are taken all physical weapons and to ignorance is given every form of brute force." The negro must work out his own destiny, and as Judge Fenner asserts, "from the standpoint of his own self-interests:" he must "form a just and definite conception of what the race problem is." But he is not to be hampered by all these varying, conflicting statements which affirm that he should say, "Hands off. This is my problem, I will solve it," and then set vigor-ously to work to declare what he shall do and what he shall not do—in short that he must solve it by a solution proposed exclusively by the whites for their own self-interest. This assumption is as unjust as it is unwise. There are two parties interested in the solution of this great problem, and the views of each must be considered.

The present seems dark to the negro and that there is an increasing discon-tent, is perfectly evident, still I am far from despairing of his success in the future. In the language of Rabbi [Gustav] Gottheil, when referring to the condition of his own people in this land, I would say of the negro, I am of the opinion that his position will continue to improve in this great country. The old prejudice against him will gradually fade away. We shall, in no distant day, have the negro figuring not only in politics and literature, but in the fine arts and in every thing that unites to harmonize and elevate mankind, just as the men of other races.

America has been and will be, despite legislation, the gathering place of the nations and races of the whole earth. Its future must be worked out by a har-monious working together of its heterogeneous population. All must be uplifted together. It must be acknowledged by all who are struggling to solve this question, that selfish expediency never makes wrong right, that injustice reaps its own reward. In time, some way and somehow, these barriers will come down—it may be brought about by all this loud and constant discus-sion, as walls of Jericho fell before the sound of trumpets in the hands of the marching Israelites. Let the thundering of right and truth come from friend or foe, and let the negro stand firm in the belief expressed by our minister to Hayti, Frederick Douglass,—"God and I make a majority." If the South and North, white and black, will unite on lines of justice and humanity to man, the race question will work out its own solution with the least friction and the best results.

Notes

1 [Matthew C. Butler (1836–1909), Confederate general and U.S. Senator from South Carolina from 1877 to 1895, proposed a bill in 1890 to send black people back to Africa. The notation (?) is in the original text.]

2 [Charles E. Fenner (1834–1911) served on the supreme court of Louisiana from 1889 to his resignation on October 1, 1893.]

3 [William Campbell Preston Breckinridge, "The Race Question," *Arena*, June 1890, page 39.]

4 [James Anthony Froude (1818–1894) was the author of *Thomas Carlyle* (London: Longmans, Green, 1882) and *The English in the West Indies* (London: Longmans, Green, 1888). Spenser St. John (1825–1910) was the author of *Hayti; or, The Black Republic* (London: Smith, Elder, 1884).]

5 *Forum* for March.

The Negro Question from the Negro's Point of View

Arena 4 (July 1891): 219–222.

In the discussion of the so-called "Negro Problem," there is, as a rule, a great deal of the sentimental and still more of the sensational. By a series of *non sequitur* arguments the average disputant succeeds admirably in proving what is foreign to the subject. This is true of writers of both sections of our country—North as well as South—but especially true of those of the South.

The recent symposium of Southern writers in the *Independent* on the Negro Question, as interesting as it was for novelty and variety of view, is no exception to the rule.[1] If the negro could be induced to believe for a moment that he was thus actually destitute of all the elements that go to make up a rational creature, his life would be miserable beyond endurance. But he has not reached that point nor does he care to reach it. Others may exclaim:—

> "O wad some power the giftie gi'e us
> To see oursel's as ithers see us;"[2]

but not the negro, if the vision must always be so distorted. The black man is naturally of a sanguine temperament, as has so often been said; and the facts in the case bear him out in entertaining a hopeful view of his own future and his ability to carve it out. I am sure that they do not warrant even our Southern friends in taking such a pessimistic view of the situation, so far as the negro himself is concerned. But facts are of little account nowadays. There is a tendency to ignore them and appeal to the prejudices and passions of men, and that, too, when it is well known that such methods of procedure prolong rather than settle the question at issue. This is the work of the alarmist—to keep things stirred up and always in an unsettled state.

I think it may be justly inferred that the average white man does not understand the black man, and that he is still an unknown quantity to many of the white people of the country, even to those who profess to know him best. Admitting this, then, it is but natural that much of their deliberation and many of their conclusions should be wide of the mark. The negro does not censure the white man for his conclusions as they are the logical consequence of his premises, but he *does* object to his premises. Our white friends make their mistake in seeming by all their movements to insist that there is but one standpoint from which to view this question, the white man's; but there is another and the negro is viewing it from that side, not selfishly but in a friendly and brotherly spirit.

Senator George was right when he said that the solution of this question should be left to time, but wrong when he further added, "and to the sound judgment of the Southern people."[3] The recent disfranchisement of the negroes of his native State shows very plainly to the thoughtful citizen that the South is not yet capable of justly handling this question, notwithstanding that they are the people "who have the trouble before them every day." This is Mississippi's fatal mistake and one that places the State in the rear of her Southern sisters, and for the present, at least, lessens the value of any suggestion from that quarter.

It is well understood that the sentiment of the American people is that enough has been done for the negro; that the country is under no obligations to look further after his interest, and that he must act for himself. Survival of the fittest is now the watchword. There is no objection to this provided the blacks are *allowed* to do for themselves,—to survive as the fittest, if it be possible,—but this they are not allowed to do. They are certainly anxious to work out their own destiny. They are tired of sentiment and are therefore impatient. They desire to show to the world that they are not only misunderstood but misjudged. They are willing to unite with either North or South in the adjustment of present difficulties.

Unlike the Indians they are sincere—neither treacherous nor deceitful.[4] They are simple, frank, and open-hearted, and are as desirous of good government as are the most honored citizens of the land. Let alone, they will give neither the State nor the nation any trouble. They feel themselves a part and parcel of the nation and as such have an interest in its prosperity as deep as those who are allowed to exercise, untrammelled, the rights of citizenship.

To keep the blacks submissive there is need of neither army nor navy. Though at the foot of the ladder they are contented to remain there, until by virtue of their own efforts they may rise to higher planes. The negro has never sought, does not now, nor will he seek to step beyond his limit. "Social equality," "Negro domination," and "Negro supremacy," are meaningless terms to him so far as his own aspirations are concerned. The social side of this question will regulate itself. It has always done so, in all ages and all climes, despite coercion, despite law. This is the least of the negro's cares. His demand for civil rights is no demand for "social equality." This is a mistaken view of the subject. It is this dread of social equality, this fear of social contact with the negro that precludes many well-meaning people from securing accurate information in regard to the aims, and purposes, and capabilities of those whom they desire to help. But there is light ahead, dark as at times it now may seem, and erroneous as are the views in regard to the negro's relation to the American body-politic.

Congressman Herbert, in his effort to show the negro's incapacity for self-government by calling attention to the defalcations, embezzlements, and petty larcenies, etc., of reconstruction times, forgets that if this is to be taken as the gauge of capacity for self-government, the same rule will apply to bank and railroad wreckers of the present day,—to every defaulter and embezzler of State and private funds, and to every absconding clerk.[5] Now we must remember that this class of citizens is enormously large, and that they are all white, as a rule. Every daily paper that one picks up devotes considerable space to this class of citizens who, according to Mr. Herbert, has shown its "incapacity for self-government," as well as the incapacity of others "who alone have acquired such a capacity" as is claimed by Congressman Barnes. Queer logic is it not? The latter should say so, for it is he who claims that "the Anglo-Saxon is the only member of the human family who has yet shown evidence of a capacity for self-government."

Again, it is said that the negro cannot attain high and rigid scholarship, and even those who have succeeded in becoming educated "if left to themselves would relapse into barbarism." Now, I cannot believe that any such statement as this can be made with sincerity. In the light of the facts it is preposterous. Flipper, while at West Point, demonstrated beyond controversy the fallacy of such a position as the first; and there is hardly a college commencement in which some negro in some way does not continue to show its falsity by distinguishing himself by his extraordinary attainments.[6] Even while I write, a letter lies before me from a young colored student, a graduate of Brown University, who is now taking a post-graduate course at the American School for Classical Studies, at Athens, Greece.[7] From all reports, he is making an excellent record, and will present a thesis in March on "The Demes of Athens." As to relapsing into barbarism, were the negro removed from white influence, the mere mention of the negro scholar, Dr. Edward Blyden, born on the island of St. Thomas, educated and reared in Africa away from the slightest social contact with people of Anglo-Saxon extraction, is sufficient proof that such a conclusion is not a correct one.[8]

What a leading journal has said in regard to the Indians may be repeated here as applicable to the negro: "The most crying need in Indian [negro][9] affairs is its disentanglement from politics and political manipulations."

Here is an opportunity for the Church, but the Church has shown itself wholly inadequate to meet the case, and because of its tendency to shirk its duty, may be said to be to blame for many of the troubles growing out of the presence of the negro on this continent. I have noted that there is more prejudice in the Church, as a rule, than there is in the State. If, as is asserted by some, neither Church nor State can settle this question, then there is nothing to be done but to leave it to time and the combined patience and forbearance of the American people,—black as well as white.

Notes

1 [The symposium was in the *Independent* on April 2, 1891, and consisted of the following set of essays: B. T. Tanner, "The Condition of the Negro—The Colored Ministry"; W. C.

P. Breckinridge, "The Race Question"; George Marion McClellan, "The Rights of Negroes"; J. E. Rankin, "Industrial Education for the African"; C. W. Grandison, "The Social and Moral Condition of the Colored People of the South"; Charles W. Chesnutt, "A Multitude of Counselors"; Henry Clay Gray, "Negro Christianity"; Luther A. Fox, "Religious Advancement of the Negro in Southern Rural Section"; A. Tolman Smith, "The Support of Colored Public Schools"; Edward Dickerson, "Negroes and Grand Jury Duty"; J. T. Gibbs, "The Southern View and the Northern View of the Negro."]

2 [Robert Burns (1759–1796), "To a Louse" (1786), stanza 8, lines 1–2.]

3 [James Zachariah George (1826–1897), Democrat and Confederate officer, was a U.S. Senator from Mississippi from 1881 until his death in 1897.]

4 [This is an odd comment for Scarborough to make, because he was part Indian through his mother. See *Autobiography*, p. 23.]

5 [Hilary Abner Herbert (1833–1919), Confederate soldier and Democrat, served in the U.S. Congress from 1877 to 1893.]

6 [Henry Ossian Flipper (1856–1940), appointed to West Point in 1873, became its first black graduate in 1877.]

7 [John Wesley Gilbert (c. 1865–1923) earned his B.A. and M.A. in Greek from Brown University and was the first black person to attend the American School of Classical Studies in Athens. See Michele Valerie Ronnick, "John Wesley Gilbert (c. 1865–1923)," *Classical Outlook* 78 (2001): 113–114.]

8 [Edward Wilmot Blyden (1832–1912), classics professor at Liberia College from 1862 to 1871, became in 1880 the second black member of the American Philological Association.]

9 [The square brackets around "negro" are in the original article.]

An Inside View of the Southern Convict Lease System

Indianapolis Freeman, December 7, 1891, p. 5.

The recent mining troubles in Tennessee have revived the interest in the Southern convict lease system. Even the South, itself, which is generally dead to all reforms, is becoming somewhat agitated over the subject, and well it may do so. There is no system of penal punishment practiced by that section that is so degrading, so inhuman, so barbarous, so revolting in all of its aspects as is the present method of punishing recreants on southern soil. A graded scale of punishments, when the Negro is in question, is an unknown thing. The stealing of the smallest trifle is classed whenever the Negro is the culprit with midnight burglary or open high way robbery. The fellow in any of these cases may be sent to the chain-gang or penitentiary from which he is leased to the highest bidder for a term of years in common with others to engage in whatever kind of labor the lessees may decide.

It is said that in Arkansas, Mississippi, and Louisiana the system is at its worst, in Tennessee it is at its best. The truth of this statement depends largely upon what my informant means by the terms "worst" and "best;" for I am sure so far as I have been able to observe the system is about as bad in Georgia, Alabama and Tennessee, a[s] it is in any other part of the South. Take it at its best it is a sort of life and death struggle with the poor, unfortunate prisoners, and therefore deserves the severest condemnation of all humane citizens at least white or black. Especially should the Negro be interested for the reason that the majority are Negroes, and if the Negro cares nothing for the Negro, pray, tell me, whom we have to plead our cause[?] The Negro[']s first duty is to the Negro whether he be high or low in office or out of office, educated or uneducated he is morally bound to protect himself, while at the same time he is looking after the interest of his race. Any colored man who will defend a white man against a member of his own household in court or out of it deserves to be ostracised by that household. The colored lawyers of our country ought to concentrate their best efforts upon some scheme to ameliorate the prison life of their brethern. Charity begins at home and he who does not

POLITICS, POLICY, AND PREJUDICE

think so is fearfully behind the times. We must come to it sooner or later, and we might as well begin now as at any time to carve out our own future, not only by what we do but by who we dare to do. The Negro is altogether too timid, unless he can foresee the outcome he fears to venture. He will never do much until he gets over this feeling. What interest have the lesse[e]s in the convicts other than the amount of money made out of their labor? None at all. In many instances the lessees sub[-]let those whom they have leased to parties as irresponsible as themselves, if not more so. Thus the man goes on from bad to worse with no one to interfere or call a halt. These poor, half fed, half clothed, uncared for creatures[;] the barbarities of their convict lives cannot be described with words. *Miserabile dictu.*

The state, of course, often gets large revenue from the lessees—amounts ranging from $50,000 to $500,000 and possible more. But again what of their condition? They are as filthy and dirty as a mule, infected with vermin and loathsome to look upon. The sight is sufficient to bring tears to the eyes of the beholder. The sick are frequently neglected in so much that no hospitals are provided for them. Sometimes the sick and the well are confined in the same cell. Often their water supply is bad and disease and sickness are the results; sometimes scarcely any water at all.

An Alabama warden is writing upon this subject and the following strong language: "To say there are reformatory measures used at our prisons or that any regard is had to kindred subjects is to state a falsehood. The system is a disgrace to the state, a reproach to the civilization and Christian sentiment of the age and ought to be speedily abandoned.["]

The convicts who have been parceled out to work on farms, railroads, in brick yards, in mines and in various other pursuits fare even worse, for in addition to the deprivation already referred to they are compelled to labor whether in the rain or in the sunshine and frequently compelled under guard to pass the night without shelter in the midst of storms and the severest cold. If they attempt to escape they are shot down like dogs wherever found. Aside from this the system of convict labor is nothing more or less than a system of slave labor a species of labor that has always been found to be detrimental to the best industrial and commercial interests of a free country and a free people. Then it is not to be wondered at that public sentiment was with the miners in their recent troubles in Tennessee. It is to be regretted that the miner did not release all the convicts and it is to be regretted the more that all did not make sure their escape. While I am opposed to lawlessness yet the time has come for action instant action of some kind on the part of the oppressed let the results be what they may. The Negro must rise from his lethargy and show himself a man and stop this constant whining and fretting.

Race Legislation for Railways

Our Day 9 (July 1892): 478–485.

The recent adoption of the separate car service for the two races in the South is not generally regarded as a wise movement. It is thought that legislation of this kind not only legalizes prejudice, but defers the era of good feeling and amicable relations between the races.

The war is over and the breach between the North and South, growing out of the rebellion, is rapidly healing up, and the two sections of our great country are gradually re-uniting. Capital is finding its way to the South in large amounts and the hitherto large wastes and barren portions of that section are being built up and beautified at an astonishingly rapid rate.

Some time ago in an editorial article in *Frank Leslie's Illustrated Weekly Newspaper*, entitled "A Step Backward," I took the opportunity to denounce the separate car service as unjust and subversive to our best interests, North and South. I attempted to show why such service was objectionable, and further stated what would be the inevitable result if the South persisted in and insisted upon legalizing such distinctions between the races.

Since that paper appeared there has been an almost universal movement throughout the South to have such legislation, providing for separate cars, enacted by all the state legislatures.

We might as well now as any other time view this matter squarely and impartially, for facts are facts. And as the matter now stands we are simply deferring the era of peace and good will, and are provoking the negroes to adopt measures for their own protection, that they would not otherwise think of, by the constant attempt to remind them that they are negroes and are, therefore, entitled to no respect whatever. Poor policy is this, and I judge that the South in a few years will admit the truth of this statement.

All the laws thus far enacted relative to the separate car movement run very nearly in the same groove.

The Tennessee law in substance is as follows: (*a*) The railroads must provide separate coaches, equal in comfort and convenience for the accommodation of the white and colored passengers; (*b*) The conductor who is by this law clothed with police powers is instructed under a penalty to see that the two races do not ride together under any circumstances, except in the case of colored nurses or servants who may have seats with their masters or mistresses in the white people's car; (c) The person refusing to go into the coach provided for his race shall not be allowed to enter any car at all, but shall be left standing on the platform, if this takes place before the train leaves the station; if the train is in motion he is to obey orders or else be put off.

This law is intended to prevent white people from riding in the negro car and negroes from entering the car set apart for the whites.

It is said that the very members of the Farmers' Alliance who were the authors of this infamous legislation are the men who fail to observe it. These men, it is said, go into the colored coach, sit down, smoke, drink, gamble and swear until the attention of the conductor is called to the matter, in which case they are usually invited out into the smoking car. This conductor, as a rule, may pass through the coach a dozen times, but he never pays any attention to them until they are pointed out to him. Here is a specific example. I quote from a reputable negro paper published in Nashville, Tenn. The writer says: "I had occasion, a few days ago, to inform the conductor that ten white men were in the colored car, five of whom were smoking. I asked him if the separate car law was in effect on his road. He replied, 'Yes, but whenever the other car is full I let them come in here and make them behave!'" This is only one of the numerous instances of this kind that might be quoted. The conductor has no right whatever to allow, even in the event of crowded cars, the members of one race to sit with those of another. The law makes no provision for the convenience of passengers in the case of crowded coaches. This is not all. In no case whatever is a man or woman who is known to have a mixture of negro blood, visible or otherwise, permitted to go into the coaches provided for the whites. It will clearly appear from the foregoing that the conductor's police powers are often discretionary in that his line of action is determined by the color of the passengers whose interests may be at stake.

The same writer just referred to tells us that on coming from Manchester, Tenn., a few days ago, he observed that the colored car was filled with white people of both sexes as there were only three colored persons on board, and that among them were two "toughs," who began smoking offensive pipes. When the conductor came in and observed it, he remarked: "You men must stop smoking; this is the darkies' car, and it is only their say so whether you white folks can stay in here anyhow. If they say you must go out, you must go." Why not let the negro remain in a decent car till his presence shall give offense to other passengers? Why this difference? Why enforce the law in the case of one and not in the case of another? These are the questions that are now beginning to agitate the negroes of the South. It is well understood that if the separate car system proves an inconvenience to the white passengers to any extent, the Act providing for such service will be repealed. But if, on the other hand, all of the inconvenience and annoyance shall come to the blacks, the probability is that the law will remain in force until by agitation public sentiment shall reach such a point as to demand that black citizens shall be treated as citizens and shall have accorded to them the rights and privileges enjoyed by other citizens. Already the negroes are taking steps to test the validity of the law in Tennessee; while in Louisiana and Mississippi similar steps are being taken. It is proposed to use every legitimate means at hand to have the Act rescinded. Test cases are to be made whenever the opportunity presents itself. The best legal talent from both races is to be engaged by the negroes, who are the plaintiffs in this case, and an effort made to show that the law is unconstitutional.

Judge Tourgée has offered to give his services in conjunction with others as soon as the negroes are ready to take up the matter.

It is due the better element of the whites to say that there are many among them that are in sympathy with the blacks and are willing to unite with them, under any reasonable pretext, to help them assert their rights and secure justice. The inconvenience to which the negroes are put, and especially the better class of negroes, is by no means overlooked by them. This, too, is aside from the humiliation which is attendant on every change the negro is compelled to make from car to car because of his color.

Whatever be the cause of this movement, it is evident, as I have already intimated, that the South is almost a unit in the matter of separate coaches for the two races. We find such laws not only in Tennessee, but in Alabama, Louisiana, Texas, Mississippi, Georgia and Arkansas as well. In Virginia the Governor recommended the passage of such an Act, but the Legislature refused to comply with the request. In Kentucky the Governor took opposite ground and when approached on the subject refused to entertain the motion, rejected the idea and threw his influence against it. As a result when the matter came up in the Legislature its opponents were greater than its friends in number and it failed of passage. The negroes themselves were implacable and were determined to defeat it at any cost, and they succeeded. In Alabama it is said that the separate car system has been in operation for many years and with good results, and so far as the railroad and street car companies are concerned that the race question is forever settled.

In South Carolina when the proposal came up in the Legislature for consideration it was defeated in the Senate and then killed. Public sentiment in this state was against it and public sentiment prevailed. In North Carolina the separate car law was likewise discussed, but without any definite action. It is barely possible that both North and South Carolina will stoutly refuse to indorse such backward movements—the outgrowth of slavery and negro oppression—and will endeavor to set an example to their less enlightened sisters of the South as to the best policy to pursue to insure peace and friendly feeling among the citizens of the respective states—white and black.

The Georgia law, which provides for separate cars for white and colored people, reads as follows:

> *Section 1.*—Be it enacted by the General Assembly of the State of Georgia, That from and after the passage of this Act, all railroads doing business in this state shall be required to furnish equal accommodations, in separate cars or compartments of cars, for

white and colored passengers, provided that this Act shall not apply to sleeping cars.

Section 2.—Be it further enacted, That all conductors or other employees in charge of such cars shall be required to assign all passengers to their respective cars or compartments of cars, provided by said companies under the provisions of this Act, and all conductors of dummy, electric and street cars, shall have and are hereby invested with police power to carry out the provisions of this Act.

Section 3.—Be it enacted, That any passenger remaining in car or compartment or seat, other than that to which he may have been assigned, shall be guilty of a misdemeanor, and on conviction thereof shall be punished as prescribed in Section 4310 of Code of 1882. Jurisdiction of such offenses shall be in the county in which same occurred. The conductor and any and all such employees on such car are hereby clothed with power to eject from the train, or car, or compartment, or seat any who may occupy seats other than those that may be assigned to them.

Section 4.—Be it further enacted, That when a railroad car is divided into compartments, the space set aside or provided for white and colored passengers, respectively, may be proportioned according to the proportion of usual and ordinary travel of each on the road or line on which said cars are used.

Section 5.— Be it further enacted, That it shall be unlawful for the officers or employees having charge of such railroad cars to allow or permit white and colored passengers to occupy the same car or compartment; and for violation of this section any such officer or employee shall be guilty of a misdemeanor, and on conviction thereof, shall be punished as prescribed in Section 4310 of the Code of 1882.

Section 6.—Be it further enacted, That the provisions of this Act shall not apply to nurses or servants in attendance on their employers.

Section 7.—Be it further enacted, That all companies using compartment or separate cars shall furnish to the passengers comfortable seats and have such cars sufficiently lighted and ventilated, and a failure to do so shall be a misdemeanor punishable under Section 4310 of the Code of 1882.

Section 8.—Be it further enacted, That all laws and parts of laws in conflict with this Act be and the same are hereby repealed.

This is the Georgia law. As an interesting relic of barbarism—pure and simple—it will be difficult to find anything in the annals of literature, ancient or modern, that surpasses it.

But the question that now arises is, Will it or any other law forbidding the intermingling of the races in railroad cars or in street cars bring about the end desired?

It is very evident that the attempt to enforce the law will produce friction between the races and possibly blood-shed. Some time ago a conductor was murdered by a negro in Florida and on one of the Florida roads for attempting to enforce a law which provides that negroes shall ride only in cars set apart for them, and in none other. The railroad officials on all of the southern lines find it difficult to enforce the law because of the negro's opposition to it and his refusal to obey orders. For this opposition the railroad companies are largely responsible, as they do not furnish either separate cars or equal accommodations. Then, too, they are to blame for permitting such legislation to be recorded upon the statute books. For if they had been as determined in their opposition to the passage of this law as were the lessees of the Tennessee convicts to prevent the Legislature from taking action against the heinous system of parceling out convicts to the highest bidder for mining purposes, the Act providing for separate cars would never have passed. For extra cars and extra expense, if there be any, the railroad companies have themselves to blame. To carry out the letter of the law, if not the spirit, would require at least four grades of cars: one first-class coach for white passengers; one for colored passengers; one second-class coach for white passengers and one for colored. Then, to meet the demands of this arrangement, there would be required a very long train. This the railroads refuse to furnish as it is not a paying investment. As a substitute the old antebellum "Jim Crow Car" system is revived and the blacks are compelled to accept quarters there or none. This is the situation that the negro is placed in. It virtually amounts to a retaliation on the part of the companies upon the negro for something over which he had no control, and for which he is in nowise responsible. Some time ago a colored [1] Bishop of the A. M. E. church, the hero of the Ecumenical Conference, held in Washington City, a gentleman and a scholar, in company with three colored college professors started for Nashville. They took seats in a first-class coach in Cincinnati and rode like other passengers and with other passengers till they reached a point within fifty miles of the Tennessee state line. Here, about four o'clock a.m., the conductor came in and informed the Bishop and his companions that at the next stopping place, which is Franklin, Kentucky, they must go into the car set apart for colored people. He further added that he was subject to a fine of several dollars if he failed to enforce the law, but so far as he was concerned he was perfectly willing that they should remain where they were. Then as if to clinch his last remarks, with a good deal of earnestness, supplemented with an oath, he added that it was a very unjust law,—to which statement all the party assented.

The law demanded that negroes should ride with negroes in a coach set apart for negroes, so the conductor's gentlemanly request was complied with, the Bishop taking the lead and the others with luggage and gripsack in hand following in single file till the negro car was reached. This coach proved to be the smoking car divided into two parts—the half next to the engine being set apart for the blacks. It was veritably a pig-pen with all the term implies, nauseating in the extreme—filthy and dirty—yet this was the "equal accommodation" provided by the laws of Tennessee. The Bishop took it calmly, as did his associates, made the most of it, and then and there resolved never to try again an open day car below Mason and Dixon's line if a Pullman car could be found anywhere near and a berth could be secured. This episode is only one of the many daily occurrences of this kind. Well-dressed, gentlemanly as well as scholarly negroes, for there are such among them, are all hustled alike into these "Jim Crow cars" and are compelled to submit to insults that stir up the Satanic side of their natures and cause them to do deeds of violence that would be otherwise unknown. This is sowing the wind and reaping the whirl-wind, and who is to blame, Ham or Shem? Shall we continue to follow this *modus operandi*, or shall we attempt to build "golden bridges" between the North and the South, between the blacks and whites—which Murat Halstead, formerly of the *Commercial Gazette*, so strenuously advocated in that great daily after the election of President Harrison? We all approved. Let us have peace. We knew that President Harrison would give the country a wise, clean and able administration, and it was the universal desire that there should be no North and no South—no blacks and no whites so far as sectional differences and race prejudice are concerned. But we were doomed to disappointment, for the South seemed bent on having its own way, whatever the consequences might be. If it is the policy to eliminate the negro from the body politic by rendering him a dissatisfied factor and thereby forcing him out of the country, the present method will hardly bring about that result.

Murder, rapine and their concomitants will, of course, follow such tactics wherever practiced. Instead of law and order, violence and confusion will reign supreme.

The colored people are now raising subscriptions throughout the country in aid of the movement to test the separate car law as it exists in some of the southern states. The success of their efforts depends largely upon the interest that they may arouse in their own behalf and also upon the drift of public sentiment as to the justice or injustice of such a law.

Note

1 Bishop B. W. ARNETT, D. D., ex-member of the Ohio Legislature.

As You Like It

Cleveland Gazette, October 1, 1892.

Not one white man out of a hundred of those who are brought or bring themselves in contact with the Negro knows how to talk to a Negro audience.

He may sit down vis-a-vis with single ones of the race and converse, exchange opinions, give advice, etc., etc., but put him before a hundred or more and he immediately proceeds to make a hopeless failure of it—at least as far as the Negro goes.

It seems next to impossible for the white man in general to divest himself of the idea of his superiority and to meet the race as man meets man. He may be philanthropic to the highest degree, good to the core, full of the "milk of human kindness" and yet fail in this particular.

The Negro as a rule listens to all that the white man has to say with courtesy and attention: but oftimes this is largely due to the possession of politeness—that innate virtue in his possession, and accorded him by all. It serves many a purpose. But this courtesy of attention does not make it true that he is made enthusiastic or even ordinarily pleased by the utterances circumstances may force him to hear.

The white man who can rise before a Negro audience and not inform his hearers that he was always a friend to "your" people; that his father or grandfather or some near relative was an ardent supporter of anti-slavery principles, an abolitionist who had suffered for his belief, or a prime mover in carrying on the operations of the underground railroad—*that man scores one point for his speech in the beginning*.

If he does not go on to inform them of the ways their fathers trod and profusely congratulate them upon their superior advantages and urge them to rise above the cabin and cotton fields (when many of those before him never saw either), *he ensures for himself greater commendation still*.

There is the speaker who means well from the bottom of his heart. They all do, but he forgets that it is some twenty years since freedom came to the Negro, and while he himself has been growing aged, a new generation has come up, and the talk that seemed so learned then and which roused the "amens" and "bless you, honey," and all that of the days when freedom was a new thing, is now just twenty-seven years too old. He means it for the encouragement and enlightenment of bright youth and young manhood before him, but it falls on unresponsive ears, because these are of another generation, and a progressive one as well.

Not long since six persons addressed a Negro audience. The first speaker was jocosely familiar and showed his spirit by frequent reference to color, while he expatiated upon black, brown, cream and white, with declarations to the effect—truthful no doubt—that curly, kinky hair might be just as desirable as straight, silky locks. The next recited the history of the fathers and grandfathers with due pathos, giving such a picture of near degradation as would have made a white audience squirm audibly.

The third arose or rose to the occasion with an oratorical effort which included a panegyric upon what the Negro race had accomplished. It took better—but he spoiled the effect by his emphatic and frequent you's and we's. Still another dwelt upon the southern outrages and his own deep-dyed hatred of such a policy. He struck a responsive chord, but even Negro audiences tire of hearing the horrid tale when the speaker has no remedy to propose and it is evident that he speaks "to be heard." The fifth speaker made a poor "out" of it, as a critic in his audience put it. He was not in sympathy with the time or the occasion and he endeavored to be honest with himself and yet conservative. He found there was no middle ground which he could consistently occupy with any degree of comfort to himself or hearers, and after floundering through a few unfortunate, incoherent, semi-contradictory statements, sat down in confusion to the relief of all parties.

The last of the company "rose for a few words." Perhaps the previous speakers had exhausted all the ammunition usual to such occasions; perhaps he was not so bright, so learned, so well-read; perhaps he really sought to say something unique. But whatever the cause, the "few words" were well chosen and expressive of the desirability of the possession of things which go to make up noble lives in general, not noble Negro lives in particular. The topics of the day which interest the world at large he seemed to judge might, should, would and could interest his hearers as well. He said nothing, he did nothing to leave the slightest impression that he stood there a sympathizer or a being of a superior scale in any sense. Yet he was sympathetic and he commanded close attention and hearty respect. It is needless to say he sat down in the midst of a tumult of applause. It would have been a question to some why he was accorded such a response, but perhaps some might have gotten an idea for the remark which expressed a satisfaction full of peculiar significance—"That man treated us white."

Imagine just for a moment what effect a speaker would have who should address an audience of white people with commiseration for the low pursuits their fathers and mothers followed, with jokes upon any characteristic they possessed as a distinctive thing—this with the idea of superiority ever in sight would not be liked at all. No people delight in hearing of their poverty, perhaps degradation, of not more than a generation back at the least. It is too near. Then why should the Negro? The poor have sensibilities which charity sympathetically avoids disturbing. Why not use this forebearance in speaking to the Negro? He, no more than other people in general, has not reached the philosophical plane of the individual who remarked that folks might make fun of his hair, his features, his form—it did not affect him; it was nature they were ridiculing; but when they came to laugh at his principles, then only were they laughing at himself. It would be a felicitous moment if all were at such a height, but that day and hour have not yet come.

The Negro as a mass prefers to be talked to in the abstract rather than in the concrete. He can appreciate the need of learning, riches, honor and virtue with all other desirable good in this world just as readily when put before him the abstract. He does not need sympathetic reference at every opportunity. The sympathy that he wants is that which is shown in actual endeavors to create a different state of things—a sympathy that does not exhaust itself in talk.

He does not want to have A or B state to him from the platform that the world will recognize him, that he is as good as anyone, that God created men free and equal, and then be met outside—men far the superior of the talker, intellectually and financially—by the same A or B in a shamed-faced, apologetic, condescending sort of way if among other white people on another occasion. The Negro does not want so much senseless palaver and musty platitudes. He has a keen scent for the meaning back of the veneer of sound, for the heart and soul of the man; yet when he recognizes these to be all right, he feels the truth of the old proverb that the truth should not be told at all times, and he applies it right to his own case.

Sometimes a man prays to be delivered from his friends. Friends have no right, acquired or hereditary, to probe wounds or uncover them, to rediscover scars or notice their presence or possession. There is no danger that the Negro will fail to remember the paths through which he has come to the present and the constant recalling of the matter in any form is entirely uncalled for in addressing him.

The white man who appears before the Negro audience must learn to individualize. He must remember there are Negroes and Negroes. He must forget that he is white and while not being effusively familiar in his attempt to embrace him as a man and a brother, he must guard himself against the offensive use of the second person of address in all its forms. This he must do if he really wishes to achieve any great results.

In short, the white man who talks to the Negro needs not only intelligence, learning and good will, but to these he must add common sense, tact and delicacy, for, if the truth must be told the Negro is a little sensitive.

The Negro Problem:
The African Ethnological Congress

Leslie's Weekly, September 28, 1893, p. 206.

Among the many auxiliary congresses of the World's Columbian Exposition,[1] none, perhaps, save one (the Parliament of Religions), has awakened such general interest and attracted such wide attention, as well as large attendance, as the Congress of African Ethnology. There are reasons for this. It was not merely accidental or a fortuitous circumstance. It was not merely curiosity. It was because Africa is no longer the dark continent in the strict sense of the term. It is now known as never before known. It will be known in the future better than now. The civilized world is turned toward it, and in such way as to emphasize the opinion that in the future Africa will be the battle-ground of the nations of the earth. In short, the result of the partition of Africa must be to put that country on the way to a higher civilization in such manner that it will tread in the footsteps of Europe onward and upward till it shall become more vigorously and more actively lighted up by the arts and sciences of the present high civilization of these contending Powers, and in the end its ancient glory shall return to it with all of this added splendor.

Mr. Frederick Perry Noble, of the Newberry Library, Chicago, and secretary of the African Congress, in an article in *Our Day,* among many other pertinent observations, makes the following significant statement:[2]

"Africa has played a great part in ancient history. The venal impression, still too prevalent, has been that in the sphere of history Africa has been a Sahara; but the view is about as correct as the old-time thought of the Great Desert. In Africa civilization had its birth. Egyptian and Hykshos and Persian and Hellene and Roman and Saracen and Frank and Turk and Saxon have in turn seized the serpent of old Nile. The Father of the Faithful and the Prince of Israel and the founder of the Hebrew theocracy sought shelter in the shadow of the pyramids. Egypt saved the Christ-child from death. Cyrene of Africa gave Simon as Africa's first cross-bearer.

The eunuch of Ethiopia was the first African to receive baptism. Apollos of Alexandria was the first African mighty in the Scriptures. Its bishop, Athanasius, saved to Christianity its faith that Christ is very God of God. Near the ancient mistress of the seas Rome and Carthage settled whether the civilization of the West and the future should be Shemitic or Aryan, enslaved and stagnant, or free and progressive. In Africa Augustine thought out the problems of fate, free will, and man's return to God. There Tertullian wrought out a theory of the church. Thus Africa was of old bound by a thousand streams of life to the currents of the world's advance, and contributed forces of its own to civilization and Christianity."

Admitting this to be the fact, we are led to inquire what are the possibilities of a country so rich in experiences, so fertile in resources, so well endowed with the skill and wisdom of ages. This question has been in a measure answered by the recent gathering of some of the world's most learned men—scientists, philologists, sociologists, explorers, diplomats, statesmen, doctors, lawyers, men of letters, theologians, missionaries, and scholars—all of whom, by investigation and research, were able to bear testimony to the magnificent possibilities of a country hitherto unknown as to its people, as to its material wealth, and as to much of its inner history.

The congress at various times reviewed the geography, history, language, the ethnology, the archæology, the paleontology, the arts and sciences, and all that go to make up the country and people. The American negro in all of his relations constituted a fertile topic for discussion. From a sociological stand-point the addresses of Dr. William Hayes Ward, of the New York *Independent*, Dr. Noble of Chicago, Frederick Douglass, Bishop Turner, Dr. [M. E.] Strieby, and Dr. [Joseph-Edmund] Roy were not only among the most notable, but were marvels of breadth and frankness of statement. Their utterances must constitute the key-note to the solution of the so-called negro problem in the United States. *Equality before the law, a fair and equal chance, must be granted to the blacks, whatever be the feeling against them.* Until this is allowed the negro question in the United States will never be settled, view the matter as one may.

It has been shown that the negro will not emigrate to Africa or elsewhere, voluntarily. It has also been shown that compulsory emigration is out of the question. Again, it needs no argument to show that colonization (Mr. Graves to the contrary, notwithstanding) in any part of the United States is impracticable. Here the matter must rest and the question be solved without change of base.

The object of the congress was a comprehensive one. It was not only to call attention to Africa and its people, but to stir up a settlement against injustice to the American blacks. How far the latter was a success, time will tell. The Belgian minister, Albert Le Ghalt, presented a valuable address on the Congo Free State. He opened with a message of sympathy from King Leopold to the congress and the United States. There can be nothing but praise for the King of Belgium, with the added words, "*Macte virtute*"—Go on in your virtue. For of all the kings and potentates of foreign lands he has taken advanced ground in his philanthropic efforts to solve the so-called African problem.

The ethnological congress was intended to supplement the work of the Berlin and Brussels congresses, or rather to do what they failed to do: *take a firmer and more vigorous stand in reference to the policy* to be pursued in relation to Africa and the African. Justice should be done there as well as here. The Africans should be treated as human beings and not as sticks and stones. Let Christianity and its civilizing influences operate there as well as here, and the results will take care of themselves. It has often been claimed that African exploration could not well be carried on without war and bloodshed and suffering. This opinion can no longer have exclusive sway, as from the lips of Mrs. Mary French Sheldon we find that this is unnecessary, and we are forced, too, to the conclusion, after hearing the many papers of those who know Africa from personal experience, that a new era of exploration has dawned upon the civilized world. Dr. [Robert Needham] Cust of England, in his "Ethics of African Geographical Explor[ation]," is of the same opinion.

Another phase of the congress of peculiar interest was the linguistic side. African philology in all its relations came up for a full discussion, and received due attention—the African tongues and dialects purely as such, and the same in relation to foreign languages, the outcome of the latter in contact with native speech. Will the African speech lose its identity by social contact with foreign tongues and blend with the same—will it become extinct, or will it drive out its rival, maintaining its own against all foreign attacks? These are all interesting questions and present a problem that may well attack future congresses of philology everywhere.

Lewis Grout, author of a Zulu grammar, in speaking of the languages and dialects of Africa, says that there are about four hundred and thirty-eight languages and one hundred and fifty-three dialects spoken in the country, making in all a little less than six hundred. This is only an approximation, as the present imperfect state reached by linguistic science in relation to African speech makes an accurate statement out of the question. The six families of these languages settled upon are classified into Hamitic, Shemitic, Nuba-Fulah, Negro, Bantu, and Hottentot Bushman. Each of these groups was analyzed and divided according to kinship[.]

Mrs. French Sheldon, a lady well qualified to speak from her standpoint as a traveler, added the result of her own observations: "Some African tribes have a sympathetic language more or less phonetic, but naturally circumscribed, as they have but few wants to express. They have no love expressions except 'I like you,' or phrases of that sort. They use a great many soft vowels like the Italian in their conversation, and the few consonants they have are harsh, like the Anglo-Saxon."

In the ample conditions fulfilled in this great gathering, the study of Africa has been presented as never before to the civilized world. The forthcoming memorial volume of the sessions will present a summary of enlightened, optimistic views of this continent and the race wherever found, that must lead to a bettering of the condition of the race such as it would be impossible to obtain by any other method than that of this gigantic scheme of discussion, so ably outlined by the secretary, F. Perry Noble, and so magnificently executed by the many learned participants.

Notes

1 [For a fuller discussion of the exposition see *Autobiography*, pp. 123–130.]

2 ["Africa at the Columbia Exposition," *Our Day* 9 (November 1892): 773–789. Frederick Perry Noble (1863–1945) was assistant librarian at the Newberry from 1891 to 1893.]

The Negro's Part
in a Presidential Nomination

Leslie's Weekly, July 30, 1896, pp. 67 and 71.

To one who has kept an eye upon the political situation in this country and the part played by the negro in political movements, and especially the one which culminated in the nomination of our next President, William McKinley, it is evident that the influence of the colored voter can neither be overlooked nor over-estimated.

From start to finish the representatives of this contingent of the Republican party were eagerly sought and their Presidential preferences ascertained. As a rule they had preferences. Generally these, in the late Republican contest for the Presidential nomination were for Major McKinley. Only here and there were found supporters of either Reed, Allison, Quay, or Morton. While the negro recognized them all as capable and honorable gentlemen, abundantly able to rescue our great commonwealth from the throes of financial ruin, he believed most in McKinley; had heard him talked of most; his name, associated as it was with the tariff movement, had become a household word, and he was very anxious to see him nominated and to risk his chances in the major's hands.

While the Afro-American is interested in all the leading issues of the day as they relate to the good of both party and country, he never loses sight of the issue in which he is specially concerned. Naturally enough this should be so. For the most part he has been a sort of happy-go-lucky fellow, contented to take things as he found them, but now he exhibits a feeling of unrest, as is apparent.

In his canvass as to the merits of the men spoken of for the Presidency, the leading question with him was: Which of them will conserve the interest of the colored man best and will aid him in his struggles for the comforts of life?

That the black man no longer in himself constitutes a distinctive national issue in any political campaign is as well known to the man of color as is the fact that the sun shines; but as a Republican he is bound to support the candidate of that party, even though he may not be his choice, and as a negro the one who he thinks will be friendliest to his interests as a citizen.

The negro is much like his Democratic brother; he talks—talks vociferously and threatens to bolt, but seldom does it. He votes, as a rule, with the party that gave him freedom, and defies his critics. He is sensible.

There was intense feeling displayed at St. Louis by the few who had other candidates than the one nominated. Thus one prominent colored leader declared that if Major McKinley did not prove true to the colored wing of the Republican party he would use the press to scorch every negro from Ohio who supported him and encouraged others to do so.

Now, so far as Governor McKinley is concerned there is no ground for fear on that line—for he is square. The writer has been honored with an intimate acquaintance with the major for years, as also with Governor Foraker, and knows whereof he speaks.[1] He knows that Major McKinley, like Senator Foraker, is all right on the race question so far as manhood rights are concerned, and that he is a friend of the oppressed wherever found—in all climes—black or white. In proof, extracts from his many speeches, delivered on many occasions, can be cited. That he is the people's candidate goes without saying.

The negro delegates at St. Louis were enthusiastic in their preferences and in their support of their candidate. These men were above the average. They could give good reasons for their faith and their choice. A bureau of Ohio colored men, with headquarters and rooms at the Laclede Hotel, did efficient service among their Southern brethren in the interest of Major McKinley. They were the guests of the celebrated Tippecanoe Club, of Cleveland, Ohio.

The negro can be trusted. He will not always sell his vote, nor will he always break his pledge nor violate his oath. I remember that while at St. Louis a colored delegate from the South was asked to cast his vote for another candidate than the one for whom he was instructed; but he indignantly refused, as a man of honor, to betray the trusts reposed in him.

Suffice it to say that the black delegates were loyal to the end to the candidates of their choice, whether McKinley, Reed, Allison, Morton, or Quay, despite influences to make them waver. These men on the whole were far superior to those of many previous conventions, and were present not for the loaves and fishes,[2] but to help nominate a man who would conserve not only their individual interests, but the interests of all the people—the interests of the entire country—best. In the nomination of Governor McKinley they believe that they have the man.

Notes

1 [See *Autobiography*, pp. 88–89, 106–108, 148–150, 192, 194, and 198.]

2 [Mark 6:30–44.]

The Negro's Duty to Himself

Indianapolis Freeman, December 30, 1899.

Advice to The Race That Will Lead it to Victory—"By Their Fruits Ye Shall Know Them"—The Negro as a Brave.

Ther[e] are duties objective and there are duties subjective. There are duties that we owe to others and then there are duties that we owe to ourselves.

When the North by virtue of the emancipation act and by force of arms made the Negro a freeman, and when by special legislation and constitutional amendments it further clothed him with citizenship, it took upon itself new duties and new responsibilities. It declared that it would see to it that this newly enfranchised people should enjoy unmolested the emoluments and blessings to which he was entitled by this new life. This it was morally bound to do, not only to the extent of special legislation, but to the retaking up of arms, if reduced to that extremity, to maintain justice.

But it has utterly failed to do this. As a result Negro citizenship, the Negro life, counts for nothing at all in legislation or its execution. Mob law, mob violence, now reigns supreme throughout the South and in many parts of the North.

The brave deeds of the black man in all the wars of the country, and especially in our most recent struggle, are either forgotten or are ignored.

It was a Negro who first spilt his blo[o]d on Bunker Hill; then, again, on Lake Erie with Perry. It was he that sacrificed his life at Milliken's Bend, Port Hudson, Fort Pillow, in that fearful crater at Petersburg in the defense of a country that now practically disowns him and that now refuses to afford him civil and political rights. It was he that saved the Rough Riders from annihilation at Las Guasi[m]as, that stormed with unparalleled bravery the heights at El Caney and swept gallantly forward in that magnificent charge up San Juan hill and won the praise of the civilized world. Yes, all this seems to have been forgotten and the colored man plays no part in the councils of the nation except as an on-looker. His heroes are not crowned by a grateful republic as are the Deweys, the Schleys, the Sampsons, the Hobsons and the Roosevelts. Nevertheless they are all heroes, with hearts as big as any that ever found lodgment in mortal breast—heroes as brave as any that ever walked on earth.

Their skin may be black, but their courage is undaunted. The pulse of patriotism beats as warmly in their breast as it does in that of the Deweys, or the Schleys. The only charge that can be brought against them is that they have the "misfortune" to be black. An ungrateful republic!!

This peculiar situation is no doubt in part due to strenuous efforts on the part of the North to placate the South, and to wipe out as far as possible all sectional differences—all reminders of the rebellion of '61. The social and commercial interests of the two sections are becoming so closely blended and allied that the two not only think alike but act alike in matters of public policy.

The South has stifled public opinion—muzzled the press, intimidated the pulpit, defied justice so long that it has things quite its own way. The few friends that the Negro has in the North are almost powerless to render him service. Southern mandates always secure a respectful hearing and too frequently a quiet acquiescence. The best test of friendship is the fruit it bears. If the South is truly the Negr[o]'s best friend it ought to exhibit that fruit. "By their fruit ye shall know them." To claim such friendship for it while it ope[n]ly or covertly engages in disfranchising and murdering Negroes is simply preposterous.

Now what is the Negro to do under the circumstances? Why, he must turn to the resources within himself—make the most of them. His duty lies nearest him. It is subjective. Too long has he been neglecting himself. Too long has he been depending upon outside assistance to carve out his future. Too long has he been pining his faith to the tricks of politics and politicians. Too long has he been seeking external influences and agencies as a panacea for his ills—when he himself might have put his rugged shoulders to the wheel and have done for himself what he has asked others to do.

Our great and good Bishop Turner is not altogether wrong. He is wiser and sees further into the future than many of his critics. While I do not agree with his emigration theory, I commend the bishop for his stalwart, vigorous defense of his people and I give him credit of having the true courage of his convictions.

Booker T. Washington is doing a splendid work in his line—one which is highly commendable and one of which we are all proud, but this is not all of it.

We must get together. We must put aside contentions, jealousies and personal differences, and act more in concert concerning all matters essential to the welfare of the race. The growth, prosperity, salvation of the Negro people should be a mutual, righteous cause that takes the precedence of all else so far as we ourselves are concerned. This is both patriotic and philanthropic.

The situation demands co-operation, possibly more so now than ever before. It demands that each should act his part and act it well; that each should lend a hand where a helping hand is needed; that each should strengthen the other in matters of business or otherwise when there is a demand for it. All may not think alike; all may not see alike; all may not agree. It is a blessing that this is the case. This is an evidence of progress. It should not be counted against us. It is not natural that we should. History furnishes no record of other people's having done so. Why should the Negro prove an exception? In all things the good of the race should be first and last. These differences as to methods should conserve the same end, making strong a people now weak. Our future depends largely on ourselves. With race united, with interests in common, we shall in a manner at least be able to help ourselves and withstand the attack from without. Conferences, conventions and conclaves properly managed are all well enough so far as they go. They are, however, simply a means to an end. Thus they should be regarded. Our future is largely in the hands of our public and professional men—preachers, lawyers, doctors, etc.—more largely than we are apt to think. They should bestir themselves and should handle their sacred trust with consummate tact and wisdom. I am not discouraged.

I believe the same God who reared the continents above the seas and peopled them with nations, who gave them freedom of conscience and of will, and who has watched their rise and fall from the dawn of creation, still guides the destinies of races and of peoples and that He

> "Standeth within the shadow
> Keeping watch above His own."[1]

Note

1 [Rev. Newell Dwight Hillis (1858–1929), "God the Unwearied Guide."]

Our New Possessions—An Open Door

Southern Workman 29 (July 1900): 422–427.

Within the past two years the United States has, perhaps unintentionally, opened many doors to the American people. In some instances, as the cartoonists have so aptly represented it, "Uncle Sam" has propped them open with official supports of promise and treaty, verbal and written, to an extent exceedingly gratifying to those who are interested in the development of our commercial relations at least, as they exist between our own country and others—doors which have been hitherto wholly or in part closed to our government.

There are doors, however, that the cartoonist has not represented. These are the ones that the armies of the United States have opened. The three wars in which this country has engaged since 1861—the Civil War, the Cuban War and the Philippine War—furnish striking coincidences along several lines, not the least important of which is that in each case a serious consideration of the dark races of the world forms a prominent feature.

In every instance in history dealing with conquest in any form, the conquered country has been thrown open by the advancing armies, and its civilization has been replaced by that of the superior forces. From the beginning of the Christian era the church, as soon as it was strong enough, followed in the wake of the soldier, and education was not far behind. To come down three decades, or a little more, we find the opportunity opened at their beginning by the Union army, improved to an extent simply marvelous, measuring the results achieved from the day the first transport carried to the Southland missionaries and teachers to the emancipated slaves.

When we compare the condition of the Negro race in this country at present with that of thirty-five years ago; when we consider the comparatively short period that has intervened between the old and new life, and the fact that the people involved were just freed from slavery, our astonishment is boundless. No matter what adverse claims are made, the workers for the moral and intellectual elevation of the Negro wrought to good purpose.

In fact the high plane reached by such a goodly number of the race emphasizes this fact while it brings more prominently into view the degradation that still exists among a large number, in the "black belts" of the South in particular.

But the Negro is too prone as a class to feel at times that the race does not go forward fast enough, that it does not have opportunities enough. Barring the all too frequent exhibitions of race hatred and prejudice, it seems a mistake to quarrel with fortune seriously because she does not lead on more rapidly; in the face of the evolution that has taken place and is still taking place we should recognize the forward strides as being all that could reasonably be expected.

The Negro has begged and is still begging, however, for opportunity to show the stuff of which he is made—all the possibilities that lie within him. This is his prerogative. He has based his plea upon manhood rights and justice, and he presses it continually with an earnestness and vigor which are sure to bring reward for merit in due season. We are looking for open doors for all the people and in all directions. We clamor for admission into the various civil and political avenues of life. Though there are many disappointments because of avenues closed to us it seems to me that sometimes we let the vision of near disappointment utterly obscure other paths farther away that might be trod, if we but turned our attention to energetic efforts in those directions. I have said that the Civil War afforded many opportunities, and not the least among them is that of doing for self—of allowing the Negro to aid in his own elevation and education when competent—in the building up of schools wherein he may test his own powers as teacher and manager. So great, however, was the opening that somewhat of a mistake was made at first in preparing him almost exclusively for teaching and preaching at the expense of other callings to which many were better adapted and better fitted by nature.

With the advent of industrial ideas and industrial training came a widening channel. That which had seemed for a moment about to be dammed up by the inrush of colored youth who thought to be helpers of their own people, was relieved by openings into other lines—the results of manual training. By this means a goodly number of young men and women are ready for positions along these avenues. The Negro has passed through much since the early days of his history; and because of a lack of outlets, and opposition on account of color there is a vague feeling of unrest taking possession of the race that is not for its best interest, especially if fostered too far. But it cannot be denied that the Negro begins to feel the stress of existing pressure that bars his progress— to feel it with a far livelier sensitiveness than formerly; while at the same time, the wise, conservative ones of the race deprecate the too frequent tone of bitterness that this sensitiveness takes on and voices in unwise speech.

But just now when the pessimist is seeing so much through a glass darkly,[1] it seems to me that there should be noted the curious coincidences mentioned—the fact that the uplifting of the darker races has been and is still one of the first things calling for consideration at the close of the three wars. It is conceded by everyone that at the present time there is a great school work to be done in these added islands. Those of our white friends who lead in such movements have already begun the work. In the *Educational Review* a few months ago we find the address of Dr. W. T. Harris delivered before the National Educational Association at Los Angeles last summer. It deals with the educational policy for our new possessions.[2]

The special features of this policy are distinctly set forth in advising the proper direction of school work, the employment of teachers, and the arrangement of work, with added suggestions as to the establishment of manual training schools or even better, special trade schools. Here, in the last named idea especially, seems to be afforded a possible opportunity for young men and women of color. Why should not the educated Negro take part in this uplifting movement in Cuba, Puerto Rico, and the Philippines? Even if the question of understanding Spanish as an equipment comes in, certainly there are some who can fill this requirement. In this connection our schools would do well to consider the advisability of adding this language to the schoolroom work, especially as a part of the equipment of industrial teachers. Even if not prepared in this respect, could not the Negro as easily learn the language for the purpose of instruction as other English speaking teachers already at work there have done—in Luzon, for instance, as Mr. Peter MacQueen states?[2] In speaking of the state of education he says that there are about 7000 children in the public schools of Manila which, as he further says, "General [Valeriano] Weyler established because he believed that the boy or girl who could read or write made a more useful slave." Here, according to the same authority, about a dozen American girls are already teaching English. This gives us a basis for the belief that some of our own could take hold of the problem with others. It would seem in truth that the colored race here is specially and providentially prepared for just such work. Education as it pertains to the race is and has been carried on in the United States as nowhere else on the globe. Here the Negro has had the benefit of long and close contact with civilization, culture, and refinement in ways for exceeding any attempt at uplift elsewhere. Here he has been allowed to begin, at least, the working out of a higher civilization of his own with the result that friends and foes alike are forced to the knowledge that strong, growing, multiplying *nuclei* of such civilization are to be found scattered throughout this country. His growing strength in education, refinement, culture, wealth, gradual but sure, gives him the right to make the plea of proper preparation, of special fitness to undertake the work indicated.

I say it seems providential that this preparation has been growing and it seems too that one sphere for the exercise of this strength is among the added millions in the islands south and far east who need to be brought to a higher plane. A people that has already passed to a certain extent through the varying phases of a "problem" as the race question is so often denominated, should possess to an important degree certain knowledge that would make it of value in undertaking the same or similar solutions in new territory.

The United States Government has placed the Negro in a position to gain experience in various ways. It took him to Cuba as a part of the army, where he showed the same bravery that disarmed a great amount of prejudice in the days of the Civil War, when it was predicted that he could not or would not fight. Las Guasimas, El Caney, and San Juan decided the matter for the second time. He has been retained in some instances as a keeper of the peace in the regions where he fought and the same authority that placed him in Cuba has transported him across the Pacific to aid in the task of quelling the insurrection in the Philippines.

The Negro, so far, has been able to take advantage of the open doors and it would be a pity if after helping to bring these various belligerent parties to a recognition at least that the United States Government first of all must be respected, without saying anything about the various perplexing questions that have arisen in this connection—it would be a pity, I say, if the Negro himself should not be able to share in the doing for these color kin-folk. We may not have the developed instinct for colonization possessed by some other races, (and that colonization, meaning isolation as a people, would be prejudicial to the rapid advancement of the race, has been and is still my belief) but this idea of aiding in the work that must inevitably be one of some continuation, judging from the past here and the material with which it is now to be undertaken elsewhere—this idea seems worth following out.

It may be extended even further than the idea of engaging in the work of instruction. The Negro's industrial training ought to find more than one outlet in this direction. There should also be those of the race possessing capital and business instinct sufficient to make it a profitable matter to cast their lot in these islands. The race needs to be fired by proper ambition, a proper spirit of adventure perhaps, to gain what may be had by the seeking, enterprising man of color.

I shall be very much mistaken and disappointed as well if a reasonable share of our soldiers do not profit by their presence in this new territory, to remain after their time is served and work out a future for themselves. Even if this is not probable the youth here who have had so much advice, so much instruction, and some experience at least as to how and what to do, as to the desirability of obtaining a foothold here or somewhere, should profit by these open doors.

I believe such possibilities as these are to have much to do with helping to solve many of the vexed questions that have arisen and that are still arising, whether we wish them to or not, because of the presence of large numbers of the race congregated in any one section. Determination, courage to face new things, enterprise, daring, will go far to help the race in making its own future.

It is a good thing sometimes, as we have hinted before, to turn attention from the things near by that only irritate as we dwell upon them, and give thought to possibilities for better things, farther removed.

This does not mean that we would advise a fanatic rush anywhere. We have not lost faith in the possibilities for a future here in these United States. It does mean, however, that we cannot afford to ignore what may be ours elsewhere under wise, thoughtful arrangement.

There is another phase of the situation that I can but touch upon here. What is to be the place of the native people of color in these islands will, I feel sure, depend in some considerable degree upon the influence brought to bear upon them by the Negro from this continent. They are disposed to take kindly to those of color from the United States, so a good authority in the Philippines states. This being so only adds another argument to the advisability of utilizing the influence here for bettering the condition there. That the lot of these millions will be better, happier, more full of promise under the guidance of this country, no matter what form that guidance may take, than it was under that of Spain is a foregone conclusion in my mind. But I feel equally positive that the higher planes to which they may attain in the future will be largely determined by the presence of men of color from this country, the aid these are allowed to give in the uplifting of these peoples, and the respect with which these are treated in the matter by those who have it in their power to help or hinder.

To endeavor to reach out into these new domains, however, will be in many ways beneficial to the race at large. It is a channel into which to turn the restless mood of the race, and it would be wisdom for all concerned to keep this open freely, even invitingly, to the Negro as well as to the white man.

Notes

1 [I Corinthians 13:11–12.]

2 [For the text see William Torrey Harris (1835–1909), "Educational Policy for Our New Possessions," *Educational Review* 18 (1899): 105–118.]

3 [Peter MacQueen (1865–1924), a former Rough Rider, was an Episcopal minister and journalist.]

Lawlessness *vs.* Lawlessness

Arena 24 (1900): 478–483.

When the American people, North and South, come to realize the fact that violence begets violence, and that no people can be safe where law is ignored or disregarded on the merest pretense, then perhaps we may look for a better state of things than can possibly exist under present conditions. To attempt to right wrongs, real or imaginary, in the present lawless way is simply to invite lawlessness in return. The negro is a human being and possesses all the attributes of human beings. As such he must be treated if peace and harmony are to prevail. Only in this way is it possible to prevent crime and disorder, with all their attendant evils.

The South is largely responsible for the condition of things now existing in that section. It has only itself to blame. We would suppose that thirty years would have taught the Southern white man that it is far better to practise the Golden Rule than to repudiate it by resorting to mob violence at any time. It has been well said that the New Orleans riot[1] supports the gloomy view that direct wreaking of lawless vengeance on helpless objects fosters a spirit of inexcusable lawlessness for its own sake, and that habitual application of lawless remedies to criminals of one race begets indiscriminate disregard for the legal rights and mere human privileges of that race as a whole. This was shown to be true in the recent riots in New York City. The further thought is added that such a state of things as existed in New Orleans could not have happened in a civilized community unless its civic virtues had been enfeebled by a long training of indulgence in acts not more lawful but less absurdly senseless.

That the time for reform in the method of dealing with negro criminals has not only come but is long past goes without saying. The law should take its course in every instance, whether North or South, whether the accused be white or black. It is a cowardly thing to refuse to give the black man a chance. It is beneath the dignity of any one calling himself an American citizen to refuse this right. The negro has rights as well as duties. I believe that, if granted the former, he will take care of the latter. As a rule, when let alone he is both law-abiding and patriotic. An insult to his country's flag is an insult to himself, and it is felt as keenly by him as by any other American citizen. It is not necessary to bring forward proof of this. History is full of examples of his bravery, his prowess. He has taken some part in all the wars of the country, from the battle of Bunker Hill to the present; and has never been found wanting. He is still ready, willing, and even anxious to shoulder a gun in his country's defense. He is neither a coward nor a traitor. All he asks is fair treatment, fair play—a human being's chance. The question rests with the American people—with their sense of right and justice.

The negro has been greatly misrepresented by emissaries from the South— so much so that his friends seem to be growing less while his enemies multiply. This is one cause of discontent and restlessness on the part of the race. The better class of colored people is no more responsible for the conduct of the hoodlum element than is the better class of white people. Hoodlums are hoodlums, whether white or black, and they should be dealt with to the fullest extent of the law. The mistake of the South lies in its tacit sympathy with these law-breakers, while there are too frequent unions in deeds of violence. Take the following as an example of this sympathy. It explains itself:[2]

> "Edward McCarthy, a young white man who came to this city from New York several days ago, appeared before a police magistrate here in New Orleans. He was arrested yesterday morning to protect him from a mob, which was endeavoring to lynch him because of some remarks he made in connection with the negro riot. McCarthy had said that negroes had white hearts—were as goods as white men— and not all of them should be lynched because of the action of two of them.
>
> "'Do you consider a negro as good as a white man?' asked the judge.
>
> "'In body and soul, yes,' replied the prisoner. He was fined $25 or thirty days in the parish prison."

This is only one of many incidents where blind, unreasoning prejudice gets the better of judgment and defeats justice. Its purpose is to degrade and intimidate, and there is a strong showing of a strain of the vengeful element permeating such acts. To fine a man for the expression of an honest opinion when he is asked for it is barbarism pure and simple. Such a judge has no business to sit upon a bench that represents justice.

It is this inability to express one's convictions in any sense if it does not accord with Southern ideas of the race, or with the idea of its inferiority wherever found, that breeds trouble. This is supposed to be a free country. In it the anarchist can air his sentiments to the verge of declared purpose to assassinate; strikers can in the hearing of officers of the law make threats, and rioters can say whatever they will, to say nothing of deeds—and what is the result? No such gagging of the mouths of these as of a man by fine, imprisonment, and bodily injury if he but dare to say that the negro is the equal of a white man. There are thousands of negroes the equal of the best white men, in body, mind, and soul, and the superior of tens of thousands who can boast nothing in a mental or moral way—yes, or in a physical way either, except that they are "white."

Such treatment as this creates the race antagonism we deplore. There are bad black people as there are bad white people, and this bad blood in the negro is aroused to that retaliatory stage where crime is committed. It is this state of things that brings it to the surface. It is not freedom *per se*, as some claim, though there may be cases of depravity as total as any found in the white race, which the negro has imitated in everything since he was placed here without his consent. There are some in all races that cannot stand alone, that need restraint; and there are those to whom freedom from oppression of any kind means simply opportunity to oppress in turn. This is seen daily in the conduct of the foreigners who come to us from countries that have held them in close subjugation. The moment they step out from Castle Garden they pounce upon the negro race as an object of contempt and hatred, and one they can exercise their license upon.

It is from cases like this, too, that the negro perceives that the statement so often made that the Southern people are the negro's best friends is false—simply a play upon Northern ears, designed to win sympathy for the South and thus let it be left to do as it pleases in reference to the race, which they in reality ardently despise. The negro as a race will never consent to leave so vital a question as this, a question that means so much to him and those near and dear to him—that means so much to his future—to people that represent a section of country in which an official dares to fine a man for saying that a negro "in body and soul is as good as a white man."

In the new outlook for the United States it is a question that will bear deep consideration—how can justice be assured the race that fought to make the country what it is and preserve its integrity, and that stands now in part as a bulwark against invaders, or willingly streams off to the Orient to protect its interests wherever they may lie? In the face of the race riots, when *no* negro is safe, and the seeming powerlessness of government to hold such in check or bring the guilty ones to punishment, there is little wonder that the darker races of the isles of the sea look with suspicion upon a people that permits such outrages to take place under the very flag we have asked them to look upon as a sign of sure protection. What guaranty have they that their fate will not be like that of the negro? What guaranty have they that, if they yield to this county's will, justice will be done them? The doctrine of State sovereignty has been carried so far that it seriously interferes with the provisions of the Constitution, and makes the amendments to that document to all intents and purposes of no force in reference to the negro. The South is permitted to do as it pleases, and the negro finds all the odds against him. His friends in the north and the few he may legitimately claim in the South are intimidated—made to feel that it is disgraceful to attempt to defend the black man or espouse his cause in any way.

Much of the lawlessness on the part of the negro, therefore, can be accounted for. With the injustice, the malice, hatred, and contempt because of color confronting him at every turn, all that is bad in the race is constantly being roused to assert itself. It is a continuous exercise of retaliation, which will grow as it rolls on unless some measures be wisely instituted looking to the protection of the race, to the meting out of justice rigidly to any one and every one—but justice most rigidly kept within the law. Let justice be done in every case, and let the best element, both North and South, fearlessly unite to demand that the country shall be governed by law, not by lawlessness. It is a serious reflection upon the white race, which can claim so many years of advance in civilization, culture, wealth—in all the power and material resources of this world—that it must confess its inability to set proper examples for the belated races of the world to follow, by allowing indulgence in the lawlessness that has recently swept as a wave over the land.

In no case has it been shown that lynching has proved an adequate remedy for crime. In no case has mob violence been productive of good. The opposite has been the rule. Retaliation has been engendered, desperadoes have been made still more desperate, and the innocent have suffered far more than the guilty. No attempt to disregard the processes of law—to defy legal authority— can bring about the desired results. Civilization itself is bound to go down before such repeated assaults upon law. The infection of lawless conduct will spread to an alarming extent, and the evil will be something terrible to contemplate unless our boasted Anglo-Saxon superiority shows itself superior to the mob, and to injustice; for until man is regarded as man, black or white, in North or South—until equality before the law is made something more than a name—we may look for such an increase in these periodic disturbances, these seasons of riot and bloodshed, as will appal the whole nation. They are bound to come, as effect from cause; and who will be responsible?

Notes

1 [In the summer of 1900.]

2 [See the pamphlet by Ida B. Wells-Barnett (1862–1931), *Mob Rule in New Orleans* (Chicago, 1900).]

The Negro's Appeal to the Nation: A Plea for Justice

Howard's American Magazine, April 1901, pp. 378–381.

As a people, the United States has reached the high-water mark in all that nations covet. It is prosperous above all others, and it has secured that which men seek most—the plaudits, the approbation of the world. Its victories over Spain, the glories it has achieved have made it a world nation, and given it a conspicuous place among the peoples of the earth—such as the Revolutionary fathers never anticipated.

All are proud of this fact, and none more so than the Negro. He has been a factor in bringing about these results. He spilt his blood freely and willingly to help make these conditions possible. As a part and parcel of this Government his interests are as great and as permanent as those of the most highly favored citizens of the Republic. Yet, notwithstanding, the relation that the Negro race sustains to all American interests, it is still regarded as an alien people, with neither rights nor privileges that white humanity feels bound to respect. Because of this it finds itself in a most unsatisfactory condition to-day. It has reached a crisis in its history unequaled in gravity since its emancipation.

Then it had a strong hold upon the Nation's sympathy and determination to right its wrongs. Public sentiment in its favor had reached such height that nothing could stem its course. The slave became a free man, surrounded, supported, encouraged by a host of friends whose enthusiastic loyalty at once manifested itself in countless ways.

Though but thirty-five years have passed, that strong current has subsided and a reaction has set in. Friendship for the race has cooled to a marked degree of indifference, while hatred has grown to such malignant intensity that it brings a struggling people again face to face with a state of things that threaten dire results. The old loyalty and friendship are things of the past. Criticism, skepticism and mere toleration have usurped their place. The community of interest has disappeared. New interests, domestic and foreign, now unite the white people of the North and the South with the black man left out. The two races have drifted apart with the years, new movements and the new generation. The points of mutual contact that once made for mutual sympathy and mutual respect have nearly ceased to exist. The gulf has widened until now it seems well-nigh impassable. The Negro finds himself alone to fight his own battles as best he can against tremendous odds. His vices are magnified, his virtues grudgingly admitted, if at all. He himself is so discussed, dissected and analyzed that he feels every movement misjudged, every motive questioned, every trait scrutinized as to its racial significance and, in short, every nerve laid bare.

In view of this situation the Negro has become restless, discouraged, despondent, almost to the verge of despair. He sees that he has reached a most critical period, a most portentous moment in his life.

The vengeance of the mob wreaks its lawless will on the black man for crimes, alike real or fancied. For trivial offenses he is sent to prison and to the chain gang, where deep degradation is forced upon the unfortunate victim, regardless of age or sex. The convict lease system of the South makes common prey of the race, while all over the land material, as well as other interests, sacrifice it to the greed and avarice and to the desire for place and power. In the public eye the Negro is absolutely a nonentity. The lynching spirit, nowise on the decline, has for sixteen long years laid violent hands upon the race. The figures show that the victim of mob violence, whether North or South, is almost invariably a black man. Out of 115 thus unlawfully executed in the year 1900, 107 were of the Negro race. According to statistics, gathered by the *Chicago Tribune*, Louisiana and Mississippi led with 20 each; Georgia had 16; Florida, 9; Alabama, 8; Tennessee, 7; Arkansas and Virginia, 6 each. Indiana, Kansas and Colorado also disgraced themselves by lynchings, while in various other Northern States repeated attempts were made in the same direction. Burning at the stake, accompanied by the most fiendish tortures—the most atrocious cruelties—is the portion of the colored man. With a word, race hatred fires mobs to run riotously mad in great cities North and South, clamoring for the blood of every Negro. He is shot down in cold blood, tracked with bloodhounds as in the days of slavery, and subjected to every form of indignity as well as persecution. Negro womanhood does not escape. It is assaulted and traduced, and the white assailant allowed to go free while the black man, guilty or nor guilty, if but suspected of a similar crime, is hunted like a beast, and dispatched without mercy. The entire country seems to have returned to an era of barbarism. Negro human life and Negro human rights are not considered worthy of either serious thought nor of common protection. Disenfranchisement is spreading throughout the South. One by one the Southern States in direct violation of the constitutional amendments are depriving the Negro of the right to vote. Every means is used to prevent the exercise of the ballot. Force, fraud, chicanery and cunning combine to cheat the race of its legal rights. Proscription meets it everywhere. Public places of amusement and of comfort, once freely opened, now turn the Negro from their doors with trivial excuse or with insult. The refined are made to suffer the same treatment as the degraded. Neither class nor condition is taken into consideration. The Negro is a Negro. Jim Crow cars are the portion of all who travel in the South, and interstate laws are as good as annulled in many sections. These same cars are even daring to enter Northern limits, and thus thrust further indignity upon an already much humiliated people. Freedom of speech and of action is exercised in the South at the risk of life. In short, the constitution is hourly trampled upon by those who seek to repeal its amendments by statutes, and do repeal them in fact by the ostracisms, the insults, the outrages and the deprivations of every right and privilege that manhood holds dear. Existence itself is made miserable for a people living under a Government whose basis is liberty, and whose corner-stone is justice and equal rights.

In such a state of affairs, for the race to remain inactive means death to the individual, death to the race itself. Some movement must be made. Problems thicken and the Nation sits like a Sphynx—immovable and silent. The Negro must speak. He must act for himself. Ten millions of black people and sixty millions of white are here together. Here together they must largely remain despite all plans and theories to the contrary. The destinies of the two races are strangely united. Their future is one of interdependence, and the character of this future largely rests upon the raising up of such forces as shall prevent a total and disastrous collapse of all friendly interest and all civil order, that shall strengthen the relations that shall make for mutual interest, and that shall shape a true and a high civilization for all concerned. To this end strenuous efforts should be put forth by every American patriot, black or white.

Shall the present deplorable condition be handed down as a legacy to be perpetuated through the twentieth century, is a vital question. The present is dark and presages a future of more intense gloom unless the consciences of the American people can be aroused to a high sense of duty, their hearts touched with a deep sympathy and their reason enlightened. To these the Negro race makes its appeal to-day. We ask where are the Christian ministers and teachers? Where are the friends of humanity? Are there no Garrisons, Lovejoys, Phillipses, Sumners, Lincolns, Douglasses, Gerrit Smiths to plead the cause of the despised Negro? Who will stand by us as we beg for justice, for our rights, for an equal chance to make a way upward and onward unimpeded by restrictions, by proscriptions, by prejudices?

Shall not this century be made indeed the "century of humanity,"[1] with race prejudice and hatred eliminated and human sympathy deepened and broadened to the utmost? The Negro needs friends to-day. He needs more avenues open to him. He urges the recognition of true manhood and worth wherever found. This is not only a necessity for his own advancement, but the Nation needs it as well, because to refuse it is to embitter further those daily galled almost beyond endurance, to make dangerous classes more dangerous, to invite lawlessness, to incite to crime and to anarchy.

The race must receive encouragement in its efforts to make the most of its opportunities and to labor for the upbuilding of character, and for the elevation of the masses. It only asks for an equal chance to share in all that lifts races and nations to high planes intellectually and morally—that it shall not be impeded in its progress, that it shall not be limited in its endeavors. The Negro makes an appeal for proper discrimination—for the recognition of the fact that there is good as well as bad in all races, and he begs not to be treated like a brute, hunted like an outlaw, scorned and avoided as an outcast—all because some are low and vile and mean. Despite all criticism, the Negro race, as a whole, is as law-abiding as any people. It does not condone crime, it does not shield the criminal; but it does plead to be allowed to live under the law, to be judged according to the law, to be made subject to the impartial execution of the law.

We appeal no longer to political parties. They have proved both apathetic and powerless. Politics is no longer a panacea for our ills. It is now purely a question of humanity, and the exercise of Christianity. In view of this, can those mighty engines of power—the platform, the press, the pulpit, which oppose so vehemently prize fights, the canteen and the saloon, Sabbath desecration and kindred evils, longer consistently remain silent concerning the terrible crimes against a helpless race—crimes that stain our country's name, disgrace its boasted civilization, and that receive the condemnation of even heathen people?

We can but feel that the South, which has so boldly and openly preached and practiced discrimination, disfranchisement, proscription, lawlessness and hideous crimes against the Negro, has succeeded in overcoming the scruples of the North so far that the two sections are united in the belief that the Negro is receiving but his just deserts. There is seemingly no North, no South now as regards the status of the Negro. He is condemned by both, ostracised by both, and by both consigned to servitude and degradation.

We do not ignore the fact that the Negro has a part to perform in bringing about a different condition so far as it relates to himself, and we call the attention of the Nation to the efforts of the race toward higher planes as evidenced in the advancement in education, in the refinement, the wealth, the industry, the growing care for its own. But at this time we need the highest moral sentiment of the whole people to co-operate with us in our efforts to bring about that state of things that will lead to a better understanding between the races and that will scatter the accumulated forces that have given birth to such intense racial antagonism and hatred as confront us to-day.

Again we make urgent appeal to the Nation to recognize the import of all these things and to rally to the defense of the right.

Again we beg most earnestly that the best and the most profound thought be brought to cope justly with the dark situation.

Again we make a fervent plea that the Nation will join hands to see that justice shall reign, that the law shall be supreme, that charity, not hatred, shall be placed above the law, that all the undeveloped races brought within the jurisdiction of this great country of ours may witness the manifestation of that spirit alone which recognizes God as the father of all and all mankind as brothers.

Note

1 [This is a phrase from Victor Hugo and was used by Eugene V. Debs in 1898 in the opening line of his speech, "Appeal to Reason."]

The Negro and Our New Possessions

Forum 31 (May 1901): 341–349.

Many theories have been proposed for the solution of the Negro problem. It is declared by some that it is a question of the South, as most of the Negroes are found in that section, and that, therefore, it should be settled there, and with reference to the people who will be most largely affected by the Negro's presence; that his education and life should be adapted to his environment; that any education tending to lift him out of his sphere, as it is put—referring, of course, to the higher training—is both harmful and destructive to the interests of both races. These views are based upon the assumption that the Negro is always to remain in the South, and that he is always to occupy a subordinate place—a presumption without an adequate basis of fact.

Colonization is offered as another solution. The black man is advised to migrate westward, to take up unoccupied territory there, to settle down, and to work out his own destiny to the best of his ability. In this way, it is argued, he can best develop the powers within him. Again, it is proposed that the race leave the congested districts of the South—scatter, diffuse itself over the whole country, and, in a sense, lose race identity, by mingling with the whites, as far as possible. And still another theory is more vigorously pressed than any hitherto mentioned. It is declared that this will produce a change operating for the good of all concerned. Its advocates unhesitatingly assert that it is best to confine the Negro largely to industrial lines, to set a limit to his education, to reserve the higher training for a few picked out here and there as capable to receive such instruction, and to make of these leaders; thus encouraging the race, as it is claimed, to maintain its place in the labor ranks.

No matter, however, what theory is proposed by which the many problems concerning the Negro are sought to be solved, and no matter what individuals have accomplished, no one will deny that the race as a whole cannot make substantial progress unless there are outlets for its capabilities and acquisitions. This fact brings up one of the most discouraging features in contemplating the subject—that here, in this country, it makes no difference what the Negro has done or may do in any line whatever, he finds few opportunities for the exercise of his gifts and powers. He must simply hope on and do the thing he can find to do next him. Hope deferred maketh the heart sick, is a saying proved true in life again and again; and it is only owing to the characteristic good spirits of the race that many of these who are ready for advanced lines of labor can sturdily hold to the thought that there may be a future in which they shall share along these lines. It is this that helps the plucky ones to push on and find niches for themselves here and there, defying dislodgment from a position that brain, and not brawn, has enabled them to fill.

As I have said elsewhere, at different times, the Negro finds everything against him just now. He meets boycott, refusal to work by his side, and closed doors of labor unions. He sees plainly a determined stand to force him back from the vantage-ground he gained and a resolve to circumscribe him, in every effort he puts forth, and to keep him within his "sphere"; where he may do only those things "of which he is capable from inherited aptitudes," as one puts it, referring to servile or industrial lines. It is a most discouraging state of things that confronts him on every hand. It is assuredly the darkest period in the progress of the race since the Civil War, not excepting the dark days of Reconstruction; for then he had more sympathy from those who looked on and who stood by him. More forbearance was exercised toward him then, and there was a greater desire to forward all his aspirations. In short, his friends were many more than now. To-day he is largely left to himself, to make his way all alone, with the odds greatly against him.

So, with proscription, disfranchisement, prejudice, hate of the lower classes all over the land, Jim Crow cars set apart as his portion without reference to individual status, whether educated or uneducated, refined or vicious, with hotels and places of amusement closed against him, with restrictions in civil and legal rights, and with lynchings on mere suspicion, how can the race look upon the present hour other than as the darkest? Such is the situation, and no one feels it more keenly, experiences more humiliation, or chafes more under the continual ban than does the educated Negro, the man or woman of culture who has fine sensibilities and high aspirations, and who wishes to make of life what he or she has been taught should be made of life—the best possible of every faculty given by the Creator.

A crisis seems to be at hand, and well may it claim the serious attention of friends and of foes—all who are interested in social and economic problems. The complications are great, and the race, with this growing against it, is thrown into a dangerous state of unrest. It is a wonder that under the circumstances the balance is kept so true—that the Negro remains the loyal, patriotic citizen that he does. But this true balance is most largely due to the wisdom of the leaders, the good sense of the higher classes, the exercise of judgment and sage counsel by the trained men and women of the race, those who keep faith and constitute the ballast bringing about proper self-control. Thus there is patient waiting to see if light will not come out of darkness, if salvation will not be afforded from what seems a hopeless situation. But while the country at large is thinking as to what it shall do with him, the Negro is feeling that something must be done and done by himself. He is thinking deeply on the situation, and his thought is turning on how he may better race conditions.

As none of the theories advanced looks toward anything else than keeping the Negro in a quasi-peasant stage, or in absolute subjection, or deporting him, they naturally do not find favor with the race at large. Colonization, meaning the isolation of the people as a whole, I firmly believe will be detrimental to any rapid advancement. But I do think that a certain amount of emigration would be advantageous; and in this connection I do not think we have entertained seriously enough the possibility of using our new possessions as an opportunity for the American Negro. It seems to me that this is forced upon the race just now, when the best in it are suffering more or less from the keen humiliation incident upon the stress of the situation and the present pressure that bars advancement everywhere. This consideration seems of vital importance.

I have had occasion to say, at other times, that a curious coincidence is to be found in connection with the three wars in which this country has engaged since 1861. In each case it is to be noted that the consideration of the darker races of the world has formed a prominent feature. While this evidently has its significance relating to the work Providence has given this land as a Christian land to do, in close connection are to be found certain indisputable facts relative to the race resident within its borders.

Despite all that is said about the lack of progress of the Negro along certain lines, it is true that he has had here the opportunities to work out a higher civilization of his own, and he has not failed to grasp them. The higher classes of the race are the results of this opportunity, and they have gathered such strength that there is a peculiar fitness in making use of their acquisitions among the darker peoples of our newly acquired territory. It may be true that in many ways the future may show, as Mr. [T. T.] Fortune says in the New York "Age," that the more dark peoples that we have under our flag the better it will be for those of us who came out of the forge and fire of American slavery. There will be outlets for the American Negro and a swifter uplifting because of interest for these new peoples.

Advices from Luzon asserts unreservedly that there is a great field for the Negro in the Philippines. The reason for such assertion is given by one whose position makes it possible for him to speak with authority. He says:

> "Though there are not many Negroes in this part of the world, those that are here are doing exceedingly well. They have no race prejudice to combat from the native, and when compared with white men of equal attainments they possess the vantage-ground over the white brother."

The same authority goes on further to say:

> "Again, the white man everywhere seeks to oppress, when possible, the dark races; and differing from the white man in this, the native soon regards his dark Occidental brother in the light of possessing affinity with himself, be he rich or poor. The Filipinos and the

Japanese especially—these two hate white people most—receive the colored man with open arms. They would deny him no opportunity —this is not speculation—and are delighted when they see or hear of a great man of color."

Now it seems to me that whether this state of things is pleasing to white people or not, this does signify much in the way of escape from some of the unpleasant situations hedging the race about in this country.

The same correspondent puts it thus:

"If the colored man of the United States will be benefited in any way by the acquisition of territory and new markets by the country, it is manifestly certain it will be in the direction of enlarged opportunities."

He feels certain of these as "evident rich fields presented by the Oriental countries to American colored men of education, push, and energy." In fact, he declares from observation that while this is especially true of the Philippines, it is also true of every country, state, or dependency of the Orient, as Japan, China, Siam, Java, Ceylon. We, here in America, do know that many of these same foreigners try to be contemptuous of the Negro when upon American soil, so that they may not be classed in any way with a despised people. It is a matter of self-preservation, of convenience, to these foreigners; and so when here they follow the fashion of the hoodlum element and attempt to show scorn whenever they come in contact with a person of color. But at home they do differently.

These facts, as presented to us by one who is where he can judge accurately—on native soil under un-American conditions—are not the observations of solely one man. There are other shrewd observers in the new possessions, who see the same thing, express the same opinion, and ask the same pertinent questions. Why not lead the Negro in America to see this too? Why not open up the way for him to have a share in doing something for these color kinsfolk?

And why should not the educated Negro, the capable Negro, take part in the movement that has just begun in the Philippines, in Cuba, in Porto Rico, in Hawaii even, for the general good of the governed in these islands? A foreign tongue need be no obstacle. The Negro has a natural aptitude for language. African history will bear me out in this statement, which is corroborated by my own experience with natives from the isles of the sea and from Africa. It does seem, as previously intimated, that the evolutionary process the race has gone through in this country would make such men and women of color of inestimable value in undertaking the evolutions which must take place in the attempt to lead out to the light and on to strength the weaker, dark races of the world, wherever found. The cry comes from the Philippines, from the natives: Why does not the United States send out colored men as school teachers, and in various other official capacities? It would seem wisdom for the government to heed this cry, and to yield to the wish in the effort that is being put forth to bring these peoples under law and government represented by the American flag. The Filipinos especially, we are told, "want Occidentalism, but want it to come through hands of a like complexion to theirs."

Under the present conditions, when the call has come for such a large number of instructors in various capacities, the question forces itself upon public attention: Why not make large choice from among members of the Negro race in America for the purpose? There are plenty of both sexes fitted for this work. With the knowledge of the limited opportunities in this country, it would seem that sincerity of purpose to help solve the race problem would demand that such be given every possible consideration, and most especially when it is known that in these possessions the sought for "Occidentalism" would be preferable coming through such channels.

It has been frequently stated that the Negro has not the "colonization instinct"; and his failures in Africa to make a way for himself are brought forward as proof. This is doubtless true. The race has not gone far enough on its road to imbibe this spirit to the extent of making it a success. But a movement looking toward our new territory need not partake of the colonization feature pure and simple, which, as before said, I should not deem advantageous if viewed as isolation. That would be a misfortune. But what is presented as most advantageous is the encouragement to extend the Negro's outlook by personal inducements offered where there is something besides pure savagery and barbarism to contend with.

From Luzon the word comes:

> "Some time ago I made an investigation among the Filipinos to determine to what extent their love for the American Negro went, and found that colonization of American blacks among them would be highly acceptable, while white people as ranchers among them could only become established by having a regiment of soldiers stationed at each white ranchman's back."

This sentiment seems to pervade every stratum of life there. And through it may not this very idea of the lack of colonization instinct be rightly gauged by trial under circumstances that must differ from those surrounding the emigrants to Africa? With such a sentiment prevalent, it would seem that here is an outlet that ought to find acceptance in some way among the thoughtful ones of the race, where the Negro's industrial as well as his intellectual training may be utilized with decided benefit to the present generation and may help on marvellously future generations. The German experiment in Africa, of utilizing trained Negroes from America, is one that might fittingly be tried in our new territory, which needs development along the same practical lines to bring it to a higher degree of civilization.

This is not said with any idea that the race must give up all thought of a future as a race right here in the United States; but a movement looking toward these new possessions would simplify the problem in a measure by reducing numbers and showing that the Negro can act for himself. I feel confident that the present dark outlook will give way in time to a brighter one—that the frenzy of hate and passionate prejudice will pass away. If not, the white race will undoubtedly reap a sowing it has little expected. But it is time for the Negro to reach out individually, as some have already done and as many should do, to take courage to face new things, to weigh, then dare (*Wägen, denn wagen*), as the motto goes.

It is not a fanatic rush of all classes into these new fields that will better matters either here or there. These Filipinos are not an uneducated people as a whole. They are not barbarous, uncivilized, poor, as a class. We have plenty of authority to the contrary. Among them, it is said, are some of the ripest scholars the world has. We cannot call them barbarians indiscriminately. The wealth of some is dazzling, and in those Oriental countries there are not a few dark-skinned millionaires. Then, again, we face the fact that these same dark people are in the trade world, first and foremost, competing with the lighter-colored races, showing a sharpness in business matters which in reality makes them marvels of that trade world. So those who would take advantage of this outlook are the men who can do something, manage something, create something.

In the idea existing among these people that the American colored man is a distant relative of theirs—and, above all, that he is not a white man, which for him "is a free passport without credentials," lies the great opportunity for the thrifty, energetic Negro. These same people have no hope, it is asserted, in a white man's country; no more, perhaps, than has the American Negro here, in those sections where the determination to dominate him is tenaciously held. But these isles cannot be said to be the white man's country, because for centuries such has been the mixture that the color line is not known—it is not drawn unless the idea is imported from those countries where prejudice has rank hold.

The color question which Spain, with other countries, was called upon to face long ago led to one thing: despite her treachery, oppression, cruelty, and misrule, she did not humiliate these peoples because of the admixture of blood of darker races. The color question should never be allowed to be injected into that part of the world. There we find places where the dark face may meet with humane treatment, with civility, even with deference, if the manhood back of it deserves it; and there this feeling of equality should be kept in its purity. It may be, as has been said, that it is a good thing for all that more of the dark races are under the American flag. There may be a lesson for all in this fact—a lesson that nothing else will teach—a lesson that man's inhumanity to man cannot forever continue, especially that inhumanity based upon color and assuming a contemptuous, dominant attitude toward it. Can there not be one place on the face of the globe where the white man does not seek complete control; where a channel may be opened up to give the broadest possible opportunity for the strengthening of the weaker races; where black manhood can stand erect and unhindered, and can enlarge respect for itself, or even create it where it does not exist? But to enter hopefully this door, open to the man of color, two things are necessary—aid and proper treatment from those who have it in their power to help or to hinder.

It would seem that our war with Spain was providential, aside from humanitarian grounds; that the great Ruler of the universe, in permitting this country to gain continuously such signal victories over the Spanish people, intended that, despite its prejudice and race hatred, it should take a leading part in the solution of some of the great problems pertaining to the darker races of mankind. Because of its Christian civilization it assuredly has the vantage-ground for taking a prominent part in this direction. It cannot honorably recede from the initiative it has already taken; and as a sequence it must handle the problems thrust upon it, with the acquisitions of these new millions, in a way that shall command, on the one hand, the respect, or, in the other, the condemnation, of the civilized world. It must deal with these people justly or unjustly. To do the latter is to show itself unequal to the task of coping with the situation; it is to weaken it at home and abroad.

The selection of the Negro for campaigning purposes in this new territory was a wise one. The only thing to be regretted is that more are not thus employed in the foreign military service of the nation. But the hope of the future is that this will be brought about. The black man has proved himself not only a brave soldier, but a patriot as well, in spite of the treatment accorded him. We need only cite as proof of this his readiness at all times to up arms in his country's defense, and his career at San Juan and El Caney. Campaigning in Cuba, Porto Rico, or the Philippines give the black man an opportunity to see and study the country for himself, to study its people as he could not under the circumstances. He is doing it, and this very knowledge gained from experience constitutes a new era, the dawn of a brighter day, for the race and its descendants. Though the Negro himself at first looked upon the idea of sending black troops to these new countries as an attempt at expatriation, yet there is hardly one of the race to-day who does not see in this new movement a great amount of good to come to those with whom those soldiers are allied at home. To my personal knowledge not a few of the best of these soldiers propose to stay in the Philippines, and to start out in life there. This of itself will have its influence upon others in America. Gradually the adventurous spirit will develop itself.

In connection with this, it sounds more like a prophecy than anything else, when we recur to the words of that gallant old soldier, Gen. Thomas J. Morgan, who knew well what it was to command Negro troops,[1] and who did not hesitate to advocate their employment. In the early days of the Spanish War, he said:[2]

> If the United States has really entered upon an era of colonization or of taking under its protection the West Indian and Philippines Islands, we must be prepared for the necessity of a large army of occupation. Such an army could with advantage be made up largely, if not exclusively, of Negro soldiers. They would be better suited for tropical or semi-tropical climates, would be more contented than

white men in that far-away service, and would not be objectionable to the native inhabitants of the islands in either ocean, so that there seems to be no special reason why there should not be given to the Negroes at least a fair opportunity to show what soldierly qualities they possess and what fitness they have for official positions."

General Morgan has touched vital points. Fair trials only are desired. A chance to determine what the black man can do when out from under the stress of prejudice is necessary to the highest development of the powers within. Let the black man have this chance under conditions which obtain nowhere in this country exactly the same. Let him be encouraged along lines that promise opportunity, and we feel confident that much of this present unrest will be a thing of the past and that his future will be assured as it cannot now be in view of existing conditions in this country.

Notes

1 [In the 14th U.S. Colored Infantry.]

2 "The Independent," June 30, 1898.

The Negro as a Factor in Business

Southern Workman 30 (August 1901): 455–459.

If every Negro now engaged in business in any part of our great commonwealth should be removed from such business—should suddenly drop out of sight—his removal would not create a ripple in business circles, so slight is his hold upon the money centers of the country. His financial value plays such an insignificant part in the commercial world that, whatever happens, he would not be missed. There are reasons for this. In the first place, the members of the race that are engaged in any kind of paying business are comparatively few. A generation is not sufficient to develop business men, and the Negro is not much over a generation old. Then again those that are thus engaged have no great financial influence as the result of their holdings—either of stock or bonds—to the extent that the market can be affected in any way, whether success or failure attends them.

We have colored business men throughout the country but comparatively few of them are doing business on a large scale. The race has made wonderful advancement in countless ways in the last forty years. All this should be placed to its credit. But marvellous as this is, there has been no point in its career when it could safely pause for even a moment. On, on, and on it has had to go, and on and on it must keep going, with ever accelerated pace, to keep up with the throbbing life and movement of civilization that now surround it. If it does not bend every nerve, grasp every opportunity toward the solution of problems which now confront it and of which it is a part, it will be hopelessly left behind. I think every thoughtful Negro is well aware of this, and therefore there is no ground for actual fear as to the future. The possibilities of the race are fully demonstrated both by its past and its present, by the achievements of its representatives in all lines of activity in which they have been and are engaged. The fact that the Negro is thinking is strong evidence that he is not unmindful of his status and of what is expected of him.

The recent gathering of Negro business men in Boston[1] under the leadership of that magnetic man, Mr. Washington, is proof positive of the thoughtful attitude of the race concerning its material development. The importance of such development is fully recognized, as is shown by those who took part in this meeting. But the Negro has hardly begun his development in the business activities of the country. It is in an embryo state as yet, as it were. This field is almost limitless. It is also an inviting one, and the black man may well turn his attention to it and fit himself by proper educational training for what lies before him there. Once entering upon it he must either make himself or fail in the attempt. The stronger he becomes as a financial factor in this active, bustling, seething world of ours, the easier it will be for him to make himself felt as a power in the interests of his own people where such power is needed and where it must do good for all concerned.

If the black man lacks in one particular more than another it is in the power of sticking. He becomes discouraged too easily. He fears risks, he fears venture. His very timidity invites failure. Then again, the fault lies in his business habits, which do not always guarantee him the success he might otherwise deserve. Many have entered upon a business career with bright prospects, but through a lack of thrift and tact and correct business habits have not succeeded. In their failure they have carried many of their fellows with them, some of whom never had courage thereafter to re-enter that life. There are others who might do better for shiftlessness. The Negro has much to learn and it will take time and patience to rid him of many of his faults.

It is not only an honor and an advantage but a necessity for a man to be so educated that he will not fear to risk the varying fortunes—the vicissitudes of life. It is an honor to be able to do whatever falls to one's lot—to do it right royally, to be a king in whatever line is undertaken. That the man dignifies his calling is more than a saying, provided that calling is a legitimate one.

"All is habit in mankind," says one writer,[2] while another declares man to be a bundle of habits. "Fixed habits are acts that take on the nature of fate—so binding us by chains self-woven that many a step is taken that yields neither pleasure nor profit." To make strong men, men of vast capacity for affairs, right habits are necessary. Once attained they are a fortune in themselves, while wrong ones hang forever upon one, clogging the wheels of enterprise and, as a rule, bringing not only disaster but ruin upon the victim. Right habits make character, which someone calls the answer to a problem in addition— "the sum total of all that we think, and feel and do". That man, whether white or black, who possesses not only knowledge and skill but character, is invincibly clad. In his hands are the keys of future success. This is what the race needs most to-day.

Prejudice with all its disadvantages has its advantages. Aside from testing character, it forces the Negro to make outlets for himself which would not otherwise have been made. The powers which would otherwise lie dormant he is forced to exercise by the goading of this same prejudice. Confidence in one's ability to do is born, strength is developed and a disposition to launch out for oneself because of the situation, is created. This is especially shown in lines of business where he is forced to face-to-face competition. Under the circumstances, then, he has been compelled to do what under different conditions would not have been done. May it not be true that God, despite the motives of men, will use these prejudices and the tremendous odds against which the race is now contending as a sort of fitting or training school for the Negro, leading to the readjustment which is sure to come?

A race that can point to representatives of great and successful enterprises, however few, may consider that it has scored a point in its favor and cannot be despised nor despaired of. Mr. Washington is a living example of what may be done in these lines. His success should encourage others to exercise their capabilities for business, and build up enterprises which shall help the whole people. A race that makes such efforts is bound to have in time creditable representatives in all business activities—representatives who will maintain their standing in competition with the business world.

It is here—in business—where the competition seems greatest, where the numbers seem largest and the fight thickest. It is a bread-and-butter struggle, and the black man, to succeed, must possess the business qualities that characterize successful business men everywhere. Touching the question of organization and business, Mr. Washington admirably states the case when he says: "I have faith in the timeliness of this organization. As I have noted the conditions of our people in nearly every part of our country, I have always been encouraged by the fact that, almost without exception, whether in the North or in the South, wherever I have seen a black man who was succeeding in his business, who was a taxpayer, and who possessed intelligence and high character; that individual was treated with the highest respect by the members of the white race. In proportion as we multiply these examples North and South, will our problem be solved. Let every Negro strive to become the most useful and indispensable man in his community. When an individual produces what the white world wants—whether it is a product of the hand or head or heart, the world does not long inquire what is the color of the skin of the producer."[2] Again he declares himself in these words: "No matter by what conditions we may find ourselves surrounded, may we ever keep in mind that the law which recognizes and awards merit, no matter under what skin found, is universal and can no more be nullified than we can stop the life-giving influences of the daily sun."

As we have said, success in any undertaking must redound to the credit not only of the individual but of the race. As in education the race is benefited in proportion to the rise of individuals out from the mass, so wherever individual men and women exhibit capacities for managing affairs and strive to train themselves for the best possible exercise of those capabilities, just so far will the race receive rightful recognition. Merit in anything will win its way, and it will not hurt the race irremediably if prejudice does compel the Negro to do a little better than others in order to receive equal rewards. It becomes a matter of satisfaction in the end that it is so, though it may gall at the time. Prejudice thus defeats its purpose by the very compulsion to supreme excellence which it insists upon. It forces on and up to that strenuous exertion that produces the great things in the world. Still, we must agree that the insistence upon superexcellence is not general. It is not met in all lines and this is a helpful and hopeful sign. In literature and art the "man's a man for a' that."[4] He must be so in business too—in all its relations.

All sides that pertain to living must be touched. The Negro must reach out. As I have had occasion to say concerning our new possessions in previous articles, this reach must extend where opening[s] are to be found and it seems to me that those possessing capital should make use of it as any other American would, not fearing to run some risk. Foresight, shrewdness and ability to calculate, must be quickened as instincts, while the necessity of being gentlemanly, fair, square—in every way honorable—must be kept well to the fore. As a people we agree that there is much to be learned, but I have faith that the patience of the race is a distinguishing characteristic that will help much in this learning, holding it in the proper attitude as it goes through educational, and disciplinary processes.

One trouble is that the moneyed men of the race—the few who have a goodly share of this world's goods—are not altogether the ones who care to establish any particular business or branch out to any great extent in those already engaged in, and which perhaps have made the fortunes possessed. Conservatism is a good thing if not carried too far, but if it checks all aspirations and throws wet blankets upon every possibility that does not plainly and unmistakably shadow forth probability of considerable success, it is positively damaging. Business men of the present day are enthusiastic over the lines that are developing, the limits which are extending and the possibilities that are being presented. The Negro must imbibe this enthusiasm and in striving to be cautious, must not be over-cautious. The race is continually saying "get religion and learning," and it has had a third necessity thrust upon it—to "get money." Legitimate business is a legitimate channel for this getting, and may build up a monument for the race in enterprises undertaken and carried out so as to attract attention and command admiration and support.

Such enterprises should be encouraged by the race itself. This encouragement is a necessity to success. If a Negro is willing to place his money and service at the disposal of the people, the race can do no less than give it patronage. Without this, little can be accomplished. But with co-operation added to other necessary requirements residing in the individual, the Negro business man or woman may look for results commensurate with the efforts put forth.

Notes

1 [The National Negro Business League met in Boston in 1900.]

2 [Pietro Metastasio.]

3 [This comes from the sixth paragraph of Booker T. Washington's address at the first meeting of the National Negro Business League, August 24, 1900.]

4 [Robert Burns (1759–1796), "A Man's a Man for A' That," 1795.]

What the Omen?

Competitor 2 (1902): 6–7.

The White Man Does Not Know the Negro.
"Mediocri[t]y is Jealous"

Among the many absorbing questions before the American people today the race question seems to hold its own. Our magazines and papers, generally,—dailies and weeklies as well as monthlies,—all feel it to be their duty to say what should be done with the Negro and to give verdict as to citizenship, his status, his future, and the sort of education best adapted to his needs as a man and a citizen. In fact no phase of the Negro's life fails of discussion at the hands of the most flippant penny-a-liner, as well as the gravest thinker. All have theories of some sort and they do not hesitate to express them, whether they are visionary or practical.

If theories alone could have solved this problem, long ere this would race friction have been removed. It would have been a question of the past. But, unfortunately for the race, unfortunately for the people at large, many of those who had no remedy for the troubles complained of, have had most to say and they have generally said it in the most reckless way, regardless of facts. Only now and then do we have a calm view of the situation with reasonable suggestions as to the best course to follow in these days of strife and unrest.

As we enter upon the twentieth century, it will be well for black and white to get together and understand one another and ascertain as far as possible what is best to do in the light of facts before us.

One thing is certain—the white man does not yet know the Negro. Strange as it may seem, the Northern white man does not know him after many years of close observation; neither does the Southern white man, for all the years gone by in which the Negro has lived in his midst. The observations of both, in fact, only leave the Negro largely an unknown quantity to either. I have claimed heretofore that there is a life that the white man knows nothing of. It is found in the hovel as well as in the cultured home, in the school and the church. It is a life in the bud-time of race-pride and another race prejudice, and it is swelling to the blossoming. *What will be the fruit?*

To know the race one must do more than visit it occasionally here and there, must see more than even a close examination of schools and churches, instructed, aided and supported by white philanthropy, will disclose. The toadying, servile representatives of the race, the politicians, the dependent ones—all must be passed by and the Negro people found. To know the Negro one must be with him and become a part of his life—see what he is doing, and, above all, *know what he is thinking.*

Go into the schools and churches where there is not a shadow of white influence to check freedom of speech or tinge thought and what do we see and hear? In every case we find those from the oldest to the youngest with some ideas upon the race question and ready to express them. Not so with the white children. They are not thinking about the color of their skin or the texture of their hair or their rights, the contempt and ostracism following them everywhere; but the Negro child, on the other hand, of every shade of color, has these almost constantly in mind, for they are thrust upon him. *He can think of little else.*

In such schools, in such communities, the field work, the social gathering, the literary society, the routine of school or church or community life, the platform—all are tinctured deeply with these ideas and thus are expressed in some form on every possible occasion. All these questions are in a large degree to the race, as far as interest is concerned at least, the *momentous, the ever-present, ever-burning topic.*

No youth of the white race feels the weight of any subject agitating the mind of the public as these colored youth feel this one. *What is the omen,* when boys and girls alike make it a common question, in some form or other for all their daily work? It has been said that the two races are growing apart, that there is as much race prejudice in the one as in the other. In many respects this is true, though the prejudice on the part of the Negro is a thing of natural growth from certain causes, not an inherent quality. The fact that the Negro is rising without anything like adequate recognition—at least other than a patronizing one—is one of these causes. As here and there the Negro comes to the white man's level, among the best he is confronted with that "Ah-you-are-here" expression, which means more than words can signify, and he straightway feels his pulse stirred to the defensive counter spirit of "I-am-and-what-are-you-going-to-do-about-it?" The result is the two mutually draw back from each other.

Among the middle classes, where the level of the whites, intellectually and financially, is more readily and more rapidly being reached by the greater number of Negroes, there is still more prejudice to be found. It is here where the Negro has his fiercest battle-ground; it is here where he finds his greatest opposition. It is only following out the idea of the French writer who said, "Mediocrity alone is jealous." The constant desire of this class of white people to rise to the highest level aggravates them upon seeing a Negro reaching out for or obtaining in any way that which they may have or may be seeking and they make it known by greater assumption of superiority, especially over those of the race who have reached their own plane of living, and here again is a creation of a counter prejudice.

Growing refinement brings with it to the Negro all that sensitiveness which is accorded to refined people wherever found, and naturally he recoils from rebuffs, insults and contumely, and holds himself aloof more and more only as business demands contact. He has no growing reason to revere the whites as a mass, and if nations are proverbially ungrateful, what more can be expected of individuals, no matter how much fine theorizing there may be upon the subject of what the Negro owes to the white man.

With this increasing prejudice, for reasons named, there is a growing race pride. This is taking firm root among the young people of the Negro race who are being taught to respect those of their own number who have obtained honor and distinction through merit. The schoolboy and schoolgirl are studying the history of their own race with eagerness. They are finding out that it is not an altogether degraded people from which they have sprung, and with the gathering evidence about them of education, refinement, even wealth, and high character, they see no good reason why they should be despised for mere color or the possession of some imperceptible drops of Negro blood, as in many cases. This is a laudable pride, based upon both past and present grievances. Think you that this thoughtfulness of the Negro youth will be without some sort of fruit? Will these not have as much influence upon their ignorant brother masses as have the whites over the ignorant masses of their own color? I repeat, *the white man does not thoroughly know the Negro. He does not begin to see all that boils and seethes and ferments in the brains of this growing class. It is well for the nation to learn wisdom from the mouths of babes and sucklings;*[1] *and when these prattle of race issues, it is an omen not to be unheeded.*

Note

1 [See Psalms 8:2 and Matthew 21:16.]

White vs. Black

Voice of the Negro 1, no. 1 (1904): 25–28.

I have lately been reading sketches of the lives and careers of some of the world's greatest Negroes, among them Pushkin, Dumas, Toussaint L'Ouverture, Frederick Douglass and Daniel A. Payne. More than once did I ask myself, wherein were these men the inferior of the white man; if there were any grounds for the claim other than that of color; if the literary, civil and military achievements of the Negro did not refute this charge?

These reflections were forced upon me by present conditions, by the attitude of the American people toward the black man and the oft repeated statement that he is of an inferior race and should be forced to occupy an inferior place. Neither history nor observation supports this theory. If there is any inferiority at all it is the result of conditions and lack of opportunities. I believe in the old saw that every man is the architect of his own fortunes, be he white or black.

Alexander Pushkin was regarded as Russia's greatest poet. He holds that place today. His place among literary men in Russia as well as among literary men generally is undisputed. The fact that he had Negro blood in his veins has not seemed to militate against him. Dumas, the French novelist, known to the reading public throughout the world, also holds high rank among the leading literary French representatives. He is spoken of as "the literary heir and successor of Walter Scott." His stories were cast in the mould of the Waverley novels, but the coloring and the mechanism were of French mode instead of the English, and they gained thereby greatly in vivacity and ingenuity of plot. Dumas' books will be read when those of any other authors of equal celebrity will have perished. Hamilton Mabie calls "The Three Musketeers" a "master piece of literature." The unbiased, the unprejudiced mind does not stop to ask the color of the writer, for that is of no concern.

Toussaint L'Ouverture, the great Haytian general, to whom Hayti owes her independence more than to any other one man, compares favorably with the best of our military leaders, either past or present, as a skilful warrior and an illustrious general and statesman. It is said that his best claim to our respect and admiration consists of the entire devotion of his varied and lofty powers to the redemption of his color from degrading bondage and its elevation into the full stature of perfect manhood. Moved by similar impulse—by hatred of Slavery—Frederick Douglass used his matchless powers of mind and soul to free his brethren from the shackles that bound their limbs. He was engaged in a struggle that means much to himself and his people. Night and day Mr. Douglas[s] appealed to the conscience of white America in behalf of his race. He consecrated his wonderful eloquence and splendid abilities to the cause of freedom. What Mr. Douglass did in a civil and political way, Daniel A. Payne did as a preacher of the Word. Like Douglass, Bishop Payne was a remarkable man—raised up of God to do the work that he did for the education of his people.

These are only a few examples of many that might be cited. But they are known to the world and serve to show the possibilities of the race and they prove conclusively that much of this talk about Negro inferiority is simply father to the wish. It may be said that these are exceptions, that they represent but a class. It is my opinion that the future of the Negro people will largely depend upon the exceptions as we find them here and there—the progress they may make. To them we must look for the solution of the problem. If they are hindered in their strivings and are prevented from attaining their highest ambitions, if their aspirations are stifled, then we must expect the race to suffer according. It is for these exceptions that I plead. I plead for a fair chance and an equal opportunity. I plead that their hopes and yearnings and aspirations may not be crushed, but that they may be given a human being's chance.

Brave words are these: "The only solution reserved for us is the adoption of these children of Africa into our American life. In spite of our race feeling, of which the writer has his share, they will win equality at some time. We cannot remove them, we cannot kill them, we cannot prevent them from advancing in civilization. * * * They are now very weak; some day they will be stronger. They are now ignorant and passion-wrought; some day they will be wiser and more self-restrained. I do not know just what form the conflict will take * * * As long as one race contends for the absolute inferiority of the other the struggle will go on with increasing intensity. But if some day the spirit of conciliation shall come into the hearts of the superior race the struggle will become less strenuous. The duty of brave and wise men is to seek to infuse the spirit of conciliation into these white leaders of white men."

Thus Prof. John Spencer Bassett states the situation in a nutshell. Would that those for whom the admonition is intended would follow it! But hardly, for the professor, because he had the courage of his conviction, is already compelled to yield his official head.[1] If freedom of speech and freedom of action are to be denied in this discussion fraught with such grave consequences, we can never hope for a peaceful and amicable settlement. It is this spirit of intolerance and lack of fair play that makes the situation so gloomy. There seems to be no disposition on the part of many, who claim to be sincere, to arrive at a common understanding. With the spirit lurking in so many hearts we may expect just what we are now having—friction. Will the country not see this?

Will thoughtful men and women shut their eyes and ears to the overtures of Justice?

It is this cursed American prejudice North and South, that stands in the way of better results on the part of the Negro people. Hampered and proscribed as they are it is impossible for them to develop the best that is in them. If the white man could only put himself in the black man's place for a time—feel as he feels, have the same impulses and yearnings, he would be better prepared to pass judgment. The spirit of intolerance is abroad throughout the land, in the North as well as in the South. This is especially true when the black man's rights are in question. It is a sad commentary upon American Christianity and the American spirit of justice when the American people cannot or will not calmly and dispassionately come to an understanding on questions so vital to both races as those now agitating the public mind.

A year ago last summer Prof. Sledd of Emory College, Oxford, Ga., was forced to resign his position because of the somewhat liberal attitude he took on the Negro question in a contribution to the Atlantic Monthly.[2] The whole country seems to be going mad over this question, putting words into the Negr[o]'s mouth that he never thought of, and thoughts into his head that he never dreamed of, and attributing to him desires that are altogether foreign to him. The Negro is simply thinking and planning for himself and for his own elevation. The educated Negro knows right from wrong. He realizes the burden he is carrying. The weight of it presses heavily upon him. Our schools and colleges are sending forth young men and women who are bound in time to revolutionize public opinion. These cannot be kept down. It is to the far-sighted, the intelligent Negro that we must look to bring about the proper solution in time. He cannot, however, do this alone. The far-sighted intelligent white man must also unite with him.

The Negro[']s great drawback lies, in the fact that he is too often misjudged as a people. It seems strange that the American people will persist in putting an estimate upon the race generally, according to the lowest standards and the lowest types, and that they wilfully refuse to consider that group of men and women such as the Congregationalist refers to when it says: "There are not less than two hundred college graduates among the colored people of Chicago. Some have acquired a good practice as physicians, while others are doing well as lawyers. Some are teaching and a few are preaching. But the majority are leading a non-professional life, and are as successful in their employment as an equal number of graduates among their white brethren * * * * Whatever the theories of eminent men as to the desirability of industrial training for most colored people, it is the opinion of the Chicago graduates that for their race thoroughly trained leaders are indispensable.["]

It was Tennyson who said,

"I hold in truth, with him who sings
    To one clear harp in divers tones,
    That men may rise on stepping stones
Of their dead selves to higher things."[2]

The Negro craves, begs for this opportunity of self-improvement as suggested by these lines that he may thus rise—that he may rise to higher things where he too in common with the rest of mankind may fulfill the object of his creation. Are the American people so heartless as to deny him this one request? Has our civilization reached so low an ebb and our Christianity become such a mockery, and have the consciences of men become so dulled as not to be moved by his entreaty?

The black man does not want the white man's pity, but he asks rather for his sympathy. He is as anxious as any body that this constant strife and struggle between man and man should cease; that all men should live as brothers—happily together—sharing the same fate and the same danger for a common country. There is no good reason why the Negro's amor patriae should not be as strong and as warm as that of any living man. But he must be properly treated. He must be accorded his civil and political rights. Where hatred, slander, abuse and foul play hold sway there can be no love on the part of those against whom these shafts of bitterness are hurled.

Some day the white man will regret the present treatment of the black man. Some day he will open his eyes to the fact that those, whom he now regards as his inferior and whom he places on the level with the brute, are men and women with souls like those of other people. Some day he will see the present proscriptive laws enacted by the states reacting to the detriment of his own progress and prosperity. Conscience is a powerful corrective when allowed to act freely. I fully believe that this whole matter will be amicably settled in time when the white man shall be brought to see the error of his way and when the Negro shall have reached that point in our civilization where he can demand respect by what he is to himself and to the nation at large.

In the mean time patience is the only role the Negro can play successfully. We may not yet have reached the depths of humiliation. The better classes, the deserving, the sensitive, may be made to drink of still more bitter waters because linked by ties of race to the criminal and the depraved. But if we can be brave to endure, if we can keep hope alive, if we can hold fast to faith and be strong to work on, the reaction will come—the day of the Negro will dawn in time. It is for that we must labor—for the future generations, for a day those now living may not see—and gird ourselves with the satisfaction of knowing that we are the pioneers in the struggle for recognition—that through our efforts, our strifes and our sufferings, peace and good-will may supplant misunderstanding and hatred and that we are preparing the way for that time when white and black shall have reached the full stature of Christian manhood which calls all peoples men and brethern.

Notes

1 Since the above was written by an action of the college authorities Prof. Bassett has been retained. [Attempts were made at Trinity College, the precursor to Duke University, to fire

Bassett in 1903 over the controversy that his article "Two Negro Leaders," *South Atlantic Quarterly* 2 (July 1903), caused. In it he ranked Booker T. Washington second to Robert E. Lee among Southerners born in the last century.]

2 [Sledd's article, "The Negro: Another View," was published in the June 1902 *Atlantic Monthly*. Sledd was a classicist.]

3 ["In Memoriam," stanza 1, lines 1–4.]

The Moral of Race Conflict

Voice of the Negro 1, no. 3 (1904): 90–93.

The pages of the world's history are sown thick with the deeds that record man's inhumanity to man. The array of pitiless facts reach from the earliest dawn down to the present. In the march of races through barbarism and civilization the stronger ones have invariably sought to enslave, to crush, to annihilate the weaker. Wherever there has been found a governing, ruling class, it has sought by every means in its power to keep another class or classes under subjection. The forms of servitude have been various, but in all, the methods used to obtain the end have tended to harshness, terrorism and brutality. On the other hand, history is also replete with conspiracies and insurrections, through which the oppressed ones have endeavored to obtain freedom and natural rights.

This shows on one side the possession of an innate desire to be one's own master which everywhere urges to revolt against oppression, and, on the other hand, there is plainly evident the mingling of the brute nature with man's, which makes men tyrannical and ferocious. And as natures grow by what they feed upon, so we see the despotic spirit growing by exercise, and ideas of superiority inflated by dwelling upon them, which irritation and unrest increased until the limit of endurance is reached.

Over and over again the lesson has been set for nations in the march of conquest, but again and again their experience has failed to impress succeeding ones. Power has always become inhuman, and the weak have been refused their rights and pushed to the wall, oftimes with fiendish delight. Nation against nation, race against race we find them pitted, until in one way or another the struggle comes to an end.

The servile wars of Rome are but an example of the point in question—wars in which some of the most bloody cruelties known to man were perpetrated. The recent sway of the Boers in Africa furnishes another illustration. These early Dutch settlers of Africa almost stamped out the very life of the French Protestants—the Huguenots who were exiled in the dark continent—forbidding them even to speak their native tongue in petition or worship, and establishing a system of espionage in every household until every vestige of national sentiment was crushed out. These same Dutch tyrants had once fought a bitter fight for political and religious freedom. As for the native African, these Boers simply made of them beasts of burden, subjecting them to most inhuman treatment, spurning, maltreating them and heaping upon them every indignity because of their color and race. Spanish misrule and tyranny for centuries crushed the weaker races in every province over which Spain has sway, until Cuba became synonymous with heartless oppression, and the reign of the same brutality in the Phillipines is a matter of history as well. The Jew, too, has been the victim of cruel injustice in every country in which he has sojourned.

Inherited tendencies to despotism, inherited prejudices and blind bigotry, together with ignorance, have all had to do with the problem of these race conflicts. Still it is not so easy to point out one moral as the one above all others to be drawn from the situation.

Two things are plainly evident, however. First, there is no safeguard for the weak, the undeveloped races of the world, except in an awakened public sentiment among the classes who can and will make use of the strong arm of the government in behalf of righteous execution of impartial justice—in punishment of wrong and protection of right; and second, the truth of the argument that Demosthenes made against Philip with such telling force—that all power is unstable that is founded upon injustice.

The corollary to this last is perhaps what concerns us directly. Here we may seek for the moral. The nation that refuses to rouse itself to high moral activity in its treatment of the weaker races, and that allows to go unrebuked, injustice, murder, rioting, lynching, unlawful assault of any kind upon a race because of its color, its nationality, its ability to make an adequate defense, invites a growing menace to the peaceful security of every class. That the mills of the gods grind surely, if slowly,[1] is a belief of which it is difficult to divest oneself in the light of history. We reap what we sow as individuals, and this is no less true of nations. The Boer who placed the iron heel on Huguenot and native African alike had to succumb to another power. Is it possible that injustice and contumely can be heaped unceasingly upon a defenseless people without a Nemesis showing its will some time in the centuries? The questions as to how, where, when, may not receive any immediate answer, but the lane is long that has no turning. The idea of retributive justice has found lodgment in the minds of nations from the days of Eschylus who portrayed it so vividly in his tragedies. Sometime, somewhere, either now or hereafter, individuals, nations, or their descendants, are believed to be recipients of an inevitable reward for ill deeds done.

Viewed both subjectively and objectively we find that inhumanity causes deterioration. Brutality, injustice, hardened natures, blunt all the finer sensibilities, sear alike those who exercise them and the victims. We have but to instance the early Sicilians whose tyrannical conduct led to that frightful insurrection[2] where the wretched city of Enna felt the vengeance of men brutalized by oppression. The other phase is shown when greed led the early slavers to fill the places in their human cargo, made vacant in any way, with their own servants or the very men who had helped them to gather the cargo.

In seeking a moral we cannot over-look the cause leading to such atrocities. And we find it in greed. Greed is the foundation of the entire course of action—selfish greed—greed for money, for power, for self indulgence—greed, well called "the nation's curse.["] This greed and the innate cruelty nourished by it govern today the treatment of races, just as in the days of Sicilian landowners and African slavers. Here we may turn to the race on American soil which experiences with the greatest force the race conflict, and we find another element added to greed, which itself takes on a peculiar form in this case. Hate is the added element and jealousy is the peculiar form which is manifested. This jealous hate is most rampant in the breasts of the ignorant and vicious, and there it is more to be feared than flood or fire or famine, for if allowed to wreak its terrible fury at will upon the hated race—the one against which this passion is conceived, it is a step to broader fields for outrages. Like a tiger, having tasted blood, it will lash itself into a frenzy on every pretext and seek to satisfy its insatiable appetite upon any object in its way. The growth of such passions has been plainly demonstrated in the many riots which have risen in such fury here and there all over the land. This passion for violence, the world over, has been able to raise a mob at a word, and at a word hurl it against individuals, or classes, against armed authority itself in the blindest, most unreasoning rage.

It is the knowledge of this that makes the soul, longing to be free from the sight and sound of it all, cry with Cowper:[3]

"O, for a lodge in some vast wilderness

* * *

My soul is sick with every day's report
Of wrong and outrage with which earth is filled.
There is no flesh in man's obdurate heart,
It does not feel for man: the natural bond
Of brotherhood is severed as the flax
That falls asunder at the touch of fire."

With the hatred of the lower classes of society to face, with the indifference and prejudice of the upper classes to withstand, with the clamor on the one hand to hold the Negro race within industrial lines, and the refusal on the other hand to admit it into labor organizations, or factories or shops; with the outcry against its higher development and the assertion that it can never rise to equal heights with other races no matter how much property, morality or intellect it possesses, this race especially is forced into a conflict that might well daunt the soul of hardier races, flung as it is from rock to whirlpool, buffeted and battered whichever way it turns.

What is the moral of race conflict? Let us ask if the nation living under the American flag will face the truth that all government is unstable that is not founded upon justice? Bugle notes here and there call the nation to consider well the situation. Carl Schurtz has blown a blast in his recent article on "Can the South Solve the Negro Problem."[4] Though his conclusion refers to a section, the final answer in considering the moral must come from the whole people—only through the sway of justice everywhere can we meet the issue of race conflict in a civilized, Christian manner. The only sentiment, I reassert, that can cope with this spirit of conflict must begin with and sway the classes everywhere who posses power and influence. These must be wide-eyed to possible impending perils if the spirit of humanity and justice does not make its force felt, rouse themselves from indifferent lethargy and spurn their baser selves that counsel resistance to right.

When nations agreed concerning the abolition of the slave trade the infamous thing trembled, concealed itself and at last died. It was when slavery had caused the evolution of a strong moral sentiment in the governing classes that the hideous bonds began to weaken, and when armies and navies stood ready to support the fiat of its doom these hateful bonds fell asunder.

But the race that has stood to receive such continuous shocks of assault has gained some things from the conflict. Out of the turmoil, the struggles, have been developed some needed characteristics. Strength, endurance, determination, high purpose, fixed resolves—all are shown in a growing element of the race which is daily forcing respect and recognition by ability and worth. It is a rising class capable of standing upon its dignity, firmly clinging to its rights and privileges as citizens of worth and intelligence, with the dregs it is not associated any more than are the higher classes of any race. Only to help uplift and purify—not to suffer the same fate as dregs. This birth of such a class in less than fifty years from slavery carries with it an argument that cannot be gainsaid, and the partial respect that it enjoys may be increased by various things to be remembered as of the actual past and probable future: patriotism that helped to keep the country undivided, that assisted in withstanding invaders, that helped to extend national possessions, and that lend a hand to avert perils in many places. Even the proudest Norman in time was forced to give the hand of fellowship to and have respect for the Saxon churl, when, making England's cause its own by valor a change of opinion concerning itself. May not the common danger found in this spread of lawlessness bring together the best elements, and by union against a common foe reduce the present conflict?

One thing is certain. The theory that the germs of individuality have been stifled by the past training in slavery is no longer tenable in regard to the Negro race. The stage has been reached where it can no longer be treated as a mass, an indivisible unit. Individuality is playing a part and a great part in the present. It will play a much more decided part in the future. If the sense of right and justice is allowed development in the breasts of the ruling classes everywhere, this nation need not trouble itself about the moral to be drawn.

Wisdom and prudence counsel all things for national safety. There is no safety in oppression which begets hate and lawlessness. The lawmaking and the executive powers rest with the higher classes. To them, North, South, East and West, we must look for the clear reading and broad comprehension of the lessons drawn from man's inhumanity to the black men.

"On God and God-like men we build our trust."[5]

Notes

1 [See Sextus Empiricus, "Against the Professors."]

2 [In 136–134 B.C.]

3 [William Cowper, "The Task" (1784), book 2, lines 1 and 6–11.]

4 [Carl Schurz, "Can the South Solve the Negro Problem?" *McClure's Magazine* 22 (January 1904): 258–275.]

5 [Alfred, Lord Tennyson, "Ode on the Death of the Duke of Wellington" (1852), stanza 9, line 34.]

The Negro and the Louisiana Purchase Exposition

Voice of the Negro 1, no. 8 (1904): 312–315.

A[t] the meeting of the American Philological Association, held at Yale University in July, 1903, it was decided to hold the next annual meeting at Cornell University, Ithaca, N. Y., in July, 1904. At a subsequent meeting of the executive committee of this Association the place was changed to St. Louis, with September as the date. This was done in order to afford the members an opportunity to attend the International Congress of Arts and Sciences to be held in this city, as many distinguished scholars from Europe and all parts of the world will be present and take part in the proceedings.

Not long ago the writer received notice of this change, and with it a circular, calling attention to the advantages of a certain hotel, the only one within the grounds. The inducements are flattering, while the offer is both generous and tempting. It is not to be supposed, however, that the hotel management means to include, knowingly, anyone of African extraction.

Following the communication referred to, the author of this paper received another letter requesting him to become a member of the International Congress just mentioned, and to take part in its proceedings. Very likely the other colored members of the Association received similar invitations, for the American Philological Association knows no color. The same may be said of the Archaeological Institute of America, as well as of a few other associations with which the writer has the honor to be connected. In these societies it is merit, not race. Brain, not color, that wins.

The writer's experience in St. Louis teaches him that the Negro will receive no consideration from any hotel not managed by some member of the race, and that he will be denied many of the privileges and advantages of the Exposition because of his color—because he is a Negro. One may expect insults, humiliations and embarrassments, if at any time he attempts to be a man or a gentleman as others. As a servant or a menial in any capacity, he may receive patronizing toleration. The sentiment in this city is avowedly anti-Negro.

In 1896, when Mr. McKinley was nominated for the first time to the Presidency by the National Republican Convention, then held in St. Louis, the writer, with eight or nine other men of color, was selected and requested by the Tippecanoe Club of Cleveland, Ohio, to go to St. Louis as a sort of vanguard, to assist whenever necessary, in lining up the forces in the interest of Major McKinley. The late Senator Hanna was the leading spirit in this movement, for he was one of the members of this celebrated club. Through him quarters were obtained for the party at one of the leading hotels of the city, despite the opposition and protest that met his first efforts. It was distinctly understood, however, that no white man should eat at the same table with the colored guests; so that when some of the Canton men—men from McKinley's own home— attempted to sit down at this table on one or two occasions, they were quickly informed that they must conform to the rules of the house or else leave. The fact was that the Negro's presence there was an innovation, and was about as much as the authorities could stand. While, therefore, this group of colored men received courteous treatment, because they behaved themselves as gentlemen, it was plainly to be seen that they were not wanted, and that it was only force of circumstances that led to their toleration.

These references, though of a personal nature in part, all have their bearing, and will serve to illustrate the point in question more fully perhaps than anything else.

Anticipating, therefore, the kind of treatment that would befall a black man at the Louisiana Purchase Exposition, the author of this article wrote the Secretary of the Treasury, the Hon. L. M. Shaw, protesting against making an appropriation to the St. Louis Fair authorities, on the ground that the black man, though a citizen of the United States and a tax-payer, would not receive proper treatment there, and that he would not only be discriminated against, but that he would be even humiliated and insulted in a variety of ways if he visited the Fair, no matter how gentlemanly his appearance and conduct. It was further urged that Congress could not justly appropriate funds out of the National Treasury to assist an undertaking where any members of our great Republic would be denied any privileges justly due them. Such an appropriation pre-supposed that all American citizens would be treated alike. If then, Congress knowing the facts in the case, granted aid to the enterprise, it would at least tacitly acquiesce in the management, whatever that might be. In reply, the Secretary wrote the following note:

TREASURY DEPARTMENT,
Washington, September 14, 1903.

My Dear Sir—Your letter of September 3d is received. An appropriation in behalf of the Louisiana Purchase Exposition was made by Congress. The Secretary of the Treasury is an executive officer, and, of course, cannot consider the matter referred to in your letter. All such communications should be addressed to Congress.

Very truly yours,

L. M. Shaw.

When the St. Louis authorities appeared again for a further raid on the Treasurer to secure additional funds through Congress in the shape of a loan, thinking it an opportune moment to renew one's protests, another letter was then addressed to the Speaker of the House, Mr. Cannon, appealing to him to come to the rescue, to make it possible to hinge the appropriation upon the proper treatment of all American citizens alike, setting forth reasons for the opposition. In reply he stated he had turned over the letter to the committee having the matter in hand for their consideration. Nothing more was heard from it. Whether the committee took any notice of it or not is still unknown. The inference is that the Negro and his rights are no longer factors in the consideration of Congressional questions.

The saddest feature of the whole matter is that the black man has no court of appeals. All avenues are closed to him. That a people—a part and parcel of the great Commonwealth—a people who helped to cut the forests, make the timber, build the cities, till the soil, and who with sweat of brow endured pain and hardship for their country's sake, should now be ignored and treated with disdain when it comes to the enjoyment of the fruits of these labors, is indeed a sad commentary upon the much vaunted American sense of justice, American civilization and American Christianity. Then, too, the Negro was here among the first of its settlers. The development of the southern portion of this Purchase is largely due to his presence and labor. He is so closely identified with it that he is an integral part of it, yet as a man or a woman a place in it is denied.

All others will have greater consideration at the hands of the American public than do those who by right are entitled to it. Thousands of people who have had nothing to do with the strenuous work leading to the growth of this territory—people of this country and also foreigners will be welcomed and accorded every courtesy. There will be Indians, Chinese, Japanese, Mexicans, Hindoos, Italians, Cubans, Hawaiians, Filipinos, even down to the Negritos of the islands in the Pacific, in whom some wiseacres have thought to have discovered the missing link—all these will be received officially and entertained as others, no notice being taken of their presence in cars, on grounds, in cafes—in fact, anywhere, unless suspicion arises in the mind of some that they belong to the wonderfully mixed race that we call the American Negro. Let this suspicion but gain a faint hold and woe to any one on whom it may be fastened. Yet, parenthetically, we may say, that there will be many there of such fair complexion as to be "above suspicion" so far as race is concerned, and who will hobnob in cars and cafes with the white multitude, all unknown as part and parcel of the Negro race. Such is the irony of the American situation.

President Roosevelt in his admirable address at the opening of the Exposition, April 30, 1903, among other things, said: "The people of these states (referring to the Louisiana Purchase) have shown themselves mighty in war with their fellow men, and mighty in strength to tame the rugged wilderness. They could not thus have conquered the forest and the prairie, the mountain and the desert had they not possessed great fighting virtues, the qualities which enable the people to overcome the forces of hostile men and of hostile nature. On the other hand, they could not have used aright their conquest had they not in addition possessed the qualities of mastery and self-restraint, the power of acting in combination with their fellows, the power of yielding obedience to the law and of building up an orderly civilization. Courage and hardihood are indispensable virtues in a people; but the people which possess no others can never rise high in the scale of power or of culture."

Now, without question, the Negro cannot be left out in this summary of causes. His labor has helped, as we have said, in the southern development, especially of this Purchase, far beyond what he is given credit for. He helped form and make the Louisiana Purchase not only possible, but one of the crowning glories of our great Republic, and no one takes greater pride in this show of results and the occasion that gave them birth than does the American black man. Again, President Roosevelt gives food for thought in his significant reminder that material prosperity is well and must be had for a foundation for a higher life, but that it "goes for very little, unless the American people do in very fact build this higher life thereon:" This is true, but what is this "higher life?" Is it not that high civilization that is based on justice and equal rights—"liberty and the pursuit of happiness"—which form the basis of our Constitution? Is it reasonable to suppose that the Negro can always remain patriotic under opposing conditions? Can the fires of patriotism always burn in his breast when he finds himself confronted by the existing conditions? Is it good for the stability of the American Republic? It would some times seem that for the universal good of this American sentiment that reaches to the "higher life" some northern city would have been better for the holding of such an exposition—a city unhampered by traditions and customs and influences—even though it were not a part of the original purchase. Many of us could wish that it might have been thus.

From Jefferson to Roosevelt is, however, only one century. We can live in the hope that the 200th anniversary of this event will see a very different state of things, that, to make an application of the President's closing words, the insistence he calls for may be placed "upon the virtues of self-restraint, self-mastery, regard for the rights of others," and that "our abhorrence of cruelty, brutality, and corruption in public and in private life alike" be clearly shown. With this carried out by all the Republic may become all we hope to see it.

Yet with all the present prejudice we feel that we can prophesy that the next century will have so added to the Negro's material possessions, to his learning and his manhood, and will have so changed the spirit manifested toward him that he will no longer be an "outsider" when we celebrate the capture of San Juan, for instance, and that color will then be unknown.

After all, a century is but a short time in the development of a people, and who knows what the next hundred years will bring forth—what marvelous changes will take place, not only in the arts and sciences, but in the attitude of one people toward another, of one race toward another—for there is already a goodly share of white blood, Indian blood, Mexican blood, to say nothing of other bloods that enter into the American civilization. While we live let us hope for the better.

The Negro's Duty in the Present Contest

Voice of the Negro 1, no. 11 (1904): 531–533.

The eighth of November this year is a day fraught with great significance to these United States. On the outcome of the presidential election hinge great potentialities. It is a question whether we shall have Republican or Democratic rule with all that the victory for the winning party may carry with it. There is a national side to be considered and a race side as well.

There are those who claim that the Negro should divide his vote between the two great parties, and every now and then we hear of a "flop" of some Negro to the Democratic side. At times this seems most largely to be done for effect—to bring some obscure person into political prominence, but very often there is the undisguised odor of "loaves and fishes" accompanying the performance.[1]

We hear a mass of heterogeneous arguments at such times—that the Negro owes nothing to the Republican party, that the race should be rewarded by offices from the party gaining its vote, that every man should look out for himself, that it is the way to get rights, that there is nothing to fear from Democratic success, that it is mere sentiment to adhere to Republicanism, etc., etc. The[s]e and similar arguments, sifted and reduced, hold but two stable elements in them—selfishness and corruption.

In the first place, no matter what mistakes individual or general that the Republican party has committed in local situations or even in national, as regards the Negro, it is perfectly impossible to say with truth that the Negro owes nothing to it, for without it his existence as a part of the body politic would not have been possible. Then as to local issues even where no great party principle is at stake there is nothing more to be considered than the fact of obtaining the highest bid for influence. As to the policy that every man should look out for self, we know that anarchy and dissolution of government would be the end of mere self-seeking. We utterly repudiate the idea that this course is a way to get rights. The Democratic party has either ignored or ruthlessly trampled upon the Negro and his rights in all its platforms and actions. As to danger from Democratic victory, the continued abrogation of rights in Southern sections of the United States is sufficient evidence that, with the party in power, these things would grow to an extent beyond the power of sentiment to keep down, and that Jim Crow cars, and proscription would multiply, while denial of right to vote would creep insidiously into every possible nook. There is more than sentiment bound up in holding to Republicanism. It has as a leader to-day a man that shows us where safety lies, where there is the least danger of meddling with constitutional rights, where the man's measure is the stature he has reached by achievement, where there is the least humiliation awaiting us, where, in short, is the vantage ground from which our battles must be fought for victory and from which we may expect the greatest things.

We are as a race the cynosure of all eyes to-day. We are the target for all shafts that malice, prejudice and vengeance can hurl. We are in the storm center of such a disturbance to-day as we have never before experienced. In some sections there is a determination to rid the body politic of the Negro's presence at any cost. No subterfuge that will aid in the scheme is overlooked. Every criminal act is magnified and multiplied. Sensational newspaper reports, many without a scintillation of truth—exaggerated speeches, vile hysterical presumptions, jealous fury—all are employed with this end in view.

A lengthy, labored, ill-tempered article, from John Temple Graves in the *New York Times*, has just recently attempted to show that the "civilization of the South is in a serious and alarming crisis," and this because of the presence of the Negro and because of the voices raised here and there in the defense of a people whom the South has always had with it from the earliest settlement at Jamestown up to the present, a people who under the most arduous, galling and tyrannical rule of bygone days, patiently bore their yoke with the hope of better days, people against whom no such slanders were hurled as now. Why this change of sentiment? Why is the race to be treated now as outcasts, threatened, despised and spurned with a hatred bordering on fanaticism? It is no more a criminal race than the whites. It has grown in intelligence and desert, and the crimes of a few should not be charged against the whole.

What are the Negroes of to-day? Count them, look at them and see the blood in their veins—blood begotten of unbridled passions of the South. Shall we exile our own? And who are these who would burn, kill, destroy, wipe out the race? There is but one answer. Those who form the bulk and backbone of the Democratic party, who know but that, who have thrust aside the Negro's friendship and his protecting arm as worth nothing, and who are now accounting everything that is vile to him. With this temper existing no Negro is safe. The educated, the cultured, the honest, the worthy—all are classed and branded as only a part of a "seventh century race," which should be dealt with by "seventh century methods"—put out of the way. God forbid that the race should ever be left to the mercy of any section advocating such sentiments and given its power through the aid of this "seventh century" race, unless the Negro desires to provide all possible means for his own swift, dark and mysterious taking off. Such hysterical shrieks, such rabid utterances do no good. Those who write thus should see it as no way for better relations. Separation is impossible. The Negro is no slave, nor the white any longer his master. The

443

future of the race cannot be settled without his consent. He cannot be ostracized, deported, or lynched by the whole-sale. It is not human nature, and the Negro is human, no matter who denies it. He cannot unite with a solid South or a party that stands for such sentiments. The truth is that the Negro is by far the more self-controlled of the two races. Any sane person can see this when whip and lash and spur are constantly applied and patiently taken. He has held himself well in hand, and it is well. But the best men of both races must unite for something beside talk and demand fair play, and the upholding of law. Not till this is done will peace come and not until there is peace is it wise to trust our fortunes out of the hands of the party that gave us freedom.

As to the odd parties, to step aside from the main ones—the People's party and the Prohibition party, the Social Democratic party and the Socialist Labor party, and the National Liberty party—let us dispose of them briefly. They have alluring names, but they are untried in performance of enticing promises and "swapping horses in the middle of the stream" is never a safe thing. But one thing can be expected of these and that is, by sophistry so persuading and dividing Negro votes where they are of great consequence that it will enable the Democratic party to sneak into power. The Negro is not ready for fooling with "Bryanism"[2] as represented by the first named, nor with liquor prohibition alone for which the second stands. He wants prohibition of illegal methods, of lynchings and burnings and the like. He is not ready to risk the Utopian communism of Social Democrats, nor should the other Socialist side in the Labor party appeal to him as furnishing a safe haven. The Negro is too busy trying to get his own millions just now. He is listening to the advice to get land and money and he certainly does not want to throw his wealth into a common purse. Then there is the latest born—the National Liberty party with a Negro as a candidate.[3] Some one has said that Kansas "can't help being crazy because of its geographical position," and we find this State stands first in a list which this party inferentially claims will give it sixty per cent of the Negro vote. It is too preposterous to think for a moment of jeopardizing what the race has by running after an *"ignis fatu[u]s"*—a wandering fire that strong, common sense tells can not be reached.

All of these parties help the Democrats. This is the whole truth in a nutshell; and while a vast amount of specious reasoning is used to appeal to the Negro's restlessness and disgust, his vanity and race pride, the fact remains that at the ballot box in November [Theodore] Roosevelt and [Alton B.] Parker will stand as the real competitors for the reins of government. Democracy with Parker will be just so largely helped as the unwise Negro voter chooses to waste the votes of the race by scattering to these five party winds that woo him. No one should delude himself with the idea that a Negro stands the ghost of a chance to be made president. Democracy laughs in its sleeve at the help such a delusion would afford.

No; the Negro's path for the present lies upward through the way blazed out by the Republican party. That is a fact too patent to need argument; and that Theodore Roosevelt with his sturdy, strenuous adherence to strong and high ideals for every man is the leader most desirable for our future weal seems plain as daylight. Then our duty is plain. We must ferret out corruption at the polls, we must warn of false prophets, we must expose illegal means to carry elections, we must argue, persuade, shame, if necessary, that the weak, the ignorant and vicious, yes, even the intelligent—who have the freedom of the ballot do not help prevent the victory of Republicanism. Its life-preservers will float us, but it is well to fear the gods bringing such gifts from any other—their sustaining weight is from iron loading and the Negro will sink.

If we are men and not selfish, cowardly or unwise we will not dare to trifle with the sacredness of the ballot. We cannot afford to have an Arnold or Judas in the race. The entire logic of past events points out our duty. President Roosevelt has stood by the race. It is our duty to stand by him at the polls this fall. It will increase respect for us, will add friends to the race, will crystallize swavering sentiment in our favor and furnish the best, most unanswerable arguments as to our stability, our intelligence, our patriotism and our power. Let us be neither mercenaries, cowards nor traitors. Let every Negro do his duty and help to keep Roosevelt in the presidential chair.

Notes

1 [See Mark 6:41.]

2 [William Jennings Bryan was a leader of and presidential candidate for the People's Party (or Populist Party).]

3 [George E. Taylor was the National Liberty Party's candidate.]

The Emancipation of the Negro

Voice of the Negro 2, no. 2 (1905): 121–125.

Forty-two years have passed since Abraham Lincoln issued on January 1, 1863, the immortal document that gave liberty to four millions of human beings held in slavery, and guaranteed to them all the rights and privileges which their new birthright entitled them to enjoy. The issuance of the Emancipation Proclamation was a war measure—a necessity growing out of the Rebellion. While Mr. Lincoln looked with disfavor upon slavery it was not his purpose to adopt any measure that would sever the Union. He frankly declared that if he could save the Union with slavery he would do so, but if not, then slavery would have to go. He well knew, however, that the inexorable logic of events would finally bring about the freedom of the slaves.

In his first inaugural address he stated his position in these words:

> "Apprehension seems to exist among the people of the Southern States that by the accession of a Republican administration, their property, their peace and their personal security are to be endangered. There has never been any reasonable cause for such apprehension. Indeed the most ample evidence to the contrary has all the while existed and been open to their inspection. It is found in nearly all the published speeches of him who now address you. I do but quote from one of these speeches when I declare that I have no purpose directly or indirectly to interfere with the institution of slavery in the States where it exists. I believe I have no lawful right to do so; and I have no inclination to do so."

It will be remembered that Mr. Lincoln issued a preliminary document warning the rebellious States what they might expect if they did not lay down their arms by January 1, 1863. These utterances were unheeded and as a result the inevitable followed—slavery was abolished.

It must be believed by every student of history and every thoughtful mind that the hand of providence was in this movement—that the time had come for doing away with a[n] iniquitous system that was bound if continued, to work the ruin of both races—that God did thus use men and measures to execute his purposes in the ripeness of the time. The result was an emancipation from slavery that had lasted nearly two hundred fifty years.

It is a long cry from 1620, when the first slave ship left its helpless cargo at Jamestown, up to 1863 when the descendants of these and all that followed were set free and given mastery of themselves and their future destiny, as it would be supposed from the fiat that went forth that New Year's day. But these centuries filled with sorrow, anguish and degradation were, after all has been said, years of preparation in which gradually the captive race assimilated to a wonderful extent, the civilization surrounding it, considering how barred out it was from that participation which could bring about the best development of any people.

Barbarism gave way to enlightenment, and Christianity though it was preached as a religion calling subservience to masters, served to soften many of the asperities of the situation, leaving its indelible impress upon natures unusually receptive to its influences. Education too, crept in despite watchful repression and legal prohibition, and then environment did its work in a thousand ways, to say nothing of the influence from heredity of white blood that Southern lust had no natural repugnance to allowing to filter down through the veins of the slave race. All of these things gave more or less cumulative advantages as a no mean start for the Negro when the fetters dropped from his limbs.

Today the old wail is still heard that the period that followed emancipation was filled with mistakes. It is easy to look back from the misty distance of forty odd years and say this or that was a mistake; that this or that was a misstep; this or that should have been done or left undone. To criticize at such long range is infinitely more simple than to face conditions then existing and which we cannot now reproduce. The Reconstruction period that followed emancipation was a war necessity also, and it was the natural order of existing conditions that the Negro should have the right of suffrage. It is impossible to conceive how it could have been otherwise. The ballot was the only safeguard the newly emancipated people had—their only weapon of defense—their only means of protection. This suffrage may have been improperly used, and the right abused, but even then it served to check political outrages and political impositions that were bound to follow in the wake of the war.

Mistakes were made, it was true. No great world movements are made without mistakes. But there were mistakes all around, those made not only by the Negro and his friends, but by those who had so recently held him in subjection. The chief mistake of the Negro was in putting too much confidence in men claiming to be his friends—in allowing himself to be wielded by the carpet-baggers that infested the South in those days, and who grew rich through his political support. These same men—those still alive—are now taking part in damning him. But the only wonder is considering all things—the heat of passion and the memories of so recently stilled active strife—the ballot was not used still more aggressively by the race. Only this race with its characteristic virtues of patience, forbearance and long-suffering would have exercised it as carefully as it did.

Among the mistakes harped upon at this time, no one is made more prominent nor so craftily used to our present hurt than the claim that the field of possibilities opened up to the Negroes at that time was too broad, that the education that had served to train and strengthen the white race was unfitted for the Negro, that he should not have been allowed to rush into such unlimited educational pastures, to strive for higher learning—that in fact all the grand scheme of education planned and carried out in the South was one terrible mistake.

It was no mistake. The forty odd years have proved it. It was a necessity of the time of the ballot and the unconditional emancipation. Those opportunities which were afforded, coupled with the eagerness for learning, have been at the root of the progress of the race—have in fact brought the Negro where he is today. Had education been limited to the rudiment as the cry goes up that it should have been done; had the race at that crucial moment held down to the idea of work with the hands as wisest and best, there would never have been the uplift in a people that has astonished the world. The ambition, the inspiration, the opportunity, combined to give us those today who have made good the standing of the Negro and have helped to prove the first thing necessary at that time to prove—*that he had a mind, that he had capabilities and could grow, and that he was not a brute.* That very education helped give race leaders without which there could not have been received the recognition that the world has been compelled to accord.

In conjunction with those earnest intelligent men who had wrung out and wrought out an education from slavery's hard experiences or in spite of them, fitting these people to be the first leaders when the chains fell to the earth, with them these younger ones, ambitious, alert, determined, trod the upward paths and beat a broad road on the long highway to that upper plane that is the goal all civilized races strive to reach. I repeat that without such advantages we would have no such leaders in the world as we claim today and no such inspiration as clings to us in spite of the effort to strip us of its possession. No; the world must never for a moment consider as a mistake this education offered to the Negro people as it emerged form slavery. *It was a necessity.*

Frederick Douglass said that the race must be measured by the depth from which it has come. I would add that a race is also to be measured by the road it has had to travel. Slavery was a fearful road for the Negro. The wonder is that he came out from the toils with as much grace and with as many virtues as he possessed in 1863. Then there was placed before him the long road which he has since traversed, and no one will deny that it has been a rough and thorny one. Freedom brought trials with the responsibilities that freedom everywhere entails. The Negro faced the condition—-sink or swim, survive or perish. He had before him the making of a race—-the setting up of ideals, the formation of homes, the overcoming of superstition, ignorance and degradation and supplanting these by enlightenment, by education, by a general uplift. With this he had to work, to learn self-support and support of others, and he had to learn to save.

Is there a truthful soul, knowing anything of that day and of this, who dares to assert that the race stands on a lower plane now than it did when freed?

What has emancipation brought to us, and what has it brought us, are two parallel questions. We built upon what we had when slavery ceased and who shall say that, considering the tools and conditions—the weakness, the poverty and ignorance, and the oppression, that as a race we have not built fairly well. Emerson's words surely apply to us: "The beginnings are slow and infirm, but 'tis an always accelerated march."[1] The unparalleled progress in these years of freedom is a story that has been many times repeated with the growing wonder by the unprejudiced observer and listener, the world over. The results of emancipation have been marvelous when we stand and see the contrast to the past in the many cultured homes of today where refinement and learning are to be found, when we view the astounding material advancement which statistics prove, when we take into consideration the civil advantages which are not to be despised, though injustice rankles deep in some channels; and when we see the multitude of humbler homes where contentment, morality and industry abide, it is and must ever be a source of pride for us and our friends as we think that less than fifty years ago, homes and firesides were few and the race did not own its own flesh and blood, that it was but a prey to the vulture propensity of the so-called superior race.

The race is not worse today. Emancipation brought the Negro out into the full light of day where all things were seen and noted. In former days the aims of the race were not noticed. Nothing concerning slaves, except a "runaway" or a suspected insurrection was deemed worthy of public notice. There was then a sure way of disposing of a "bad Negro," and the world was none the wiser when crimes or indiscretions connected with them occurred. *Today the bad we do is shouted from the housetops, and the good is buried deep in the valley of Silence.* The vicious are called "the race," and the refined and cultured, the honest and industrious are all commanded to suffer with them under a common ban.

Are we then to be pointed out as pariahs—all of us—because of the crime of a few, because base passions find lodgment in some brutish beasts? Emancipation has not yet made a saint of the Anglo-Saxon though he has had freedom for nigh one thousand years. Why should so much be expected of the Negro in less than a half a century? No one denies that the Negro imbibed much that is bad, but we do claim that much of the evil passion set stirring in his breast and working out in assaults and conflicts is the natural result of expressions of hatred and opposition flaming out in violent language at every opportunity and showing itself in those fearful deeds of mob violence that vie with the most fiendish of heathen countries and ancient times. The Vardamans and the Tillmans are to blame for much of the evil wrought by the ignorant and vicious of the race. Ranting does not prove that a race is worse, and reason shows the proof to be on the other side.

Verily, Emancipation has a wide meaning—emancipation from iron chains and the overseer's whip, emancipation from ignorance, poverty and degradation, emancipation from wholesale, unmerited abuse, from unjust discrimination, from unrighteous treatment, from invisible bonds that forbid one to live freely, to act freely, to enjoy freely. *We are not yet emancipated in full.*

Forty-two years ago our papers of citizenship were issued but we have had to fight every inch of the way to the present. The fighting has not been in vain. It has developed our manhood and caused a settled determination in our breasts to live free or die like freemen and not like slaves. We have tasted some of the fruits of freedom and its gall and bitterness for those who have climbed somewhat the heights of experience taunts, jeers, sneers, to be thrust aside, scorned, denied common courtesies, humiliated, even cursed. It is a poor argument for the sickly sentimentalist to say that it would have been better never to have emancipated this people or never to have opened the higher avenues to them as it creates "delusive hopes," and "damns with impossible ambitions." It is a detestable argument for the white race to use and a sorrowfully pessimistic one for the Negro to adopt.

The fact is we need today new moral leaders in the "ranks of aggressive reform," to quote the expression of a strong present day writer—more perhaps than in the days of chattel slavery, but these are needed for the supposedly emancipated people. We need friends with backbone enough to say they are friends when out in the forum and to act their friendship—not shrink at the opprobrium our enemies would mete out to a "Negro's friend." We need every bit of optimism that can be thrown in our way, that we may see through the present darkness and detect the least glimmer of light beyond the dead wall of opposition and apathy that confronts us, and we need to take hope and comfort in what has been achieved already by the race, for it undeniably stands on higher ground.

To me there breaks a light ahead, however, when I recur to the thought of that one dauntless man in the White House who in 1863 had the courage to free four million slaves, and then again when I compare with him that other man who stands at the head of the nation and who has dared, even when his own political future was in the balance to say *that nothing would make him close the door of hope against the ten millions struggling upward.* And more—a growing faith possesses me that in the stupendous, overwhelming voice of the people that spoke in November we may see that the bug-a-boo of race does not really affright them after all and that saner views are seizing them, that there is a tendency to abatement of intolerance, to lessening of prejudice, to allowance of a fair chance for all, the Negro included.

May we not find in it an indication that there will be less opposition and more encouragement, less malice and more human sympathy, less of the spirit that works for evil and more of that which works for Christian brotherhood? May we not hope that our full emancipation "dawns up the sky?"

"Lean out, our souls, and listen."

Note

1 [See Ralph Waldo Emerson (1802–1882), "The Sovereignty of Ethics" (1878).]

Our Pagan Teachers

Voice of the Negro 2, no. 6 (1905): 404–406.

Out of the world problems are evolved the world's lessons. Vexed questions have confronted both civilization and barbarism, and these have passed on down from generation to generation in some form from the beginning of time—a gift from the garden and the first created pair. No matter how chary the world may have been of profiting by the teachings that accompanied them, it has been compelled time and again to give a listening ear to the instructions thus forced upon it. But while some have listened, some have mocked at the teachers and teachings. While some have learned wisdom and gladly acknowledged the debt, some have meted out scorn, persecution and even death to nation or individual that dared to teach new manners, new philosophies, new religions. Socrates was rewarded with the cup of hemlock for his efforts in practical didactics, yet today we are forced to acknowledge both his wisdom and power, and would gladly welcome another who could but "bend his bow," though he be a pagan. But Socrates appealed to the intellect solely, and truth to tell he had a mixed mass of intellects to deal with, mostly "one-story, some two-story, or three-story" perhaps, with but a very few of the "skylight" order. And today if we were forced to judge of the present by the impression made through more recent pagan teachers, we might face the necessity of reaching a similar conclusion concerning the modern intellects.

This has been borne in upon me by an excerpt from the *Boston Congregationalist*. Speaking of an incident of the war in the East between Christian Russia and pagan Japan, it indulges in the following suggestive exclamations: "How these Japanese pagans do heap coals of fire on their enemies' heads!" The reference was made to the fact that the municipality of Nagasaki had voted $3,500 to be expended in entertaining Russian prisoners enroute through the city.

The fact and the preliminary remark have given us a basis for a strong moral lesson—a living lesson in ethics, and it has a double edged application. Aside from the bravery, skill and endurance of the Japanese, one other thing has been very noticeable, the ethical bearing of this pagan people at war with a Christian nation. Not only have they exhibited remarkable fighting qualities, but these have been equalled if not surpassed by their humane and courteous treatment of the conquered forces. This people may know nothing of Christianity in our sense of the word—as we profess it—but in the majority of cases on record they seem to have practiced quite fully what the Great Teacher taught and what we are so used to hear preached—conduct that we have learned to regard as inseparable from the Christian spirit.

The Japanese have not stopped to argue with the world as to whether they were yellow or white, red or black; they have simply forged ahead in this battle for their rights in spite of prejudice against them, and have depended upon the righteousness of their cause and their conduct for the approval of the world. *Neither taunts, nor jeers, nor slander, nor misrepresentation have made them swerve in the least from the line laid out by themselves.*

Their enemy has been arrogant, tricky and merciless. In view of the means taken to defeat them and the odds against them, one would look for a pagan people to lose no opportunity nor time to get even at any cost. But they have not done so. Though occupied with one chief thought—victory, to save their country—at no time do we hear of inhuman treatment, of savage retaliation, not even of scoffing when the defenseless have been at their mercy a prisone[r] in their hands. On the other hand, forbearance, courtesy, gentleness have characterized every act. They have shown a Christian nation how a Christian should do. They have set an example for all other nations to follow in war or in peace. They have done more: they have set a standard for internal relations and they have given the white and the black alike of this country something to ponder upon.

And now when the rumors that the "bear" may be about ready to sue for peace reach us in vague whispers, we almost question whether the lesson has continued long enough to make the right impression upon the world—to lead to such an application as to bring about needed reforms at home. The question is: "Shall it be lost upon our own civilization in its double application?" Will our foes as a race parade with praise these virtues of the Japanese and refuse to practice them toward the people in its midst—a people at its mercy in many respects as much as the Russian prisoner, or conquered force is at Japan's mercy?

"With malice toward none" seems to have been written in the Japanese code of action and on their hearts as a people. This is the gist of the lesson to be learned by us all here, white and black alike.

The Negro race has been balancing on a pivotal point for some time. It has seen in the past few years especially so much of rage and hatred assailing it with its virulence for no righteous cause whatever, that there is danger of the balance being destroyed and the descent taking place on the wrong side. There is danger of retaliation by bursts of malice on those who smite so heavily. Yet this is the most unwise thing in which to indulge. Sane reasoning will see that, situated as we are, this indulgence would result in loss of great advantage to us. As a race noted already for its patience under great trials, it is absolutely necessary in view of all our surroundings that we make our claim good to this characteristic—that we seek to restrain rather than to inflame. We must put into practice the return of good for evil, the smothering of prejudice in our own breasts, and influence the ignorant masses to this end. God is not dead; conscience is not dead; and a steady pursuance of the path that leads to elevation and the right, reaching out for what is ours with no thought of malice, but in a spirit of manly patience; this will do more for us than by "tearing passion to tatters"[1] at every opportunity, ranting and threatening. We must believe that the pagan teaching before us cannot be lost wholly upon the stronger people about us.

These Japanese pagans are quiet and reposeful as a people, but they act. They are free from that swagger, brag and bluster which we find so common among us. Doing is the thing that tells after all, and effective doing is what we need to practice. I would not have the black man appear cowardly or clinging, or bereft of any manly qualities that tend to fix his status as a man and elevate him in the sight of the world, but I would have him shed those characteristics that impede his progress. I believe that he may take this nation so recently admitted among civilized nations as a teacher in many things and learn valuable lessons. He need not yield that which has cost him years to acquire; he can stand sturdily for right and show that behind his black skin is a soul to be admired.

It took an Ebed-Melech, a black-skinned Ethiopian, to show it to a king of apostate Judah, when he dared intervene for the Prophet Jeremiah's safety, but he knew how to win his cause with respect, and he received his reward in this life; Jehovah saw to it that he was delivered when Jerusalem was destroyed.[2]

The race wants deliverance from many things, and if pagans can afford us lessons through their victories, the least we can do with the added advantage of a Christian civilization is to try the same path to victory. Let us try more and more the heaping of coals. Prejudice and opposition may find this melting heat more effectual than all else in the end.

Notes

[1] [See *Hamlet*, act 3, scene 2, "It offends me to the soul to hear . . . . a robustious periwig-pated fellow tear a passion to tatters."]

2 [See Jeremiah 38:7.]

The Negro Criminal Class—How Best Reached, Part I

Voice of the Negro 2, no. 11 (1905): 803–804.

The criminal Negro is one of the heaviest burdens that the race has to carry today. Not that the Negro criminal is worse than any other criminal; nor that it can be proven that there is a larger proportion of criminals in this race than we find in any other races; nor that as yet there has been any special exhibition of great aptitude among Negroes for crime that amounts to genius. In fact the showing is in our favor in these respects, but notwithstanding this, we as a race are laboring under such serious disadvantages that we are not able to bear the extra burden of criminality with the same ease and indifference as representatives of other races.

We have to take cognizance of everything that threatens our welfare as a people. The world at large does not differentiate sufficiently as to the Negro. It refuses to see what President [Frank G.] Woodworth of Tugaloo University has endeavored to make clear—that there are ["]*Negroes and Negroes: crude, cultured, shiftless; thrifty, grotesque, urbane; immoral and grossly debased; clean and living the life of the Spirit.*" The Vardamans of the world know no distinctions, make no discriminations, brand all alike as a lower order of creation. Therefore Negro criminality cannot be ignored by us. We must not only ever strive to keep the upper classes ever moving on, but we must make strenuous efforts to rid ourselves of this incubus that weighs us down, clinging as tenaciously for our general destruction as did the Old Man of the Sea to Sinbad the Sailor, and equally necessary to our safety to be dislodged.[1]

It falls to the Negro to do this work. No one else understands the conditions as well as he. It cannot be left to the courts to handle and meet our punishment. The philanthropists and the sociologists of the white race are unable to grasp all the elements of the problem and see their real relations. We alone know all the phases of Negro life, situation and environment that escape the most observant of other races; we alone know the Negro's soul, his struggles, the seeming hopelessness of endeavor at times, and the consequent despair that assails and drags so many down in its darkness.

First of all, not every Negro who commits crime is to be regarded as a criminal. Public sentiment has too often forced members of the race into deeds classed as criminal, but these are not real criminals. The press, the pulpit and the mob have far too many times helped to *make* criminals among us. There are those in the criminal ranks who are criminals by instinct, and those who have been made so by environment. On the other hand, many are forced into criminal paths because of the censure, the prejudice, the scorn and contempt poured out upon the race; because of the refusal to treat it as made up of human beings with any claims to consideration or respect; because it has been hunted and harried—innocent and guilty alike—at the slightest intimation of possible guilt on the part of the vicious or irresponsible among the whites. The result has been that the weak and ignorant Negroes, forbidden aspiration, falsely accused, restive under injustice and discouraged, have become desperate and have often viciously resolved to live DOWN to the reputation forced upon them. The white people then must be blamed for a share of Negro criminality. All things that are designed to degrade a race, have a tendency to instill into it a disregard for law and order. So criminals are frequently made by those who villify and arouse antagonisms. It is the Dixons who go into hysterics over every advance that the Negro makes—seeing in it nothing but danger to the Saxon, sounding notes of warning because Negroes are counselled to become employers and independent—these constitute a most dangerous class of men. They may wear the livery of ministers of the Gospel and pose as friends of the Negro, but such men who inflame passions and invite classes and colors to war against each other, are the worst of anarchists and are our most vicious foes.

Beginning with such as these men of education and going on down until the jealous poor white is reached, we see everywhere hatred and vindictiveness evinced in words and deeds that go a long way to help increase Negro criminality. Coupled with this the Southern white man's preference for Negro women, as shown by the numerous cases of cohabitation, and we have another element equally as strong that tends to lead to crime among Negro men.

With this preface which makes no excuse for crime other than to throw upon the proper ones the *onus* or the burden for a certain amount of it, we now turn to the direct consideration of the criminal.

In this century when the individual counts for so much, when we have repudiated the idea that the work of the world must be done with the masses as such, we know that we must seek for that cure which will reach each case, never forgetting that the Negro is a man, and that every effort toward the reform of the hardened criminal must be accompanied by an undoubted interest in the MAN, himself, by a recognition of the manhood spark when found in the most degraded, and by an endeavor to arouse that self-respect which the villifiers of the race seek to stifle. The Negro must be made to feel that crime hurts self more than any one else.

The efforts that are being put forth in penal institutions for reform are in general good, but the hardened criminal Negro needs to feel that the cure undertaken is because of an interest in himself, the man; he wants to be reached by the personal touch, to understand that sermons, lectures, entertainments, are not mere amusements.

Today, the medical world is considering insanity, drunkenness, tuberculosis—various ailments and conditions of mankind with a view to ascertain the best treatment for all of them as *diseases,* and the question has been raised, "Is not crime too a disease?" At least kleptomania is so considered. With no attempt to go into this subject from any expert standpoint, we all admit that there is some sort of contagion in crime, and this possibility of contagion enters in when we consider the hardened criminal who should not be allowed to infect others. So aside from the appeal to the subverted moral nature to make itself clean and move on higher levels which must ever have a place, there should be laws that will segregate the hardened criminal prisoner from those not yet steeped in crime. We would go still further and hold with some of our sociological experts that after individual study reveals the fact that there is no hopeful basis for reform and that viciousness is too deep-seated to correct, then there should be given no opportunity for the return of these parties to old ways or to corrupt others.

But the pardoned prisoner is to be reached—the convict when he faces the world again with every door leading to a better life closed against him. For this purpose we need Shelters and Homes such as the Salvation Army maintains, where the fallen may receive a welcome, a kind word of encouragement, and a chance for a new life. The more rapidly we become men who can employ our own people, the more aid we can give in a noble endeavor to keep those who see no future and who seem to care for none.

In close connection with this comes the thought of the need to exert ourselves by voice and pen to secure justice for the accused Negro; for where injustice presses in conviction for crime it is almost impossible to find the individual criminal able to listen to *moral* appeals. The criminal as well as any other class of men desires to see *works,* and laws must be sought that will treat all alike. So much in passing for the hardened criminal class.

Note

1 [See Richard Burton (1821–1890), *Book of One Thousand and One Nights* (1855–1858), the fifth voyage of Sinbad.]

The Negro Criminal Class—How Best Reached, Part II

Voice of the Negro 2, no. 12 (1905): 867–869.

But there is a class that gives far more concern for the future—the class of young people—children and youth—in a fair way to become recruits for the criminal army because of criminal environment. It seems to me that our greatest work lies right here. We must diminish criminality by not adding to its ranks. Here the task is prodigious, for it is scattered—in a process of growth—in every slum of every, city, and every degraded home that exists. Here it is that the Institutional system—the Social Settlement idea—that has planted so many centers of higher life in these plague-spots, makes one of the best weapons to fight the evil. If we could have such agencies wherever our people congregate in numbers, much criminality might be reached and much averted. Such reformatory institutions as those planted by Professor [Albert Bushnell] Hart and Dr. [John H.] Smythe in their respective sections are also of the greatest value in uprooting criminal tendencies, in training to upright lives, in imbueing with high motives wayward youth, and in affording proper incentive to honorable action. We need a score or more of just such institutions, and if they could be largely modeled after the famous George Junior Republic in New York State which takes black and white alike and seeks to make good citizens by a wisely directed scheme of self-government, I feel that we would make use of the strongest means possible to lower the criminal record of the race.[1] It is Preventive after all that we must most largely seek— Preventive that includes the reform of the young in a plastic state.

This all calls for educators of the right sort—the best brain of the race—to push forward the work of educating *out of crime* as it were; and here our efforts must also make a center. Negro men and women of self-sacrificing lives must come forward to take up the burden, and our schools and colleges must teach something more than the mere love of knowledge. There should be inculcated a home missionary spirit. We are too apt to be more concerned, like Dickens' Mrs. Jellyby, about Borrioboola-Gha, in Africa, than about our children of the home. Schools must teach Negro youth to see that there is much to be desired in a life that spells "*self-sacrifice.*" We have but comparatively few young men and women, ready to lay themselves on any kind of altar for the good of the race. They are too much concerned with self alone. A great responsibility rests upon us here in the matter of education of the whole race that the rank of educators may be kept full of those who are devoted to the profession and who understand what education means—who think more of the formation of character in the young lives about them than of merely imparting knowledge, those who look upon teaching as a sacred duty—a golden opportunity for shaping youth, making it honest, clean-minded, and morally sound and healthy, and at the same time instilling into it the cosmic moral element that makes each human being a humanitarian in the widest and best sense—a true lover of his fellows. This is the root of the whole matter. Unless we have these workers who will teach and direct aright, creating new lovers of work for the race, we cannot expect much reform of either the hardened criminal or the growing class. After all the matter resolves itself into a matter of broad education. These teachers must do the work in slums, in institutions, in reformatory schools. They must go further in house to house efforts, helping to keep boys and girls from the streets, finding work for idle hands. When we can make the majority of parents understand and accept their responsibility for the behavior of their children we shall see a great improvement in the race and a diminution of crime.

In this connection one thing must not be overlooked, and that is the power the clergy should exert in frowning upon all forms of vice, in both the folds of the churches and in society at large. Upright ministers of the Gospel can do much to keep the Negro people in the right path, but the Negro minister himself must follow the upright path in a rigidly straight course if he is to have influence over those who go astray, and whom he would lead in right paths. An ungodly, immoral clergy as leaders will be far worse for any people than to be without leaders. Then the respectable element of the race must not countenance vice by placing in society at their side who lived lives of sin. No race can uplift itself, or can hope to eliminate or reduce criminality when there is no distinction in society between the vicious and the virtuous. Christian brotherhood calls for all possible Christian sympathy and aid but it does not call for such equality.

It is also necessary that such a race sentiment be created that will refuse to harbor criminals or shield them from justice, and this must begin with the higher classes and permeate the whole as far as possible. We need have no fear of too much education or of the theory that it makes dangerous criminals—a theory that our enemies are striving with might and main to apply to the Negro, and to the Negro alone. We can dismiss it with the pertinent words of one of the editors of Harper's Weekly—that while education is not to be considered as a moral panacea, there is plenty of expert testimony that by developing intelligence it *makes for the promotion of right conduct.*

To sum up then what must be done for the Negro criminal class we say, let the white people endeavor to see the good in us and not provoke to crime. Let us as a race join hands in educational circles, in society and in church to put the ban upon crime of every grade, setting up a high ideal of conduct, and instilling into the minds of the young people not only right ideas as to the same, but also a responsibility for their fellows which will result in raising up workers necessary to all organized efforts for reform. Then we are to adopt all the material means which serve to help up the fallen of any race, and to stifle crime in its incipiency, guard the youth in homes, agitate for legislation that will render equal justice to all and enforce respect for law and order, plead for that general exercise of Christian f[e]llowship that will lead to confidence and respect for self and others—working, in brief, to spread that teaching wide that shall bring about a correct understanding by all nationalities as to what is true success in life, by means of godly preachers, self-sacrificing, intelligent teachers, devoted philanthropists and earnest students of sociology.

The wide world everywhere is awakening to the dangers confronting society at large. When such a noted corporation lawyer for great Trusts as James B. Dill—a man I am proud to claim as a college class-mate—has raised his voice in warning against the dangers of the times—against "*pretence, graft and the easy dollar*," and has left his lucrative position for a judgeship in New Jersey; when such an educator as Dr. [Arthur Twining] Hadley, of Yale, has sounded a note of warning concerning ideal *success*; when President Roosevelt has spoken plainly of the "*pursuit, possession and perils of money*;" when even in the heart of the South a courageous Atlanta clergyman tells his people that the man who does not admit and live up to the fraternity of the Negro *is not a Christian*—when such as these "*light beacons and set danger signals*," then there is hope of help from the *outside* in solving some of our problems, leaving us to that work which we must do for ourselves.

But it must be work; it must not be talk; we must do. It is the time when *doing* counts, when glittering generalities must give way to *working out* prosaic specific details, when projects must be boldly launched and carried forward with zeal and determination, when we must cease being selfish and give the best of ourselves to the study of how to meet our difficulties and then bravely, manfully, cheerfully, gladly face and overcome them.

There will never be a time until this earth is regenerated when crime will disappear from its face. We are simply to aid Providence in all possible ways to better our portion of the world. If by vigorous use of means suggested we can block the wheels of crime, and keep the race from slipping further into criminality, we have done our part toward casting off the burden and making the future one full of hopeful possibilities.

Note

1 [The philanthropist William R. George (1866-1936) founded the first of several communities for wayward youth in 1895 in Freeville, New York.]

The Negro's Program for 1906

Voice of the Negro 3, no. 1 (1906): 47–49.

With the consensus of opinion that the Negro question is a problem, the irrefutable fact that the race is facing new, vicious forms of antagonism, and the sentiment clearly understood, as voiced by the Boston Congregationalist, that in both Church and State today there is less solicitude for the Negro as such—with these confronting us, our future movements constitute an important question. That we must look far ahead, plan wisely and act discreetly are foregone conclusions. If we cannot forge ahead as rapidly as we would like, we must at least determine upon a course by which we may maintain our own in all lines pertaining to our best interests as a race.

Our fortunes in the realm of politics have been varied in the past. We have been misled, slandered, abused and routed wherever possible to such an extent that as a profession it is to be shunned. Still, we cannot abandon politics altogether. There is too much at stake. It would be unjust to ourselves. As citizens and as taxpayers we have a duty to perform. We should never be content to rest as a disfranchised people, not even if the price in the South be its reduction of representation. Such a plan amounts to acquiescence in our position there, and is a loophole for further attempts to curtail our rights. This we must plan to resist. At the same time we must see to it that there is a greater development of morality in politics. We must stand more upon principle. It is not going to pay us to bend hither and thither, becoming shifty politicians, following the loaves and fishes until spewed out from all parties as unreliable. We cannot afford to build up the reputation of being a purchasable people. Such a course is inexpedient for even temporary gain in power or position. We must keep a watchfull attitude in respect to a legislation tending to degrade us and wrestle our rights from us, and plan to attack all such laws. We must know our rights and maintain them. To this end we must unite in definite understanding as to the best policy to pursue.

Here is where radical organization should find its *raison d'[ê]tre*. System is necessary, discussion is fruitful, counsel is wise, union is strengthening to any cause. Strong state organizations federated into a truly national one would do the best possible service. But its composition must be kept along with the able, the thoughtful, the serious, the cautious—those who put the interests of the race above personal preferrment, jealousies, and antipathies. Exploitation of any individual or furtherance of local ambitions for leadership will destroy usefulness, and greater opposition will be aroused if they foster the spirit of antagonism between the races, seeking to widen the already dangerous breach. With a determination to promote harmony, to work patiently, to make wise selection of all instruments meant to push forward our interests, but yet maintaining a sturdy manhood in all things, a national organization must make for progress. It can be made a power, helping to guide the race in the many perplexing, humiliating and dangerous situations that threaten us more and more as the Vardamans and Tillmans and Dixons strive to stir up the clamorous mobs against us.

There are two things, however we must get and keep getting—property and education. They are to be our two great levers. We cannot have too much of either. We must have that before which the world has always bowed—wealth and learning. They are our keys to future progress. We are too largely an easy-go-lucky people, spending as we go. We are industrio[u]s as a whole, but we have not learned well the art of saving. We must cease indulging in so many childish gratifications; we must preach against excursions, especially those that build up the railroads so largely that in turn treat us to Jim Crow cars and Jim Crow usage, against entertainments, against dress beyond our position, against high living—all a waste to our savings. We must urge and encourage by every possible means the love of possession, of home ownership. There is no danger of making misers of the Negro just now. This is largely an undeveloped instinct among us. There is a close connection between our voting rights—our civil rights generally—and this matter of property. We will perforce be in a position to demand more when we possess more. With money we can get much more consideration from the law which though it may be twisted to our hurt at times, must still be looked upon as our bulwark, our rock of safety.

As to our program in education there is but one answer—we must continue to educate in the broadest sense of that term; education is to be our salvation. To reduce illiteracy is not only to reduce criminality, but to open doors, make channels, new paths, force recognition. The education of the Negro should have afforded a topic for much discussion in the past few years, and we have nearly been swept into a chasm, by the whirlwind of opinions on the subject, which would set up a distinctive education for us that would end in making the race a purely industrial one. It speaks well for our growing acumen that it is being seen more and more as a danger to be avoided. With this warped conception crushing inspiration and aspiration, oppressed by material necessities, facing shut doors for opportunity, our enemies are about to become victorious; aided by our blind friends who lament the education of the race above the spheres it may occupy and then lend aid and countenance to the limitation of those spheres. We cannot, must not, will not agree to be mere hewers of wood and drawers of water—an inferior class laboring for a superior. We need industrial training, along all lines needed by other races, but we must never cease to push forward to higher planes all those who have a visage of talent or aspiration. We must do more—we must look on myriad ways to the possible creation of such talent and aspiration. "Industrial education for all, primary education for many, college education for the few"—Bishop [Charles Betts] Galloway's utterance at the Inter-Church Federation Council in New York—should be changed to "Primary education for all, industrial education for the many, higher education for all whom we can inspire to reach upward to higher spheres." We must get a clear perspective of our life as it should be—our future as we would have it, an eagle's view as it were, which will help to set up an ideal to which we must work and which no race can afford to be without. There is no future of great things for any race that is merely an industrial one, or purely a money-getting one. Neither one alone, nor the two combined can do for our future only that which they may do for any race—assist in its material development and the production of brawn. We must produce great men—poets, philosophers, linguists, scientists—men and women who can live and express the higher life in all its forms. "No man is really free who has not the spirit and art to reproduce himself ideally in some form," asserts a Southern writer in the Independent, and this writer even further declares that the Negro's "hope and great salvation lie in the realm of art"—"his great opportunity";—and *not in the industrial world.* The world knows this to be the truth and we must not let sophistry blind us to the fact. Education is our strong line of advance and the higher lines are surest to lift us to a higher rank as a people.

Along with this we must take another part in shaping educational matters; we must obtain a more equitable division of school funds, plan for longer terms in out of the way school districts, and we must insist rigorously upon efficiency in teachers, demanding professional training, putting down sham and superficiality, refusing ignorant and blatant leaders. Lastly, we must educate ourselves to look the race squarely in the face, to find its predominant faults, vices, weaknesses in mental and moral lines and seek earnestly for measures leading to their eradication.

All of this necessary elimination, all of this forward striving, must come through the wise efforts of the combination of these four forces I have sketched. Politics, property, racial organization and education must work hand in hand. They are inter-dependent, calling for strong support each of the other. They are the great instruments for self help, and self help is what we are to rely upon in large part in the future. After all the real growth of any people must be endigenous—from within.

English Principle vs. American Prejudice

Voice of the Negro 3, no. 5 (1906): 346–349.

A great Irish orator in speaking of Irish liberty once remarked that "he had rocked it in its cradle and had followed it to its grave."[1] The words came from the depths of an Irish heart filled full of despair at the thought of the utter futility of the long struggle to obtain manhood rights. He had seen the ground slipping from beneath the feet of Ireland's sons and had recognized that the power of oppression backed by prejudice was to push them into the gulf at last.

Were this Irish patriot living today I am sure he would know how to sympathize with the Negro in America, though all Irishmen are not sympathetic as one would expect them to be after their long struggle for their rights. But though England was then crushing Ireland in her iron grasp, at the same time, the English heart was responding to the suffering of the race in chains on this side the Atlantic. Life is full of just such inconsistencies, and it is not our purpose here to discuss the motives that led a long line of English statesmen down to the present time to be blind to wants and sufferings as they have long existed in the Emerald Isle. England is not the only country that sees more clearly at a telescopic range than at a microscopic one.

We here are facing the fact that in more than one Negro's heart these sad words of the Irish speaker fall with a chill of prophesy as we see rights, privileges, friends slipping away from us, and as we realize that unless we can turn the tide we too shall see the vision of our own liberty sinking into its grave. But England has been a defender of the slave in very large measure, and if we separate political England from social England we shall find that no matter how the former felt toward Ireland, the Negro and his wrongs appealed keenly to the latter. From the day when those two noble women—Ellen and Anna Richardson from their home in Newcastle-upon-Tyne, conceived the idea of freeing Frederick Douglass—buying himself for himself—from that day to this the Negro has known a bond of union with the "mother country." From that day of ransom the race has had countless reason and opportunities for discovering that social England at least frowns upon the prejudice that withers us in America. We have been able to count upon its sympathy, its aid and thorough support through all these years. The question that arises at the present time is: *Will England be able to withstand the American invasion of snobbery and prejudice?*

The American who bases his claim of superiority upon the unstable foundation of Saxon purity of blood possesses in some channels the pioneer instinct in an exaggerated form. He is aggressive beyond tolerance. He is looked upon with suspicion in foreign lands because of this dominating aggressiveness. Commercially he is persistent beyond expression. He has pushed his way into every nook and corner. He has set up his advertising boards on the Roman Campagna, and even dared to announce the merits of his goods upon the face of the Alps. His trolley cars reach out for the boulevard of the Nevskey Prospect in Russia's capital and his "tubes" bore through underground London. To all this we have no objection and no criticism. We are able in spite of our ostracised situation to view such achievements with patriotic pride. But there are limits that should be maintained in the invasions the white American contemplates. There are spheres outside of which the intended Americanization should pause. When American prejudice is carried abroad and attempts made to foist it upon foreign nations to the Negro's hurt, then it is time to call a halt with all possible vigor.

The determination of a certain class of Americans to instill this poison into the veins of foreign cities, and to impose the practices of this prejudice upon other people almost by force and arms,[2] is very evident. These persons are settled upon one course—to pursue the man of color to his death, to leave no stone unturned to make others take the same attitude. With Dixon spewing out of his mouth at every opportunity such filth as can only be compared to that proceeding from error, so vividly portrayed in Spenser's famous allegory,[3] and with echoes here and there of applause at the virulent attacks upon us as a race, and with the deadly quiet of our friends when such miscreants would make the world believe us to be fiends and brutes—with all this in mind it is like turning to the mountain breezes after being forced to pass through vile sewers, when we contemplate English principle in these matters.

This English principle is as yet untouched. In England though we are men and women yet we must be watchful. We hear again and again of this attempt to change English sentiment, illustrating the same hate that impelled to an incident that took place in London when the great Methodist Ecumenical Conference met there in 1901—an incident of which papers on both sides of the Atlantic took cognizance. It illustrates both the prejudice and the principle of which we speak. By the impertinent demand of a few white Americans at one of the most fashionable of the West End hostelries, an audacious attempt was made to regulate the customs of an English hotel and inject prejudice. This demand accompanied by a threat to leave the hotel unless complied with, insisted upon the turning out from the hotel of a party of colored guests, representatives of the African Methodist Episcopal Church. In America we well can imagine what would have been the result of such a piece of snobbery—the colored guests would have been asked to seek entertainment elsewhere. But they do things differently in England, God be praised.

These prejudiced Americans took no thought or care as to the status of these colored guests who were all people of distinction—three of them bishops of the church and one connected with societies of learning on both continents.

But it was a Waterloo for the snobs, for the proprietor, Mr. Harry Richardson, cooly met their ultimatum with the manly assertion that his house knew no distinction on account of color, and that he should not insult his colored guests by complying with such demands, though all his white guests should decide to leave the hotel in a body.[4]

Two or three white color mad people left, but the colored guests all remained. In fact their number was augmented later, when the English committee on entertainment learned of the incident; for the arrangement that was to provide for these delegates at another palatial hotel was modified to leave this company at St. Ermins so that English principle should not suffer from American prejudice. There were many other incidents coming under the writer's personal observation and connected with the great Convention of Methodist bodies from the world over, that could be given to illustrate the efforts of certain white members of the American contingent to insult and humiliate the colored delegates, *but English principle was at stake and they were never successful though the endeavor was plainly apparent.*

As the proprietor of St. Ermins said to the writer, these same Americans who objected to colored people, cottled and ogled East Indian guests of color, who lolled upon the same divans with them in unmentionable attitudes and apparel and with equally unmentionable manners. He could not understand the prejudice. It was no wonder that the London press gleefully grasped the opportunity for most sarcastic remarks on the boasted freedom of America "*at this display,*" as it put it, "*of the democratic spirit among the champions of freedom and the equality of man;*" and it reached the climax of satirical irony when one newspaper contrasted this exhibition of prejudice with the conduct of the manager of the hotel, who, it said "*took his stand upon the slavish principle of our effete and benighted country [England][5] that as long as a man behaved himself and paid his bills he should not be kicked into the street.*" The italics are ours, but the irony is England's own. Would that it had cut sufficiently deep to prevent any further attempt to create prejudice in England. But such hate is hydra-headed, and it springs up in foreign lands wherever the prejudiced Americans set their feet. These seem to feel that it is necessary to show their prejudice in order to mark themselves as superior. *They forget that it is bad breeding for guests to attempt to regulate the customs of their hosts.*

We have this to meet and every man of color has the welfare of the race to keep in mind when before people of other nations. It is the question of keeping or losing ground that must be ever before us here and elsewhere. The English principle must be kept alive, by every art known to us, by our best representation and by our determination to hold fast to our liberties as men and women.

And here is the point of our criticism. We have friends, who disapprove of this virulent spirit, but so few will take the stand necessary to prevent the subtile changes this vicious element seeks to make in any sentiment which its finds to be in our favor. So many of our friends fear too greatly offending personal prejudices by doing the right thing for us. They lack both grit and grace—a most necessary combination to the maintenance of the principle of human rights which if destroyed weakens the whole people. Injustice, long practised, strangles any nation in the coils of its own weaving.

If our individual friends and the friendly press would simply refuse to be swayed by such intolerance, we would ask nothing more.

As long as prejudice and injustice are exhibited and tolerated so long shall we have these questions to consider. We ask for a sturdy stand on principle, not maudlin sympathy. We beg the exhibition of that strength of manhood and womanhood which shall dare to treat us as men and women—the only real "square deal" we ask or need. Were the Irish orator living today he might see in England's change of attitude toward Ireland cause for something of renewed hope. He might believe that the "Eternal years of God" do after all belong to *Truth*, but he would know by experience as well that it is hard to keep that Truth *constantly uttered* so that Hope *may* "spring eternal" in the breast of the oppressed races.[6] If we can as a race do this thing we may hope that it will not be ours to follow our liberties to their grave.

Notes

1 [Scarborough takes this quotation from a speech given by Frederick Douglass in January 1883 and printed in James Monroe Gregory's *Frederick Douglass, the Orator* (Springfield, Mass.: Willey, 1893), chapter 6. The Irish orator may be John Philpot Curran (1750–1814).]

2 [For examples of the Ciceronian phrase *vi et armis*, see Cicero's speeches *Pro Milone*, 27.73, and *Pro Sestio*, 36.78.]

3 [See Edmund Spenser (c. 1552–1599), *Faerie Queene* (1594), canto 1, stanza 1, lines 1–9.]

4 [On this incident see also *Autobiography*, pp. 164–165, 173, and 175.]

5 [The square brackets around "England" are in the original.]

6 [See William Cullen Bryant (1794–1878), "Battlefield" (1839), stanza 9, lines 1–4: "Truth, crushed to earth, will rise again; / The eternal years of God are hers; / But error wounded writhes in pain; / And dies among her worshippers." See also Alexander Pope (1688–1744), "An Essay on Man, Epistle I," (1733), line 95.]

A Subsidized North

Voice of the Negro 4, no. 1 (1907): 31–34.

If we were to be called to strict account according to the dictionaries for the use of the word "subsidized" in the title of this paper, we might be criticized in regard to the validity of the charge which our use of the word implies. But it must be acknowledged that even the primary sense of the word involves the purchasing of the assistance of anyone by giving aid or subsidy in return, and certainly its modern use in this day of trusts and graft is clearly the securing of co-operation by the buying over one whose services are desired in exchange. No one need be over critical, however, as to its use. The facts are before us.

We assuredly have a section of country this side of Mason and Dixon's line that has gradually retreated from its former position of independent thought and action and is found patting and smoothing, bowing and kow-towing to, condoling and sympathizing with a section of country which less than two decades ago it dared to criticize if wrong, to defy its boasted power, to disagree with its lawless assumption, and to deny its right to dictate what should be thought, said and done by the country at large. There is no fact more apparent than this:—the change in the mind and the attitude of the North in all lines touching matters of public policy, and especially that policy which in any way relates directly to the Negro race.

Just after the Civil War when the two sections of this country were rent asunder and when gloom, despair and demoralization hovered over the entire land there was large sympathy in the North for the emancipated slave; friends of the Negro were in evidence everywhere, and not afraid to disclose their sympathy and friendship. They contributed largely of their means to aid schools and churches for the poor "freedman." The best classes went South to teach and to help the newly enfranchised race. In fact the heart of the North was so fired with sympathy and good will that nothing was left undone that could be done to reach and improve the condition of the recently enslaved people.

Then came Reconstruction and the ballot was given the race and other safe guards were thrown about it to insure it (as was supposed at that time) protection in its civil and political rights; and the 13th, 14th and 15th Amendments to the Constitution were meant to settle irrevocably the question of slavery, of citizenship, of the ballot, for all time to come.

But has the question been settled? Were the safeguards sufficient to protect the Negro people? Did the Amendments make them really citizens? Did even the Emancipation Proclamation free the Negro in reality?

I say, No; only in part and for a time. The white South from start to finish never intended to submit to what these enactments were designed to bring about. Its seeming acquiescence at first was merely a matter of expediency and because it was right up against the inevitable. It knew how to wait and to work for the opportunities it craved. These came one at a time, and now forty and more years afterwards we face the results of the efforts to achieve its purpose through manipulation of Northern sentiment[,] thought and action.

From the days of Reconstruction there has been a continuous appeal to the North for sympathy for the white South. The South has kept its hand on the pulse of the North and its heel on the neck of the Negro, coaxing the former into abettal of its plans and driving the latter back into the next thing to slavery—*peonage*. It has declared that it loved the Negro and knew best how to deal with him and begged to be let alone to do so and we know how it has dealt with him. It has courted Northern capital to help its commercial and educational interests and securing it, the two sections became cemented in closer union; for where a man's money is there is his heart also. With this same end in view the South has sought to extend its domestic relations by intermarriage between the sections, and thus strengthen the bond. It has made the most it could out of the appeal of Anglo-Saxon brotherhood. With all this it has kept before the world the Negro's mistakes, and heralded with gross exaggeration the vices of the individual, claiming them as racial. It has made no discrimination between good and bad, ignorant and educated, offensive and inoffensive, innocent and guilty. It has bunched all the race as one— a thing to be maligned, slandered, misrepresented continually that it might make the world believe it as thoroughly black as painted, something to be spurned, scorned, hissed, and spat upon by all. It has been a most apt pupil in following Chateaubriand's political direction: "*Throw mud, throw mud continually; something will be sure to stick.*" Getting bolder by boasting which receives no countercheck and by deeds that are only faintly condemned, the Vardamans, the Tillmans, the Dixons, the Hok[e] Smiths and men of that clas[s] have not only vaulted into the saddle in their own section, but are now riding rough shod over the entire country, bound upon but one errand—to create sentiment against the Negro and strengthen their own cause as represented by themselves. Such emissaries as these are unwearying in their determination. What have they accomplished? I say "The subsidization" of the North. Friends have been diverted in sympathy or rendered indifferent. The North has grown silent and has held hands off in matters pertaining to our welfare. For fear of bringing about abuse, losing trade, disturbing domestic peace and tranquility, the North has grown to dislike or fear to take up our cause, no matter what injustice we suffer. It is far cheaper to bewail the sufferings of the Russians or of the Cubans. It dreads the charge from the South of having greater love for Afric-blood than Anglo-Saxon, and dislikes to have it said that it is disrupting the sentiment of union. The North has reached the point where it is ready to echo almost anything the South chooses to assert. It is afraid of hurting the feelings of the white South. It thinks the early education of the Negro a mistake, the ballot a blunder, the Negro a fiend. It has placed its opinions at the feet of the South and its mind entirely at the South's suggestive influence. Sectionally it has become hypnotized by the assiduous efforts of these men who with others have succeeded in muzzling the press, muzzling the pulpit, muzzling the platform—muzzling the mouths of nearly all who in the past saw any good in the Negro people.

The result of their activity has been such that in many instances the Negro in the North now finds himself deprived of facilities for moral, intellectual and social improvements which he once enjoyed. He is denied the right of becoming a member of the Y. M. C. A. because of Southern patrons. He is shut out from the church because of Southern membership. He is even debarred from hotel and restaurant accommodations because of Southern guests. He is refused admittance to many schools of learning, notably Princeton, because of Southern white students. He is not even allowed the privilege of bathing in the ocean, notably at Atlantic City, because of white people from the South who, as guests, object to it. Thus churches are closed, schools, hotels, restaurants—all places of culture and elevation and comfort are closed to the race and even those of amusement except as *a rule the dive, the brothel, the saloon and prize-ring*; and now since [Joe] Gans won in the last named, Baltimore is trying to see to it that he shall not meet a white man there again if it is possible to prevent it.[1]

So the North unites with the South to make criminals out of the race and then unites in blaming it because it becomes criminal.

This same pernicious activity, which we have mentioned as determined to invade the North to imbue it with its sentiments, almost forced the Jim Crow car into the very doors of Philadelphia and did actually sen[d] them across the Ohio river, even into the capital of the state—Columbus. But we have some friends not yet subsidized. In this last case, Gov. [George K.] Nash drove them back to Southern limits, when as president of the Ohio Colored League I had the honor to ask his intervention, and I must admit that when I made a public protest because of the discrimination which refused Mr. Wilder, a distinguished colored citizen of South Carolina and Ex-postmaster of Columbia, and myself a glass of soda water at Ocean Grove, [New Jersey,] the authorities quickly put an end to such proscription at this place.[2]

But I repeat, that these men of the South have come North with their theories and beliefs. They are to be found in all professions and business activities here. So much under the influence are the majority of the newspapers of the North to-day that it is difficult for a black man to get the hearing that he demands. They will not listen to him.

Money talks it is said and the South knows it well. It has obtained its foothold and it proposes to use its power to carry out its mission—to keep the Negro down, push him into the brothel, keep him an inferior—*make him a criminal.*

Some one in writing for the *California Outlook* has chosen to see a wholesome effect in the Gans-Nelson prize fight on the race problem and says that the Negro prize fighter is of moral and commercial good to the race—asserting that a colored minister, orator, or editor could not accomplish in a few short hours in his profession what Gans did in the same length of time.

This brings a long train of pertinent suggestions with it. Are we to be forced to conclude that the weapons of evil are to be more potential in the adjustment of the race question than Christianity? I am not ready to accept this conclusion, but it is a sad commentary on the Christianity of our white brethren that the Negro gets more consideration in the saloons, in the brothels, in the dives, in the prize ring than in the churches; and it is not surprising that so many of the race are to be found in these places of evil. For this the white clergy are largely to blame. Fearless men in the pulpit could do great good in influencing their hearers to see the right and do the right, in averting clashing and trouble; but Ah,—sad to say,—men of the cloth seem to have allowed themselves to be subsidized with the rest of the world.

And n[o]w we hear the frantic appeal of John Temple Graves, that Atlanta editor who, with Messrs. Hoke Smith, and others of that city, were the real instigators of the disgraceful and infamous riot that has fired all our hearts with indignation. By constantly denouncing the race, they sought for selfish ends to excite race antagonism, and now dare cry aloud to the North to sympathize with them. It is to be hoped that this last outrage upon the Negro will open the eyes of the North and deter it at least from uttering maudlin sentiments over the South in this case, if it does not make it ashamed as well of upholding a section that will stoop to such conduct. The North will do the South its best real service if it denounces such barbarism and sternly impress the lesson couched in the words of one who has declared that the South *fails to read her problem aright, if she permits lynching and torture and bloodshed to prevail to the debauching of her youth and to the desperation of her blacks—that in short her blood will be on her own head, for as surely as she sows cruelty, she shall reap horror.*

I saw with deep conviction that the North has become *a subsidized section.* All the facts and conditions go to prove it. What can we do about it[?] In the face of our present situation it seems a necessity to make a fresh appeal to this part of the country to regain its clear head, to look forward to the end, to discern right from wrong, to call unflinchingly for justice, to discriminate between the criminal individuals and the race as a whole so largely innocent, industrious and law-abiding, aspiring but to possession and enjoyment of homes, education and wealth. Since this last awful tragedy in Atlanta it is borne in upon all thoughtful persons of either race that such criminal lawlessness cannot continue.

It must receive a proper check. The Negro as a race does not uphold the criminal class. We are striving to root out crime, but we do demand the protection of the law. The best white men say they cannot control the mobs that riot and kill innocent and guilty indiscriminately. Then how can they, who are so powerless with all the law's machinery at their command, expect the best men of color to control the brute element of color without assistance of any kind, and we may add without the encouragement that comes from protection of the innocent? The proper check of crime can only come when it is realized that forcing the race apart from all that is high and good is forcing it into crime, when it is seen that false charges, must in the very nature of events, come home to roost like curses, when it is understood that retaliation never settles any problem, when both North and South, the white people, are willing to acknowledge that the race is worth conciliating, and that the hoodlum white element must be taken sharply in hand when it sets out on a rampage of Negro hunting.

This work should begin right here in the North, which must be made to feel that it is *particeps criminis* with the South in the making of Negro criminals, when it sanctions by voice, by pen or silence the determination of the South to force the Negro to the wall. The North must awake to its situation and cease to echo every view set forth by the South because the South says so. It must refuse to countenance anything that panders to race prejudice if it would show itself free from Southern influence. All incentives to mob violence, such as false charges, exaggerated reports, racial abuse in the newspapers and the production of such plays as the infamous "Clansman" must not only be denounced, but forbidden, if possible. The abuse of the race by Tillman and his class must be stopped. The strenuous objections of the members of the race accomplished this in one instance in Dayton, Ohio, where the Y. M. C. A. asked this Negro hater at the request of the colored people, not to touch the Negro theme, and surprising to say he really consented to do so. Somebody must move with determination in such matters.

It is intimated that the race is not wanted in the South as laborers. Wisdom should lead both sections to cultivate a little more of the telescopic vision than the microscopic—a long range of sight that see[s] far ahead all things and their relation, the vision of the eagle that sees more than the beetle with its short range, that confines the sight to one thing close at hand and magnifies it out of all proportions to other things. The right conception of truth, right and justice requires that we look well to the future advantages. We are needed in the development of this country and this country should never repudiate the Negro. The country that can take in and assimilate the vast foreign element that swarms to America on every ship—an element with so much viciousness and ignorance, selfishness and lawlessness—this country should not hesitate to protect and deal justly with the millions of Negroes born here, native to its customs, its religion and its laws, a race that has been so long-suffering, peaceful, forgiving, and one that has given its life blood for the Union.

Will the North heed our cry and our protest? Will it regain its ascendancy and lead toward the path of peace between white and black? We need its active interference and it should begin soon. The Negro people stand ready to cooperate with those who will stand with them for law and order, for peace and fraternity, for right and justice. There is but one path to peace we declare to both North and South—to use the law for the protection and the punishment of both white and black alike, to practice the true Christianity that is preached and to leave the door of hope open to the Negro as to any other people.

WILL THE NORTH SHAKE OFF THE HYPNOTIC INFLUENCE OF THE SOUTHERN FRENZY, THE INFLUENCE THAT HAS BEEN SO SUCCESSFULLY EXERCISED OVER IT—AND LEAD FOR PEACE—FOLLOW LIGHT AND DO THE RIGHT?

Notes

1 [The African American boxer Joe Gans (1874–1910) was declared victor over Oscar "Battling" Nelson (1882–1954) in a match fought at Goldfield, Nevada, in 1906. Nelson won the rematch held on Labor Day in Colma, California, in 1908.]

2 [See also *Autobiography*, pp. 162–163.]

Race Integrity

Voice of the Negro 4, no. 4 (1907): 197–202.

This age is regarded as one of great enlightenment. Yet with all its knowledge, there is a vast deal of ignorance or wilful blindness manifested along some lines. This state is born of many things, but when based upon traditional ideas, deep rooted, not only in error, but in prejudice and malice, there we find the most insensate manifestations.

Cherished beliefs, no matter upon what founded, have always resulted in rearing idols to be worshiped. Before such *icons* the world has bowed again and again. Religion has had its share of them, but the religious world also raised idol-breakers—the Iconoclasts who set to work in the eighth and ninth centuries to shatter them as did the Protestants in the Netherlands in the sixteenth century. Dogmas have crept into every phase of human life and endeavor, and no doubt will continue to do so, while mankind exists with its passions, its prejudices and its weaknesses, its preconceived notions and its obstinacy; so the labors of the Iconoclast have been and will be demanded for the sake of progress.

Among the multitude of cherished superstitions to which world-masses cling at one time or another, there are none more erroneous, more mischievous than that included under the unctuous expression, "Race Integrity." Here is heroic, legitimate work for the Iconoclast. Here his labors are an absolute necessity. But we are aware that to lay hands upon this idol, to tear it from its place, will covenant profaning the holy altar itself; that there are those who, viewing such an act, will fear that punishment to follow that overtook Uzziah when he sought simply to steady the ark on the memorable journey from Kirjathjearim.[1] There is no doubt whether that if the ranting Dixons and Tilmans and Vardamans and men of that ilk could become avenging fates, any one who dared attempt to shatter this idol would suffer instant annihilation.

But in the progress of civilization those who would overthrow cherished superstitions have had to suffer. Galileo's idea of the world systems ran counter to set theories, and under awful penalties he had to recant, though he whispered under his breath "E pur si muove." "It moves for all that." Luther, Cranmer, Latimer and countless other martyrs have suffered when seeking to pull the bandage from eyes so long blinded, and let in the light of truth. Today no one disputes Galil[e]o's claim; and theological freedom of thought and expression agrees with Luther and others of his school.

These men had to suffer I say; but they did good service and accepted the stake, or dungeon, or ban, bravely for the sake of truth. They shattered falsity; and the Iconoclast of today will render equally good service in dissipating the errors of the present, none of which, I repeat, is worse than the hydra-headed dogma that masquerades under the alluring title of Race Integrity—the one of all of Errors' vile brood, most fitly designed to perpetuate race discrimination, race hatred and race conflict.[2]

To the task of an Iconoclast I propose to devote this article, with the postulate that there is no such thing as "Race Integrity."

In the first place, to believe the theory of purity of race, of unmixed blood, as the term is interpreted to mean today, is to go back to first principles and to deny that of one blood God created all nations—to deny the unity of the human race. But of those who contend for more centers of creation than one, we demand proof; and of those who hold to the Darwinian theory of animal descent for some men or all men, we again call for proof—for the missing link that turned some peoples or all peoples into what we are pleased to call mankind. We know that the ages have asked this in vain. It has never been deduced and the *onus probandi* still rests upon its advocates.

On the other hand [Gottfried] Leibnitz, [George Louis] Buffon and [Daniel Paul] Schreber, [Johann C. P.] Erxleben and [Wilhelm von] Humboldt, [Johann F.] Blumenbach and [Georges] Cuvier and a long array of scientists stand ready, as the result of investigation of both physical and moral characteristics of the races of men, to affirm that all are identical in species and God their Creator. Therefore, to maintain that there is no such thing as Race Integrity is to maintain not only the unity of the human species, but at the same time to repel the "cheerless assumption of superior and inferior races." That there may be backward ones we admit, as all have been backward at some period of their existence.

What the first type of man was in form and color is not absolutely known; but enough is shown by history, Ethnology, analogy and reason to conclude that the primitive man was not light colored, that he had his origin in a warm climate, (possibly in Africa as is now being asserted) and that the type no longer exists. Even if we accept the premise that man began his migrations in early ages from Central Asia—as has been so long held, we can trace him with Dr. [John] Bachman, and find proof for our claim. Here the human family is followed through four diverging lines—southeast, southwest, northeast and west, and at every step we discover changes of climate and growth of varieties differing in color, form and language. We follow continually varying types of men until we have met with the so-called Mongolian on the northeast, the African on the south and the white man on the west. On the route we are carried insensibly from center to extreme, not being able to mark the differences in the links of the chain that binds all these peoples into one. Everywhere neighboring races have blended. This all goes to prove that no race is indigenous to the soil—unmixed, pure. Even when that first great migration took place the people knew not the home of their ancestors—they, too were in a strange land—they had come from some unknown center which we must leave the coming scientists definitely to determine.

If we turn to the European peoples alone, we find the historian Tacitus in error when he refers in his Germania to the Germans as indigenous—offspring of the soil.[3] We discover growing proof every day that the Germans, like all the cultural people of the old world, have no right to be called, as the Greeks also erroneously denominated themselves—autochthonous—children sprung from the land they inhabit. No, none of the races are indigenous. For centuries Germany gave shelter to Gallic tribes and by all the consequent commingling, Germany must be more Gallic in descent than many other races that have claimed such. In fact, Prof. Sergius of the University of Rome, in his new work, claims that the entire primitive population of Europe originated in Africa, from which three great stocks sprung—African, including Egyptians, a Mediterranean variety and a Nordic one, that spread over northern Europe. The claims are often conflicting, but all the research serves to shatter all claims of Race Integrity.

Then if we turn to France, M. Jean Finot's recent "Romance of the French Race" affords other telling points. He says the French are not direct descendants of the Gauls, but that, noting invasions and irruptions the Germanic blood runs freely in French veins, and in fact that France has been the grave of men of all sorts of races because of these invasions and irruptions; and he cites Russian Mongols, Semitic Arabs, Germans, Normans, Visigoths, Burgundians, Franks, etc., up to some fifty great varieties and some smaller ones, including the Tziganes, who are of such puzzling origin. *Nor does he forget to add that the early existence of the Negro has also been traced in France.*

What has happened in France has happened everywhere with variant races. The history of the world is the history of migratory nations, who from the first have simply swarmed over the face of the earth, possessed themselves of the fairest spots and safest habitations, and as they roamed they lost to a greater or less extent their race integrity. The story of every individual people partakes of the same characteristics—wars, invasions, captives, amalgamations—all have been taking place since the world began with man upon its face.

But to turn to our present day boaster of boasters—the white man who prides himself on his Saxon origin. What "race integrity" has he to keep? To hunt up the ancestry of an individual is a dangerous thing and full of unexpected surprises; and the haughty Dixons and Tillmans and Vardamans and Tom Watsons individually might not only find convict fore-fathers and wanton fore-mothers, but farther back they would surely find the rudest of barbarians. Our Anglo-Saxon brother has only to thank God for the law of change which has made it possible for him to improve upon that type which was then a mixture of Celts, Goths, Danes and Saxons. This Saxon serf ancestor, it is true, had qualities that commended him to the proud Normans who though he spurned his Saxon slave at first, amalgamated with him at last after the loss of Normandy. As for the Normans themselves they were simply drifters, a composite of Scandinavian and French, and who the French were, we have already stated.

"Race Integrity," forsooth! In view of the facts it is a myth, and the term a misnomer. Mr. Wm. B. Smith in his book, "The Color Line [1905]," which is intended to be an hysterical plea for pretended "Race Integrity," has made use of a term far more fitting to the situation. He speaks of "Mongrelization" as a thing to be feared; while the truth is there is nothing but mongrelization to which we can point in the life of the entire world. Yes; the Caucasian (so-called), who boasts of his still more remote Aryan descent, has a very weak reed to lean upon, for the Aryan dogma is another idol that stands in danger of complete destruction from the vigorous and philosophical attacks now being made upon it. Professor [Robert] K. Hartmann with others have reached the conclusion as they express it that the so-called Aryans never existed as a primitive people, except in the imagination of "arm-chair scholars," and they proceed to show that the Aryan language idea, so ably set forth by Max M[ü]ller, is a mistake in view of continuous discoveries.[4]

No! if any one people could with any vestige of historic backing boast of "Race Integrity" it is the Jew. It is agreed that the Jews' religious rites have conserved to keep them distinctly apart with the least admixture of foreign blood for over 2,000 years. But even then we have but to trace Biblical history and note the long, long list of unions with idolators to the destruction of both kingdoms, Israel and Judah, and see what this fact must mean as to purity of blood. Strains of Semitic blood must have ever been percolating through other veins for many a century since the time of Abraham, while at the same time their own race suffered similar changes. Jebusites, Amorites, Girgashites, Hittites, Hivites and Perrizites—all of them were not at all, per se, averse to inter-marrying with the Israelites. Solomon himself married an Egyptian princess. In fact, both social and political relations were so exceedingly close at times in Biblical history that it may be reasonably inferred that neither Solomon nor his Egyptian bride possessed any vaunted "race integrity." Today the Jew, brought into the air of freedom, has entered such a diversified life, and has grown so in intelligence and broadened so in view that there is a pointing toward the breaking down of the barriers by which the race has kept itself somewhat aloof. Mixture is going on, a most noted example having taken place quite recently in New York high life.

The truth is that the term "Caucasian" has little or no meaning as it is now used. The word itself is a conventional term given at the first by [Johann] Blumenbach to designate what he considered the highest type of the human family, shown by a skull from Mount Caucasus. When we attempt to trace those who would claim the name as an expression of their superiority we find the type has disappeared. There is no pure specimen now in existence. And if we ask what is "white" we can only say, "that it is a term used to designate the absence of color"—that is all, and no sign whatever of "race integrity." We have already indicated that science and investigation point to the fact that primitive man was not white. It is no new theory, but it has seemed convenient for the Saxon to let it rest as much as possible in discrete oblivion. Bishop H. M. Turner of the African Methodist Episcopal church has often promulgated it in his own inimitable way, and Moncure D. Conway has also declared that the white people of the world today are only a reflex leprosy and that the natural color is brown or black. History, remote yet unquestioned, teaches that the primitive inhabitants of Greek countries were not white. Then we have to the credit of Negro scholarship that admirable monograph from Bishop Tanner[5] showing that Solomon did not belong to the so-called white race. And it is this matter of changing color, of gradations, of tints among the people of the earth, that must be one of the strong proofs of the lack of "race integrity." Henry tells us that every complexion is still found in Egypt—"the yellowish Copt, supposed to represent the ancient Egyptian, the swarthy villager, the dark wild Arab, the dead, dusky black of the Nubian, the coarser, more jetty black of the Negro, and still further, the weather-blacked, spirited and often finely chiseled face of the southern Arab." And he goes on to remark further that the natives of Egypt are generally dark, and far southward toward Ethiopia, almost black; yet those of high rank, being protected from the sun are pretty fair, and would be reckoned such even in Britain.

Humboldt and Muller and Linnaeus and others refer constantly to these gradations, not only of tint but of physiognomy—all of which must be the outcome of un-numbered ages of migratory, wide geographical extension, destruction, admixture, climate and surroundings, and variants in descendents. All these have most certainly united with the more prolonged sojourn in localities as civilization advanced, to affect color, form and feature, and thus make the changes seen to-day changes that will continue to go on under any like combined influences and in future ages result in still greater complexities, just as difficult to trace, but all going to prove the fact that "Race Integrity" did not exist in the past, does not exist today and cannot in the future.

It is a most extensive subject that we have but touched upon—so extensive that we can only hint at the ideas advanced by archaeologists, ethnologists and geologists as to the changes in the world's peoples. All details must perforce, in a brief discussion be omitted, as it is not our present purpose to prove or disprove theories as to origins—but only to set forth enough to show that "race integrity" as the term is used, has no meaning whatever.

If we turn to this country and narrow our investigation to the Saxon, as found here, we have abundant proof that the same is true in his case as in that of other peoples—his blood is far from pure. The white man has voluntarily mingled his blood with the Negro's for 250 years, and so interwoven together are the two that if the truth were admitted, and the facts publicly known, a large proportion of the white element so-called would be found to possess some strains of Negro blood. To our regret as a people we are virtually compelled to admit relationship of every degree to these very Tillmans, and Vardamans and Dixons of the South. Then as to the old saying that "blood will tell," down goes another idol before the image-breaker; for Dr. [Pearce] Kintzing, after repeated experiments, tells the world the Negro blood can be no more told than other blood—that it is a fallacy that admixture with the

Negro will even always result in race characteristics. So the Iconoclast's work goes on and the world is forced to say it cannot tell black from white, cannot draw the line of blood—does not know Negro from Saxon. Thousands who possess Negro blood have declared themselves white unchallenged and are even now mingling with the whites, passing for white, marrying for white. We know many of them. We know their mothers and their fathers. We pass them every day but we remain silent inwardly smiling at the claim of "race integrity." The actual truth is that the white people of this country, many of them, have more of the Negro blood than they have of any other mixture in their veins. But they would deny it and make most frantic searches to disprove it, preferring to admit any other claim. Some time ago a North Carolinian was found sueing to compel a board of education to admit his six fair daughters to a public school in an endeavor to disprove Negro blood by making boasts of a bright colored Portuguese as an ancestor.

But the ridiculous demand for "race integrity" still goes on and it is not confined alone to the white side of the house. The Negro too is guilty of adopting the Shibboleth. So contagious is it to shout with the mass "Great is Diana of the Ephesians," and so the race too cries, "Let us preserve our 'race integrity.'" And what have we to preserve in the light of the facts deduced from history and present situation? Surely no more in the past than any other race variety, far less in the present and in this country. It is very doubtful whether the type brought from Africa can today be found here unmixed. That type, even, has been destroyed and it has taken only 250 years to make us what we are—people presenting every gradation of tint from white to black, and every variation of feature. In our veins runs most largely the vaunted Saxon blood, but we possess as well, Indian, Celtic, German, Japanese, Chinese, Italian—yes, some of every nation that has set its foot upon these shores—all have mingled with us until we are the highest possible present-day example of complex mixture on the earth. *So mixed are we that we know not who we are or what we are, and cannot even agree upon a suitable name for ourselves—so mixed that if all were counted to us who bear our blood we would have at least twenty-five rather than ten millions charged up to our census account.*

It is the height of absurdity for the Negro to adopt this cry, accepting with it the position of an outcast, ostracized people; and why should we be feared as a people or be set aside in this manner? Note the shifty sophistry in the replies. They tell us our forefathers were slaves. We answer, "So were yours." But they continue, Your race is an inferior one. We deny it. Backward we may be, but not inferior. The unity of the human family forbids this claim. We hold with Johannes [Peter] Muller in his *Physiologie des Menschen* [1833–1840] that there are families of nations as we see them today more highly civilized, more enobled by mental culture than others, but not in themselves more noble—and what brought these families to a higher state will bring the Negro people there. Races are always going up or down. No race is always at the top; and we point to the incontrovertible fact that we are on the uphill grade. We are old, too, with a past. We had great names then, and the ages have never failed to yield some examples of black greatness. Ovid makes

Sappho the Lesbian sweet singer say[,] "Brown as I am, an Ethiopian dame."[6] [Henri] Gregoire furnishes us with a list of distinguished Negroes and mulattoes, who were an honor to the race to which they belonged. Then we come down to Pushkin, our Russian poet; to Banneker, and Phillis Wheatley, to Dumas and L'Ouverture, until we reach the present, starred with a galaxy of names to our credit—poets, painters, linguists, orators, educators. As to the future it will take care of itself on the world-old-principle of growth and development.

But we are vicious, claims another voice. I reply we have our virtues as well as vices—as many of the former I venture as have other races, and no more vices. May we purge ourselves of them!

But you seek "social equality" comes the final heart-rending shriek. At last the great fear is revealed, which is no fear at all in view of the social equality that has been practiced since we came to these shores. The term is simply another bugbear to fan hatred and alienate further the races.

And here I pause to say that it is to be lamented that we have among us those who so truckle to Southern prejudices as to make haste to deny that the Negro wants "social equality." "I am a man," I say with Terence, and with him I consider nothing foreign to me that relates to a man, and the right to individual opinion is every man's right.[7] No one man can speak for a race in matters belonging solely to the individual. Social equality concerns individuals and individuals must and will determine their social matters.

Let "social equality" take care of itself. But in this last frantic charge against us, the Southern white man seems to have eaten of the "insane root" that "takes the reason prisoner."[8] A certain class has arisen with neither logic nor memory—denying us a past, striving to rob us of a present, and forbidding a future—a class that is endeavoring by playing upon such terms as "social equality," and "race integrity" to wipe us from the face of the earth. And why? *Because we are living witnesses of the falsity of their claims to race integrity, and because we are troublers of their conscience and because we are competitors for world success. Hence the inconsistent unreasoning attitude.*

God grant that our eyes may be kept open to every subtle movement that tends to keep us back, to every form of philanthropy that offers stones for bread; God grant that we may not lend an iota of effort or acquiescence to further cries that would consign us to the depths.

I am ready to affirm that as a race we should not be feared as an integral part of American life. This country is wide enough to hold the millions that are mounting up in our population and there is not a race entering it but may contribute something of benefit to American life and character. Unquestionably America is to be the theater of the greatest commingling of races known to the world. This commingling has been going on since the discovery of this new world. Just as waters rising above dykes are bound to overflow the land, so without hindrance no King Canute can sweep back this tide; nor can priests ban it by bell, book or candle. Some time in the future we are all to be amalgamated into this American body politic. Despite the stress of the present situation, every thinking person must see that this country, by this union of races, will be the future abode of a typical American who will be neither black, white, red, yellow, as we use these terms and who will laugh at his ancestors who so strenuously shouted for "race integrity." Yes, as Bishop Hamilton rightly declares, "These great grandchildren of the present age will be partly Chinese and Japanese, partly Hebrew and Negro, partly Caucasian and Southern European,"—and [I] will add, with many other strains entering into their blood.

It is for America to think of this—to make every effort to suppress the anarchists of society (such as the author of the "Clansman"),[9] who would inflame the passions of the mob and burn the Negro at the stake. Charity begins at home, and instead of giving all its pity to the terrible situation of the Jew in Russia, America should see to it that no fanning of the flame of race hate is allowed here at home. No more than in the past, is either the present or great moral future of this country to be limited to ethnic origins, for as Prof. [Napoleone] Co[l]ajanni of the Naples university tersely puts it, "It is not in ethnic factors but in physical, moral and social constitutions that we must look for the causes of a nation's greatness or decadence." Andrew Carnegie voiced the same idea when he said before the immigration commission in reply to a remark about "purity of blood:" "It is not purity of blood you want, for it is the mingling of the different bloods that makes the American." And the Negro cannot be left out of consideration. Commingling has gone on too far for this. We must break the idols worshipped so long, and free ourselves one and all from the influence of that abominable and intolerable stupid dogma of "race integrity."

As terms have only that meaning that is attributed to them—whether "Saxon or Negro," "white" or "black," race integrity or what not—we should for ourselves seek a new and better meaning for this term. "Race Integrity" needs to be translated as meaning for all races the task of rising, by looking well to morals—to the cultivation of the highest possible character, to reaching out with every intellectual and economic force toward prosperity and greatness. With this meaning to the Shibboleth, national and racial boundaries will fade away far more quickly than through wars and bloodshed.

But while we are working and waiting as a people we must not lose hope in ourselves, but hold persistently and rigidly to the faith that Walt Whitman, the "most American of poets"—has thus phrased:[10]

> "Each of us inevitable,
> Each of us limitless—each of us with his or her right upon the earth,
> Each of us allow'd the eternal purports of the earth,
> Each of us here, as divinely as any are here."

Notes

1 [See 1 Samuel 7:2, 2 Samuel 6:6, and 2 Kings 15:1–7.]

2 [See Edmund Spenser (c. 1552–1599), *Faerie Queene* (1594), canto 1, stanza 1, lines 1–9.]

3 [See Tacitus, *Germania*, chapter 2, "ipsos Germanos indigenas crediderim."]

4 [See Robert Hartmann (1832–1893), *Die Nigritier* (Berlin: Wiegandt, Hempel & Parey, 1876.)]

5 [*The Color of Solomon.*]

6 [This is Alexander Pope's translation. For the Latin, see Ovid, *Heroides*, 15.36–37: "candida si non sum . . . fusca colore."]

7 [See Terence, "Heautontimorumenos," act 1, scene 1, line 25: "homo sum humanum nil a me alienum puto."]

8 ["Or have we eaten on the insane root that takes the reason prisoner," said by Banquo in Shakespeare's *Macbeth*, act I, scene 3.]

9 [Thomas Dixon Jr.]

10 [Walt Whitman, "Salut au Monde," stanza 11, lines 223–226.

An Appeal to Colored Voters

Cleveland Journal, October 19, 1907.

To the Editor of The Cleveland Journal:

I wish through your columns to urge every Negro voter in Cleveland to do his whole duty in the coming municipal election to give Mr. Burton his warmest and most enthusiastic support.[1] The Negro can not afford to do otherwise. If he does he will dig his own grave and will be buried in it. Mr. Burton is a splendid type of America's best manhood, and an able and fearless standard bearer, a man of high character, splendid ability and sterling worth, one in whom all can trust. He is a gallant leader and stands squarely upon justice to all men.

I have known Mr. Burton for many years, and have always found him every inch a man. I appeal to the colored voters especially to do their whole duty, to help give this republican leader and champion of good government and fair play a rousing vote, such as is befitting his eminent life and services. Democratic success even in a municipal election is dangerous, and is not to be thought of, and I hope that every Negro voter in the great city of Cleveland will be found in the Burton band wagon. Remember that it is only in states under democratic control that we find those abominable "Jim Crow" cars and all forms of legislation and proscription, subversive of the Negroes' best interests, humiliations of a most degrading character. Only in the states of the Tillmans, the Vardamans, the Dixons, the Jeff Davises and that class of obstructionists. A democratic victory in the north, whether it be that of a city or that of a state, encourages these men to continue their deviltry.

Therefore I warn you to beware of the Greeks, even though they offer presents.[2]

Notes

1 [Theodore E. Burton (1851–1929), Republican politician and graduate of Oberlin College (1872), was a U.S. representative for many years and then a senator from 1909 to 1915 and 1928 to 1929.]

2 [See Virgil, *Aeneid*, book 2, line 49: Laocoon says, "timeo Danaos et dona ferentes."]

Race Riots and Their Remedy

Independent, August 18, 1919, p. 223.

There is but one remedy for race riots, and that is, justice—a willingness to accord to every man his rights—civil and political. This is the only solution of the vexed question called race prejudice, which is at the bottom of all the race troubles in all sections of our country.

Riots at all times are to be deplored and rioters themselves punished; and nothing I say in this article must be construed as an apology for lawlessness or crime.

The negro is the unfortunate victim in all these outbreaks—unfortunate because of his color, and unfortunate because the odds are against him, and because few people, nowadays, seem to think that he has rights that other men are bound to respect. This is the situation as we face it today.

The spirit of the negro who went across the seas—who was in action, and who went "over the top"—is by no means the spirit of the negro before the war. He is altogether a new man, with new ideas, new hopes, new aspirations and new desires. He will not quietly submit to former conditions without a vigorous protest, and we should not ask him to do so. It is a new negro that we have with us now, and may we not hope also that we have new white men? The war has revolutionized the entire world. It has changed our mode of thinking and our mode of action. New peoples with new thoughts must come to the front now.

When that horde of crude, unlettered and uncultured negroes was brought from the South—drafted against their will—disfranchised and representing nothing—when they were thrust into the cantonment to be converted into soldiers, little did the War Department think that it was creating a new race problem that would have to be dealt with later. This act transformed these men into new creatures—citizens of another type—that which they could not get in times of peace, came to them in times of war. I verily believe that it was providential. Many of these returning soldiers will not go South, but those who do so will demand a change in the treatment of their race.

It was rather unfortunate that the greatest of all wars—the World War— should have found the South in the saddle. It was an opportunity for that section and it made the most of it, so far as the black man is concerned.

The policy of the Administration has been against the black man. The avowed purpose of the Federal authorities, from the beginning of the war till its close, was to make the negro feel that he is a negro and must occupy a negro's place. This spirit was taken by the white men in uniform across the seas, where every effort was used to have the Allied people understand that the negro had no standing on this side of the Atlantic.

If the negro had not been sent to camp—if he had not been trained in common with the white soldier; if he had not gone across the seas, and if he had not gone "over the top," and made good; and if he had not expected better treatment on his return to his native land at the hands of those who drafted him and sent him to the trenches, I am sure that he would not be so exasperated over the situation.

He feels the injustice keenly. The negro officers and men now returning have but one story to tell, and they tell it with bitterness and in tears. Yet there is no redress, there is nothing that the negro can do, but wait. He dares not— he must not take the law into his own hands. That is anarchy and leads to riots and lawlessness. The higher and better classes of colored people, like the higher and better classes of white people, are not in sympathy with mob law or anything that is destructive of good government.

The war is now over, the negro soldier has returned. Note his treatment on the railroads, all of which are under Government control. Many of these men in going to their homes with laurels of victory won in their country's defense are not permitted to ride in other than the Jim-Crow cars. Many of them have been assaulted and thrown off the cars by Government officials—notwithstanding their record across seas—simply because of their color. Many of them have not only suffered in this way, but have met death, because they sought better treatment. This is a terrible chapter in our American life, and only the negro's love for good government prevents serious trouble.

The negro is law-abiding and only occasionally shows a retaliatory spirit. Will not the American white people come halfway—put aside their prejudices and play fair with this people that has done so much to help win this war? Negroes are not rioters, but can be made so. It is a burden they carry. They ask no favors, but simply a man's chance in the race of life, and an opportunity to develop the powers that God has given them.

Farming

Optimisms in Negro Farm Life

Opportunity (February 1926): 65–67.

Virginia, like other Southern states, is largely agricultural. More than 19,000,000 acres of its territory are in farm lands. Of its people, three-fourths live in the country and in rural districts (see census of 1910). From the same source we learn that the total number of farmers (white and black) was 184,018 and in 1920 the number was 186,242, a gain of 2,224 in ten years. In 1910, of this number 135,904 were white and 48,114 were black. In 1920, white farmers numbered 138,560 and colored 44,786, a falling off on the part of the Negro farmers, but an increase of white farmers. This decrease of colored farmers, no doubt, was due to migrations of the blacks from the country to the cities and to northern industrial centers.

Statistics show that there are 926,708 Negro farmers in the United States. Of the Negro land owners there are at least, 30,908 in the State of Virginia.

Any phase of the successful Negro farmer's life offers food for reflection. He has a vocation and an avocation. His vocation is his farm at seed and planting time and at harvest. His avocation is the spending of unoccupied time in numerous outside activities whereby he may add to his fortune. This is so throughout the South.

It was a typical southern fall day that the writer happened at an early hour in a typical southern farming town to stop at the terminal of a southern railroad. The number of empty cars, the bustle and noise, the general activities, the result of men and boys getting ready for the day's work not only attracted his attention but interested him greatly. The cars had been brought down by trainmen the evening before and had been left on the siding to be filled with Negro farm products by Negro producers and owners of the same for shipment. It was an interesting sight to observe wagon after wagon, dozens of them, wagons and carts loaded with peanuts to be shipped to various points. The drivers of the teams were of both colors, though in the South. All day long this activity continued, white men and black men working together side by side and doing business together without friction.

On inquiry it was learned that the motive power back of this big business was a Negro, a large land owner and a man of large means. He had sold his harvest of peanuts to the peanut buyers of the state and was now shipping the same for cash. It is said that this is an annual occurrance. It was quite evident to the writer, from the large transactions of the day that business is business and money knows no color.

The shipper was only one of many groups of prosperous and successful Negro farmers found not only in the State of Virginia but throughout the South. His character and financial standing gave him great prominence and power in his community. He was a man of substantial worth as a citizen and meant much to the people with whom he was associated in business and otherwise. W. B. Turner, the man referred to, is the owner of 1,020 acres of land, 400 acres of which are tillable and 618 are woods. Two acres surround the house as yard and grove. In the earlier days when land was cheap, varying from $2.00 to $5.00 an acre, many Negroes looked far enough ahead and were wise enough to take advantage of an opportunity to become land owners. They bought many acres and continued to increase the number. Those who could hold it became rich and independent and those who could not, of course failed. It is not a rare thing now to find a black man in the South owning land varying from 500 to 3,000 acres. Mr. Turner's five sons, all prosperous farmers, cultivate their own land given them by their father. The father's example of activity and thrift proved to be a great inspiration to the sons. Mr. Turner lives in a style in keeping with his wealth but is often found working with the hired help or with his sons with coat off, either wielding an axe or a pick or loading a car with lumber cut from his own woods.

The first day's experience was so encouraging and so delightful that a second visit was made to this railroad terminal for further observation. On arrival, many open cars were found awaiting consignments of lumber on contract, lumber owned by Negro farmers. Thousands and thousands of feet of timber of all shapes and sizes filling many cars were being shipped to various parts of the state and country for various uses, some of which the railroad people bought for themselves for uses of the road, while many other shipments were made to Northern centers. Checks of large amounts were received by these black men for material shipped. The writer was told that when the season was dull or when the crops were laid by, some of these men made in addition to the receipts from their crops sums varying from $2,000 to $3,000 annually, buying and selling logs. Logging among them is quite an industry.

In this particular instance the owner was one of three brothers, the Tennessees, named for the state from which they migrated in an earlier day. They proved to be good citizens and good farmers, attentive to their work and duties, becoming very prosperous. Only one of them had attended school for any length of time. He was a graduate of Hampton Institute. In a letter to the writer he says:

"The property owned by me here in Adam's Grove, the real estate varies from two hundred to three hundred acres, and my personal property is valued at about $25,000. I had much more property than this but sold down to these figures.

"The improvements made since owning it have been as follows: Cut and cleared land for cultivation 55 acres—built two tenement houses—one with five rooms, and another with four at a cost of $1,500 each. Insurance amounts to $1,700 each. Built one store house at a cost of $1,000 and insured it for $700. I built a blacksmith shop in order to continue my trade at a cost of $500. The house in which I live cost me $3,000 and is insured for $1,200. I have six minor outer buildings that cost me $100 each. I hold policies in the Mutual Benefit Life Insurance Co., Newark, N. J., and in the North Carolina Mutual Life Insurance Co., Durham."

This is not all the property Mr. D. C. Tennessee owns. There are some smaller portions of land that he has not mentioned. This, however, is a good showing for a colored man of forty-five years.

Paul Sykes is another remarkable character, the owner of much land and a most successful farmer. An uneducated man—a man of unusual native ability and hard sense, he has accumulated large means. Three or four banks hold his funds and his credit is good wherever he is known. He usually spends from $1,000 to $3,000 annually for fertilizers alone, some being for his renters and tenants with ample time for payment for the same. He has a most interesting family of five children of whom three are young men and like their father successful farmers. He does no active work himself now but leaves his five hundred acres to the care of his sons to look after and till.

One Henry Scott, whom the writer often met while he was living was a peculiar character—quite eccentric in fact. He owned three thousand acres in his state and carried accounts in several banks. He was regarded as one of the most substantial farmers of his time. He built churches and contributed to charity but paid little or no attention to his own personal appearance.

Other names that might be mentioned are H. E. Smith, Emmett Broadnax, J. L. Claud and the large family of the name of Rick. Such examples of thrift and enterprise are most encouraging and may be regarded as rifts in the clouds, showing a brighter day ahead, evincing the Negro's ability to succeed under handicaps.

Help From Farm Loan System

Until recently the Negro farmers of the South have been greatly hampered in securing funds to meet their demands, because they have been unable to secure the advantages accruing from the Farm Loan System. They have, for the most part, been unable to get their applications properly considered, and this is still true in a large portion of the South. The difficulties in the way are many and are hard to overcome. In a few instances it has been due to ignorance as to mode of procedure but in the majority of cases, to the prejudices of the section in which they lived. As no special records are kept by the banks of the Farm Loan System of colored borrowers, it has been impossible up to date to get the number of Negroes benefited by this System. Of the twelve

Regional banks which responded to communications it was learned that there was no discrimination on account of color as the color of the borrower was not known. The trouble is with the local Farm Loan Associations which exclude the Negro from membership, thus making it impossible for him to get recognition. Because of this discrimination the black farmer has suffered greatly in many instances and has lost valuable property.

When it was learned that the obstacle was entirely local, steps were at once taken to meet the situation in the country in which the writer found himself. Some two hundred names of deserving Negro farmers were transmitted to the local white associations and duplicates of the same were sent to the Federal Land Bank in Baltimore.

> "I wrote the Secretary and Treasurer of Southampton County, N. F. L. A. a few days ago, asking him to give special consideration to the needs of the colored farmer, stating that if delay was due to the fact that we were limited in funds that we would make special effort for additional allotment of funds for his county, in order that we might take care of those whom you mentioned, asking him to give special attention to their needs."

Again, another letter:[1]

> Dear Sir:
> I was glad, this morning, to receive your communication and furthermore am pleased to state that since your visit to the office we have loaned considerable sums of money to the colored people of Southampton County, Virginia. We are doing what we can to assist the farmers of that county, but it appears that both the white and colored farmers are so greatly in need of money that it is difficult to get sufficient funds to meet all the demands.
> I want to assure you again that we will do everything we can to assist the colored farmers as referred to by you.
> Yours very truly,
> C. R. Titlow,
> Secretary.

As the result of this correspondence loans varying from $200 to $10,000 (to a single individual) were made to Negro farmers wishing for such assistance either for improvements or for enlarging their acreage.

An Advocate at Court

The Negro farmer needs an advocate at court and since he has no representative of his own group this advocate must be the friendly white man—the white man who is able and willing to help him in his struggles. He must depend upon him for a helping hand and for sympathetic co-operation until the time shall come when the color line is less sharply drawn and race prejudice less acute.

The following figures from the Bureau of Census will explain themselves:

Negro farmers constitute 8.9 per cent of the total Negro population while the white farmers represent but 5.8 per cent of the total white population.

Although the Negro population forms but 9.9 per cent of the total population in the United States, the Negro farmers form 14.7 per cent of all farmers.

Of the 926,708 Negro farmers in the United States, 218,612 are owners; 2,026 are managers and 705,070 are tenants.

In 1920 these farmers operated 41,432,182 acres of which 27,926,900 were improved. The value of the land and buildings amounted to $2,257,645,325, or an increase in ten years which represents an average of $11,124,397 every thirty days.

Of the 705,070 tenant farmers, 701,471 were in the sixteen southern states, led by Mississippi with 137,679 and Georgia with 113,929. Other states having more than 50,000 each were, in the order named, South Carolina, 86,063; Alabama, 77,873; Arkansas, 56,811; Texas, 59,945; North Carolina, 53,040; and Louisiana, 50,969.

Of the 218,612 owners, 30,909 were in Virginia; 23,519 in Texas; 23,130 in Mississippi; 22,759 in South Carolina; 21,714 in North Carolina; 17,201 in Alabama; 16,040 in Georgia; 15,369 in Arkansas; and 10,975 in Louisiana. In no other states were there as many as 10,000 Negro farm owners.

Between 1910 and 1920 Negro f[ar]mers increased at the rate of 3.7 per cent; native white farmers at the rate of 3.1 per cent; while foreign born white farmers decreased at the rate of 13.2 per cent.

Of the 581,050 foreign born white farmers in the United States only 40,801, or 7 per cent were located in the 16 southern states.

These figures make interesting reading and clearly show that the part that colored farmers are playing in rural districts and in our agricultural life is by no means small. It is quite possible then that here on southern soil and on southern farms the outlook for future success is more optimistic than elsewhere. The Negro farmer is the back-bone of the South. It is upon his success and his prosperity that the prosperity of that section largely depends. The South will yet awake to the fact that in the ill treatment of the colored farmer it is making the mistake of its life. Conditions are bound to change. The acquisition of land and the accumulation of money will be powerful levers in bringing about these changes.

The Negro should be brought into closest touch with the Department of Agriculture. A Bureau should be established to the end that the best trained minds of the race in scientific and Agricultural lines may operate for their own group as others of another race cannot do.[2] This bureau should constitute the point of contact between the Government and the field as it pertains to the Negro farmer. We already have trained specialists and experts who could meet these conditions and who could furnish the Government with valuable information making for the good of the Department of Agriculture and the country.

There is much now that cannot be known because it cannot be gotten at except through scientifically trained *Negro* investigators.

The Negro farmer is now too potential to be longer ignored and neglected.[3]

Notes

1 [Titlow's letter is found in Scarborough's *Autobiography*, p. 295.]

2 [Scarborough tried to set up such a bureau: see *Autobiography*, p. 297.]

3 [Aaron Douglas's drawing of a man working in the field accompanied the original article on page 66.]

Index

response to mob vengeance, 411
"Utility of Studying the Greek"
(Scarborough), 161–165

V

vaudeville, 266
vengeance
of mob, 410–412
of oppressed, 434
Vergil. *See* Virgil
Virgil, 274, 275, 276, 278, 282, 285–286,
292, 294, 306, 331, 482
Virginia, 487
railway law, 384
Virgule, 165
Volapük, 246
voting, 482. *See also* political rights
division of blacks, 359
and education lever, 461–462
federal election law need, 361–368
federal surveillance need, 358
Harrison, Benjamin (president) on,
362–363
in Mississippi, 361–362, 377
and property lever, 461
seeking suffrage, 102
South Carolina population numbers,
364–366
suffrage rights, 447–448
unconstitutionality of voting curbs,
366–367
Washington, Booker T., on, 88

W

Ward, William Hayes, xxxi, 96, 220
Ware, Edmund A., 29
"Warren G. Harding: A Brand New
President. . ." (Scarborough),
xxxiii, 137–140
wars overview, 433–434
Washington, Booker T., xxiv, xxxi, xxxv,
87–89, 193–194, 207–212, 217,
398, 423, 424, 432
West, Andrew Fleming, 314
Western Authors and Artists Club,
Kansas City, xxxviii
West Indies, 252–253
What Should Be the Standard of the

University, Normal School, Teacher
Training and Secondary Schools
(Scarborough), 178–184
"What the Omen?" (Scarborough),
425–427
whites
American superiority claim, 464
belief in black inferiority, 429
and black audiences, 388–390
future regrets, 431
individualizing blacks need, 390
middle-class battleground, 426
mob control need, 471
and "Negro problem," 369
premises about blacks, 377–378,
425–427
self-belief in superiority, 429
social contact fear, 377
understanding of blacks, 376–377,
425–427
violence by, 336–337, 408, 443, 470
"White *vs.* Black" (Scarborough),
428–431
Whitman, Walt, 480, 481
Whitney, W. D., xxxii, 239
Whittier, John Greenleaf, 28
"Why I Am a Republican"
(Scarborough), 20–23
Wilberforce University, xxiv, xxvi, xxvii,
xxxiii, xxxviii, xxxix–xl, xl,
173–174, 182
Williams, George Washington, 7
Wolf, F. A., 302, 303
World War I, xxvi, xxvii, 483–484
Wright, Richard R., xxiii, xxxiii
writing, invention of, 39, 302–303

X

Xenophon, 50, 287, 320, 329
"Xenophon or Andocides, —Which?"
(Scarborough), 284

Y

Y.M.C.A., 469, 471
Young, Charles, xxvi

Z

Zeus, 274–275, 276